THE FOUNDATIONS OF ECONOMIC POLICY
Values and techniques

Nicola Acocella

Translated from the Italian
by Brendan Jones

CAMBRIDGE
UNIVERSITY PRESS

CAMBRIDGE UNIVERSITY PRESS
Cambridge, New York, Melbourne, Madrid, Cape Town, Singapore, São Paulo

Cambridge University Press
The Edinburgh Building, Cambridge CB2 2RU, UK

Published in the United States of America by Cambridge University Press, New York

www.cambridge.org
Information on this title: www.cambridge.org/9780521584074

Originally published in Italian as *Fondamenti di Politica Economica*
by La Nuova Italia Scientifica 1994
and © La Nuova Italia Scientifica

First published in English by Cambridge University Press 1998
as *The Foundations of Economic Policy*
Reprinted 2000
English translation © Cambridge University Press 1998

A catalogue record for this publication is available from the British Library

ISBN-13 978-0-521-58407-4 hardback
ISBN-10 0-521-58407-8 hardback

ISBN-13 978-0-521-58638-2 paperback
ISBN-10 0-521-58638-0 paperback

Transferred to digital printing 2005

THE FOUNDATIONS OF ECONOMIC POLICY

This is the first English-language adaptation of Professor Nicola Acocella's best-selling undergraduate textbook *Fondamenti di politica economica: Valori e tecniche*, originally published in 1994. Aimed at intermediate and undergraduate students who have completed an introductory course in Economics, *The Foundations of Economic Policy* is a class-room tested book which brings an exciting new approach to the teaching of economics by taking subjects which are normally compartmentalised within welfare, macro, micro and applied economics and considering them within a unifying framework based on the persistence of market failures and the full range of issues connected to them, including public intervention and regulation. *The Foundations of Economic Policy* is the most comprehensive, user-friendly and innovative economics textbook currently available.

Professor Nicola Acocella is based at 'La Sapienza' at the University of Rome

To Annamaria

Contents

Contents

PART III **NORMATIVE AND POSITIVE THEORY OF ECONOMIC POLICY**

* Sections marked by an asterisk and the appendices contain more difficult material that make the book useful to more advanced students.

Preface

Some 35 years ago there were rather simple and commonly accepted justifications for government intervention in the economy. At a microeconomic level these were mainly the existence of monopoly, externalities and public goods, and income inequalities. At the macroeconomic level intervention was justified on the basis of the Keynesian analysis of aggregate demand and subsequent developments.

Market failures at both levels were considered so widespread and deep as to justify programmed action by government. In the late 1940s authors such as R. Frisch, J. Tinbergen, H. Theil and others began to develop the so-called 'theory of economic policy'. On the basis of fixed targets or a social preference function, as well as an analytical model of the economy and the assumption of rational policymakers, the consistent levels of policy instruments were derived for static and dynamic settings.

However, a difficulty remained in justifying the social preference function, which had been proved to be difficult to link to individual preferences by Arrow and others. This difficulty was overcome rather artificially by Tinbergen and Theil by referring the social preference function directly to policymakers.

Two main attacks were made on these justifications of public policy: the first was advanced by Coase, the second by Friedman and other monetarists of subsequent generations. At the methodological level, critics of public policy were able to reaffirm the virtues of the 'invisible hand' at both the micro and macro level by microfounding the latter on the theory of general equilibrium, which was assumed to be solid enough to support the entire edifice.

Moreover, a revival of the Kaleckian concept of the political business cycle, set in a different perspective, tended to underscore numerous 'non-market failures'. At the beginning of the 1980s the prevailing attitude of economists had clearly shifted against public intervention, advocating the scaling-down of government to a bare minimum.

Nevertheless, developments in public economics in the 1970s and 1980s largely sought to reaffirm the limits of the market that had already been pointed out and to identify new ones. The possible existence of fundamental non-convexities, imperfect and asymmetric information, incentive incompatibility, imperfect competition, strategic complementarity and scale economies confirmed the conclusion that a large set of market failures indeed exists. And yet, some of these situations may also involve government failures.

The picture is now quite complicated, and it seems appropriate and necessary to provide a clear statement of the various arguments for and against both the market and government, preliminary to any discussion of the techniques of public intervention. In turn, any such a statement requires a discussion of the principles by which market and non-market failures can be assessed, in particular different efficiency and equity criteria.

The first part of the book is devoted to a discussion of such criteria: how they can or should be developed, with or without reference to individual preferences or external – even absolute – principles. More specifically, the principle of ethical individualism in the presence of endogenous preferences is critically discussed. In general, a theory of justice external to current individual preferences is shown to be necessary for the existence of a complete social ordering. This analysis allows us to underscore some limitations of the Pareto principle.

The concept of Pareto optimality is used in the second part of the book to determine some of the implications of the two fundamental theorems of welfare economics in the space of actions. A careful analysis of the theorems provides arguments both for and against the market. The analysis of microeconomic failures is completed by a discussion of market failures that, given the present state of the discipline, can be best analysed from a macroeconomic standpoint. These are involuntary unemployment, inflation, balance of payments disequilibrium and underdevelopment.

The third part of the book is devoted to presenting the 'classic' normative theory of economic policy developed by Frisch and others and to examining criticism of this position, from the Lucas critique to the theory of political business cycles and the theory of bureaucracy. Non-market failures are then discussed and, to a certain extent, compared with market failures.

Taking both market and non-market failures into account, an analysis of specific policy targets and instruments follows in part IV (microeconomic policies), part V (macroeconomic policies in a closed economy) and part VI (macroeconomic policies in an open economy). The analysis in these parts is concerned with the role of institutions in influencing the performance of an economic system and the interplay of different agents in shaping social institutions.

The final part of the book is devoted to the analysis of problems of consistency in economic policies (time consistency, internal and external coordination). These issues are discussed at the end of the book because some such problems – those of coordination – can be only be dealt with satisfactorily once the economic policies in an open setting have been analysed.

This textbook is intended for students who have completed at least a full year's study of both micro- and macroeconomics. However, sections that have been marked by an asterisk and the appendices contain more difficult material that make the book useful to more advanced students as well. No calculus is required except for some of these sections and appendices. Each chapter is completed by a summary and a list of key concepts. A detailed subject index makes the book a helpful resource for consultation by the educated public in general. A list of symbols used in the text is provided at the beginning of the book.

In preparing this work I was greatly assisted by the advice and criticism of many friends and colleagues. A list of all those who helped me with the Italian edition would take up far too much space, but I cannot fail to thank those who read various parts of this version and helped eliminate many errors and inconsistencies: Guido Cozzi, Giancarlo Corsetti, Giuseppe De Arcangelis, Debora Di Gioacchino, Silvia Fedeli, Paolo Leon, Riccardo Martina, Luciano Milone, Amedeo Panci, Giuseppe Pennisi, Diego Piacentino, Gustavo Piga, Fabio Ravagnani, Stefanio Rossetti and Luigi Ventura. I owe special thanks to Giuseppe Ciccarone, who courageously accepted the challenge of reading the entire manuscript and offered many invaluable suggestions that have improved the book in many points. My greatest debt is to Federico Caffè, who in the early 1960s introduced me to the fascinating world of welfare economics and economic policy.

I owe the idea for an English-language edition of the book to Marcello De Cecco. Giacomo Becattini, Peter Hammond, Guido Rey and Jaime Sempere all contributed in various ways to making this edition possible. The entire project would have been impossible without the financial support of the Banca di Roma in meeting the costs of translation. I give my heartfelt thanks to all.

Sabrina Zukar ably prepared the figures. Simona Mabellini contributed her time and effort with generosity. Brendan Jones translated the book with care and skill.

The debt to my wife and children that I contracted in writing the Italian edition has now accumulated interest.

Nicola Acocella
University of Rome 'La Sapienza', March 1997

Symbols

a	coefficient measuring sensitivity of investment to the interest rate
A	autonomous expenditure
b_t	benefits at time t
B	total discounted benefits; in a different setting, public debt
B_t	total budget deficit or surplus
BMB	bank monetary base (bank reserves)
BP	deficit or surplus on the balance of payments in real terms
BP_m	deficit or surplus on the balance of payments in monetary terms
c	marginal (and average) propensity to consume
c_t	costs at time t
C	total discounted costs; in a different setting, consumption
Cg	government consumption
CA	current account in real terms
CA_m	current account in monetary terms
CR	loans
D	deposits
DCE	domestic credit expansion
e	nominal exchange rate
e_r	real exchange rate
ε_m	import elasticity
ε_x	export elasticity
g	gross mark-up rate

G	government expenditure
Gp	primary government expenditure
GDP	gross domestic product
h	ratio between currency in circulation and deposits
i	nominal interest rate
I	private investment
Ig	government net investment
INT	interest on public debt
IRR	internal rate of return
j	ratio between bank monetary base and deposits
k	fraction of income held as monetary balances
K	capital
KA	net capital movements
L_s	money supply
L_s^1	outside money
L_s^2	inside money
LF	labour force
M	imports
m	propensity to import
M_w	Rest of the World imports
m_w	Rest of the World propensity to import
MB	monetary base
MRS	marginal rate of substitution
$MRTS$	marginal rate of technical substitution
MRT	marginal rate of transformation
N	employment
NPV	net present value
p	price or absolute price level (in the home country)
$\dot{p}$	inflation rate
p^e	expected price
$\dot{p}^e$	expected inflation rate
p_a	participation rate
p_m	import price expressed in terms of foreign currency
p_x	export price expressed in terms of domestic currency
p_w	price of foreign goods in terms of foreign currency
P	population

PMB	the public's monetary base or currency in circulation
π	average labour productivity
q	quantity consumed or supplied in a given period
q_x	quantity exported
q_m	quantity imported
Q	quantity produced since the beginning of production
r	real interest rate
R	profits
S	savings
t	time; in a different setting, tax rate
T	time horizon; in a different setting, total transactions; in still another setting, taxes or current revenues; sometimes used to indicate taxes less transfers
Tr	total government transfers
Tr_c	current transfers less interest
Tr_k	capital transfers
Tr_h	transfers to households
TT	terms of trade
u	utility function (or level); in another setting, income multiplier; in still another setting, unemployment rate
U	total unemployment
v	sensitivity of speculative demand for money to the interest rate
V	money velocity of circulation
w	wage unit or unit labour cost
W	welfare function (or level); in a different setting, wages
X	supply or consumption of a good in a microeconomic setting; exports in a macroeconomic setting
Y	income as output or demand; sometimes, tax base, Y_s = output, Y_d = demand
Y_n	natural rate of employment income
Y_w	Rest of the World income
$\bar{Y}$	Full employment income
z	money multiplier

1 Introduction

1.1 Economic policy

The reader about to embark on the study of economic policy will very probably already be familiar with the principles of economic analysis, and it is to this discipline that we will turn to introduce our subject.

Economic analysis examines the individual or aggregate decisions of private economic agents about what they produce, exchange and consume. These decisions are taken with specific objectives in mind, objectives that represent criteria for ordering the various possible situations in which agents might find themselves. For example, according to neoclassical theory consumers choose the combination of goods that maximises their utility, while entrepreneurs choose the quantity of output and the combination of inputs for each good that maximise their profit.

Economic analysis does not usually examine the behaviour of 'public' economic agents, which are attributed with collective aims. The choices of the latter – for example, government decisions regarding the level of expenditure or taxation – enter the macro- and microeconomic models of economic analysis as simple data. At most, alternative hypotheses regarding the level of government expenditure or taxation[1] are considered in order to acquire some indication of what changes there would be in the performance of individual economic agents or the economy as a whole. Our study of economic policy must therefore complete many aspects of this analysis on three different levels.

1 First and foremost, we must seek to understand the process by which government makes its choices, taking as given its objectives and the roles and scope of

---

[1] In this case the variables are said to vary parametrically.

1

different institutions[2] and assuming that we know how the economy functions. This is the '*current*' *choices* level.

2 A second level of analysis concerns the very existence and respective structures of government and the market. In standard economic analysis both of these institutions are considered 'natural', the latter perhaps more so than the former. The scope of each is given and possible areas of overlap and relationships of substitutability or complementarity do not emerge. In other words, economic analysis does not address questions about the extent to which government replaces the market – and vice versa – or the degree to which government is necessary for the market or reinforces it. Beyond the specific case of government and the market, a more general issue regards the types of higher-level economic institutions that are necessary or useful in governing a society. This is the level of *institutional (constitutional) choices*, which we reach once we know society's objectives and how the economy functions under different possible institutions.

3 The final level of analysis concerns the identification of socially desirable goals. A similar problem is dealt with in economic analysis when the firm is realistically conceived as a combination of diverse interests rather than in terms of the classic figure of the entrepreneur (who is both owner and manager). Simplifying, it can be argued that a firm is composed of the owner, who seeks to maximise profits; the manager, who instead seeks to increase the firm's size (sales) or its rate of growth, since his income, power and prestige (the manager's ultimate objectives) depend on these variables; and workers, who are primarily concerned with the level of their real wages. An attempt to define a preference function for the firm must take account of the preference functions of the economic agents that operate within it. Similarly, for society as a whole we seek to derive a system of preferences (and hence objectives) from the preferences (objectives) of the various components of the community. This level of our study of economic policy therefore seeks to identify social goals (the *social choices* level).

We shall see that this is only one of the ways of determining society's objectives. It is in fact an indirect approach: society's assessment of reality only emerges from individual preferences. An alternative approach would be to establish direct social 'rankings' of possible situations rather than ones mediated by individual preferences.

Without going into further detail here, we can define economic policy as the discipline that studies public economic action, inasmuch as it studies all three levels: the 'current'

---

[2] The term 'institution' has been given a variety of meanings in the social sciences. However, these can be reduced essentially to the following two. First, the term may indicate a set of 'rules' that regulate, in a lasting manner, the relationships within a group of agents; in this sense, for example, marriage, private property and the market are all institutions. A second meaning extends the definition to include the agents involved in implementing the rules and the resources necessary to do so; in this second sense, the government, the family and the Mafia are all institutions. We will use the term in both senses.

choices of the government, the choice of higher-level institutions (i.e., the definition of society's 'economic constitution') and the identification of social preferences or objectives. Economic policy thus complements the analysis of the behaviour of economic agents and the functioning of economic systems conducted in economic analysis. Economic policy and economic analysis have in fact been conceived as separate disciplines for the sake of convenience within the more general framework of economic science to enable a more in-depth analysis of the issues involved. Just as in economic analysis it is essential to understand government action, drawing from the discipline of economic policy, in the latter it is equally crucial to understand the functioning of the private economic system, borrowing this knowledge from economic analysis.

Two clarifications are in order. First, economic policy can serve as a guide to public action only with the help of a variety of disciplines: in addition to economic analysis, these include philosophy, political science, constitutional and administrative law, statistics, econometrics and many others. With this in mind, we must caution that the knowledge provided by economic analysis cannot usually be used as a guide to action without the qualifying and mediating contributions of these other disciplines.[3]

The second clarification regards the possibility (or necessity, as some would argue) of widening the definition of economic policy to include any conceptualisation that uses the knowledge of economic analysis (and other disciplines) as a guide to action for any economic agent whatsoever, especially the largest and most powerful. This would comprise not only government and other public bodies but also big business and industrial associations or lobbies, as well as 'big labour' (Caffè, 1966, vol. I, pp. 13–14). Such a broad range of study would correspond to the second of the two ultimate tasks of economic science identified by Knight (1952): first, understanding and explaining certain phenomena, and, second, using that understanding to guide our action.

This broader definition has only recently received significant attention, but it will be largely reappraised in the light of the approach we adopt in chapter 9, where we characterise economic policy as a *strategic game*.

1.2 Economic reality and social preferences

A question that will recur throughout this book is why and under what conditions do we require the presence of an economic agent with social or collective objectives in an economic system composed of individuals who essentially pursue their own interests. The need for such an agent is clearly related to the possibility that the operation of the economy may be judged unsatisfactory in some way; that is, it fails to satisfy certain wants. Such a judgement requires a comparison of reality and desires: if, for example, we

---

[3] For example, in Keynesian economic theory an increase in investment, whether public or private, causes income to increase by some multiple. Income could be increased by raising public investment. However, the precise amount of such investment can only be established if we know the value of certain parameters, which calls for statistical or econometric investigation; at the same time, the feasibility of increasing public investment must be assessed in both political terms (the possibility of winning parliamentary approval) and administrative terms (the possibility of effective and timely implementation).

have (involuntary) unemployment in a system based entirely on private action and this state of affairs is considered socially undesirable, intervention by an agent that pursues social aims is required.

This text has no intention of explaining further how economic systems work. Although we will draw on the relevant areas in economic analysis, our focus will be on social (or public or collective) *desiderata*, especially the way in which these are (can be, must be) formulated, which is the subject of social choice theory. We can then proceed with a comparison of desires and reality to derive society's institutional choices (what role to assign to different institutions) and government's current choices (the specific economic measures to be taken).

Bear in mind that the validity of many of our conclusions regarding institutional and current choices closely depends on the validity of the analytical tools employed, in particular the theories adopted to explain the performance of the economic system. At least as much as other sciences, economic analysis does not offer, nor can it offer, a body of objectively true statements (Myrdal, 1953, 1958). Each economic theory highlights certain more or less important aspects of reality, and the economic policy scholar must exercise special care in choosing a reference model. More specifically, we will see that two opposing 'visions' underlie the different theories: one that casts its gaze on economic reality through 'Panglossian' lenses, emphasising the 'harmony' and the ability to adjust (perhaps hidden but undoubtedly present) of certain institutions, such as the market; and another more pessimistic (or simply more realistic) view that underscores the negative aspects of those institutions in terms of 'failures' and instability.

1.3 Outline of the text and organisation of the discipline

In introducing the issues of economic policy, the three levels of choice examined by the discipline were presented in the following order in section 1.1: current choices, institutional choices, social choices. Note, however, that the logical order of these issues is precisely the reverse. No institutional or current decision can be taken without first establishing social preferences; given these, institutional choices at the various levels can be taken. Once our higher-level institutions have been established, current choices can then be made.

The text normally follows the logical order. More specifically, in part I (chapters 2, 3 and 4) we examine the process of identifying social objectives. Part II (chapters 5, 6 and 7) deals in a highly abstract way with the institutional choices consequent upon the various possible social aims, principally with reference to the government–market dichotomy. We frequently return to the question in more realistic fashion later in the text. In general, the first and second parts cover the branch of economic policy known in the literature as *welfare economics*.

Part III (chapters 8 and 9) and part VII (chapter 19) also examine general issues regarding institutional choices. More specifically, part III examines policy models: given the social preferences that are to guide public action, as well as the analytical models developed by economic analysis, we must deal with the problem of planning, i.e., coordinating the use of available tools to satisfy those preferences, achieving the

Table 1.1. *An overview of the discipline of economic policy*

Part of the discipline	Subject matter	Parts and chapters of the book
1 Welfare economics	1 Identification of social preferences	Part I Chapters 2, 3, 4
	2 Identification of optimal institutions at the constitutional level	Part II Chapters 5, 6, 7
2 Theory of economic policy	1 Planning criteria (design and structure of public intervention)	Parts III and VII Chapters 8, 19
	2 The actual process of public decision-making	Part III Chapter 9
3 Theory of current decisions (corrective and structural)	1 Microeconomic decisions	Part IV Chapters 10, 11, 12
	2 Macroeconomic decisions	
	2.1 in a closed economy	Part V Chapters 13, 14, 15
	2.2 in an open economy	Part VI Chapters 16, 17, 18

multiple objectives of government action. This (normative) approach to public intervention is then compared with the actual process of public decision making (the 'positive'
theory of economic policy). Part VII seeks to establish the characteristics and the
optimality requirements of government decisions that involve a number of time periods
or that are entrusted to separate political authorities.[4] Both parts belong to the *theory of
economic policy*, which addresses questions regarding the definition and structure of
government intervention.

Current choices can be divided into:

(a) 'structural' choices (such as those regarding the type of financial system), which
    are decisions on institutional, but not constitutional, matters; and
(b) 'corrective' choices (for example, a change in income tax brackets).

The *theory of current decisions* is examined in the remainder of the book. In parts IV,
V and VI we will examine, respectively, microeconomic policies (chapters 10, 11 and 12),
macroeconomic policies in a closed economy (chapters 13, 14 and 15) and macroeconomic policies in an open economy (chapters 16, 17 and 18).[5]

An overview of the content of the discipline is given in table 1.1. The plan of the book
and its division into parts and chapters is also presented here.

---

[4] The treatment of this point does not follow the strict logical order. For reasons of clarity, we have
chosen to defer to the final chapter issues that in purely logical terms should be examined in part III.
[5] Obviously, the division shown here contains areas of overlap at the borders between sections,
especially with regard to institutions.

1.4 Summary

1 Strictly speaking, economic policy is the discipline that studies public economic action. It examines the process through which social preferences are formed (social choices), the choice of institutions and the current decisions of government.

2 More generally, the field of economic policy comprises any discipline that uses the knowledge of economic analysis and other disciplines as a guide to action for any economic agent.

3 The question that recurs at each of the levels noted in point 1 above is that regarding the foundations of a social (or collective) point of view distinct from individual preferences.

4 These foundations are to be sought in economic analysis and other social sciences.

5 The parts of this book are arranged in decreasing order of abstraction. The first part deals with the process through which social preferences are defined. The second concerns the implications of those preferences for social institutions, in particular the choice between government and the market. (These two parts constitute welfare economics.) The third part outlines the structure of rational public action and provides a more realistic picture of the agents that form society and the process of defining and implementing government action. Parts IV, V and VI examine government action in various fields at both the micro- and macroeconomic levels and in closed and open economies. The final part returns to the analysis of the rational organisation of government economic action.

1.5 Key concepts

Institution
Institutional, constitutional choice
Current choices
Social choices
Economic constitution
Welfare economics
Theory of economic policy
Theory of current decisions

PART I

DEFINING SOCIAL PREFERENCES

2 Individual preferences and social preferences

2.1 Welfare economics

Two approaches can be taken in identifying a society's preferences and/or objectives: one positive, the other normative. ← *key word.*

The *positive approach* seeks to identify the preferences and objectives effectively held by a given society in a certain period. Since every community is the expression of varied *leads to* rather than monolithic interests, we must tackle the problem of identifying and, if necessary, synthesising multiple and possibly conflicting preferences. In the abstract, there are a variety of solutions to this difficulty, but in a democracy it seems appropriate to begin by considering policymakers[1] as the persons that express (or should express) the preferences of society as a whole. Examining policy guidelines independently provided by policymakers, reviewing their consultations with technical experts[2] and/or identifying preferences 'revealed' through their actual choices[3] are essentially the methods we have at our disposal. We can, of course, debate if and to what extent we are *What public* dealing with the true preferences of a *society as a whole*, or if politicians pursue the *does.* interests of only a part of society, or even their own private goals. Such issues are important (and we discuss them later), but they can be set aside at this stage. The positive approach is of interest when we wish to determine the specific content of public intervention. It has therefore been suggested that economists should identify the preferences that society reveals through its representatives in order to provide advice on the appropriate measures to be taken by government.

Such an approach will prove useful in dealing with the problems examined in part III

---

[1] For the moment it is not important to identify the specific institutional referent of this term (parliament, government, political parties).

[2] As suggested by Frisch (1959).

[3] This method can be borrowed from economic analysis, which uses it to construct consumer preference functions.

9

(chapters 8 and 9). In parts I and II, however, we look for a criterion for assessing the performance of an economic system from the point of view of the goals that its members wish to assign to it.

The second approach, the *normative theory of social choice*, seeks to identify the preferences and objectives that a society *should* have on the basis of some ethical or political postulate – introduced or borrowed by economic policy scholars – about the meaning of 'collective interest' or 'public good'. We can use such a postulate – or the social preferences derived from it – to assess the 'optimality', or lack thereof, of alternative institutions.[4] In particular, we might be able to establish whether an economic system featuring certain institutions (e.g., the market) rather than others (e.g., government ownership) is more or less capable of satisfying certain social goals or preferences.

The normative approach is none other than welfare economics. In aiming to define an overarching criterion or objective of economic policy, welfare economics enables us to give systematic unity to economic policy itself and provides a point of reference for dealing with specific problems. It therefore represents *the logic of economic policy* (Caffè, 1966, p. 86).

Welfare economics became the central and relatively abstract nucleus of economic policy when economists, borrowing from philosophy,[5] turned their attention to defining the idea of public interest. They thus introduced concepts such as total welfare, economic welfare and social welfare, which define criteria of social choice and have been used to assess the performance of economic systems founded on the pursuit of individual interests. This has cast light on areas of market 'failure', where the intervention of an agent with collective goals might produce greater social welfare.

Such areas of market failure have normally been analysed with reference to microeconomic issues (resource allocation, personal distribution of income). This book will extend the definition of failures to include macroeconomic dysfunctions associated with the 'instability' of economic systems, as revealed by the existence of involuntary unemployment, inflation and so on.

In abstract, then, welfare economics is primarily concerned with defining the criteria of social choice. At a more practical level it uses such criteria to assess economies based on different institutions (principally government and the market) in order to identify the most desirable.

This chapter will discuss criteria of social choice. Chapter 3 will be devoted to the analysis of one of these: allocative or Pareto efficiency, with a brief discussion of the conditions required to satisfy this principle. Chapter 4 will analyse additional criteria and offer some details regarding the corresponding optimal social states, without however making specific reference to institutional aspects. Chapters 5, 6 and 7 will take up the discussion of optimal institutions; that is, rules that incorporate the various possible criteria of social choice.

---

[4] Following Sen (1970a), we mention two other possible applications of social choice criteria: (a) the theory of committees, which we briefly discuss further on; (b) social criticism or the assessment of social policy, which postulate principles of social choice that are not satisfied by existing mechanisms.

[5] More specifically, they drew on the branch known as 'public philosophy' or 'civic philosophy', which deals with questions involving the individual as a citizen.

2.2 Constructing a social ordering

We have so far spoken of social preferences, objectives and choices. More generally, the issue of social choice can be approached in a number of ways aimed at defining one or another of the following concepts: social ordering, collective choice rule, social decision function, social preference function, social objective, policy objective. There are numerous differences between these concepts and we cannot analyse all of them in detail in this book.[6] Deferring to chapter 8 our definition of a policy objective, which we have used in an intuitive fashion up to this point, for the moment we will confine our discussion to clarifying the meanings of 'ordering' and 'social preference function' (also known as 'social utility function' or 'social welfare function').

A *social ordering* is a ranking of the possible situations (*social states* or *states of the world*[7]) in which a society may find itself. It identifies situations that, from the social point of view, are either *indifferent* between themselves, *preferred* to others or *worse* than others. An ordering must normally have certain properties, including transitivity (if social state *a* is preferred to social state *b*, and *b* is preferred to *c*, then *a* is preferred to *c*). The ordering may be incomplete, in the sense that it does not rank all possible states of the world. Some states may not be comparable under the rule governing the ranking. For a more detailed discussion see Sen (1970a, chapter 1).

If certain conditions are met (see Sen, 1970a; Mas-Colell *et al.*, 1995, chapter 22), the social ordering can be expressed as a function, known as a 'social welfare function' (SWF).

Each social state is a complete description of the situation in which society finds itself in relation to one or more human actions or natural events. Although we are especially interested in the economic features of each state, at least in principle we cannot ignore other aspects of social life, such as individual liberties and rights.

For example, in a society composed of two individuals, social state *a* represents a certain allocation of resources (let us suppose one member of society has 10 bushels of wheat and 20 sheep and the other has 15 bushels of wheat and 8 sheep) and some attribution of individual rights and liberties (both individuals have the right to cultivate the land and tend their livestock on separate plots; both also have equal political rights). In a possible social state *b* all resources and rights could be controlled by one individual while the other has nothing and must comply with the decisions of the former. Obviously, there are an infinite number of possible states in which a society might find itself. As in the preceding example, some of these may differ considerably; others might differ less markedly: in a hypothetical social state *c*, conditions might be exactly the same as in *a*, with the sole difference that the first individual has 1 peck less of wheat and the second has one more.

The problem of constructing a social ordering of the various possible states of the world is formally similar to that faced by a consumer in neoclassical theory, who must order possible alternatives (essentially, baskets of potentially consumable goods) into a

---

[6] Some of these are defined in Sen (1970a; 1982, pp. 285–6).
[7] The former term is that used in Arrow (1951); the latter has been used more recently in the context of social choice theory by some authors (Boadway and Bruce, 1984).

ranking of preferences (or indifference relations). However, the construction of a social ordering is a much more complex task.[8] Whereas individual preferences can only be expressed directly over social states, in the case of a social ordering the following issues must also be addressed:

1 choosing between direct and indirect social orderings; and
2 choosing between different methods of aggregating individual preferences in the case of indirect orderings.

We will tackle these issues in the following two subsections.

2.2.1 Choosing between direct and indirect social orderings

The first problem that arises in defining a social ordering concerns the role to give to individual preferences over social states. The social ordering may be *directly* related to social states on the basis of some external principle. For example, accepting an equality principle might prompt us to judge the various states of the world in relation to the value of some index of inequality: social state *a* will be preferred to state *b* if and only if the value of the Gini coefficient[9] – or some other inequality indicator – in state *a* is less than its value in state *b*.

By contrast, a social ordering is *indirect* if, again on the basis of some (different) external criterion, it is constructed exclusively in relation to the preferences of individuals: the social preference is a mere reflection of the latter. As we shall see, welfare economics makes more frequent use of indirect orderings, which appear to be consistent with the tenets of liberalism. More precisely, they are based on the principle of *ethical individualism* ('*welfarism*', as Sen terms it; see, for example, Sen, 1987), i.e., the view that (i) each individual is the best judge of his or her preferences and (ii) the value of possible social states is determined by the individual's perception of these states (and the satisfaction obtained). This is the only allowable basis for assessing social states, and anything not considered relevant by the individual must not be assessed by society as a whole.

There are two types of objection to indirect orderings.

1 First, one can object to the idea that the social ranking must only take account of the satisfaction effectively enjoyed by individuals at a certain point in time, ignoring other aspects of the social state that might be worthy of consideration, such as the existence and ability to exercise rights and liberties and the quantity of goods actually available to the different members of the community. Some argue that these other aspects may have social value in and of themselves, regardless of how they are valued (at a certain point in

---

[8] We set aside the fact that the social ordering may not necessarily be expressed in terms of a social preference function.

[9] This is a statistical measure of the concentration (or inequality) of some feature (in our case, income) of a population. Its value can range from zero, corresponding to a perfectly equal distribution, to one, indicating complete concentration of the feature in one individual.

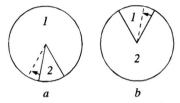

Figure 2.1

time) by individuals. For instance, consider (following Sen, 1982) a redistribution of income in relation to two alternative starting positions, *a* and *b* (see figure 2.1).

In both cases the redistribution is made in favour of individual 2 at the expense of individual 1: at the level of the two individuals' satisfaction the cases are therefore similar in some respects. They could nevertheless be judged differently because the person adversely affected by the redistribution has a different starting income in the two cases. Some might look favourably on the redistribution in case *a* and disapprove of case *b* (although individual 1 suffers a reduction in satisfaction in both instances) inasmuch as (relatively) little is taken from someone with plenty in case *a*, while a (relatively) large amount is taken from someone with little in *b*. However, in judging the two situations in this fashion, we take account not only of the *consequences* of the social states with regard to the satisfaction of the two individuals but also of other aspects of the states themselves (in this case, the initial distribution of income), a possibility denied to us under ethical individualism.[10]

The example given here refers to the distribution of income, but as noted earlier social states also differ in the rights and liberties guaranteed to members of society. There are two conceptions of liberty, as Isaiah Berlin (1969, p. 131) distinguishes in his classic essay: *negative liberty*, defined as 'the absence of coercion' by other individuals or the state; and *positive liberty*, which consists in the ability 'to be somebody, not nobody', to be a 'thinking, willing, active being, bearing responsibility' for one's choices and able to explain them by references to ones own ideas and purposes. This second concept of liberty, which may conflict with the first, is closely linked to the availability of essential goods and hence to the distribution of income. An adequate supply of goods may well be a necessary, if not sufficient, condition for individuals to enjoy positive liberty.

---

[10] The contrast is between utilitarianism, which leads to welfarism, and the absolute rights of the Kantian view (Boadway and Bruce, 1984, p. 176).

   According to some, if rights are considered as part of the social state, they can become the object of preferences (of a higher order than those regarding other aspects of the state of the world) (see Pattanaik and Suzumura, 1994; Hammond, 1995). This would eliminate any *a priori* definition (considered arbitrary) of the content of the rights, which would be tied to the preferences of individuals.

   We cannot undertake what would be a very complex discussion here. Let us simply note the possibility of justifying a direct ordering of social states on the basis of a belief in absolute rights or on the basis of the fact that the preferences revealed by individuals in some context (such as in the social contract: see section *4.5) might require that we ignore individual preferences expressed in another context (e.g., for current decisions).

2 The second objection to indirect orderings regards the fact that in reducing the situation of society to the satisfactions of individuals, the latter's preferences are often considered to be given. This is particularly the case with the neoclassical school, which usually accepts the canons of *methodological individualism*, according to which every proposition about a group of individuals is reducible to propositions concerning the behaviour of separate individuals, without going into the factors that formed it, especially the influence of the environment and the attitudes and judgements of groups and so on (Schumpeter, 1954, p. 889). In reality, individual preferences and the behaviour of individuals do not emerge independently of the economic and social context, but are instead affected by many factors, including other people's habits (Duesenberry, 1967), fashion and social 'norms' or habits (Leibenstein, 1950; Etzioni, 1985), which expose preferences to manipulation, especially by firms. In other words, individual preferences, which are supposed to guide social choices through indirect orderings, are in fact themselves shaped by other forces (*endogenous preferences*). There is thus a risk that indirect orderings do not reflect the original, 'genuine' preferences (or at least the interests) of all individuals in a society, but rather the final preferences of some fraction of them.

Advocates of ethical individualism consider direct ordering unacceptable since the preferences of individuals are replaced by those of one person (for example, a philosopher or social reformer) – perhaps not even a member of the community – with paternalistic or authoritarian consequences. Such a risk undoubtedly exists, but it can be practically eliminated by setting out which features of the social state, such as certain rights and liberties, must be preserved by granting them constitutional status. This can safeguard individuals not only from external forces but also from forces within the community itself, perhaps to even a greater degree than would the use of indirect social orderings. Given the potential for manipulating preferences, indirect orderings do not protect individuals from the action of others at all; they simply make the manipulation more subtle compared with that reflected in direct orderings.

2.2.2 Aggregating individual preferences

If we choose to construct an indirect social ordering, we must tackle the problem of how to aggregate individual preferences when they differ, as they usually do, i.e., when each individual has his own ordering of possible social states.

To clarify the problem, consider the following example. The possible social states are shown in table 2.1. We can assume that individual 1 prefers state *b* to state *a* and *a* to *c*. In state *b* he would own all the available resources, whereas he would receive only part of them in *a*; in situation *c*, he would have somewhat less wheat than in *a*. Conversely, we can suppose that 2's preference ranking would be *c*, *a*, *b* (in decreasing order).

Note that the individual preferences are different. If both individuals had the same preference ranking (say, *b*, *a*, *c*), the social preference would be identical to the individual preferences. However, differing individual preferences make it difficult to determine an aggregate preference function.

Table 2.1. *Endowments of two individuals in different social states*

	Individual 1		Individual 2	
Social states	Wheat	Sheep	Wheat	Sheep
a	10	20	15	8
b	25	28	0	0
c	9	20	16	8

Aggregation has at least three controversial aspects. They involve:

1 the representation of individual preferences, with particular regard to the *measurement* of satisfactions;
2 the possibility of *comparing* the positions of different individuals;
3 the *aggregation rule*.

Let us consider these in order, limiting ourselves to an intuitive discussion of the issues.

1 There are at least two ways to measure individual satisfactions: ordinal measurement and cardinal measurement. The former was used in the previous example to express the preferences of the two members of our hypothetical society with regard to the social states *a*, *b* and *c*. This is how we are accustomed to indicating consumer satisfactions when we use Pareto's indifference curves. An alternative method is to assign cardinal rather than ordinal numbers to the satisfactions associated with the various social states: for example, the first individual might derive a utility of 50 from state *a*, 120 from state *b* and 49 from state *c*.

Opinions differ as to the possibility – or appropriateness – of using one or the other type of measurement. In particular, some share Pareto's belief that we only have ordinal 'information' regarding such preferences, and that is sufficient for the economist. Others, such as Pigou and the utilitarians, opt for cardinal measurement of individual satisfactions. The issue of measuring individual satisfactions is not of great importance in itself, but rather in relation to the position we take with regard to comparability, as we will see shortly.

2 There are also differences regarding the possibility of making interpersonal comparisons of utility: some are willing to admit such comparisons, arguing that different individuals have equal 'ability to experience' and thus their satisfactions are 'commensurable'; others, however, deny that such interpersonal comparisons are possible.

The value content of the different positions on interpersonal comparability is clear: those who start from egalitarian premises are more likely to admit such comparability, while those who base their views on other values tend to avoid any explicit comparison. Note that in both cases value judgements are introduced, i.e., ethical or political assessments are formulated not only by those who are willing to compare utilities but also by those who argue for non-comparability.

Interpersonal comparability of utilities was accepted by the utilitarians and was adopted by the English economist Pigou in *The Economics of Welfare* (Pigou, 1920). Although its publication does not necessarily mark the founding of the discipline, the work both sanctioned the field's official name and gave substance to a particular *theoretical orientation*. Beginning with Robbins (1932), this stance was opposed by subsequent authors who, on the basis of the position sustained by Pareto even before Pigou's work appeared, argued that economics was not able to pronounce on the interpersonal comparability of utilities.

Robbins' essay provoked a wide-ranging debate that gave rise to an attempt to reconstruct welfare economics on a non-utilitarian foundation, in particular denying the assumption of equal capacity for satisfaction used by Pigou but discarded by Pareto. This strand (known as 'new' welfare economics) accepted the foundations of Pareto's analysis but sought to overcome some of its limitations.

Comparability is not independent of the type of information we have about the utility of individuals: it would not make much sense (if not in special cases) to assume the comparability of one person's satisfaction (or change in satisfaction) with that of another if it could not at least in theory be measured cardinally. If we were in fact to do so, we could state, for example, that a certain fact gives rise to a benefit (in terms of satisfaction) to an individual that is greater than the disadvantage caused to another individual without knowing how much one or the other has gained or lost in cardinal terms; but this would not be logically consistent. The opposite is not true, however: someone who accepts the cardinal measurement of individual preferences might not necessarily accept the possibility of interpersonal comparisons.

A more rigorous analysis of the problems in points 1 and 2 above is given in section *2.3.

3 The last problem to be addressed in constructing a social ordering is that of selecting a method for aggregating individual preferences. One option is to sum satisfactions, which can be done in certain circumstances (briefly, when individual satisfactions can be measured cardinally and are comparable), but not in others. When this method can be used there are a variety of other aggregation functions available (see section 4.2). If preferences are measured ordinally and interpersonal comparisons are not possible, the aggregation method is, as we shall see, a special one and enables us to construct partial social rankings only (the Pareto principle; see section 3.1). If we set aside mathematical or logical rules in favour of institutional and procedural methods, we can aggregate individual preferences through voting procedures, which we will examine in section *3.6.

The reader should now have a general idea of the many difficulties we face in formulating direct or indirect social orderings. It should also be clear that the solutions to these problems depend to a great degree on subjective assessments of what is considered appropriate. In other words, they require us to make *value judgements*; that is, personal preconceptions, beliefs and ethical, religious or political judgements that express subjective views about *what should be*.[11]

In some cases the introduction of value judgements is manifest, as when we attempt to formulate a direct ordering of social states. In other cases it is less evident and, as such, more insidious; this is the case not only in old welfare economics but also in its newer version. To construct indirect orderings, new welfare economics uses the principles of ethical and methodological individualism and, in the Pareto variant, rejects the interpersonal comparability of utilities. These views are not always explicitly stated. Even when they are, there is still a risk that the social ordering will reflect not the genuine preferences of individuals (and with them the original value judgements) but rather those of social 'persuaders', precisely because, as mentioned in section 2.2.1, the process by which tastes and values are formed is not analysed.

*2.3 'Information' about individual utilities and interpersonal comparisons

Having clarified the serious limitations and distortions involved in any social valuation of states of the world that incorporates a 'welfarist' premise, we can now turn to the additional difficulties that arise within this approach, which, despite some criticism, has many adherents.

The problems regard the so-called *invariance requirements*[12] and concern:

(a) measuring individual utilities; and
(b) comparing individual utilities.

The 'information'[13] available in both cases can come in different forms. In measuring utilities, we have information related to:

1 ordinal measurability;
2 cardinal measurability;
3 ratio scale measurability;
4 absolute scale measurability.

---

[11] By contrast, factual judgements are statements about *what is*. In using the distinction between value and factual judgements we do not wish to lend support to the view that they can be separated in the field of economic analysis, which the positivists argue is the branch of economic science dedicated to the study of *what is*. In this respect we largely agree with Myrdal's position (Myrdal, 1953, 1958). The text refers instead to the social orderings that must guide economic policy decisions, and in this regard nearly all economists are now willing to acknowledge, at least in abstract, that such orderings must be oriented by some point of view (or objective) having the nature of a value judgement, even if some often seem to think that broad or unanimous acceptance of a certain value judgement causes it to lose this quality and become instead an 'objective' proposition.

The current nearly unanimous acceptance of the need to use value judgements in constructing a social ordering follows on the failure of new welfare economics to construct social orderings without external value judgements or based on widely shared beliefs.

[12] As will become clear, invariance requirements refer to the allowable transformations and comparisons of the different measures of utility.

[13] The various meanings that can be given to this term will be clarified later in the section.

1 *Ordinal measurability*, so called because it shares the properties of ordinal numbers, requires minimal information. It is used to construct Pareto indifference curves. It enables us to compare the utility levels of a single individual but not the magnitude of changes in those levels. An ordinal utility function is *invariant* up to an increasing monotonic transformation. In particular, the utility function of individual i, u^i, can be replaced by the function $f^i(u^i)$, where $df^i/du^i > 0$, without any loss of information and therefore without effect on the ordering of social states from the individual point of view.[14]

Such a function allows us to determine only the *sign* of the change in utility caused by a variation in the goods available; that is, it only allows us to say whether the bundle of goods a provides greater, less or equal satisfaction than bundle b: if we have $u^i(b) > u^i(a)$, a and b will retain the same order when we use some increasing monotonic function of u^i, $f^i(u^i)$; that is, $f^i(u^i(b)) > f^i(u^i(a))$. In this case, if the individual possesses the bundle of goods b rather than a, his utility is greater but we cannot say by how much. We cannot say if it increases by a large or small amount, or if in shifting from bundle a to bundle b the utility of i increases more or less than it would if i shifted from b to another possible bundle c, such that $u^i(b) > u^i(c)$. In other words, ordinal measurement does not necessarily provide us with the sign of the second derivative of the utility function (which compares the relative size of the two increases). An ordinal measurement can be obtained from an individual by asking him about his preferences with regard to various alternative positions.

2 *Cardinal measurability* of utility provides more information, allowing us to compare changes in a person's utility caused by variations in the bundle of goods at his disposal. The cardinal utility function is defined up to a positive affine transformation; i.e., y^i and z^i are equivalent cardinal measures of the individual's utility if $z^i = a^i + b^i y^i$, with $b^i > 0$. Temperature scales are an example of cardinal measurement: if y indicates the temperature in Celsius, the corresponding value on the Fahrenheit scale is given by $z = 32 + 1.8y$.

This form of measurement allows us to compare changes in utility caused by variations in the quantity of goods available and ensures that the ratios between the variations in utility produced by such changes do not vary with respect to the scale; in other words, it preserves the sign of the second derivative (which is important in defining risk aversion). Specifically, cardinal measurement enables us to say, for example, that person i gains more utility moving from bundle a to bundle b than in moving from b to c, because a positive affine transformation would preserve this information. Suppose that a consists of 10 units of a single good (for simplicity), b of 11 units and c of 12 units: a cardinal utility function would allow us to affirm (reject) the principle of decreasing marginal utility of that good for individual i if the increase in utility obtained in moving from a to b was greater (less) than that obtained in shifting from b to c.

This kind of measurement was extensively used in economic analysis before Pareto

---

[14] More generally, we have invariance with respect to every strictly increasing transformation and not just differentiable transformations with positive derivatives.

and is still used today, especially in studying choices made by economic agents under uncertainty. Von Neumann and Morgenstern (1944) showed that if certain axioms about consumer preferences are satisfied, then under uncertainty these preferences can be represented by cardinal utility functions. Thus, in such a context doubts regarding the possibility of actually obtaining information in cardinal terms could be resolved.

3 *Ratio scale measurability* offers even more detailed information about an individual's utility. In this case, utility is measured like weight, in pounds or grams, with a fixed ratio between scales having the same origin (zero on one is equal to zero on the other). Utility is defined up to a positive linear transformation: $z^i = b^i y^i$, with $b^i > 0$.

This would enable us to compare not only absolute changes in utility – as with cardinal measurability – but also proportional changes, i.e., rates of growth, in a way that is independent of the measurement scale. It is easily shown that with ratio scale measurability if

$$\frac{y^i(c) - y^i(b)}{y^i(b)} > \frac{y^i(b) - y^i(a)}{y^i(a)}$$

then we also have

$$\frac{z^i(c) - z^i(b)}{z^i(b)} > \frac{z^i(b) - z^i(a)}{z^i(a)}$$

4 Finally, *absolute scale measurability* involves assigning a unique real number to each satisfaction and offers the maximum information possible regarding individual utilities.

Let us now turn to comparing utilities between different individuals (point (b) at the beginning of this section). Three types of information are possible: *non-comparability*, *partial comparability* (limited to only a part of the information on individual utilities, such as changes rather than levels) and *full comparability* (comparability of all information on individual utilities).

Our assumptions about comparability may not be independent of those about measurability. For example, it is difficult to imagine comparing changes in utility between different people that are not comparable for a single individual owing to the availability of purely ordinal indicators only.[15] By contrast, if utility is measured on an absolute scale, we are assured of full comparability of utilities precisely because we have assumed the existence of a single evaluation scale that allows us to assign a unique real number to each situation: since they are unambiguously determined, the real numbers thus obtained can be compared among themselves (Boadway and Bruce, 1984, p. 145). Note that the greater the comparability assumed among the utilities of different individuals, the easier it is to order the various social states for society as a whole.

In this section we have discussed 'informational requirements' with regard to measurability and comparability, just as we examined 'information' in terms of utility or other aspects of a social state in the previous section. We must now ask what sort of

---

[15] A possible exception is that represented by Rawls' criterion (see section *4.5).

information are we talking about when we refer to measurability and comparability: is it 'knowledge' about factual states obtained with appropriate measurement techniques (in which case we would be dealing with more or less easily acquired *objective* information) or rather an 'indication' of the value judgements adopted by those – economists or economic policymakers – who propose to construct a social welfare function? (ibid., p. 168). Much of the difference between 'old' welfare economics and utilitarians, on the one hand (Bentham, Mill, Edgeworth, Pigou), and Pareto and new welfare economics, on the other, lies with differences of opinion about measurability and comparability. For the former, a person's utility can be ascertained in cardinal terms and different individuals have the same capacity to 'feel'. By contrast, Pareto and the new welfare economists argue that:

(a) personal utility cannot be measured cardinally in principle, stressing that even those who argue that it can could only measure utility ordinally in practice;

(b) the positions of different individuals are fundamentally non-comparable; even if it were possible in principle to compare them, there would be no way to do so in the real world.

Following Sen (1982, pp. 265ff.), it cannot be denied that interpersonal comparisons of utility may have some *descriptive* content, in addition to being an expression of the value judgements of those who seek to construct a social ordering.

2.4 Summary

1 Economic policy may seek to:
learn the preferences and/or objectives actually present in a given society (the positive approach);
identify the preferences that the society should have on the basis of some ethical or political principle regarding the meaning of public interest (the normative approach).

2 Welfare economics is concerned with the normative approach and represents the theoretical core (logic) of economic policy, through which it is possible to judge the results obtained with different institutions, in particular the market and government.

3 Normative theory seeks to define a ranking (or ordering) of social states. The ordering can be obtained directly, on the basis of some external ethical or political principle, or indirectly if – accepting the liberal principle (ethical individualism) – it is founded solely on the preferences expressed by individuals with regard to the different social states.

4 Indirect orderings overlook aspects of social states such as rights and liberties except when and to the extent that these are reflected in individual preferences; indirect orderings usually consider individual preferences as given (methodological individualism), thus ignoring the possibility that they might be distorted by some other agent (endogenous preferences).

5 The choice between direct and indirect social orderings corresponds to the choice between an explicit external principle (which is at the basis of the direct ordering) or an external principle surreptitiously introduced by 'persuaders' when they distort individual preferences (which in this case would constitute only the formal basis of an indirect ordering).

6 The decision to construct an indirect ordering requires us to solve the difficulty of aggregating individual preferences, which involves:
   (a) the way individual preferences are represented;
   (b) the possibility of interpersonal comparisons;
   (c) the aggregation rule.

7 Individual utilities may be measured either cardinally or ordinally.

8 We can either accept or reject the comparability of individuals' satisfactions.

9 Individual utilities that can be measured cardinally and are comparable can be aggregated by summation or some other mathematical operator. Aggregating non-comparable ordinal preferences is an entirely different process.

10 All social orderings, whether direct or indirect, involve the use of value judgements, which are particularly evident in the case of interpersonal comparisons and the choice of the aggregation rule.

*11 The ordinal measurement of satisfactions is invariant up to an increasing monotonic transformation, which only allows us to determine the sign of the change in utility; cardinal measurement is defined up to a positive affine transformation and allows us to compare absolute variations in utility; ratio scale measurement is defined up to a positive linear transformation and also enables us to compare rates of change in utility; using an absolute scale involves assigning a unique real number to each satisfaction.

*12 We can have full comparability, partial comparability (i.e., limited to certain aspects of satisfactions) or complete non-comparability of utilities.

2.5 Key concepts[16]

Positive, normative approach to social choice
Collective interest
Logic of economic policy
Market failure
Social ordering
Social objective
Social preference function (social utility function, social welfare function)
Social state (state of the world)
Direct, indirect social ordering
Gini coefficient

---

[16] The terms marked with asterisks refer to sections so marked.

Ethical individualism
Welfarism
Methodological individualism
Endogenous preferences
Aggregation of individual preferences
Ordinal, cardinal measurement of preferences
Utilitarianism
Interpersonal comparability of satisfactions
New welfare economics
Aggregation rule
Value judgement
Empirical (factual) statement
*Invariance requirements
*Informational requirements
*Increasing monotonic transformation
*Positive affine transformation
*Positive linear transformation
*Ratio scale measurability
*Absolute scale measurability
*Non-comparability
*Partial, full comparability

, usefulness.

3 The Pareto principle and 'new welfare economics'

How do we attach a value, to individual utilities that are non comparable.

3.1 Aggregating non-comparable ordinal preferences and the Pareto principle

(cannot be aggregated.

We have seen the many problems that arise in constructing an indirect social ordering. In particular, we can aggregate individual preferences (the only elements allowed by the postulate of ethical individualism) in a variety of ways depending on the information we have about the measurability and comparability of utilities.

If we assume that individual utilities are ordinally measurable and non-comparable, the task of aggregating them appears arduous. We cannot resort to the simplest form of aggregation – summation – because it is an operation on cardinal rather than ordinal numbers and because it requires commensurable addends, which is ruled out by the assumption of non-comparability. Even under these conditions, however, aggregation is possible in the *special sense* given by the following propositions:

1 *A group of individuals increases its welfare by moving from state b if all the individuals are more satisfied in b than in a.*

2 *The group of individuals increases its welfare in moving from a to b if at least one individual is better off in b and no individual is worse off.*

Proposition 1 is the 'weak' *Pareto criterion* or *principle*; proposition 2 is its 'strong' version (Arrow, 1951, pp. 36 and 96). They allow us to construct a social ordering of *a* and *b* if individual preferences are ordinally measurable and non-comparable.

It should be emphasised that both propositions are value judgements; they are valuation *criteria* that might not be shared by everybody.[1] For example, before accepting one or the other proposition, we might want to know something about who will

---

[1] Sen (1970a, p. 57) argues that a value judgement remains a value judgement even if nearly everyone in a society accepts it.

23

benefit (e.g., whether the beneficiary is rich or poor), or how much some individuals (e.g., the rich) might expect to benefit. However, the postulate of ethical individualism does not allow us to take account of such additional information. Despite its status of value judgement, the Pareto principle has an important role in economic science in that it represents a concept of *efficiency*: the possibility of one or more individuals obtaining more of something (in our case, utility) without forcing other individuals to do with less. Notwithstanding the special nature of the concept of efficiency given by the Pareto principle, it is a widely used criterion, especially in neoclassical theory. We will discuss its limitations in section 3.2.

From the concept of the Pareto *principle* we can derive that of a Pareto *optimum*.[2] For simplicity, we will refer to the strong version of the principle. A social state *a* is Pareto 'optimal' if in moving from that state to any other state it is not possible to increase the welfare of one member of society without worsening the condition of at least one other.

We should note that the term 'optimum' is an entirely unsatisfactory choice of terminology (see Cornwall, 1984, p. 402). Since it is derived from the Pareto principle, the so-called Pareto optimum carries with it all of the limitations of the principle itself, limitations that are masked by the use of a term ('optimum') that implies desirability. We will see that such an association is not well-founded. The use of a less value-loaded term, such as 'Pareto efficiency', would have been more appropriate.

3.1.1 Consumption efficiency

The Pareto principle and the Pareto optimum can be illustrated in diagrammatic form with reference to a pure consumption economy. For the moment we will not consider the problems of the efficient allocation of resources for production, deferring our discussion of this issue to the next subsection. As we have implicitly done so far, assume that output (which is taken to be perfectly divisible) is given and that it is to be divided between two individuals, Alice and Bob, for consumption. Obviously, there are *infinite* possible consumption 'allocations' (or 'lists' of quantities of goods assigned to each consumer) within the limit of total output and each of these allotments corresponds to a utility pairing for Alice and Bob, which can be shown in the plane of their respective utility functions (see figure 3.1)[3] as a set of points bounded by the *utility possibilities curve* (UPC). Points above the UPC cannot be attained for a given level of output, no matter how goods are allocated among individuals.

The Pareto principle allows us to say that the society formed by Alice and Bob prefers the allocation at point *b* to that at *a*. Hence, *b* is better than *a* on this criterion. However, neither *b* nor *a* are Pareto optimal because it is possible to move to another state and increase the welfare of at least one of the two members of society without making the other worse off. By contrast, the infinite number of points along the UPC are all Pareto

---

[2] Pareto, developing an idea of Walras, first enunciated his concept of 'maximum ophelimity' for a society, later known as 'Pareto optimality', in 1894 and developed it more fully in his *Manual* of 1906. See Pareto (1906).

[3] This is possible even if the functions are only ordinal. Those who have read section *2.3 will know that these are defined up to a positive monotonic transformation.

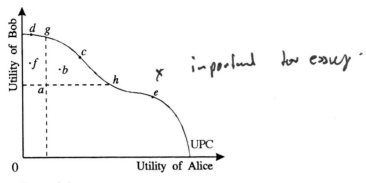

important for essay

Figure 3.1

Table 3.1. *Possible allocation of consumption between the two members of society*

Goods	Alice	Bob	Total
Bread	35	7	42
Cloth	37	30	67

optimal, since no matter where we move from each, it is not possible to improve the situation of one of the two individuals without worsening that of the other.

The existence of points such as c, d and e is immediately understandable: moving from d to c or e may simply be a consequence of Bob gradually receiving less of one or more goods. Points like a and b show that the utility of both individuals can increase by moving north-east (up and to the right) from any point within the area bounded by the UPC. Since we have assumed that total output is given, the economy can be in such a state only as a result of a 'poor' division of the total bundle of goods between the two individuals.

For example, suppose that there are only two goods (bread and cloth) and that consumption is allocated as shown in table 3.1.

Assume that the marginal rate of substitution (MRS) between cloth and bread at the given endowments is four for Alice and two for Bob. This means that Alice is willing to give up (or receive) one unit of cloth in exchange for four units of bread, leaving her overall utility unchanged, while Bob is willing to give up (or receive) one unit of cloth in exchange for only two units of bread. In a certain sense, Alice has received 'too much' bread and 'not enough' cloth, while Bob has received too much cloth and not enough bread.

If the allocation of consumption were that shown in table 3.2, both individuals would enjoy greater welfare.

In this situation, Alice would receive three fewer units of bread in exchange for one additional unit of cloth, which is more than enough to ensure a level of welfare equal to that enjoyed in her starting position; in fact, she would be willing to accept one unit of cloth in exchange for four units of bread, whereas she has only given up three units. Similarly, Bob would have one fewer unit of cloth and three extra units of bread, when

Table 3.2. *Alternative allocation of consumption between the two members of society*

Goods	Alice	Bob	Total
Bread	32	10	42
Cloth	38	29	67

he would have been willing to give up 1.5 units of cloth for three units of bread (since his MRS between cloth and bread was two). We can see that the allocation of consumption can be Pareto improved as long as the two individuals have a different MRS. When the rates are equal it is not possible to reallocate goods between the two members of the society in a way that improves the situation of one without worsening that of the other.

We can thus conclude – with some generalisation – that in an economic system where output is given and preferences satisfy certain properties,[4] the efficiency condition (Pareto optimality) requires that the marginal rates of substitution of all the members of society for each pair of goods be equal. All the points along the UPC in figure 3.1 are characterised by such equality, whereas points inside the curve are not.

The diagrammatic representation of the Pareto optimum used so far only considers the positions of individuals in terms of utility and does not reveal the combinations of goods associated with the different utility levels. Consumption-efficient allocations can also be shown with the aid of an *Edgeworth box diagram* (figure 3.2) as a set of points of tangency between the indifference curves of the two individuals (the *Pareto set* or *contract curve*).[5] This representation is made in the plane of goods, and not utilities, as in the UPC. It therefore shows the allocations of goods between the two individuals, distinguishing optimal from non-optimal ones.

Let the total quantities of cloth and bread be $0A$ and $0C$ respectively. If the allocation of the two goods between Alice and Bob is that at point a (where Alice has $0D$ units of cloth and $0E$ units of bread, and Bob has BF units of cloth and BG units of bread), the efficiency condition is not satisfied: the indifference curves of the two individuals intersect and the MRSs are different. Alice or Bob, or both, could increase their utility (reaching a higher indifference curve) if the goods were allocated as they are at any one of the points between h and g, where the indifference curves are tangent and therefore have equal MRSs. Each point on the contract curve is a Pareto efficient consumption allocation, since any move away from it will increase the utility of one individual only by reducing the utility of the other. Points a, g and h in figure 3.2 correspond to points a, g and h in figure 3.1.

Note that reaching one optimal state rather than another by means of one or more Pareto-improving actions depends crucially on the initial distribution of goods. In figure 3.2 the infinite number of points of the segment gh are Pareto optimal allocations that can be obtained starting from the initial distribution a.

---

[4] In particular, they must be differentiable, monotonic and convex (see, for example, Gravelle and Rees, 1992).

[5] Alice's indifference curves are drawn in relation to the origin 0, while Bob's are drawn with respect to B.

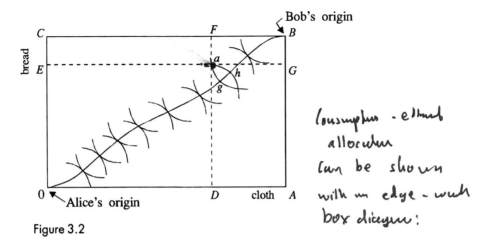

Figure 3.2

[handwritten note in right margin:] Consumption - efficient allocation can be shown with an edge-worth box diagram:

3.1.2 Efficiency in a production economy

Until now we have assumed that output is given. In the real world, however, efficient resource allocation does not involve solely the allocation of final consumer goods (*consumption efficiency*) but also regards:

- (a) the use of the various inputs in the production of different goods, i.e., the choice of technique (*production efficiency*);
- (b) the supply of inputs by each individual (*input supply efficiency*);
- (c) the choice of output levels for the various goods ('*general*' efficiency).

For simplicity we will disregard point *b* and begin by looking at *a*.[6] Assume we have given quantities of two inputs for the production of bread and cloth. Let the production functions be given and have the standard textbook properties. Our task is to determine the quantity of the two inputs to be used in producing the two goods; that is, the allocation of inputs among the possible uses. Using an approach similar to that adopted in section 3.1.1 we can show that the allocation of inputs is Pareto efficient when the marginal rates of technical substitution (MRTSs) between the two inputs in the production of the two goods are equal: if the inputs are labour and iron, the ratio in which iron can replace labour for a given level of output must be the same in both the bread and cloth industries.

We can use the Edgeworth box diagram to show the conditions for an efficient allocation of inputs. Referring again to figure 3.2, we can reinterpret it as follows: the axes now measure the quantity of inputs, labour and iron; 0A and 0C are the given quantities of inputs rather than final goods and instead of indifference curves we have production isoquants. The allocation of inputs for the production of bread and cloth at point *a* is inefficient, since it is possible to increase output of at least one of the two goods without diminishing production of the other. All of the points of tangency between the isoquants are efficient. These are points where the MRTS for bread, which represents the slope of the isoquant for this good, is equal to the MRTS for cloth. The set of all such

[6] The interested reader can consult a text such as Gravelle and Rees (1992).

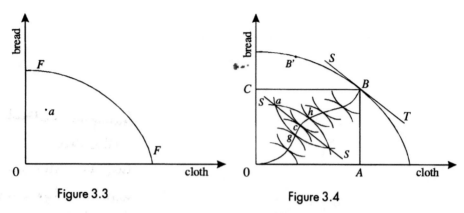

Figure 3.3   Figure 3.4

points gives us the *input contract curve*. Production efficiency is ensured at points on this curve, since an increase in the output of cloth can only be obtained by reducing that of bread, and vice versa. If we transfer the quantities of bread and cloth corresponding to each point of tangency of the isoquants on to another diagram – that is, if we move from the plane of factors of production to that of goods – we obtain the *transformation curve* or the production possibilities curve (shown by FF in figure 3.3).[7]

By construction, all the input allocations along the input contract curve correspond to quantities of the two goods that are on the curve FF, while allocations off that curve – such as that at a in figure 3.2, reinterpreted as an Edgeworth box diagram for the efficient allocation of inputs – correspond to points inside the transformation curve (such as a in figure 3.3), which are obviously inefficient.

Let us now consider the problem of efficient output choice. Assume that the total quantities of inputs and the production functions are given. As the transformation curve shows, we need to reduce bread output by some amount in order to increase cloth output by one unit. The marginal rate of transformation (MRT) specifies the terms of this reduction, which differ according to the quantities of the two goods that are produced. The choice of the level of output should be made by taking account of production possibilities and consumer preferences simultaneously. Let the MRT between bread and cloth be five and the MRS be two. This means that we can obtain five units of cloth by forgoing one unit of bread, whereas both Alice and Bob would be equally satisfied if they received only two additional units of cloth. Recall that consumption is efficient when all consumers have the same MRS. Under these conditions consumers will benefit if firms produce less bread and more cloth. Pareto efficiency in the choice of output, also called 'general' efficiency, is therefore obtained when the MRS between the two goods (the same for all consumers) is equal to their MRT.

Efficient output choice is shown diagrammatically in figure 3.4. We have general efficiency when cloth output is $0A$, bread output is $0C$, and the quantities consumed are those indicated at point c, where the slope of the indifference curves of both Alice and Bob, given by SS, is equal to that at point B of the transformation curve, given by ST. In the figure only one such point is shown, but in general there may be many.

---

[7] More on the properties of this curve can be found in any microeconomics textbook.

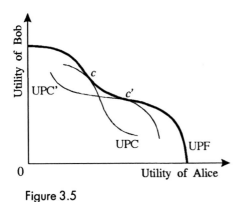

Figure 3.5

A formal demonstration of the Pareto efficiency conditions that also takes account of the variability of inputs is given in section *3.7.

*3.1.3 The utility possibilities frontier

It may be helpful to consider the points on the contract curve in terms of Alice and Bob's utilities. Section 3.1.1 introduced the utility possibilities curve (UPC) in an intuitive fashion, later specifying that it corresponds to the utility enjoyed by the two consumers at each point of the contract curve.[8] We must now add detail to this picture. Referring to figure 3.4, we assume that output is given at *B*; the various allocations of consumption along the contract curve (each of which satisfies the *consumption* efficiency conditions) produce utility pairings for the two individuals, which can be shown with a curve like the UPC in figure 3.1. We have used the same letters in order to emphasise that the points on one curve correspond to those on the other (and that points off one curve are also off the other). Note, however, that only some points on the UPC (e.g., point *c*) also ensure 'general' Pareto efficiency when output is at *B*.

Now suppose that output of the two goods is at point *B'* of figure 3.4 rather than *B*. This new output combination of bread and cloth corresponds to different consumption possibilities and a different contract curve, with different utility levels for the two consumers.

The new utility pairings for Alice and Bob obtained when output changes can be shown on the same diagram. Consider figure 3.5: the UPC corresponds to the contract curve for point *B* in figure 3.4. We have consumption efficiency at all the points on the UPC, but general efficiency is ensured only at some points, such as *c*. We can say the same for UPC', where *c'* is one of the points at which both consumption and production are efficient. We can draw a utility possibilities curve for each of the infinite number of points along the production frontier and on each curve there will be one or more points representing general efficiency. The set of points that meets the conditions for general efficiency – that is,

---

[8] The ordinal measurability of personal utility (which underlies the contract curve), characterised by invariance up to a positive monotonic transformation, enables us to derive the UPC, whose sole requirement is a negative slope.

the *envelope* of the various utility possibilities curves (UPC, UPC′ and the infinite number of other possible curves) – is called the *utility possibilities frontier* (UPF).

It is important to note that if utilities are ordinally measurable the only property of the UPF that can be demonstrated is that it has a negative slope. Since resources are allocated efficiently, one of the two consumers can increase his utility only if the utility of the other decreases. The possibility of rising sections of the UPF arises only in the presence of externalities.[9] The concavity of the UPF can be established only if we have more information about utility functions (see Graaff, 1957, chapter IV) and, in particular, if we have cardinal measurability.

3.1.4 The limits of the theory of general equilibrium

The analysis conducted in sections 3.1.1 and 3.1.2 has a number of limitations, in particular:

(a) its static nature, which means that the points on the UPC are points of static efficiency;

(b) the maximisation hypothesis, which some argue does not hold in a world of uncertainty;

(c) the exogenous nature of preferences, which are considered as given under the canons of methodological individualism;

(d) the high degree of abstraction, which excludes aspects of considerable importance for characterising the operation of an economic system.

These limitations are typical of neoclassical theory and, more specifically, the theory of general equilibrium as formulated by Walras, Pareto and Cassel, however much we might admire the elegance and grandeur of its analytical construction.[10]

It is important to be fully aware of these limitations, as well as those inherent in the postulates underlying the Pareto principle,[11] in order to better understand the development of the analysis we will conduct later, especially when the theory of general equilibrium is used to assess the performance of a capitalist economic system.

3.2 The limitations of the Pareto principle and the attempt to overcome them: new welfare economics

It is worth pausing a moment to review our progress so far. Our first step was to introduce a widely adopted criterion for the indirect ordering of social states, the Pareto principle, and, in its wake, the principle of Pareto optimality or efficiency. We then identified the conditions that an economic system must meet to satisfy the Pareto efficiency principle, making use of concepts borrowed from the theory of general

---

[9] These are positive or negative effects induced by the action of one agent on the situations of other agents, with no corresponding payment (see section 6.3).

[10] For other limitations of this theory, see Eatwell (1987).

[11] We will discuss their consequences at length in the next section.

equilibrium. Both steps involved the introduction of concepts or hypotheses that raise questions only partly addressed here.

The limitations of general equilibrium theory were briefly outlined in section 3.1.4. Let us now consider the limitations of the Pareto efficiency criterion.[12] These are related to the postulates that underlie the criterion itself (ethical individualism, ordinal measurement and non-comparability of utilities), which:

1 ignore important aspects of the various states of the world; and
2 provide only a partial ordering, which can give rise to a 'tyranny of the status quo'.

1 We have said that the Pareto principle is based on the premise of ethical individualism, since it takes individual preferences as the sole basis for social preferences. As it does not consider liberties and rights, however, it may conflict with other principles. For example, it is inconsistent with the principle of 'minimal liberty', which guarantees the existence of a sphere of personal preferences that each individual wishes to safeguard: if someone prefers reading *Lady Chatterley's Lover* to some other activity, society should respect that preference. However, if a second person places the banning of Lawrence's book at the top of his list of preferences, the Pareto principle, which gives greater priority to *unanimous* orderings of preferences, may conflict with the sphere of personal liberty (Sen, 1982, chapter 13).[13] The 'impossibility' of a Paretian liberal seems paradoxical, since many consider the ethical individualism incorporated in the Pareto principle to be a guarantee of liberties.[14]

The criterion also ignores other aspects of a social state, such as the quantity and distribution of goods, and this can considerably limit the use of the Pareto principle, especially in situations of great inequality.

The illiberal nature of the Pareto criterion prompted Sen (1982) to suggest that we

[12] Sen has made a penetrating critique of the consequences of the focus placed on the Pareto principle by traditional welfare economics: on the one hand, this has confined welfare economics 'into a very narrow box and has, on the other hand, given it a sense of ethical invulnerability which does not seem to survive a close scrutiny' (Sen, 1970a, p. 200).

[13] More precisely, let us assume that the views of the two individuals about reading the book are different. We have three alternatives: x, y and z, where x is the situation in which only individual 1 reads the book; in y only individual 2 reads it and in z no one reads it. Let us suppose that the preferences ranking of the first person, a prude, is z, x, y, while that of the second, a more lascivious fellow, is x, y, z. The preservation of a sphere of individual preferences that are *decisive* in orienting social choice is the essence of the liberal principle. In order to respect the decisive preferences of the prude, we could require that no one read the book (z must be preferred to x); to respect the same essential preferences of our more lecherous fellow, we should allow him to read the book (y) rather than forbid it to all (z). (Note the preferences of individual 2: he prefers x to y simply because he takes pleasure in the idea that the book can be read by the prude, but in any case he would like to be able to read the book himself and considers this preference decisive over banning the book.) In order to respect the liberty of both individuals, society should prefer z to x and y to z; the best solution would be y and the worst x. However, according to the preference rankings of the two individuals, x is Pareto superior to y since both persons prefer x to y.

[14] The paradox disappears if we consider the failure to satisfy the Pareto principle – i.e., the existence of inefficiency – to be a consequence of each individual's right to interfere with the utility of others. We will see later that this corresponds to the creation of externalities.

simply abandon it, while the irrelevance of income distribution has led Sen, Rawls and others to propose different social choice criteria, which we will discuss in sections 4.2 and 4.6.

2 The Pareto principle allows us to construct only a *partial* ordering of social states. Referring to figure 3.1, we saw that from a society's point of view state c is preferred to b and both are preferred to a, but it is not possible to construct a ranking for states c, d and h; nor can states such as a and d (or e) be ordered, despite the fact that a is clearly not efficient. In more general terms, not only can we not define an ordering among efficient social states, we cannot even construct one between certain inefficient states and other efficient ones.

The limitation imposed by partial ordering is clear: such an ordering cannot rank all the possible alternatives and is therefore of little use. In the case of the Pareto principle, this is due to the value judgements (or type of 'information') that it expresses; in particular, the assumption that personal utilities are non-comparable.

An important consequence of these limitations of the Pareto principle (and the Pareto 'optimum') is the so-called tyranny of the status quo. Since our scope for making comparisons is limited (that is, it does not extend to all possible states of the world), there is a tendency not to move from any given state, whether efficient or not, to others. This does not necessarily occur because the other states are 'worse' (or less efficient), but often simply because they cannot be compared with the initial state, which may therefore prevail due to inertia.[15]

For an example, refer to figure 3.1. Assume we are at c. The partial nature of the Paretian ordering means that we cannot determine whether d (or e) is better than c, and so there is a tendency to remain at c, given that there are always inertial factors at work in the real world associated with the material (and psychological) costs involved in any change. Likewise, if we are at point d we cannot say whether c or e is better, and so society tends to remain at d, and so on.

The influence of the initial position on choices based on the Pareto principle is clear even if we begin in inefficient states. We still find the tendency to remain relatively close to the initial position: starting at a, for example, the Pareto principle might allow us to reach b, but not d or e; by contrast, d could be reached if we began at f. In other words, different initial positions admit different sets of Pareto superior positions. This should be borne in mind to balance the claim that the Pareto principle is an 'ideal' rule by virtue of the fact that it produces unanimous decisions. The principle can be conservative in nature, imposing the tyranny of the status quo.

Economists have sought to overcome the limitation of the incompleteness of Paretian orderings without abandoning the basic premises of the Pareto principle or the principle itself by introducing additional conditions or axioms. This is essentially the approach taken by the school of new welfare economics, which, erroneously considering the Pareto principle to be objective and uncontaminated by value judgements, sought to extend its application.[16] In particular, the compensation principle – which has attracted

---

[15] Note that the status quo prevails for practical rather than logical reasons.
[16] This was examined at greater length in section 2.2.2.

the attention of many prominent economists – is a proposal for introducing additional conditions that broaden the set of social states for which an ordering can be constructed. We will examine this approach in the following two sections. A more general attempt to construct complete orderings on the basis of the Pareto principle and additional widely accepted axioms was made by Arrow (1951). We discuss his work in section 3.5.

3.3 The compensation principle

The need to extend the set of socially 'rankable' states of the world without abandoning the Pareto principle prompted a search for additional conditions or principles for judging the desirability of moving from one social state to another despite the presence of benefits for some people and disadvantages for others. Kaldor (1939) developed the original formulation of the *compensation principle*.[17]

Kaldor argued that a change that led to an increase in productivity, and therefore in society's real income, would increase the welfare of society as a whole, since those who benefited from the change would be able to compensate those who were worse off while retaining a net benefit. The *possibility* of paying compensation would be enough to judge the change favourably. If the compensation were actually paid, the change in question (in combination with the compensation) could be assessed on the basis of the Pareto principle alone, without the need for an extended version.

For an example of the compensation principle as formulated by Kaldor, let us refer to figure 3.6.

Take states *a* and *e*. For the reasons given in the previous section it is not possible to construct a social ordering of the two states on the basis of the Pareto principle, since moving[18] from one to the other would, depending on the case, reduce the utility of either Alice or Bob. If the initial position is *a*, we cannot say that *e* is Pareto superior to *a* because Bob will be worse off at *e*. Kaldor's principle states that if the gain enjoyed by Alice in moving from *a* to *e* is large enough to allow her to compensate Bob and still have a net gain, then the change from *a* to *e* is desirable, i.e., *e* has a higher position in the social ordering. In order to see that this is the case in our example, recall that the utility possibilities curve is obtained by efficiently reallocating output in every possible way. It would therefore be possible for Alice, the beneficiary of the move from *a* to *e*, to give part of her endowment in *e* to Bob. We could thereby move from *e* to *h*, where Bob would be fully compensated for the change and Alice would have a higher utility level than she did at *a*.[19]

---

[17] Kaldor's contribution came within the framework of the wide-ranging debate sparked by Robbins' 1932 essay and dealt specifically with the repeal of the Corn Laws in England in 1846. Harrod (1938) had argued that the measure could be judged favourably only if the different individuals were in some way equal. The debate that followed Kaldor's work involved a variety of economists, including Hicks (1939).

[18] In order to favour the reader's intuitive understanding of the problem, we use terms such as 'moving' which can give the impression that we are in a dynamic setting. Be warned that our analysis is purely static.

[19] In fact, Alice could 'overcompensate' Bob and still enjoy a residual benefit up to point *g*, where Bob would be 'overcompensated' and Alice would have the same level of utility as she had in situation *a*.

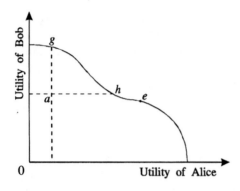

Figure 3.6

Kaldor's proposal was the subject of considerable debate and heated criticism. Leaving aside the modification we discuss in the following section, the questions that were raised concern: *→ what will be the compensation?*

(a) the effective payment of the compensation; and
(b) the more general problem of whether the change from one social state to another can be evaluated solely in terms of its effects on total income, overlooking the actual distribution of wealth. *Health!*

Little (1949) pointed out that the desirability of such a change could not be decided on the basis of the *potential* superiority of one situation over another, ignoring the *effective* consequences of the change on distribution; that is, we cannot separate efficiency from equity and ignore the latter. This is what happens if we limit ourselves to determining the mere possibility of paying compensation, taking no interest in its actual payment. A common-sense view would find it difficult to accept the idea that a change which made the rich richer and the poor poorer should be evaluated positively if it *could* satisfy the (*potential*) compensation principle even though the compensation was not actually paid: many would agree that the net increase in income did not correspond to greater welfare (Gravelle and Rees, 1992).

Once again, ranking social states with the use of criteria purged of value judgements has proved to be unrealistic and dangerous.

*3.4 Scitovsky's 'double' criterion

Scitovsky (1941) noted a logical difficulty with Kaldor's reasoning, which we can illustrate by referring to figure 3.7. The latter is derived from figure 3.5 (the UPF is not shown and, for simplicity, only two utility possibilities curves are given, UPC and UPC'). Recall from section *3.1.3 that: (a) there are an infinite number of utility possibilities curves, one for each point on the transformation curve; and (b) the curves intersect.

The difficulty pointed out by Scitovsky arises whenever the two states to be compared are on opposite sides of the point of intersection of two utility possibility curves.

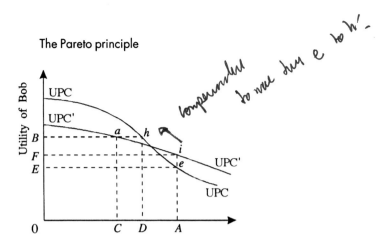

Figure 3.7

Consider a move from point *a* to *e*, states in which different quantities of the various goods are produced, corresponding to different points on the production frontier.[20] In the new state, *e*, Bob could be compensated and Alice would still be better off. This can be seen in the figure: once we have moved from *a* to *e*, which implies different total output, we *could* use compensation payments to move along the UPC to a point such as *h*, where Bob would not be worse off than he was in *a* (he would still have a utility of 0*B*) and Alice would improve her situation (increasing her utility level from 0*C* to 0*D*).

However, if the compensation were not actually paid, we would remain at *e* (rather than going to *h*) and Bob would suffer a utility loss equal to *BE*. But, being at *e*, Bob would seek to return to the initial position *a*, arguing that from *a* it would be possible to move along the UPC with appropriate transfers of resources (compensation) to arrive at a point such as *i*, where Alice would not be worse off than at *e* (enjoying the same utility 0*A*), and Bob would have a higher level of utility, 0*F*, than at *e* (0*E*), the position to which he would have been relegated by the initial uncompensated move. Note that the transfers (or compensation) are only potential. It therefore does not cost Bob anything to ask to return to *a*. Once we know that the compensation is only potential, Bob's request to move to *a* only makes it clear that, *beginning at e*, a return to *a* is desirable. Thus, once we were at *e*, Bob could cite Kaldor's principle of potential compensation to argue for a return to *a*. But, having returned to *a*, we would be back where we started and the process could be repeated all over again.

The economic system could therefore oscillate indefinitely between *a* and *e* if, given potential compensation, we did not adopt a double criterion:

(a) in moving from *a* to *e*, Alice can compensate Bob and still be left with a net benefit (as proposed by Kaldor); *and*

(b) Bob cannot pay Alice to remain at *a* (as he could do in our example).[21]

---

[20] This means that more of one good is produced and less of another; consequently, with a given initial assignment of resources, the person with a greater preference for the more abundant good will derive more utility for any given level of utility of the other.

[21] The reader can imagine situations in which one or other of the cases (and the second in particular, which is the innovation introduced by Scitovsky) occur.

The reasoning underpinning Scitovsky's criterion has a parallel in a situation well known in the theory of index numbers, where the effect of a change in output on national income may differ (either positively or negatively) according to whether the prices used are those of the initial or final (or some other) year. We might then face the following paradoxical situation:

$$\sum p_1 q_1 < \sum p_1 q_2 \qquad (3.1)$$

$$\sum p_2 q_1 > \sum p_2 q_2 \qquad (3.2)$$

where p_1 and p_2 are prices in the initial and final years and q_1 and q_2 the quantities of goods and services produced in those years.

This could also happen in the case of compensation if we think of the initial and final years as the initial situation a and the alternative e. Since condition (3.1) holds, we can say that income in situation e is greater than that in situation a if the distribution selected – which is reflected in prices – is that of a. It will therefore be possible for the better off to compensate those who find themselves worse off in such a way as to return them to the previous distribution while retaining a net benefit. However, since (3.2) also holds, income at a is greater than that at e if the distribution considered is that of the second state. Thus, we cannot state either that a is superior to e or that e is superior to a. It would be a different matter if, given (3.1), we had not (3.2) but rather:

$$\sum p_2 q_1 < \sum p_2 q_2 \qquad (3.3)$$

which would establish the 'definitive' superiority of the bundle of goods and services produced in period 2 over that produced in period 1. Equations (3.1) and (3.3) together are equivalent to Scitovsky's formulation of the compensation principle.

Satisfying Scitovsky's double criterion does not, however, eliminate the general reservations concerning the compensation principle (see the end of section 3.3).

3.5 Arrow and the impossibility theorem

In order to overcome the partial nature of Pareto orderings, Arrow (1951) takes a different approach to that adopted by the proponents of the compensation principle. He tries to construct a complete social ordering axiomatically by supplementing the Pareto principle with other widely accepted axioms having the nature both of ethical norms and procedures satisfying them.[22]

For example, consider a set of alternatives a, b and c. Let us suppose that all consumers prefer a to b, but some prefer c to a and others prefer a to c; similarly, some prefer b to c and some c to b. If we apply the Pareto principle, the unanimity of individual preferences for a over b allows us to construct a social ordering of a and b; in other words, society will prefer a to b. However, the Pareto principle does not allow us to order c with respect to a and b. Arrow attempts to construct a complete ordering by employing the Pareto principle with additional conditions that enable us to order

---

[22] It will not escape the reader that the selection of many assumptions implies the use of value judgements.

Pareto non-comparable states as well. These additional conditions can be expressed in axiomatic form. The normative content of the axioms used by Arrow is underscored in Mueller (1989, chapter 20). The axioms also have a procedural counterpart; i.e., there are voting procedures (majority voting, for example) that satisfy the axioms, as we will see in section *3.6.

Take the weak version of the Pareto principle, which states that society must prefer social state a to social state b if all its members prefer a to b.[23] In order to extend this ordering and make it complete and 'rational', it seems necessary (or reasonable) to supplement the Pareto principle with the following conditions:

1 *An* unrestricted domain *condition: the 'rule' for constructing a social ordering out of individual orderings must be defined for all possible sets of individual orderings. In other words, the 'rule' for the social ordering of individual preferences holds whatever these preferences may be, as long as each system of individual preferences is not contradictory.*

2 *An* independence of irrelevant alternatives *condition: in choosing between a and b, we must only take account of individual preferences with regard to those alternatives, ignoring individual orderings of other possibilities. This hypothesis is introduced in order to econom- ise on the information necessary for social ordering, but it also enables us to exclude insincere expressions of preferences made for strategic reasons.*[24]

Following Arrow, it can be demonstrated that with this set of hypotheses the Pareto principle enables us to obtain a complete social ordering. However, this can only happen if the preferences of one individual are *decisive*; that is, if the choice of one individual determines society's choice, regardless of the preferences of the other members of society (i.e., there is a *dictatorship* in determining social preferences).

The practical significance of this result is of considerable importance: the members of a community that wish to construct a complete social ordering satisfying the conditions of unrestricted domain and independence of irrelevant alternatives, as well as the weak Pareto principle, must necessarily accept the preferences of one individual regardless of those of the others. Under these conditions, rejection of dictatorial choices makes it impossible to define a complete ordering that overcomes the partial character of the Pareto principle while still applying the principle itself. This is the *Arrow impossibility theorem*.[25]

Various attempts have been made to get around the 'impossibility' result by eliminat- ing one or another of the axioms that Arrow thought necessary for constructing a complete social ordering. Special attention has been directed at assumptions regarding

---

[23] The Pareto principle does not imply that society must prefer a to b *only* if all its members prefer a to b. If this were the case we would require the *unanimity principle*, giving a veto to each individual (see section *3.6).

[24] For example, under certain circumstances a person who prefers a to b might declare that he preferred b to a in order to ensure that a third alternative c, which he prefers to both a and b, is ranked higher in the social ordering (see also section 3.6.1).

[25] The result is an 'impossibility' or 'possibility' theorem, respectively, depending on whether the axioms on which the ordering is constructed include or do not include non-dictatoriality.

the information we have on individual satisfactions (measurability and comparability). We saw in section 3.1 that the Pareto principle is founded on the specific 'informational' postulates of ordinal measurability and non-comparability. It has been shown that the other axioms introduced by Arrow also rule out cardinal measurability and/or interpersonal comparability of utilities (see, among others, Mueller, 1989, chapter 20). Some have argued that these are the key hypotheses and that removing them would allow us to construct a complete social ordering.

Abandoning simple ordinal measurability does not enable us to avoid the impossibility result, however (Sen, 1970a). A complete, non-dictatorial social ordering can be obtained if, in addition to cardinal measurability, some degree of interpersonal comparability is admitted. In particular, if we allow full interpersonal comparability in addition to cardinal measurability of individual utilities it is possible to construct a simple or generalised utilitarian SWF (see section 4.2).

*3.6 Voting theory

We have reviewed the main problems that arise in the axiomatic specification of a social ordering based on individual preferences. The axioms normally reflect value judgements, which may be more or less acceptable. This apart, the axiomatic approach is a purely logical exercise and apparently almost entirely ignores the procedures normally used in the real world to aggregate individual preferences, i.e., forms of voting.

This section will show that:

(a) different procedural methods are based on different value judgements;
(b) there is a correspondence between the criteria used in logical schemes for the construction of social orderings and voting procedures;
(c) it is difficult to construct a social ordering in a democratic society.

Voting theory therefore enables us to extend the analysis of the previous sections.

Every voting situation presupposes a set of rules of varying complexity, each of which is the product of choices that have significant effects on the results of the vote itself.

One group of rules regards the choice of who can vote and the number of votes each participant will cast; this calls for the same sort of interpersonal comparisons as those used in the axiomatic construction of the social ordering and for the selection of a dictator.

A second group of rules concerns the voting procedures and involves establishing:

(a) the proposals to be put to a vote (in particular, deciding who can formulate the proposals);
(b) the voting procedure proper; this can be either a *binary* rule (in which pairs of alternatives are voted on) or a *plurality* rule (in which more than two alternatives are voted on simultaneously);
(c) the order of voting, which is important in cases where not all the alternatives are voted on at once.

The influence of value judgements in determining the procedure for formulating proposals is clear, but we will shortly see that they are also involved in the other procedures.

A final group of rules concerns the procedure for determining the outcome of the vote: for example, we can choose between unanimous or majority voting. The degree to which individual preferences are respected in social choices differs in the two cases. In the two following subsections we will concentrate on the problems connected with this last group of rules.

3.6.1 The unanimity rule

Under unanimous voting a community decides to choose state *a* over state *b* *if and only if* all the members of that community prefer *a* to *b*. The basis of unanimous decisions is the idea that the liberty of every individual must be safeguarded. This is therefore the ideal democratic procedure for a liberal society. Unanimous decisions meet the Pareto criterion: by definition receiving unanimous consensus leads to choices that no voter has an interest in blocking.[26] The unanimity rule satisfies the four conditions that lead to Arrow's impossibility theorem[27] and, indeed, it does not give a complete social ordering in all cases.

By its very nature, this rule is best suited to a community or organisation whose members have sufficiently homogenous preferences and to decide questions in which considerations of efficiency outweigh distributive concerns. When this is not the case, unanimous voting will maintain the status quo. For example, let *a*, *b*, *c* and *d* be feasible states to which the two members of society have assigned the utilities shown in table 3.3.

If we put all the situations to a binary vote, no alternative will receive the votes of both voters. No matter what the initial state is, the lack of unanimity means that the status quo will prevail. The difficulty created by applying the Pareto principle is thus accentuated. In the case of different individual rankings, the unanimity rule effectively gives each voter a veto, which inevitably preserves the status quo. The Pareto principle in itself does not imply that the status quo will prevail: if we are on the contract curve, the principle does not allow us to choose among the various states and the persistence of the status quo is simply due to the costs involved in any change.

Another important aspect of the unanimity rule is that the final outcome is influenced by the *order* in which the alternatives are voted on if, as occurs in the real world, pairs (or some other subset of alternatives) are voted on at any one time. Starting from the same point, the final result of the vote may differ depending on the voting path selected.[28] For

---

[26] The result of voting is part of the so-called *core*, which is the set of points on the contract curve in which no voter or coalition of voters is able to obtain a better outcome starting from a certain initial allocation (see section 3.1.1).

[27] As Van den Doel and Van Velthoven (1993, p. 94) put it, 'alternatives are not excluded a priori; as long as the group members agree, that is also the group decision; at each decision the individuals will always present their best alternative; and there is no dictator'.

[28] The number of voters is often relatively small. In this case we speak of 'committees' and the analysis of voting problems is called the *theory of committees*. In this case, which we will return to later, the voting order is largely decided by the committee chairman. There may also be rules that to some degree govern the path to be taken, which is more often the case when the number of voters is large or the voting takes place within a public body.

Table 3.3. *Utility of the two members of society in different social states*

Social states	Alice's utility	Bob's utility
a	6	5
b	7	4
c	8	3
d	5	8

Table 3.4. *Utility of the two members of society in different social states*

Social states	Alice's utility	Bob's utility
a	6	5
b	11	6
c	7	9
d	9	12
e	14	8

example, let *a, b, c, d* and *e* be feasible states to which Alice and Bob assign the utilities shown in table 3.4.

If we have binary voting with *exclusion* (that is, the defeated proposal cannot be reconsidered in a subsequent round of voting), beginning at *a* and voting on *b* and *a, b* will win; in subsequent rounds, *b* will be selected over *c* and *d*, but will be defeated by *e*, the final winner in the voting process. By contrast, if *a* is initially set against *c*, the final outcome will be *d*.

In addition to manipulation related to the order in which alternatives are voted on when this is decided on a discretionary basis (in the case of a committee, by its chairman), we must also consider the actions of the other committee members. They may not vote according to their true preferences in order to ensure a superior result. Let us return to the previous example, assuming, for simplicity, that proposals will be put to a (binary) vote in alphabetical order. Let us also assume that Bob decides to vote insincerely for 'strategic' reasons. In the first vote, *b* loses to *a* if Bob votes against *b*, stating falsely that he prefers *a*. If both voters express their preferences truthfully in the subsequent vote, *c* is selected over *a* and *d* defeats *c*; in the final vote, *e* loses to *d*. By voting against *b*, Bob made possible the final victory of *d* over *e*, which would have won if he had voted sincerely at the outset. Bob has thereby gained more utility than he would have had he voted truthfully (12 rather than 8).[29]

The effect of strategic voting is shown in figure 3.8, which plots the utilities of the

---

[29] In doing this, he will have exploited a property of the *core* (see note 26): once a point in the core has been reached, every voter blocks any shift away from it: moving from one point to another on the contract curve (see section 3.1.1) means that the increase in the utility of one of the two consumers can only occur at the expense of the other, who therefore takes action to block the move.

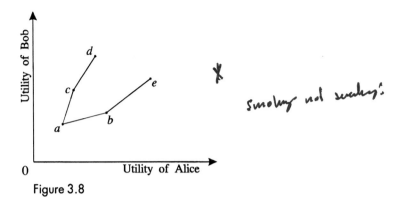

Figure 3.8

various alternative positions for the two voters. We begin at *a*. It is clear that the best positions for both voters are *d* and *e*; at *d*, Bob's utility gain is greater than it would be at *e*, and vice versa for Alice. Thus, Alice will seek to reach position *e* and Bob will try to reach *d*. It is immediately clear that the first vote is decisive for the final outcome: if Bob can cause *b* to lose, he avoids the path leading to *e* and opens the way to the final victory of *d*; he thus exploits the *path dependence* property of unanimous voting.

3.6.2 Majority voting

We have seen that unanimous voting does not eliminate the possibility of manipulation. Perhaps the greatest defect of this procedure is that it tends to favour the status quo, since the difficulty of achieving complete agreement between voters on possible changes increases as the number of voters rises. Moreover, the search for a compromise solution that would satisfy all the voters can require time and effort and is therefore costly.

It may be appropriate, then, to set aside the unanimity criterion, together with the principle of interpersonal non-comparability of preferences. Democratic principles can be safeguarded equally well by a majority voting rule.[30] Such a rule meets a number of requirements of voting procedures (for example, speed: see Mueller, 1989, chapter 4) and protects voters with regard to the uncertainty of their future preferences in the various situations that may occur (Rae, 1969; Taylor, 1969).[31]

---

[30] Obviously, under majority voting the alternatives that are unanimously preferred by individuals will still be preferred by society, but such a system also enables us to order states about which individual preferences diverge or conflict.

[31] Barry (1965, p. 312) offers the following example. Five people are in a train compartment in which they can decide whether or not to allow smoking. The problem is to find a rule to decide whether they will be allowed to smoke or not. It is assumed that each person is uncertain regarding his (or her) preferences (whether he will want to smoke or not) and that, should someone decide he wants to smoke, he would suffer due to the ban imposed by non-smokers as much as he would if he were a non-smoker and smoking was in fact permitted. Under these conditions, it can be shown that majority voting maximises the expected utility of each person.

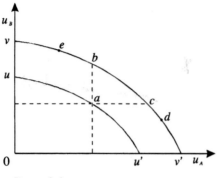

Figure 3.9

Since the majority voting rule abandons the principle of interpersonal non-compar-ability, voting outcomes more frequently lead to redistributions of income.[32] An example is given in figure 3.9. Let A and B be two different-sized groups of voters. Preferences are unanimously shared within each group. The initial position a is on the utility possibilities frontier uu'.

Let us consider a decision about whether to proceed with, for example, the construc-tion of some public work to be financed with contributions from all members of a community. The project will increase everyone's utility, shifting the UPF from uu' to vv'. However, the actual position on the new curve will depend on how the burden of the financial contribution is distributed among the community members. The use of unani-mous voting means that the final position can only be located on the segment bc of the new frontier. Majority voting opens the way to alternatives such as d or e, with the actual outcome depending on which group (A or B) is more numerous (see Mueller, 1989, pp. 58–9).

That majority voting may lead to unsatisfactory or ambiguous results has long been known, with the debate over its characteristics going back more than two centuries (see Borda, 1781; Condorcet, 1785). For example, assume that there are at least three alternatives (e.g., a, b, c and d) and we are using a plurality rule. Each voter (suppose there are 21) indicates a single complete ranking of the available alternatives; the alternative chosen by the society (or committee) will be that ranked highest by the largest number of voters. We also assume that the preferences of the voters are those shown in table 3.5, which is drawn from Moulin (1988).

Three voters prefer a to b, b to c and c to d and so on. With eight votes, a ranks first, ahead of b (seven votes) and c (six votes); however, a is in fact the worst outcome for the majority of voters, being ranked last by $7 + 6$ voters. We must therefore – as Condorcet, Borda and others have done – abandon or amend the majority rule in order to identify a single, satisfactory winning proposal in place of a.

---

[32] However, we cannot simplistically deduce from this that small social groups are at the mercy of larger groups. For example, if the former are wealthier, they can influence the latter in a variety of ways (with coercion or bribes based on their greater power, manipulation of preferences with a distorted use of information, etc.).

Table 3.5. *Voter preferences for different social states*

	Number of voters that prefer the order indicated			
Preference order	3	5	7	6
1st	a	a	b	c
2nd	b	c	d	b
3rd	c	b	c	d
4th	d	d	a	a

Among others, the following solutions have been suggested:

1 In a system of plurality voting, for n alternatives being put to a vote, each voter assigns zero points to the least preferred alternative, one point to the penultimate alternative and so on up to the most preferred alternative, which receives $n - 1$ points. Summing the points for each alternative, we select that with the highest score (the *Borda count*). This procedure always produces a unique winner: in our example, b would receive 44 points, compared with 38 for c, 24 for a and 20 for d. Nevertheless, the rule calls for obvious subjective judgements when the *ordinal* measurement of individual preferences is replaced with *cardinal* numbers: the result could change depending on the number of points assigned to the different placings in the preference ranking.[33] The outcome could also change as a result of strategic voting.

2 Another possibility would be to adopt a binary voting procedure for the different alternatives, choosing the proposal that defeats all the others in a series of binary votes (the *Condorcet solution*). Using the numbers from table 3.5, c would be the overall winner while a would finish last.[34]

Condorcet was aware of the limitations of his proposed solution, i.e., the possibility that no clear majority emerges for any proposal (unlike the Borda count). While allowing us to order all social states by pairs, binary majority voting does not necessarily generate a *transitive preference ordering*: for example, with only three alternatives, a may be preferred to b and b to c, but c may be preferred to a.

This produces a cyclical majority; that is, it does not identify a clearly superior outcome even if individual preferences meet the normal conditions of rationality, including transitivity. Let there be three alternatives a, b and c. The orderings of the voters (1, 2 and 3) are those given in table 3.6.

Voting with a binary system, a is preferred to b by two of the three voters and b to c by the same margin, from which we should be able to deduce that a is preferred to c if

[33] Using the same example try assigning a much higher number of points – say, 24 or more – to the top-ranked proposal on each voter's ballot, 2 points to the second, 1 to the third and 0 to the last. The winning alternative will be a rather than b. The reader can imagine other rankings and other weightings that bear out this observation.

[34] Between a and b, a loses since it is preferred by $3 + 5 = 8$ voters, while b is preferred by $7 + 6 = 13$ voters. Voting between b and c, we have b losing by $3 + 7 = 10$ votes to $5 + 6 = 11$ votes. Finally, in c against d, d loses by 7 to $3 + 5 + 6 = 14$ votes.

Table 3.6. *Voter preferences for different social states*

	Voters		
	1	2	3
Order	a	b	c
	b	c	a
	c	a	b

transitivity held for the committee as well. However, transitivity is not respected since *c* defeats *a* in a head-to-head vote. The intransitivity of the ordering under Condorcet's majority voting procedure therefore violates one of the conditions of a social ordering. Since the majority voting rule satisfies Arrow's axioms (weak Pareto principle, unrestricted domain, independence of irrelevant alternatives, non-dictatorship), we have a clear example of the validity of his impossibility theorem. There is no alternative that is superior to all the others and the majorities are cyclical (the *Condorcet voting paradox*).[35]

It is legitimate to ask how likely this situation is and if it would not occur at all under certain conditions.

In response to the first query, we can demonstrate that the probability of the Condorcet paradox occurring increases as the number of alternatives and/or voters increases: for example, the probability is slightly more than 1/20 in the case of three proposals and three voters and slightly more than 1/3 with 7 alternatives and 11 voters (Fishburn, 1973, p. 95).

As to the second problem, Black (1948, 1958) set out sufficient conditions under which majority voting on binary proposals would produce a transitive social ordering. Let the society be composed of *n* members, where *n* is an odd number. Individual preferences are expressed with regard to a single dimension (one-dimensional preferences), i.e., they concern, for example, only the amount to be spent on some project (for instance, the amount needed for the construction of a swimming pool) and not other matters, such as voting on both the level of expenditure *and* the use of the funds (swimming pool, day-care centre, road, etc.) or on how the financial burden is to be distributed among voters. In addition, we assume that each voter has only one most-preferred alternative among those being voted on and that satisfaction increases as we approach this alternative and decreases after it; i.e., preferences are *single-peaked*.[36] Under these

[35] Cyclicity could be avoided by excluding losing proposals from subsequent voting rounds. In our example, the vote between *a* and *b* comes out in favour of *a*, and *b* is excluded. We then vote on *a* and *c* only, where *a* loses and *c* is the final selection. However, we should bear in mind that here, too, as in the case of the unanimity rule, the final outcome depends on the order in which the alternatives are voted on, which means that the procedure is open to manipulation.

[36] If preferences are expressed with regard to only one question, the requirement for single-peaked preferences may appear easy to satisfy (see, however, Osborne, 1995). It is more difficult, in any case, when there are two or more elements relevant to the preferences themselves (see Mueller, 1989, p. 67). Voters who have only one best alternative when the vote regards one question only

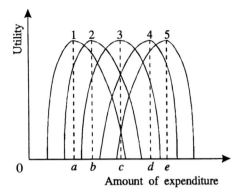

Figure 3.10

conditions a majority vote over two alternatives will produce a unique, well-defined social preference, which will be that of the voter whose most-preferred alternative is in a median position (the *median voter theorem*).[37]

Let there be five voters and five alternatives (for example, different levels of expenditure for a swimming pool) arranged in increasing order, *a*, *b*, *c*, *d* and *e*, such that $a < b < c < d < e$. Voter 1 prefers *a* to all the other possibilities, voter 2 prefers *b* and so on. The median voter is voter 3, whose preferred alternative, *c*, divides the values of the alternatives into two groups of equal size: one that includes *a* and *b*, which are less than *c*, and a second including *d* and *e*, which are greater. In figure 3.10 the expenditure levels are shown on the horizontal axis and preferences are indicated on the vertical axis.[38] The alternative preferred by voter 3 (*c*) will receive a majority of votes. Suppose we vote between *c* and *b*. While *b* will only receive the votes of 1 and 2, *c* will receive those of the other three voters, who prefer it to *b*. No other alternative among the remaining four enjoys equal or greater consensus than that chosen by the median voter.

(for example, how much to spend for a certain well-defined purpose with a specified method of contribution) may have more than one equally preferred alternative if there are a number of matters to be decided (for example, not only the amount to be spent but also the purpose of the expenditure or the division of the financial contribution): in this case, for instance, spending 100 on a swimming pool or 200 on a day-care centre may be equally preferred.

Some argue that the essence of politics is the fact that opposition parties tend to raise new problems and suggest new alternatives (see Riker, 1982). Some of these can breach the previously unanimous front of the governing parties and receive approval. One example is offered by the United States in the nineteenth century, with the introduction of slavery as a subject of political debate at the national level. This threatened the coalition of expansionist agrarians, which was ultimately defeated (Riker, 1982, chapter 9).

[37] Given an ordered set (for example, in increasing order) of *n* values, the median is the value below and above which there is an equal number of values. If *n* is odd, it is easy to identify the median: it is the value with $(n - 1)/2$ values to its left and the same number to its right; if *n* is even, it is the arithmetic mean of the two adjacent central values.

[38] For simplicity, infinite possible levels of expenditure have been considered (even if each voter has only one preferred expenditure level). In the real world, spending levels are discrete, which causes the preference functions to appear discontinuous. The reader can verify that voter preferences in Condorcet's voting paradox are not single-peaked, which can explain the absence of a most-preferred proposal.

Referring to Arrow's impossibility theorem, note that in the case just considered majority voting has produced a social ordering (which is complete and transitive, although we have not discussed these characteristics) by violating the unrestricted domain condition, since limits were placed on the type of individual preferences allowed (they were assumed to be single-peaked). The sufficient conditions for producing a well-defined – and acyclical – social preference are thus particularly restrictive.

Work done since Black's contribution has sought in particular to do away with the postulate of one-dimensional choices and has identified other necessary and/or suffi-cient conditions for a definite (acyclical) outcome.[39] Nevertheless, under certain condi-tions it is still possible to arrange voting procedures strategically so as to obtain one outcome rather than another, even under the majority voting system examined here. The *Gibbard–Satterthwaite theorem* states that if there are more than two alternatives to be voted on, no non-dictatorial voting procedure is immune to the manipulation of preferences through insincere declarations by voters (Gibbard, 1973; Satterthwaite, 1975).

To sum up, there are difficulties in constructing a social ordering in a democratic regime. They regard, in particular: (a) insincere voting for strategic purposes; and (b) 'multi-peaked' individual preferences.

Political institutions can nevertheless be arranged in such a way as to reduce or even eliminate these difficulties by skirting the conditions under which they arise. For example, strategic voting can be reduced if participation in votes on specific alternatives is voluntary, which in practice limits the vote to people interested in those (and not other) alternatives. In addition, despite the existence of multipeaked preferences (which is often a consequence of the fact that choices are multidimensional), we can still apply the median voter theorem if voting regards 'slates' of proposals, candidates or parties. What is more, while cyclical majorities can emerge from single votes, multiple votes on different questions might avoid them (see Ingberman and Inman, 1988). We will not extend our analysis of actual political institutions here since we wish to keep this part of our discussion on a more abstract level. Such an analysis in any case lies within the domain of political science. The last 40 years have seen the emergence of a new approach, the *public choice school*, which deals with the economic study of non-market decisions, or simply the application of economics to political science. Its subject matter is the same as that of political science (theory of the state, voting procedures, theory of parties, theory of democracy, etc.) but its methodology is that of economics, especially neoclassical theory (Mueller, 1989, pp. 1–2). Space limitations prevent us from examin-ing these issues in greater detail, but we will return in chapter 9 to certain aspects of the problems this discipline addresses.

Our objective in this chapter has been to show that:

1 All the procedures in the construction of a social ordering through voting constantly reflect value judgements about the best action to take; these judge-

---

[39] Among others, see Davis, De Groot and Hinich (1972); Chichilnisky and Heal (1983) and Gans and Smart (1996). For a survey, see Osborne (1995).

ments lead to the selection of one or another of the possible alternatives and therefore benefit one or another of the members of society.

2 There is a correspondence between the value judgements underlying the voting rules and the conditions that make the aggregation of individual preferences possible.

3 It is difficult to define a social ordering in a democratic regime. It was shown that using either unanimous or majority voting rules as an aggregation procedure for individual preferences:

(a) does not guarantee that a well-defined social preference will be expressed;

(b) can lead to different results depending on the circumstances (in particular, on voting procedures); social preferences can therefore be altered by voters and/or those in charge of the voting if special measures are not taken to avoid this.

*3.7 Appendix: A formal demonstration of the Pareto efficiency conditions

Alice and Bob (for simplicity, A and B) have utility functions with normal properties (continuity, monotonicity, etc.), u^A and u^B:

$$u^A(q_p^A, q_t^A, l) \quad u^B(q_p^B, q_t^B, m), \tag{3.4}$$

where q_p^h and q_t^h are, respectively, the quantities of potatoes and tea consumed by individual h (for $h = A, B$), and l and m are the quantities of the two inputs supplied by A and B respectively.[40]

The production functions are also defined

$$q_p = f_p(l_p, m_p) \quad q_t = f_t(l_t, m_t), \tag{3.5}$$

where q_p and q_t are, respectively, the quantities of potatoes and tea produced, while l_p, m_p, l_t and m_t are the inputs used for the production of potatoes and tea.

Equality conditions between consumption and output of final goods must also be satisfied:

$$\sum_h q_p^h = q_p \quad \sum_h q_t^h = q_t \quad h = A, B \tag{3.6}$$

as well as the equality of the total quantity of inputs used and the quantities available:

$$l_p + l_t = l \quad m_p + m_t = m \tag{3.7}$$

The Pareto optimality conditions for the efficient allocation of resources are obtained by maximising the utility of one consumer with respect to the quantity of goods and factors, subject to the constraint that the utility of the other consumer is given and the conditions (3.5), (3.6) and (3.7) are satisfied.[41] The first-order maximisation conditions are obtained using Lagrange multipliers for the various constraints.

---

[40] We will consider the supply of inputs to be variable rather than given.
[41] A non-negativity constraint on all decision variables should also be satisfied.

Hence, for max $u^A(q_p^A, q_t^A, l)$ subject to $u^B(q_p^B, q_t^B, m) = \bar{u}^B$ and (3.5), (3.6) and (3.7), we write the Lagrangean:[42]

$$L = u^A(q_p^A, q_t^A, l) - \mu_1[\bar{u}^B - u^B(q_p^B, q_t^B, m)] - \mu_2[q_p - f_p(l_p, m_p)] +$$
$$- \mu_3[q_t - f_t(l_t, m_t)] - \mu_4\left[\sum_h q_p^h - q_p\right] - \mu_5\left[\sum_h q_t^h - q_t\right] + \qquad (3.8)$$
$$- \mu_6[l_p + l_t - l] - \mu_7[m_p + m_t - m]$$

where the μs are the Lagrange multipliers of the various constraints.

Assuming non-corner solutions, the first-order conditions obtained by differentiating the Lagrangean and equating to zero are the following:

$$\partial L/\partial q_p^A = \partial u^A/\partial q_p^A - \mu_4 = 0 \qquad (3.9)$$

$$\partial L/\partial q_t^A = \partial u^A/\partial q_t^A - \mu_5 = 0 \qquad (3.10)$$

$$\partial L/\partial l = \partial u^A/\partial l + \mu_6 = 0 \qquad (3.11)$$

$$\partial L/\partial q_p^B = \mu_1(\partial u^B/\partial q_p^B) - \mu_4 = 0 \qquad (3.12)$$

$$\partial L/\partial q_t^B = \mu_1(\partial u^B/\partial q_t^B) - \mu_5 = 0 \qquad (3.13)$$

$$\partial L/\partial m = \mu_1(\partial u^B/\partial m) + \mu_7 = 0 \qquad (3.14)$$

$$\partial L/\partial q_p = -\mu_2 + \mu_4 = 0 \qquad (3.15)$$

$$\partial L/\partial q_t = -\mu_3 + \mu_5 = 0 \qquad (3.16)$$

$$\partial L/\partial l_p = \mu_2(\partial f_p/\partial l_p) - \mu_6 = 0 \qquad (3.17)$$

$$\partial L/\partial m_p = \mu_2(\partial f_p/\partial m_p) - \mu_7 = 0 \qquad (3.18)$$

$$\partial L/\partial l_t = \mu_3(\partial f_t/\partial l_t) - \mu_6 = 0 \qquad (3.19)$$

$$\partial L/\partial m_t = \mu_3(\partial f_t/\partial m_t) - \mu_7 = 0 \qquad (3.20)$$

together with the constraints (3.5), (3.6), (3.7) and $u^B(q_p^B, q_t^B, m) = \bar{u}^B$.

With the appropriate calculations,[43] we obtain the following conditions:

$$(\partial u^A/\partial q_p^A)/(\partial u^A/\partial q_t^A) = \mu_4/\mu_5 = (\partial u^B/\partial q_p^B)/(\partial u^B/\partial q_t^B) \qquad (3.21)$$

$$-(\partial u^A/\partial l)/(\partial u^A/\partial q_p^A) = \mu_6/\mu_4 = \partial f_p/\partial l_p \qquad (3.22)$$

$$-(\partial u^A/\partial l)/(\partial u^A/\partial q_t^A) = \mu_6/\mu_5 = \partial f_t/\partial l_t \qquad (3.23)$$

$$-(\partial u^B/\partial m)/(\partial u^B/\partial q_p^B) = \mu_7/\mu_4 = \partial f_p/\partial m_p \qquad (3.24)$$

$$-(\partial u^B/\partial m)/(\partial u^B/\partial q_t^B) = \mu_7/\mu_5 = \partial f_t/\partial m_t \qquad (3.25)$$

$$(\partial f_p/\partial l_p)/(\partial f_p/\partial m_p) = \mu_6/\mu_7 = (\partial f_t/\partial l_t)/(\partial f_t/\partial m_t) \qquad (3.26)$$

[42] We could have written an analogous Lagrangean for consumer B, obtaining the same final conditions.

[43] For example, we can obtain (3.21) by bringing the μ in (3.9), (3.10), (3.12) and (3.13) to the right-hand side and then dividing term by term (3.9) and (3.10), on the one hand, and (3.12) and (3.13), on the other.

$$(\partial u^A/\partial q_p^A)/(\partial u^A/\partial q_t^A) = (\partial u^B/\partial q_p^B)/(\partial u^B/\partial q_t^B) =$$

$$= \mu_4/\mu_5 = (\partial f_t/\partial l_t)/(\partial f_p/\partial l_p) = (\partial f_t/\partial m_t)/(\partial f_p/\partial m_p) \tag{3.27}$$

Condition (3.21) shows the equality of the MRSs between the two goods for the two consumers (efficient consumption allocation). In fact, $(\partial u^A/\partial q_p^A)/(\partial u^A/\partial q_t^A)$ is simply the MRS between potatoes and tea for $A(-dq_t^A/dq_p^A)$, as we can see by totally differentiating A's utility function and assuming that the change in utility is equal to zero (i.e., she is moving along a given indifference curve ($du^A = 0$)). Similarly, the right-hand side of (3.21) gives the MRS between potatoes and tea for B.

Conditions (3.22)–(3.25) show the equality of the MRSs between each input and each good, with the marginal productivity of the input considered in terms of the good (efficient supply of inputs).

Condition (3.26) shows the equality of the MRTSs for the two goods, indicating an efficient allocation of inputs (production efficiency).

Finally, (3.27) shows the equality of the MRS between the two goods and the MRT between the two goods ('general' efficiency).

3.8 Summary

1 The Pareto principle states that the welfare of a group of individuals increases in moving from state a to state b if all of the individuals are better off in b, or if at least one individual is better off and no one is worse off.

2 A Pareto optimum is, consequently, a state from which any move to another state does not improve the utility of someone without worsening that of at least one other individual (Pareto efficiency).

3 In a pure consumption economy, Pareto efficiency is achieved when output is allocated among individuals in such a way that the MRSs for each pair of goods are equal for all individuals (optimal consumption allocation).

4 In a production economy, three further problems must be tackled:
(a) the choice of production plans (production efficiency);
(b) the choice of the supply of inputs (input supply efficiency);
(c) the choice of output levels ('general' efficiency).

5 Production efficiency is achieved when inputs are allocated among various uses in such a way that the MRTS for each pair of inputs is equal for all uses.

6 'General' efficiency is obtained when the MRS and the MRT are equal for all pairs of goods.

*7 The utility possibilities frontier is the envelope of the various utility possibilities curves and denotes not only consumption efficiency, as does each utility possibilities curve, but also 'general' efficiency.

8 The concept of Pareto efficiency is based on general equilibrium theory, which in its standard form suffers from a number of limitations (static analysis, maximisation postulate, exogenous nature of preferences and abstraction from important features of real-life economic systems). These limitations join those of the postulates underlying the Pareto criterion itself (ethical individualism, ordinal measurability and non-comparability).

9 An additional limitation of the Pareto criterion is that it only allows us to construct partial, rather than complete, orderings of social states.

10 Attempts have been made to overcome this limitation with the compensation principle and the axiomatic construction of a social welfare function.

11 The compensation principle states that any change that increases productivity would allow those who benefit from the change to compensate those who would be worse off while retaining a net benefit. Such a change should therefore be considered socially desirable. However, the mere possibility of compensation does not enable us to judge the change. In order to do so, we need to evaluate the desirability of the distribution that would result with and without actual compensation.

12 Supplementing the Pareto principle with other widely accepted axioms does not enable us to construct an actual social ordering without dictatorial choices (the Arrow impossibility theorem). Admitting some degree of interpersonal comparability as well as introducing cardinal measurement of utilities is one way of getting around the impossibility result and constructing a complete ordering.

*13 Social decisions have procedural aspects associated with some of the postulates or criteria examined earlier. Unanimous voting systems have a strong tendency to favour the status quo, and the final outcome of the voting may depend on the voting path chosen.

*14 If interpersonal comparisons are allowed, we can adopt majority voting as a decision procedure. This does not guarantee defined outcomes except under certain conditions (the median voter theorem).

*15 The difficulties of constructing a social ordering in a democratic society can be reduced or eliminated by selecting appropriate political institutions.

3.9 Key concepts

Strong, weak Pareto principle	Marginal rate of substitution
Pareto efficiency	Edgeworth box
Pareto optimum	Pareto set or contract curve
Consumption efficiency	Production efficiency
Allocation	Input supply efficiency
Utility possibilities curve	General efficiency (efficient output choice)

Marginal rate of technical substitution
Input contract curve
Transformation curve
Marginal rate of transformation
*Utility possibilities frontier
*Envelope
General equilibrium
Partial, complete ordering
Tyranny of the status quo
Impossibility of a Paretian liberal
Potential, effective compensation
Scitovsky's 'double' criterion
Universal or unrestricted domain
Independence of irrelevant alternatives
Decisive preferences
Dictatorship
Arrow impossibility theorem

*Binary, plurality voting rule
*Unanimity, majority voting
*Core
*Theory of committees
*Voting with exclusion
*Strategic voting
*Path dependence property
*Borda count
*Condorcet solution
*Transitive preference
*Cyclical majority
*Condorcet voting paradox
*Single-peaked preferences
*Median voter theorem
*Gibbard-Satterthwaite theorem
*Public choice

4 Theories of justice, welfare functions and the social optimum

⟨ 4.1 The need for a 'theory of justice'

In section 3.5 we said that it is impossible to construct a complete social ordering based on the Pareto criterion and certain other widely accepted axioms. There have been many vain attempts to develop alternative solutions based on the Pareto principle. As we have seen, however, it is possible to construct complete orderings if we abandon the postulates of ordinal measurability and non-comparable individual utilities that under-lie the Pareto principle itself.

The outcome of Arrow's attempt to construct a complete social ordering put an end – with little or nothing to show for its efforts – to the scientific programme initiated by Robbins' 1932 essay (the starting point, if not the 'manifesto', of new welfare economics), which sought to go beyond the utilitarianism of Pigou and, more generally, to eliminate recourse to interpersonal comparisons of utility and value judgements.[1] The attempt to direct welfare economics towards the exclusive study of problems of efficiency, separated from those of equity, was thus a failure.

Given the necessity of using some sort of interpersonal comparison to define complete social rankings, we must specify the principle that will enable us to evaluate all possible alternative situations, especially in cases where opting for one or another state means improving one person's situation while worsening that of another.

Such a criterion of distributive justice can be part of a broader system of social justice criteria. The central problem of distributive justice consists in defining principles for judging the desirability of alternative ways of: (a) assigning the participants in the productive process (more generally, the members of a society) the benefits of that activity; and (b) apportioning the related costs.

Obviously, such criteria depend on each individual's view of the world. It is therefore

[1] The specific importance of Robbins' essay was discussed in section 2.2.2. We should bear in mind, however, that Arrow's analytical aims were quite different from those pursued by Robbins.

no surprise that economists attempting to construct social orderings have often taken their inspiration from principles of social or political philosophy (as with Pigou, who adopted certain principles of utilitarianism) or study these disciplines directly (Harsanyi and Sen, for instance); in a number of cases, principles of distributive justice have been developed by social philosophers themselves (such as Nozick and Rawls).

When the need for criteria to evaluate distribution became clear to economists, efforts to construct a social ordering thus found many points in common with contemporary social or political philosophy, which carries on the work begun by modern moral philosophy with partly new concepts and methodologies.

In section 4.2 we examine the main criteria of distributive justice that incorporate the postulate of ethical individualism and can be expressed in the form of a social welfare function (SWF). Section 4.3 examines how to identify the social optimum for a given SWF. We then take a more detailed look at two of the most well-known justice criteria that can be expressed in terms of a SWF: the utilitarian criterion (section 4.4) and Rawls' theory of justice (section *4.5). In section 4.6 we briefly discuss two other justice criteria that are not formulated in terms of a SWF and that reject ethical individualism (Nozick and Sen).

4.2 Interpersonal comparisons, justice criteria and social welfare functions

If we want to aggregate individual utilities or positions in order to construct a SWF, or rank situations from a distributive point of view, we require additional postulates beyond that of the comparability of individual utilities or, more generally, individual situations.

Let us first examine the construction of a social welfare function. Assume that we accept the idea that social welfare must only reflect individual preferences with regard to the various states of the world (ethical individualism or 'welfarism'). If we allow interpersonal comparisons of utility – in order to overcome Arrow's impossibility theorem – we still have to define the aggregation rule. This consists in choosing a mathematical operator (e.g., summation) to convert individual preferences into a single social preference. The aggregation rule is not a purely mechanical process since it also reflects value judgements about interpersonal relationships; in other words, distributive justice criteria. We will be able to verify this as we investigate the most important and frequently adopted social welfare functions:

(a) utilitarian SWFs;
(b) Bernoulli–Nash SWFs;
(c) the Rawls SWF;
(d) the Bergson–Samuelson SWF.

4.2.1 Utilitarian social welfare functions

These are the most simple and intuitive forms of SWF. Given individual utilities, u_i, if these are comparable and we assign the same (unit) weight to the H individuals, the

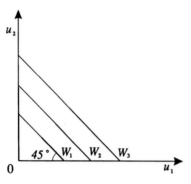

Figure 4.1

social utility of social state x, $W(x)$, can be expressed as the sum of the $u_i(x)$:

$$W(x) = \sum_{i=1}^{H} u_i(x) \tag{4.1}$$

Equation (4.1) is the *simple utilitarian SWF*, also known as the Benthamite SWF (from Jeremy Bentham, founder of the classical utilitarian school, who was inspired by the work of the British philosopher Francis Hutcheson and the Italian political scientist Cesare Beccaria).

Assuming for simplicity that there are only two individuals, we can show this SWF in diagram form using indifference curves similar to those adopted in the marginalist analysis of consumer decisions. Here, the curves are called *social indifference curves* or *isowelfare curves* and are represented by negatively sloped parallel 45° lines such that $W_1 < W_2 < W_3$ (see figure 4.1).

A more general utilitarian SWF can be obtained by assigning different non-negative weights, a_i, to different individuals:[2]

$$W = \sum_{i=1}^{H} a_i u_i \tag{4.2}$$

This SWF, known as the *generalised utilitarian SWF*, was derived in axiomatic form by Harsanyi (1976). For two individuals it can be shown as a map of social indifference curves represented by parallel lines with a negative slope equal to the ratio of the weights assigned to the two individuals (see figure 4.2).[3]

4.2.2 Bernoulli–Nash social welfare functions

One alternative to summation is multiplication. The *simple Bernoulli–Nash SWF* is:

$$W = \prod_{i=1}^{H} u_i \tag{4.3}$$

where Π stands for the product operator.

---

[2] For simplicity the indication of the dependence of social welfare and individual utilities on the state of the world will be omitted in this and subsequent SWFs.
[3] The slope, given by the tangent of the angle β, is equal to $-(a_1/a_2)$.

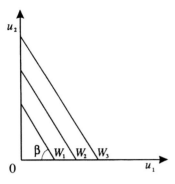

Figure 4.2

The *generalised form* introduces the weights a_i as exponents of the individual utilities:

$$W = \prod_{i=1}^{H} (u_i)^{a_i} \tag{4.4}$$

Multiplication accentuates the egalitarian nature of the aggregation rule, since a more equal income distribution produces greater social welfare (summing utilities is not egalitarian unless we make the specific hypothesis of decreasing marginal utility). Let us examine why this is the case. Assume that:

(a) there are two individuals;
(b) the only relevant aspect of social states is income;
(c) income to be distributed is given and constant, equal to, say, 10;
(d) the two consumers have equal capacity for satisfaction, which means that an equal weight (for simplicity, 1) is given to each consumer's preferences;
(e) preferences can be measured cardinally and, for simplicity, the marginal utility of income is constant and equal to 20.

Let us consider two alternative distributions, one egalitarian, the other non-egalitarian.

1 If income is distributed equally, each consumer's utility will be equal to 100. In this case, the (simple) utilitarian SWF will record social welfare of 200 and the (simple) Bernoulli–Nash SWF will give welfare of 10,000.
2 If income is not distributed equally, so that individual 1 receives, say, six and individual 2 receives four, the total utility of 1 will increase while the utility of 2 will diminish. As we have assumed that the marginal utility of income is constant[4] and equal for the two consumers, the increase in 1's utility will be exactly equal to the decline in 2's (20); i.e., we have $u_1 = 120$ and $u_2 = 80$. In this situation, the level of social welfare (200) given by the utilitarian SWF is unchanged from the previous situation. If we multiply rather than sum utilities,

---

[4] We can eliminate this assumption without any loss of generality; in fact, the alternative hypothesis of decreasing marginal utility would accentuate the result we wish to show.

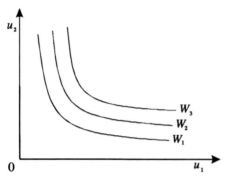

Figure 4.3

however (the Bernoulli–Nash SWF), the second situation turns out to be worse
than the original state,[5] with social welfare equal to 9,600.

A Bernoulli–Nash SWF can be shown in diagram form with hyperbolic isowelfare
curves (see figure 4.3).

4.2.3 The Rawls' social welfare function

An even stronger egalitarian premise underlies the Rawls SWF, which measures social
welfare exclusively in terms of the utility of the worst-off individual. For example, if
individual 1 has utility of 100 and individual 2 has utility of 80, social welfare is equal to
the utility of individual 2.

This can be expressed as:

$$W = \min(u_i) \quad i = 1, 2, \ldots, H \tag{4.5}$$

Note that an alternative position in which the utility of individual 1 increases from 100
to 120 while that of 2 remains at 80 does not produce a higher level of social welfare,
since social welfare is defined as the utility of the worst-placed individual, which has not
changed. In other words, Rawls' SWF[6] gives a precise indication of social choice: the

---

[5] The fact that the Bernoulli–Nash SWF penalises distributive inequalities can be understood more
clearly if we consider that it is not additive with respect to the two utilities but rather with respect to
the logarithms of the utilities. The sum of the logarithms of two numbers whose total is given is
maximised when the two numbers are equal and tends to decline as the difference between the
numbers increases.

[6] We use a formulation of Rawls' position widely adopted in the literature (however, compare with
Sen, 1982, p. 29). Rawls does not in fact speak of a social welfare function, nor does he appear to
introduce the postulate of ethical individualism. He prefers to speak about the 'expectations' of
individuals, which can be interpreted as a synonym of 'utilities' (see Rawls, 1971, pp. 75 ff.). His
yardstick for inequality is the quantity of 'primary' social goods available to individuals: rights and
liberties, opportunities and powers, income and wealth (ibid., pp. 90 ff.). While aware of the
difference, we have preferred to use a version of Rawls' justice criteria expressed in terms of a social
welfare function as we do not feel this conflicts with his position. This approach has already allowed
valuable comparisons that will be investigated more fully later (section *4.5).

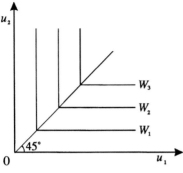

Figure 4.4

welfare of the society increases (is maximised) only if the *minimum* utility increases (is maximised); for this reason the Rawlsian SWF is called the *maximin* SWF. In diagrammatic terms, the Rawlsian isowelfare curves are L-shaped, with their vertex along the bisector of the first quadrant and sides parallel to the axes (see figure 4.4).

The shape of the curves means that an increase in the utility of an individual does not increase social welfare if the utility of the least-advantaged individual does not change. Thus, the horizontal part of the social indifference curve shows that an increase in the utility level of individual 1 does not increase social welfare (which remains at W_1 or W_2 or W_3) if the other individual's utility does not increase. The vertical part of the curve shows that an increase in the utility of individual 2 will affect social welfare in a similar way. There is no *trade-off* between the utility of one person and that of another, as was the case with the SWFs described above. On the contrary, the utilities of the two individuals are perfectly complementary.

4.2.4 The Bergson–Samuelson social welfare function

This SWF has the most general form of all:

$$W = W(u_1 u_2, \ldots, u_H) \tag{4.6}$$

and can be specified in a variety of functional forms, such as the additive form of the utilitarian SWF, the multiplicative Bernoulli–Nash form or the Rawls SWF. In any case, the function *normally* has the following properties:

(a) it is defined with respect to individual utilities; i.e., it accepts the welfarist postulate;
(b) individual utilities are comparable;
(c) the strong Pareto criterion is satisfied;[7]

---

[7] Recall that an increase in the utility of one member of society increases social welfare as long as no other member's utility is decreased. In the Bergson–Samuelson SWF, the Pareto principle is used simply as a hypothesis of social non-satiability: social welfare increases as the satisfaction of each individual increases, *ceteris paribus*. The criterion does not imply, however, that individual positions are non-comparable, which is explicitly rejected by hypothesis *b* (Gravelle and Rees, 1992, advance a similar argument).

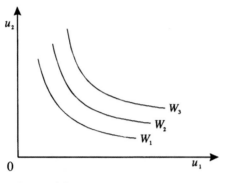

Figure 4.5

    (d) social preferences are convex or strictly convex (indicating a preference for the diversification of utilities among different individuals rather than concentration of utility with one person only).

These properties allow us to construct a map of convex or strictly convex social indifference curves (figure 4.5). Property (a) permits us to define W in the plane (u_1, u_2); (b) ensures that we can define *social* indifference curves, i.e., *we treat society as an individual*; property (c), together with certain other conditions, ensures that the indifference curves are decreasing; and (d) establishes their convexity or strict convexity. The Rawls' SWF does not satisfy property (c). According to Rawls, in fact, if the utility of anyone except the worst-off individual increases, social welfare does not increase.

4.3 Choosing the social optimum

When the justice criterion can be expressed in the form of a SWF, as in the cases above, the social choice can be made in a manner similar to that followed by the consumer when choosing the optimal bundle of goods to consume: the SWF is maximised subject to the constraint faced by a society, which is given by the utility possibilities frontier introduced in section *3.1.3. For readers who omitted this section, the utility possibilities frontier (UPF) in a two-person society indicates the maximum utility one individual can enjoy, given the utility of the other, for *all possible optimal resource allocations*. The concept of the UPF is very similar to the utility possibilities curve (UPC) discussed in section 3.1.1, from which it is, in fact, derived. The UPF and the UPC coincide in a pure consumption economy. The UPF and the UPC are decreasing, unless the action of one individual to increase his utility also has positive effects on the other individual that the latter does not have to pay for (positive externalities or external economies). In such cases the increase in one person's utility can occur without reducing that of the other, given the society's resources. The curve is certainly concave if utilities are cardinally measurable.

    In figure 4.6 the social optimum is at a, where the slope of the UPF is equal to the slope of a social indifference curve, i.e., the marginal rate of social substitution. The

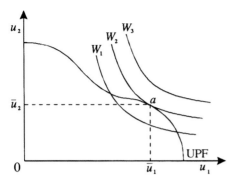

Figure 4.6

utilities of the two individuals at a are $\bar{u}_1$ and $\bar{u}_2$. The optimum may not be unique if the UPF is not concave.[8]

Obviously, point a in figure 4.6 does not immediately give us the optimal social state, since the SWF and the UPF are expressed in terms of the utilities of the two individuals. However, since the utilities are defined with respect to social states, it is always possible to identify the social state associated with the utilities of individuals 1 and 2 that maximise the SWF. An additional problem, which is of no great interest at this stage of our analysis, regards the actions to be taken to reach the optimal social state. In the following section we will see how it is possible to move from utilities to social states and, to a certain degree, actions.

4.4 The utilitarianism of Pigou

The founding father of classical utilitarianism was Jeremy Bentham. Major contributions in the field of economics came from Henry Sidgwick, a student of Bentham's, and Arthur C. Pigou. Similar arguments (hence 'neo-utilitarian') have been advanced more recently by John Harsanyi.

Bentham defined the happiness of the nation as the sum of the satisfactions of each citizen and advocated that institutions and public action be directed towards obtaining 'the greatest happiness of the greatest number' (Bentham, 1789), a progressive attitude compared with public policies of the time, which were still not based on democratic principles.

Pigou took up the thread of classical utilitarianism more than a century later, purging it of many philosophical elements, and defined *total* (or *aggregate*) *welfare* as the sum of the utilities of the members of society obtained from the various sources of satisfaction.

---

[8] Although multiple equilibria complicate the life of the analyst (and the student), they can be useful in the real world. Recall that, by construction, all such equilibrium points are efficient, since they are on the UPF, differing only in the different utility levels of the various individuals, which are largely attributable to distribution differences. The existence of multiple efficient equilibria therefore allows us to choose between different distributions on the basis of external considerations (for example, political feasibility).

In doing so, Pigou postulated that individual utilities were cardinally measurable and fully comparable[9]. Total welfare can therefore be expressed by the simple utilitarian function:

$$W = \sum_{i=1}^{H} u_i(x) \tag{4.7}$$

where x represents all the features of the possible states of the world that determine satisfaction (availability of economic goods, natural beauty, love, etc.). Pigou did not analyse total welfare, however, but only the part of welfare stemming from sources that can be measured in monetary terms,[10] or what he called *economic welfare*, assuming that, subject to contrary proof, changes in economic welfare will correspond to changes of the same sign in total welfare.[11]

Limiting our discussion to economic welfare, the non-economic factors included in x drop out, leaving only the quantities of the various economic goods *available* to each individual.[12]

The term 'available' can be interpreted in a number of ways: faced with an infinite time horizon it would be appropriate to refer to consumption only, since consumption over an infinite horizon can satisfy all the economic objectives of individuals. However, faced with a finite time horizon, the problems of an individual's position in the future and of each generation's interest in future generations arise. Therefore, consumption in the period considered would not be the only source of economic utility: this would also depend on the wealth accumulated at the end of the time horizon available to individuals or to future generations, which should therefore be considered an additional argument of the utility function. So, referring to a realistic finite time horizon, Pigou correctly considers national income[13] – that is, the sum of consumption and saving by society over a certain time period – as the indicator of economic welfare. All other things being equal (in particular, distribution), since each person's utility is an increasing function of his income, it can be argued that economic welfare increases as the total of individual incomes (i.e., national income, or product) rises.

This argument assumes a constant income distribution. If an increase in national income were accompanied by changes in the distribution, an increase in economic welfare would not be assured. In order to take account of changes in the distribution Pigou introduced another hypothesis in addition to cardinal measurability and

---

[9] Pigou's fundamental work is *The Economics of Welfare* (1920). An earlier edition was entitled *Wealth and Welfare* (1912). Pigou's original arguments were repeated in subsequent editions of *The Economics of Welfare* (the fourth and last edition came out in 1932, but it was reprinted in 1952 with additional appendices) and in a later paper (see Pigou, 1951).

[10] This holds if we assume there is a clear dividing line between what can and cannot be measured in monetary terms, which is not always the case. For example, the enjoyment of natural beauty, which would be a free good, is often tied to the availability of economic goods that enable us to move to beautiful locations.

[11] Cases in which economic and total welfare diverge occur, for example, when economic welfare is accompanied by pollution or unethical behaviour.

[12] We are assuming that resource endowments are given.

[13] Pigou used the term 'national dividend'.

comparability: decreasing marginal utility of income. Together with the other assumptions, nthis principle enables us to state that the utility of the last penny for a rich person is less than the utility of the last penny for a pauper, if the marginal utility functions of the two are not too dissimilar (equal at the limit). Note that the hypotheses of cardinality and comparability allow us to compare changes in utility for two different people as if they were the same person. With these postulates, the principle of decreasing marginal utility of income, which is normally used in relation to changes in the income of a single individual, can be applied to changes in the income of two people as if we were dealing with the income of the same person.

Accordingly, an increase in national income with no change in distribution will increase welfare. The same holds for an increase in national income associated with an 'improvement' in the distribution, which – given our decreasing marginal utility assumption – means an increase in the income of the poor. If, however, an increase in national income were accompanied by a 'worsening' of the distribution through a reduction of the income of the poor, the increase in utility for the rich would be counterbalanced by a reduction in the utility of the poor and the net result would be uncertain unless we were able, *in practice* and not just in principle (as supposed by Pigou), to measure the cardinal utility of the individuals involved.

Similar reasoning enables us to state that a redistribution of income from the rich to the poor is certain to produce an increase in economic welfare if it is not accompanied by a reduction in national income. If there were a reduction, it would be necessary to actually measure individual utilities in order to be able to calculate the net result.

Thus, a definite outcome is only assured in the cases provided for by the following two propositions of Pigou, which are *sufficient* conditions for an increase in economic welfare:

1 *Economic welfare increases if the size of national income increases without 'worsening' the distribution, i.e., reducing the income of the poor* (efficiency condition).

2 *Economic welfare increases if the distribution 'improves' and the size of national income does not decline* (equity condition).

Our discussion from the previous chapter highlights the evident limitations to Pigou's approach. However, since we know that value judgements must be introduced if we wish to construct a social ordering, we can only decide whether we share the value judgements on which Pigou's analysis is based.[14]

[14] The practical consequences of the Pigovian analysis are worth discussing even if we do not deal with the relationship between social orderings and institutions (government and the market in particular) at this stage.
   Pigou's first proposition opens the way to public policies aimed at maximising national income; that is, policies intended to improve economic efficiency. One aspect of such policies was noted by Pigou himself: they call for the removal of the causes of the divergence between private product and social product. The latter cannot be maximised if, for example, agents do not take account of the benefits or harm their actions may cause others. Situations of this sort are a consequence of *externalities* (or *external effects*) associated with the actions of individuals. As we mentioned above,

*4.5 Rawls' theory of justice

In Rawls' theory, a given distribution is just when it is fair, in the sense that it offers everyone the same opportunities.

Rawls arrives at his position by way of a thought experiment in which individuals find themselves in an *original position* in which they decide as free and equal persons the structure (rules) of a just society (in other words, the basis of their *social contract*).[15] Each individual ignores how the various alternatives can influence himself and decides on the basis of general considerations only, since he is covered by a *veil of ignorance* with regard to:

- (a) his current and future position in society, particularly his class and social status;
- (b) the distribution of endowments, natural abilities such as strength, intelligence and so on;
- (c) his personal preferences, especially his aversion to risk; and
- (d) other circumstances such as the political and economic situation, his age group, etc.

In such conditions the members of this society would unanimously accept the following two principles of justice:

1 'Each person is to have an equal right to the most extensive total system of equal basic liberties compatible with a similar system of liberty for all.'

2 'Social and economic inequalities are to be arranged so that they are both: (a) to the greatest benefit of the least advantaged . . . and (b) attached to offices and positions open to all under conditions of fair equality of opportunity' (Rawls, 1971, p. 302).

The second of these is of particular importance to our discussion. With it, Rawls introduces what he calls the *difference principle*, according to which inequalities in life

externalities are the advantages or disadvantages caused to other agents (producers or consumers) by the activity of a given agent (producer or consumer) for which the latter does not, respectively, receive or pay a price. We will discuss this at length later on, but it is worth mentioning also here not only to acknowledge Pigou's use of externalities – a concept introduced by Marshall for analytical reasons (see section 6.3) – in economic policy matters, but also to provide an idea of the possible implications of the category of economic welfare. As we said, in the presence of externalities the UPF may have increasing segments, which in intuitive terms means that it is possible to reallocate resources in a way that increases the utility of both individuals. Nevertheless, the economic agent that causes positive externalities may hesitate to take actions that produce positive effects that he cannot appropriate entirely, since part of these accrue to others. Hence the need for intervention to stimulate such activities.

The second of Pigou's propositions constitutes the theoretical foundation of income redistribution policies. The postulates on which it is based clarify the type of information and/or value judgements that are needed to support them.

[15] Rawls generalises and raises to a higher level of abstraction the social contract theory of Hobbes, Locke, Rousseau and Kant. The concept of the original position had already been introduced by Harsanyi (1953). On this subject, see also Binmore (1989).

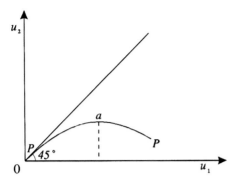

Figure 4.7

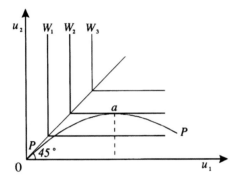

Figure 4.8

prospects are justifiable only if we can associate them with a benefit for the worst-off individual (ibid., pp. 76–8). For example, suppose there are two individuals, 1 and 2, and that the former is the better off of the two. As long as a state or action will improve the position of 2, that state or action is considered fair and desirable, whether or not it improves the position of 1.

We can show the situation in terms of the utility of 1 and 2 as in figure 4.7.[16]

From the origin 0 to point a the difference principle is satisfied. At this point the Rawlsian SWF is maximised, as we can see in figure 4.8, where the curve of possible utility distributions is tangent to the social indifference curve W_2 at a.

This position differs from the one that would result from other theories of justice: each of the other SWFs we have examined would place the social optimum somewhere to the

---

[16] The curve PP corresponds to the UPF introduced in sections *3.1.3 and 4.3. The first part of the curve is increasing, conveying the idea that, given the resources available to society, the increase in the utility of an individual can initially take place without disadvantaging the other, instead improving his position owing to positive externalities. In other words, society can establish cooperative arrangements that are advantageous for all of its members, at least within certain limits.

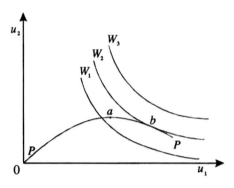

Figure 4.9

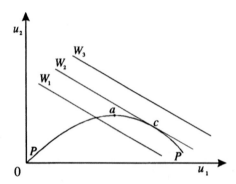

Figure 4.10

right of a,[17] with the distance from point a increasing as the slope of the social indifference curve increases. Consider figure 4.9, in which b is the point of tangency with an indifference curve derived from a Bernoulli–Nash SWF. In figure 4.10 point c, again to the right of a,[18] is the maximum obtainable with respect to a utilitarian SWF.

As noted above, the Rawlsian SWF is markedly egalitarian. Nevertheless, it is not entirely so; in fact, it may express a preference for a less-egalitarian situation if this benefits the worst-off person the most in *absolute* terms (Stiglitz, 1988).

For example, let individual 1 have a utility (or income) of 100 and individual 2 one of 50. Let there also be two alternative situations:

(a) the utility of individual 1 increases to 1,000 and that of 2 rises to 55;
(b) the utility of individual 1 increases to 200 and that of 2 rises to 54.

[17] This is clear if we consider the fact that: (1) point a is the maximum for u_2; therefore at a the curve PP has a slope equal to zero; (2) the only indifference curves with horizontal sections are those of the Rawlsian SWF. All the other SWFs have decreasing indifference curves, which can be tangent to the OP curve only at points to the right of a.

[18] This assumes that the scale for measuring utility does not change. However, even assuming this it is not possible to say in general whether b is to the right of c or not.

According to Rawls, alternative *a* is preferable since the increase in the utility of the worse-off person is larger, even though relative inequality is greater in *a* than in *b*.

4.6 Non-welfarist principles of justice

The SWFs we have examined so far all accept the principle of ethical individualism; they are therefore essentially appraisals of social states mediated by individual preferences. Among the philosophers and economists who reject ethical individualism are Nozick and Sen, whose justice criteria we now consider. In addition to rejecting ethical individualism, Sen also seems to discard the postulate of methodological individualism.

4.6.1 Nozick's theory of justice

Nozick (1974) develops the so-called *entitlement theory*, which has numerous forebears (among the most recent, see von Hayek, 1960).

The theory assesses distributive justice not with regard to results (e.g., the quantity of goods available to individuals or the utility each enjoys), but rather with regard to procedures (*procedural* or *formal justice*). Under this approach, any distribution is considered just if individuals' fundamental rights have been respected. Regardless of levels and differences in individual utilities, these rights include the right to life and the products of one's labour and freedom of choice. They are inalienable rights, being independent of, and antecedent to, all forms of social organisation. They are also absolute, in that they are not subject to any constraint other than the duty to respect the fundamental rights of others.

This sort of theory of justice aims only to guarantee liberty and the exercise of rights, not to satisfy preferences. The yardstick of justice is not individual utility, i.e., the consequences of a certain social state for an individual, but rather the exercise and respect of rights.[19] For Nozick individual utilities are not the appropriate yardstick for assessing whether the justice criterion (safeguarding rights) has been satisfied.[20] It is up to the reader to decide whether such a vision of the world is desirable. What is clear, however, is the distance between Nozick and ethical individualism and, hence, any form of ordering based on such a postulate, from the Pareto principle to SWFs.

4.6.2 Sen's theory of justice

By introducing the innovative concepts of *functionings* and *capabilities*, Sen (1980b and 1985) succeeds in merging consideration of material aspects and the results achieved by individuals, on the one hand, and rights and liberties, on the other. He begins by observing that both the quantity of a good (food, for example) and the utility generated

---

[19] It is precisely the refusal to take account of the *consequences* of an action or fact in evaluating its desirability that prompts Nozick to reject ethical individualism, which, by contrast, requires that we consider the consequences of the action or fact (in terms of individual utility).

[20] According to Nozick, the market cannot be defended on the grounds of efficiency but only as a manifestation of the exercise of individual rights.

by its use are inadequate indicators of the welfare of an individual or a community. The total quantity of food is inadequate as a guide since some may not have access to it.[21] Nor is utility any more successful as a criterion, since it is a psychological indicator that is incapable of (fully) revealing certain effects. For example, the effects of malnutrition – intended as either a shortfall or excess of food – are not always perceived by the individual: one may take pleasure in a single crust of bread, but the lack of certain fundamental nutrients may scar one's body for life.

There are in fact non-psychological aspects of goods that are central to evaluating their advantages to people and society. Goods have characteristics that people may use to perform certain functionings[22] and it is the achievement of these functionings (being well-nourished, healthy, able to move, having self-respect, being respected, being able to take part in the life and progress of the community, etc.) that indicates the benefit enjoyed by people, allowing them to exercise *positive liberty* (see section 2.2.1). More-over, it is not only the effective performance of certain functionings that is important, but also the very possibility (the 'capability') of performing them, even if they are not actually performed. For example, it is important to have the right to move without legal or material obstacles, even if a person should decide not to move. Similarly, freedom of speech is a capability, in that it allows everyone to express their views: it does not 'require that a person should be continuously speaking, but that he should be able to speak if he were to so choose'. Obviously, for basic 'capabilities' such as feeding oneself adequately, enjoying good health or acquiring an education, the element of choice may be unimportant, since people will normally take advantage of them when possible. In this case, the capability of performing certain functions corresponds to their effective performance and the distinction between capabilities and functionings largely disap-pears; in other cases, however, the distinction remains important (Sen, 1982, pp. 29–31; see also Sen, 1992, chapter III).

The ideas of Sen and other scholars who have moved in the same direction (for example, Desai, 1990; see also Nussbaum, 1992) have found an application in the study of poverty and human development indicators; in particular, purchasing power, educa-tion and health are proxies of 'capabilities' used to construct indicators of human development (see section 7.5).

---

[21] At a personal level, some of the food produced may be unavailable if it is used as seed or to obtain other essential goods and services (clothing, medical care), or due to the inappropriate distribution of what is available to a family among its members; at the level of society as a whole, food may be produced but still be unavailable to some of its members if they do not have the necessary purchasing power. This seems obvious, but it is overlooked by those who focus on per capita food supplies, aiming only to verify the groundlessness of Malthusian predictions. As a result, in many Third World countries millions of people have died because of their lack of access to essential goods (Sen, 1984). On the consequences of inequality for malnutrition, see also Dasgupta and Ray (1986).

[22] In relating 'functionings' to the characteristics of goods, Sen follows the strand in the literature that reduces goods to their characteristics (see Gorman, 1956; Lancaster, 1966).

Table 4.1. *Summary of correspondence between postulates, types of ordering and specific criteria (or SWFs)*

Postulates (P)	Types of social ordering (O)	Specific ordering criteria (OC) or SWFs
P_1: Various (e.g., distributive equality; right to life, education, health; civil and political liberties; participation in social life)	O_1: Direct	OC_1: Non-utilitarian criteria: 1 Nozick (requires P_1: respect of fundamental individual rights, right to life, to the fruits on one's labour, freedom of choice) 2 Sen (requires P_1: respect of functionings and capabilities)
P_2: Ethical individualism (only individual preferences count)	O_2: Indirect	OC_2: Pareto principle (requires P_2, P_3, P_5)
P_3: Ordinal measurability of utilities		SWF_1: utilitarian or Bernoulli–Nash SWF (requires P_2, P_4, P_6)
P_4: Cardinal measurability		SWF_2: Rawls SWF (requires P_2, P_3 [or P_4], P_6)
P_5: Interpersonal non-comparability		SWF_3: Bergson-Samuelson SWF (requires, among other things, P_6, OC_2)
P_6: Comparability		

Table 4.1 provides an outline of the relationship between postulates, types of ordering and specific ordering criteria (or SWFs).

4.7 Summary

1 The need to use some form of interpersonal comparison to define complete social rankings prompts us to choose criteria of distributive and social justice.

2 There are various justice criteria based on the postulate of ethical individualism and the interpersonal comparison of utilities. However, they differ in the aggregation rule they use. Summation is used for the utilitarian SWF. Multiplication is used for the Bernoulli–Nash SWF. An even more egalitarian option is to equate social welfare with the utility of the worst-off individual (the Rawls SWF). The Bergson–Samuelson SWF is a very general social welfare function.

3 The social optimum is obtained by maximising the selected SWF under the constraint of the UPF.

4 Within the utilitarian strand of welfare economics, Pigou identifies the maximisation of economic welfare as a policy objective. National income is an indicator of economic welfare, both in terms of its size and its distribution. The sufficient conditions for increasing economic welfare are the following:
   (a) an increase in national income that is not accompanied by a worsening of its distribution (the efficiency condition);
   (b) an improvement in the distribution that is not accompanied by a reduction in national income (the equity condition).

*5 Rawls views justice as fairness, in the sense of offering the same opportunities to all. This result emerges as the outcome of a social contract agreed upon by individuals in the 'original position', each covered by a 'veil of ignorance'.

6 A rejection of the welfarist postulate underlies the theories of justice proposed by Nozick and Sen.

7 Nozick argues for a form of procedural justice, considering situations to be just as long as the fundamental rights of individuals have been respected.

8 Sen argues that it is necessary to guarantee people's access to the goods that enable them to perform certain functionings.

4.8 Key concepts

Theory of justice	Bergson-Samuelson SWF
Efficiency, equity	Social optimum
Social welfare function (SWF)	Total (aggregate) economic welfare
Simple, generalised utilitarian SWF	*Original position
Social indifference curve	*Social contract
Isowelfare curve	*Veil of ignorance
Simple, generalised Bernoulli-Nash SWF	*Difference principle
Decreasing marginal utility of income	Entitlement principle
Rawls' maximin SWF	Formal (procedural) justice
Primary social goods	Functioning
Trade-off	Capability

PART II

SOCIAL CHOICES, GOVERNMENT AND THE MARKET

5 Social preferences and institutions

5.1 The role of the market and government

Chapter 4 concluded our analysis of the part of welfare economics that deals with criteria for ordering social states, thereby enabling us to identify possible objectives for a society. Our discussion helped us clarify the conditions for constructing social orderings. We ruled out the possibility of deducing them on purely logical grounds, showing instead the necessity of employing value judgements, i.e., ethical and political principles, especially with regard to distributive justice.

The second part of the book addresses the problem of how different economic institutions – i.e., different 'rules' or procedures governing economic interactions among individuals – enable society to best satisfy those principles and the objectives derived from them. Limiting our discussion to the 'constitutional' aspects of economic institutions (setting aside consideration of current choices), we find two principal 'rules' of social interaction: the *market* and *government*. Obviously, other institutions may also have economic importance, such as *firms*[1] and *non-profit organisations* other than households and government. Focusing on the market and government, we intend to direct our attention to the extreme aspects of the contrast between institutions oriented towards the pursuit of individual and collective interests, respectively. In reality, the contrast concerns other institutions as well. There are organisations, such as firms, that in their most abstract form also pursue private aims, or other organisations with social ends that do not share the features of government, such as voluntary non-profit groups.

The second part of the book offers a preliminary examination of how and under what conditions the economic results that can be achieved through the market (intended as a

---

[1] Firms do not play any substantial (realistic) role in general equilibrium theory, even if this formally takes account of them. The problem was first raised by Coase (1937) and, more than half a century later, we still do not have a comprehensive framework for the analysis of the market, the firm and other institutions.

specific expression of private interests) or government (intended as a particular expression of collective interests) ensure that the principles of efficiency and equity we examined in the first part are respected.

At this point in our analysis the distinction between market and government can only be conducted with regard to the private or public nature of the interests represented by the institution. Later we will also consider the difference between the two in terms of the nature of the allocative mechanism and, more generally, the decision process typical – but not exclusive – of the institution: voluntary in the case of the market, coercive in the case of government (see, among others, Hirschman, 1970; Stiglitz, 1989; Holcombe, 1994).

To begin we will refer to the principle of efficiency as given by the Pareto criterion.[2] The reason for this will be immediately clear.[3] The correspondence between Pareto optimality and equilibrium in a perfectly competitive market has been demonstrated in the economic literature. This correspondence will enable us to transfer that efficiency criterion, which we have until now defined in purely abstract terms in relation to individual utilities, to the level of institutions or to that of the actions to be taken to maximise social welfare, and thus in terms more closely related to possible social states.

The correspondence between competitive equilibrium and the Pareto optimum is based on the set of hypotheses, conceptual tools and methodologies of general equilibrium theory. In many respects, the correspondence is thus a development of Adam Smith's 'invisible hand' aphorism, which underscores the virtues of the market in achieving the 'public good'.

Sections 5.2–5.5 examine the theorems that establish the equivalence of perfect competition and Pareto optimality. Section 5.6 takes a critical look at the relationship between the equivalence asserted by the first of these theorems and the concept of the invisible hand. Section 5.7 investigates the precise meaning of the second theorem and the problems it raises.

 ## 5.2 The fundamental theorems of welfare economics

Economic theory has proved that there exists a double correspondence between the market and Pareto optimality, enunciated in the following two 'fundamental' theorems of welfare economics:

1 *In an economic system with perfect competition and complete markets, a competitive equilibrium, if it exists, will be Pareto optimal.*
2 *If there are complete markets and certain conditions are met regarding individual utility functions (convex indifference maps) and production functions (convex production sets),*

---

[2] We have seen that even utilitarianism assigns an important role to efficiency (see the first of Pigou's two propositions in section 4.4).
[3] We are not arguing that the principle of efficiency should be given greater weight than fairness or other criteria. Note that although we begin our discussion with the Pareto principle we will also examine other possible social choice criteria.

every Pareto-optimal state can be realised as the outcome of a competitive equilibrium through an appropriate redistribution of resources (initial endowments) among individuals.

The first theorem is *descriptive*, since it shows the consequences of a well-defined market situation in terms of a given social ordering criterion.

The second theorem is *prescriptive*, in that it specifies the conditions regarding allocation and distribution that must be satisfied in order to reach a certain desired state (in terms of utility).

5.3 The first fundamental theorem

In order to understand the implications of the first theorem we need to provide a precise definition of the central concepts it expresses.

By *perfect competition* we mean a regime in which there are:

    (a) homogeneous goods;
    (b) a large (hypothetically, infinite)[4] number of agents;
    (c) no agreements between agents;
    (d) free entry and exit;
    (e) full information about prices.

While we will give greater space to this subject later (see chapter 6), let us first take an intuitive look at what these conditions mean in relation to achieving a Pareto-optimal state. The condition of homogeneous goods enables us to define markets precisely. Together with the requirement for a large number of agents, the absence of agreements and free entry and exit, it also ensures that agents regard market prices as given (i.e., they are *price-takers*). Full information on the set of prices in all markets is a transparency requirement needed to avoid market segmentation and ensure that a single price holds over the entire market for a given good.

Complete markets imply the absence of *externalities*, which by definition (see section 4.4) would place agents in a relationship that does not involve an economic exchange and for which, therefore, there would be no market. [5]

A (Walrasian) *competitive equilibrium* is a price vector and an economic allocation (consumption and production vectors) which satisfy conditions of utility and profit maximisation as well as market clearing (no excess demand for each good). An equilibrium certainly exists if agents' utility functions have the standard properties (continuity, non-satiability of preferences, etc.) and increasing returns to scale are ruled out (production sets are convex).[6] Note that increasing returns to scale mean constantly decreasing long-run average costs, which would be an obstacle to the presence of more than one

---

[4] This assumption is usually termed as the 'existence of a continuum of agents'.
[5] We will see later that the problem is more general, since it includes the case of public goods, transactions costs and asymmetric information (see sections 6.3–6.7).
[6] The conditions were formulated, among others, by Arrow and Debreu (1954) and by Arrow and Hahn (1971). Although Arrow is reluctant to exclude convexity, note that in an economy in which each agent accounts for an infinitely small part of the market (more precisely, there is a continuum of agents), convex production sets are neither required nor consequent (see Farrell, 1959; Duffie and Sonnenschein, 1989).

firm in the market since each firm would seek to increase its size until it saturated the market.[7]

There can also be more than one competitive equilibrium position. This creates analytical difficulties for anyone attempting to identify a single equilibrium point[8] but can prove useful from the standpoint of economic policy, providing a range of efficient positions that can be chosen on the basis of other criteria, such as equity or political feasibility.

The most problematic aspect of a competitive equilibrium concerns its stability, e.g., the possibility of reaching and maintaining such an equilibrium. There is still no satisfactory proof that ensures such an outcome (see, in particular, Kirman, 1989; see also Hahn, 1982, pp. 73 ff; F. M. Fisher, 1983).

Briefly reviewing the ground covered in section 3.1, Pareto optimality in an exchange and production economy requires:

(a) the efficient allocation of consumption, which is obtained when the MRS for each pair of goods is equal for all consumers;
(b) the efficient allocation of production inputs, which is obtained when MRTSs for each pair of inputs in the production of all goods are equal;[9]
(c) 'general' efficiency, which is obtained when the MRS between each pair of goods for all consumers is equal to the MRT.

The proof that all these conditions are satisfied in a competitive equilibrium is fairly intuitive. We have efficient consumption if the *law of one price* holds. In this case the ratio between the prices of any two goods (bread and cloth, say) will also be unique and, since the equilibrium of *every* consumer in a perfectly competitive market is found at the point where the consumer's MRS between bread and cloth is equal to the unique ratio between the market prices of the two goods, the MRS between the two goods for *all* consumers will be equal.

Similarly, we can see that the law of one price ensures an efficient allocation of inputs. Each producer of final goods (bread and cloth, in our previous example) will minimise his costs using the combination of inputs that equalises the MRTS between labour and machinery and the ratio between the prices of labour and machinery. However, since there is only one price for each input in a perfectly competitive market, the ratio between the prices of the two inputs will also be unique; therefore, in equilibrium the MRTS between labour and machinery in the bread industry will be equal to that in the cloth industry.

---

[7] The numerosity of agents (one of the conditions for perfect competition) requires that there are no increasing returns to scale. The presence of numerous agents means that each represents a small fraction of the market. In particular, each firm reaches its equilibrium point at a relatively low level of output. The cost curve is therefore initially decreasing and then increasing or constant. This would be impossible in the case of increasing returns to scale. In this case Pareto efficiency would require that the price be equal to marginal cost, but the steady decline in unit costs implies that they are higher than marginal cost at each point. Meeting the efficiency condition would therefore require the price to be lower than average costs, i.e., the firm should operate at a loss.

[8] In reality, the problem is more complex; for example, the existence of multiple equilibrium positions might make comparative statics practically irrelevant.

[9] If inputs are not considered given, other conditions must be satisfied to have efficient supply.

To demonstrate that the MRS and the MRT are equal in a perfectly competitive market, recall that the firm maximises its profit by producing the quantity at which price is equal to marginal cost; or, to express this condition in a different way, the firm uses an input up to the point where the ratio between its price and its marginal productivity is equal to the price of the final product.[10]

From the latter condition it follows that the ratio between the price of bread and the price of cloth is equal to the ratio between the marginal productivity of labour (or machinery) in terms of cloth and the marginal productivity of labour (or machinery) in terms of bread. This second ratio gives the MRT between cloth and bread, which will therefore be equal to the MRS between the goods.

5.4 The second fundamental theorem

As we will see in more detail in section 5.6, the scope of the first fundamental theorem is fairly limited, not only because the conditions for the existence (and stability) of a competitive equilibrium are very restrictive, but also because of the special nature of Pareto 'optimality' itself.

It has been demonstrated that perfectly competitive markets can produce equilibrium situations that are Pareto efficient but in which some consumers do not have the resources necessary for survival (Coles and Hammond, 1995) or which are dictatorial; even slavery can be Pareto efficient (Bergstrom, 1971). Thus, Pareto 'optimality' does not assume or imply any judgement about the desirability of a given situation. To say that a certain state of the economic system is Pareto optimal does not mean that it is 'good', but only that it ensures production efficiency, consumption efficiency and 'general' efficiency *in relation to a given initial distribution of resources.* As Sen (1970a, p. 22) argues, a social state can be Pareto optimal but still be 'perfectly disgusting'. We cannot therefore say that we must – or that it is desirable to – work towards achieving a Pareto optimum, or that a change is desirable only if it satisfies the Pareto principle. Different initial endowments of resources can lead to different Pareto states; these are not comparable since each one presents a different distribution of final goods and, hence, different utility levels for individuals.

An example can help clarify these points. Consider the UPF in figure 5.1. We know that every point along the frontier is Pareto optimal. This includes points u and u', where individual 1 and 2, respectively, have zero utility. Let us suppose that the initial position is z (or some point very close to it). Imagine that (almost) all machinery has been assigned to individual 2, who combines it with his labour in a less-than-efficient way in production but nevertheless derives considerable satisfaction from the arrangement. Individual 1 is a disabled person who can hardly work at all; since he owns (almost) no machinery, his final output and utility is (almost) nil. By hypothesis, this position is Pareto inefficient. If, however, individual 2 combined his inputs more appropriately, the system could reach point u, which is Pareto optimal. Almost no-one would consider this final position, which is conditioned by the starting point, to be desirable even if it is undoubtedly optimal in a Paretian sense.

---

[10] Although expressed differently, the two conditions are equivalent: if one is satisfied, so is the other.

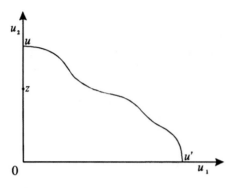

Figure 5.1

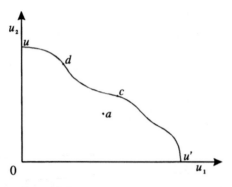

Figure 5.2

The question then arises of whether a social planner who judges certain Pareto optimal states with sharply divergent utility levels to be undesirable can avoid them and reach more egalitarian positions through the market mechanism. The second fundamental theorem of welfare economics enables us to say that he can. As we have said, every Pareto optimal state can be obtained as a competitive equilibrium if certain conditions are met and as long as resources are redistributed appropriately. This should be carried out with transfers that do not interfere with the properties of the market as a mechanism for resource allocation.

The usual interpretation of the second theorem is shown in diagrammatic terms in figure 5.2. We again examine the UPF uu'. Point d represents a social state with considerable inequality in utility levels, since the utility of individual 1 is very low and that of 2 is very high. If the planner feels that it would be more equitable for 1 to receive a higher level of utility, taking society to a point like c on the UPF, he can reach the new state (given the conditions we have set) by redistributing initial endowments between the two members of society – e.g., from d to a – and allowing the competitive market mechanism to operate, which it is assumed will reach equilibrium at point c or some similar position.

There would therefore be a clear division of roles between government and the market: the former would have a redistributive function while the latter would have an allocative function.

5.5 Extending the theorems

The competitive equilibrium in the two fundamental theorems is a special one, being a one-period equilibrium that excludes any consideration of uncertainty. Can the theorems be extended to overcome these two limitations? In fact, they can and the extension is relatively simple,[11] although, as we will see, not very meaningful.

If we consider a time horizon of some finite number T of periods,[12] there are no additional problems and the extension of competitive equilibrium (as well as the associated properties of Pareto optimality) to an intertemporal setting is immediate. We simply consider 'dated' goods and treat a good at different times as a different good. If there are m types of goods in a single period and economic activity continues for T periods, the total number of goods is $m \times T$. The same good in different periods will have different prices; thus, the price in period $t + 1$ will be equal to the price in period t plus the real interest rate for one period: we can exchange one unit of the good at time t with $1 + r$ units in period $t + 1$, where r is the real interest rate in terms of the good. From the point of view of production, with the available resources a producer can elect to sacrifice one unit of good x in period t in order to produce $1 + r$ units of the same good in period $t + 1$.

This extension clearly enables us to analyse the decisions of economic agents at the beginning of the first period in relation to all the T periods in the time horizon with regard to the supply of and demand for goods and inputs. For example, at the initial date each consumer can decide how much bread and cloth to consume at time t, how much at time $t + 1$, etc., so as to maximise his overall utility over the time span considered. Similarly, each firm can plan the output to be delivered in each period.

In the next section we will discuss the realism of the intertemporal equilibrium. For now, note that the model imposes stringent information requirements. We have to know all prices for all goods for the T periods, which means that in the initial period (when agents have to make their decisions) all of the markets for those goods must exist: both the markets for the m goods to be delivered in the initial period (*spot markets*) and those for the goods to be delivered in each of the subsequent periods (*forward markets*), whose prices need to be known in the initial period in order to guide agents' intertemporal allocation of resources.[13]

This intertemporal extension of the competitive equilibrium is not dynamic: individual decisions are still made at one time, not sequentially. The only new element is the lengthening (and division into periods) of the time horizon taken into consideration by agents.

We can also extend the model of competitive equilibrium (and the related Pareto optimality properties) to account for uncertainty by introducing *contingent markets*, in which a good is defined by its physical nature, by the period in which it will be available *and* by the situation that will occur in the period itself: e.g., not only are umbrellas

---

[11] The extension of the theorems is due to Arrow (1953).
[12] The number of periods is arbitrary, but there are problems when $T = \infty$.
[13] Less stringent conditions have been considered, but for simplicity we will not examine them here (see, for example, Boadway and Bruce, 1984, p. 88; Mas-Colell *et al.*, 1995, pp. 694–708).

available now and those available at time t considered as different goods (as in the case of intertemporal decisions under certainty) but also those available at time t should it rain or not.

Contingent markets are particularly important, since they allow agents to 'hedge'; i.e., to insure themselves against the occurrence of certain events. Ordinary insurance policies are one form of contingent market: one party (the customer) pays a premium to the other party (the insurer) to 'purchase' the right to a quantity of money (or more generally, certain goods or services) conditional on the occurrence of a certain event (survival, death, injury, illness, etc.).

The second extension of the fundamental theorems of welfare economics also raises a number of problems that we cannot examine here. However, note that in the real world forward and contingent markets are rare and information on the related prices is therefore not available. Diamond (1967) showed that, under certain conditions, a stock market can provide the same exchange opportunities as a complete system of contingent markets, but the conditions imposed are extremely restrictive.[14]

5.6 The first theorem as a clarification (of the limits) of the 'invisible hand'

5.6.1 The 'invisible hand' and the first theorem

It goes without saying that the founder of economic science, Adam Smith, was an enthusiastic advocate of the virtues of competitive markets. His 'invisible hand' aphorism captured the ability of the market to ensure that the economic choices made by each agent in the pursuit of his personal interests and satisfaction would have beneficial effects for society as a whole:

As every individual, therefore, endeavours . . . to employ his capital . . . and so to direct that industry that its produce may be of the greatest value; every individual necessarily labours to render the annual revenue of the society as great as he can. He . . . neither intends to promote the publick interest, nor knows how much he is promoting it. . . . he intends only his own gain, and he is in this . . . led by an invisible hand to promote an end which was no part of his intention (Smith, 1776, Book IV, chapter II, p. 456).[15]

The first theorem of welfare economics can be interpreted as a development of the invisible hand aphorism, specifying:

(a) the characteristics of markets that produce positive results for the entire economy;

(b) the theoretical hypotheses and methodological approach that allow us to establish the connection between markets and those results;

[14] We would also have to consider the role of expectations in the stock market and the possibility that speculation is destabilising. Incompleteness of financial markets is the subject of Magill and Quinzii (1996).

[15] An interesting, albeit unconventional, interpretation of how Adam Smith viewed the invisible hand is given in Rothschild (1994).

(c) the criterion used in evaluating the favourable (or optimal) nature of the results themselves.

However, at the same time these very clarifications underscore the limits of the invisible hand, which are connected with the way the three points listed above are interpreted in the first theorem and their interactions. We will examine these limitations in the following subsections,[16] which serve as an introduction to issues we will examine in greater detail in chapters 6 and 7.

5.6.2 The limits of markets in the real world

The first theorem of welfare economics specifies perfect competition as a market regime capable of producing a Pareto optimum. We should bear in mind that the concept of competition used by the classical economists was much vaguer and less restrictive than that employed in general equilibrium theory (see section 5.3). Precision, although analytically fruitful (as it allows us to proceed in rigorous fashion to a definite result, that of the first theorem),[17] is achieved at the expense of realism.

Section 5.3 set out the conditions of perfect competition. A quick glance at the list shows just how unrealistic they are. A detailed analysis of the divergences between the features of actual markets and the assumptions defining 'perfect competition' is given in section 6.2.

The first theorem also states that complete markets, i.e., the existence of markets for all goods and services, can ensure a Pareto optimum. However, markets are not complete in the real world, due to the presence of externalities, public goods, transaction costs and asymmetric information. We will investigate these aspects in detail in sections 6.3–6.7.

Incomplete markets and market regimes other than perfect competition are special cases of situations in which the equilibrium output of each industry differs from that predicted by perfect competition in an Arrow–Debreu model: equilibrium quantities are positive in monopoly, or in any other form of non-competitive market, but nonetheless different from those in perfect competition;[18] they might be zero (or, rather, undefined) in the case of incomplete markets. In general we can simply refer to divergence of real markets from perfectly competitive markets, including disparities due to both non-competitive and incomplete markets.

It could be argued that: (a) divergences between real-life markets and those postulated in the model underlying the first theorem are small; and (b) small differences between reality and the theoretical model leave the results virtually unchanged, ensuring that the outcome is broadly optimal.

[16] The order we will follow is purely expository and reflects that used later in the text. The logical arrangement and order of importance of the various limitations is exactly the reverse.
[17] Those who argue that the modern concept of perfect competition is missing the fundamental idea of classical thought, that of competition as a 'process', do not necessarily regard this precision as an advantage.
[18] In the case of partial equilibria, one can also say that output under (non-discriminating) monopoly is less than that in perfect competition.

With regard to the extent of divergences from reality, we have already said that the assumptions underlying perfect competition seem entirely unrealistic. We can now add that the pervasiveness of externalities and the scarcity of forward markets contribute even further to the unrealistic nature of the model. However, the most interesting aspect of the question does not regard the size of the divergence between market reality and the abstract assumptions[19] but rather the institutional consequences of even small divergences. From this point of view the complete markets of perfect competition appear to be an '*absolute*' condition for Pareto optimality to hold: either all markets exist, thus ensuring an optimal outcome, or the lack of even one market means that to obtain the feasible 'optimum' we must abandon perfect competition altogether (see the discussion of the theory of the second best in section 6.8). This means that the first theorem of welfare economics is not 'robust', i.e., it does not survive even small variations in the underlying hypotheses.

5.6.3 The limitations of general equilibrium theory

The first theorem is based on general equilibrium theory, which is characterised by the adoption of methodological individualism and by its static nature. Both of these features are, in our view, open to criticism.

Methodological individualism, which normally considers individual preferences as given without referring to the factors underlying those preferences (environment, social conventions, etc.), ignores the role of 'persuasion'. There are versions of neoclassical theory that admit endogenous preferences and this undoubtedly enhances its explanatory power. Nevertheless, these variants cannot be used for normative purposes together with the Pareto principle: the presence of 'persuasion' threatens to 'undermine the fundamental argument in favour of the market, i.e., that each individual is the best judge of his own interests' (Franzini and Messori, 1991, p. 21).[20] A particular instance of this is the existence of 'merit wants' (see section 6.10), but the problem is much more general.

The second limitation of general equilibrium theory is its static nature.[21] This means that general equilibrium theory is only able to interpret the static aspect of the Pareto criterion,[22] which at least in principle is open to a dynamic interpretation since it is possible to conceive the allocation of resources – the central concern of the Pareto

---

[19] It might not be possible to measure such divergences; that is, we may not be able to say whether the difference is large or small, as this assumes we are able to identify the real world situation exactly, or objectively. This possibility is denied by those, such as ourselves, who reject a positivist approach. Nevertheless, we feel it is possible to use the term 'small' in a special sense, meaning the number of real-life markets that diverge from perfect competition.

[20] The two authors raise the following question: 'Which preferences of the "persuaded" individual must be considered in evaluating the optimality of the resulting situation? The original preferences, assuming these are known, or those following persuasion?'. Their answer shows that the Pareto criterion becomes 'useless' (Franzini and Messori, 1991, p. 22). The problems posed by endogenous preferences are also analysed in Harsanyi (1955) and Hahnel and Albert (1990).

[21] As noted in section 5.5, the intertemporal extension of general equilibrium theory is not truly dynamic.

[22] A more optimistic position is held by Hahn (1982, p. 82).

criterion – as a dynamic problem; that is, in such a way as to ensure a temporally efficient arrangement of production and consumption.

The static nature of general equilibrium theory and its unsatisfactory treatment of uncertainty mean that it cannot account for types of efficiency (such as the 'adaptive' efficiency of Alchian, 1950) that incorporate a learning process leading to the gradual understanding of problems and 'correct' responses. These and other limitations of the theory also explain why it does not enable us to identify the market failures that give rise to the 'instability' of capitalism. We will discuss these at length in chapter 7.

5.6.4 The limitations of Pareto optimality

The limitations of Pareto optimality are a consequence of the hypothesis of non-comparability and the postulate of ethical individualism. Both prevent us from considering the distribution of income as relevant to social ordering (see section 6.9).

In addition, ethical individualism does not allow us to take account of either (a) rights and liberties or (b) the availability of goods considered socially useful regardless of the utility that individual agents may actually derive from them (merit wants).

We have already discussed rights and liberties to some extent and we will not examine them further. Merit goods will be discussed in section 6.10. Here we wish to emphasise that the satisfaction effectively enjoyed by an individual is a clearly distorted indicator of social welfare if preferences are endogenous rather than exogenous. In this case the foundation of liberalism turns out to be extremely fragile: any effort to ensure that social preferences reflect individual preferences, aimed at protecting society from external interference, is undermined by the fact that individual preferences are not 'genuine', since some individuals are influenced by others. The central problem of a democracy is to find institutional arrangements that at least partially offset this interference.

5.7 Market and government in the light of the second theorem

We said that the second fundamental theorem is 'prescriptive' and that it enables us to deal with distributive issues, which are not considered by the first theorem. The solution of distributive problems is not entrusted to market mechanisms but rather to government intervention. Thus, according to the usual interpretation of the second theorem, the operation of the invisible hand (the market) should be flanked by the action of a 'visible hand' (the government). Under the conditions postulated, the market would ensure the efficient allocation of resources and the government would be responsible for redistribution. Only if markets were not perfectly competitive would it make sense for the government to participate in the allocative process as well.

The practical significance of the second fundamental theorem can be assessed from the point of view of (a) its prescriptive content in favour of the market and (b) the separability of the allocative and redistributive functions. We will examine these aspects in the following subsections.

5.7.1 The weak prescriptive content in favour of the market

The weakness of the second theorem's prescription in favour of the market stems from the following two considerations:

1. in addition to sharing all the limitations of the first theorem, the second also has its own;
2. government can also play a role in the allocative process, a task which the usual interpretation of the second theorem assigns to the market.

1 The second theorem is a product of the same analytical process as the first, sharing many of the same premises (Pareto principle, general equilibrium theory, complete competitive markets) and, therefore, the limitations discussed in section 5.6. The principal difference is that while, strictly speaking, the first theorem only requires *private* information regarding initial endowments,[23] tastes and technology, the second theorem, as we will see in section 5.7.2, requires that at least one group of agents, including the government, have *full information* on such characteristics.

2 Even if we fully accept the above limitations, the second theorem's prescription in favour of the (capitalist) market[24] is still quite weak. Every Pareto optimal state *can* be reached through the operation of competitive markets, given an appropriate redistribution of initial endowments by the government. However, the advocates of *market socialism* (Lange, 1936; Lerner, 1934, 1937, 1944)[25] argue that the same outcome can be achieved with a different institutional arrangement.

Let us take a closer look at how a market socialist system might function according to Lange. The means of production, except for labour, would be owned by the state. Consumer preferences, revealed by demand prices, would guide resource production and allocation. Supply prices would be decided by the managers of public-sector firms. Supply and demand determine the equilibrium level of output. There would be no market for producer goods and services, and their prices would be pure accounting indices established by the central planning office (through trial and error) to ensure that supply and demand match. Given these prices, the managers would determine in each industry: (a) the quantity of inputs to use, by choosing the amounts that minimise average cost; and (b) the level of output, setting it at the point where marginal cost equals price.

---

[23] The agent's situation is known only to himself and not to other agents or the government.
[24] It should be noted that the hypotheses regarding the *market structure* do not in themselves imply specific hypotheses about the *production and distribution system*; however, in speaking of the market implicit reference is often made to a capitalist system of production and distribution. This is characterised by private ownership of the means of production and wage labour.
[25] For a fairly recent restatement of the case for market socialism see Roemer (1994a); on this topic see also Stiglitz (1994).

Any distributive inequalities would be eliminated through government action. In purely economic terms, whether such a system might actually work would depend on solving the problem of calculating the prices of producer goods and that of agent incentives (see section 6.7).

Such problems are not specific to this institutional structure. In fact, they also arise with regard to the effective operation of a (hypothetically) competitive market. The reader familiar with general equilibrium theory will recall that equilibrium prices in a competitive market are announced by an 'auctioneer' after examining the possible decisions of agents in relation to alternative sets of prices.[26] This is exactly the same process as that the central planning office would have to follow in an equally hypothetical system of market socialism in order to choose the prices that would guide the production of capital goods.

Furthermore, note that both utility functions and technological possibilities (which determine agents' decisions) must be known to the government (i.e., it must have full information) in order for it to perform its redistributive function. Without this information, the government could not determine precisely the transfers to be made to some and the taxes to apply to others.

We are thus faced with a paradox. The second theorem is normally interpreted as assigning an allocative role to the market and a redistributive role to the government. This second function cannot be performed if the government does not have exact knowledge about the reactions of the market. However, if the government did have such knowledge, it would also be able to implement the desired allocation directly, leaving the market without a role (Dasgupta, 1980, p. 111).

For example, consider figure 5.2 again. Let d be the initial position and c the desired end state: the standard interpretation of the second theorem is that the government redistributes resources from d to a and lets the market reallocate them in such a way as to move from a to c. The problem we have just raised is that if the objective is to move to state c, the government must carry out an *appropriate* redistribution, i.e., one that ensures that the subsequent operation of the market will bring the system to c. However, in order to do this the government must know how the market works; that is, it must have exact knowledge about the initial resource endowments, technology and preferences that underlie the behaviour of agents that will lead the system to c. Otherwise, the government will not know which redistribution to implement; i.e., it will not know whether to redistribute resources so as to bring the system to a or to some other point. However, if it did have such complete information about the action of the market, the government would be able to replace the market in the allocative process as well.

A problem of incentives would certainly arise under market socialism, since the managers of firms, not being owners, would have no special interest in maximising

---

[26] Note that the prices actually applied must be only the equilibrium prices. One might think that the market, starting from disequilibrium prices, could converge towards a system of equilibrium prices through an iterative series of adjustments; however, there is no guarantee that this would happen (stability is not ensured).

profits (or minimising costs).[27] But to a certain extent a similar problem exists in capitalist economies, where the separation of ownership and control is typical of large 'managerial' firms (Marris, 1964). Incentives may also play a role in the perverse sense of construing markets as constraints on public action, as we will see in the following subsection.

5.7.2 The separability of allocation and redistribution

The most interesting aspect of the second theorem is its claim that initial endowments can be redistributed through both positive and negative taxation[28] in a way that does not distort the allocation of resources. As we saw in section 5.4, this would imply that the redistributive and allocative functions are separable. However, more extensive analysis shows that such separability is not possible.

In general, a tax is *non-distortionary* if and only if it does not prompt agents to circumvent it (or secure it, if it is a subsidy). In a situation of private information this can occur if the tax induces agents to reveal the truth about their characteristics, i.e., endowments, preferences and technologies, when they take account of the effect of their revelations upon the allocation of economic resources (*individual incentive compatibility*).[29]

It is commonly argued that distortion can be avoided with *lump-sum taxes*. Such taxes are independent of agents' level of economic activity, however expressed (income, consumption, supply of services, etc.), and, therefore, invariant with respect to their economic decisions. They should instead be related to the very existence of a person (as in the case of a poll or head tax) or to personal characteristics that are insensitive to the tax (age, eye colour and so forth). However, even these taxes could be distortionary under some conditions; for example, a poll tax can distort individual decisions as it may influence decisions to migrate, have (more) children, etc.

Nevertheless, the important point is that the problem is not simply one of the distortionary effects of a tax. If the problem was only that of generating a given level of revenue, it would be possible to impose taxes with limited distortionary effects. It is true that even a poll tax can distort decisions but these distortions are certainly less severe than those caused by an income or consumption tax, and on the whole they are of little significance. However, we are interested here in the use of taxes for redistributive purposes: to redistribute resources, the government must be able to apply positive taxes to some and negative taxes (or subsidies) to others. However, if the redistribution is not to interfere with market allocation, how can we tax some and subsidise others without knowing beforehand the outcome of the market process? In order to identify those who will be taxed or subsidised, our decision must be based at least in part on variables such as income or consumption, that are endogenous to the allocative mechanism and can thus be affected by our decisions. The values of these variables are also difficult to

---

[27] Ways of tackling this problem have been suggested (see Roemer, 1994a).
[28] The latter are subsidies.
[29] The concept of individual incentive compatibility was introduced by Hurwicz (1972).

identify *a priori*, partly because individuals may have an incentive to conceal the necessary information.[30]

Let us clarify these issues with an example. Suppose that the desired objective is a more equitable distribution of income. To this end, we introduce:

(a) a positive tax of, say, £2,500 on individuals with an income of at least £20,000;
(b) a £2,000 subsidy for those with an income of less than £20,000.

The distortionary effects will be limited for many people, at least in the sense that either they can do nothing to avoid the tax or there is no incentive to do anything to obtain the subsidy or not pay the tax. However, the decisions of some will be influenced by the measures: in particular, those whose income lies just above the dividing line between subsidy recipients and taxpayers may have an incentive to reduce their efforts in income production or to conceal their income.[31]

The reader will have realised that the lack of non-distortionary redistributive tools has important consequences.

1 First, in distorting the allocation of resources with respect to the Pareto optimal allocation, redistributive policies reduce efficiency; that is, they reduce the utility of at least one of the two individuals in our hypothetical society. This is shown diagrammatically in figure 5.3, where the distortionary effect of redistribution lowers the UPF from uu' to vv'. The curve vv' has only one point in common with uu', the starting point d: only in the absence of redistribution are there no distortionary effects on the allocation of resources; any redistribution will generate distortionary effects and lower the UPF.

2 Second, one can ask whether the market is the most efficient allocative mechanism when a redistribution is effected. In terms of figure 5.3, vv' is the UPF associated with the distortionary redistribution from d to a, *followed by the operation of the market*. We can

---

[30] Obviously, these considerations hold in a (realistic) context of private information. The literature on the distortionary effects of distributive measures in the case of private information is extensive. In particular, see Hammond, 1979 (who introduces the concept of multilateral incentive compatibility to rule out the possibility of a coalition of privately informed agents manipulating an economic allocation), Stiglitz (1987) and Hammond (1990). Lerner (1944) was the first to point out the distortionary effect of lump-sum taxes; see also Samuelson (1947).

[31] This gives a rough idea of the problem. In reality, it could be argued that the tax should be imposed on the basis of the information available on initial resource endowments (inherited or otherwise available goods, and ability to work). However, even here our argument would hold. Assuming equal material wealth, the redistribution should be based on the other initial resource, ability to work. People would have to be classified according to their ability and taxed (the more capable) or subsidised (the less able) in order to equalise incomes, which would call for perfect knowledge on the part of the redistributive authority. If we assume this condition is satisfied, the redistribution might still have distortionary effects on the allocation process: the incentive to increase one's capacity for work through, for example, education and professional training may be weakened. The assumption of full information is also unrealistic since abilities to work are not easily observable and individuals, who possess such information, have no incentive to reveal it; with private information, any redistribution is impossible or difficult. Thus, either the redistribution is possible (when we have full information) but distorts the allocation of resources, or it is impossible or difficult (when information is private). We will explore this issue further in chapter 11.

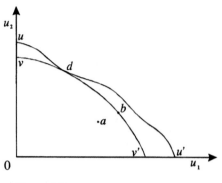

Figure 5.3

ask where the frontier will be if, assuming that the redistribution has to be implemented, the allocation is carried out *by means of some form of public action* (for example, government spending). Will it be inside or outside *vv'*? A satisfactory answer to this question cannot be given in abstract terms.

Some recent work offers an unconventional reply that changes commonly held views of the roles of the market and government. We said above that the redistribution of initial resources can only be carried out with mechanisms that distort the allocation of resources. In particular, it may require the use of instruments such as taxes, rationing or multiple prices that may provoke reactions from agents (e.g., they may turn to *side markets* such as 'black' or 'underground' markets) aimed at evading or avoiding the redistributive measures. In this case markets would not function as an efficient *instrument* for resource allocation but rather as a *constraint* on the implementation of an economic policy aimed at promoting both efficiency and fairness (see Blackorby and Donaldson, 1988; Hammond, 1987, 1990). The market mechanism could therefore leave society further below the UPF than would an economic system in which production and distribution were assigned to the government or, in any case, where there were limits on the operation of markets.

For example, consider a case in which the government wished to redistribute endowments in favour of the sick. Given private information on the health of individuals, cash transfers (and/or taxation) – with legal markets for health and pharmaceutical services – will distort the allocation of resources, as everyone will have an incentive to qualify as infirm. In-kind transfers, e.g., direct provision of treatment and medicine (with a ban on the resale of the latter) would have less severe (or no) distortionary effects because the services (medical treatment) are impossible to resell and the resale of drugs is presumably limited since it is illegal. In both cases, the presence of (legal or illegal) *markets* is a constraint on public action that reduces its effectiveness and makes it possible to achieve a lower-level optimum only: the market lowers the efficiency frontier with respect to that where the allocation of medical treatment is carried out directly by the government and there is no way to exchange goods and services in a market. We will examine this issue further in section *11.8.

5.8 Summary

1 There are two main institutions, in the sense of 'rules' of social interaction: the market and government. The relative merits can be assessed in the light of the principles of efficiency and equity that we have examined so far.

2 A good starting point for our analysis is the Pareto efficiency criterion, as there exists a correspondence between the equilibrium allocation of a perfectly competitive economy and a Pareto optimal allocation.

3. This correspondence is expressed by the two fundamental theorems of welfare economics. The first theorem states that with perfect competition and a complete set of markets a competitive equilibrium (if it exists) is a Pareto optimum. The second theorem states that under certain conditions every Pareto optimum can be achieved as a competitive equilibrium with an appropriate redistribution of initial resources.

4 If the two theorems, obtained in the framework of general equilibrium theory, are extended to incorporate a time horizon of more than one period and uncertainty, they ensure an efficient intertemporal allocation of resources.

5 The theorems are a development of the concept of the 'invisible hand' introduced by Adam Smith, which underscores the virtues of the market in achieving the 'public good'. However, the unrealistic and restrictive nature of the hypotheses on which they rest is indicative of the limits of this concept.

6 With specific reference to the first theorem, the limitations regard:
   (a) the markets that allow us to obtain Pareto-efficient results (there must be a complete set of perfectly competitive markets);
   (b) the theory that allows us to establish a link between those markets and those results (general equilibrium theory);
   (c) the criterion used to assess the desirability of the results (Pareto efficiency).

7 With regard to the second theorem, we must first note its weak prescriptive content in favour of capitalist markets. The same Pareto optimum could be achieved with a different institutional arrangement (market socialism).

8 Again referring to the second theorem, the separability of the allocative and distributive functions asserted by the theorem depends on the existence of full information. With private information, redistributive measures have to satisfy the individual incentive requirement; the market, far from guaranteeing the desired outcome in terms of efficiency and equity, can act as a constraint on public action.

5.9 Key concepts

Market
State
Firm
Voluntary organisation
Non-profit organisation
Invisible hand
Fundamental theorems of welfare
   economics
Complete markets
Perfect competition
Price-taking
Competitive equilibrium
Existence of an equilibrium
Multiplicity of equilibria
Stability of an equilibrium
Continuity of a function
Non-satiation
Convexity

Law of one price
Intertemporal equilibrium
Spot, forward and contingent markets
Competition as a 'process'
Realism of hypotheses
Robustness
Persuasion
Adaptive efficiency
Visible hand
Market socialism
Market structure
Production and distribution system
Non-distortionary taxation
Lump sum transfer
Individual, multilateral incentive
   compatibility
Side market

6 Market failures: microeconomic aspects

6.1 Introduction

We have seen that the principal result of specifying the conditions which must be satisfied for the 'invisible hand' to produce a social optimum (as well as identifying it with the Pareto optimum) is negative. Indeed, the conditions are so restrictive, and the nature of the optimal state that can be achieved under them is so special, that one could say the first theorem of welfare economics clarifies the reasons why the market does *not* usually guarantee an efficient and equitable social state. Table 6.1 summarises these reasons.

This chapter will examine the reasons for *market failures* at the microeconomic level. The following chapter will deal with failures at the macroeconomic level, which the literature does not normally include in the category of market failures. Almost all economists use this term to refer to the situations in which the conditions of Pareto optimality are not satisfied (thus excluding failures associated with distributive inequalities and merit goods), and in any case exclude any consideration of macroeconomic aspects. We prefer to follow Stiglitz (1988) and broaden the category of market failures to include those that arise when the conditions of Pareto optimality are satisfied and macroeconomic performance is involved.

6.2 Perfect competition and markets in the real world

We have already pointed out the unrealistic nature of the assumptions of perfect competition. Real-life markets feature imperfect or monopolistic competition, oligopoly and monopoly. In all of these real market situations the condition that ensures Pareto optimality under perfect competition, i.e., equality of price and marginal cost (see section 5.3), is violated.

The following section will examine the realism of the various conditions of perfect

Table 6.1. *Limitations of justifications of the market economy based on the first theorem of welfare economics*

Underlying hypothesis of first theorem	Reason for criticism	Level of failure	Reference in the book
1 Complete competitive markets			
1.1 Competitive markets	1 Non-competitive regimes	Microeconomic	Section 6.2
1.2 Complete markets	1 Externalities	Microeconomic	Sections 6.3–6.4
	2 Public goods	Microeconomic	Sections 6.5–*6.6
	3 Transaction costs and asymmetric information	Microeconomic	Section 6.7
2 Theory of general economic equilibrium			
2.1 Methodological individualism (exogenous preferences)	1 Merit wants	Microeconomic	Section 6.10
2.2 Static analysis and other hypotheses (certainty, absence of money, etc.)	1 'Instability' of the system	Macroeconomic	Chapter 7
3 Pareto principle			
3.1 Non-comparability of utilities	1 Income distribution	Microeconomic	Section 6.9
3.2 Ethical individualism	1 Rights and liberties	Non-economic	
	2 Income distribution	Microeconomic	Section 6.9
	3 Merit wants	Microeconomic	Section 6.10

competition. In section 6.2.3 we will digress with a discussion of other concepts of efficiency suggested by the earlier subsections.

6.2.1 Numerosity of agents and returns to scale

Let us first examine the case in which the requirement for a large number of agents is not met on the supply side. In particular, suppose we have a monopoly situation that does not depend on historical or legal factors or on barriers to entry but solely on the nature of the *returns to scale* in the industry. If returns are increasing, we face what is called a *natural monopoly*: minimising costs for the quantity demanded by the market can only be achieved when there is one firm.[1] This is shown in figure 6.1 (DD = demand function; AC = average cost; MC = marginal cost, which is assumed to be constant).[2]

---

[1] If there were two or more firms, they would have an incentive to merge; or each could seek to increase output in order to reduce costs.

[2] Any decrease in unit cost is therefore due to the existence of fixed costs.

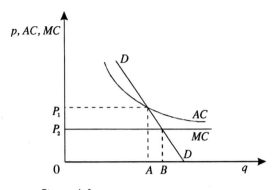

Figure 6.1

Let us examine what price the monopolist will set with an eye to the possibility of achieving an efficient allocation. If it chooses price P_2, equal to marginal cost, producing the quantity $0B$ (which would satisfy the condition for Pareto efficiency) the firm would suffer a loss, as unit costs are higher than marginal costs. The only way to avoid a loss without distorting the allocation of resources is to set the price equal to marginal cost and cover the loss (equal to fixed costs) by charging all consumers of the good a lump-sum (and hence non-distortionary) fee.[3] But how is the firm to divide the total extra payment among its customers? Assume that the number of consumers is not known before the firm is established. If there were only one consumer, that person would have to bear the entire fixed cost; if there were two, they would each bear half the cost; n consumers would pay $1/n$ of the total surcharge. The firm could estimate a minimum number of consumers, n^*, among whom it will divide the fixed cost, charging any additional consumers a price equal to marginal cost only, if it is not to be distortionary.[4] Having already covered fixed costs with the surcharge imposed on the first n^* consumers, subsequent consumers will not have to bear the extra burden. However, given these conditions it is possible that no consumer will want to be one of the first n^* consumers who must pay the surcharge. Each consumer will have an incentive to engage in *free riding* behaviour.

It is equally unlikely that a firm can discover who its customers are by committing them to purchasing a given quantity of goods before it begins production; consumers will avoid signing one of the first, more expensive, contracts (see also Inman, 1987, p. 659).[5]

The free rider problem could only be avoided if the firm were in a position to set discriminatory prices. This would require:

[3] We know from chapter 5 that a truly non-distortionary tax only exists under very restrictive conditions (taxation of exogenous variables, full information). To pursue the argument we are interested in here we can assume that these conditions are satisfied.

[4] In practice, the charge for fixed costs in addition to the marginal cost is paid by all consumers, but this is not an efficient solution either.

[5] This failure, pointed out by Dupuit (1844) and later by Marshall (1890) and Pigou (1920), was re-examined in great detail by Hotelling (1938). We will return to this issue in section 6.5, which will present an important parallel between market failures due to increasing returns and those caused by public goods.

(a) the necessary information to set an appropriate price for each consumer, taking account all the factors (preferences, income, etc.) that determine the price elasticity of each consumer's demand;

(b) no possibility for consumers to resell the goods on secondary markets.

However, these are difficult conditions to meet.

In conclusion, we can say that it is not possible for the 'natural' monopolist to set its price equal to marginal cost. Nor would it be profitable. Apart from the above considerations, we know from elementary microeconomics that a monopolist maximises its profit when marginal cost is equal to marginal revenue. Decreasing costs therefore lead to market failure, making it impossible to satisfy Pareto optimality.

Another problem emerges if scale economies are not so great as to lead to monopoly but give rise to oligopoly instead. In this case, rather than responding automatically to the prices set by the market, as in perfect competition, firms are involved in a game in which they set their prices and level of output by taking account of the reaction of their competitors, thus engaging in 'strategic' behaviour,[6] with the consequence that not all possible equilibria will be Pareto efficient.

With natural monopoly or oligopoly, market failure can be eliminated or reduced by government action in the form of regulation (antitrust legislation, price controls, etc.) or the creation of state-owned firms. We will discuss these measures in section 10.6.

6.2.2 Free market entry and exit

Economies of scale have traditionally been considered the most important cause of market failure. Recently, some authors (see Baumol, Panzar and Willig, 1982) have argued that equilibria similar to those produced by competitive markets are possible even in a monopoly or oligopoly situation created by the existence of increasing returns to scale. This result depends on the 'contestability' of markets, i.e., the *possibility* that firms can enter and exit a market freely and without costs.

Assume that the (small number of) firms in the market earn *extra* profits, setting their prices above average cost. If entry and exit are free and costless, new firms will enter the market. They can divide part of the extra profits with the existing firms, gaining market share by setting a lower price until the existing firms react by lowering their own prices. In order to avoid the losses of a possible price war, the new entrants can always exit the market (by assumption, at no cost) having earned net extra profits in the meantime.

The 'hit and run' tactics employed by the new entrants would be possible if entry and exit were completely free and costless; this, then, would be the main condition for competition, and ensuring it would produce outcomes similar to those obtained under perfect competition, despite the presence of scale economies. These tactics would in fact induce incumbent firms to set a price no higher than average cost, thus eliminating any extra profit; it would also reduce costs to a minimum.

---

[6] This is a difficult term to define for those who are not familiar with game theory. Briefly, we can say that strategic behaviour is any behaviour that takes into consideration the possible decisions of others and also seeks to influence them, which is not possible in perfect competition.

Two comments are in order. First, the condition of total absence of entry and exit costs is not satisfied in the real world,[7] where these costs are quite significant. For example, take the specificity of capital (whether human or physical), which gives rise to training, design and adaptation costs for the performance of specific functions; take also the costs involved in promoting specific products. All such costs are *sunk costs* if capital (even its most apparently fungible components) is re-employed in a different use.[8] This means that markets are hardly contestable in real life.

Second, we must stress that if markets were contestable there might still be a distortion in the allocation of resources. Recall that Pareto efficiency requires that price equal marginal (not average) cost. The efficiency that can be achieved in contestable markets differs from Pareto efficiency and consists simply in the fact that the monopoly firm sets output at a level implying absence of profits and minimisation of costs.

Only in a special case will this situation be Pareto efficient. This is shown in figure 6.2, where the demand curve intersects the unit cost curve at its lowest point, and hence in correspondence to marginal cost. In other cases (figures 6.3 and 6.4) this does not occur: the equilibrium positions are efficient, in the sense that we have production efficiency (minimisation of costs), but they are not Pareto efficient, since price is not equal to marginal cost. The equilibrium in figure 6.4 is efficient (in the sense we have discussed) but is not stable. The incumbent cannot produce $0Q_2$ setting price at $0P_2$; if the market is contestable, new competitors will enter, trying to satisfy part of the demand at a lower price. Nevertheless, given the pattern of costs, there is no room for more than one firm: however output is divided, two firms will have higher costs than a single firm. This can be illustrated very clearly by imagining a market in which one firm produces $0Q_1$ and the other produces Q_1Q_2 (equal to $0A$). The area $0Q_2EP_2$, which gives the cost of producing $0Q_2$ for a single firm is less than the sum of the areas $0Q_1CP_1$ and $0AFB$, which give the cost of producing $0Q_1$ and Q_1Q_2 ($=0A$) respectively. This will hold for any division of $0Q_2$.[9]

Even if contestable markets are not sufficient to ensure Pareto efficient outcomes, considering the other positive features of these markets it may be desirable for the government to seek to reduce entry and exit barriers as much as possible. This is especially so for legal barriers such as licenses and authorisations to engage in an activity, when these requirements have no other well-founded justification. This is particularly important when alternative solutions, such as nationalisation, are considered inappropriate (for example, because of budget difficulties or the incentive problems arising with public-sector managers). We must bear in mind, however, that in many cases entry and exit barriers such as advertising costs, are a part of firms' strategies. In this case it may be necessary to control the behaviour of dominant firms through antitrust legislation.

[7] Only in this case, and assuming (unrealistically) that the incumbent reacts slowly to the new entrant, would hit and run tactics work. A relatively simple exposition of this point is given in Vickers and Yarrow (1988). This is a case of 'non-robustness' of the model to even small changes (in a more realistic sense) in the hypotheses (see section 5.6.2).

[8] In some cases these costs can be partially recovered by appropriately managing human and physical capital.

[9] Obviously, this outcome depends on the exact shape of the cost curve and the level of output. If output were significantly more than $0Q_2$, this would no longer be valid.

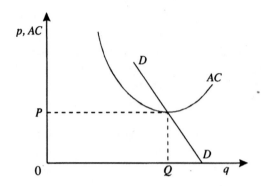

Figure 6.2

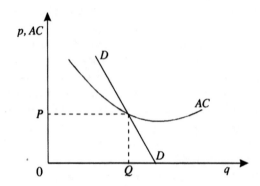

Figure 6.3

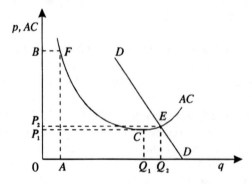

Figure 6.4

6.2.3 A digression on concepts of efficiency

We have so far examined the correspondence between real-life markets and the assumptions of the first and second theorems of welfare economics regarding the type of market needed to achieve Pareto efficient states. We have emphasised this concept of efficiency because it has been used to clarify the idea of the 'invisible hand' (see section 5.6). This does not mean that it is the only or even the most important concept of efficiency. The existence of other concepts should be clear from the previous subsection, in which we spoke of efficiency in terms of minimising average cost. We can now add two further concepts of efficiency: X-efficiency and dynamic efficiency.

The concept of *X-efficiency* was introduced by Leibenstein (1966) to indicate the ability of firms, rather than markets, to allocate resources efficiently (by equalising the MRTS and the ratio of factor prices) and select technically efficient production plans. Economic theory normally assumes such ability as a corollary of profit maximisation, without examining the organisational aspects of a firm. However, it has been pointed out that this assumption does not always hold in firms that do not face competitive pressures.

Dynamic efficiency is an important concept but is less precise than allocative Pareto efficiency about the conditions that make it possible. At a microeconomic level it could be defined as the ability to reduce production costs over time (i.e., increase the productivity of inputs) as a consequence of process innovation.[10] According to Schumpeter (1943), innovation is greatest in monopolistic markets, where the stimulus to invention comes from the prospect of reaping its fruits in full. This incentive is missing in competitive markets, where an innovative firm would immediately be imitated by others and would not earn any extra profits. This position has been criticised on theoretical grounds and the empirical evidence is contradictory (see Scherer, 1980). In any case Schumpeter's position is indicative of the fact that different optimality criteria (and different theoretical hypotheses) can lead to different conclusions about the desirability of the various market regimes.[11]

We could say that non-competitive market regimes are Pareto inefficient, but they may be efficient in the sense that under certain conditions (contestability) unit costs can be minimised; or they *may* stimulate innovation and hence dynamic efficiency. There are therefore arguments both for and against non-competitive markets. The presence of public enterprises in industries facing increasing returns to scale could help reconcile these different aims. We will discuss this issue in section 10.6.4

6.2.4 The other assumptions of perfect competition

Briefly examining the other conditions for perfect competition, note that the presence of a large number of agents does not ensure a competitive market if there are *agreements*

---

[10] At a macroeconomic level, dynamic efficiency corresponds to the economy's capacity to grow.

[11] Vickers (1995) has stated different concepts of competition and correspondingly different ways through which it can promote economic efficiency (through *incentives* to reduce organisational inefficiency, *selection* of efficient organisations and *stimulus* to innovation).

between them to limit competition. This indicates another possible task for the government: preventing such agreements, which is normally done through antitrust legislation.

The requirement for *homogeneous* goods may not be met, first because of company strategies aimed at differentiating products so as to create specific markets for a given firm's goods in which it holds a monopoly position. Differentiation is accentuated by advertising, which should therefore be controlled by government intervention when it does not convey any real information. Others argue that it is a form of free speech (rather than an instrument of persuasion) and as such merits protection. [12]

Full information about the prices set in the various transactions involving the same good is an equally, if not more, important requirement for perfect competition. Partial information creates one or more largely independent sub-markets for the same good (*market segmentation*) and gives rise to the possibility of excess demand in some and excess supply in others, with no tendency towards equilibrium. Section 6.7 examines in detail one aspect of partial information often encountered in the real world: asymmetric information.

6.3 Incomplete markets and externalities

The first fundamental theorem of welfare economics postulates the existence of complete markets, i.e., markets for all existing goods and services at a given time (in a one-period equilibrium) or in all periods covered by the decision horizon (in the intertemporal equilibrium). However, in the real world markets may be incomplete (or missing) due to: (a) externalities; (b) the existence of public goods or (c) the absence of some spot or forward markets due to transaction costs and asymmetric information in a world of uncertainty (Magill and Quinzii, 1996).

In this section and in section *6.4 we examine externalities. Sections 6.5 and *6.6 look at public goods. Section 6.7 investigates the consequences of transaction costs and the asymmetric nature of information.

The definition of externality allows us to deduce that the absence of payment for the benefit (positive externality or *external economy*) or harm (negative externality or *external diseconomy*) caused to others signifies the absence of a market. This may be due to:

1. The lack of individual *property rights*[13] over certain goods, which are instead 'common property'; this may induce each individual user to over-exploit[14] the goods and to act as a free rider, ignoring the common rights of other individuals and raising these individuals' access costs to the common property: think of air and water and their use in travel, hunting or fishing;

---

[12] The reader might find it interesting to verify the actual information content of the advertising we are exposed to.

[13] 'A property right is a socially enforced right to select uses of an economic good' (Alchian, 1987, p. 1031) or any other good, we might add.

[14] The standard of comparison is the use an individual would make of the good in a certain period if there were individual property rights; this use might be moderated by a variety of considerations, such as the depletion of the goods and maintenance or repair costs.

2 Jointness in production or consumption: an individual produces or consumes, creating a benefit (or disadvantage) for others owing to the way in which the activity is carried out. Typical cases of negative externalities caused by joint consumption (*consumption externalities*) are the noise pollution caused by someone listening to a radio at full volume or the air pollution produced by automobiles;[15] examples of activities that can give rise to external consumption economies are tending one's garden or getting an education. Production diseconomies include factory waste disposal (industrial pollution), while examples of external economies are the technological knowledge imparted by staff training programmes, the free dissemination of technological information or the construction of communications infrastructure open to all (*production externalities*).[16] A now famous example of production external economies is that of the reciprocal advantages accruing to the bee keeper and fruit farmer operating on neighbouring plots of land (see Boadway and Bruce, 1984).[17]

In general, the effect externalities produce with respect to the Pareto efficiency conditions is to require different MRSs between the various individuals (consumption externalities) and, similarly, different MRTSs across industries (production externalities).

Take consumption externalities for example. Let the goods being consumed be bread and compact discs. Owing to the condition of her stereo (which can only play at high volume), Alice's music playing causes significant noise pollution for Bob, while his music has no external effect on Alice's utility. If Alice chooses her bundle of consumption goods only with regard to her own utility function (*private* welfare),[18] she will set her MRS between CDs and bread equal to the ratio of their market prices and will have no incentive to move from this position. However, she will thereby consume 'too many' CDs from Bob's point of view, reducing his utility: each of her CDs is a cause of disutility for him. Taking a social point of view would mean changing perspective: each person should take account of all of the effects of his choices, both the impact on his individual utility and that on the utility of others. Hence, in choosing her consumption bundle

[15] This externality, like the others we will examine shortly, can also be attributed to the lack of individual property rights. The two causes of externality are not mutually exclusive; they can in fact be considered as two aspects – one legal, the other economic – of the relationships that can exist among the members of a society.

[16] These and similar reasons are why, according to Marshall, it would be possible for an industry to produce at decreasing costs while the individual *firms* in that industry face increasing costs: think of the reciprocal advantages created in 'industrial districts' – areas specialising in a particular line of business, which are still important in a number of countries, such as Italy (see Brusco, 1986; Pyke, *et al.*, 1990; Sengenberger and Pyke, 1992). For Marshall, then, external economies made perfect competition consistent with the reality of scale economies at an industry level. However, apart from the case of industrial districts, Marshall used externalities as a purely analytical expedient in order to continue to use a competitive framework even if in the real world the number of industries facing increasing returns to scale was rising, which undermined one of the conditions for perfect competition (numerosity of agents).

[17] The small selection of examples presented here does not give a true picture of the pervasiveness of externalities, which has been underscored by authors such as Hunt (1980).

[18] That is, we assume that she takes no account of the consequences of her choice on Bob's utility.

Alice should also consider the noise pollution suffered by Bob. This would cause her to reduce her consumption of CDs below the level she would choose if she were to take account of her utility alone. The fact is that Alice has no incentive to take account of the harm her consumption of CDs causes Bob, as she does not have to pay a price for that harm; instead, acting on purely private criteria, she equalises the MRS between CDs and bread and the ratio of their prices.

We can show that the condition for an efficient allocation of consumption in the absence of externalities leads to an inefficient allocation if there are externalities. Referring to the previous example, starting from a situation in which the MRSs of the two individuals are equal and are also equal to the price ratio and the marginal rate of transformation (MRT) – e.g., four units of bread against one CD – the utility of at least one of the two could increase. In particular, if we took one disc from Alice and gave it to Bob in return for an extra four loaves of bread for Alice, Alice's utility would remain the same while Bob's would increase, as he would be less bothered by Alice's music. We can conclude that:

(a) the initial allocation was not optimal, as Bob was able to increase his satisfaction at no loss to Alice; and

(b) since everyone's endowment of goods has changed, the MRSs are not equal in the new Pareto-superior situation.

We can add that an efficient allocation of consumption requires the MRS between CDs and bread for the person causing a diseconomy to be higher than the price ratio and the MRT. Let us return to our example. Acting on the basis of social criteria (i.e., taking account of externalities), Alice should reduce her consumption of CDs. Doing so, her MRS between CDs and bread increases, since the MRS is decreasing as the consumption of CDs rises. Since the price ratio and the MRT are unchanged, the MRS for the person causing a diseconomy (which was equal to the other person's MRS, the price ratio and the MRT in the purely private situation) is now higher than this common value. In the case of a positive externality, the MRS would instead be lower than the other person's MRS, the price ratio and the MRT.[19]

Similar considerations hold for production externalities. Achieving Pareto efficiency in the presence of production externalities requires that the MRTS between the two factors in the production of the different goods be different. This is easily seen if we apply the reasoning we used with consumption externalities.[20]

We can express the same concept in another way. Externalities cause divergences between private costs and social costs or, equivalently, between the *marginal private product* and the *marginal social product*. In the presence of external economies, the

[19] A simple formal demonstration of some of these propositions is given by Mueller (1989, pp. 25–7). The reader can derive all of them by following the same maximisation procedure as that given in section *3.7, provided that $u^B = u^B(q_p^B, q_t^B, m, q_t^A)$, if A's consumption of good t causes an externality for B.

[20] Take the same example and replace bread and CDs with labour and machinery and the utilities of A and B with products a and b (e.g., oil and fish), assuming that the output of fish is negatively affected by the quantity of machinery used to produce oil.

marginal private cost is greater than the marginal social cost. By contrast, external diseconomies result in higher marginal social costs than marginal private costs. The opposite holds for the marginal product.

This has important consequences. Take the example of a polluting factory. The polluter does not have to bear the social cost of the pollution and, therefore, in equalising his (private) marginal cost and price he will produce a higher level of output than he would if the social cost of pollution were also included in his calculations. The opposite would occur in the case of external economies. We can thus conclude that industries that generate negative externalities produce more than the social optimum, while those generating positive externalities produce less.[21]

Government intervention can remove the divergence between social and private cost (or product) by internalising the cost or benefit to society caused by the activity of a firm or individual. It can do this in a variety of ways, which we will discuss more fully in section 10.3. In particular, the government can levy taxes (known as Pigovian taxes, as they were initially suggested by Pigou; see Pigou, 1920, chapter XI; 1928) on those who create external diseconomies or can use regulation to prevent the creation of diseconomies.

6.4 Externalities and the Coase theorem

It has been pointed out that both forms of government intervention (taxes and regulation) assume that some members of society have a right and others do not (for example, citizens have a right to breathe clean air, while firms do not have a right to pollute). This particular assignment of property rights is not apparently controversial today with regard to externalities generated by pollution, but disagreement can arise over other forms of externality.

For example, let us take a problem that has served as the basis of innumerable westerns: the relationship between farmers and ranchers. If property rights are assigned to farmers, the passage of a herd of cattle over a planted field constitutes an injury caused by the rancher to the farmer and therefore calls for corrective public intervention (e.g., a tax on cattle). Were property rights assigned to ranchers, trampling a crop would not give rise to a diseconomy for farmers; in fact, if the cultivation of the land were to hinder the passage of the herd, a diseconomy would arise for ranchers. Hence, the very existence of uncompensated disadvantages or advantages and the identity of those who cause them depend on how property rights are assigned.

According to Coase, the real problem a society must solve is the choice of institutions, and therefore the criteria for assigning property rights. In his view, institutions should be designed so as to guarantee the maximum possible efficiency. In this regard he makes the following two propositions:

---

[21] This argument was originally advanced by Pigou in his discussion of the factors determining the size of the national 'dividend'.

1 *If a number of conditions are satisfied (including prior assignment of property rights and absence of* transaction costs),[22] *agents affected by externalities can reach mutually beneficial agreements without government intervention; moreover, if there is only one position that maximises social wealth, the agents involved will reach that position regardless of the way property rights were assigned.*

2 *If there are transaction costs, the possibility of reaching the most efficient position through the market can depend on how property rights are assigned; therefore, property rights should be assigned in such a way as to ensure that the most efficient position (which is not necessarily unique) will be reached (see Coase, 1960).*

Stigler (1966) labeled proposition 1 the 'Coase theorem'; this is the most well-known and debated element of Coase's arguments. In addition to the prior assignment of property rights and no (or negligible) transaction costs, the other necessary conditions for this proposition to hold are: the presence of an external authority that ensures the performance of contracts, and a freely transferable *numeraire* good, such as money. Given these conditions, the only role for the government in dealing with externalities should be to assign property rights and ensure contracts are honoured. In reality this is not a minor role,[23] since the assignment of property rights, which would in any case require a governmental political mechanism, will determine the final distribution of wealth.

We can illustrate the theorem with the following example. Let there be a rancher and a farmer. All other things being equal, if each could operate alone their net earnings would be 100 and 240, respectively. If they operate at the same time, however, especially if the cattle must cross the farmer's fields, there will be damage of 30 to take into account.

Let us now examine Coase's propositions in relation to the possible situations, which may differ as regards:

(a) the assignment of property rights (to the farmer or the rancher);
(b) the existence or absence of transaction costs;
(c) the existence or lack of technologies to limit the damage caused to the crop by the herd.

In the first four cases shown in table 6.2, we assume there are no transaction costs (the Coase theorem). In the first two we also assume there is no way to prevent the damage. In cases 1 and 3 property rights have been assigned to the rancher; in cases 2 and 4 they have been assigned to the farmer.

If the right to use the land is assigned to the rancher, no compensation will be paid for the damage caused by his herd and the farmer's earnings will therefore be 210 (situation 1). If, however, property rights are assigned to the farmer, he must be compensated by

---

[22] These are costs for establishing and using markets as a mechanism for resource allocation; they include costs for discovering quoted prices, goods available and the potential partner to a transaction as well as those of negotiating, drafting and enforcing contracts.

[23] Coase does not give much importance to this role, since his aim is only to find the most efficient institutions.

Table 6.2. *Efficiency and equity in relation to the attribution of property rights*

	Rancher's earnings	Farmer's earnings	Total earnings
	1st Coase proposition		
1 Rancher has property right, no transaction costs	100	210	310
2 Farmer has property right, no transaction costs	70	240	310
3 Rancher has property right, fencing used, no transaction costs	100	220	320
4 Farmer has property right, fencing used, no transaction costs	80	240	320
	2nd Coase proposition		
5 Rancher has property right, fencing used, transaction costs = 11	100	220	320
6 Farmer has property right, fencing used, transaction costs = 11[1]	(a) 69 (b) 70	240 240	309 310
7 Rancher has property right, cowboys used, no transaction costs	100	230	330
8 Farmer has property right, cowboys used, no transaction costs	90	240	330
9 Rancher has property right, cowboys used, transaction costs = 11[1]	(a) 100 (b) 100	219 220	319 320
10 Farmer has property right, cowboys used, transaction costs = 11	90	240	330

[1]Solution (a) represents taking action to prevent damage; solution (b) represents paying compensation.

the rancher and, consequently, his earnings will be 240 while the rancher's will fall to 70 (situation 2).

Let us suppose for the moment that we can reduce the damage to the farmer's crops by fencing the fields, which we assume costs 20. It is immediately clear that fencing raises the net total earnings of society as a whole: we can prevent damage valued at 30 at a cost of only 20. We still have to decide who is to pay for the fencing, but this is only a *problem of distribution, not efficiency*. What we can show is that however property rights are assigned, fencing will be used.

If the rancher holds the property rights, he will not be concerned with the damage caused by the herd and will earn 100 in any case; having no property rights, the farmer will instead find it advantageous to fence his crops (situation 3 in table 6.2). [24]

If, however, the farmer owns the property rights, it is not in his interest to fence his

[24] In this case his freedom to cultivate the land could be in doubt. We assume that property rights are defined as giving a right of precedence in the use of the land, so that the person possessing them is exempted from paying any compensation to other users of the land, who may use it on the condition that they do not cause harm to the owner of the rights.

crops since he can simply demand compensation of 30 from the rancher. In this case, we will remain in situation 2. This is a suboptimal state, however, since the rancher would gain by paying the full cost of 20 to fence the crops: this is still less than the compensation he would otherwise have to pay. The rancher will therefore seek to reach agreement with the farmer to pay for the fencing of the crops.[25] There will be no obstacles to the agreement if, as we have assumed, transaction costs related to the agreement are negligible.[26] This leads us to situation 4, which is superior to 2.

We have seen that with no transaction costs, with or without fencing, the optimal allocation of resources is invariant to the assignment of property rights and the most efficient allocation is chosen. However, *this does not mean that the income distribution is the same in the two cases.* On the contrary, this is clearly influenced by the way property rights are assigned: the user with exclusive rights to a good – or a right of precedence in its use – will be favoured.

Let us now examine Coase's second proposition, which regards the possibilities open to society when there are transaction costs, as is the case in the real world. For simplicity, we assume that these costs are borne entirely by the person without property rights.

According to proposition 2, transaction costs can have a significant impact on the possibility of producing an efficient allocation of resources. If transaction costs are low, their impact will be negligible, but if they exceed the potential net benefit they will discourage those who do not have property rights from proposing an agreement to adopt measures to prevent the damage when cooperation from the other party is neded.

Let us return to table 6.2. Assume that transaction costs are equal to 11. If the rancher holds the property rights, transaction costs are irrelevant, since the farmer will in any case benefit from fencing his crops. This is situation 5 in table 6.2, which is exactly the same as situation 3. If, however, the farmer possesses the property rights, the rancher could prevent damage to the crops by paying the cost of fencing (20) plus transaction costs (11), which would reduce his net earnings to 69 (= 100 − 31; situation 6a). However, this is less attractive than simply paying compensation to the farmer (100 − 30; situation 6b).

Let us now examine what happens if there is a more efficient way to prevent damage than fencing, such as exercising closer control over the herd with cowboys. Let the cost of this technique be 10. If the rancher holds the property rights, it will benefit the farmer to hire cowboys if transaction costs[27] are low or nil. If there are no transaction costs, we find ourselves in situation 7 in table 6.2. If the farmer holds the property rights, it is in the rancher's interest to hire the cowboys instead of fencing the crop, regardless of the existence of transaction costs (situation 8).

If, however, the rancher holds the property rights and transaction costs are 11, the

---

[25] The fencing costs are borne by the rancher in his own interest: he would otherwise be required to compensate the farmer, as he does not own the right to use the land.

[26] These costs generally regard the search for the owner who is willing to reach an agreement (in the case of many agents), the specification of the way the agreement is to be carried out and clauses to ensure that the agreement will be performed.

[27] These must be borne since the rancher must agree to have his herd monitored by cowboys.

farmer would spend a total of 21 to prevent damage with cowboys, with net earnings of 219 (situation 9a). This would offer no advantage over fencing, which costs 20, with net earnings of 220 (situation 9b). Thus the most efficient solution will not be adopted. In the presence of transaction costs, the less expensive technique will only be adopted when property rights belong to the farmer (situation 10). In this case total earnings will be higher (330) than in any of the other situations in which there are significant transaction costs.

This argument supports the first part of proposition 2, which states that in the presence of significant transaction costs, the possibility of achieving the most efficient allocation of resources for a society – which in this case is obtained using cowboys rather than fencing – depends on how property rights are assigned (in our case, they would have to be held by the farmer). In other words, the way in which property rights are assigned is not irrelevant to efficiency; it would be so only if there were no transaction costs, which is not the case in the real world.

The importance of Coase's work cannot be overstated. First, it underscores the fact that the Pigovian analysis of externalities and the proposed policy (taxation) implicitly assume a specific institutional context (i.e., a certain assignment of property rights), without examining the problem of whether an alternative assignment of rights could enhance efficiency.[28] Second, Coase's work underpins the now extensive literature on property rights covering a vast range of institutional issues (see, for example, Pagano, 1992). Nevertheless, his work has received criticism, especially from those who have focussed on the interpretation given to it by Stigler, which is based on proposition 1 (the 'Coase theorem').[29]

One important criticism of Coase's work is that the theorem is tautological (Calabresi, 1968). Consider it again: if we assume that agents act rationally and that there are no transaction costs or legal barriers to exchange, in a situation where property rights have been assigned any inefficient resource allocation will be completely eliminated through agreements between economic agents. This statement is tautological if by inefficient allocation of resources we mean (as we normally do) a situation that can be improved for some without worsening the condition of others: such an improvement is always obtainable through bargaining if there are no transaction costs.[30]

A second criticism (Cooter, 1982) regards the possibility that, in the absence of an authority to force individuals to negotiate, they might adopt reciprocal hostile posi-

[28] However, with reference to pollution, if we have the polluter pay compensation for the damage caused (and therefore grant other people a right to clean air) it is not only for historical reasons, but also because we feel that this institutional solution is more efficient than the other (attributing property rights to the polluter): in short, we feel it is less costly for society to solve the problem at the source rather than downstream (e.g., by wearing gas masks). The value of Coase's work is that of having demanded explicit – and therefore clearer and more effective – consideration of the terms of the problem.

[29] Coase himself sought to clarify a number of erroneous interpretations in one of his rare but penetrating essays (see Coase, 1988).

[30] Regan (1972) notes that the Coase theorem also establishes the invariance of the final position with respect to the assignment of property rights. However, this invariance is ensured only if certain specific hypotheses are satisfied (for example, 'quasi-linear' preferences; for the significance of this hypothesis see Varian, 1987).

tions like those envisaged by Hobbes (threats, attacks, attempts to eliminate adversaries, etc.) rather than cooperative behaviour. This criticism apparently misses the mark, since Coase does not argue that, even with no transaction costs, we can do without the government, which among other things would be entrusted with protecting individual rights. However, there is one sense in which Cooter's critique is on target: cooperative behaviour among the members of a society may not only depend on the possibility of procuring economic gain for oneself; there might be no cooperation even when there is an economic gain for the cooperating agents if other, non-economic, considerations prevail. In addition, cooperation can depend on the overall distribution of income.[31]

A further problem concerns the effects of the way property rights are assigned. This is relevant *only* for distributive purposes when transaction costs are absent (compare situations 1 and 2, or 3 and 4). It is relevant for *both* distribution and efficiency in a world where there are transaction costs. Compare cases 9b and 10, where property rights are assigned differently: both the size and distribution of income are different in the two cases. The important policy problem arising in this context concerns the objective to which the assignment of property rights should be geared. In the case we have considered, an incorrect interpretation of proposition 2 would suggest assigning the rights to farmers, since this would lead to the most efficient position. This is not so, however, as the distributive effects should also be taken into account, following our discussion in chapter 4.

The last and most important question raised by the Coase propositions regards the possibility that they (especially proposition 1) can be interpreted as a way of limiting the effects of market failures caused by externalities. Coase's argument is not unattractive and underscores clearly interesting problems (especially proposition 2); however, the most important issues arising from the existence of externalities are:

(a) that they conflict with the conditions required by the second fundamental theorem of welfare economics (convex production sets); and

(b) that externalities create analytical difficulties that can jeopardise the existence of a market equilibrium, since they can give rise to discontinuities in the supply functions of goods.

In this regard it is important to examine the phenomenon of 'fundamental non-convexities' pointed out by Starrett (1972) and Laffont (1976). Suppose there is an external diseconomy (smoke) for which tradable pollution permits are granted, as suggested by Coase. Now take a laundry. Obviously, it can produce and sell laundry services; in addition, it can sell its pollution permits[32] to nearby factories (up to some maximum) if the associated property rights are assigned to it and it is not engaged in a

---

[31] The sign of the relationship is uncertain. There are reasons to support both a direct and inverse relationship between the degree of cooperation and the degree of inequality of incomes.

[32] We will discuss such permits in much greater detail in section 10.3. For the moment, we can say that once the maximum pollution level has been established, 'rights' to pollute up to that level are assigned to firms, which the holder of the right can either use directly (if the business generates pollution) or sell to others who engage in a polluting activity.

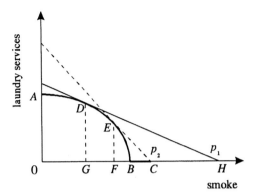

Figure 6.5

polluting activity. Let us first consider the conditions of production, referring to figure 6.5 (see Cornes and Sandler, 1986, pp. 36 ff.).

The quantities of labour and capital inputs for the production of laundry services are given. Suppose first that the maximum quantity of smoke permitted is $0B$. As the quantity of smoke produced by nearby factories increases, the quantity of laundry services that can be produced declines, as shown by the production frontier (or transformation curve) AB, which bounds a convex set. When the quantity of smoke produced is equal to $0B$, the laundry, 'drowned' in smoke, no longer finds it profitable to provide its services and exits the market.

Suppose now that the permitted level of smoke emissions extends up to $0C$, which is greater than $0B$. An increase in smoke output beyond B, which is now possible for the factories if they buy permits from the laundry, would not reduce the output of laundry services any further, as they are already nil at B, and therefore the segment BC is also efficient in terms of production and belongs to the production frontier. The complete production set, which is bounded by the line ABC, is no longer convex, as it was when the transformation curve was given by the line AB.

Let us now examine the implications of fundamental non-convexities. The laundry chooses the quantity of services and pollution permits it will supply on the basis of the relative price of the two 'goods' (laundry services and smoke). Let p_1 be the ratio between the price of pollution permits and the price of laundry services. At this price the optimal combination of the two goods is at point D. Assume that the price of permits rises, but stays between p_1 and p_2. The supply of permits increases and that of laundry services decreases. This moves the optimal combination to somewhere between D and E on the transformation curve. When the price reaches p_2, the laundry will be indifferent between point E and point C.[33] But if the relative price increases even slightly above p_2, the firm will exit the laundry market and sell all its pollution permits. The output of laundry services will now be zero, while the other firms will produce pollution up to $0C$ using the pollution permits they have purchased. Obvious-

---

[33] Remember that BC is part of the transformation curve.

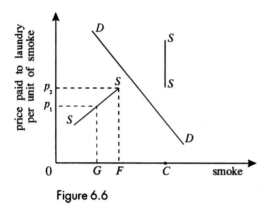

Figure 6.6

ly, subsequent increases in the relative price cannot further reduce the supply of laundry services, which is already zero.

This creates a discontinuity in the supply function for pollution permits. Referring to figure 6.6, the supply of permits (and smoke) rises continuously from 0 to F as their relative price rises (up to p_2), but jumps to $0C$ when the price rises above p_2 and remains at that level for any price $p > p_2$. The supply curve for pollution permits is the discontinuous SS line.

The presence of a discontinuity in the market supply function means that there will be no equilibrium in the pollution-permit market if the demand curve passes through the discontinuity, as shown by DD.

We asked earlier if the market can at times act as a constraint on public action. In the light of our discussion, we might well ask instead whether the market is simply not a feasible alternative to public action under certain circumstances.

6.5 Public goods

In the competitive markets considered in the theorems of welfare economics, goods are characterised by *rivalry* in their use (for consumers and producers): the use of a good by one person restricts the availability of the good for another. In real-life markets, however, there are also non-rival goods; that is, goods for which an increase in one person's consumption does not reduce its availability for others ('more for you means no less for me'). These are known as *public goods*. Examples of public goods are national defence, monuments, street lighting, lighthouses or radio and television broadcasts. In all of these cases the use of the good by an additional person raises the cost of providing it by (virtually) nothing, i.e., the marginal cost is (virtually) zero. In some cases, such as pollution, it would probably be more accurate to speak of public 'bads', but we will generally use the term public goods.

Public goods are a special form of externality, since the producer of such goods does not benefit himself alone but also benefits others, who can use it *for free*: if, for example, a shipping line builds a lighthouse to guide its ships through a dangerous stretch of water,

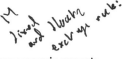

fixed theatre and exclang rule:

it also creates a benefit for all the ships that sail through the area without receiving any payment from other ships.

Every good or service produces some externalities, but in many cases these have little impact, such as the admiration or envy the colour of my neighbour's car might arouse (in which case we speak of private goods). In cases such as the lighthouse the external effect is much more significant, perhaps accounting for the entire value of the good. These are public goods.[34] There is a broad spectrum of goods between these two extremes. Curing contagious diseases, road building, parks and sports facilities are all goods with varying degrees of public and private characteristics.

A public good, then, has only fixed costs. Take the lighthouse. Construction and running costs are largely invariant to changes in the amount of services provided to ships.[35] This is in fact an extreme case of increasing returns to scale. We saw in section 6.2 that the existence of increasing returns to scale owing to high fixed costs in a natural monopoly can lead to market failure; considering the dominance of fixed costs in public goods, the two forms of market failure can be thought of as one. In both cases it is the presence of fixed costs and decreasing average costs that leads to market failure (see Foley, 1970; Heller, 1972; Starrett, 1988; Mueller, 1989), creating an incentive for a cooperative solution: if the supply of one unit of a good to individual A and another unit to individual B cost twice as much as it costs to produce one unit for A (or B), there would be no reason to cooperate: each consumer could choose *independently* whether or not to acquire that good and there would be no benefit from a cooperative decision to provide (consume) the good (Mueller, 1989, p. 11). Cooperation is in principle profitable only if provision (consumption) of two units of the good costs less than twice as much as one unit. In practice, cooperation is difficult to obtain since private agents have an incentive to free ride.

We can state the reasons for market failure in the case of public goods even more clearly: if A bears the fixed cost for the production of a public good, B would benefit, since in a competitive economy he could not be charged more than the marginal cost, which for a pure public good is equal to zero. However, in this case A would pay the full cost of the public good, which may well reduce (or eliminate) any incentive to produce the good. In such conditions, each agent will prefer to act as a free rider, waiting for others to produce the good.

There is another aspect of public goods to consider. In some cases it is impossible to exclude others from the use of public goods owing to the nature of the goods themselves and/or technical reasons: national defence and lighthouses are examples. It is possible to exclude some from using other goods, such as television signals, but exclusion adds to the cost.

---

[34] This is the meaning of non-rivalry: the full value of a public good can be used by everyone. For example, let the value of the lighthouse be F. The utility (or profit) function of other ships will include the full value F. By contrast, the colour of my neighbour's car is a negligible factor in the car's value, and I can easily omit it from my utility function.

[35] Note that we have defined the amount produced in terms of the number of services rendered to other ships. A taller or more powerful lighthouse might provide more services, but the effective variability of the size and power of the lighthouse is in reality relatively limited; in any case, for a given size and power, costs do not vary however many ships pass through the area.

is each agent a consumer: why should the govnt provide public goods.

The difficulty or impossibility of exclusion accentuates the free rider problem and the impracticability of the market,[36] making the production of public goods a less attractive proposition. If others could be excluded from consumption of a public good,[37] the benefits accruing to its supplier would be equal to any direct benefit from the good itself plus the amount paid by others for the use they have been *allowed* to make of the good. By contrast, if it is not possible to exclude others the only benefits will be those deriving from the direct use of the good.

In other words, since the decision to produce a private or public good by a private economic agent depends on the existence of a non-negative expected profit, by reducing expected profit, non-excludability makes the production of public goods by private agents less attractive. In fact, everyone will have an incentive to free ride, seeking to use the public good that others might decide to produce. This becomes increasingly likely as the number of agents who would benefit from the good increases.

Non-excludability is important because it can explain why some natural public goods are ruined: this is the 'tragedy of the commons', i.e., the over-exploitation of common property such as air, water and other natural resources (see Hardin, 1968; Cornes and Sandler, 1986). The two properties of public goods – the essential condition of non-rivalry and the non-essential but very common condition of non-excludability[38] – provide the justification for government intervention to produce such goods directly or stimulate production by others and to finance their production through taxation or to regulate their use in order to prevent the plundering of natural resources.

*6.6 A formal treatment of public goods

The nature of a public good can be formally represented by the condition

$$x_i \leq \bar{X} \quad i = 1, 2, \ldots, H \tag{6.1}$$

where $\bar{X}$ is the output of the good and x_i is the consumption of the good by individual i. By contrast, the condition for private goods is

$$\sum x_i \leq \bar{X} \tag{6.2}$$

---

[36] Oakland (1987, p. 486) stresses that 'while the inability to exclude costlessly exacerbates the efficiency problem of private provision of public goods, it is not essential for market failure'. We can add that exclusion, although possible in some cases of public good, is not desirable because consumption of the public good by an individual does not preclude consumption by another (apart from possible problems of congestion). There is therefore no reason to set a price (a form of exclusion) for the public good (at least as long as congestion is not a problem). More precisely, since the marginal cost of using a public good is zero, making the marginal user pay a price greater than zero (i.e., practicing some form of exclusion) would violate the conditions of Pareto efficiency in a competitive economy, where price is equal to marginal cost.

[37] Obviously, the ability to exclude also means the ability to demand payment for the use of the good if one wishes to do so.

[38] Public goods with both characteristics are called pure public goods. If exclusion is possible, they are called *impure* or *mixed public goods*. Those who consider both non-rivalry and non-excludability to be necessary conditions of public goods define mixed or impure public goods as those that lack *one* of the two characteristics (not necessarily non-excludability).

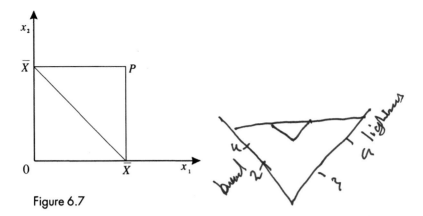

Figure 6.7

Inequality (6.1) means that each individual can consume *all* of the public good produced; he will consume less only if exclusion is feasible and his consumption is thereby limited. Inequality (6.2) shows that it is the *sum* of personal consumption that is limited by the amount of the good supplied. This difference is further illustrated by figure 6.7, which shows the possible consumption of a public or private good (of which quantity $\bar{X}$ is available) by the two members of a hypothetical society.

Consumption of a private good can only take place within the isosceles triangle $0\bar{X}X$. In particular, if the sum of the individual amounts consumed is equal to the supply $0\bar{X}$, greater consumption by one person is only possible at the expense of the other and consumption is given by the points along the hypotenuse, where $x_1 + x_2 = \bar{X}$.

By contrast, consumption of a public good can occur anywhere within the quadrilateral $0\bar{X}P\bar{X}$ if exclusion is possible. If exclusion is not possible, both members of society will consume $0\bar{X}$ and the level of consumption is indicated by point P.

As demonstrated by Samuelson (1954), the conditions for 'general' Pareto optimality in the presence of public goods are different from those we presented in section 3.1.2 (the MRS between two goods for all individuals equal to the MRT). Assume there exist only two goods, bread and a lighthouse. With a MRT of 2, we could give up two units of bread in order to build a lighthouse. To obtain 'general' Pareto efficiency it is not necessary for each consumer to be willing to reallocate consumption of the two goods in the same proportion, i.e., to have a MRS equal to 2: if there are four consumers, it is sufficient for each to give up 0.5 units of bread in order to have an additional lighthouse with no change in his utility. More precisely, the condition that must be satisfied for 'general' efficiency in the allocation of resources in the presence of public goods is not $MRS^i_{a,b} = MRT_{a,b}$, but rather $\sum_i MRS^i_{a,b} = MRT_{a,b}$, where i denotes individuals and a and b are the goods.[39]

We can present the substance of our discussion so far in terms of a simple 'prisoner's

---

[39] Given the similarities between externalities and public goods, it is not surprising that a similar condition holds in the case of external economies. The reader might find it helpful to consult Mueller (1989, p. 27).

Table 6.3. *Prisoner's dilemma and public goods*

			B	
			Build	Don't build
A	Build	1	(8, 8)	4 (5,11)
	Don't build	2	(11, 5)	3 (6, 6)

dilemma' game (table 6.3).[40] Let there be two shipping lines, A and B, that have the same number of ships operating a given route. Each assesses the consequences of its decision to build or not to build a lighthouse and, at the same time, of the possibility that the other will build it (or not). The first number of each pair shown in the cells of the matrix in table 6.3 indicates the net benefit to A from the four possible combinations of the two strategies that A and B can follow. The second number gives the net benefit to B. Thus, if they adopted a *cooperative strategy* and both decided to build they could share the costs and reap a high net benefit (8 each). However, this is not an equilibrium solution *in a private system* because each can expect to benefit more from a non-cooperative strategy. For example, A finds it profitable not to build, since by doing so (i.e., acting as a free rider) he would gain 11 (rather than 8) if B decides to build and bear the entire cost of the construction. On the other hand, A would gain 6 if B also decided not to build (compared with a gain of 5 if he decided to build and B did not). A's payoff from playing 'Don't build' is in both cases higher than that from playing 'Build'. The same holds for B[41] and, therefore, both find it advantageous not to build (cell 3), although this outcome is Pareto inefficient compared with that produced by the cooperative solution (cell 1). The latter cannot be reached except through cooperative action that can only be enforced (or facilitated) by the intervention of a third operator whose objective is to

[40] The game was initially used to illustrate the situation of two prisoners who cannot cooperate, i.e., they cannot make a binding commitment. Take the case of two prisoners accused of the same crime in a situation where the prosecutor is not sure of obtaining a conviction. Each prisoner is told that if he confesses he will receive a reduced sentence while the other will serve the full term; if both confess, they will receive a less-than-full sentence but the penalty will still be longer than if only one were to confess. If neither confesses, both might be convicted of lesser crimes only. Given these conditions, both prisoners have an incentive to confess. The reader can use the matrix shown in the text, replacing 'Build' and 'Don't build' with 'Confess' and 'Don't confess' respectively, and taking the results of the game to be the length of the sentence.

Public goods can give rise to (or be represented by) different games from that shown (for example, the game of 'chicken', where cooperation is again better than non-cooperation). For both games, see Rasmusen (1994).

[41] In the technical jargon of game theory we would say that the non-cooperative solution ('Don't build') is dominant for both players. In other words, each has an incentive not to build because the benefit of this strategy is greater no matter what the other decides to do.

maximise the benefit for the entire society, i.e., a public body.[42] This provides a justification for government financing or production of public goods, funded by tax receipts rather than the payment of a price.

We must still deal with the problem of the optimal output of the public good, which is difficult to establish for two major reasons: the complexity of mechanisms for measuring preferences and problems of congestion.

As regards the revelation of preferences, if it is not possible to exclude users there is no way to discover the value of the public good for individuals through the price they are prepared to pay. To encourage truthful revelation of preferences, a number of alternative mechanisms have been devised; they are, however, complex and open to manipulation by coalitions (see Clarke, 1971; Boadway, 1979; Green and Laffont, 1979). We will return to this issue in section *10.5.

As regards congestion, we have already said that there are public goods for which non-rivalry is absolute (hence the problem of congestion does not arise). However, there are also public goods for which use by one does not hinder use by another only up to a certain point, beyond which the utility to initial users may decline, probably owing to a decline in quality.[43]

When congestion is particularly severe, i.e., when it becomes a problem for a relatively small number of users, it may be profitable to produce the good through a decentralised system of relatively small communities, such as local authorities (see Tiebout, 1956) or even clubs, hence the name *club goods* given to goods such as swimming pools, tennis courts, etc. (Buchanan, 1965). Each person can choose among the different levels and qualities of public goods and the different financial contributions in the various communities, *voting with one's feet*, i.e., by moving to the community that offers the best conditions (Tiebout, 1956).

6.7 Transaction costs and asymmetric information

Since the seminal contribution of Coase (1937),[44] economists have been aware of the existence of transaction costs. Such costs are pervasive but they are of special relevance for forward markets.

In forward (especially contingent) markets transaction costs may be substantial owing to the high degree of uncertainty about future contingencies which make some of them 'uninsurable'. That is why in the real world we find very few forward and contingent markets (commodity forward markets, credit, insurance). In both spot and forward markets, transaction costs are greater in the presence of asymmetric information.

---

[42] Cooperative outcomes may emerge spontaneously when the game is repeated an infinite number of times. Such outcomes are linked to the possibility that an agent will adopt non-cooperative behaviour in response to similar behaviour on the part of others (see, for example, J. Friedman, 1990; and Fudenberg and Tirole, 1991).

[43] However, it is often difficult to distinguish between a reduction in the quality of a public good and a reduction in its quantity.

[44] Later contributions include, among others, Demsetz (1968), Williamson, O. E. (1975, 1985, 1989). The approach inaugurated by Coase has been mainly interested in analysing the relative performance of alternative institutions such as markets and firms. We will see in chapter 9 that an application to public institutions has also been suggested.

Asymmetric (or *private*) *information* refers to the different amount of information available to the two parties to a transaction, one of whom is called the *principal* (the party without full information) and the other is called the *agent* (that with full information). The terms were coined in order to convey the idea that the party without full information relies on the other to carry out transactions with hidden features. Problems of asymmetric information are also known as *agency problems*.

Asymmetric information can give rise to two different situations: (a) *adverse selection*; and (b) *moral hazard*.

Adverse selection occurs when one of the parties (the principal) is unable to observe the situation of the agent or important *exogenous* characteristics of the agent or the good involved in the transaction. It is important to emphasise that the characteristics referred to here already exist at the time the decision to undertake a transaction is made; this is why they are called exogenous.

One problem of adverse selection was first noted by Akerlof (1970) with reference to the used car market, where there is considerable asymmetry of information. Very few buyers have the knowledge to assess the condition and reliability of a used car. When they do have such knowledge, they may still find it difficult to spot hidden defects, unlike the owner, who has gained a thorough knowledge of the car through use. Suppose the market price of a used car refers to one in average condition, with an average number of defects, etc. Only owners of cars in equal or worse condition will have an incentive to sell their cars, thus lowering the average condition of cars. The person assessing the value of used cars will consequently adjust the price of an average car downwards, lowering the standard even further and so on, until there are only 'lemons' left or the market disappears altogether. This is a Pareto inefficient situation, because it is likely that the missing transactions would have been mutually beneficial: in other words, there are people willing to purchase a car with certain characteristics at a price (demand price) that is higher than that at which others are willing to sell (supply price). Similar difficulties arise in the exchange of technological knowledge. Here, too, the market fails to carry out its role of fostering mutually beneficial, and hence efficient, transactions.

Similarly, insurance companies cannot distinguish between risky and less risky customers or events, which may 'empty' some markets.[45] The same thing can occur when patients are unable to distinguish between competent and incompetent doctors, or when financial intermediaries are unable to assess the insolvency risk of potential customers.

Let us take a brief look at bank lending. Suppose that banks are unable to determine the riskiness of specific borrowers and that they charge a uniform interest rate that includes a

---

[45] The reader with some knowledge of actuarial mathematics can consider a standard life or health insurance contract offered on fair terms to customers with a different probability of having an accident, falling ill, etc. in the case where each person is perfectly informed about his or her own probability of experiencing such an event but where the insurance company does not know the individual probabilities of any given customer having an accident, falling ill, etc. Those with a lower risk will not insure themselves, which raises the average probability of the event occurring for the remaining people and thus increases the premium rate charged by the insurance company. The effect is to reduce the number of insured people even further. This goes on until the premium rate (including administration costs and a profit margin) is so high as to discourage even the riskiest person.

premium to cover the risk of insolvency. Assume also that the potential borrowers expect a uniform rate of profit net of the risk premium, with higher expected gross returns for riskier lines of business: under these conditions, only customers in the riskiest undertakings will find it profitable to borrow from the banks, thus inducing the latter to raise the risk premium. Each rise in the interest rate (either due to this mechanism or to some exogenous factor such as a credit squeeze) discourages loan demand from less risky customers. An increase in the interest rate would thus have a perverse effect on banks, one that they seek to avoid by closely evaluating the economic and financial condition of their customers and by placing a ceiling on credit supplied to each customer or denying credit to some borrowers, thus rationing credit this way rather than by raising its price (i.e., the interest rate). The behaviour of banks can have a negative effect on the allocation of resources: we cannot assume that the bank allocates credit to projects with the highest expected return (see Stiglitz and Weiss, 1981; Ordover and Weiss, 1981).

The second problem of asymmetric information, the moral hazard (or incentive) problem,[46] arises when the principal is unable to monitor the actions carried out by the agent or the characteristics of the good conferred (controllable by the agent) following the decision to go ahead with the transaction in a situation where the agent has no incentive to act in the principal's interest. We will give only three examples: (a) the failure of a holder of an insurance policy to take appropriate risk reduction measures; (b) *shirking* by a worker (or manager) in the performance of a contractual duty; (c) the incentive for borrowers to undertake riskier projects as an effect of higher interest rates.

There are various steps that can be taken by private agents to avoid the negative consequences of adverse selection: contracts in which payment is linked to approval of the quality of the good or to the results obtained using the good; pledges of collateral; quality *certification* by professional associations; establishing a reputation (e.g., through trademarks); *signalling* the characteristics of the good or one's own qualities (e.g., being willing to accept conditional contracts that provide for repayment in the case of malfunction). A solution to moral hazard is the use of incentives (e.g., partial insurance, so that the agent has an interest in preventing fire, illness, etc.; higher wages to raise the expected loss of workers to prevent shirking). One solution to the problems raised by both forms of asymmetric information is to abandon prices as an instrument of rationing and make recourse to direct rationing (e.g., credit rationing). However, it is highly doubtful that these or other private solutions can systematically overcome the incompleteness of markets caused by asymmetric information. Take product certification: this has all the characteristics of a public good, giving individual agents an incentive to engage in free riding behaviour (Inman, 1987, pp. 660–1).[47] In some cases

---

[46] This is sometimes called the hidden action problem.

[47] Certification has been compared to network externalities, i.e., the external effects created in situations such as telephone networks, where the advantages of joining the network increase as the number of people already connected increases. No one has an incentive to join a network with few users, as this would mean bearing a large share of fixed costs.

   Private networks are limited to very large-scale projects, in which, however, there are initially a relatively small number of participants and other circumstances also work to counter the problem of free riding (personal ties, location, etc.). For more on the concept of network externalities see Economides (1996).

private solutions to asymmetric information can have negative effects, such as in the case of credit rationing or in that of unemployment caused by high wages (see section *7.4.6).

The solution is therefore public action in various guises, ranging – in the field of microeconomic actions – from regulation imposing certain behaviour in order to produce better information to the creation of government-owned enterprises to produce public goods or to overcome asymmetric information. There are many examples of such intervention around the world in the areas of insurance,[48] banking[49] and certification.[50]

6.8 The theory of the second best

We have frequently remarked on the divergence of real-world conditions and the hypotheses used to obtain certain results, such as the first theorem of welfare economics.

Of course, any scientific proposition must to some degree abstract from certain aspects of reality: to take an example from geography, a 1:1-scale map of the world would not give us a better understanding of reality; it would be a description rather than an attempt to identify key features and, in our field, important connections, causes and effects. Such a map would be at least as awkward as reality itself. The key to scientific abstraction is to set aside features that are less important for the purposes at hand (whether analytical or prescriptive), so that the conclusions reached with the simplified model broadly correspond to the aspects of the economic system that we wish to emphasise or influence. We can thus accept theories that use unrealistic hypotheses where the perspective chosen justifies this choice.[51]

A corollary of this argument is that 'small' changes in real life and/or in the theory do not modify greatly the conclusions of the model, which remain attached to the 'core' of reality: the model is 'robust' with respect to small variations in the hypotheses.[52]

---

[48] Various forms of public insurance are common in many countries (life insurance, export credit, deposit insurance, etc.).These also partly serve a redistributive purpose in favour of certain categories (small savers, exporters, small depositors, etc.) (see Stiglitz, 1988, pp. 121–2).

[49] Examples are public financial intermediaries, subsidised loans, government-guaranteed student loans and so forth.

[50] For example, the rules and public bodies for supervising weights and measures, quality certification and the certification of financial statements.

[51] According to Friedman (1953) the realism of hypotheses is irrelevant and what counts is the predictive power of the model. This position has been widely criticised, especially by Samuelson (1963), who argues that it is necessary to use realistic assumptions in any case. The position taken here is very similar to that of Sen (1980a), who, after asserting that the description (analysis) of a phenomenon calls for the selection of its most important features, correctly argues that correspondence with reality is neither a sufficient nor a necessary condition for the description (analysis) of the phenomenon. For example, the statement 'Michelangelo produced the statue of David' is not true, since quarry workers and others also played a role, but it is nonetheless useful since it gives us information about the source of the inspiration expressed in the statue, which is the most interesting aspect of a sculpture.

[52] If the analytical purpose of the statement concerning the person responsible for the David is to show the source of inspiration, our argument in note 51 would remain valid even if Michelangelo had delegated part of the execution of the sculpture to others.

The central idea of the first theorem of welfare economics is that a competitive equilibrium is Pareto optimal. We could therefore argue that small divergences from perfect competition do not lead us far from the Pareto optimum, and that the smaller any divergence is the less we stray from Pareto optimality.

The *theory of the second best* argues the exact opposite: it is not true that 'a situation in which more, but not all, of the optimum conditions are fulfilled is necessarily, or is even likely, to be superior to a situation in which fewer are fulfilled' (Lipsey and Lancaster, 1956, p. 12).

Let us try to understand why. First we must emphasise that where at least one of the conditions necessary for Pareto optimality is not met, we will have an inferior outcome; that is, we can only achieve a second-order optimum with respect to a 'first best' Pareto optimum. Hence the term 'second best'.

Let us consider a situation in which, for simplicity, we wish to assess only one aspect of the general efficiency of an economic system, production efficiency. We know that profit maximising firms in a competitive economy will achieve such efficiency; that is, they will allocate scarce resources among various uses in the most efficient way. One of the ways the conditions of production efficiency can be expressed in a perfectly competitive market is the equality of price and marginal cost (see section 5.3). To say that firms fulfil this condition means that they will use resources in the production of a good until the value of the resources used to produce an additional unit (i.e., marginal cost) is equal to the value society assigns the good (i.e., price). If this condition is met throughout the economy, given consumer preferences, the price of each good (say, bread) will exactly reflect the resources necessary (wheat, transportation services, energy, etc.) to obtain the good itself (or rather, the last unit produced); in turn, resources will have been produced following analogous criteria.

If perfect competition in a sector is 'unattainable' (for example, owing to the impossibility of eliminating monopoly in the provision of transportation services),[53] it is clearly impossible to achieve a Pareto optimal situation. However, we might think that the second best outcome would require that optimum conditions for resource allocation be met in the other $n - 1$ sectors (where n can be very large). The theorem of the second best tells us that this is not the case and it is easy to see why.

Let us consider bread production. If the level of bread output were established by equalising price and marginal cost, too few resources might be used in the production of bread: the cost of transportation services used in making bread is high, not because of the natural scarcity of these services (or the resources needed to produce them) but because providers of these services can exercise their market power. Underproduction of bread would mean that a distortion in one sector unconnected with any scarcity of resources has been allowed to curtail output in another sector. In our example, if there are no other goods, achieving the social optimum would necessitate setting the output of bread at a level where marginal cost is higher than the market price; this position can be achieved with government subsidies for bread production. We can apply the same

---

[53] We will return later to the nature of such a distortion.

reasoning to problems regarding substitutability in consumption rather than comple-mentarity in production.[54]

Our example shows how divergence from *one* of the efficiency conditions causes a divergence from *all* the other conditions, in some *non-specifiable* way, given the numer-ous and complex relationships of complementarity and substitutability among goods. This conclusion is of great importance in the analysis of Pareto efficiency in markets where there are even small divergences from the conditions for perfect competitive equilibrium: the fundamental theorems of welfare economics are not robust.[55]

Nevertheless, the reason a sector may feature an *irremovable* divergence from perfect competition may not be equally clear. The problem is to determine if government intervention can eliminate the divergence and if that intervention should be aimed at this goal, rather than at encouraging (or discouraging) the production of other goods. Let us assume that the cause is in fact 'irremovable': for example, natural monopoly.[56] It could be argued that nationalisation or regulation allow the state to guarantee non-monopolistic behaviour, even when the causes of the monopoly cannot be removed; for example, efficiency would be ensured if a government-owned monopoly determined output by setting price equal to marginal cost.

Only if the government could not or would not act to achieve this end would we need a generalised divergence from perfect competition in other sectors in order to ensure a second-best situation. There are in fact many reasons why the government might be unable or unwilling to establish, for example, a public enterprise: an excessively high level of public spending, large budget deficits or problems of management control.

An entirely different application of the theory of the second best involves public action itself. With reference to our earlier example, let there be two government agencies, one of which is responsible for competition policy (in particular in the transportation sector) and the other for the supply of essential goods (bread). The problem is whether the two agencies can act separately; that is, can they take decisions in isolation from each other, implementing *piecemeal* policies? We can ask if the bread supply agency can act in isolation from the other agency to ensure that the efficiency condition (price equal to marginal cost) is met in its sector regardless of the actions of the other agency, which might in turn seek to fulfil the same conditions in its own industry. In the light of the theory of the second best, the answer is, in general, clearly no. 'Separability' conditions for which the distortions in one sector do not affect the Pareto optimality conditions in

[54] Suppose that there exists an irremovable monopoly in the supply of road transportation services only. What is the efficient pricing policy for the railways, supposing that there are no other industries? Given the substitutability of the two services, we could argue that the purchase of rail services should be encouraged by setting rail prices below marginal cost.

There is a large literature on the theory of the second best. Some contributions were made before the Lipsey and Lancaster article and regard problems with the theory of customs unions (see Meade, 1955; Viner, 1950), 'optimal' production (see McKenzie, 1951) and excess burden of taxation (Corlett and Hague, 1953).

[55] A similar conclusion is reached if we consider the incompleteness of markets, as we saw earlier, especially with regard to externalities (see section *6.4).

[56] The reader will recall that this exists when a single firm is able to produce at lower cost than that at which two or more firms would produce any level of output. We will discuss natural monopoly at greater length in section 10.6.2.

others have been identified, but they are extremely restrictive. Nevertheless, these conditions are important for dealing with a number of practical questions of economic policy, such as cost–benefit analysis of projects (see chapter 12).

6.9 Income distribution and equity

Having concluded our microeconomic analysis of the causes of market failure due to failure to respect the Pareto optimality conditions, we must now present the remaining two causes, which may occur even when a state is Pareto optimal. In this section we examine issues relating to equity.

Before beginning, we must note that '*equity*' can assume a variety of meanings. For example, we can distinguish between the ability (or productivity) principle (which invokes equality of opportunity or equal starting points) and the need (or redistribution) principle (which seeks to equalise outcomes). Liberal doctrine adopts the former, underscoring the need for common rules (procedures) and for everyone to be able to participate in the game, which, however, can end with different outcomes for the participants according to their abilities and their determination. Socialist and catholic doctrines emphasise needs, underscoring the desirability of equal welfare (or in any case a levelling of certain outcomes) for the members of society, regardless of abilities or procedures.

These are two extreme views that influence to varying degrees the positions actually taken by individuals, political parties and governments in Western democracies. Both visions are part of the 'culture' and ideology of these democracies and any differences, as great as they may be, are nevertheless only differences of degree.

We are particularly interested in the economic aspects of equity (i.e., economic equality). One indicator of this is the distribution of income. Even a partial acceptance of the principle of need, in economic terms, means that we must pay attention to the distribution of economic 'values' (i.e., income, wealth, consumption, etc.) among different individuals.

Deferring our discussion of some other indicators of 'values' to our examination of development (section 7.5), we will limit ourselves here to a consideration of some data on the degree of income inequality between 'rich' and 'poor' countries and within the 'rich' countries themselves.

In 1990 some 3 billion people (58 per cent of the world's population) had a per capita income of $600 or less (World Bank, 1992, table 1). Moreover, inequality does not seem to be disappearing. On the contrary, it has actually increased in the last three decades, as can be seen in table 6.4.[57]

Inequalities within individual countries are, obviously, much less marked.[58] The main, but certainly not the only, reason for inequality is unemployment, which fuels a

[57] Nevertheless, it is important to note that among the poorest countries there have been large differences in the growth rate of GDP.

[58] Income inequalities within developing countries are usually greater than in the developed world, although the differences can be quite significant even in the latter.

Table 6.4. *World income inequality, 1960–89*

	Percentage of world income			
Year	Received by poorest 20%	Received by richest 20%	Income of richest/ income of poorest	Gini index
1960	2.3	70.2	30	0.69
1970	2.3	73.9	32	0.71
1980	1.7	76.3	45	0.79
1989	1.4	82.7	59	0.87

Source: United Nations (1994).

large segment of poverty especially in countries that do not have a system of income support for the unemployed. In the United States, which although it does not have the highest per capita income is unanimously considered the most economically advanced country in the world, fully 38.1 million people (or 14.5 per cent of the population) were living below the poverty line in 1994. The percentage of poor people was up from 11.1 per cent in 1973, but down from 22.4 per cent in 1959 (see United States, 1993, 1996).[59]

Government redistributive action can be carried out through public spending (in particular transfers to households and/or firms; see chapter 11), taxation (especially progressive taxes; see chapter 11) and price controls (fixing both minimum and maximum prices; see section 10.7).

6.10 Merit wants

We have already presented the criticism of welfarism (section 4.2), showing among other things that very few people in modern Western society would be prepared to support fully the idea that each person is always the best judge of his own needs under all possible circumstances. For example, there is broad agreement that this assumption does not hold for minors or the mentally infirm. The replacement of individual choices with those of some external entity (the essence of *paternalism*) can be extended to other situations. Such an approach can be justified on two counts:

(a) people may not have information about important aspects of the situation needed to make á choice, or their information (and preferences) may be distorted by advertising or other external influences;

[59] The US official poverty line was defined in the mid sixties on an absolute basis, reflecting the different consumption requirements of households based on their size and composition. The poverty thresholds fixed in monetary terms are updated every year to reflect changes in the Consumer Price Index.

By contrast, the European Commission, following the approval of the first Community Action Programme to Combat Poverty (see Commission of the European Communities, 1989), has indicated a *relative* poverty line, equal to 50 per cent of the average disposable income per equivalent adult in the member country in question.

(b) their decision-making processes do not follow the normal canons of rationality.

Paternalism is a feature of much government action, especially through regulation in areas such as safety (mandatory crash helmets, seat belts, grounded sockets, earthquake-proof construction techniques, etc.); health (ban on use of narcotics or, during Prohibition in the United States, alcohol); education (compulsory school attendance up to the age of 16); art (conservation of artistic heritage, art subsidies, etc.). Government-run compulsory insurance schemes also have a paternalistic foundation.

Needs whose satisfaction the government wishes to promote regardless of individual preferences are known as 'merit wants' (Musgrave, 1959). Goods that enable satisfaction of merit wants are called 'merit goods'.[60]

Note that the paternalistic argument in support of government intervention in these areas may be supplemented by other forms of justification, such as the presence of externalities or of public goods (as is the case of compulsory education or the prohibition of alcohol consumption). In countries with a system of social insurance, a similar justification given for individual safety regulations is the desire to reduce public expenditure – and thus the negative effects on other people – needed to cope with the consequences of injuries (medical care, disability pensions and so on). Some might be willing to support certain measures only when this second level of justification predominates. For example, laws such as the prohibition on driving while drunk (given the risk of injuring others) might be acceptable but not those that primarily or exclusively safeguard the health of the individual concerned (e.g., seat belt requirements).

Merit goods:

6.11 Summary

1 Microeconomic market failures can be associated with:
   (a) divergences between real-life markets and those postulated by the first theorem of welfare economics (competitive markets, complete markets).
   (b) rejection of the postulate of ethical individualism, which underlies the Pareto principle (merit goods and income distribution), and/or the postulate of methodological individualism, which underpins the theory of general economic equilibrium (merit goods).
   (c) rejection of the postulate of interpersonal non-comparability of utilities, which underlies the Pareto principle (income distribution).

2 The existence of non-competitive markets can be attributed to the invalidity of the assumptions of perfect competition. Two differences are of particular

[60] The shift in focus from individuals' needs to objects (goods) is, however, open to criticism: it is claimed that in many cases what is safeguarded is the (consumption of) the good, when in most cases we wish to (or should) promote the welfare of the individual.

importance: the small number of suppliers, owing to economies of scale, and barriers to entry or exit from the market.

3 It is not profitable for a private monopolist to set price equal to marginal cost, which means that the Pareto optimality conditions are not met.

4 According to the theory of contestable markets, free market entry and exit is the most important factor in ensuring quasi-competitive market results; however, entry and exit costs make it difficult for a potential entrant to 'hit and run'.

5 (Allocative efficiency is not the only concept of efficiency. Other significant forms are 'X-efficiency' and 'dynamic efficiency', which can in some way be related to Pareto efficiency.)

6 Incomplete markets are associated with externalities, public goods, transaction costs and asymmetric information.

7 Externalities cause a divergence between private costs (or benefits) and social costs (or benefits). The conditions for achieving Pareto efficiency in the presence of externalities differ from those that hold without externalities and meeting them requires public intervention.

8 According to Coase, government intervention is not necessary to reach the most efficient state: if there are no transaction costs, it will be possible for agents to reach mutually beneficial agreements. However, if there are transaction costs, government intervention is needed to assign property rights in such a way as to ensure that the most efficient outcome is reached. There have been many specific criticisms of Coase's position. The most general criticism underscores the fact that the theorem does not narrow the range of market failures: the presence of externalities conflicts with the second theorem since it implies non-convex production sets and jeopardises the very existence of a market equilibrium.

9 Public goods, characterised by non-rivalry and non-excludability in use, are a special category of externality. Non-rivalry gives rise to free riding behaviour, which leads to market failure and the need for government intervention for the production, financing or regulation of such goods.

*10 A prisoner's dilemma game can be used to illustrate the nature of public goods.

11 Private, asymmetric information gives rise to agency problems in the form of 'adverse selection' and 'moral hazard', which can prevent the formation of both spot and forward markets (by raising transaction costs) and thereby hinder the efficient allocation of resources. Incompleteness of markets can be overcome by public intervention.

12 (Even small disparities between reality and the hypotheses used in the fundamental theorems of welfare economics can give rise to very large modifications

of the conditions needed to achieve a Pareto optimum and, in particular, can reduce the desirability of perfect competition).

13 The free operation of the market does not ensure acceptable income distributions. Acceptability can be judged on the basis of different principles that influence government action to varying degrees.

14 Rejection of the welfarist assumption introduces the final example of (microeconomic) market failure: it may be felt necessary to act on behalf of individuals regardless of their preferences (merit wants).

6.12 Key concepts

Returns to scale
Natural monopoly
Free riding
Strategic behaviour
Contestable markets
Entry, exit barrier
Sunk cost
X-efficiency
Dynamic efficiency
Agreements among firms
Homogeneous good (commodity)
Market segmentation
External economy, diseconomy
Property right
Marginal private, social product
Consumption, production externality
Industrial district
Internalisation (of externality)
Coase theorem
Pure, impure (mixed) public good
Rivalry
Excludability
Tragedy of the commons
*Prisoner's dilemma

*Cooperative strategy
*Dominant strategy
*Congestion
*Club good
*Voting with one's feet
Transaction cost
Asymmetric, private information
Principal
Agent
Agency problem
Adverse selection
Moral hazard, hidden action
Incentive problem
'Lemon'
Empty market
Shirking
Signalling
Certification
Network externality
First, second best
Fairness
Merit want, good
Paternalism

7 Market failures: macroeconomic aspects

7.1 The instability of a capitalist market economy

The conclusions reached in chapters 5 and 6 prevent us from using the first theorem of welfare economics in defence of real-life markets for at least three reasons, which lie at the heart of 'classic' microeconomic market failures. These are:

(a) the numerous divergences of real-life markets from those postulated in the theorem make it impossible to achieve a Pareto optimum;

(b) the methodological individualism of the theory underlying the theorem is too strong a constraint with respect to the needs judged to be worthy of satisfaction;

(c) the optimality criterion used in the theorem is only one of a number of possible 'success criteria', and it is not necessarily the most important (see section 5.6 and table 6.1).

However, a more complete assessment of the ability of real-life markets to act as an 'invisible hand' cannot neglect numerous recurring 'crisis' situations of unemployment, inflation, external payments imbalances or underdevelopment, which do not appear to be immediately explainable in terms of the classic microeconomic market failures. These situations are manifestations of the 'instability' of capitalist market economies.[1] Instability here does not simply mean the failure of the economy to converge towards equilibrium but also the possibility that the economy may evolve along a non-optimal path from the point of view of efficiency and/or equity and may remain in such a non-optimal state.

These aspects of reality are difficult to model using general equilibrium theory and, often, even with other existing microeconomic theories. Let us examine some of the reasons for this conclusion, focusing on general equilibrium theory.

[1] See, among others, Robinson (1962b); Minsky (1975).

It is difficult to believe that persistent mass unemployment, often experienced by market economies, is a voluntary phenomenon. *Involuntary unemployment*, however cannot arise in models of general competitive equilibrium: if all markets are in equilibrium, the labour market will also be in equilibrium and any unemployment must be voluntary.

Microeconomic theories explain relative prices, not the absolute price level; they have never succeeded in modelling a monetary economy in a satisfactory way. For these reasons they cannot take account of inflation.[2]

Since models are developed in real terms, such theories have limited explanatory power in dealing with problems of imbalances in the balance of payments, since this is expressed in monetary terms.

Finally, problems such as underdevelopment are difficult to tackle with static theories like general equilibrium theory.

Advocates of the virtues of the invisible hand have attempted to account for some of these features of reality (unemployment, for example) using general equilibrium theory and introducing hypotheses that explain the malfunctioning of prices (price rigidity); in this context a central role has been given to the assertion that government intervention has contributed to this rigidity and, therefore, to the crises we are examining.

A more convincing analysis has been advanced by others who have argued that the cause of the instability is to be sought in structural features of the markets that prevent them from operating in the way and with the results predicted by general equilibrium theory. The structure of the Walrasian model of general equilibrium in fact excludes a number of essential characteristics of market capitalism. They are:

1. factors and circumstances, such as uncertainty, change and disequilibrium, closely connected with dynamic problems (see, in part, section 5.5 and, in more detail, Vercelli, 1991);
2. historical and institutional factors such as:

   the existence of different social classes or groups (savers and investors; wage earners and capitalists; unions; internal or external pressure groups) on which certain behaviour and economic outcomes depend;

   the existence of money, payment systems and financial institutions, which are in some respects the product of the context in which economic activity takes place (uncertainty, incomplete information) and in part are a consequence of the existence of well-defined social groups or classes (e.g., the existence of a financial market is connected with the separation of saving and investment).

Some argue that the instability of market capitalism can be demonstrated by using a theory that abandons the microeconomic standpoint of individual agents and markets and instead considers relationships between economic aggregates.

Results at the macroeconomic level can differ from those generated by micro-economic models. For instance, in the case of Walrasian equilibrium the central problem of market economies, understanding how different agents coordinate their decisions

---

[2] In particular, consider that (the rate of change in) the absolute level of prices is an indicator of inflation.

in a market economy, is often circumvented by resorting to *ad hoc* hypotheses.[3] Specifically, the difficulty in addressing this problem consists in the fact that the behaviour of one agent is a function of the behaviour of other agents. Agents are not negligible (infinitesimal) entities, but rather are significant (discrete) elements of the market, and therefore adopt strategic behaviour aimed at influencing the choices of others. Prices can give misleading or inadequate signals of other agents' intentions; the time sequence of signals can also be interpreted in different ways.[4]

A microeconomic model, even a non-Walrasian model, finds it difficult to account for such aspects of reality. Although non-Walrasian micro-models have led to interesting analytical results shedding light on the instability of capitalism, studying the operation of an economy in aggregate terms has its own foundations that cannot be completely reduced to existing microeconomic theory. In other words, we can speak of a *macroeconomic logic* that does not entirely correspond to the logic of microeconomics, meaning, for example, that the system may be in equilibrium even if individual agents are not (Fitoussi, 1983). We will see later that the recent attempt of neoclassical macroeconomists to reduce macroeconomics to purely microeconomic (Walrasian) foundations can largely be considered a failure (see Vercelli, 1991). For the moment at least, macroeconomics is an autonomous discipline that appears able to say something more than and different from microeconomics about the problems of instability under capitalism.[5]

Adopting this approach, we will define as *'macroeconomic' failures* those failures associated with the instability of market economies. More specifically, unemployment, inflation, balance of payments disequilibria and underdevelopment can be considered macroeconomic market failures for the following three reasons:

(a) they are *failures*, since they reflect the presence of inefficiencies and/or injustice, raising the same problems we encountered in our analysis of microeconomic failures;

(b) they are *market* failures, since they are intrinsic to the working of actual markets, as we will show in the following subsections; there can also be government failures of the kind emerging in relation to the political business cycle, but these

---

[3] In the case of the Walrasian model, the *ad hoc* assumption is the fictitious auctioneer.

[4] For example, a given sequence of prices can give rise to the formation of different expectations about future prices.

[5] Hahn has taken a different position, arguing that macroeconomics 'is simply the project of deducing something about the behaviour of such aggregates as income and employment from the micro-theory which we have' (see Hahn, 1985, p. 5). The real problem, in his view, is the search for microeconomic bases at least as rigorous as the Walrasian model that enable us to derive results of the type obtained by Keynes in order to account for the structures and instability encountered in market economies. Similar ideas have been recently expressed by Greenwald and Stiglitz (1993). The position of all these authors seems acceptable in principle at the analytical level. For the purposes of economic policy, it nevertheless seems necessary to choose, among the different *existing* models, those most suitable for representing the instability of capitalism. Such models currently adopt a macroeconomic logic that cannot be entirely reduced to that of microeconomics. More recently, Hahn and Solow (1995) have argued that it is untenable to hold both that macro-models should be the exact aggregation of a micro-model and that the only micro-model is Walrasian. On this issue see also Colander *et al.* (1996).

are of a different nature and we defer our analysis of them until chapter 9;

(c) they are *macroeconomic* failures, since the theory that best explains them currently appears not to be a micro-theory, but rather a macroeconomic one.

The macroeconomic aspect of failures connected with 'instability' should not be misleading, preventing us from associating them with the more traditional microeconomic failures.[6] In the light of point (a) above, we can see that the problems arising from the operation of the market are much the same and can always be expressed in terms of inefficiency and injustice, even if some are microeconomic in nature and others are macroeconomic.

It is with reference to these problems that it seems justified to speak of welfare economics as the logic of economic policy (see section 2.1); that is, as a unified set of criteria for assessing the validity of public action.

Let us now examine in greater detail the main forms of instability both individually and in relation to each other.

The following two sections describe the characteristics of unemployment and inflation, clarifying the problems of efficiency and equity they are associated with. Section 7.4 presents the main economic theories that have dealt with these phenomena in a short-run framework and that identify the roots of such kinds of instability in the operation of the private or public economic system.

Section 7.5 deals with the problems of slow growth and underdevelopment from a purely descriptive point of view; the explanations for this form of market failure and its consequences for employment are analysed briefly in section 7.6. For expository reasons, the definition and description of the balance of payments is given in section 16.1 and the discussion of the underlying theories is deferred to chapter 17.

7.2 Unemployment

By unemployment we essentially mean involuntary unemployment. This arises when there are (potential) workers willing to accept employment at, or even slightly below, the prevailing (real) wage rate (Keynes, 1936), but the demand for labour is insufficient to provide them all with jobs: the supply of labour is therefore 'rationed'. We will not discuss either *voluntary* or *frictional unemployment*.[7]

In the post-war experience of market economies we can distinguish two different phases of employment and unemployment: before 1973 (the year of the first oil crisis) and after 1973. In the pre-1973 period, unemployment was in steady decline in various countries; in the subsequent phase, it increased significantly, the most notable exception being that of the United States (table 7.1).

---

[6] The need to use the more traditional concepts of welfare economics (especially equity) in assessing and solving macroeconomic problems has recently been pointed out by Drèze (1995).

[7] On Keynes' definition, voluntary unemployment occurs when, for various reasons, a worker does not accept a wage rate equal to the marginal productivity of his labour; frictional unemployment is caused by errors of calculation, unexpected changes, etc. that give rise to temporary imbalances in the supply and demand for labour in given fields and areas. The data available are not normally able to distinguish the various types of unemployment.

Table 7.1. *Unemployment as a percentage of the total labour force in selected industrial countries*

Year	Canada	France	Germany	Italy	Japan	Sweden	United Kingdom	United States
1950	3.6	2.3	8.2	6.9	1.9	1.7	2.5	5.2
1955	4.3	2.4	4.3	7.0	2.5	1.8	2.1	4.2
1960	6.8	1.8	1.0	3.9	1.7	1.7	2.2	5.2
1965	3.6	1.3	0.5	5.0	1.1	1.2	2.2	4.4
1970	5.6	2.4	0.6	4.9	1.1	1.5	3.1	4.9
1975	6.9	4.0	3.6	5.8	1.9	1.6	4.3	8.3
1980	7.5	6.2	2.9	7.5	2.0	2.0	6.4	7.0
1985	10.5	10.2	7.1	9.6	2.6	3.0	11.2	7.1
1990	8.1	8.9	6.4	10.3	2.1	1.8	6.9	5.6
1995	9.5	11.6	8.2	12.2	3.1	9.2	8.7	5.5

Sources: Maddison (1991), until 1975 and OECD (1996) for subsequent years.

Unemployment in market economies is certainly well below the levels seen during the Great Depression, when the unemployment rate[8] reached 24 per cent in the United States (1932) and 20 per cent in Great Britain (January 1933). Nevertheless, the return to double-digit unemployment rates is an indication of the relevance of a problem that many had thought solved from both an analytical and a policy point of view.

The existence of involuntary unemployment represents a loss of efficiency in static and dynamic terms. In static terms, it means that it is possible to improve the situations of some individuals (the unemployed themselves) without making others worse off.[9] Moreover, unemployment of human resources for a prolonged period may cause these resources to deteriorate: the deterioration of skills is one of the reasons why the probability of an unemployed person finding work declines as the period of unemployment lengthens (examine figure 7.1, which refers to France). Although the various curves refer to different years and reflect the different macroeconomic conditions prevailing in each year, they are all clearly decreasing, indicating a decline in the probability of finding a job as the period of unemployment lengthens.

In addition to causing a loss of efficiency, unemployment usually increases the inequality of income distribution. The economic and social consequences of unemployment can be eased at an individual level by government action to redistribute income, such as paying unemployment benefits or guaranteeing a minimum income.

Although unemployment benefits have been introduced in all developed countries, both their level relative to wages and their duration vary markedly across countries.[10]

[8] The unemployment rate is defined as the ratio between the number of unemployed and the labour force (people who offer their services in the labour market and find – or do not find – employment). If U denotes the unemployed, N the employed and LF the labour force, $LF = N + U$. The unemployment rate is $u = U/LF$.

[9] At least some of the unemployed have a marginal productivity that is higher than the '*reservation wage*', i.e., the wage they are willing to accept.

[10] A fairly comprehensive survey of unemployment benefits in various countries is provided by Layard, Nickell and Jackman (1991, tables A1 and A2, pp. 514–16).

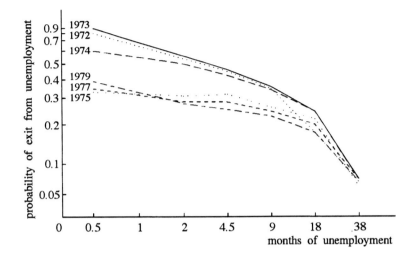

Figure 7.1
Source: Malinvaud (1984).

No basic-income system has so far been introduced. We will discuss the effects of such a system in terms of efficiency and equity in chapter 11.

When unemployment benefits are sufficiently high, it is easier to fire or lay off workers, as the benefits reduce the cost of these actions both to the worker and the firm. Although the latter bears part of the cost, it faces less worker resistance. Unemployment benefits are therefore both an instrument for supplementing personal incomes and for increasing the flexibility of the economic system and industrial relations, i.e., relations between employers and employees. Some economists oppose unemployment benefits because they supposedly create labour supply disincentives. However, according to the available evidence, only the maximum duration of benefits, not their relative amount, seems to have an impact on the labour supply and, then, on the duration of unemployment and the effectiveness of unemployment in reducing wages (Barr, 1992).

Unemployment represents an economic cost for society as a whole in terms of lost output. This cost must be added to the non-economic costs of unemployment, which come in the form of frustration, social exclusion and the possibility of social unrest and higher crime levels.[11] The existence of all these costs explains the commitment to achieving 'full' employment taken on by the governments of many market economies in the post-war period, partly under the influence of solutions suggested by Keynesian theory.[12]

Nevertheless, this commitment was hedged by at least two considerations:

[11] We could also add worker's greater dependence and vulnerability to blackmail by employers. However, this is not a net cost to society, since it is offset by a benefit to employers. It is nevertheless an important feature of unemployment, since it plays a role in the 'disciplinary' function of unemployment, which we will discuss shortly.

[12] This occurred in the United Kingdom with the White Paper on employment policy of 1944 and in the United States with the Employment Act of 1946. These important changes in public policies reflected the work not only of Keynes but also of other reformers, such as William Beveridge.

1 First, the term 'full' employment was not intended literally as 100 per cent of the labour force. The commitment regarded involuntary unemployment in excess of frictional unemployment, since the latter was considered a normal consequence of 'imperfections' in the markets. In reality, frictional unemployment corresponds to vacancies that would be extremely difficult to fill immediately owing to a lack of information and short-term inertia (e.g., the time needed to change jobs, which frequently involves moving from one place to another).[13]

2 The full employment position is akin to a 'precipice': 'The point of full employment, so far from being an equilibrium resting place, seems to be a precipice over which, once it has reached the edge, the value of money must plunge into a bottomless abyss' (Robinson, 1937, p. 24). One explanation is that the effects of the pressure of demand for goods operate on supply, which in full employment is completely inelastic. Perhaps more important is another argument emphasised by Robinson: the incompatibility of full employment with the traditional wage system of liberal capitalism (Robinson, 1962b, p. 118). Such incompatibility is associated with the 'discipline' exerted by unemployment on wage demands (Marx, 1867; Kalecki, 1943; Shapiro and Stiglitz, 1984; Bowles, 1985). The absence of a (large) pool of unemployed able to compete with employed workers lessens fears of redundancy and, thus, undermines worker effort while encouraging demands for wage rises. In other words, it is possible for the objective of full employment to conflict with 'factory discipline' or the social and political stability of the market economy. Such conflict tends to emerge in the form of inflation, which we examine in the following section.

7.3 Inflation

It is well known that the term inflation normally refers to a (sustained) rise in the general level of prices and, therefore, a decline in the value of money. There are many types of inflation, which can be distinguished by:

(a) their immediate causes: demand-pull inflation, financial inflation, credit inflation, supply inflation, cost-push inflation, profit inflation and imported inflation;

(b) the pace of price increases: creeping inflation, moderate inflation, galloping inflation, hyperinflation.

Demand-pull inflation is caused by the pressure of demand exceeding supply when the economy is making full use of its physical and human resources.[14] Financial and credit inflation are forms of demand-pull inflation triggered, respectively, by an increase in government deficit spending (i.e., without a corresponding increase in tax revenues) and

---

[13] There are other situations in which unemployment coexists with vacant jobs. For example, there may be *mismatching* between the supply and demand for certain skills, which can only be eliminated with (re)training.

[14] If there are no sectoral supply bottlenecks (as there are in real life), the rise in prices should begin to emerge only when aggregate demand exceeds supply.

by excessive bank lending when the economy is operating at the full employment level.[15]

Supply inflation is a consequence of shocks that reduce supply (natural disasters, war, major restructurings of production that temporarily reduce productive capacity).[16]

Cost-push inflation consists in the shift of higher production costs (in particular, variable costs) on to prices. *Profit inflation* is specifically associated with an increase in *profit margins* made possible by imperfectly competitive markets. An effective way to analyse the effects of changes in costs and profit margins on prices is offered by the full cost principle (mark-up theory).[17]

Imported inflation has various possible roots: a prolonged increase in a country's exports fuelled by excess foreign demand (which may give rise to inflation in the foreign country, hence the term *imported* inflation); a large capital inflow that expands monetary base and stimulates demand; or, finally, an increase in the prices of imported raw materials and semifinished goods due either to autonomous decisions by their producers (as in the oil crisis) or to a currency depreciation.

The distinction between the various types of inflation should not be overemphasised, since there are often situations in which the various causes interact, as is the case with cost-push and demand-pull inflation: an increase in aggregate demand, in addition to provoking a rise in prices on its own, brings the labour market closer to full employment, thereby causing a rise in wages[18] that further boosts prices.

---

[15] The best-known example of this occurred in 1929 in the United States, when bank credit fuelled stock market speculation that ended in October of that year with the collapse of share prices. For more on this type of inflation and the related problems, see Minsky (1975).

[16] One important case occurred around 1990 with the destruction of productive capacity in Eastern European countries in the wake of institutional and political upheaval, the opening of markets, the abandonment of price controls and industrial reconversion and restructuring.

[17] The full cost principle states that prices are formed by adding to variable (or direct or prime) costs (unit labour costs, or the ratio of labour costs to average labour productivity; raw materials; energy; specific taxes) a gross *mark-up* rate including the normal industry-wide (net) profit margin as well as provision for indirect (fixed) costs (depreciation, etc.). If for simplicity we consider unit labour costs only, we have $p = (w/\pi)(1 + g)$, where p is price, w is unit labour costs, π average labour productivity and g the gross profit margin or gross mark-up rate. Taking the logarithms of the two terms of the price equation and differentiating with respect to time, we have the following relation: $\dot{p} = \dot{w} - \dot{\pi} + (1 \dotplus g)$ where the dot over the variable indicates the rate of change of the variable per (infinitesimal) unit of time, e.g., $\dot{p} \equiv (dp/dt)/p$. The same relation holds approximately for discrete changes.

The reader not familiar with calculus can consider that for any variable z which is the product of two other variables, x and y (i.e., $z = x \cdot y$) it is true that $\dot{z} \cong \dot{x} + \dot{y}$, where $\dot{z} \equiv (\Delta z/\Delta t)/z$ and, similarly, the dot on each of the other variables indicates the percentage rate of change of that variable. This can be demonstrated rather easily if we first put $z_{t+1} = z_t + \Delta z$ and similarly for the other variables. If $z_t = x_t \cdot y_t$ is subtracted from $z_t + \Delta z = (x_t + \Delta x) \cdot (y_t + \Delta y)$ and the difference is divided by $z_t = x_t \cdot y_t$, we obtain $\dot{z} = \dot{x} + \dot{y} + \dot{x}\dot{y}$, where $\dot{x}\dot{y}$ is a higher-order term, negligible for small changes in the variables. Similarly, one can show that, if $z = \dfrac{x}{y}$, $\dot{z} = \dot{x} - \dot{y}$, approximately.

From the combination of these two rules (the one for a variable that is the product of two other variables; the other for a variable equal to the ratio of two other variables) the expression indicated above for changes in prices can be obtained.

[18] According to the Phillips curve, a reduction in the unemployment rate causes an increase in the *rate of change* in money wages.

As regards the rate at which prices increase, we can categorise inflation as:

> *creeping*, when prices rise slowly (say 2–3 per cent annually);
> *moderate*, if the rate of increase is less than 10 per cent annually;
> *galloping*, when prices rise at double or even triple digit rates; and
> *hyperinflation*, for an annual rate of at least 300 per cent.[19]

Inflation can be measured with one of the various price indices available:[20] the *implicit GDP deflator* or its components (*consumption deflator, investment deflator*, etc.), *wholesale prices, producer prices, consumer prices*, etc. As we know, these indicators refer to different baskets of goods.[21]

Inflation in the post-war period has been very different in the industrial and developing countries. In certain of the latter (for example, in Latin America) galloping inflation or even hyperinflation are usual, although they do not necessarily cause the value of a currency to collapse, creating the need for its replacement, i.e., the need for another instrument able to act as a medium of exchange. Except for the years immediately following the second world war, inflation in the industrial countries was normally of the creeping sort, at least until the first oil crisis. The increase in oil prices caused inflation to rise almost everywhere, although it has never evolved into hyperinflation (table 7.2).

By contrast, there were many cases of galloping inflation prior to the second world war. Moreover, periods of inflation were frequently followed by periods of deflation (especially before 1914), an example of the 'classical' cycle in which prices rise during expansionary phases before falling during recessions. Since the end of the war, not only have the (rare) recessions not been accompanied by falling prices, but there have even been situations in which stagnant demand and inflation have coexisted (hence the term '*stagflation*').[22]

Inflationary pressure emerges whenever the recipients of money income (wages, profits, rents) seek to increase their own share of real income at the expense of others (i.e.,

---

[19] These figures are indicative only. Cagan (1956) offers a study of the most important cases of hyperinflation. For an analysis of inflation in Germany after the first world war, which in November 1923 saw prices reach 1,422.9 billion times their pre-war level, see Bresciani Turroni (1937).

[20] We must bear in mind, however, that certain potentially inflationary situations are imperfectly measured by changes in prices. For example, excess demand, rather than raising prices, may be reflected in an increase in imports or activate other rationing mechanisms (e.g., lines at the cash register or delivery delays). This is called '*repressed*' or '*hidden*' inflation.

[21] Each indicator can be worked out differently to emphasise the dynamics of inflation over time. For example, we can divide the change in the index in the last year (e.g., from April 1995 to April 1996) by the value of the index at the beginning of the period (April 1995) to calculate the *twelve-month (end-of-period)* rate of change; if the change in the index in the last 12 months (from May 1995 to April 1996) with respect to the previous 12 months (May 1994 to April 1995) is divided by the average value of the index in these 12 months (May 1994–April 1995), we obtain the *average* inflation rate for the last year.

[22] In comparing the figures in tables 7.1 and 7.2, note that after 1973 many countries have recorded a rise in both unemployment and inflation. See Acocella and Ciccarone (1994, 1997) on stagflation as a breakdown in the classical cycle and the regularities underlying the Phillips curve.

Table 7.2. *Average annual percentage change in consumer prices in selected industrial countries*

Year	Canada	France	Germany	Italy	Japan	Sweden	United Kingdom	United States
1950–5	2.5	5.4	1.9	1.9	6.4	5.6	5.5	2.1
1955–60	1.9	5.9	1.8	1.7	1.5	3.7	2.6	2.0
1960–5	1.5	3.8	2.8	4.9	6.2	3.6	3.6	1.3
1965–70	3.9	4.3	2.6	2.9	5.4	4.5	4.6	4.2
1970–5	7.3	8.8	6.1	11.3	11.5	8.0	13	6.7
1975–80	8.6	10.5	4.2	16.6	6.6	10.5	14.1	8.4
1980–5	7.4	9.6	3.9	13.7	2.7	9.0	7.2	5.4
1985–90	4.5	3.1	1.4	5.7	1.4	6.3	5.9	4.0
1990–5	2.2	2.2	3.5	5.1	1.4	4.4	3.4	3.1

Sources: Our calculations from sources quoted in table 7.1.

consumers).[23] The resistance of others and/or constant real output (which may be physically impossible to increase in the short run) causes an increase in prices. This definition of inflation covers the basic types of inflation: cost-push and demand-pull inflation. It shows that inflation is a symptom of social conflict and, at times, in its more extreme and uncontrolled forms, of social collapse.

The struggle for income distribution of which inflation is an expression is never neutral, in the sense that it always involves some change in the distribution itself, since an increase in the general (or absolute) price level is always accompanied by a change in relative prices: some can only keep their prices unchanged (if they are exposed to fierce competition) or succeed in raising their prices by less than the average rise, while others are able to raise their prices by more than the average. At a more aggregate level, the links between changes in prices and changes in the incomes of different economic agents (essentially workers and capitalists) will be examined more fully in section 15.2.

---

[23] Obviously every income earner is also a consumer. Nevertheless, one may try to be a free rider, since the benefit he receives from an increase in income may be greater than his loss as a consumer.

For example, take a 10 per cent increase in wages in the bread industry, which for simplicity we assume is not accompanied by an increase in productivity. If bread factory owners do not want to see their profit margins reduced, the wage rise originates a 10 per cent rise in bread prices in the absence of other direct costs, as we can see from the full cost principle. This increase harms all consumers, including workers in the bread industry. The latter, however, receive a net benefit, since their incomes have increased by 10 per cent while their costs have risen by less. The 10 per cent rise in the price of bread causes the cost of a typical basket of goods to rise by less: for example, if spending on bread accounts for 20 per cent of overall consumption expenditure, then the increase in spending is equal to 20 per cent × 10 per cent = 2 per cent.

We can present the same argument in another way. By definition, redistributing income means that the advantage to some is equal to the disadvantage of others. Even though the agent responsible for the redistribution can be both beneficiary and victim, the redistribution may still be worthwhile if the benefit accrues to a relatively small number of agents while the cost is spread over a larger number. Obviously, this is likely to be the case if the changes regard a single industry and are not transmitted to other sectors. Nevertheless, even if transmission is likely, any single agent may find it profitable to try and increase his income, acting as a free rider.

Not only income but also wealth is redistributed by inflation. For example, the value of a bond with a fixed nominal value declines in real terms in an inflationary setting, to the advantage of debtors (typically firms and, often, the government) and the detriment of creditors (typically households).[24]

Obviously, the extent of the redistribution of income and wealth depends on many factors, including the degree to which inflation has been anticipated by agents and their bargaining power[25] and, therefore, their ability to adjust the price of the good they offer. In order to protect themselves from unexpected rises in the general price level, some agents are able to introduce *indexation* mechanisms that link their income to changes in the general price level, as sometimes occurs with money wages and yields on securities.

The costs to some agents of the redistribution of income and wealth caused by inflation are cancelled out for society as a whole because they are offset by gains for others. There are therefore no net costs from inflation for the whole economic system as far as redistributive aspects are concerned. Some have even argued that moderate inflation can benefit the entire economic system owing to the stimulus it gives to investment: firms, which are generally debtors, see the cost of the capital they raise in the financial market decline in real terms and, at the same time, the rise in prices enables them to increase total revenue (turnover), while other costs may not rise to the same extent owing to inertial factors.[26]

Inflation has positive net costs for society as a whole, however, since it gives rise to specific costs generated by the need to adjust price lists or automatic payment machines (called *menu costs* and *slot machine costs*, respectively) or by the reduction in real money holdings, due to the increase in interest rates that normally accompanies an increase in the inflation rate, thereby raising the opportunity cost of holding money. People therefore make more frequent visits to the bank to withdraw cash, incurring what are known as *shoeleather costs*. Some argue that these costs, while perhaps small in themselves, cause inflexibility that has harmful effects in terms of unemployment.

Furthermore in an open economy inflation leads to a loss of competitiveness, with consequent balance of payment problems (see section 17.1 for a more extensive discussion).

Apart from these considerations, the costs to society of creeping or moderate inflation are relatively modest, especially compared with those associated with unemployment, with which there can be a trade-off. On the other hand, reducing inflation can become an economic policy objective for essentially two reasons:

---

[24] Government can also benefit from inflation if it imposes progressive taxes ('fiscal drag': see chapter 14).

[25] This is a function of all the elements of the productive structure that determine effective competition. The international openness of the economy *can* have some influence.

In reality, in certain cases (such as the government and other public bodies) we cannot speak of bargaining power, since their power is based, for example, on a direct ability to affect prices – e.g., through fiscal or monetary policy – that cannot properly be considered to fall within the framework of negotiations.

[26] A rapid survey of the literature that, for various reasons, has pointed out the advantages of a positive inflation rate is given by Drèze (1993, pp. 32–3).

(a) to reduce the social conflict associated with it;
(b) to reduce the risk of experiencing the uncontrollable growth of prices in the form of hyperinflation.

The social costs of hyperinflation are certainly much larger, and there is also a risk that an economy afflicted by hyperinflation might even have to do without the benefits of money, which would not be able to fulfil its essential functions as a unit of account, medium of exchange and store of value.[27]

7.4 The short-run analysis of unemployment and inflation

This section examines unemployment associated with the level of aggregate demand from a short-run perspective as well as inflation that can emerge in the same short-run time frame. We defer a short analysis of the long-run causes of unemployment to section 7.6.

7.4.1 The re-equilibrating abilities of the market in 'classical' macroeconomic theory

Macroeconomics – as we understand this term today – essentially began with Keynes. If by the 'classics' we intend – as he did – all those who preceded him (i.e., the 'classical' economists proper plus the neoclassical or marginalist school),[28] it is clear that a true 'classical' macroeconomic theory does not exist precisely because macroeconomics came into being with Keynes. Nevertheless, we can use the term with reference to a *reconstruction* of classical thought in terms of aggregate variables. This is in part an arbitrary operation, both as an *ex post* reconstruction and as a summing together of a wide variety of schools. For example, our discussion does not apply to the work of Malthus, Marx and Sismondi, who did not at all believe that the capitalist economic system was immune to economic crises.

First of all, it is important that we understand the 'vision' of 'classical' macro-economics, which is very similar to that underlying Smith's invisible hand: a capitalist system is driven by forces, generated by individual interests, that on their own can produce an equilibrium showing some kind of optimality. On this view, economic phenomena appear as the manifestations of natural laws (Vercelli, 1991) rather than the product (at least in part) of the existing institutional context, which is reduced by the 'classical' economists to the operation of a pure *barter economy*. With reference to the concepts introduced in section 7.1, according to this vision the economic system has a natural order that gives it 'stability', especially in the sense of ensuring full employment of resources.

We said that the market is virtually the only institution considered by the 'classics'. Obviously, they were aware of the existence of money, but they believed that the essence of the functioning of the *real* economy could be represented without considering money

---

[27] See Dornbusch and Fischer (1994, section 17.4) on the costs of galloping inflation and hyperinflation.
[28] The interested reader is referred to, respectively, Hollander (1987) and Henry (1990).

itself. *Say's law*, which asserts that supply creates its own demand, certainly holds in a barter economy: saving is in itself an act of investment which ensures equilibrium in the goods market. In a *monetary economy*, Say's law no longer holds,[29] for reasons we will examine in the next subsection. Planned saving and investment in a monetary economy could still be considered to match if we thought there was a mechanism to rebalance them, i.e., to coordinate the related decisions. That is, we could assume the existence of a price for saving (the interest rate), whose movements would balance planned saving and investment. However, in section 7.4.2 we will see that in a monetary economy there are problems with attributing this role to the interest rate.[30]

The existence of opposing social classes (workers and capitalists) is sharply drawn in the work of the classical economists proper, while it is almost entirely absent in the neoclassical school, which paints a picture of 'fungible' individuals, in the sense that any individual can fill the role of worker or entrepreneur. Nor are there institutions representing the two classes (e.g., unions or business associations). The terms of the opposition between workers and capitalists are also simplified by the idea that the *real wage* (which in equilibrium is equal to the *marginal product of labour*) is set directly in the labour market.[31] This is clearly consistent with the barter economy hypothesis but is in sharp contrast with reality, where only the *nominal wage* is set in the labour market, while the real wage is determined by taking the ratio of the nominal wage to the general price level (which is determined in the goods market). The classical hypothesis has clear implications for the ability of the system to ensure equilibrium in the labour market, which is certainly greater when the real wage is set directly in this market.

We noted earlier that the 'classics' were well aware of the existence of money. However, they simply considered it a veil over the operation of the real economy, since its role is limited to the determination of the general price level. The 'classical' theoretical system therefore has a *dichotomous* structure (monetary aspects are separated from real aspects) in which, according to the quantity theory of money, the money supply has the sole function of determining the absolute level of prices, remaining *neutral* with regard to the real economy.[32]

7.4.2 The critique of Keynes and Kalecki

Keynes' *General Theory* (1936) is the crowning achievement of decades of research, stimulated by the problems of his time, on the fundamental and distinctive features of an economic system based on competition and private capital accumulation.

---

[29] Say's law can be seen as one of the first analytical statements of the concept of the invisible hand.

[30] A critical examination of the mechanism for coordinating savings and investment decisions in neoclassical theory is offered by Ravagnani (1994).

[31] We are referring to the 'marginalist' version of the 'classical' position. As is well known, the classical economists proper considered the real wage to be at the subsistence level.

[32] More precisely, a dichotomous system is one in which there is a separation between the conditions and variables that represent the real equilibrium, on the one hand, and the conditions and variables of the monetary equilibrium, on the other. The former include preferences, initial resource endowments and relative prices (in particular, the real wage and the interest rate); the latter include the nominal quantity of money and the absolute price level. See Patinkin (1956, chapter VIII) for more on dichotomy.

Throughout his work Keynes underscores the importance of the existing social structure and the institutional arrangements created by human beings to solve the problems they encounter. He identifies the two essential features of a capitalist system:

(a) a monetary economy, which is largely the product of conventions or rules that have emerged over time;
(b) social classes (workers, capitalists/entrepreneurs, *rentiers*), which are affected by price movements in different ways and, therefore, react differently to actual or expected changes in wages, interest rates and other prices.

The analysis in the *General Theory* incorporates a number of simplifying assumptions, of which we should mention:

(a) the existence of a closed economic system, or a situation in which net exports are zero; this assumption was later dropped by other authors;
(b) a short-run outlook, which means that productive capacity and technology, consumer preferences and the degree of competition are given. As a result, behavioural functions and certain parameters (propensity to consume, liquidity preference, propensity to invest), which are more or less sensitive to changes in expectations, are also given.

Keynesian analysis focuses on the changes in employment caused by changes in aggregate demand and behavioural parameters.

Compared with the classical argument that changes in *relative* prices would always be able to ensure that aggregate demand was at the full employment level, the Keynesian view is that *nominal* price movements are slow relative to changes in quantities. The *stickiness* of *nominal* prices (especially their downward *rigidity*) is a consequence of the distributive conflict between the various classes of income earner: each individual will tend at least not to reduce the price of the good he supplies, fearing that the prices of the goods he purchases will remain unchanged or will rise. Paradoxically, a monetary economy makes it more difficult to coordinate the decisions that determine the income distribution.

Nevertheless, this should not lead us to think that ensuring greater price flexibility would enhance the ability of the system to re-establish equilibrium. Take the rigidity of money wages. According to the 'classics', the flexibility of real wages, obtained by reducing money wages in conjunction with a (less-than-proportional) reduction in prices, would allow an economy to attain a full employment level of income. However, apart from the stability problems that can arise, this position is based on an incomplete vision of the real wage that focuses on its role as a cost (to the firm) while neglecting its role as income (for the worker). This is an unjustifiable extension of a proposition valid at the microeconomic level to the system as a whole.[33]

According to Keynes, a reduction in money and real wages will increase employment only if aggregate demand does not fall, which depends on the effect of the wage reduction on the variables that determine demand: the propensity to consume, the

---

[33] For an individual firm or industry the reduction in monetary wages shifts the supply curve to the right and produces a new equilibrium at a lower price level and a higher level of output and demand.

marginal efficiency of capital and interest rates. Changes in money (and real) wages affect these three variables in many ways. It is worth reviewing the most important arguments, since they give us an idea of the complexity of Keynes' analysis of a matter that is often dealt with in a schematic and over-simplified way.

1 The fall in real wages causes a redistribution of income from workers to other classes, including *rentiers*, that have a lower propensity to consume.
2 The reduction of wages in a country relative to foreign wages improves the international competitiveness of its goods.[34]
3 The reduction in prices associated with the fall in money wages causes the real value of debts to rise, with the consequent possibility of bankruptcies or, in any case, a reduction in investment demand.[35]
4 The fall in real wages may induce expectations of either further reductions or, by contrast, an increase in subsequent periods. This will have corresponding negative or positive effects on investment.
5 The reduction in money wages accompanied by some reduction in prices lowers the transactions demand for money associated with the payment of wages themselves. If the nominal quantity of money remains unchanged, this is equivalent to an increase in the real money supply, which leads to a fall in the interest rate. This should have a positive impact on investment unless it triggers expectations of future rises in long-term interest rates and wages owing to the increase in investment (Keynes, 1936, chapter 19).[36]

In general, the multiplicity of effects produced by changes in the real wage raises doubts about the ability of this mechanism to ensure equilibrium in the labour market. The inadequacy of the real wage as a price capable of returning the labour market to equilibrium is compounded by the inexistence of a price that can match saving and investment decisions. In a monetary economy saving is separated from investment and the two functions are carried out by two correspondingly distinct classes of agents, unlike the barter economy of the classical world, where saving and investment always coincide because at every moment one decision exactly corresponds to the other. In a monetary economy, the separation of saving and investment decisions introduces an element of uncertainty about the likely return on the new capital (investment). This return is linked to *expectations* about many aspects of the future, such as the level of demand and cost

[34] This is one of the few cases in which Keynes goes beyond the hypothesis of a closed economy in the *General Theory*. Strictly speaking, we should ignore these effects, but they are significant in economies with a high degree of international openness.
[35] At the same time, there may be an increase in the propensity to consume of agents with a surplus of savings (creditors), but it is unlikely that this increase can offset the decline in investment for many reasons, which include: greater awareness on the part of entrepreneurs of the effects of price changes; the 'epidemic' nature of the fall in investment, including that due to bankruptcies (the *Fisher effect*). Note that the effect described by Fisher (1932, 1933) implies a direct relationship between aggregate demand and the price level. The reader should be aware that some authors give a different content to the Fisher effect, referring to Fisher's analysis of the relationship between interest rates and inflation (e.g., see Summers, 1983 and note 77 to this chapter).
[36] The increase in investment could generate expectations of future price rises.

conditions. Thus the decision process behind investment choices depends on the expectations underlying the marginal efficiency of capital as well as on the 'animal spirits' of entrepreneurs.[37] On the other hand, saving decisions are largely tied to the volume of income. Hence 'the propensity to save and ... the schedule of marginal efficiencies [of capital] are two curves which do not intersect anywhere, since they are not in pari materia and do not relate to the same variables' (Keynes, 1935, p. 552).

In a monetary economy the capital value of financial wealth is also intrinsically unstable. This introduces a further source of uncertainty, which may induce individuals to avoid holding wealth in forms that do not allow them to protect its value; that is, they may attempt to remain 'liquid' (i.e., demand money). As Keynes points out, in this framework the interest rate 'is the reward for parting with liquidity' for a certain period of time and is therefore the price that brings demand for and supply of money into equilibrium. The interest rate has little to do with saving decisions and therefore cannot function as the price that equilibrates saving and investment. Saving decisions are prior to and independent of the interest rate, which depends on the financial form of saving: 'if all savings were retained in money, the saver would not receive any interest at all' (Vicarelli, 1984, p. 138).

What is the source of the instability in the value of financial wealth? As is well known, it is due to expectations of possible fluctuations in the interest rate.[38] This underscores the entirely *conventional* nature of this variable. The interest rate is the compensation demanded by someone in return for not holding his wealth in liquid form; it will rise as the number of people who think that in the future its level will be high increases; on the other hand, '*any* level of interest rates which is accepted with sufficient conviction as *likely* to be durable, *will* be durable' (Keynes, 1936, p. 203).[39]

For all of these reasons, aggregate demand and employment in a capitalist system are unstable and may be far below the full employment level. In Keynes' view, government intervention through monetary policy and, above all, fiscal policy is the only force that can bring the system to full employment.

The tools of Keynesian analysis have helped to explain not only shortfalls in aggregate demand and unemployment, but also situations of excess demand, providing specific recommendations on how to avoid inflationary pressures. In his pamphlet *How to Pay for the War* (Keynes, 1940), Keynes himself analysed such situations in relation to the problems caused by the second world war.

Under wartime conditions, demand tends to increase excessively, primarily owing to the stimulus of military expenditure, which, together with ordinary consumption and investment demand, usually gives rise to excess demand and inflation. This had happened during the first world war: government deficit spending was initially financed by

---

[37] As is well known, investment in Keynes normally depends on the interest rate, *given* the marginal efficiency of capital. Here we have sought to underscore the uncertain character of the assessments that generate the latter variable. Shortly we will deal with the uncertain and conventional nature of the former.

[38] In particular, the idea that the interest rate might rise in the future generates fears of capital losses from holding unredeemable fixed-interest securities.

[39] The conventional nature of the interest rate is examined, for example, in Ciocca and Nardozzi (1996).

issuing bonds, while authorities sought to curb private spending with higher interest rates. The attempt to avoid or contain inflation was not successful, however, as overall spending was not reduced at all: financing the war effort with public debt coupled with a restrictive monetary policy increased households' disposable income (thanks to the interest they received), thereby sustaining a high level of consumption and causing price inflation. It also increased the public debt burden. Governments were thus induced to finance their deficits with monetary base. However, the small rise in nominal interest rates that resulted, together with high inflation, reduced the real interest rate and, therefore, provided an incentive to invest, stimulating demand through this channel as well. The increase in the quantity of money together with the constraint on output growth imposed by the full employment of resources therefore had further inflationary consequences.

Keynes' suggested recipe during the second world war was to ration private consumption, prohibit certain uses of savings (such as the purchase of durable or luxury goods and the securities of firms producing civilian goods) and channel savings into bank deposits, which would be used to subscribe government securities issued at low interest rates in order to reduce financing costs.[40]

Before concluding this subsection, we must take a short look at the work of Michal Kalecki (1933), which has many points in common with that of Keynes. The analysis of the Polish economist, who could boast some precedence (never claimed) in introducing the principle of effective demand (Robinson, 1964, p. 95), is unjustly ignored in most macroeconomics and economic policy textbooks. There is in fact considerable convergence between Keynes and Kalecki,[41] beginning with their analysis of social classes and the separation of saving and investment decisions, and including their understanding of many of the characteristics of a monetary economy, such as the fact that workers are paid in monetary rather than real terms. The central themes of Kalecki's analysis can be shown in diagram form. In figure 7.2, the line DD' shows how the marginal productivity of labour (MPL) changes as the number of employed workers, N, changes. If the number of workers in a given period is L, equal to full employment, and the current real wage is $0W$, the value of output, $DEL0$, will be distributed between workers (who receive $EL0W$) and capitalists (who receive the remainder, equal to DEW).

Now suppose, for simplicity, that the workers consume all of their income and capitalists do not consume anything, investing instead.[42] If investment is exactly equal to profits (DEW), demand will be equal to output at full employment. However, nothing guarantees that this will happen: investment could be less than profits if the outlook for future profitability is poor. In this situation a fall in money wages that was not accompanied by a proportional fall in prices (for example, owing to monopoly production in the goods market) could also contribute to reducing effective demand further,

[40] This technique of channelling savings was called the 'monetary circuit'.

[41] The main difference is that Kalecki does not make use of the multiplier; however, his analysis of the business cycle and price formation is much richer than that offered by Keynes. Sebastiani (1994) gives an excellent presentation of Kalecki's work.

[42] This hypothesis, typical of the classics, is compatible with the Keynesian hypothesis that the marginal propensity to consume of the system as a whole is less than 1.

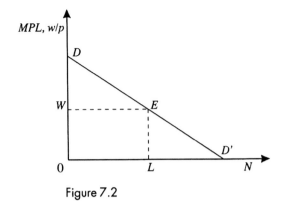

Figure 7.2

since it would depress the level of the real wage, $0W$, and, by hypothesis, the level of consumption.

Kaleckian investment theory is particularly important not only for its analysis of the business cycle but also for its examination of the long-run tendency towards stagnation in capitalist economies. According to Kalecki, the dynamics of capitalist systems depend primarily on the investment decisions of firms. These are mainly financed by realised profits, which also serve as an indicator of future profits. Investment increases productive capacity more than demand and the difference between them widens as the degree of monopoly and the share of income accounted for by profits increase. However, investment is limited by self-financing and does not depend on the long-term interest rate, which is stable (Kalecki, 1954).

This analysis is shared by other economists, such as Steindl (1952, 1981), and to a certain degree has influenced post-Keynesian investment theory. The reader might find it useful to compare Kalecki's analysis of growth with Harrod's position (section 7.5.1).[43]

Keynes' analysis contains a wealth of considerations on the functioning of a capitalist economy and, as we have seen, shines light on the many fundamental reasons why it is difficult to believe that the *normal* condition of such an economy is one of full employment. Many economists have sought to identify specific situations that can give rise to (involuntary) unemployment, casting it as the result of *exceptions* and *imperfections* with respect to a normal state of full employment.

The absorption of Keynes' thought into orthodox 'classical' theory began just a few months after the publication of the *General Theory* with the work of Hicks (1937), to whom we owe the *IS-LM* model familiar to anyone with at least an elementary grounding in macroeconomics. In this model, only a liquidity trap could prevent the system from reaching full employment. The liquidity trap would render monetary policy ineffective, making it necessary to use fiscal policy to return the economy to full employment.

---

[43] The differences between the two approaches and the links between Kalecki and post-Keynesian theory are highlighted in Boitani (1984).

The *IS-LM* model is an excellent teaching tool for arriving at an initial approximate characterisation of the functioning of an economy in the short run and of the effects of using various instruments of macroeconomic policy. This is one of the reasons why the model has gained such wide acceptance. Indeed, we too make use of it, given the lack of more satisfactory models that would enable us to express at least some of the most significant aspects of the Keynesian analysis in formal terms.

The *IS-LM* model was the starting point for the so-called 'neoclassical synthesis'. Many authors contributed to its development, with a leading role being played by Modigliani (1944), who identified the rigidity of nominal wages as an additional special case that would give rise to unemployment.

The absorption of Keynes' thought into the 'classical' framework continued with Patinkin's work. This provided the analytical foundation for the monetarist models rejecting the effectiveness of Keynesian policies. We will examine this development in the next three subsections. A different strand of analysis has been developed more recently by a number of economists linked in some way to Keynesian thought (the New Keynesians), who pursue the analysis of market 'imperfections' or, more generally, situations that give rise to involuntary unemployment. This group frequently employs concepts introduced and used in microeconomics, such as scale economies, market power and informational asymmetry, thus explaining unemployment in terms of certain types of microeconomic failure. We will examine this line of analysis in section 7.4.6

7.4.3 Reasserting the economy's re-equilibrating capacities: Pigou and Patinkin

We have seen that with Modigliani (1944) the rigidity of nominal wages comes to occupy a central role in the explanation of unemployment. The 'accommodation' of Keynes' analysis with the 'classical' approach is accomplished by emphasising the role played by the flexibility of wages and, more generally, prices in ensuring full employment. There appear to be two decisive steps in this classical accommodation, that taken by Pigou, before Modigliani's article appeared in 1944, and that taken later by Patinkin.

Pigou (1941), who does not have excessive faith in the optimal properties of the operation of market economies,[44] notes however that there is a theoretical possibility that the economy will always return to full employment if the *absolute price level* is perfectly flexible. Consumption is assumed to be sensitive to the *real value of money balances* in addition to the level of current disposable income. If an economy in a full employment equilibrium is affected by a shock that produces a situation of insufficient effective demand, the general level of prices will decline, since these have been assumed to be flexible. This will lead to an increase in the real value of money balances, which rises above the previous level (by hypothesis, the desired level). Consumers will consequently spend the difference between the effective and desired value of real money

---

[44] Recall Pigou's contribution to welfare economics.

balances.[45] This fuels aggregate demand, thus returning the system to full employment. In other words, it is always possible for the general level of prices to fall enough to increase the value of real balances above the desired level so as to cause an increase in consumption that will ensure full employment.[46]

Pigou acknowledges that this effect has limited practical significance, as a number of empirical studies show (see Mayer, 1959). Others (see Tobin, 1980, pp. 28–9) find that for the effect to operate it might require such a sharp and prolonged fall in prices as to negatively affect expectations about the equilibrating capacity of the system.

The theoretical aspects of the operation of this mechanism are developed further by Patinkin (1956), who calls it the *Pigou effect* and generalises it, placing it at the centre of his model. His approach seeks to develop the analysis of the interrelationships between monetary and real phenomena and to demonstrate the automatic readjustment capacities of perfect competition with fully flexible prices.

Patinkin analyses the logical structure of the 'classical' economy and compares it with that of the Keynesian economy. We said earlier that the classical model is dichotomous, in that it separates the real and monetary aspects of the economy; we also said that money is neutral in that model. Keynesian analysis goes beyond this dichotomy and the neutrality of money. Patinkin seeks to demonstrate that, under the assumed conditions,[47] the introduction and generalisation of the Pigou effect eliminates the 'classical' dichotomy,[48] while reaffirming the neutrality of money asserted by pre-Keynesian economists.

This reaffirmation is based on the argument that the Pigou effect is always (theoretically) capable of returning the economy to full employment. If the money supply increases, there is an increase in the real value of money balances (*real balance effect*). Unlike the original Pigou effect, this rise is not produced by a reduction in the general price level (with unchanged nominal money balances) but rather by an increase in the nominal quantity of money (with an initially unchanged absolute price level). The resulting increase in real money balances above the desired level gives rise to an increase in consumption; but, since the system is at full employment, excess demand causes prices to rise until real balances return to the desired level (i.e., that preceding the increase in money supply), which occurs when prices have risen in proportion to the increase in the money supply: if, for example, the money supply doubles, the price level will also double.

---

[45] For example, assume that every consumer has initial money holdings equal to 1,000; if the general price level is equal to 10, this means that each consumer holds 100 units (or 'baskets') of consumption, each costing 10. Further, assume that 100 is the desired value of money holdings in real terms. If, owing to the weakness of aggregate demand, prices fall to 5, the real value of money balances doubles to 200; a consumer wishing to keep his money holdings at the same level as before will consume the excess of effective money holdings over the desired level (200–100).

[46] The Pigou effect therefore implies an inverse relationship between aggregate demand and the price level, which conflicts with the direct relationship between these variables implicit in the Fisher effect mentioned in section 7.4.2. The dominance of one or the other is discussed in Tobin (1980, chapter I).

[47] He also postulates no uncertainty or *money illusion* and, as we will see, a special type of money.

[48] In fact, a monetary variable (the quantity of money itself) is present in the real part of the system, helping to determine the level of consumption together with income.

This reaffirms the argument for the neutrality of money put forward by the 'classics' while bridging the dichotomy between monetary and real phenomena.

Patinkin's analysis has been criticised, not only because of its postulates, which distance the model considerably from the features of an actual economy, but also because of the implicit assumption regarding the type of money considered in his model.

This second critique is levelled by Gurley and Shaw (1960), who introduce the distinction between *outside money* and *inside money*. The former is money created by an external authority (the government, for example) and given to the private sector (households and firms) in exchange for goods and services purchased from the private sector itself, for which it represents a net financial asset. Changes in the price level in the presence of outside money give rise to the expansionary effects noted by Pigou, and an increase in the supply of outside money will trigger a proportional rise in prices, therefore remaining neutral. Only when this is the sole form of money in the economy can the Pigou effect occur, preserving the equilibrating capabilities of the economy and the neutrality of money itself. However, outside money is not the only type of money.

Inside money is created within the private sector through the banking system: deposits are inside money, representing an asset for some agents (consumers, etc.), largely[49] corresponding to bank loans, which are a liability for other agents (firms, etc.). This money simultaneously denotes a credit and debit position within the private sector. A decline in the general price level will increase the real value of both assets and liabilities, if we ignore distributive effects between creditors and debtors.[50] This means that overall private sector spending will not change. Therefore, price changes can influence aggregate demand only through changes in the interest rate, and not through the effect of real balances on consumption.

In reality, outside money and inside money co-exist. In this case neutrality no longer holds, as we will see in more detail in section *7.4.7 and as Patinkin (1956, 2nd edition) himself recognises, unless there is a mechanical link between one type of money and the other such that an increase in one is accompanied by an increase in the other, thereby maintaining a constant ratio between them.

The path chosen by Pigou and Patinkin to re-establish the substance of certain 'classical' propositions is therefore impracticable. The monetarists take a different road. We will discuss their approach in the following two subsections.

---

[49] As we will see later in chapter 13, the fundamental equilibrium of the bank balance sheet is: $BMB + CR = D$, where BMB is the monetary base held by banks, CR denotes loans and D deposits. For simplicity, we assume that there are no *open market operations* (sale or purchase of securities in exchange for monetary base).

[50] In other words, we assume that the increase in the real value of the asset will increase spending by creditors by the same amount it reduces spending by debtors owing to an equal reduction in the real value of the liability (i.e., there is no Fisher effect). This appears to conflict with reality, where an increase in the real value of debt tends to lower spending, as debtors tend to have a greater propensity to spend than creditors.

7.4.4 'Natural' unemployment and the limits of government according to Friedman

Friedman and the monetarists conceive the market economy as intrinsically stable, unlike Keynes and the Keynesians.[51] They do not deny the instability shown in numerous real-life situations, but they attribute it to government action rather than to the private sector.[52]

Friedman revives the *quantity theory of money*, adapting it to take account of Keynesian innovations. This theory (of which the Fisher equation – also called the quantity equation – is the most complete expression) postulates a causal, direct and proportional relationship between the quantity of money and the price level, assuming a constant level of money velocity (i.e., a constant demand for money) and of transactions (which corresponds to full employment). Friedman argues that changes in the money supply are the principal systematic determinants of the growth of nominal income.[53] Nevertheless, the seemingly greater openness of neo-quantity theorists to the possibility that money does not affect just prices but also real income is in practice very limited, as we will see shortly.

One important building block of Friedman's analysis is the *permanent income* hypothesis, according to which consumption depends on the income an individual expects to earn on average over his lifetime.[54]

Furthermore, Friedman considers money as one of various forms of wealth. It is not, as it is for Keynes, an alternative to fixed-interest securities only, but rather to the entire spectrum of assets, both financial (of various maturities and forms) and real (individual durable goods like land, houses, gold, firms' assets). Within this framework changes in the nominal quantity of money – at initially given prices – will cause changes in the real quantity of money, changing spending on securities and real goods. It is precisely the real balance effect that serves as the transmission mechanism of monetary policy according to Friedman. The presence of real goods in the port-

---

[51] It is possible to argue that a homogeneous Keynesian strand of analysis does not exist. Although well aware of the large differences of positions, we feel it is still possible to use the term.

[52] For example, Schwartz (1975, 1981) argues that the depression of 1929 is largely attributable to the Federal Reserve's excessive concern about stock market speculation, which prompted a monetary tightening. For a rebuttal of this position, see Temin (1976).

[53] Consider the identity known as the *equation of exchange* or the *Fisher equation*: $L_s V = pT$, where L_s is the quantity of money, V velocity, p the price level and T transactions. If we exclude financial transactions from T – money is defined as the medium of exchange for goods and services – and consider the structure of the real economy as given (especially the degree of vertical integration), we can replace T with income, Y (which the reader will recall is equal to market output net of the double counting for intermediate goods). In this case V would no longer denote the *transactions* velocity of money, but rather the *income* velocity of money. In addition, if we replace velocity with the fraction of income individuals desire to hold as money balances, k (the inverse of velocity), we can rewrite the Fisher equation as $L_s = kpY$. If k is constant (as Friedman basically assumes), changes in L_s will be reflected in nominal income, pY.

[54] The permanent income hypothesis leads us to include real balances among the elements of the consumption function, for reasons we cannot examine here. This is important for understanding the monetarists' conception of the operation of monetary policy. We will examine other consequences of the hypothesis shortly.

folio of assets that are a substitute for money means that monetary policy is not neutral. Nevertheless, Friedman (1968) argues that these effects are normally temporary and associated with inflation. More precisely, he argues that monetary policy cannot peg the market interest rate[55] or the current (or market) unemployment rate below the natural interest rate and the natural rate of unemployment, respectively, for more than very short periods without triggering rising inflation. Let us see why.

First, we must clarify the meaning of a number of concepts introduced by Friedman. The *natural interest rate* is basically the equilibrium price between the demand for capital (investment) and the supply of capital (saving). The *natural rate of unemployment* is that where the number of job vacancies is in a certain equilibrium relation with the number of unemployed; since there is a broad balance between supply and demand for labour, wages tend to remain constant. The natural unemployment rate is determined by structural factors, such as the level of economic development, the value placed on leisure and the characteristics of the labour market (e.g., flexibility, segmentation, availability of job information). Friedman (1968) emphasises that 'natural' does not mean constant over time or that economic policy cannot influence the natural rate, but simply that government action can only be directed at the structural factors that determine it. As we will see shortly, monetary or fiscal macroeconomic policies do not affect these structural elements.

Imagine that the market interest rate and unemployment rate are at their natural levels; the goods market and the labour market are therefore in equilibrium. An increase in the quantity of money, causing an increase in the level of real balances, will initially lead to a reduction in the interest rate and an increase in the demand for goods, especially capital goods, with an accompanying rise in output. At the same time employment will rise, owing to the simultaneous rise in supply and demand for labour. This is apparently a contradiction: the increase in the demand for labour can only occur if we assume a *decline* in the real wage; while an increase in the supply of labour occurs only if there is a *rise* in the real wage. We can overcome the inconsistency by assuming that:

(a) expectations are adaptive (i.e., agents adjust them on the basis of the past value of the reference variables);[56] and

(b) the various agents have different information and reaction times to information: in particular, firms are better informed than workers of past or current price increases. Firms expect a fall in the real wage (valued in terms of their

---

[55] It is more accurate to speak of an interest rate structure, given the variety of financial assets.

[56] More precisely, under this hypothesis, expectations for a variable are revised in each period in proportion to the difference between the actual value of the variable in the previous period and the value expected for the same period, i.e., in proportion to the error in the forecast made in the previous period. In formal terms, the expected price at time t can be expressed as: $p_t^e = p_{t-1}^e + \gamma(p_{t-1} - p_{t-1}^e)$, where p_{t-1}^e is the expected price at time $t-1$, while p_{t-1} is the actual price and $0 < \gamma < 1$ is a constant. If, in place of the price level at time t, p_t, we consider the inflation rate in period $t, \dot{p}_t$, expectations regarding the inflation rate in period t are adaptive if: $\dot{p}_t^e = \dot{p}_{t-1}^e + \gamma(\dot{p}_{t-1} - \dot{p}_{t-1}^e)$. In the special case where $\gamma = 1$, we have: $\dot{p}_t^e = \dot{p}_{t-1}$; i.e., the expected inflation rate for period t is equal to the actual rate in the previous period (static expectations). This simple relation will be used shortly.

product) and correspondingly increase investment and their demand for labour. For their part, workers, noting an increase in nominal wages and not in prices (i.e., incorrectly predicting the increase in the prices of consumer goods), expect an increase in real wages and therefore increase their supply of labour.

However, the money illusion of workers is only temporary and in the long run the unemployment rate should rise to its natural level. At the same time, the market interest rate will rise due to the increase in prices, until it is again at its natural level.

Let us examine in detail the behaviour of the market unemployment rate using the 'expectations-augmented' Phillips curve. The original Phillips curve (which was statistically observed in Phillips, 1958, and is widely used by Keynesians) is the inverse relationship between the rate of change in money wage rates, $\dot{w}$, and the unemployment rate, u: $\dot{w} = \phi(u)$, with $\phi' < 0$. According to Friedman, this relation is unlikely to remain stable over time.

To understand the reasons why the curve tends to shift, Friedman first draws attention to the fact that workers are not interested in the nominal wage but rather in the real wage. Therefore if they want to ensure a certain increase in the real wage (say, 5 per cent), they will be satisfied with a 5 per cent increase in the nominal wage only if they expect no rise in prices. The original Phillips curve implicitly incorporates the hypothesis that the expected rise in prices, $\dot{p}_t^e$, is nil (or that the nominal wage rate matters). However, this hypothesis is not necessarily valid. In our example, it certainly does not hold if the 5 per cent increase is inflationary[57] because the consequent increase in prices will affect expectations about future price changes.

Hence, we can replace the equation $\dot{w}_t = \phi(u_t)$ with the more general equation: $\dot{w}_t = \phi(u_t) + \dot{p}_t^e$. We therefore cannot speak of a single Phillips curve, but rather a map of (short-run) Phillips curves, each with a different value for expected inflation. If the expected inflation rate for period t is equal to the effective inflation rate in the previous period, $\dot{p}_{t-1}$, substituting we have $\dot{w}_t = \phi(u_t) + \dot{p}_{t-1}$.

This relationship is shown in figure 7.3, where for simplicity we have drawn only two Phillips curves. Assume that in period zero the system has been at u_N for some undefined time: the rate of wage change in the current period is $\dot{w}_0 = 0$; since $\dot{w}_{-1} = 0$ as well, if we assume $\dot{\pi}_{-1} = 0$ and $(1 \dotplus g)_{-1} = 0$, we have $\dot{p}_{-1} = 0$ and, therefore, $\dot{p}_0^e = 0$, for the specific hypothesis of adaptive expectations. Hence, $\dot{w}_0 = \phi(u_N) + \dot{p}_{-1} = 0 + 0 = 0$ and $\dot{p}_0 = \dot{w}_0 - \dot{\pi}_0 + (1 + g)_0 = 0 - 0 + 0 = 0$.

This situation will last as long as there are no shocks. An expansionary monetary policy would shift the system from u_N to $u_1 = u^*$ in period 1, causing a wage increase $\dot{w}_1 = \dot{w}^* + \dot{p}_0$. If $\dot{w}^* = 5\%$, then $\dot{w}^* = 5\% + 0 = 5\%$. Hence, in period 1, immediately following the monetary action the system moves along the initial Phillips curve ww. If we

---

[57] The possibility that the wage increase is inflationary can be analysed in terms of the full-cost principle (see section 7.3), according to which $\dot{p} = \dot{w} - \dot{\pi} + (1 + g)$. Since we can, as a first approximation, consider $\dot{\pi}$ and $(1 + g)$ as constants, we can express the rate of change in prices as a function of the rate of change in wages alone: $\dot{p} = \dot{w} + $ constant, and, if the rate of change in wages depends on the unemployment rate (as in the original Phillips curve), we can write $\dot{p} = f(u)$. This relation is called the *derived Phillips curve*. In our example, we will assume for simplicity that $\dot{\pi} = (1 + g) = 0$, hence $\dot{p} = \dot{w} = \phi(u)$.

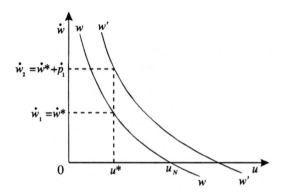

Figure 7.3

continue to have $\dot{\pi}_1 = (1 + g)_1 = 0$, we will have $\dot{p}_1 = \dot{w}_1 = 5\%$. This means that if the system remains at $u_1 = u^*$ in period 2, we have $\dot{w}_2 = \phi(u_1) + \dot{p}_1 = 5\% + 5\% = 10\%$. Since this holds for every value of $u \neq u_N$, it follows that in period 2 the valid Phillips curve is the initial curve augmented by inflation expectations, i.e., the curve $w'w'$. Summarising, the variables would have the following values in the various periods:

t	$\dot{p}^e$	u	$\dot{w}$	$\dot{p}$
0	0	u_N	0	0
1	0	$u^* < u_N$	5%	5%
2	5%	$u^* < u_N$	10%	10%

In this light, we can also understand how – according to Friedman – monetary policy can trigger a self-fuelling inflationary process. Is there a limit to the rise in the inflation rate? Actually, such a limit must exist. Recall that the process was triggered by the rise in real balances caused by an increase in the money supply with prices (initially) un-changed. When prices have risen by as much as the money supply (if the rise was a one-time increase) the expansionary effect of real balances will dissipate and there is therefore no reason for the unemployment rate to be less than the natural rate. If, however, there has been an increase in the *rate* of money supply growth, the expansion-ary effect of real balances will end when the *rate* of increase in prices has risen by the same amount.[58] Nevertheless, at that point, since an inflationary process is already under way (at a rate equal to the growth in the money supply), agents will expect prices to rise at the same rate in the future and the rate of wage change will also be positive (and equal to the expected inflation rate), despite the fact that the unemployment rate is at its natural level.

We can draw the following conclusions from our analysis.

    1 According to the modern quantity theorists, monetary policy is effective only in the short term; it can keep the market unemployment rate below the natural

[58] At the same time, workers will have noted the increase in the inflation rate.

unemployment rate for a short period only. Doing so for a longer period would require the quantity of money (or its rate of growth) to be increased even further, which will generate inflation higher than that initially anticipated by workers, thus creating scope for holding the unemployment rate below the natural level. Therefore, we can guarantee an unemployment rate below the natural rate only at the cost of rising inflation.

2 Again according to the monetarists, the long-run Phillips curve is vertical; i.e., for any inflation rate unemployment will remain at its natural rate. There is therefore no trade-off between unemployment and inflation, except in the short run.

What positive role do neo-quantity theorists attribute to monetary policy? In the words of Friedman (1968), it must keep the economic machine 'well-oiled': the change in the money supply must be equal to the average variation in money demand, which, if there is no change in the velocity of circulation, is equal to the change in real income in a stable price environment.[59] Therefore, if aggregate demand grows by an annual average of 3 per cent over a sufficiently long period, the money supply must also increase by 3 per cent annually.[60] This is the essence of the so-called *simple rule* (a case of predetermined government behaviour or, as we will see in section 8.4, an automatic rule), which Friedman contrasts with discretionary intervention by monetary authorities, especially the use of counter-cyclical monetary policy, which consists in policy measures decided on a case-by-case basis by the authorities: when demand is weak, the central bank takes expansionary action; in situations of excess demand it adopts a restrictive stance.

The superiority of automatic rules over discretionary measures is not solely due to the temporary nature of the effects of discretionary policy on employment and its cost in terms of inflation,[61] but also to the possibility that it might have perverse effects, owing to the length and variability effect of the time lag of monetary policy, i.e., the delay with which the effects of this policy feed through to the economy: the economy could start responding to a monetary expansion or contraction in a phase of the business cycle that is completely different from that in which the policy action was originally undertaken.

Friedman is equally sceptical of fiscal policy. First, a change in government spending can turn out to be ineffective even in the short run if it is perceived to be temporary. In this case the change would have no effect on permanent income and therefore on consumption. Even if it were effective in the short term, it would not be so in the long run, since an increase in deficit-financed government spending without issuing money

---

[59] Taking the version of the quantity theory presented in note 53 of this chapter ($L_s = kpY$), we have $\dot{L}_s = \dot{k} + \dot{p} + \dot{Y}$. If $\dot{k} = 0$, i.e., the velocity of circulation is constant, since we want $\dot{p} = 0$, then $\dot{L}_s = \dot{Y}$, as we have argued.

[60] Friedman had initially suggested a 2 per cent annual increase in the money supply, assuming a decline in velocity of 1 per cent per year. This hypothesis seemed to be supported by econometric evidence (although this was later refuted) and was consistent with the conception of money as a luxury good, i.e., a good with income elasticity of demand greater than unity.

[61] Friedman argues that one of the greatest costs of inflation is a consequence of the difficulty of gauging relative prices, which can give rise to an inefficient allocation of resources.

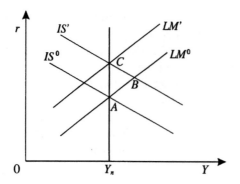

Figure 7.4

would crowd out interest-rate-sensitive private spending, i.e., investment. By shifting the IS curve (from IS^0 to IS' in figure 7.4), the increase in public spending would initially raise income above the corresponding natural level of unemployment (Y_n in Figure 7.4) but would also cause:

(a) an increase in the interest rate (see point B in the figure), given that the money supply is constant while income increases, reducing the money available to meet speculative demand;

(b) an increase in the price level or inflation rate for the reasons given in our discussion of the expectations-augmented Phillips curve. Inflation reduces the real money supply, causing LM to shift to the left, thus determining a further rise in interest rates, until demand returns to the level corresponding to the natural rate of unemployment (C in figure 7.4).

The dual conception underlying the monetarist position is:

(a) the private economic system is intrinsically stable, obeying forces that return it to full employment (or to the 'natural' rate of unemployment) even if hit by external shocks; important stabilising factors are the exogenous character of money,[62] the long-run outlook of consumption decisions (based on the permanent income hypothesis) and the 'adaptive' nature of expectations;

(b) in contrast, government action is ineffective beyond the short term and does not affect the structural features of the economic system. For example, lowering the market unemployment rate does not lower the natural unemployment rate: in fact, government action may even be destabilising if, for example, it causes an increase in prices that reduces agents' ability to assess their situation.

As we will see in the following subsection, this view of the operation of the private economic system and government action is carried to extremes by the so-called second-generation monetarists, the theorists of new classical macroeconomics. We will

---

[62] That is, money is determined in a rigid way by some external authority.

therefore not criticise Friedman's monetarism here, reserving our critique for the next subsection with reference to certain aspects of his position shared by the monetarism of new classical macroeconomics.

7.4.5 The ineffectiveness of government intervention in new classical macroeconomics

New classical macroeconomics (NCM) shares and in fact strengthens the first-generation monetarist approach, basing its arguments on even more optimistic hypotheses about the intrinsic re-equilibrating capacity of a market economic system and, on the other hand, reaching even more pessimistic conclusions about the effectiveness of government intervention in the economy. It is founded on two essential hypotheses:

(a) agents form their expectations rationally;
(b) markets are constantly returned to equilibrium by the movement of perfectly flexible prices.

Agents form their expectations rationally in the sense that they use all available information, which is not necessarily complete (Muth, 1961). For example, an agent may know the price of his own product, but not those of other products; there is, in other words, asymmetric information between different islands.[63] In making decisions, the agent will form his expectations of the relevant variables (in the previous example, of the prices of the other products) using all information at his disposal. A rational prediction will be correct *on average*. The agent can make errors, but these will be random, not systematic. The presence of systematic errors would imply a less-than-complete use of certain information, especially past prediction errors, which is excluded by the rational expectations hypothesis (REH).

Expectations of this sort are forward looking, rather than backward looking as in the case of adaptive expectations. The introduction of rational expectations is equivalent to the hypothesis that agents act *as if* they knew the theory underlying the model. From this point of view, the REH is necessary for the consistency of the model (the agents whose decisions underpin the model cannot forecast results different from those predicted by the model). However, the process by which agents form rational expectations, i.e., the way they learn the functioning of the economic system and thus the model that represents it, is not clear. Moreover, it is implicitly assumed that the economic model does not change, or that it has adapted to every possible past change (the *stationarity condition*), which necessarily makes the rational expectations theory a long-run theory (B. Friedman, 1979).

The introduction of rational expectations into an economic model is a powerful tool, ensuring that agents' expectations are consistent with the results generated by the

---

[63] This hypothesis, utilised by Lucas (1973), is exemplified by a reference to a situation in which each agent lives on his own island and knows the price of his good and not those of goods produced by other agents on other islands.

model. In a model that incorporates the REH, the 'vision' underlying the model is extremely important. If the model adopts a 'classical' viewpoint, i.e., it postulates the existence of a more or less 'natural' equilibrium, then the REH reinforces the existence of a natural equilibrium. If, however, the model views the private economic system as unstable, the REH makes economic policy even more effective, as we will see shortly.[64] Thus, of the two hypotheses put forward by NCM, the REH does not appear to characterise the school's stance since it is also now used by economists who hold very different views.

Moving to the second, and key, hypothesis, NCM postulates the existence of markets that are rapidly clearing or always in equilibrium. In particular, the labour market is always in full employment equilibrium and any unemployment is voluntary. Unemployment can decline if there is an *unexpected* increase in the general price level that is noted only by firms and not by workers. For example, assume that there is an unexpected increase in demand. The prices of goods will tend to rise, reducing the real wage level expected by firms, thus increasing their demand for labour and, at the same time, the supply of goods. The increase in the demand for labour causes expected money and real wages to rise, since workers are unaware of the simultaneous rise in prices; they will be willing to increase their supply of labour services, which will reduce (voluntary) unemployment. But these effects cannot last.

Let us take a closer look at the effects of an expansionary monetary policy. The situation in the goods market is shown in figure 7.5. Similarly to what happens in a market for a single good, suppose that we can define an aggregate[65] demand curve, AD, and an aggregate supply curve, AS. Y_0 is the long-run equilibrium, where actual and expected price levels coincide; the unemployment rate is the natural rate. Now imagine there is an *unexpected* increase in the money supply; this causes aggregate demand to increase, shifting AD to the right from AD_0 to AD_1. As a result, the price level for all goods rises above the expected level, but, since we have asymmetric information,[66] each agent initially perceives only the increase in the price of the good he sells and will therefore increase the amount of the good he is willing to supply. Equilibrium output will therefore rise from Y_0 to Y_1.

However, the expansionary effect of an increase in demand and prices is due to the element of surprise. It cannot last, since not only the price of each agent's own good is at an unexpected level, but also the prices of other goods and labour, and the discrepancy will induce agents to modify their expectations. The only consistent equilibrium is therefore that where expected prices equal actual prices. If the increase in the money supply is *transitory*, after the initial surprise output will return to a level corresponding to the natural rate of unemployment. Agents will maintain their expectations regarding prices – leaving the position of AS unchanged – and, since in subsequent periods the

---

[64] It can be argued that it is difficult to imagine how rational expectations could be formed in this case (Davidson, 1982–3).

[65] These have become a normal feature of major macroeconomics textbooks (see, for example, Dornbusch and Fischer, 1994), even if they are based on debatable hypotheses about the functioning of the economy.

[66] Recall the 'islands' example mentioned earlier.

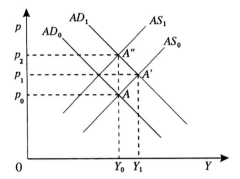

Figure 7.5

money supply will return to the normal level, the AD curve will return to AD_0. So, output is still that corresponding to the natural rate of unemployment, Y_0, and prices are at the initial level, p_0. In summary, if the increase in the money supply is *unexpected but transitory*, it will raise employment and prices, but only temporarily.

If, however, the increase in the money supply is permanent, sooner or later agents will revise their price expectations upwards, shifting the supply curve to the left, as shown in figure 7.5.[67] Thus, the positive effects in real terms of an *unexpected but permanent* increase in the money supply will be short lived, with the only long-run effect being an increase in the price level to p_2.

By contrast, an *expected* increase in the money supply will not have any effect on output because it *simultaneously* generates expectations of an increase in the prices of other goods and therefore induces agents (firms and workers) to safeguard their income by raising the price of their product. If everyone raises their prices, the general price level rises, thus confirming expectations. This can be illustrated by referring again to figure 7.5. The only result of the increase in aggregate demand from AD_0 to AD_1 is the rise in the price level from p_0 to p_2, with no change in real income from its initial level at Y_0, which corresponds to the natural unemployment rate, since there is a simultaneous shift in aggregate supply from AS_0 to AS_1. The difference with respect to the case of an unexpected but permanent increase in the money supply is that there are no real effects even in the short run.

Fiscal policy also fails to produce real effects. If fiscal measures are expected – either because they are announced by policymakers or simply deduced on the basis of available information – they leave the general equilibrium of the system unchanged, immediately affecting prices alone. The Phillips curve is vertical not only in the long run but also in the short run. An expansionary fiscal policy will therefore be entirely ineffective or even harmful due to resulting inflation. Only fiscal measures that are unexpected and, note, unpredictable, given available information, can be effective, but

---

[67] To understand the reasons for this last shift, consider that each agent, for each given price level of his good, expecting a general increase in the price level of other goods and labour as a result of the increase in demand, will be willing to supply less of that good.

this success would necessarily be sporadic. Such a policy could not be systematic,[68] since agents would otherwise incorporate their knowledge of the habitual behaviour of policymakers into their information set, rendering government action predictable: a one-off surprise effect is allowed, but the REH makes it impossible for policymakers to surprise (or fool) agents systematically.

In this light, the implications of NCM for economic policy are drastic and negative: there is no systematic possibility for economic policy to change the level of output and employment. In other words, we have *policy neutrality* or *policy invariance*.

The theoretical approach of NCM is in many respects a clear advance, thanks to its introduction of refined and innovative conceptual tools and analytical techniques. However, some of the basic hypotheses and the underlying vision of the economic process are essentially the same as those of the 'classical' economists, and as such are open to the same criticisms. In particular, we refer to:

(a) the continuous re-equilibrating tendency of markets, as in general Walrasian equilibrium, despite the imperfect flexibility of prices[69] in the real world (see the next subsection for more on this problem);[70]

(b) the type of information available (as postulated in the island parable), which seems very peculiar and, once again, at odds with reality: quite often agents can learn of changes in the general price level at the same time, or even before, they learn of changes in the price of the good they sell;[71]

(c) more generally, the simplistic approach to the numerous problems associated with the real-world scarcity of information, the limitations of our calculating and optimising abilities and the complexity of learning the parameters of the model. These are essential matters, and different approaches entail different consequences for economic policy. For example, NCM's neglect of learning processes conflates the long run with the short run; as a result, conclusions valid only for the long run are also attributed to the short run, where they are unacceptable. Introducing rational expectations into macroeconomic schemes based on Walrasian general equilibrium thereby renders neutral, and hence innocuous, the expectations themselves;

(d) the fact that the economic system depicted by NCM appears to reproduce the operation of a stationary society and the behaviour of individuals whose rationality excludes 'the highest, specifically human form of rationality: creative rationality [which] aims at transforming the environment into more satisfactory forms, necessarily violating the conditions of stationarity which

---

[68] Policy would have to be systematic if it were aimed at certain objectives: for example, if the government wants to ensure an unemployment rate of 5 per cent, it must act systematically, i.e., increase (reduce) demand when the actual unemployment rate is higher (lower) than the target rate.

[69] As an alternative to perfect price flexibility, one could argue that the price elasticities of supply and demand are high enough to ensure the readjustment of markets. Nevertheless, the empirical evidence on elasticities does not appear to support values high enough for this to occur.

[70] This Panglossian vision of economic reality is criticised in Buiter (1980).

[71] The island model – initially proposed by Phelps (1970) – seems appropriate for a society where the most rapid form of communication is a floating coconut (see Maddock and Carter, 1982).

the new classical economists consider indispensable for the applicability of rational expectations' (Vercelli, 1991, p. 105).

Obviously, with such hypotheses and such a vision of the economic process it is possible to obtain results that border on the absurd: 'we are asked to believe that three and a half million unemployed, give or take half a million searchers, are to be explained by their desire to substitute present for future leisure' (Hahn, 1985, p. 16).

7.4.6 Some recent theories of involuntary unemployment

We have said that one of the main macroeconomic problems is involuntary unemployment. This is a salient feature of the 'instability' of market capitalism underscored by Keynes.

Despite the lively, penetrating and technically sound criticisms levelled by the neoquantity school and NCM at the Keynesian analysis, this central problem remains. We have seen that the first- and second-generation monetarists focus instead on voluntary unemployment and its variations. However, voluntary unemployment is *not* the problem. Economists, workers and the public want to understand why someone is involuntarily made redundant or cannot find a job, even if he is willing to work at the current wage rate. We are less interested in understanding why someone else might resign voluntarily (or in any case not work) in order to sit in the sun in the Bahamas or otherwise have more leisure.

The inability of monetarists to come to grips with the problem of involuntary unemployment – as with other aspects of the instability of a market economy – can be explained (as we noted in section 7.1) by the failure to consider those aspects of the system, such as the insufficient re-equilibrating capacity of prices, uncertainty, etc., that, despite being an essential element of its practical operation, are automatically eliminated from the analysis of long-run equilibrium positions.

At the time the efforts to restore the 'classical' approach were in full bloom, awareness of these problems led to a number of attempts to formulate new analytical approaches. Some of these adopt the vision of Keynes and Kalecki, while others limit their scope to removing certain of the hypotheses of orthodox neoclassical models; still others take a sharply different tack, agreeing on the underlying problem (the causes of involuntary unemployment), but giving it a very different explanation.

The main themes of research are the following:

1 the operation of an economy with essentially fixed prices;
2 the explanation of the rigidity of prices and wages;
3 the explanation of the high level of real wages as a possible cause of involuntary unemployment;
4 the identification of strategic complementarities between individual decisions that could lead to a long-run equilibrium with involuntary unemployment.

1 The *fixed price* or *disequilibrium models* first introduced by Clower (1965) and Leijonhufvud (1968) have been refined in more recent years. They mark a move away (at least

in a short-run perspective) from the concept of Walrasian equilibrium, especially in their elimination of the auctioneer who ensures that decisions are coordinated and transactions carried out at equilibrium prices only. If prices are rigid, it is possible that some agents will find themselves 'rationed'; i.e., they cannot effectively express the demand or supply that maximises their position. And this can happen simultaneously in different markets, especially the goods and labour markets, creating an interdependence between excess demand (or supply) in both. If, for example, prices are too high with respect to wages, a vicious circle of excess supply of goods and excess supply of labour is created, which corresponds to Keynesian unemployment: in a decentralised economy, it is possible that no one will have an incentive to act so as to return the system to full employment (see Barro and Grossman, 1971; Malinvaud, 1977; Benassy, 1992).

2 Explaining the rigidity of prices and wages (*nominal rigidities*), to which the economists of the neoclassical synthesis (as well as Pigou and Patinkin) attribute the existence of unemployment (see section 7.4.3), plays an important role in the new-Keynesian research programme. It has been noted that there can be considerable resistance to price changes under imperfect competition, even when the costs involved are very low, such as those incurred in changing price lists or adjusting automatic payment machines (see Mankiw, 1985; Blanchard and Kiyotaki, 1987).

The *theory of implicit contracts* (Baily, 1974; Azariadis, 1975) can account for wage rigidity, but it has difficulty in explaining unemployment. This theory assumes different degrees of risk aversion and informational asymmetry between workers and firms. Workers are also assumed to have less access to insurance markets. Under these conditions both groups of agents have an incentive to agree to labour contracts that incorporate a form of insurance from the firm, which agrees to pay an essentially constant wage regardless of the economic situation. The worker gives up part of his potential wage when economic conditions are good in exchange for a commitment from his employer to pay the same wage in less favourable conditions, when the worker might otherwise lose his job and, consequently, receive no wage at all. The reduction in the wage initially received by the worker constitutes the premium paid to ensure he is not fired later. However, the insurance contract is *implicit*, not explicit. Firms prefer implicit contracts when there is informational asymmetry: for example, in order to avoid shirking by workers, which would be more likely if there were an explicit contractual guarantee against redundancy and the firm could not effectively monitor the effort made by the worker (moral hazard).

Nevertheless, by its very nature this approach does not account for unemployment very well. In fact, it is intuitively clear that implicit insurance agreements in labour contracts would tend to reduce unemployment in otherwise negative social states as compared with the level that would prevail in a competitive labour market. There could therefore even be 'socially excessive' (i.e., inefficient) employment. Rosen (1985, p. 1155) has noted: 'the only way a risk-averse worker can partially insure against the utility loss of layoff and unemployment in this problem is by working in circumstances where it is socially inefficient to do so'.

3 Depending on the circumstances, high real wages may or may not create unemployment, as we know from Keynesian analysis. However, it is also important to understand the possible causes of high real wages, in addition to their effects. Among the many such causes, we will limit our discussion here to two: efficiency wages and the insider–outsider problem.

The hypothesis of *efficiency wages* (see, among others, Shapiro and Stiglitz, 1984) is based on the idea that the wage level influences the productivity of workers: not in the fairly obvious sense in which a higher wage increases the physical and psychological capabilities of the worker by raising his standard of living, but rather that it induces the worker to refrain from shirking since it raises the value of the income the worker would have to forgo as a result of the inevitable loss of his job if the shirking were discovered. The higher wage results because the worker and the firm have asymmetric information about the worker's effort (the worker has private information), which means that it is difficult for the firm to monitor the worker's performance. The firm therefore has an incentive to increase his wage, which acts as both an incentive and deterrent for the worker, thus inducing him to make a greater effort in performing his job. If this behaviour is practised by many firms, the higher wage level can create unemployment (in the long run or, in an open economy, even the short run).

Insider–outsider models (Lindbeck and Snower, 1984; Blanchard and Summers, 1986) attribute high unemployment to the high wage level imposed by employed workers (*insiders*).[72] These workers can force firms to pay higher wage rates than those requested by unemployed workers (*outsiders*) for two major reasons: first, there are hiring, training costs and redundancy costs, which segment the labour market; second, insiders can decide to cooperate among themselves but not with would-be outsiders hired to replace fired insiders. Firms respond to the higher wage rate imposed by insiders by moving along the labour demand curve, thus reducing the level of employment.[73]

This model has a number of important consequences. In particular, it implies that there is little worker turnover: both the employed and unemployed tend to remain employed or unemployed and there is little movement between the two groups. If employed workers behave as the model assumes and do not have an interest in defending the unemployed, deflationary policies (or external shocks of the same sign) cause a fall in employment and an increase in unemployment for any given level of inflation; the equilibrium unemployment rate therefore tends to rise. The effect can be accentuated by a prolonged reduction in aggregate demand, which leads to an increase in the proportion of long-term unemployed. This increases the power of insiders, since in practice the long-term unemployed are not effective competitors of those with jobs (see section 7.2). The increase in the equilibrium unemployment rate can explain the persistence of unemployment (*hysteresis*) even when there is an increase in aggregate demand if this occurs after prolonged deflationary policies.[74]

4 There are many theoretical hypotheses based on the existence of *strategic comple-*

---

[72] Others, such as McDonald and Solow (1981) emphasise the role of unions.

[73] This might not happen if workers' utility functions take account of both their wage and the level of unemployment.

[74] Relationships between hysteresis and the natural rate hypothesis are examined in Cross (1988).

mentarities in otherwise imperfect markets.[75] They emphasise the existence of *reciprocal external economies* among the decisions of the various economic agents: one agent tends to do what the other does; for example he increases or reduces production if others do the same. A model of strategic complementarities is offered by Weitzman (1982). The presence of *increasing returns to scale* means that firms are large relative to the size of their market and therefore face a decreasing demand curve with respect to price. Each firm, whether an existing firm or a new one created with unemployed factors, fears saturating the market with its output and therefore seeks some way to limit production. But if all the firms took a bolder approach and increased their output in a coordinated manner, the demand of each firm would create a market for the others and the economy could attain full employment.

Despite their considerable diversity, the explanations of unemployment offered by these theories concur in arguing that real-life markets can have adverse effects on the level of employment, making corrective government action necessary.

Some of the approaches discussed here develop ideas and results in the spirit of Keynes and Kalecki (especially the Weitzman model). Almost all offer explanations of the possible causes of unemployment that might be relevant to certain countries or historical periods. However, their generality and analytical development do not yet appear satisfactory. Nevertheless, they are a good starting point for resuming the debate on the reasons for the instability of capitalism following the rehabilitation of market economies by the monetarists with models generally based on the assumptions of complete markets, full information, no transaction costs and representative economic agents (see Kirman, 1992; Greenwald and Stiglitz, 1993).

An especially interesting element of these analyses is that they are all conducted in microeconomic terms, drawing inspiration from the microeconomic failures analysed in chapter 6, and seek to overcome at this level some of the restrictive hypotheses employed by the monetarists. Some of these analyses could be used to provide appropriate microeconomic foundations to theories of involuntary unemployment. As mentioned, however, their current development seems insufficient, and until more progress is made we think it is legitimate to continue to use macroeconomic models that are not based on microeconomic foundations.

Although at the moment there is no comprehensive and widely accepted Keynesian theory (see Romer, 1993), we think that the discussion so far shows that the Keynesian vision of capitalism appears to be the most suitable for explaining some market failures at the macroeconomic level, specifically unemployment, and the need for government intervention to mitigate, if not eliminate, its effects. Friedman's monetarist school is to be lauded for having clarified, or emphasised, factors and mechanisms that can contribute to understanding inflation: among the factors, the creation of an 'excessive' money supply; among the mechanisms, expectations of future inflation.

In the coming chapters devoted to employment and monetary stability policies we will primarily make use of Keynesian models. These will be subsequently adapted to take account of the problems that arise in open economies.

---

[75] On this approach, and the opposite view of strategic substitutability, see Cooper and John (1988).

*7.4.7 A formal exposition of the major analytical models

It might be useful to provide a summary comparison of the main analytical models examined in the previous subsections. Since we wish to highlight the points already dealt with in macroeconomics texts, all of the models – especially those of Patinkin, the monetarists and new classical macroeconomics – are presented in simplified form.

The 'classical' model

Equilibrium in the goods market

$$Y_s = Y_d \qquad\qquad (7.1a)$$

$$Y_s = g(N_d) \qquad\qquad (7.1b)$$

$$Y_d = C(r) + I(r) \qquad\qquad (7.1c)$$

Equation (7.1a) specifies the equilibrium condition for the goods market, which requires that supply, Y_s, equal demand, Y_d. Equation (7.1b) is a production function in which capital is given, as assumed in a short-run analysis.[76] The relation (7.1c) shows the components of aggregate demand (consumption and investment), both of which are functions of the real interest rate, r. Substituting (7.1c) into (7.1a), we have $Y_s = C(r) + I(r)$, or $Y_s - C(r) = I(r)$, which can be expressed as $S(r) = I(r)$, where $S(r)$ is saving. To identify equilibrium in the goods market, we can then use the relation $S(r) = I(r)$. Changes in the interest rate equilibrate the goods market at a full employment level.

Equilibrium in the labour market

$$N_d = g_d(w/p) \quad g_d' < 0 \qquad\qquad (7.1d)$$

which is the labour demand function;

$$N_s = g_s(w/p) \quad g_s' > 0 \qquad\qquad (7.1e)$$

which is the labour supply function.

$$N_d = N_s \qquad\qquad (7.1f)$$

Changes in the real wage ensure full employment in the labour market. No role can be played by the government.

Equilibrium in the money market

$$L_s \cdot V = p \cdot Y \qquad\qquad (7.1g)$$

The classical model is dichotomous. The equations from (7.1a) to (7.1f) determine the real variables (including the real interest rate, r, and the level of income, Y); given V and Y, (7.1g) determines the price level, p, as a function of the money supply, L_s. Given the dichotomous nature of the model, money must be neutral.

---

[76] One specification of this is $Y_s = \pi N$.

The Keynesian model
In the version given by Hicks, the model is as follows.

Equilibrium in the goods market

$$S(Y) = I(r) \tag{7.2a}$$

$$Y = g(N) \tag{7.2b}$$

The difference with (7.1a)–(7.1c) is well known from elementary macroeconomics texts.

Equilibrium in the labour market

$$w/p = g'(N) \tag{7.2c}$$

Keynes accepts the classical position that the marginal productivity of labour, shown here as $g'(N)$, must be equal to the real wage in equilibrium.

Equilibrium in the money market

$$L_s/p = L_d(Y, i) \tag{7.2d}$$

$$i = r + \dot{p}^e \tag{7.2e}$$

Equation (7.2d) gives the monetary equilibrium, while (7.2e) is the relation suggested by Fisher,[77] which defines the nominal interest rate as being equal to the real interest rate, r, plus the expected inflation rate, $\dot{p}^e$, which can be considered as given. If prices are assumed to be given, $r = i$, and (7.2e) can be eliminated.

This model is clearly not dichotomous. Macroeconomics texts give a full explanation of why money is not neutral.

The Patinkin model, mark I
This model does not make the distinction between inside and outside money (as does the Patinkin model, mark II), assuming instead that all money is outside money.

Equilibrium in the goods market

$$S(Y, L_s/p) = I(i)^{78} \tag{7.3a}$$

The difference between (7.3a) and the Keynesian model is the introduction of real balances, L_s/p, in the consumption function (and hence the saving function).[79]

$$Y = g(N_d) \tag{7.3b}$$

[77] This is sometimes called the 'Fisher equation'; it shows what is sometimes called the 'Fisher effect' of changing the nominal interest rate according to changes in the inflation rate. We have followed another strand of the literature in giving these two terms different meanings (see notes 53 and 35, respectively, in this chapter).

[78] For some features of the Patinkin model there is no distinction in equilibrium between the real and nominal interest rate.

[79] Our purpose here is to underline Patinkin's contribution to the 'neoclassical synthesis' through the introduction of the real balance effect in a Keynesian-type model. We therefore omit the interest rate as an argument of the saving function. Inclusion of this variable would fully correspond to Patinkin's thought and would strengthen our conclusions.

This relation equates demand and supply, which is a function of employment, as in the previous models.

Equilibrium in the labour market

$$N_d = f_d(w/p) \tag{7.3c}$$

$$N_s = f_s(w/p) \tag{7.3d}$$

$$N_d = N_s \tag{7.3e}$$

As we can see, Patinkin makes no change on the classical model regarding the labour market.

Equilibrium in the money market

$$L_S/p = L_d(Y, i) \tag{7.3f}$$

The model is no longer dichotomous, since money balances appear in (7.3a), but money is neutral. It is easily verified that if we move from L_s to $2L_s$ (doubling the nominal money supply), doubling p (i.e., passing from p to $2p$) leaves the system in the initial equilibrium position: in both (7.3a) and (7.3f) we would now have $2L_s/2p = L_s/p$.

Again, it is easy to verify that doubling L_s must lead to a doubling of prices if we have full employment. In this case, the increase in nominal balances at the previous price level causes the real value of money balances to increase, which increases demand for consumer goods. If we are at full employment, prices will rise proportionally to the increase in nominal balances: they cannot rise by less, since in that case there would be a further stimulus to demand; they cannot rise by more for the opposite reason.

The Patinkin model, mark II

This model distinguishes between inside and outside money (L_s^1 and L_s^2, respectively). Only the former is included in the consumption function, while both determine the money supply.

Equilibrium in the goods market

$$S(Y, /L_s^1 p) = I(i) \tag{7.4a}$$

$$Y = g(N_d) \tag{7.4b}$$

Equilibrium in the labour market

$$N_d = f_d(w/p) \tag{7.4c}$$

$$N_s = f_s(w/p) \tag{7.4d}$$

$$N_d = N_s \tag{7.4e}$$

Equilibrium in the money market

$$\frac{L_s^1 + L_s^2}{p} = L_d(Y, i) \tag{7.4f}$$

Suppose we move from L_s^1 to $2L_s^1$. If prices double, equilibrium in the goods market will remain the same, since $2L_s^1/2p = L_s^1/p$. Now take the monetary equilibrium. If L_s^1 doubles, and L_s^2 does not (increasing, for example, by 50 per cent only), while prices double, there will be a reduction in the real money supply. We have

$$\frac{2L_s^1 + 1.5L_s^2}{2p} < \frac{L_s}{p} \qquad (7.4\text{g})$$

As a result, money cannot be neutral. A purely proportional effect on prices of the given changes in the outside money supply does not re-establish the initial equilibrium; conversely, that change in the money supply does lead to changes in the interest rate and, hence, income.

Let us now examine the relationship between L_s^1 and L_s^2. If there were a constant ratio between these variables, condition (7.4g) could not hold. Recall that L_s^1 is the money created by the monetary authorities (monetary base) to pay for goods and services, while inside money primarily comprises bank money (deposits). We will see later (chapter 13) that if the deposit multiplier is fixed, a doubling of monetary base (outside money) will be followed by a doubling of deposits (inside money) as well. However, if the multiplier varies, a situation like that in our earlier example will occur, with L_s^2 increasing less (or more) than L_s^1. In this case, money is no longer neutral, as pointed out by Gurley and Shaw.

The monetarist model

Equilibrium in the goods market

$$S(Y,r) = I(r) \qquad (7.5\text{a})$$

$$Y = g(N_d) \qquad (7.5\text{b})$$

The two relations are similar to those of the Keynesian model, although saving now depends on the real interest rate as well as income.

Equilibrium in the labour market

$$N_d = f_d(w/p) \qquad (7.5\text{c})$$

$$N_s = f_s(w/p^e) \qquad (7.5\text{d})$$

$$N_d = N_s \qquad (7.5\text{e})$$

The relations are those seen in the classical model, but labour supply now depends on the real wage rate calculated on the basis of the expected price level.

Equilibrium in the money market

$$L_s/p = L_d(Y, i) \qquad (7.5\text{f})$$

$$i = r + \dot{p}^e \qquad (7.5\text{g})$$

These also correspond to the relations in the Keynesian model.

Additional conditions

$$\dot{p} = \alpha(Y - \bar{Y}) + \dot{p}^e \tag{7.5h}$$

$$\dot{p}^e_t = \phi(\dot{p}^e_{t-1}, \dot{p}_{t-1}) \tag{7.5i}$$

Equation (7.5h) is a derived 'expectations-augmented' Phillips curve under the simplified hypothesis of $\dot{\pi} = (1 + g) = 0$. In this equation $\bar{Y}$ is the natural rate of unemployment income. Recall that if the original Phillips curve is augmented by expectations, it can be written as $\dot{w} = f(u, \dot{p}^e)$; if the labour force is given, (7.5b) allows us to write this expression as $\dot{w} = \varphi(Y, \dot{p}^e)$ or, specifying the function φ in linear terms, as $\dot{w} = \alpha(Y - \bar{Y}) + \dot{p}^e$, with $\alpha > 0$. Finally, with the simplified hypothesis of $\dot{\pi} = (1 + g) = 0$ we have $\dot{p} = \dot{w}$, or $\dot{p} = \alpha(Y - \bar{Y}) + \dot{p}^e$, which is (7.5h). Finally, (7.5i) shows that expectations are adaptive.

One way to see the connections between the various parts of the model is the following: the money market equations determine i and r, given (in addition to L_s, which is exogenous) Y, $\dot{p}$ and $\dot{p}^e$; these three variables are obtained from conditions (7.5a), (7.5h) and (7.5i), given $\dot{p}^e_{t-1}$ (exogenous) and r. Relation (7.5b) specifies N_d, given Y. The three relations for the labour market equilibrium enable us to determine $\dot{w}$, $\dot{p}$ and N_s. If the long run is defined as the period which makes $\dot{p} = \dot{p}^e$, it follows from equation (7.5) that $Y = \bar{Y}$; monetary policy is totally ineffective with respect to income and can only cause inflation.

The new classical macroeconomics model
The main equations are the following:

Equilibrium in the goods market

$$Y = \psi(r) + V_1 \tag{7.6a}$$

$$Y = Y_n + \gamma(p - p^e) + V_2 \tag{7.6b}$$

$$p^e = p + V_3 \tag{7.6c}$$

Equation (7.6a) corresponds to the *IS* curve of the Hicks version of the Keynesian model and expresses the demand for goods as an inverse function of the real interest rate and a zero-mean stochastic error, V_1.[80] Equation (7.6b) gives supply, which is equal to the income corresponding to the 'natural' rate of unemployment, Y_n, corrected by a factor that expresses the surprise effect of a difference between the actual price and the expected price (*price surprise*): i.e., current output deviates from its natural level only in response to unexpected changes in the price level $(p - p^e)$. If there is no error, supply corresponds to 'natural' output up to a stochastic disturbance, V_2. Equation (7.6b) is known as the *Lucas supply curve*. Equation (7.6c) incorporates the REH, according to which the expected price is equal to the actual price up to a stochastic disturbance, V_3.

Equilibrium in the labour market

---

[80] All the stochastic terms in this model are white noise.

$$N_d = f_d(w/p) + V_4 \tag{7.6d}$$

$$N_s = f_s(w/p) + V_5 \tag{7.6e}$$

$$N_d = N_s \tag{7.6f}$$

Equations (7.6d), (7.6e) and (7.6f) correspond to (7.5c), (7.5d) and (7.5e), with the addition of the stochastic terms V_4 and V_5.

Equilibrium in the money market

$$L_s = \phi(Y,i) + V_6 \tag{7.6g}$$

where V_6 is a stochastic term.

Equation (7.6g) corresponds to the *LM* curve in the Keynes–Hicks model.

From (7.6c) we can see that p^e will be equal to p on average. If we bear this in mind in (7.6b), it is easily seen that the term $\gamma(p - p^e)$ is eliminated on average and, since V_2 is also zero-mean, on average aggregate supply will be equal to Y_n (i.e., its natural level), which should correspond to that in a Walrasian intertemporal general equilibrium under uncertainty. This means that it is impossible for any systematic policy to have an influence on income and employment.

ⅹ 7.5 Growth and development

Growth is an increase in the income and material wealth of a country. *Development* is a more general concept that usually includes growth but also considers other aspects of economic and social change. Development occurs when human well-being improves.

The distinction is important, since growth does not always imply development and development does not always imply growth. In the most backward countries there is a high risk that an increase in total income, or even in per capita income, may not be accompanied by a reduction in poverty or improvements in health, life expectancy, education, the environment, etc. However, there are also considerable differences in definitions of development (see Desai, 1991).

The considerations of the United Nations (see United Nations, 1990) seem especially well founded. They are based on the Aristotelian idea that societies should be judged according to the extent that they promote 'human good'. This leads to a definition of human development as a 'process of enlarging people's choice', which amounts to expanding human 'capabilities' (see section 4.6.2).[81] The United Nations report underscores the reasons why income cannot be considered a good criterion for measuring our range of choice:

1 Income is a means, not an end; it may be used equally for essential medicines and superfluous or even harmful goods (such as illegal drugs).
2 Experience provides examples of high levels of human development at low income levels, and vice-versa.

---

[81] Desai (1989) first used the idea of capabilities to develop a poverty index. The difference between Sen's theory and alternative ethical approaches is discussed in Crocker (1992).

3 Present income of a country may be a poor indicator of its future prospects for growth, which largely depend on how much is being invested in human capital.

4 Current measures of per capita income, which are often used for comparisons through time and across countries, often hide major problems: first, as they are averages, they do not take account of inequalities in income distribution; second, expressing per capita income in terms of a common currency (dollars, for example) overlooks purchasing power differences, which are not reflected in market or official exchange rates.

Measuring human development therefore requires the use of a range of indicators. Nevertheless, for reasons of simplicity and the availability of data, the *human development index* (*HDI*) concentrates on three essential elements of human life: longevity, level of knowledge and living standards. Longevity is indicated by life expectancy at birth; knowledge is measured by adult literacy and the average number of years of schooling; living standards are given as the logarithm of per capita income at purchasing power parity.[82]

The level of development of countries as given by the HDI differs considerably from that suggested by the traditional GDP (or GNP) indicator. The most striking examples (on 1990 data) are Sri Lanka, Vietnam and China, which rise by 44, 41 and 41 places respectively according to the new index, and Gabon, Saudi Arabia and Libya, which fall by 65, 53 and 47 places respectively.

Beyond this, we must recall the large and growing gap in per capita incomes between countries noted in section 6.9. We also remarked that domestic income disparities are less marked than those between countries. We can add that inequality is greater in developing countries than in the industrial world.

From a dynamic point of view (which underlies concepts such as growth and development), the problems of employment are especially insidious. It is not sufficient to compare actual income with the full employment level of income in a certain time period: even if the two are the same during that period, it does not mean that they will remain so over a longer span. In particular, it is not enough to maintain the same level of effective income in order to ensure continued full employment. In dynamic terms the full employment level of income is a moving target, expressed by the concept of *potential GNP* (or *output*) introduced by Okun (1962), which is an important extension of the

---

[82] The use of logarithms is based on the idea that there are 'decreasing returns' in the transformation of income into human capabilities. In other words, people do not need excessive financial resources to ensure themselves a decent standard of living. The logarithmic transformation was partially abandoned in subsequent United Nations reports in favour of a more complex transformation, partly based on a formula developed by Atkinson (see United Nations, 1993, pp. 110 ff.; Atkinson, 1970).

To calculate dollar income at purchasing power parity (PPP), we do not use market or official exchange rates, i.e., the price of a currency, say the dollar, in terms of another currency, say the yen, expressed by the foreign exchange market or set by policymakers. We instead use the exchange rate – whether higher or lower – corresponding to an equal level of domestic purchasing power of the two currencies of the countries being compared (i.e., the exchange rate thereby obtained – called the *purchasing power parity exchange rate* – should strictly reflect the ratio between the general domestic price levels in the countries concerned).

Keynesian concept of full employment income.[83] More precisely, potential output is that which can be obtained in a given time period by making 'full' use of physical and human resources. The term 'full' refers to a 'normal' level corresponding to a system operating without strains or bottlenecks,[84] which may mean (frictional) unemployment of, say, 4 per cent for a given country and time.

The variability of potential output over time is clear if we consider that the level of 'full' employment under the above definition, the labour force and average labour productivity change. We can define:

$$Y = \pi N \tag{7.7}$$

where Y is output, π is average output per employed person (average labour productivity) and N the number of employed.

Equation (7.7) can also be written as:

$$Y = \pi \cdot \frac{N}{LF} \cdot \frac{LF}{P} \cdot P \tag{7.8}$$

where N/LF is the complement to 1 of the unemployment rate,[85] LF is the labour force, P is the population and LF/P is the labour force participation rate. Equation (7.8) emphasises the variables associated with the variability of potential output over time: average labour productivity, the unemployment rate, the labour force participation rate and population.[86] Obviously each of these variables changes in relation to many factors, which we do not have space to examine here.

Equation (7.8) shows why a change in income and a change in the unemployment rate are not proportional: first, if income and the participation rate are constant, the ratio between employment and the labour force declines owing to the simple fact that productivity and population tend to rise over time. The decline in the ratio between employment and the labour force means that the unemployment rate rises. Income must increase more rapidly than the sum of productivity and population growth (which represents the long-run growth trend in income) in order for unemployment to fall.

This is the essence of *Okun's law*. It is not in fact a law but rather an empirical regularity that links the unemployment rate with the variation in real GDP. For example, the ratio between the percentage change in GDP (above the long-run growth trend) and the change in the unemployment rate for the United States has been estimated at about 2.5 to 1 (initially 3 to 1): i.e., GDP must grow by 2.5 percentage points more than its long-run trend in order to reduce the unemployment rate by 1 percentage point.

[83] This became one of the objectives of US economic policy connected with the 'New Frontier' programme of President Kennedy in the 1960s. Tax reduction was used as a new instrument in achieving this goal.

[84] This means that reference to a 'normal' level of employment is a way of expressing both an employment objective and an inflation objective.

[85] Note that this is not the employment rate, which is defined as the ratio between the number of employed and the (active) population.

[86] Multiplying the participation rate by the population gives the labour force; we can therefore write (7.8) as $Y = \pi \cdot (N/LF) \cdot LF$; we have chosen the version given by (7.8) since it shows more clearly the variables that change over time.

7.6 Market failure in growth theories

In the few pages that remain in this chapter we analyse market failures in relation to problems of economic growth. We do not deal explicitly with economic development issues, not because we think that these are less important, but rather for reasons of brevity and because we think that the widespread conviction that the market can solve growth problems (and more so than it can development problems) is erroneous. In the following subsections we intend to show that there are many possible market failures related to growth (and development).

7.6.1 The Harrod–Domar growth model

The analysis of growth problems began with the birth of economics and, therefore, with the work of classical economists. Both for reasons of space and the fact that they are presented in a number of works that we will discuss, we will not deal explicitly with classical growth theories, to which Smith, Ricardo and Marx made particularly important contributions.

Modern growth theory is largely based on the work of Harrod (1939) and Domar (1946, 1947), which sought to complete the work of Keynes in dynamic terms and in a longer-term perspective. In order to overcome the short-term outlook of Keynesian analysis, investment must be considered not only as a component of aggregate demand (as in Keynes) but also as a factor in the creation of productive capacity and, therefore, supply. Harrod identifies the ratio between the average propensity to save, s, and the capital output ratio, v, as the *warranted rate of growth* (i.e., the rate of increase in investment that will maintain equilibrium in the goods market), noting however that nothing guarantees that actual investment will equal the investment needed to meet the actual increase in demand.

If all firms expect demand to grow at the warranted rate and invest appropriately to meet that demand, then their expectations will be fulfilled. If, however, they expect demand to grow more quickly than the warranted rate, the actual *rate of growth* will be greater than the expected rate and there will be excess demand. By contrast, if expectations are pessimistic, the actual rate of growth will be less than the expected rate and there will be excess supply. This is the essence of *Harrod's instability*, which can be considered a statement of the implausibility of a market economy ensuring dynamically stable conditions of equal supply and demand.[87]

A further problem has been highlighted by Harrod's analysis. If the labour force is growing at the rate n, in the absence of labour-augmenting technical progress the actual rate of output growth cannot exceed n (the *natural rate of growth*). With technical progress the natural rate of growth is equal to $n + \lambda$, where λ is the rate of output growth per employed person due to technical progress. The second problem identified by Harrod consists in the fact that there are no mechanisms in a capitalist market economy that can also ensure that the warranted and natural rates of growth will be equal. Therefore, there is no guarantee that the labour force created through natural popula-

---

[87] We have presented the problem of Harrod's instability following Sen (1970b).

tion growth and technological innovation (with the consequent rise in labour efficiency) can be absorbed in a long-run dynamic context (technological unemployment).

7.6.2 Neoclassical and post-Keynesian growth models

The problem of the existence of automatic mechanisms for ensuring the convergence of the warranted and natural rates of growth was the object of theoretical work until relatively recently.

Neoclassical economists identified the variation of the capital–output ratio as just such a mechanism. In their view such change is induced by the substitutability of productive factors associated with changes in their relative prices. As in general equilibrium theory, price flexibility in perfectly competitive and complete markets would ensure the attainment of an efficient position, which in this case would be the maximum growth rate possible given the dynamic constraints on the availability of resources. Removing Harrod's assumption of a fixed capital coefficient, Solow (1956) shows that the warranted rate of growth would tend to converge to the natural rate. However, Solow assumes that investment decisions are always based on the relative availability of capital and labour and not on firms' expectations about the future. Under such a hypothesis, the goods market can never be in disequilibrium, thus removing the problem underlying the Keynesian analysis (i.e., the independence of investment decisions), which in its dynamic version gave rise to Harrod's instability.

'Post-Keynesian' growth theories tend to develop the analysis of the relationship between capital accumulation and income distribution.[88] They solve the problem of convergence between the warranted and natural rates of growth by assuming the possibility of changes in the average propensity to save caused by changes in income distribution. However, by specifying the convergence condition in this way, post-Keynesian analysis does not introduce – as does neoclassical theory – hypotheses that deny the existence of a problem of effective demand. Joan Robinson (1962a) argues that capital accumulation is the driving force of capitalist economies, since it permits the creation of jobs and profits. Nevertheless, its erratic nature – strongly emphasised by Keynes – is the principal limitation of market capitalism.

In the effort to identify factors that can limit the growth of the manufacturing sector and the world economic system as a whole, Kaldor (1976) considers the inability of the terms of trade (i.e., the relative price) between manufactures and primary products to rebalance the growth rates of their respective industries.[89] This incapacity is attributed to the fact that while the prices of primary products vary with changes in relative demand, the prices of manufactured goods are independent of demand and obey the logic of oligopoly (*administered prices*). Consequently, the burden of adjustment of an

---

[88] In addition to the economists we will mention later, other contributors to this strand of analysis are Garegnani, Harcourt and Pasinetti. The latter in particular has analysed the problems of economic growth (most recently, see Pasinetti, 1981, 1993).

[89] The rates of growth in the two sectors are linked by *sectoral interdependencies*: for example, agricultural and industrial raw materials are inputs for the manufacturing sector, while the primary goods sector uses industrial goods such as plant and machinery.

imbalance between demand and supply lies entirely on the prices of primary products (commodities). However, large swings in these prices tend to have a depressive effect on the demand for industrial goods. This is fairly clear in the case of a reduction in commodities prices, which, since it reduces the purchasing power of producers in those industries, also reduces demand for industrial goods. The depressive effect also emerges in the opposite case of a rise in commodities prices, since this creates scope for a more than proportional increase in the prices of industrial goods and, therefore, profits. The increase in profits may have a dampening effect on aggregate demand, since it is not normally accompanied by an equally large increase in spending. On the other hand, the inflation triggered by the rise in commodities prices is not tolerated by the political authorities of the industrial countries, who intervene with restrictive measures.

7.6.3 Endogenous growth theories

Regardless of their differences, the theories discussed in the previous two subsections share a common approach: they argue that the long-run rate of growth of an economy is equal to the natural rate and make no attempt to investigate the forces that determine long-run growth, assuming them to be known and given (*exogenous growth*). This is one limitation of these theories.

A second limitation specific to the neoclassical growth theory is the unrealistic nature of the consequences of this theoretical approach. Neoclassical growth theory implies, in clear contrast with reality, the long-run convergence of different economies towards the same growth rate and, if saving propensities are the same, the same level of per capita income.

In order to overcome these limitations, in the last ten years there have been numerous contributions to what are known as theories of *endogenous growth*. They draw their name from the attempt to explain the various, and often complementary, factors that determine the growth of an economy. Among these, technological progress plays an important role. Endogenous growth models develop, in a particular setting, some concepts used by earlier economists, such as Smith (1776), Young (1928) and others. A central role is played by the explanation of technological progress as the outcome of 'learning by doing', along the lines developed by Arrow (1962).

According to Romer (1986), who has developed this theoretical approach to growth in recent years, learning gives rise to increasing returns to scale, which are incompatible with the assumptions of perfect competition. He thus revives the problem already tackled by Marshall (see section 6.3) and his explanation is very similar to that proposed by Marshall himself: individual firms are assumed to face production functions with constant returns to scale while the economy as a whole faces increasing returns to scale owing to the external economies unintentionally generated by the past accumulation of knowledge. Government spending can reinforce technological progress and the increase in productivity produced by private investment. This is one justification for government intervention aimed at fostering growth: since it is not possible for private-sector agents to capture all the benefits of the accumulation of knowledge, the growth rate of a market economy is lower than the socially efficient level, which can only be reached with the aid of government intervention.

In later endogenous growth models, this form of technological progress is supplemented by the progress generated by specific research and development activity aimed at appropriating all of the benefits deriving from a monopoly on knowledge (Romer, 1987, 1990; Grossman and Helpman, 1991), along lines reminiscent of Schumpeter (1934). In this context the possibility arises of a conflict between two different ways of accelerating the introduction of technological progress into an economy: that produced by the search for *new* knowledge, which gives rise to monopoly positions, and that of the diffusion of *available* knowledge and, consequently, the erosion of existing monopolies. A possible role for government would be to mediate between these opposing needs by creating a framework of rules and incentives to encourage new knowledge without hindering its diffusion, thereby maximising the rate of productivity growth.

Human capital plays an important role in endogenous growth. It is simultaneously the result of a productive process and the source of technological progress. Assuming that human capital is reproduced with a technology yielding constant returns to scale, it can be shown that capital itself and the economy have a positive rate of growth (Lucas, 1988). While Lucas argues that the market is capable of ensuring an efficient accumulation of human (and physical) capital, the most recent literature (see, for example, Glomm and Ravikumar, 1992; Galor and Zeira, 1993; Bénabou, 1996; Cozzi, 1997) has underscored the many market failures associated with its formation: imperfect information; the influence of cultural, religious and social factors that often act cumulatively to produce virtuous or vicious circles; lack of the means needed to form human capital; imperfections in the financial markets to which agents could, in theory, turn in order to supplement their insufficient personal resources. Again, government intervention may therefore be necessary to foster human capital formation in such a way as to increase an economy's rate of growth. And, for the reasons we have cited, in many cases this would require income redistribution, which would have the dual effect of increasing equity and the dynamic efficiency of the economy.

7.7 Summary

1 A complete assessment of real markets cannot ignore a number of important phenomena that are not immediately apparent at a microeconomic level or in any case are difficult to account for with general equilibrium theory. We refer to the instances of 'instability' in market economies: involuntary unemployment, inflation, balance of payments disequilibria, underdevelopment.

2 According to some theories, these phenomena – which imply inefficiency and inequality – are to be attributed to structural features of markets that prevent them from operating as implied by the abstract hypotheses of the theory of general equilibrium. We therefore refer to them as 'market failures'. Since these phenomena are best described by macroeconomic theories, we call them 'macroeconomic market failures'.

3 Involuntary unemployment is an especially important example of instability, implying inefficiency and inequality.

4 Whatever form it takes, inflation represents a competition for the distribution of income. It normally gives rise to a redistribution of income and wealth and costs for society as a whole, which will be large or small depending on the level of inflation.

5 The 'classical' macroeconomic vision is very similar to that underlying the 'invisible hand': a market economy has a natural order that endows it with stability. In particular, full employment is assured by re-equilibrating movements in interest rates and real wages.

6 Keynes calls into question the capacities of market economies to re-equilibrate through changes in relative prices, especially the interest rate and the real wage rate. The uncertainty that pervades a monetary economy creates instability for new capital formation (investment) and the capital value of financial wealth, with possible negative effects on aggregate demand and employment.

7 Patinkin reassesses the re-equilibrating capacity of the market economy, reasserting the neutrality of money, but Gurley and Shaw demonstrate that this holds in certain situations only.

8 Friedman and the monetarists conceive the market economy as inherently stable. Monetary policy is effective only in the short run; in the long run there is no trade-off between inflation and unemployment (the Phillips curve is vertical). On the other hand, fiscal policy crowds out private expenditure. This view of the operation of a market economy is brought to extremes by the theorists of NCM, who postulate rational expectations and markets that are always in equilibrium. The Phillips curve is vertical in the short run as well. Fiscal and monetary policy are therefore at best useless, and may even be harmful owing to the inflation they generate.

9 The conclusion that government action is 'neutral' reached by the NCM school and Friedman's monetarists is the result of a simplistic and misleading treatment of the many problems of the real world related to the scarcity of information, limits on individuals' powers of calculation and optimisation and the complexity of learning processes.

10 There have been many attempts to find new approaches to explaining involuntary unemployment. They have regarded:
   (a) examining the operation of an economy with rigid prices;
   (b) explaining the rigidity of prices and wages;
   (c) explaining the high level of real wages;
   (d) identifying strategic complementarities between the choices of various agents that might lead to a long-run unemployment equilibrium.

11 An increase in income is an indicator of growth. Development is a different concept that considers other causes of economic and social progress. The Human Development Index suggested by the United Nations is an indicator that seeks to measure the capability of people to choose.

12 In a dynamic framework, the problems of employment can be addressed by referring to the concept of potential output: the objective of long-run full employment income leads us to attempt to minimise the divergence between that level and actual production.

13 The analysis of the problems of economic growth has underscored the possibility of numerous market failures. First, Harrod's instability is a reformulation in a dynamic framework of the problems pointed out by Keynes, stemming from the autonomous nature of investment decisions. In addition, Harrod shows that it is unlikely that the warranted rate of growth will be equal to the natural rate of growth and, therefore, that a growing labour force will be able to find jobs. Neoclassical and post-Keynesian economists offer different answers to the possibility that there are mechanisms ensuring that the two rates of growth converge. Endogenous growth theories identify numerous cumulative factors that explain technological progress and economic growth (unintentional learning, intentional R&D activities, human capital formation) and determine the possibility that market economies will grow at an insufficient rate.

7.8 Key concepts

Instability
Macroeconomic failure
Voluntary, involuntary unemployment
Frictional unemployment
Rationing
Labour force
Employment
Unemployment rate
Reservation wage
Layoff
Vacancy
Mismatch
Demand-pull inflation
Financial, credit, supply inflation
Cost-push inflation
Profit inflation
Imported inflation
Full cost principle
Direct, variable cost
Unit labour cost

Wage rate
Mark-up (rate)
Profit margin
Indirect, fixed cost
Open, suppressed (hidden) inflation
Creeping, moderate, galloping inflation
Hyperinflation
Implicit GDP deflator
Consumption, investment deflator
Wholesale, producer, consumer (retail) price
Period-average, twelve-month rate of inflation
Stagflation
Menu cost, slot-machine cost, shoe-leather cost
Say's Law
Barter, monetary (money) economy
Nominal (money), real wage
Coordination of choices

Dichotomy
Neutrality
Relative prices
(Absolute) price level
Stickiness, rigidity of prices
Flexibility
Competitiveness
Fisher effect
Expectation
Animal spirits
Marginal efficiency of capital
Conventionality of the interest rate
Monetary circuit
Stagnation
Self-financing
Neoclassical synthesis
Real balances
Pigou effect
Money illusion
Outside, inside money
Distribution effects
Open-market operations
Monetarism
Quantity principle
Fisher equation, equation of exchange
Velocity of circulation of money
Permanent income
Degree of asset substitutability
Natural, market rate of unemployment
Natural, market rate of interest
Adaptive expectation

Original Phillips curve
Derived (price inflation version of the)
    Phillips curve
Expectations-augmented Phillips curve
Simple rule
Luxury good
New classical macroeconomics
Rational expectation
Policy neutrality, invariance
Island parable
Nominal rigidity
Implicit contract
Inside, outside worker
Hysteresis
Efficiency wage
Strategic complementarity
Growth
Development
Human Development Index
Market exchange rate
Purchasing power parity exchange rate
Potential output
Okun's law
Warranted, natural, actual rate of growth
Harrod's instability
Capital–output ratio
Exogenous, endogenous growth
Learning by doing
Diffusion of technical progress
Human capital

PART III

NORMATIVE AND POSITIVE THEORY OF ECONOMIC POLICY

8 The normative theory of economic policy

8.1 The government as a rational agent

In chapters 6 and 7 we identified market failures at both the microeconomic and macroeconomic levels, thus showing the need for intervention by an agent that, having collective motives and objectives, would be able to transcend these failures.

Our analysis in this chapter focuses on the abstract potential for action by such an agent in a market economy with the aim of correcting the market's operation or replacing it altogether. We develop a theory about what this agent, acting rationally, *should* do to compensate for market inadequacies. From this point of view, we will be in a position similar to that held by much of neoclassical theory, which deduces the optimal (maximising) behaviour of various (private) agents on the basis of certain postulates.

In chapter 9 we examine the actual behaviour of government, comparing it with the abstract structure we intend to sketch out here, so as to identify 'non-market' failures in the same way we illustrated market failures in our earlier discussion.

Both steps – i.e., the formulation of both a normative and a positive theory of public involvement in the economy – are necessary if we wish to reach some sort of conclusion regarding the relative roles to assign to government and the market in 'regulating' the economic activity of individuals. In particular, the normative theory is needed as a yardstick for assessing the reality of government intervention and the possibility of improving the way it is carried out and its results. This theory has helped raise the debate about government involvement in economic life above the level of slogans, as one of its progenitors had hoped (see Tinbergen, 1956). In addition, the development of a logical structure to verify the internal consistency, and therefore the rationality, of a system of economic policy ensures that it is not based solely on intuition, experience and the forecasting abilities of policymakers.

8.2 Planning

8.2.1 Meaning and foundation

Planning means taking coordinated and consistent economic policy decisions. In the area of government intervention this means avoiding piecemeal measures and considering the full range of policy aims (targets or objectives) and the set of possible actions (instruments) for every problem.

The need for coordinated action is a consequence of at least three factors:

1 There is normally a variety of instruments available to achieve the various possible objectives. Choosing the appropriate instrument for each objective involves considering the relative effectiveness of each alternative, the time required for the effects of each instrument to operate and the presence of any constraints on their use.

2 The existence of multiple objectives and the fact that each instrument can influence more than one (even all of them; see section 8.5.2) means that in general policy problems are interdependent. In solving one problem (or hitting a target) the instrument will also affect other issues (other targets), and not necessarily in the desired way. Accordingly, the various policy problems must generally be solved *simultaneously*, as we will see. A special case in which it is possible under certain conditions to solve individual problems separately (or in a *decentralised* manner) will be examined later (see chapter 19 on the 'appropriate' assignment of instruments to objectives).

3 Policy problems are intertemporal. The solution of a problem in the present is tied to the solution of the same problem in subsequent periods. An especially important aspect of planning in this context is the 'time consistency' of public choices. We will examine the precise meaning of this term in chapter 19.

8.2.2 The constituent elements of the plan

We have already referred to the elements of a plan in section 8.2.1, mentioning two of them explicitly: targets (or objectives) and instruments. More precisely, a *target* is an economic policy aim that we can usually measure in terms of an economic variable, such as income or employment. An *instrument* is a 'lever' – represented by another variable – that policymakers can use to achieve the target, i.e., to change the value of an objective variable in the desired way. We will see later the characteristics that an economic variable must have in order to be used as an instrument.

The ability of instruments to influence targets is inferred from economic analysis, which identifies the relationships between economic variables, thereby giving us an idea of the possibility that adjusting certain variables (the instruments) will have an effect on others (the targets). The 'structure of information' on the relationships between economic variables can be expressed as a mathematical model that describes the functioning of the economy at an aggregate level (a macroeconomic model) or a disaggregated level (a microeconomic model). Obviously, the *analytical model* will differ according to the school of economic thought that most influences the economist.

In summary, a plan (or programme) is formed of three elements: targets, instruments and an analytical model. In the coming pages we will examine each in detail.

8.2.3 An example

We have seen that the essence of planning is the coordinated use of multiple instruments to achieve a variety of objectives. We will return to the problem of coordination later, after having introduced additional concepts. For the moment we will show how a simple economic policy problem involving only one target can be framed and then solved. This case will serve as an introduction to the subsequent analysis of more realistic situations in which policymakers wish to pursue multiple objectives.

Observing real-life situations allows policymakers to identify the aspects of reality that they consider to be unsatisfactory and whose correction could become a policy objective. Using the lens of economic analysis, they will also be able to identify the causal relationships between different economic variables (analytical models).

In examining the world around them, policymakers may decide, say, that employment is too low, which reduces social welfare. In such a situation, policymakers will propose specific targets for employment (N), which can be expressed in a number of ways: as increments of N (ΔN) or as a fixed value of N ($N = \bar{N}$). We will here assume that the target is expressed as $N = \bar{N}$.

For their part, economists will have developed a model of the sort shown by (8.1), which specifies the variables on which employment depends (e.g., following the Keynesian approach, the components of autonomous demand, A):

$$
\begin{aligned}
Y &= \pi N \\
Y &= C + A \\
C &= cY
\end{aligned}
\tag{8.1}
$$

In model (8.1), Y is income, π is average labour productivity, C and A denote consumption and autonomous expenditure, respectively, and c is the average and marginal propensity to consume. Substituting the second and third equations into the first, (8.1) can be rewritten in the following way, which specifies N as a function of the other variables:

$$
N = \frac{1}{\pi} \cdot \frac{1}{(1-c)} A
\tag{8.2}
$$

Our next step is to identify the instruments, i.e., the variables in (8.2) that can be adjusted by policymakers to influence the target variable.

Examining (8.2), more than one variable emerges as a possible candidate for the role of instrument: they may be variables that can be considered true instruments under policymakers' control, or others that are not true instruments but, for simplicity, can be

considered as such since they reflect, with varying degrees of immediacy and effectiveness, movements in the real instruments.

For example, A is composed of, among other things, government consumption and
investment spending, G, which is directly controllable, and private investment, I, which
we will initially take as given but which can be indirectly influenced by controlling
liquidity (see chapter 13). However, even c can be considered a policy instrument, since it
reflects income redistribution induced by government action, which could influence the
marginal propensity to consume of the economy as a whole if the propensities to
consume of individuals, groups or classes are different (see section 8.5.1).

In our example, in abstract terms we have certain degrees of freedom in choosing the
instrument. Once we have established which instrument should be used, we can solve the
policy problem. If we assume that only one instrument will be used (for example,
government expenditure), I and c will be considered given and the policy problem
consists in finding the value for G that will generate the desired value of N, i.e., that will
yield $N = \bar{N}$.

We first rewrite (8.2) as:

$$N = \frac{1}{\pi} \cdot \frac{1}{(1-c)} (\bar{I} + G)$$ (8.2′)

and then write the instrument, G, as a function of the target, N:

$$G = [\pi(1-c)N] - \bar{I}$$ (8.3)

Equation (8.3) tells us in general how G changes as N changes, with the other variables
taken as given.

Finally, we assign N the desired value $\bar{N}$:

$$G = [\pi(1-c)\bar{N}] - \bar{I}$$ (8.4)

This gives us the only value of G consistent with the data and the desired target ($N = \bar{N}$).
In the real world, then, knowing the values of $\bar{I}$, π and c, as well as that of the target, we
can immediately determine the level of G that, given our hypotheses, will allow us to
reach the employment target.

8.3 Economic policy objectives

The individual policy objectives were identified in the previous chapters. They belong to
microeconomic or macroeconomic policy. Expressing them is the task of politicians,
who are accountable to the public for their choices.

The importance of the political system in defining the relationship between policymakers' preferences and individual preferences is clear. The problem lies in identifying the objectives to pursue and the weight to give to each. If it were possible to
construct an indirect ordering without having recourse to criteria of distributive justice,
direct reference to individual preferences would enable us to solve the problem without
having to favour some preferences over others. However, we know from chapter 3 that
this is not possible. The choice of certain justice criteria rather than others by pol-

icymakers can reflect the preferences of at least a part (preferably a majority) of the electorate to a greater or lesser degree. This depends to a considerable extent on the operation of the democratic political mechanism. For the moment we assume that such a mechanism exists and functions perfectly. We also assume that there are no bureaucratic barriers or distortions in the implementation of the policies adopted to achieve the objectives. We will drop both of these assumptions in chapter 9.

There are four ways to express targets:

(a) the fixed target approach;
(b) the priority approach;
(c) the flexible target approach with a variable marginal rate of substitution (MRS); and
(d) the flexible target approach with a constant MRS.

We first examine these approaches in diagrammatic form before proceeding to a more rigorous analytical treatment.

8.3.1 Fixed targets

The first method for expressing policy objectives was developed by Tinbergen (1952, 1956) and consists in assigning fixed values to the variables chosen as economic policy targets.

Let the targets be income in two geographical areas (call them North and South): Y_N and Y_S; the possibility of producing income with existing resources in the two areas is expressed as $Y_N = f(Y_S)$, which is shown in figure 8.1 as a 'transformation' curve.

Expressing the objectives as fixed targets is equivalent to taking a point on the curve, such as A, where

$$Y_N = \bar{Y}_N \qquad Y_S = \bar{Y}_S$$

If the pair of desired values for the two income levels were outside the transformation curve, the politician would have to decide between two alternatives: either reduce the value of at least one of his targets or attempt to shift the transformation curve up (i.e., ease the constraint). Given that the second option may take time to achieve, even a stubborn and far-sighted politician could well decide to choose the first option, at least until he was able to engineer a shift in the transformation curve.

A second example of a fixed target problem is reconciling an employment target (expressed in terms of the unemployment rate, u) and monetary stability (expressed in terms of $\dot{p} \equiv (\Delta p/\Delta t)/p$, the rate of change in prices per unit of time, or the inflation rate). These two targets can be linked by a relation or 'transformation' curve, $\dot{p} = f(u)$, shown in figure 8.2 (the 'derived' Phillips curve). As we saw in chapter 7, this is a much debated relationship; we use it here to illustrate one possible type of constraint on economic policy choices.

Expressing the desired objectives as fixed targets means selecting a point on the derived Phillips curve (B, for example) where $\dot{p} = \dot{p}^*$ and $u = u^*$.

The analytical design of a planning problem with fixed targets is given in section 8.5.

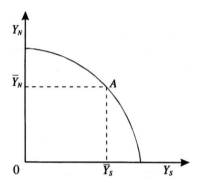

Figure 8.1

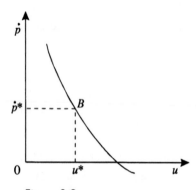

Figure 8.2

8.3.2 The priority approach

Setting fixed targets may not be feasible if policymakers do not know the exact position of the 'transformation' curve (or, more precisely, the relationship that links one target with another). In this case it may be more appropriate to specify priorities in reaching objectives. For example, policymakers may wish to ensure a certain volume of income in the less-developed area of the country (the South), then seek to maximise income in the more advanced area (the North) consistent with the actual position of the transformation curve. With reference to figure 8.3, the transformation curve can either be at A or B. However, policymakers want $Y_S = \bar{Y}_S$; they then wish to maximise Y_N, which will be $\bar{Y}'_N$ or $\bar{Y}''_N$, depending on the position of the transformation curve.

If employment and price stability are the objectives and policymakers wish to give priority to the former, they will set a certain unemployment rate as their target and then seek to minimise the inflation rate. We leave it to the reader to diagram this case.

In analytical terms, the operation involves maximising (or minimising, if we are dealing with a 'bad') the value of the non-priority target, subject to the desired value of the priority target and the constraint of the transformation curve or the model that represents the functioning of the economy.

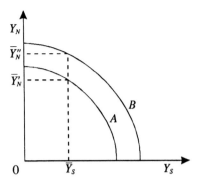

Figure 8.3

8.3.3 Flexible targets: social welfare function with variable MRS

Approaching a policy problem in terms of flexible targets is equivalent to the way the consumer problem is set in standard microeconomics.[1]

The consumer, rather than setting the quantities of goods and services he wishes to consume in rigid terms (or rather than setting priorities), indicates his objectives in flexible terms by expressing his preferences. Referring to a map of indifference curves representing those preferences, the consumer compares the map with the budget constraint (or 'transformation' curve), thereby determining his choices (i.e., the quantity of goods and services that he must acquire to maximise his utility) at the point of tangency, rather than specifying them a priori.

Similarly, the policymaker, perhaps with the help of an economist, will construct a map of 'social' indifference curves reflecting the preferences of society (a social welfare function, SWF).[2] He will superimpose the map on the transformation curve between the variables that are arguments of his utility function, thus determining the choice of objectives. Figure 8.4 shows the map of social indifference curves between Y_N and Y_S and the transformation curve introduced in figure 8.1. Obviously, the solution to the problem is given at the point of tangency, C.

As we can see, in this case the indifference curves associated with the SWF are identical to those associated with the consumer's utility function. If the arguments of the SWF were 'bads' (such as unemployment, u, and inflation, $\dot{p}$) rather than 'goods' (such as Y_N and Y_S), the indifference curves would be represented differently.[3]

First, the preference order would differ: clearly, the lower the level of one 'bad' for a given level of the other, the higher the utility. Thus, curves closer to the origin represent

---

[1] It is no surprise that this approach is due to Henry Theil (in particular, see Theil, 1954, 1964), who had absorbed the ideas of Tinbergen while working in the Dutch central planning office in the early 1950s, and had written his doctoral thesis on the theory of consumer demand. The remark is from Hughes Hallett (1989).

[2] The difference with the SWF defined in section 4.3 is that this one expresses a direct ordering and hence has as its arguments government objectives, rather than individuals' utilities.

[3] Instead of a welfare function to maximise we would have a 'loss function' to minimise. A specific case of a loss function is the misery index we will examine in section 8.3.4.

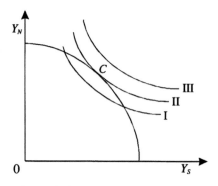

Figure 8.4

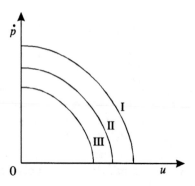

Figure 8.5

higher levels of utility (figure 8.5). Second, the curves are concave rather than convex, indicating that the MRSs are increasing rather than decreasing.

However, here too the economic policy problem has a solution, which can be found by comparing the social indifference map with the transformation curve (figure 8.6). *D* is the point of highest social welfare.

For both goods and 'bads', the arguments of the SWF are the economic policy targets. However, unlike the fixed-target approach, in this case the targets are determined endogenously as the values that maximise social welfare, given the constraint. This is an 'optimising' approach, in contrast to the fixed-target approach.[4] The reason this method is called the *optimising approach* to planning should be clear: the values of the targets are not predetermined; rather, they are defined by the optimisation process (by way of maximisation or minimisation) with the constraint given by the transformation curve or, more generally, by the model of the economy. By contrast, the values *assigned* to the objectives in the fixed-target approach, are simply satisfactory, not optimal. An analytical treatment of the optimising approach to an economic policy problem is given in section 8.5.

---

[4] The priority approach is an intermediate method.

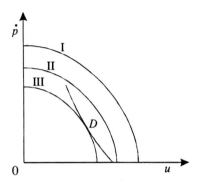

Figure 8.6

8.3.4 Flexible targets: social welfare function with constant MRS

This case corresponds to a SWF that has been linearised for simplicity, and therefore has a constant MRS.[5]

Take our example of targets for regional income distribution. The SWF can be written as:

$$W = aY_N + bY_S$$

where a and b are the weights assigned to income in the two areas. These can take any value, reflecting the preferences of the person or group that defines the SWF.[6] In this case, a and b are constant for any value of Y_N and Y_S. Consequently, the MRS between Y_N and Y_S, given by b/a, is constant.[7] We can therefore represent the policy choice problem in terms of figure 8.7. Given the assigned weights, point D determines the optimal level of income in the two areas.

Let us now look at another example that offers an interesting connection with Okun's so-called *misery index*. If the arguments of the SWF with a constant MRS are $\dot{p}$ and u, we have the function:

$$W = a\dot{p} + bu$$

where a and b are negative constants. An increase in $\dot{p}$ or u means a decrease in welfare, or an increase in misery. If we choose to measure welfare on the scale of negative values, and hence take misery (and not welfare) as our reference point, a and b are positive

---

[5] A SWF with a constant MRS is a good approximation to the true SWF only in the neighbourhood of the point at which the true SWF has a MRS equal to the one we have assumed as constant.

[6] For example, we could have $a = 1$ and $b = 2$, or $a = 1.5$ and $b = 1$.

[7] Assume $W = \overline{W}$ (i.e., choose an indifference curve); we therefore have $\overline{W} = aY_N + bY_S$, from which we can derive Y_N as a function of Y_S:

$$Y_N = \frac{\overline{W}}{a} - \frac{b}{a}Y_S$$

This is a linear function with a constant slope, $-b/a$. The MRS is equal to the absolute value of the slope of the indifference curve, i.e., b/a.

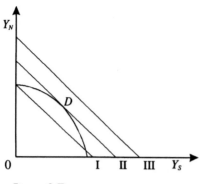

Figure 8.7

constants. In the special case where $a = b = 1$, we have Okun's misery index, which is the sum of the unemployment rate and the inflation rate.

This index is sometimes used to compare economic situations over time or in different places in order to obtain a summary view of economic conditions in one country or compare them across countries (see, for example, Bank for International Settlements, 1983; Coricelli, 1990). For example, table 8.1 gives the misery indices for the major industrial countries in various years, showing the considerable divergences between them even in restricted and relatively integrated areas like the European Union. The disparity is a symptom of the considerable differences in structural conditions and their evolution. In all likelihood, however, the differences also depend on the broad diversity of preferences and policies, which calls into question the validity of the basic hypothesis used to construct the index, i.e., the equal weight assigned to the two 'bads' (in all countries, in our case).

This indicator of welfare has been criticised for a number of reasons, which we can summarise as follows.

1 As mentioned, the misery index reflects preferences that might not be shared, since unemployment and inflation are given equal weights ($a = b = 1$). In other words, a 1 percentage-point increase in unemployment is assumed to have the same value for policymakers as a 1 percentage-point increase in inflation.

2 One consequence of the preceding observation is that the decline in welfare associated with a 1 point increase in unemployment is always compensated by a 1 point fall in inflation, and vice-versa, *whatever the starting point*. In terms of our discussion, this means that the MRS is constant (and equal to 1); this is difficult to accept, unless we remain in the neighbourhood of some given point. If the starting point for inflation and unemployment changes considerably, in general there is also a change in the ratio with which one is prepared to exchange increases in one variable for decreases in the other, leaving welfare unchanged. For example, if unemployment is 3 per cent and inflation is 20 per cent, we may be willing to accept a 1 per cent increase in unemployment in order to reduce inflation by 2 percentage points. However, if unemployment is

Table 8.1. *Misery indices in selected OECD countries**

	1970	1975	1980	1985	1990	1995
United States	9.3	16.5	17.9	10.8	10.7	7.8
Canada	9.2	17.5	17.5	14.2	12.4	11.1
Japan	8.3	13.1	9.5	4.9	4.7	2.6
Germany	4.4	9.6	8.7	8.9	7.5	10.2
France	7.5	15.8	19.6	16.0	11.7	13.2
Italy	10.3	22.4	27.9	18.6	16.5	17.9
United Kingdom	8.9	28.0	22.6	16.5	12.4	11.3
Total OECD	8.2	16.1	18.6	14.5	12.3	12.2

Note: *The indices have been calculated by adding the unemployment rate (standardised for the purposes of comparison across countries) and the private consumption deflator. *Sources*: Our calculations on data from Maddison (1991), until 1975. and OECD (1996) for subsequent years.

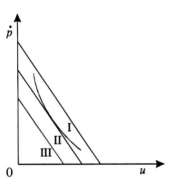

Figure 8.8

8 per cent and inflation is 6 per cent, we may be willing to accept an additional point of unemployment only if inflation falls more drastically, say by 4 percentage points.

Figure 8.8 shows the terms of the trade-off between unemployment and inflation when the SWF has a constant MRS.

8.4 The instruments of economic policy

8.4.1 Definition

A variable can be defined as a policy instrument if the following three conditions are satisfied:

1 Policymakers can control the variable; that is, they can decide what value it should have and fix it directly with their own actions (*controllability*).

2 The variable whose value has been fixed by policymakers has an influence on other variables, which are assigned the role of targets (*effectiveness*). In the simple case of one target and one instrument linked by a functional relation, effectiveness can be measured as the derivative of the target with respect to the instrument, dy/dx, where the target is y and the instrument x. With multiple targets and instruments, measuring effectiveness with derivatives is more complicated (see Tinbergen, 1956).

3 It must be possible to distinguish the variable from other instruments in terms of its degree of controllability and, above all, effectiveness: two instruments with the same effects on all targets are not really two separate instruments (*separability* or *independence*).

As defined here, an instrument appears to be a variable whose sole function is to influence other variables, which are those relevant for policymakers' preferences. However, in the real world this is a rare occurrence, since some economic variables may also have an intrinsic value in addition to their instrumental value. In other words, the arguments of policymakers' preference functions can include target variables proper and other variables that normally have an instrumental role for the attainment of the target variables. For example, public expenditure is an instrumental variable, since it influences the level of numerous policy targets such as income, employment, the balance of payments, etc. However, policymakers may also assign an intrinsic value to the amount of public expenditure or the ratio between public spending and national income (the degree of government involvement in the economy).

The lack of a sharp distinction between targets and instruments does not create excessive difficulties for dealing with economic policy problems. Theil generalised the social welfare function to include the case in which its arguments include instrumental variables (see Theil, 1964).

On the other hand, difficulties may arise if there are constraints (floors or ceilings) on the use of instruments. These can be a consequence of institutional factors: i.e., the constitution, the laws or the customs (which can sometimes have the force of a law) that regulate the behaviour of the government or the central bank of a country (for example, a balanced-budget requirement or prohibition on the monetary financing of a deficit; see chapter 14) may inhibit the use of certain instruments or combinations of instruments.

When the causal relationship that links certain instruments to the (final) objectives is complex, it can be helpful to introduce the concepts of policy indicators and intermediate targets. We will discuss these at length in chapter 13 in relation to monetary policy.

8.4.2 The different types of instrument

There are different ways of classifying policy instruments. One of these, suggested by Tinbergen (1956), distinguishes between quantitative, qualitative and reform policies. *Quantitative policies* are those that involve changing the value of an existing instrument (e.g., changing the level of government expenditure); *qualitative policies* involve the introduction of a new instrument, or the elimination of an existing one, without causing significant changes in the economic system (e.g., introducing a ceiling on bank lending or a new tax). *Reform policies* (or reforms) consist in the introduction of a new instrument or the elimination of an old one that does cause a significant change in the features of the economic system and the rules governing its operation. Reforms have a considerable institutional impact and include, in addition to the nationalisation (or privatisation) policies mentioned elsewhere: measures that define property rights, especially the degree of public or private involvement in firms and industries; the structure of the financial system (e.g., the 'separation' of short-term lending from medium- and long-term lending); and regulation of the economic structure or the conduct of firms in the marketplace (e.g., antitrust legislation). Reforms may have constitutional importance depending on the level at which they are implemented, which partly depends on historical and political factors.

We can also distinguish between *direct* and *indirect control measures*. Direct control measures aim to achieve certain objectives by imposing a given behaviour on certain categories of agents (for example, setting import quotas to reduce the trade deficit). Indirect control measures do not seek to achieve objectives by imposing a specific behaviour on agents, but rather by influencing the variables that guide agents' decisions (for example, in order to reduce the trade deficit, we could introduce a tariff on imports, which normally raises their prices, thus discouraging the consumption of foreign goods). There are many direct measures in addition to import quotas, including rationing consumption, lending ceilings, selective credit controls, wage and price controls, establishment of public-sector enterprises and various forms of regulation (e.g., requiring scrubbers on coal-fired power stations, prohibiting the sale of meat from 'mad' cows, antitrust legislation, etc.).

The three main indirect measures are fiscal policy, monetary policy and exchange rate policy. Fiscal policy regards the level of government expenditure and/or taxation. Monetary policy operates on the liquidity of the economic system through changes in monetary base and/or the required reserve ratio. Exchange rate policy seeks to influence the exchange rate, i.e., the quantity of one currency needed to purchase one unit of another currency.

A further important distinction can be made between *discretionary measures* and *(automatic) rules*. Discretionary measures are policy instruments that can be adjusted at the policymaker's discretion in a case-by-case assessment of the situation. Rules are policy instruments that operate without the need to observe and decide on a case-by-case basis. One example of a rule is Friedman's proposal to increase the money supply by a fixed annual percentage (see section 7.4.4), rather than assessing the situation periodically and deciding the measures to adopt.

A set of rules can act as a *monetary* or *fiscal constitution* if the breadth and range of the measures establish the fundamental principles of government intervention in the two areas. Adopting a certain monetary regime (e.g., the gold standard) is an example of a monetary constitution (see chapters 16 and 17).

A specific class of rules is represented by *automatic* (or *built-in*) *stabilisers*, which help to smooth the cyclical fluctuations of the economy. Examples of these are unemployment benefits and progressive taxation. Both of these instruments, which were primarily introduced to reduce the inequality of personal income distribution, also counter the cyclical tendencies of the economy, limiting the decline in aggregate demand during recession and dampening the effect of an increase during expansion. The stabilising properties of progressive taxation will be examined in detail in chapter 14.

One advantage of automatic stabilisers, which were mainly introduced after the second world war, is that they make government intervention more rapid, since they eliminate the *observation* (or *recognition*) *lag* and the *administrative* (or *decision*) *lag*, although the *effect lag* remains.[8]

The superiority of automatic stabilisers over discretionary measures from the point of view of lags does not mean that the latter do not have an important role to play in countercyclical policy, mainly due to the extent of the adjustment that is necessary in certain situations. There are also many ways to reduce the lags associated with discretionary measures, ranging from increasing the speed of data gathering to the creation of a 'project fund' for extraordinary government spending to be drawn on if a rapid fiscal expansion is needed.

8.5 The model

The pages that follow have an eminently technical purpose. They seek to clarify certain general aspects of the structure of an economic model and the modifications that a model must undergo in order to be used for policy purposes (a *policy* or *decision model*). In this context, the theoretical foundation of the models used (whether Keynesian, post-Keynesian, monetarist, etc.) is not important.

Let us briefly review the steps we took in the example in section 8.2.3.

Once employment was identified as the objective, we considered an explanatory model of the variables that influence it (see model (8.1)); this is an analytical *model in structural form*.

The structural form model was transformed through a series of mathematical steps in order to identify the variables on which employment ultimately depends, thus obtaining a *reduced form model* (equation (8.2)).

We then inverted the relationship between N and autonomous spending, thereby obtaining the *inverse reduced form* (see equation (8.3)); assigning a given value to N ($\bar{N}$), we solved the equation for G (equation (8.4)).

We will now examine each of these steps.

---

[8] The observation lag is the time interval between the moment at which the event requiring action occurs and that when the need for intervention is recognised. It is essentially a statistical lag. The administrative lag is the interval between the recognition of the need for action and the moment the decision to act is taken. This lag is due to the time needed for policymakers to study and discuss the situation and select the most appropriate response. The time it takes to undertake a policy action – which includes both the observation and administrative lags – is called the *inside lag*. The effect lag is the interval separating the adoption of the measure and the emergence of its effects. It is also called the *outside lag*.

8.5.1 The structural form of the model

Recall that an analytical model is a set of relations, usually expressed in mathematical terms, that represents the economic process in an abstract and simplified form. A structural form model presents the relationships between variables as they are suggested by economic analysis.

The model is a simplified representation of reality and therefore captures only certain features of the actual economic system. Different policymakers may be interested in different aspects of reality. Therefore, for practical reasons it is necessary to construct a variety of models, each of which is intended to highlight specific features of economic life (see Tinbergen, 1956). Thus, we have micro- or macroeconomic models, static or dynamic models, deterministic or stochastic models, closed-economy and open-economy models, etc.

For the purposes of economic policy it is essential that the model be specified or modified in such a way that it can be used as a *decision model*: in other words, the variables that can be given the role of either fixed or flexible targets and those that can be used as instruments must be identified.

A model in structural form is composed of equations of various types:

    (a) definitional equations;
    (b) behavioural equations;
    (c) technical equations;
    (d) equilibrium equations;
    (e) institutional equations.

Sometimes the same equation can be interpreted in a variety of ways.

The first equation in (8.1) is normally considered to be a technical equation, since it represents a special case of the production function $Y = f(K, N)$ – where K is the amount of capital goods available and N the supply of labour – when K is given (as is assumed in short-term analysis), so that income grows only when employment rises. In reality, since it is expressed in value terms rather than physical terms, the equation represents the behaviour of various agents (government, workers, firms, etc.), which is reflected in prices, and therefore is not a true technical equation.

The second equation in (8.1) is an equilibrium equation showing the relationship between output (supply) and the components of demand. With different specifications of the model, the equation could be considered a definitional equation of aggregate demand.[9]

The last equation is a behavioural equation.

Institutional equations, which (8.1) does not have, express relationships and constraints deriving from the need to comply with laws or custom. An example of these is the prohibition on monetary financing of deficits in the Maastricht agreements, which regulate the process of European Monetary Union. This can be written as:

$$\Delta G = \Delta T + \Delta B$$

[9] In this case aggregate supply would also be defined and another equation would represent equilibrium between demand and supply.

where G, T and B are, respectively, government expenditure, taxes and public debt. It expresses the rule according to which an increase in spending can only be financed with taxes or the issuing of government securities, not with monetary base.

Endogenous and exogenous variables

The variables in the structural form model can be classified as exogenous and endogenous.

Exogenous variables are those that determine other variables but are not in turn influenced by any variable; variables that fall into this category are data (in model (8.1) they are c and $\bar{I}$)[10] and instruments (G, according to the hypothesis in the example).

Endogenous variables are those that can determine the value of some other variable but whose value in any case depends on other variables. Endogenous variables include objectives (in (8.1), N) and irrelevant variables (C and Y).[11] The reader can check that the variables indicated are endogenous variables: for example, C influences income but is also affected by it.

We can now say that the structural form of a model is the form in which endogenous variables are expressed as a function of other endogenous variables as well as exogenous variables. Indicating endogenous variables with y and exogenous variables with x, the structural form can be written as:

$$y = f(y, x)$$

8.5.2 The reduced form model

Fixed targets

Solving an economic policy problem expressed in terms of fixed targets requires that we first proceed from the structural form model to the reduced form, and then to the inverse reduced form.

---

[10] A further distinction is sometimes drawn between *parameters* and *data* proper. In this case, data would be the exogenous variables that, although they can have different values in themselves (also as a result of public control), have a specific value in the model. Parameters are variables that indicate the sensitivity of certain variables to others in behavioural functions. These should be stable; i.e., they should be considered given (however, see the Lucas critique in section *8.8). When the model (i.e., the analytical perspective) changes, it sometimes becomes possible to explain such variables in terms of others; they therefore become endogenous variables. For example, in model (8.1), as later amended by substituting $A = \bar{I} + G$, c is a parameter (while $\bar{I}$ is a datum). However, if we added the following equation to the simple consumption function in (8.1):

$$c = c_1 \frac{W}{Y} + c_2 \left(1 - \frac{W}{Y}\right)$$

where W denotes aggregate wages, c would become an endogenous variable, which can be influenced by income redistribution measures (e.g., an incomes policy).

The reader should note, however, that there is no consolidated terminology on the meaning of the term 'data' and 'parameter'. Sometimes, as we do in chapter 13, parameter is used with reference to constants that can be changed through government action.

[11] The variables C and Y are irrelevant only with respect to the target of the decision model, N. This does not mean they are irrelevant in general.

The *reduced form model* is obtained from the structural model by eliminating through substitution all the irrelevant variables and expressing each residual endogenous variable (i.e., each target) in terms of exogenous variables only. There will therefore be as many reduced form equations as there are targets. This will prove helpful later in understanding the 'golden rule' of economic policy.

Equation (8.2) is the reduced form of the structural form model (8.1). Since there is only one target, the reduced form has only one equation. If the target is generically labelled y and the instrument x, equation (8.2) has the form $y = f(x)$.

With two targets, y_1 and y_2, and two instruments, x_1 and x_2, the reduced form model is:

$$y_1 = f_1(x_1, x_2)$$
$$y_2 = f_2(x_1, x_2)$$

(8.5)

The *inverse reduced form* is obtained by expressing the instruments as a function of the targets. In the case of a single target this means finding the inverse of $y = f(x)$, or expressing x as a function of y: $x = f^{-1}(y)$; hence the name 'inverse reduced form'. In the case of two targets and two instruments the operation is similar, producing a system of the type:

$$x_1 = \phi_1(y_1, y_2)$$
$$x_2 = \phi_2(y_1, y_2)$$

(8.6)

Having expressed the instruments as a function of the targets, we need to assign a value to the latter in order to solve the policy problem, i.e., in order to determine the values of the instruments, which are unknowns. Thus, setting $y_1 = \bar{y}_1$ and $y_2 = \bar{y}_2$, we have:

$$x_1 = \phi_1(\bar{y}_1, \bar{y}_2)$$
$$x_2 = \phi_2(\bar{y}_1, \bar{y}_2)$$

(8.6')

However, to obtain the inverse reduced form a number of conditions must be met.

Recall that a necessary condition for solving a system of equations such as that given by (8.5) is that the number of unknowns be equal to the number of equations. Bearing in mind the fact that in an economic policy problem the unknowns are the instruments and the number of equations of the reduced form is equal to the number of targets, we can derive the *'golden rule' of economic policy*, which we owe to Tinbergen: in the case of fixed objectives, the solution of an economic policy problem requires that the number of instruments be at least equal to the number of targets.

If the number of (independent) instruments is exactly equal to the number of targets, the system is *determined*. If the number of instruments is greater (less) than the number of targets, the system is *underdetermined* (*overdetermined*), i.e., there are multiple solutions (no solutions).

Imagine that we have one target and two instruments: it is possible to assign an arbitrary value to one instrument and determine the value of the other by solving the inverse reduced form. There are, therefore, an infinite number of solutions, one for each of the values assigned to the first instrument; in general, if there are m targets and n instruments, with $m < n$, we say there are $n - m$ *degrees of freedom.*

If, however, there are two linearly independent targets, one instrument is not sufficient to ensure their attainment. In general, there are a number of possible responses where the number of instruments is less than the number of targets:

(a) drop the excess targets; if we have m targets and n instruments, we must drop $m - n$ targets;

(b) find new instruments with different effectiveness from available instruments with respect to at least one target. The number of new instruments must be $m - n$;

(c) abandon the attempt to set the policy problem in terms of fixed targets in favour of a flexible target approach.

Before leaving the fixed-target example, two remarks are in order.[12] The first regards the reduced form (8.5). Note that the instrument x_1 influences both targets, as does the second instrument, x_2. In general terms, each instrument will influence both targets and it will not be possible to adjust a single instrument in order to influence a specific target without affecting other targets as well. Thus, as we mentioned at the beginning of section 8.2, in general it is necessary to determine the value of the instruments simultaneously, which tends to favour centralised policy control, thereby ensuring that decisions are coordinated. Nevertheless, there are situations where decentralised solutions (for example, independent management of monetary and fiscal policy) are possible or even desirable. We will return to this issue when we discuss the appropriate assignment of instruments to objectives in section 19.2.

Our second remark regards the number of available instruments. The existence of numerous market failures may mean that the government will try to achieve multiple objectives. The possibility of attaining the objectives is linked to the availability of an equal number of instruments, if we wish to use fixed targets. Therefore, any inhibition on the use of certain instruments deriving from preconceived positions and political, social or ideological constraints does not facilitate the government's job.

Some such restraints are codified as laws or institutions, while others clearly go against both the letter and the spirit of laws or international treaties. In any case, they can create serious obstacles to the rational design and solution of economic policy problems. There are many situations in which these impediments occur: the willingness of a government to devalue or revalue its currency, resistance to direct controls, whether with reference to either domestic relationships (e.g., rationing or lending ceilings, price controls) or foreign ones (e.g., quotas, restrictions on capital movements) and so on.

Flexible targets

A flexible objective problem is framed in terms of maximising or minimising a social welfare function subject to the constraints given by the relationships of the model, which

---

[12] Appendix 1 at the end of this chapter shows the structural form model in the case of two objectives, income and investment, and two instruments, government spending and liquidity control. We then derive the reduced form and the inverse reduced form.

represent the functioning of the economic system. With two generic targets, y_1 and y_2, we have:

$$\max[W = f(y_1, y_2)]$$

subject to

$$y_1 = f_1(x_1, x_2)$$
$$y_2 = f_2(x_1, x_2)$$

As we said earlier, this problem can be solved even if the number of instruments is less than the number of targets (for example, if we only have the instrument x_1 and not x_2). Clearly, in this case the value of the social welfare function that can be obtained will be lower. Gaining access to a larger number of instruments as a result of scientific progress or overcoming inhibitions and constraints will therefore have a positive effect on social welfare.

8.6 Limits and extensions of the classical approach

In the preceding pages we have set out the fundamental features of modern economic policy, whose founding fathers were Frisch, Tinbergen, Meade, Leontief, Hansen and Theil.[13]

The key feature of this approach is its global vision of policy problems, which is reflected in the consideration of the diffuse effects of manoeuvring each instrument, i.e., effects that influence not one target only, but rather a number of targets, or even all of them.

At the practical level, this conceptual apparatus enables us to approach real problems rationally, since we can calculate 'exact' solutions, i.e., the values of the instruments that will achieve certain objectives or maximise a social welfare function.

However, the reader must not be lulled into thinking that all problems can be solved in this way. The approach has a number of limitations; some (such as its static and certain nature) can be removed by specifying the model appropriately. We examine this aspect later in this section.

Other criticisms are of a logical nature, but they can also have a crucial impact at the empirical level (e.g., the Lucas critique). We discuss these in the next two sections.

Still others regard: (a) the realism of characterising policymakers as 'representatives' of indistinct citizens; and (b) the problems associated with the cost and the political or administrative feasibility of the solutions generated by the models. These difficulties will be discussed in the next chapter.

Let us take a brief look at the problems associated with the static and deterministic

---

[13] See Frisch (1949, 1950, 1959), Tinbergen (1952, 1954, 1956), Meade (1951, 1955), Leontief (1964, 1976), Hansen (1958), Theil (1954, 1956). More recently, see Heal (1973), Johansen (1977, 1978), Preston and Pagan (1982), Hughes Hallett and Rees (1983), Petit (1990).

nature of this approach.[14] These limitations can be overcome, although at the cost of reducing the tractability of the model.

Considering a dynamic model raises a number of specific problems that are worth mentioning. First, let us clarify some consequences of the 'golden rule' of economic policy. We saw that in the case of fixed objectives in a static context, the necessary condition for the existence of a solution is that the number of instruments should at least be equal to the number of targets. This condition does not hold in the case of a dynamic model where we seek, for example, to attain one or more fixed targets in the future.[15] Even if we have a smaller number of instruments than targets, under certain conditions it is possible to reach these objectives by extending the time necessary to achieve them. The 'golden rule' regains validity when we wish to maintain control of the target or targets over time; that is, when we desire to keep the economy moving along a given growth path.[16] A dynamic approach may also raise problems regarding the time consistency of decisions; this will be discussed in section 19.1.

A different matter, which we mentioned earlier, regards situations where a policy problem involving a number of targets and instruments can be solved separately, i.e., in a decentralised way, rather than simultaneously, i.e., in a centralised way. We will discuss this in sections 19.2 and 19.3.

8.7 The Lucas critique

In decision models the behaviour of private agents (consumers, entrepreneurs, etc.) is assumed to be predictable on the basis of a given specification of the behavioural functions and the identification of the (fixed) parameters. Policy decisions are determined by setting certain objectives and taking into account the relationships between these objectives and policy instruments based on the behaviour of private agents. However, this approach ignores the feedback effect of government decisions on the behavioural *functions* of private agents.

We are not arguing that a decision model does not consider the reactions of private agents to government action at all. This would not be consistent with what we have said so far. If, for example, government influences national income (through government spending on consumption and investment) or disposable income (through taxes and transfers in addition to government consumption and investment), private consumption will be affected by fiscal policy: if $C = c(Y - T + Tr_h)$, where T are taxes and Tr_h are transfers to households, fiscal policy will affect C through G (which acts on Y), T and Tr_h, and therefore the model accounts for consumers' reactions to government action. Rather, we wish to argue that changes in policy regimes (or the rules governing policy choices) can influence the *parameters* of private behavioural functions (in our example,

---

[14] In addition, we are dealing with a linear model. Overcoming this limitation requires advanced techniques that are not appropriate to our discussion here.

[15] This problem is known as a *target point controllability* problem and the target is also called a 'point target'.

[16] This is a problem of *perfect* or *target path controllability*. On this and target point controllability, see Preston and Pagan (1982).

c), i.e., the sensitivity of private agents to government decisions, or the functional *form* of private agents' behaviour. This is the substance of the critique advanced by Lucas (1976) against the classical model of economic policy.[17]

The analytical models used as a basis for decision models are normally the product of econometric analysis that establishes the exact specification of the form of behavioural functions and the independent variables as well as the value of the parameters. Econometric tests are based on available data about the relevant variables in past situations (characterised by the presence of certain external shocks, certain types of policy, etc.). The tested model is then used to forecast the consequences of certain policies, e.g., an increase in government spending, and design an optimal policy. However, this is accomplished by taking as given and invariant the estimated values of the parameters and the form of the behavioural functions of private agents (e.g., the propensity to consume and the form of consumption function) in the new situation. This might not be the case. Suppose that government spending has not been adjusted in previous years or that any adjustment in the past involved different forms of spending, for example, investment rather than government consumption or transfers, or certain types of government expenditure (teachers' salaries) rather than others (student canteens). A change in the volume and/or content of public expenditure may give rise to new private behaviour. For example, a programme to increase the number of student canteens might change students' propensity to consume so that it differed from that estimated with econometric models based on data collected before the number of canteens was increased.

If the model parameters change, reflecting a change in the behaviour of the system, and the 'old' model is taken as a constraint in the government decision model, the ensuing policies will not be optimal at all: they would be so only if private behaviour did not change. In other words, the constraint underlying the design of government action is not a real constraint, but rather changes as government behaviour itself changes.

The Lucas critique is undoubtedly well-founded and raises both practical and theoretical problems. At the practical level, the amount by which parameters change in response to the change in economic policies is important: if the change is small, designing policy on the basis of previously estimated values will be broadly reliable. Obviously, reliability also depends on the data set used to estimate the parameters: the larger the set and the more it encompasses situations in which different policies were in use, the less the parameters will vary and the greater the reliability of the model's indication of optimal policies will be. In the 1970s many macroeconomic relationships broke down as a consequence of major changes in the policy regime, since agents adjusted their behaviour to the new environment (Chrystal and Price, 1994).

From a theoretical point of view, the Lucas critique underscores the presence of reciprocal interactions between the behaviour of private agents and government. In particular, the private sector plays an active rather than passive role, changing its

---

[17] Another limitation of the structure of the models we have examined goes beyond the hypothesis that private agents have behavioural functions that do not change in response to changes in government behaviour: it derives from the implicit hypothesis that private agents have no power and are unable to influence government behaviour with their actions, which is clearly unrealistic.

behaviour as expectations about government behaviour change. The critique is a response to the fact that traditional analytical models do not admit this sort of interaction. In order to overcome these limitations, we need to change the type of model we use. For example, we might make use of game theory, since it is specifically structured to model strategic interactions between agents.

*8.8 A formal treatment of the Lucas critique

In order to gain a thorough understanding in formal terms of the nature and significance of Lucas' critique, as well as possible answers to the problems he raises, we initially follow the analysis of Cuthbertson and Taylor (1987).

Assume the following behavioural function of private agents at time t:

$$y_t = \alpha x_t + \beta E(z_{t+1} | \Omega_t) + \eta_t \tag{8.7}$$

where y_t, the dependent variable, is a function of another variable, x_t, as well as the expected value at time $t+1$ of a third variable, z (conditional on the information set Ω_t available at t) and a stochastic disturbance, η_t.

Assume also that z_t is stochastically dependent on the values of z in the previous two periods, i.e., it follows a second-order autoregressive process:

$$z_t = \phi_1 z_{t-1} + \phi_2 z_{t-2} + \varepsilon_t \tag{8.8}$$

where ε_t is white noise, with $E(\varepsilon_t | \Omega_{t-i}) = 0, 0 < i < t$. The rational expectation of z_{t+1} is then:

$$E(z_{t+1} | \Omega_t) = \phi_1 z_t + \phi_2 z_{t-1} \tag{8.9}$$

Substituting (8.9) into (8.7), we have the true model of the economy *if* (8.8) *holds*:

$$y_t = \alpha x_t + \beta(\phi_1 z_t + \phi_2 z_{t-1}) + \eta_t \tag{8.10}$$

The econometrician will actually estimate a function of the form:

$$y_t = \alpha x_t + \gamma_1 z_t + \gamma_2 z_{t-1} + \eta_t \tag{8.11}$$

which is equivalent to the 'true' model of the economy.[18]

The policymaker takes an estimate of (8.11) and defines the optimal policy, and this remains valid if implementing the policy does not change the form of (8.8). This may not be the case, especially if changes are made in the *rules* of government decisions. For example, imagine that the intermediate target of monetary policy (see section 13.9) is changed from the money supply to the interest rate. This may alter the nature of the autoregressive process that generates z_t, which might be better represented in some other way. For example, assume that z represents the money supply. If the intermediate

[18] 'Estimates of γ_1 and γ_2 are in fact estimates of non-linear functions of the 'deep parameter β' and the historically contingent, possibly policy-dependent, parameters ϕ_1 and ϕ_2, since $\gamma_1 = \beta\phi_1$ and $\gamma_2 = \beta\phi_2$' (Cuthbertson and Taylor, 1987, p. 254).

target of monetary policy is the money supply, we can show z_t as being affected by the values of z in the previous two periods. If, however, the intermediate target is the interest rate, the money supply at time t can be represented better by a *random walk* process, which is a specific *autoregressive process* of order 1:

$$z_t = z_{t-1} + \varepsilon_t \tag{8.12}$$

If this is the case, the description of the economy's behaviour given by (8.11) is no longer accurate and, in order to obtain an appropriate policy, should be replaced by another relation, obtained by substituting (8.12) into (8.7):

$$y_t = \alpha x_t + \beta z_t + \eta_t \tag{8.13}$$

However, the choice between (8.11) and (8.13) as the constraint on the optimisation process leading to the policy decision (and therefore the selection of the intermediate target) obviously cannot be made if we do not already know the outcome of the decision, since the behaviour of the economy changes in response to the government decision. We are thus faced with a situation where we do not know the right model.

There are a number of ways to redefine the public decision process in a more satisfactory fashion, at least at the theoretical level, so as to circumvent Lucas' critique. One way is to estimate the *deep parameters*, such as β in (8.7), which can ensure the stability of the relation. Deep parameters are those that appear in the functions describing consumer tastes and technology, which should not change in any systematic way as a result of changes in countercyclical policies (Lucas, 1977).[19]

Estimating such parameters involves practical problems that need to be studied and solved in a more appropriate forum. Our aim here is to provide a brief discussion of the strategic interaction between the behaviour of public and private agents. We have seen that private agents base their behaviour on expectations about future government action. However, once we recognise the fact that the behavioural functions of private agents can themselves change in relation to public choices, both categories of agent must consider the reciprocal effects of their decisions. The natural way to model this type of interaction is offered by the theory of dynamic games.

*8.9 Appendix 1 Structural and reduced form models in the case of two targets

Consider the case of two targets: the level of income, Y, as a short-run target, and the level of investment, I, as a long-run target.[20]

We can show the variables on which income and investment depend with a simple Keynesian model. The structural form model is:

---

[19] For an opposing view, see Vercelli (1991, section 8.5), who argues that even tastes and technology are not really invariant to changes in economic policy rules.

[20] Our underlying hypothesis is that a large volume of investment contributes to a high long-run rate of growth.

$$Y = C + I + G$$
$$C = cY$$
$$I = I_0 - ai \qquad (8.14)$$

$$\frac{L_s}{p} = kY + L_0 - vi$$

We have already seen the first two equations of (8.14). In the third, investment is represented as an inverse function of the interest rate, i, and is equal to I_0 when the interest rate is zero. The fourth equation gives the equilibrium between the real money supply (L_s is the nominal money supply and p the price level, which for simplicity is assumed to be given) and money demand (kY is transactions demand and $L_0 - vi$ is speculative demand).

In this model, G and L_s can be used as instruments.[21]

To obtain the reduced form, we take the value of i from the fourth equation and substitute its value into the third. We then substitute the second and third equations into the first to obtain:

$$Y = \frac{1}{(1 - c + ak/v)}\left[I_0 + G + \frac{a}{v}\left(\frac{L_s}{p} - L_0\right)\right] \qquad (8.15a)$$

We again take the value of i from the third equation and substitute it and (8.15a) into the fourth. With additional substitutions we have:

$$I = I_0(1 - B) + \frac{a}{v}\left(\frac{L_s}{p} - L_0\right)(1 - B) - BG \qquad (8.15b)$$

where

$$B = \frac{ak}{v}\frac{1}{(1 - c + ak/v)}$$

The equations (8.15a) and (8.15b) are the two reduced form equations for the two targets. Note that the targets are expressed in relation to data and instruments only. Moreover, Y and I depend on both instruments, G and L_s.

The solution to (8.15) is obtained by computing the inverse reduced form, expressing G and L_s as a function of Y and I and then setting $Y = \bar{Y}$ and $I = \bar{I}$.

*8.10 Appendix 2 The decision model in matrix form

The model is expressed in linear form.[22] Let $\mathbf{y}$ be a vector $(m, 1)$ indicating the target variables; $\mathbf{z}$ is a vector $(r, 1)$ of irrelevant variables; $\mathbf{x}$ is a vector $(n, 1)$ of instruments; and $\mathbf{u}$

---

[21] As we will see in chapter 13, the actual monetary policy instrument is not the nominal money supply, L_s, but some other aggregate, such as monetary base, which contributes to determining L_s. Obviously, we have assumed that the nominal money supply is the instrument in order to avoid complicating the model any further.

[22] Economic policy models are often formulated in terms of linear relations between variables. It is generally possible to linearise non-linear relations. However, it must be borne in mind that this operation can highly distort the analysis.

is a vector $(s, 1)$ of data. Let $\mathbf{A}$, $\mathbf{C}$, $\mathbf{B}$ and $\mathbf{D}$ be matrices of order $(m + r, m)$, $(m + r, r)$, $(m + r, n)$ and $(m + r, s)$, respectively.

The *structural form* is written as:

$$\mathbf{Ay} + \mathbf{Cz} = \mathbf{Bx} + \mathbf{Du} \tag{8.16}$$

Appropriately decomposing the matrices by rows, (8.16) can be written as:

$$\begin{aligned}
\mathbf{A}_1\mathbf{y} + \mathbf{C}_1\mathbf{z} &= \mathbf{B}_1\mathbf{x} + \mathbf{D}_1\mathbf{u} \\
\mathbf{A}_2\mathbf{y} + \mathbf{C}_2\mathbf{z} &= \mathbf{B}_2\mathbf{x} + \mathbf{D}_2\mathbf{u}
\end{aligned} \tag{8.17}$$

where the first expression represents m of the $m + r$ equations and the second represents the remaining r equations.

Given certain conditions,[23] it is possible to eliminate the irrelevant variables and write the same system as:

$$\mathbf{A}^*\mathbf{y} = \mathbf{B}^*\mathbf{x} + \mathbf{d}^* \tag{8.18}$$

which is a system of m equations where the matrices with asterisks are associated with those in (8.17) by the relations: $(\cdot)^* = (\cdot)_1 - \mathbf{C}_1\mathbf{C}_2^{-1}(\cdot)_2; \mathbf{d}^* = \mathbf{D}^*\mathbf{u}$.[24] The dimensions of the matrix and the vectors in (8.18) are:

$$\mathbf{A}^*{:}(m, m) \quad \mathbf{y}{:}(m, 1) \quad \mathbf{B}^*{:}(m, n) \quad \mathbf{x}{:}(n, 1) \quad \mathbf{d}^*{:}(m, 1)$$

This equation represents the target variables alone as a function of the instruments and the data. For simplicity, we will omit asterisks in the remainder of this appendix.

The necessary and sufficient condition for the existence of defined solutions with respect to $\mathbf{y}$ is that $\mathbf{A}$ is non-singular[25] and, therefore, invertible.[26] We can then solve the system (8.18), obtaining the *reduced form*:

$$\mathbf{y} = \mathbf{A}^{-1}\mathbf{Bx} + \mathbf{A}^{-1}\mathbf{d} \tag{8.19}$$

If we set $\mathbf{A}^{-1}\mathbf{B} = \mathbf{M}$ and $(\mathbf{y} - \mathbf{A}^{-1}\mathbf{d}) = \mathbf{y}'$, where $\mathbf{y}'$ is the vector of deviations of the endogenous target variables with respect to the constant values $\mathbf{A}^{-1}\mathbf{d}$, we can write:

$$\mathbf{y}' = \mathbf{Mx} \tag{8.20}$$

$\mathbf{M}$ is therefore a matrix of order (m, n) of multipliers, which give the effect of changes in the instruments $\mathbf{x}$ on the target variables $\mathbf{y}$. From (8.20) we can easily verify that $dy_i/dx_j = m_{ij}$, where m_{ij} is the generic element of $\mathbf{M}$.

Solving the policy problem with fixed objectives (i.e., $\mathbf{y}' = \bar{\mathbf{y}}'$), which requires that $\mathbf{M}$

[23] The matrix $\mathbf{C}$ must be of rank r, and in particular the matrix $\mathbf{C}_2$ must be of full rank (i.e., not singular), and therefore invertible.

[24] This step simplifies the presentation but it is not essential (see Preston and Pagan, 1982, section 1.1).

[25] Recall that the matrix $\mathbf{A}$ is of order (m, m). The non-singularity of the matrix implies that the targets are independent of each other, i.e., that none is a linear combination of the others.

[26] In other words, matrix $\mathbf{A}$ has the same rank as matrix $[\mathbf{A}, \mathbf{Bx} + \mathbf{d}]$ (see Sydsaeter and Hammond, 1995).

be invertible, is possible if and only if the rank of the matrix $\mathbf{M}$ is full and equal to that of the matrix $[\mathbf{M}, \mathbf{y}']$ (weak existence condition), or the number of independent instruments is equal to the number of independent targets (strong existence condition, valid for any vector of targets: see Preston and Pagan, 1982, section 1.3). Solving (8.20) for $\mathbf{x}$, we have:

$$\mathbf{x} = \mathbf{M}^{-1}\mathbf{y}' \tag{8.21}$$

or

$$\mathbf{x} = \mathbf{B}^{-1}\mathbf{A}\mathbf{y} - \mathbf{B}^{-1}\mathbf{d} \tag{8.22}$$

System (8.22) is the *inverse reduced form* of (8.16). We also could have obtained it directly by solving (8.18) for $\mathbf{x}$.

We leave it to the reader to present and solve the model in appendix 1 in matrix form.

8.11 Summary

1 The identification of numerous 'market failures' suggested the need for intervention by an agent that, having collective (public) motives and objectives, would be able to transcend these failures.

2 The normative theory of government intervention aims to provide the conceptual apparatus for the adoption of coordinated and consistent economic policy decisions (planning).

3 The need for coordination is a consequence of the multiplicity of instruments, each of which can influence all of the objectives (albeit each in a different way), and of the interdependence between decisions in different periods.

4 An economic policy plan (decision model) comprises objectives, an analytical model and instruments.

5 In a rational approach to economic policy, objectives are identified by policymakers and reflect the preferences of the public. They can be expressed as: fixed targets, priorities, flexible targets with a constant or variable MRS. In the case of the flexible target approach, policymakers formulate a SWF whose arguments are the objectives and sometimes the instruments.

6 An instrument is a controllable, effective and separable (independent) variable.

7 We make a distinction between quantitative, qualitative and reform policies; direct and indirect control measures; discretionary measures and automatic rules.

8 Structural form models present the relationships between variables as suggested by economic analysis. They are composed of technical, definitional, behavioural, equilibrium and institutional equations. The variables in the models are exogenous (data, instruments) and endogenous (targets, irrelevant variables).

9 Reduced form models are obtained from structural form models and express targets as a function of exogenous variables alone.

10 In the case of fixed targets, the solution to the planning problem can be obtained with the inverse reduced form model (derived from the reduced form) by assigning the desired value to the targets and solving for the instrumental variables. A solution is possible if the 'golden rule' of economic policy is satisfied: the number of instruments must be at least equal to the number of targets. If this is not the case, we can: (a) increase the number of instruments; (b) reduce the number of targets; (c) change the design of the policy problem and express the objectives as flexible targets.

11 A flexible target problem involves maximising a SWF, subject to the constraint imposed by the relations of the model.

12 The classical approach to rational economic policy has many limitations. One of the most important was identified by Lucas (the Lucas critique), who argued that it ignores the feedback effects of policy regimes on the behavioural functions of private agents, which are assumed to be invariant.

*13 The existence of reciprocal interactions between the behaviour of private and public agents means that we should change the analytical model adopted and use the techniques of game theory.

8.12 Key concepts

Planning (programming)
Interdependence among objectives
Simultaneous solution
Decentralisation
Target (objective)
Instrument
Analytical model
Fixed, flexible target (objective)
Priority approach
Optimising approach
'Transformation curve'
Loss function
Misery index
Controllability
Effectiveness
Separability (independence)
Degree of government involvement
Quantitative, qualitative policies, reforms
Direct, indirect control

Fiscal policy
Monetary policy
Exchange rate policy
Discretion
Rule
Monetary, fiscal constitution
Automatic (built-in) stabiliser
Observation (recognition) lag
Administrative (decision) lag
Inside lag
Effect (outside) lag
Policy (decision) model
Structural form model
Definitional, behavioural, technical, equilibrium, institutional equation (relationship)
Exogenous, endogenous variable
Data, parameter
Irrelevant variable

Reduced form (policy) model
Inverse reduced form
Golden rule of economic policy
Determination, overdetermination,
  underdetermination
Degree of freedom
Target point controllability
Perfect (target path) controllability
Lucas critique

Autoregressive dynamics
Random walk
Deep parameters
*Matrix
*Order
*Singularity
*Rank
*Inverse matrix

9 'Non-market' failures: elements of a positive theory of economic policy

9.1 Representing social groups

In section 8.6 we discussed the limitations of the normative or 'classical' theory of economic policy in general terms. In this chapter we will analyse the limitations associated with the *normative* character of the theory.

The *normative theory* of economic policy is a 'theory of the public interest' and ignores the problem of the realism of the hypotheses on which it is based, in particular with reference to the nature of individuals and the behaviour of policymakers. In this sense it suffers from the same limitations that typify the conceptual apparatus of neoclassical theory, on which it draws considerably. Much of the neoclassical approach is constructed in axiomatic form: the behaviour of individuals is deduced from a set of postulates. The normative theory of economic policy postulates the existence of an agent (the policymaker) who acts in the interests of somewhat indistinct individuals, incorporating the 'will of the people' into a social welfare function (Downs, 1957).

This approach largely neglects the following aspects of reality:

(a) the economic system is not composed of indistinct individuals;
(b) policymakers are not anonymous, as the theory assumes.

In this section we address the first aspect before moving on to the second in the next section.

The normative theory of economic policy in its most extreme form assumes that individuals are virtually anonymous, albeit possessing specific (abstract) preferences and different initial endowments of resources. Within this framework, government action should seek to improve efficiency (and therefore the relatively undifferentiated position of 'individuals') and, possibly, the personal distribution of income, reflecting a view of

203

the 'public interest' that is sustained by the idea of generic individuals. Such individuals ('the people') suggest their preferences to policymakers, who include them in the SWF.

The 'people', however, is not composed of indistinct members. We can aggregate these individuals into classes or groups with shared interests, needs or ideas, which tend to act jointly through their organisations – *interest groups, lobbies, cartels, unions, political parties*, etc. – in order to ensure that their preferences prevail over those of other groups.[1]

These classes or groups have different levels of power, which are expressed in both reciprocal economic relationships and the influence they can exert on the construction of the 'social welfare function', i.e., in determining the weight to be assigned to the various policy objectives. From this point of view, the problem of the personal distribution of wealth, which was the only apparent difference between individuals in neoclassical theory, becomes a key point of conflict between different social groups. It is therefore of special importance to know how 'similar' individuals organise themselves to achieve common objectives within a society, including their use of 'public' action. What would otherwise be a largely 'anonymous' SWF thus begins to acquire texture and definition.

Economics, at least in the version given by the mainstream neoclassical school, does not provide appropriate conceptual categories to tackle some of the problems we have raised: for example, the concepts of power and class (or group) are missing or play a limited role, and private institutions other than the market are virtually non-existent.

By contrast, the concepts of power, class and institution are at the centre of other social sciences, especially political science (Alt and Chrystal, 1983). In the last two decades this has given rise to a new approach to economic problems, called *political economy* or *political economics*, that gives greater importance to such concepts. The approach still lacks a clear and unifying conceptual structure but offers valuable guidelines for a more realistic treatment of economic policy problems.[2]

Keynesian macroeconomics, adopting in part the classical approach of Smith, Ricardo, Marx and others, innovated on the traditional neoclassical framework by introducing a systematic differentiation of individuals into different classes (capitalists–wage earners; savers–investors). Nevertheless, the implications of Keynesian economic policy broadly apply to society as a whole: especially in a model with fixed prices, in some situations achieving full employment can improve the situation of all of society's members, whether wage-earners or capitalists, savers or investors. Similar results can be obtained if we consider other macroeconomic objectives such as the balance of payments or economic growth. Introducing inflation into this framework is more difficult. Inflation is the outcome of a competition between different categories of economic

---

[1] In referring to classes or groups the existence of well-defined preferences shared by group members is usually assumed. However, it has recently been shown that, in practice, in many policy problems preferences can be unstable, uncertain and founded on inadequate information. This has important consequences for the role that can be played by institutions in debating and forming preferences (see Gerber and Jackson, 1993).

   On the other hand, Sen (1995) has noted that solving many vital problems of the contemporary world requires forming values through public discussion.

[2] In some cases it appears more the product of a fad. For a survey of the various strands of political economy, see Staniland (1985).

agents, and in fostering or dampening inflation government will likely fail to remain neutral between these groups.

More recently, *interest group theory* (or *capture theory*) has recognised the existence of groups of individuals with shared interests (and/or values) and sees government action to some extent as a reflection of the pressure of such groups.[3] This theory, which has roots in the Marxian idea that capitalists control social institutions and in the work of political scientists at the beginning of the twentieth century, has been reformulated in the post-war period by the *public choice school*, which was founded by Downs (1957), Olson (1965) and Buchanan and Tullock (1962). It also includes a number of other economists such as Becker, Niskanen, Peltzman, Stigler and Tollison, mainly affiliated with the universities of Chicago and Virginia. This school has a clear free-market orientation.

The traditional figures of capitalists and wage earners have thus emerged in the role of social agents, no longer as individuals but as institutions representing them (unions, political parties, etc.). Even consumers, particular categories of firms (e.g., financial and non-financial enterprises, firms exposed to international competition and those sheltered from such competition) and workers (employed and unemployed, skilled and unskilled) have appeared in a different light when they have been represented as seeking to solicit government intervention in their favour through specific organisations.

Each of these groups may wish to influence government action in a number of circumstances:

(a) in general policy attitudes such as the adoption of expansionary or restrictive policies; the choice of some kinds of policy instruments that may have different consequences for various groups;

(b) in more specific actions involving selective intervention (different tax rates, sectoral or regional incentives, protection of specific sectors, etc.).

Obviously, more general intervention is sought by larger groups capable of stimulating wide-spread support, while specific, 'sectional' actions are solicited by smaller groups (see Olson, 1982, p. 48). For example, a political party or confederation of industries or labour unions might advocate expansionary or restrictive policies; progressive or flat-rate taxation (see chapter 11). By contrast, a company or local union might ask for support for individual firms or sectors, through tax exemptions, incentives or protection specific to a company or industry.

There are numerous ways in which groups exercise their influence on government authorities. They include: voting, personal connections, opinion campaigns of varying degrees of openness, corruption and promises to politicians and bureaucrats of a lucrative career when they leave government service.

The new types of private agent that we have identified certainly make the concept of society richer than that obtained by considering a set of indistinct individuals alone. However, it is obviously not enough to crowd the stage with a variety of characters in order to achieve a better representation of the realities of social life and the way public

---

[3] The term reflects the idea that politicians, who were initially seen by economists as promoting the public good, are in fact 'captured' by groups and induced to take positions and decisions that favour these particular groups.

decisions are reached. What we really need at this point is a macroeconomic and macropolitical theory that incorporates hypotheses about the behaviour of social groups and their interactions.

The premises for such a theory exist and can be found, in our opinion, in the Keynesian methodology and in the growing body of work in other social sciences, especially political science. In addition, game theory seems to provide a powerful methodology, albeit not a robust one,[4] for analysing social interactions, especially under uncertainty and informational asymmetry.

9.2 Agency problems: the objectives of politicians and the political business cycle

The identity of policymakers is entirely ignored in classical theory. Much like firms in the theory of general equilibrium, policymakers in classical theory could be replaced by a computer. They have no identity and their role as *agents* of the indistinct individuals or social groups that they should represent is not recognised. They have no personal ideas about the desirability of the various solutions and they have no personal or other interests to pursue apart from a generic 'public interest'. There is therefore no need for institutional constraints or incentives to induce them to pursue the public interest (or even the interest of a social group).

In addition, in pursuing the economic policies deemed appropriate, they do not have to overcome any obstacles either in the social context in which they work or in the executive apparatus. With specific reference to the latter, the people responsible for defining policy objectives in turn face no agency problem in implementing the policies needed to secure those objectives, even if implementation is necessarily overseen by others. Hence, the role of these people as 'agents' of those who have been charged with defining public objectives is not recognised either.

In order to underscore the anonymous character of the people to whom classical theory attributes the task of formulating objectives and taking the actual public policy measures, we have spoken generically of *policymakers* or 'public authorities'. From our discussion it is now clear that this indistinct government apparatus is composed of two categories of person, *politicians* and *bureaucrats*. The former, who are elected, define the objectives of government intervention. The latter, who are employees, translate the guidelines of the politicians into reality. For both politicians and bureaucrats an incentive problem arises.

On a stage no longer populated by amorphous 'actors' but rather by groups of individuals with specific features, it is natural that we also seek to characterise each category of policymaker. It is reasonable to think that each policymaker has specific values and interests and, in addition, interacts in different ways with the other social agents we have identified. In this section we will deal with politicians; in the next, bureaucrats.

---

[4] We refer to the fact that the conclusions reached in using game theory are often very sensitive to the particular hypotheses adopted to model the games.

The mid 1970s saw the formulation of the so-called political business cycle theory (Nordhaus, 1975, Lindbeck, 1976, MacRae, 1977, and others), which made specific reference to 'politicians', i.e., elected representatives responsible for public decisions.

Actually, the first formulation of a political business cycle theory was offered by Kalecki (1943),[5] who argued that it was impossible for a capitalist system to pursue full employment in the long run: the elimination of the business cycle with expansionary demand policies and the creation of a *welfare state*[6] would reduce worker discipline owing to the removal of the threat of unemployment. Inflation and restrictive policies would result, which would have thus given rise to a political business cycle.[7]

Nordhaus' political business cycle is not the secondary effect of policies with other goals (as it is in Kalecki and Robinson), but rather the result of the hypothesis that the decisions of politicians are an expression of their *own* preferences. In other words, Nordhaus' basic hypothesis is that politicians, like other people, can be characterised by their status and that they express preferences and interests accordingly. More precisely, the primary objective of politicians is to remain in office. They therefore attempt to steer the economy in such a way as to maximise the number of votes they can expect to receive.

Nordhaus' second hypothesis is that election results are significantly influenced by the current economic situation. In particular, he assumes that voters, as though affected by memory loss, give most weight to the performance of the economy in the period closest to the election and, by contrast, are short-sighted and unaware of the negative long-term consequences of the economic measures implemented during electoral periods.

A third hypothesis regards the government's ability to expand the economy using monetary and fiscal instruments in the short run, even if the expansion is not sustainable in the long run except at the cost of higher inflation. This may occur since the inflationary consequences of expansion are delayed, thus giving politicians scope to increase their popularity at election time.

Nordhaus' model can be shown in fairly simple terms with figure 9.1.

S_1, S_2, S_3 and S_4 are short-run Phillips curves, while LL is a long-run Phillips curve (not completely vertical);[8] curves marked P represent the social preference function, with those furthest from the origin being associated with lower levels of welfare.[9] The equilibrium point for the politician who acts in the long-term public interest is A (the point of tangency between the long-run Phillips curve and a social preference curve). Assume the system is at A. The politician will be induced to choose the initially more popular solution B_2, which is on the short-run Phillips curve that passes through A. This, however, is not a sustainable position, since such a Phillips curve, if price

---

[5] See also Robinson (1943).

[6] Both Kalecki's and Robinson's work emerged in relation to the preparation of the Beveridge Report, which set out the foundations of the welfare state.

[7] A similar sort of political business cycle was proposed by Glyn and Sutcliffe (1972).

[8] As with other economists, Nordhaus accepts the idea that the long-run Phillips curve is steeper than the short-run curve, but, unlike the monetarists, argues that it does not become vertical.

[9] They are in fact 'iso-vote' lines: each shows the combinations of inflation and unemployment that give rise to the same percentage of the vote for the incumbent. As we saw in chapter 3, voting can be considered as an indication of social preference.

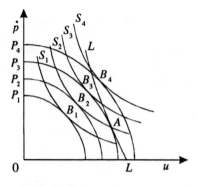

Figure 9.1

expectations are incorrect, will shift upwards to S_3, then to S_4 and so on.[10] This means that in a subsequent election, feasible points will be on social indifference curves further away from the origin, with consequently lower social welfare. As a result, long-run inflation in democratic countries is higher than the socially optimal level. An additional consequence is that unemployment tends to decline during election periods.

Some of the hypotheses adopted by Nordhaus are plausible:

(a) the idea that politicians attribute considerable (if not primary) importance to being re-elected;
(b) the dependence of voter 'mood' on the current economic situation.

Less convincing is the argument that politicians are always able to influence the short-run performance of the economy in the desired direction: for example, this is unlikely in a small country open to international trade in the midst of a global recession. Probably the strongest (implicit) hypothesis is that of the 'indistinct' politician seeking to orient equally 'indistinct' private agents. This hypothesis was discarded with the introduction of the *'partisan' politician* (from which the partisan theory of the political business cycle; see Hibbs, 1977, 1992; Madse, 1981; Alesina, 1987).

According to this theory each political party assigns different weights to different economic objectives for ideological reasons and/or because it represents different interests and social groups. With respect to a given situation different solutions will be proposed by the various parties, even if they share the same information. The alternation of parties in government therefore implies different economic policies and gives rise to a business cycle that, given its political origins, can again be called a 'political' business cycle.

Taking the United States as an example, suppose that the Democrats give greater weight to reducing unemployment than to reducing inflation (as in fact they do); the opposite holds for the Republicans. A change of party at the helm of government will lead to a change in the direction of economic policy: the replacement of a Republican

---

[10] The reader will note that moving from A to B_2 and B_3 gives rise to a business cycle triggered by the actions of politicians.

administration with a Democratic one will lead to an expansion of economic activity, a reduction in unemployment and an increase in inflation; the return of the Republicans would turn this trend around.

The cyclical behaviour of the economy is suboptimal, but inefficiency can be eliminated if the parties commit to a common cooperative policy rule, which would make both the social groups they represent better off in the long run. Even without binding commitments, the parties can improve the outcome of discretionary policies with actions that enable them to acquire a reputation (for example, for anti-inflationary rigour; see Alesina, 1987).

The range of applications of models that postulate some interaction between political dynamics and economic dynamics has broadened considerably in recent years. Rogoff and Sibert (1988) and others have sought to explain the apparent irrationality and suboptimality of voter behaviour in reaction to, for example, election period tax cuts that are then followed by fiscal tightening or inflation after the elections. According to these authors, such behaviour is entirely understandable in a situation of asymmetric information, where the government has a privileged position and seeks to signal the positive performance of the economy by means of tax cuts.

Long-run problems have also been tackled, such as the growth in public deficits,[11] which some attribute to a divergence between the preferences of current voters and those of future voters or to the uncertainty of electoral outcomes;[12] others explain it as a function of the characteristics of the electoral and political system.[13]

Finally, it has been suggested that competition between political parties not only leads to different economic policy proposals but also to different theories about the functioning of the economy. Such theories, which are usually attributed to the difference between the conservative and progressive ('liberal') visions, can emerge as a 'strategic' device to further the specific interests of different social groups or classes. For example, one can argue that the elasticity of the labour supply to the income tax rate is high (low)

---

[11] This is a different problem from the 'classic' problem of the rise in public expenditure, which has also been analysed by drawing on politics, sociology and the theory of organisation (theory of interest or pressure groups, theory of bureaucracy). A summary but complete survey is given by Mueller (1989, chapter 17).

[12] It is realistically assumed that the preferences of future voters are uncertain. This prevents current voters from knowing how public expenditure will be distributed in the future. They will then seek at least to direct current spending in their favour and thus to increase it, even if this gives rise to a budget deficit (Tabellini and Alesina, 1990).

Alesina and Tabellini (1990) argue that public debt can be used strategically by a government to influence the decisions of future governments, as there is no incentive to internalise the burden of debt service (for interest and repayment of principal), given the high level of uncertainty regarding the identity of the politicians that will be elected in the near future and differences in political orientation.

[13] Roubini and Sachs (1989) find a clear tendency towards larger deficits in countries with short-lived governments and large numbers of parties in governing coalitions. Similar results were obtained by Grilli, Masciandaro and Tabellini (1991). McCubbins (1991) explains the US public debt in the 1980s as the product of the government being divided between a Republican president and a Democratic majority in Congress ('cohabitation'): the vetoes of each side over the spending plans of the other were overcome only through compromise solutions and log-rolling, which resulted in an increase in the public debt.

simply in order to obtain the votes of those in favour of low (high) tax rates and a correspondingly low (high) level of government expenditure (Roemer, 1994b).

The available empirical evidence seems to give only partial support to the various political business cycle models, lending more weight to the 'partisan' version. In particular, there do not seem to be significant pre-electoral effects on economic variables of the sort predicted by Nordhaus (1975). Among other things, this may be the result of:

(a) the difficulty with which the government can influence economic variables, depending on external constraints;
(b) the fact that, contrary to the central hypothesis of the Nordhaus approach, politicians do not attempt to win voter favour with expansionary policies.

Empirical studies show that the second hypothesis does not hold, since there is some evidence of a *political budget cycle*, i.e., expansionary fiscal (and monetary) policies in the run-up to elections (Alesina, Cohen and Roubini, 1992).[14]

The evidence gathered so far must be carefully studied and assessed in the light of more satisfactory models of the interactions between politics and the economy that leave room for the special characteristics of individual countries. The conditions in which opportunistic fiscal and monetary measures by the government can take place need further analysis. On the one hand, if the government feels certain to win the elections, it will have no reason to implement such measures. On the other, the probability of winning will depend on a variety of factors, including the 'naiveté' or 'myopia' of voters, which differ across countries and over time.

In conclusion, we should note that stressing the existence of politicians' own objectives, or in any case objectives that differ according to social group or class, weakens the emphasis on public (rather than private) interest as the defining feature of the government and accentuates the importance of another of its attributes: the power of coercion (most recently, see Holcombe, 1994).

9.3 Agency problems: bureaucracy

The bureaucracy is composed of the (unelected) individuals who implement the measures decided by politicians. Here, too, tasks are delegated by someone to someone else and agency problems arise, as they do in the relationships between voters and politicians.

Various authors, including Tullock (1965), Downs (1967) and above all Niskanen (1971, 1975) have emphasised the fact that the behaviour of government officials can be

---

[14] One embarrassing result of Alesina, Cohen and Roubini appears to emerge in relation to the presence of a *monetary policy cycle* in Germany. The embarrassment is linked to the fact that the Bundesbank is almost unanimously considered to be the central bank with the greatest independence from political authority. However, expansionary monetary policies implemented before elections would seem to counter this view, showing that the Bundesbank has an interest in favouring the government in power. An explanation for this could be the presence of representatives of states (Länder) in the governing body of the Bundesbank. In any case this would undermine the idea that the Bundesbank is highly independent of the government.

explained if we assume that they seek to maximise their own utility. This behaviour can depend on a variety of factors, which certainly do not include only, or even mainly, the pursuit of the public interest. Rather, it includes the satisfaction of bureaucrats' personal aspirations for income, prestige, power, etc. According to Niskanen, many of these factors are linked to the size of the department, enterprise or agency in which the government officials work. The result is a bias in bureaucratic conduct towards increasing the size of government. This is made possible by the centralisation of bureaucratic functions and, therefore, the monopoly position of various departments with respect to both citizens (as suppliers of public goods and services) and politicians, who, in turn, have exclusive use of the departments themselves (*bilateral monopoly*). We know from economic theory that in this form of market the result (in our case the level of government activity)[15] depends on the bargaining power of the two parties and cannot be said a priori to be in favour of one or the other. Nevertheless, in reality the situation favours the bureaucrats, owing to the incompleteness of the information on administrative activity available to politicians. Thus, the tendency towards a steady expansion of the public sector is fuelled by the personal interests of bureaucrats in addition to those of the politicians (which we discussed earlier; see note 11 in this chapter).

Other authors have noted that bureaucracy tends to generate high costs owing to operational inefficiencies. This is largely attributable not only to the peculiarities of administrative work compared with normal productive activity, such as the relative scarcity of innovations,[16] but also to the difficulty of measuring results, the ambiguity of technologies and the multiplicity of objectives (which are typical characteristics of government activity). Moreover, government bureaucracy often places excessive emphasis on quality owing to the weight of the opinions of experts, who are not very interested in the production cost of the goods and services provided.

Although these analyses contain some elements of realism, they have also been criticised. In particular, it has been remarked that there is no positive correlation between the centralisation of departments and the growth of bureaucracy. Moreover, in the long run the possibility of creating multiple departments to carry out the same administrative work would undermine the situation of bilateral monopoly, replacing it with monopsony. Migué and Bélanger (1974) have argued, contrary to Niskanen's position, that there are elements of conflict (substitutability) between the size of a department and the personal interests of bureaucrats: an expansion of the supply of government goods and services reduces the resources available to pay bureaucrats' salaries. Efficiency would still be a problem, since the level of bureaucrats' pay could in a certain sense be too high, but this difficulty differs from that identified by Niskanen.

Apart from modifications of the emphasis placed on the various aspects of the

---

[15] In Niskanen's original contribution, the preference functions of politicians and bureaucrats differ: the former tend to maximise the difference between benefits (in terms of the budget's size) and the production costs of public services; the latter seek to maximise the size of the budget subject to the constraint of covering costs. The result is a tendency for bureaucrats to increase the size of the budget beyond the level of maximum satisfaction for politicians, where cost is equal to marginal benefit. For a simple presentation of Niskanen's model, see Mueller (1989, chapter 14).

[16] These are common to both private- and public-sector bureaucracies.

behaviour of government bureaucracy, the real problem lies in the differences in the analogous behaviour of private-sector bureaucracies. Certainly, empirical studies can contribute to identifying the existence and extent of the differences. However, studies conducted so far do not offer clear conclusions, although most indicate better results for the private sector (see, with different emphasis, Stiglitz, 1988, and Mueller, 1989). The feeling that government bureaucracy is inefficient is even more widespread than empirical results would suggest (Stiglitz, 1988).

Apart from differences in private-sector bureaucracies, in a policy perspective it is important to identify the fundamental problems that arise when one wants to improve the performance of government bureaucracies, which are the following:

(a) specifying individual tasks in a way that is consistent with the information handling abilities of each bureaucrat;
(b) ensuring that each bureaucrat conscientiously carries out the tasks assigned by politicians.

With regard to the second problem, the aims of politicians are to avoid *shirking*, the *corruption* of government employees by individuals who could benefit from the action of the bureaucrat[17] and the formation of *bureaucratic oligarchies* that favour the special preferences of government employees over those expressed through the democratic process. These goals can be achieved in two substantially different ways:

1 through the establishment of sufficiently rigid administrative procedures: once the interests to be safeguarded have been identified, the actions of bureaucrats to satisfy those interests are guided by specifying the procedures to be followed, including the publicity of certain acts, and sanctions (i.e., a 'negative' incentive) for deviation from the prescribed procedures;
2 through the introduction of explicit 'positive' incentives, such as incentives linked to 'output', reliance on competition between bureaucrats or on consumer action.

The choice between the two approaches to obtaining the desired behaviour depends on many factors, especially uncertainty about the reactions of bureaucrats, which can limit the scope for explicit positive incentives. Nevertheless, in general it is widely acknowledged that control of the bureaucracy forms part of the larger framework of agency problems and that first-best solutions, i.e., measures that guarantee perfect observance of the instructions of the principal without additional costs, do not exist.

More generally, the entire process of forming and implementing government decisions has been modelled in terms of agency relationships with the aid of game theory, and the most recent developments tend to identify a variety of 'ultimate' principals (for example, consumers and firms[18]) or 'second-order' principals (for example, the president and the legislature, in presidential systems). Spiller (1990) presents a game between consumers, industry, legislators and bureaucrats, in which consumers, thanks to their

---

[17] There is an extensive literature on this issue. For an original approach, see Franzini (1993).
[18] The partisan model of the political business cycle is also based on the idea of differentiated principals.

large number, tend to have greater influence over legislators, while industry influences bureaucracy by altering its system of incentives. Alt (1991) illustrates a different game in which the monetary authorities (the US Federal Reserve Board) are the 'agent' of three 'principals' (the President, Congress and the financial community).

Modelling agency relationships has served not only to analyse bureaucratic activity but also to suggest the most efficient solutions. This second line of research is still in its infancy but appears to promise interesting applications (Tirole, 1994; Martimort, 1996; Dixit, 1997).

9.4 Social groups, institutions and economic policy

Our analysis of the actual functioning of the government has revealed a decision process that differs from the ideal model presented by normative theory. We have seen that this process does not necessarily operate in the general interest but may instead serve the interests of politicians and bureaucrats (moral hazard). A more careful examination has revealed that politicians' and bureaucrats' actions can also reflect the interests of the largest or most powerful social groups. In any case, we must revise the view of government as an undifferentiated representative of the 'will of the people' (i.e., the preferences of citizens) that has underpinned much of the normative theory of economic policy.

Can we conclude that this theory is useless? There is no doubt that, as a normative theory, it retains its validity once we have postulated the desirability of government intervention. In some sense, the richer analysis of political economy that we have been discussing in this chapter tends to enhance that postulate, since this analysis shows that society is composed of groups of differing power: this may create a need for the government to intervene in order to prevent some distributive failure. The aspect of the classical theory of economic policy that seems to collapse here is the idea (which, in reality, only a few defend) that public action must and can tend towards a general improvement. Instead, we must accept the idea – which is much more consistent with the analysis of welfare economics[19] – that every public action has different effects on different social groups. For example, an employment policy has different effects from an anti-inflationary policy, not only on their explicit objectives (employment and inflation) but also on other objectives, especially income distribution in all of its many aspects. This fact is much clearer once we have diverse 'characters', i.e., different social groups, in our tale instead of undifferentiated individuals. In the end, the government is simply one of the institutions of a society and, while it reflects its history and the current economic and social structure, it tends either to sanction its preservation or shape its change.

This occurs under the impulse of the various social forces and in theory it is possible for all social groups to influence the formation and implementation of public choices through a system of controls and incentives for politicians and bureaucrats.

Depending on the degree of cohesion between social groups public policy will be more

---

[19] We have seen that no proposition about the desirability of a change can avoid value judgements, which represent ideals or interests.

or less inclusive. In other words, in a tightly knit society the social groups will act cooperatively and government policies will in fact be aimed at the public interest;[20] in a society with considerable conflict between its various groups, 'public' policies will be directed in favour of one or some groups in the struggle against others and every measure will be contested by one force or another.

The question we have to ask now is whether the government can be trusted as an instrument capable of implementing policies for efficiency and redistribution, or if it would be better to rely on markets and private institutions. The next section deals with this question.

9.5 Market and 'non-market' failures

The 1980s and early 1990s saw the emergence of widespread opposition to extensive government involvement in the economy in favour of a drastic reduction, or confinement with constitutional restraints, of its role. This shift was strongest in Great Britain and the United States, finding political expression with the election of Margaret Thatcher and Ronald Reagan. In practical terms, in these and other countries both the allocative and distributive functions of the government were reduced, sometimes drastically. In some cases, intervention has assumed new forms: for example, wider use has been made of instruments that mimic the market (such as the assignment of tradable rights, instead of taxes) or in any case require its presence (such as cash transfers instead of direct government provision of goods and services); public-sector enterprises have also been privatised and some of their functions have been entrusted to regulation.

The origins of free-market opinion movements are to be found both in the changes in the operation of the economy in the 1960s and in a number of influential theoretical contributions that in some cases were inspired by those changes. The poor performance of governments in some countries explains such movements further.

The main change in economic tendencies in the 1960s concerned the behaviour of economic agents, essentially as a consequence of the emergence of virtually full employment conditions in all the developed countries. The expectations-augmented Phillips curve conceived by Phelps and Friedman can be seen as an expression of those behavioural changes. The altered operation of the economy gave rise to problems that were difficult to manage with existing institutions and often led to frequent but ineffective government intervention.

An influential contribution that, unlike Phelps' and Friedman's, does not appear to have evolved in parallel with changes in economic reality but rather to have emerged autonomously, was made by Coase (1960).

In the view of some (Romani, 1984, pp. 30 ff.) another doctrinal contribution that

---

[20] This does not mean that *every* policy measure must necessarily be to everyone's benefit or provide for compensation for those harmed by the measure. Government action effectively aiming at the public interest can result in a multiplicity of measures, which in all likelihood will benefit the various social groups in turn, ensuring 'such a division of benefits that most persons in every part of the country would be better off by reason of the program as a whole' (Hotelling, 1938, p. 259).

played an important role in changing attitudes towards government involvement can be traced to the work of Simon. According to Romani, Simon (1976) shows the limitations of substantive (as opposed to procedural) rationality, thus reassessing positions such as Hayek's (see, for example, Hayek, 1945) that, within the framework of an evolutionary rather than Cartesian or Enlightenment approach, view the market as the most suitable institution for exploiting knowledge.[21] Without attempting to discuss the merits of such philosophical and epistemological problems,[22] it must be acknowledged that this approach has contributed (and in some cases rightly so) to the movement against government intervention.

A final cultural root of the free-market movement is the 'public choice' school, which attempts to apply economic methodology to the process of forming and implementing policy decisions, in particular introducing the assumption that all agents, including politicians and bureaucrats, pursue their own interests. As we have seen, this school underscores the inefficiency and injustice that can accompany government action as a consequence of this behavioural assumption.[23]

Waste, erroneous calculations, the abuses of politicians and bureaucrats, and the influence of sectional interests, together with the difficulty of reacting to new problems and to problems that we know about but which may appear in a different context are a frequent occurrence and justify a significant reform, if not reduction, of government intervention. From this point of view, the essential problem is whether these *non-market failures* (or *government* or *state failures*) can be assessed in the same way as market failures and, furthermore, whether they can be overcome or not.

In order to tackle the first question, it is important to note that market failures are largely posed at a very high level of abstraction and constitute a logical as well as an empirical problem (consider, for example, externalities, public goods, merit goods, inequalities, adverse selection, insufficiently flexible prices).

At a lower level of analysis there are problems associated with moral hazard that lead to both market and non-market failures. This incentive problem is typical of all hierarchical organisations, both private and public. From this point of view – and at this level of analysis – it might be appropriate to make use of the transaction costs approach in future analysis for choosing between alternative governance structures (Dixit, 1996).[24]

The existing literature underscores three points in comparing the importance of moral hazard in private and public institutions: (a) the measurability of targets; (b) the

---

[21] Romani (1984, p. 37) considers 'presumptuous the attitude of the economist, and social scientist in general, who, when faced with an economic policy problem, thinks that the only way to solve it is to be given the desired ends by the politicians and to discover the most appropriate means to achieve them with the help of his personal substantive rationality'.

[22] Salvati (1985, pp. 142–3) notes, for example, that an evolutionary approach should be used with caution in relation to human societies. Moreover, according to the advocates of this approach themselves, the outcomes of the evolutionary process are usually 'satisficing', not optimal, which leaves the door open for improvement through external intervention.

[23] Despite the many contributions to this issue, there is still no satisfactory unified theory of public sector failures, apart from the attempts of Wolf (1979, 1988) (see Le Grand, 1991).

[24] The meaning of transaction cost was explained in section 6.7.

extent and nature of agency situations; (c) the impact of complementary institutions in solving agency problems.

As to the first problem, it is usually argued that it is easier to monitor private managers because the target they are assigned, i.e., profit, is more easily measured than those assigned to policymakers. This not true in a strict sense, since there are many measurable success indicators of government economic action, ranging from the literacy rate and average life expectancy to the employment rate, etc. However, it is also true that the multiplicity of government targets could cause some monitoring difficulties even if all the targets were measurable, simply because of the many facets involved.

With regard to the second question, the incentive problem is in fact more severe with government action because of the existence of multiple agency situations involving the electorate, politicians and bureaucrats (those at different levels too: national, regional and local); in addition, there are often common agency relationships (e.g., politicians beholden to, or bureaucrats answerable to, multiple interest groups) (Dixit, 1996, 1997).

As to the impact of complementary institutions, it has often been asserted that incentive problems with private managers can be more easily solved because in addition to monitoring by (incumbent) owners, they are also subject to the discipline of the market, which may force the firm into bankruptcy or impose the replacement of the incumbent managers following a takeover, should the firm be poorly run. This point is not well-founded, however. There is, in fact, an extensive literature on the limits of supervision and control that can be exerted by the stock market. Singh (1971), for example, shows that takeovers can involve profitable concerns as well as badly managed or unprofitable firms (see also Scherer, 1980). Stiglitz (1991) argues that the wave of takeover activity in the 1980s benefited managers – who exploited confidential information to reap enormous gains – rather than shareholders. In contrast, Dore (1992) points out the considerable influence and control exercised not by 'anonymous' stock markets but by other organisations (universal banks) in economies like Japan and Germany. On the other hand, it must also be noted that effective monitoring of private managers depends on institutions that are conceived at the government level (e.g., trade law).

Summing up, moral hazard is a problem shared by both private and public governance structures. Not all the reasons for saying that the incentive problem is more acute for the latter are well founded, but two of them seem of particular importance: the larger number of layers where the agency problem arises and the multiplicity of goals and, therefore, success indicators for the government.

There are ways to tackle moral hazard in government action. Stiglitz suggests a number of reasons why public-sector enterprises can provide their managers with the same incentives as private enterprises with a broad shareholder base (Stiglitz, 1994, chapter 5). In the next chapter we examine some incentive mechanisms that have been suggested for public-sector enterprises.

The discretion of politicians and bureaucrats can be reduced by the introduction of appropriate rules. Some authors have suggested setting limits on budget deficits or making the central bank independent of the government, in both cases in order to limit inflationary impulses that might be imparted by politicians and bureaucrats. Such rules would also reduce the discretionary power of policymakers to counter unexpected negative shocks. Setting such rules involves a choice between different policy objectives. In principle, however, rules can be devised that reflect the values of anyone (or the majority of citizens).

The need for a formal rule arises when there is deep social division. Unwritten rules or customs, often formed over decades or centuries as a part of a spontaneous process or the result of patient education, can be suitable in more cohesive societies. In any case, policymaking must be seen as a dynamic process that seeks to develop rules and organisations to cope with various limitations on participants' information and actions (North, 1990; Dixit, 1996). In this respect effective policymaking requires the participation of citizens and social groups in political life and administrative activity. The cooperation that they can offer and the control they can exercise are indeed difficult to replace with written rules and are often at the root of unwritten ones.

9.6 The process of defining government intervention

In the following we assume that moral hazard problems in the public sector can be tackled with the same degree of success as in the private sector.

Our objective is to construct a normative theory of government intervention that takes account of the existing alternatives and the multiple effects it produces in a varied social environment. The following are the various stages of defining a programme of public action:[25]

1 *The origins of government action.* These are to be sought in politicians' awareness of the existence of a problem, either because of their own convictions or as a result of public debate or pressure from individuals and interest groups.

2 *Analysing the operation of other institutions.* The existence of a problem does not necessarily mean that government intervention is required. It can be justified on the basis of the following conditions:

(a) there is a failure of the market or other private institutions (e.g., private voluntary organisations or firms, although a broader definition of the market would include the latter);
(b) the government can obtain better results than other institutions in at least one respect (the result desired, e.g., employment; the cost of the intervention; or the different distributions of income generated by the various institutions), all other conditions being equal.

3 *The choice between alternative measures.* In many cases government intervention can make use of a variety of instruments, which have different costs and results that must be carefully evaluated and compared. This operation precedes the choice of whether to

[25] To a certain extent, we draw on Stiglitz (1988, chapter 9), generalising some of his arguments.

intervene or not: satisfying condition 2(b) above implies that the most desirable type of intervention has already been identified.

The choice of the type of measures must take account of the following elements:

(a) political and bureaucratic feasibility;[26]
(b) the reactions of the market and other institutions;
(c) the nature of the consequences, both microeconomic (the various types of efficiency, personal distribution of income, satisfaction of merit wants) and macroeconomic (employment, inflation, balance of payments, development, functional or regional distribution of income).

9.7 Summary

1 The 'normative' theory of economic policy is a 'theory of the public interest', which does not address the problem of the realism of its basic hypotheses or the behaviour of the public authorities that they imply.

2 In reality, the economic system is not composed of anonymous agents but rather of classes or groups of individuals with shared characteristics or needs. They organise themselves into interest groups, cartels, unions, political parties, etc., in order to ensure that their preferences prevail over those of other groups, as highlighted by the 'political economy' approach.

3 The category of 'policymakers' can in fact be divided into politicians and bureaucrats. Both are faced with agency (and therefore incentive) problems.

4 With specific reference to the actual behaviour of politicians, a number of theories have been proposed that seek to explain the existence of expansionary and restrictive phases (in relation to elections or the alternation of different parties in government) and the growth of government expenditure and public deficits in terms of asymmetric information.

5 The problems of government bureaucracy have also been dealt with in similar terms. They do not differ greatly from those arising with private-sector bureaucracies. Solutions to the problems of government bureaucracy may involve the introduction of explicit positive incentives, as in the private sector, or the establishment of compulsory procedures, including requiring that certain acts be public, with sanctions for those who do not comply.

6 The positive theory of economic policy rejects the idea that government action must and can tend towards a general improvement of everyone's position. It has contributed to inspiring political movements that have sought to underscore the failures of government action and, therefore, the need to reduce the influence of the government or change its style of intervention. These failures

---

[26] Kanbur and Myles (1992) argue for political constraints to be integrated into the policy formulation process rather than being faced at the implementation stage.

differ from most market failures, sharing only the problems arising from moral hazard, albeit in different form and to a different extent.

7. In constructing a normative theory of government intervention that takes account of the existing alternatives and the multiple effects of government action in a varied society, special attention must be paid to:
   (a) the interests involved and the reasons for government action, especially whether there is a market failure or not;
   (b) the superiority of the outcome of government intervention over the performance of other institutions;
   (c) the choice between different alternative programmes, with special regard to their feasibility and their expected outcomes.

9.8 Key concepts

Classical, normative theory of economic policy

Positive theory of economic policy

Citizens

Class

Interest group, lobby

Cartel

Political economy

Interest group theory, capture theory

Policymaker, politician, bureaucrat

Non-market (government) failure

Political business cycle

Welfare state

Iso-vote line

Partisan politician

Divided government ('cohabitation')

Political budget cycle

Monetary policy cycle

Takeover

(Political) feasibility

PART IV
MICROECONOMIC INTERVENTION

10 Microeconomic policies for efficiency

10.1 Targets, instruments and models

Microeconomic policy consists of measures to:

(a) ensure the existence and operation of markets when they are able to produce the desired optimum;
(b) correct the many inefficiencies of the actual operation of markets shown by microeconomic theory;
(c) ensure an equitable personal or household[1] distribution of wealth and guarantee the supply of merit goods.

Policies aimed at ensuring the existence and operation of markets (point (a)) represent the *minimal state*; or what the strongest advocates of the market feel are the (minimal) functions that should be performed by the government. We discuss this in section 10.2.

Corrective policies (point (b)) are used to compensate for the existence of externalities and public goods (even in a hypothetically perfect market), as well as for divergences in actual markets from the ideal model of perfect competition (in particular, those caused by economies of scale, collusive agreements and entry and exit barriers). We discuss these policies in sections 10.3–10.6.

Redistributive policies and those aimed at ensuring the provision of merit goods (point (c)) are examined in chapter 11.

The concepts underlying these policies are essentially those of welfare economics, discussed in chapters 5 and 6. The reference model, with all its merits and faults, is usually that of general equilibrium under perfect competition.[2]

---

[1] Personal or household distribution is the only type of income or wealth distribution that can be considered in taking account of equity in a microeconomic framework.
[2] The analytical instruments used are those of neoclassical economics. Only recently has the problem of market failure, especially with regard to public goods, begun to be analysed within the framework of other economic paradigms. See Parrinello (1993).

In chapter 8 we said that an analytical model normally contains variables that in a decision model serve as targets and others that serve as instruments. Instrumental variables have often been used in analytical models to represent the behaviour of an agent, the government, considered essential to understanding the functioning of the economic system.[3] This can be done within the framework of both macroeconomic and microeconomic policies.

Nevertheless, the reference model for microeconomic policies – which represents market equilibrium – is frequently not designed to reflect government action.[4] It must therefore be adapted by introducing additional variables (for example, regarding taxes and subsidies) or even new relations that were not initially contemplated, or by introducing *ad hoc* interpretations of existing relations.

In some cases the reference model, although belonging to the neoclassical tradition, is of a partial equilibrium kind as it describes the equilibrium for a single market or even for a single firm, such as when we consider government intervention in relation to positions of market dominance.

10.2 Making the market work: the minimal state

The need for government intervention is often a source of disagreement among economists, not so much because the existence of market failures is denied but rather because of the possibility that government intervention might also fail, albeit for different reasons. There is, however, one area of government action that excites practically no controversy because it is considered necessary for civil society and even the very existence of the market itself.[5] Nozick (1974) argues that what he calls the minimal state is morally legitimate, but that no more extensive state could be morally justified.

In this view, the minimal duties of government are assigning rights, protecting against force, theft and fraud, and enforcing contracts and rights. These are essential conditions for the existence and proper functioning of the market itself, for a variety of reasons. First, assigning rights (legislative activity), especially property rights, is the very foundation of the market. The way rights are assigned will also produce different results in terms of distribution and efficiency.[6] However, the mere assignment of abstract rights is

---

[3] Obviously, an analytical model can only *assume* a given government behaviour. However, alternative assumptions are possible, i.e., we can postulate parametrical variations in the behaviour of the government (e.g., in tax rates). By contrast, a decision model must *determine* the optimal behaviour of the government.

[4] The reasons for this are to be sought in the evolution of economic thought: microeconomic models, especially the general equilibrium model, have long tended to show the virtues of the market in its purest form, automatically excluding any consideration of external intervention. By contrast, macroeconomic models, which were developed (essentially within the framework of Keynesian analysis) precisely to show that the performance of a market economy could be improved by government intervention, had to be formulated in a way that explicitly considered variables representing government action.

[5] Certainly, the specific content of government action – e.g., the type of laws enacted – will differ in relation to the extent of the market; nevertheless, the performance of the functions that we will shortly list is in any case necessary.

[6] Recall Coase's theorem (see section 6.4).

not sufficient. Respect for rights must also be guaranteed. This requires that the same authority that assigns rights must take responsibility for interpreting them in relation to real-world situations (judicial activity) and ensuring that holders of rights are protected from others within or without the community who might threaten their enjoyment of such rights (police action).

Performing these functions requires the attribution of other subsidiary functions. For example, since legislation, justice and protection all involve expenditure, citizens must make some form of financial contribution, normally through taxation. We deal with taxation in the next chapter.

10.3 Externalities and public policies

We said that externalities create an inequality between private and social cost (or product), if we are dealing with production externalities, or between marginal private and social utility in the case of consumption externalities. These divergences cause inefficiencies that can be eliminated by removing the divergences themselves, i.e., by internalising the social cost or benefit with the originating agent.

This can be accomplished in a number of ways. In particular, we can:

1 tax (subsidise) activities that give rise to external diseconomies (economies);
2 provide incentives to eliminate external diseconomies;
3 introduce tradable rights (permits) to create external diseconomies;
4 regulate the behaviour of economic agents.

We will deal with these in order, referring primarily to external diseconomies. However, much of our discussion holds equally well for external economies (with the appropriate adaptations, i.e., subsidies instead of taxes, etc.).

10.3.1 Taxation

It is intuitively clear that if a productive activity creates external diseconomies (economies), the difference between marginal private cost (benefit) and marginal social cost (benefit) can be removed by introducing a positive (negative) tax.[7] Thus, in the case of an external diseconomy if a tax equal to the value of the externality were added to the original marginal private cost, the firm would bear a new, higher marginal private cost equal to the marginal social cost, and would be induced to take its production decisions in relation to the latter. If the taxes are set as a fixed amount per unit of product, a tax a would be added to the marginal private cost, MC, of firm i generating the externality. The firm would then set output where $MC + a = p$, with p being the price of the good.

Referring to figure 10.1, let us now imagine a monopolistic firm that generates

---

[7] In the case of a diseconomy, we have a true tax; a 'negative tax' is a subsidy. These taxes are called Pigovian taxes.

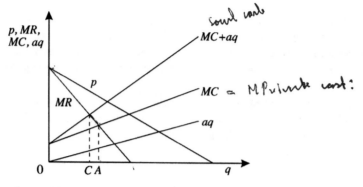

Figure 10.1

external diseconomies of *aq per additional unit of product.*[8] Without government intervention, the firm would produce $0A$. If the externality were internalised by imposing a tax of $a \cdot q$ per additional unit, marginal private cost (including the tax) would equal marginal social cost and output would decline to $0C$.[9] If a firm generating an external economy is subsidised, it will raise its output. The reader is invited to present this in diagram form.[10]

10.3.2 Incentives for eliminating external diseconomies

Now look at figure 10.2, which is simply figure 10.1 with a number of additions. The firm produces $0A$, whereas the socially efficient level is $0C$. Rather than setting a tax of $a \cdot q$ per additional unit of output, it would be possible to induce the firm to produce the socially efficient level by granting it a subsidy, equal to DE (which is the value of the diseconomy at the social optimum) for each unit of output reduction below $0A$. The marginal cost of production for the firm would therefore rise by DE for each unit of output. If the firm continued to produce $0A$, its cost would be AB, equal to the effective cost of production plus DE, which is the subsidy forgone by continuing to produce at the previous level. The same can be said for each lower level of output. The marginal private cost curve is therefore PMC with a fixed subsidy equal to DE for the reduction in output. The result is the same as that obtained with a tax per unit of output: the firm will position itself at D and produce $0C$.

Note that the incentive to reduce output is different from the incentive to use plant, materials and so on in such a way as to reduce substantially the external diseconomy. Suppose the diseconomy is pollution. It is true that using cleaner technology, made

---

[8] More simply, the diseconomy could be fixed, equal to *a* for each unit of product, as in the previous example. We have chosen this other hypothesis to elucidate a number of differences between various policies for correcting externalities.

[9] The reader can imagine situations in which the externality increases more or less than proportionally with respect to output and, correspondingly, the unit tax varies with the variation in output.

[10] Pigovian taxes or subsidies could be extended to consumers if they were to generate externalities.

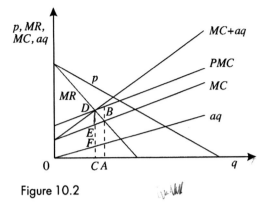

Figure 10.2

possible by the subsidy, would reduce the external diseconomy. However, output would still be greater than the socially efficient level because the firm has its production cost reduced by the subsidy. The firm uses the pollution-reducing technology but will keep output above the socially efficient level, i.e., where marginal social cost equals price (see Stiglitz, 1988).

10.3.3 Tradable permits to produce diseconomies

Tradable discharge permits were first introduced in the 1980s as a response to pollution. They work as follows. The 'optimal' level of the external diseconomies created by different industries in a given environment is first determined. For each industry, this corresponds to the level of output $0C$ in figure 10.1. 'Pollution rights' are then assigned (for example, by auction) up to the established level. All firms (as well as conservationists) can participate in the auction. They can use the rights themselves or can stop polluting (if an appropriate technology becomes available) and sell their pollution permits to others.[11] Firms will pay a maximum price equal to the value of the right, which is the value of pollution that corresponds to output $0C$, i.e., DE (or CF). The firms' marginal cost curve will therefore rise by DE, as in the case of the subsidy for reducing output (see figure 10.2), and each firm will produce $0C$.

One effect of a system of pollution rights – like taxes – may be to stimulate investment in pollution abatement technology, since under this system pollution is costly. Another shared advantage of tradable rights and taxes over subsidies is that they are a source of revenue for the government. The magnitude of the effect on the level of pollution is more predictable with rights than with taxes, since in the former case the level is specifically predetermined rather than estimated, as in the case of taxes.[12]

---

[11] For details, see Dales (1968).
[12] Taxation acts on the price imputed to the external diseconomy, leaving it to the firm to decide the quantity. With the pollution right system, however, the level of the diseconomy is set and the market fixes its price. Obviously, this holds if the administrative apparatus used to set and monitor pollution levels is efficient.

10.3.4 Regulation

An alternative to taxes is regulation, a direct control measure that normally imposes certain obligations or prohibitions on economic agents: for example, requiring firms to use pollution abatement equipment or certain production methods, or forcing home-owners to keep the sidewalk in front of their house clear of snow, etc. As we will see, regulation can be aimed at eliminating external diseconomies (the most frequent case) or creating external economies.[13]

The results of regulation can differ from those produced by taxation. They are not greatly different in static terms, since they are aimed at eliminating external diseconomies and, therefore, increasing efficiency. In fact, the results are quite similar if the same information is available for the two policy options and administrative costs are assumed to be the same.

In reality, however, information is always incomplete and any policy measure will be ineffective if founded on inaccurate data or erroneous calculations. Nevertheless, regulation and pollution permits seem preferable to taxes and subsidies for pollution abatement if the reaction of firms is uncertain. Administrative costs are probably lower for (uniform) regulation than for taxes (or subsidies) and permits.

A 'dynamic' advantage of taxes and tradable rights is that all firms have an incentive to reduce pollution in order to reduce the costs associated with taxes or the purchase of rights. In the case of regulation, the incentive exists only for those firms that are not in compliance with the established standards when they are introduced. The measures also have different effects on the distribution of income. For firms, regulation is less costly than taxation. If subsidies for reducing output or for investing in pollution abatement techniques are used instead of taxes or pollution permits, the cost to the firm is reduced even further.

The range of applications of the various policy instruments for increasing allocative efficiency in the presence of externalities is extremely varied. In the United States, a core of legislative measures (for example, the Clean Air Act from the early 1970s) has been supplemented with a system of pollution permits created by the Environmental Protection Agency to ensure that the standards are reached. The proposal to introduce a carbon tax, advanced by the European Union in 1991 as a tool for countering the greenhouse effect, met with fierce opposition from the United States and Japan, as well as industry.[14]

The problem of protecting transnational commons is of special importance. It requires the international coordination of individual country policies and the creation of suitable institutions, which can be of the same type as those operating at the national level (pollution permits, regulatory agencies, etc.). We will deal with the problems encountered in coordinating national policies in more detail later (see chapter 19).

---

[13] We will see later that regulation can also be used for other purposes. The objectives, techniques and substitutes for regulation are considered in Waterson (1988), Spulber (1989) and Kay and Vickers (1990), among others. An interesting reformulation of the 'capture' theory of government decision-making – with specific applications to regulation – is given by Laffont and Tirole (1991).

[14] On the effects of this tax see Carraro and Siniscalco (1993).

However, we can say now that the difficulties of coordinating environmental policies can be reduced or eliminated if countries negotiate not only in terms of pollution levels but also use some other instrument (e.g., trade policy, foreign debt, development aid) to induce other countries to cooperate.

The reasoning shown in diagram form above can be presented in more formal terms with a simple decision model in which the policy objective is production efficiency and the analytical model captures the aspects of the operation of the economy most relevant to our discussion here (a producer creating external diseconomies and another producer harmed by the diseconomies are taken into account). The model is given in the next section.

*10.4 A decision model for production efficiency with externalities

Let there be two price-taking firms, 1 and 2, in two different industries with the first firm creating a diseconomy for the second. The harm to firm 2 is a direct function of the output of firm 1. Let the output of firm 1 and firm 2 be q_1 and q_2, respectively; prices in the two industries are p_1 and p_2 and total costs are $c_1 = c_1(q_1)$ and $c_2 = c_2(q_1, q_2)$, with all derivatives positive.

We wish to maximise the total profits of the two firms, Π, by choosing output appropriately. The problem is therefore:

$$\max_{q_1, q_2} \Pi = [\Pi_1 + \Pi_2]$$

subject to

$$\Pi_1 = p_1 q_1 - c_1(q_1)$$
$$\Pi_2 = p_2 q_2 - c_2(q_1, q_2)$$

The first order conditions are:

$$\partial \Pi / \partial q_1 = p_1 - dc_1/dq_1 - \partial c_2/\partial q_1 = 0 \qquad (10.1)$$

or

$$p_1 = dc_1/dq_1 + \partial c_2/\partial q_1 \text{ and} \qquad (10.1')$$

$$\partial \Pi / \partial q_2 = p_2 - \partial c_2/\partial q_2 = 0 \qquad (10.2)$$

Equation 10.2 gives the equality of price and marginal cost for firm 2. However, the efficiency condition for firm 1 requires that price be higher than marginal cost, since we have assumed that $\partial c_2/\partial q_1$ is positive because firm 1 creates a negative externality. Firm 1 must therefore set output below the level where price equals marginal cost if, as we have assumed, marginal cost is increasing. In other words, efficiency requires that output be less than the optimal level with no externalities.

Since firm 1 has no incentive to reduce output on its own, government intervention is needed to obtain an efficient solution by:

(a) levying a tax equal to $\partial c_2/\partial q_1$ for each additional unit of output;
(b) introducing a subsidy equal to $\partial c_2/\partial q_1$[15] for each unit of foregone output below the level that would have been produced in the absence of government intervention;
(c) auctioning rights to produce the externality, for which the firm will be willing to pay up to $\partial c_2/\partial q_1$ in correspondence with the socially efficient point q_1^*; or
(d) prohibiting the creation of external diseconomies above a certain level. Suppose, for example, we are dealing with pollution. Setting a limit on the quantity of pollution is the same as introducing a constraint such that $q_1 \leq q_1^*$ in the short run. In the long run, the effects of introducing a limit on pollution levels can be examined in terms of a decision problem for firm 1 between alternative production processes that generate different amounts of pollution, subject to the constraint that the level generated is less than, or equal to, that laid down by the regulation.

*10.5 Public goods and their financing

The problem of supplying a public good is threefold and involves:

(a) determining the socially efficient amount of the good;
(b) financing the good;
(c) producing the good.

The first two aspects are closely linked. In fact, the reason for determining the socially efficient amount of the good (which is not done by the market) is that private agents are reluctant to finance it, preferring to engage in free riding behaviour. The third aspect can be dealt with separately. Let us begin by examining the first two problems.

According to Wicksell (1896) and Lindahl (1919) both the problem of the optimal quantity of public goods and that of financing the related expenditure can be solved on the basis of the individual preferences expressed by consumers for the goods themselves. We can ask each individual to indicate his demand for the public good at some hypothetical price, or with regard to some distribution of the taxes needed to meet the cost of supplying the good. If the value (equal to the cost) of the public good is G and the share of financing borne by individual i is t_i, we have $\sum_i t_i = 1$; t_i can be thought of as a 'personalised' price for the public good. Suppose $i = 1, 2$. In order to find the level G of the public good common to both individuals,[16] we construct their demand curves for the good (figure 10.3).

---

[15] If the subsidy is a fixed amount per unit, $\partial c_2/\partial q_1$ must be calculated at the point of social efficiency, q_1^*.

[16] The amount of the public good provided must be the same for both since both can consume the entire value of the good. According to Wicksell and Lindahl, the joint indication of the value of the public good associated with the willingness to pay would ensure that there is no free riding.

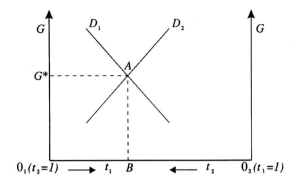

Figure 10.3

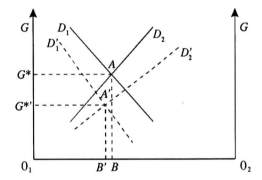

Figure 10.4

The origin of the axes for person 2 is at $t_1 = 1$, where his share of cost G is $t_2 = 1 - t_1 = 0$. At point A both individuals demand the same quantity, G^*, of the public good, with person 1 being willing to pay $0_1 B$ and person 2 being willing to pay $0_2 B$. Point A (*Lindahl equilibrium*) is Pareto efficient, since both demand curves (along which the maximisation conditions for both consumers are satisfied) pass through it.

The problem with the Lindahl equilibrium is that it assumes that the consumers consider the 'personalised' prices as parameters that are independent of their declared preferences. This is entirely unrealistic, since each consumer will have an incentive to shift the costs of supplying the public good on to the other by declaring a lower demand for the public good at each price. Consequently, the quantity demanded will be underestimated and output will be too low (if the good is produced at all). This is shown in figure 10.4, where D_1 and D_2 are the 'true' demand curves and D'_1 and D'_2 are those expressed for strategic reasons (i.e., to avoid paying the cost of the public good) by free riding consumers.

It is important to understand that when the consumer demands a certain quantity of the public good at a given price, this very act creates a positive externality, precisely because the good he is paying for is a public good. This is what induces him to demand less than the socially efficient amount. However, the problem can be avoided if the externality is internalised by paying each consumer a 'premium' equal to the value of the positive externality declared by other consumers.[17] The individual is thereby induced to act on the basis of social criteria, i.e., to choose the amount of the public good so as to maximise the social objective. With this system of incentives (known as the *Clarke–Groves mechanism*) we could in principle induce each consumer to reveal his preferences accurately. There are, however, considerable implementation problems (Inman, 1987, pp. 699–700).

We can determine the amount of the public good to produce and, at the same time, the division of the related cost with other mechanisms, such as voting. However, each raises some kind of difficulty (see Cornes and Sandler, 1986, part III).

In practice, the methods used to measure demand for public goods make use of both market and non-market data. With the former, we gain indirect information on individuals' willingness to pay for the public good or its close substitutes (e.g., spending on trips to less polluted areas). Methods based on non-market data make use of interviews or experiments. Needless to say, we cannot insist on scientific precision with such methods, but we can obtain responses that provide reasonable approximations of the optimal amount of the public good. Once output has been determined, some government body will provide for its financing using funds from its budget and/or specific contributions from private consumers.

The third aspect of the problem of public goods regards the actual production of the good. The fact that the government must take responsibility for determining the optimal level of output and financing production does not mean that it must also produce the good itself. There may be reasons why the private sector can produce the good more efficiently: once the problems of financing and optimal output have been solved, the problem of production can be tackled separately.[18] Since some of the discussion of public-sector firms in the next section is relevant to this issue, we will postpone our analysis until then.

10.6 Market power, regulation and public enterprises

10.6.1 Increasing potential and effective competition

The existence of monopoly or oligopoly raises numerous questions regarding the orientation of public policy. As we saw in chapter 6, such market situations give rise to (static) allocative inefficiency. However, some argue (like Schumpeter, 1943) that situations of economic concentration generate better performance from a dynamic point of

[17] In reality, each consumer would pay a price equal to the 'value' of the public good minus the 'premium' received, which would equal the positive externality of the good declared by others. The 'value' of the good is defined as the sum of the values declared by consumers for the least preferred alternative public good. A very clear example of the way this preference revelation mechanism works is given in Mueller (1989, pp. 124–5).

[18] However, bear in mind that if the value of the public good has been set equal to its cost, the problem of production should be solved *before* determining the optimal level of output, which depends on its value and, therefore, its cost.

view.[19] According to Schumpeter, a powerful stimulus to innovation, and therefore growth, comes, on the one hand, from the prospect of reaping the extra monopoly profits expected from innovation and, on the other, from the more abundant resources generated by such extra profits. By contrast, others have argued that the stimulus to innovation could come from the pressure of competition on a firm (Cyert and March, 1963). However, since the empirical evidence is contradictory (see, for example, Scherer, 1980 and Martin, 1993) we must suspend judgement about the general effects of monopoly on *dynamic efficiency* and assess the specific circumstances that can influence the outcome in individual cases. In general, therefore, we limit our discussion to examining static allocative efficiency.

What chance is there of obtaining greater *potential* or *effective competition* in monopolistic or oligopolistic situations? Let us first consider potential competition. As we said in chapter 6, increasing contestability (greater potential competition) certainly contributes to increasing the efficiency of the market (although not necessarily its allocative efficiency) and can be achieved by removing government barriers to entry and exit[20] (when they are not sufficiently justified for other reasons, such as the need to ensure specific skill levels, health requirements, etc.) and by controlling the strategic behaviour of firms, which can be accomplished through regulation. Nevertheless, contestability will never be perfect simply because some entry and exit barriers cannot be eliminated. As we mentioned earlier, these are associated with sunk costs, which make it impossible for potential competitors to 'hit and run'.

We might also argue that the government should or must seek to create *effective competition* in addition to or in place of potential competition. Let us consider two measures that can be used for this purpose.

First, assume that the production and demand conditions are those shown in figure 6.2. Without government intervention there would be only one firm, with unit costs equal to $0P$. Let us now assume that the government compels the monopoly to split itself into a number of smaller firms, as was done with ATT in the United States in 1982. In the place of the single monopolist we now have a number of independent firms, which could create effective competition between them.[21] This would both reduce firms' ability to

---

[19] *Economic concentration* measures the degree of dispersion of production (or capital, workers or other variables) among the various firms in an industry. *Financial concentration* measures the degree of dispersion of these variables among financial groups in the economy as a whole. A financial group is a group of firms linked by equity interests. *Technical concentration* refers to the degree of dispersion of production (or other variable) among productive units (or establishments) in an industry. Since some firms (especially larger firms) have more than one establishment, technical concentration tends to be less than economic concentration (and the dispersion of productive units greater than that of firms).

[20] This can also include the liberalisation of foreign trade and capital movements. However, the long-run outcome of liberalisation is not necessarily greater (effective) competition but rather, in some circumstances at least, less competition.

[21] In fact, in the ATT case, competition is low and is limited to long-distance telephony since the so-called Baby Bells operate in different regions. However, it was thought that independent local telephone companies in a separate segment of the industry would reduce the incentive to favour one long-distance carrier over another.

exploit market power and increase their internal efficiency. However, each of the new companies would produce some fraction of $0Q$ at a unit cost higher than $0P$, with the additional cost rising as the number of firms increases. Since the rise in unit costs is virtually certain (thus generating production inefficiency), this alternative cannot be considered except in cases where the economies of scale are not very strong compared with the extent of the market, or for those specific production tasks in which there are no appreciable economies of scale.

The second possibility for increasing effective competition even in the presence of scale economies consists in auctioning the right of access to the market ('*competition for the market*' or '*competition for monopoly*'). The underlying reasoning is as follows. Although producing at the minimum average cost compatible with demand in the presence of scale economies implies the existence of a single firm, the monopoly profits generated by this firm could be appropriated by the government by auctioning the right to produce the good to potential market entrants (a form of *franchising* suggested by Demsetz, 1968).[22] In some cases this mechanism would achieve efficiency without placing an undue burden on the regulatory authorities. However, the characteristics of most industries are such that competition for monopoly cannot work, for many reasons. We mention two:

(a) there is a risk that the participants in the auction might collude; the risk increases as the number of firms in the auction decreases;

(b) it is possible that one firm has a strategic advantage over the others. For example, a firm might already have experience in the field; knowledge thus acquired would allow it to offer a higher price, perhaps even dissuading others from competing for the franchise (in greater detail, see Vickers and Yarrow, 1988, pp. 111 ff.). Such conditions are highly likely in industries with large static and dynamic (learning) economies of scale.

We can therefore conclude that the scope for increasing potential competition is limited by the existence of irremovable entry and exit barriers. Strengthening effective competition is also difficult to achieve, owing to the impracticability of auctions aimed at appropriating monopoly profits, and may not necessarily be desirable, since it means giving up the low costs tied to scale economies.

Rather than aiming at the impossible, ineffective or damaging goal of increasing potential or effective competition, anti-monopoly policy could instead seek to ensure that the market power associated with scale economies and entry and exit barriers (or

---

[22] The price set by the monopolist would still be higher than marginal cost, meaning that the conditions of allocative efficiency are not met. The auction would only allow the appropriation of the monopolist's surplus profit. There is, however, an alternative approach to the auction that would both secure allocative efficiency and appropriate the monopoly profit. First, regulation can be used to force the firm to set its price equal to marginal cost. This would give rise to a loss, since in a natural monopoly marginal cost is lower than average cost, but the loss could be offset by the government with a subsidy. An auction could then be used to ensure that the subsidy is not excessive: the right to produce the good in a natural monopoly – but with price equal to marginal cost – would be assigned to the firm bidding the lowest subsidy.

any other factor)[23] is not exploited. The instruments available are essentially the following:

(a) regulation of private-sector monopolies, which can take the form of:
   antitrust legislation;
   price controls;
(b) public enterprises.

We examine these alternatives in the three following subsections.

10.6.2 Antitrust legislation

Regulating the market power of private-sector firms[24] with *antitrust* (or *anti-monopoly*) *legislation* has at least three objectives:

(a) safeguarding economic liberty, especially that of small firms to enter the market and survive, thus allowing the exercise of free enterprise;
(b) controlling the economic and political power associated with economic concentrations, which may be used in a variety of ways to jeopardise economic and political democracy;
(c) increasing allocative efficiency.

We will pay particular attention to the latter objective. We know that the allocative inefficiency of a particular market structure is caused by:

1 agreements to limit competition (collusive price fixing, market quotas, etc.);[25]
2 abuse of a dominant position (setting low purchase prices or high selling prices, price discrimination, adoption of strategic barriers to entry);
3 mergers or takeovers that adversely affect potential and effective competition.

These practices either pave the way for creating 'monopolistic' conditions (the practices mentioned under points 1 and 3) or represent the exploitation of such conditions (point 2). Some argue that firms can use these practices to obtain increases in production efficiency (through static and dynamic scale economies) that offset the loss of allocative efficiency. Obviously, this argument does not exclude the need for antitrust legislation, partly because greater allocative efficiency could itself give rise to greater production efficiency (by means of 'χ'-efficiency). However, it does strengthen the argument for examining the effects of these practices on a case-by-case basis.

The antitrust legislation introduced since the end of the last century, beginning with the Sherman Act of 1890 in the United States, forbids conduct aimed at restraining trade or creating a monopoly. In some cases, as with the Sherman Act, the legislation has had little to do with economic efficiency, being passed mainly to control the economic and political power of concentrations.

---

[23] The presence of many firms in an industry does not guarantee competitive results; for example, the firms could still collude to raise their price.
[24] This can also be applied to public enterprises if for some reason it is feared they will imitate private sector firms.
[25] Small- and medium-sized firms can also enter into collusive agreements.

The US legislation makes illegal 'every contract, combination in the form of trust or otherwise, or conspiracy in restraint of trade', as well as monopoly secured by any other means. The federal government is empowered to enforce the legislation and violation of its terms is a misdemeanour offence. Determining the meaning of terms such as 'restraint of trade' and 'monopoly' has been left to the courts, which have changed their interpretation over time.

Nearly all other anti-monopoly legislations around the world have been modelled on the Sherman Act, but some significant differences are worth noting. Article 85 of the Treaty establishing the European Community (since 1 November 1993, the European Union, EU) declares void any agreements that undermine competition within the common market, but allows those aimed at promoting technical progress or improving the production and distribution of goods. Article 86 prohibits any abuse of dominant positions that affects trade between member states. According to Council Regulation of 21 December 1989, mergers and acquisitions that create or strengthen a dominant position giving rise to significant barriers to effective competition in the common market are incompatible with the common market.[26] Ascertaining the illegality of sanctionable acts is the responsibility of the European Commission.

The laws of individual member states normally complement EU legislation, fully accepting its underlying principles. This is especially true in the case of Germany and Italy. It is less so for France and the United Kingdom, whose basic position is that competition is essentially neutral, with either positive or negative effects according to the circumstances. The main difference between EU rules and French law regards the control of concentrations, with France placing considerable emphasis on what it perceives as a need to strengthen its national productive system. The United Kingdom also gives weight to forms of efficiency other than allocative efficiency. The differences between the criteria adopted in these countries and those at the EU level have, then, a number of foundations, ranging from the pre-eminent role assigned to non-allocative efficiency (and the partial acceptance of the Schumpeterian argument regarding the advantages of monopoly) to only partly economic considerations (the need for 'national champions' to ensure the independence of the economy from the domination of foreign capital).

Obviously, in the case of a conflict EU rules prevail over national legislation. However, EU legislation and national legislation have some relatively distinct and non-conflicting areas of application, leaving room for laws based on different criteria. In fact, European rules only prohibit restrictive agreements and abuses of dominant positions that affect trade between member states, which excludes almost all such practices in the services sector and many in agriculture and industry. Moreover, the existence of a minimum threshold for economic concentrations to be considered at the European level introduces an even sharper separation between the two spheres than the rules governing collusive agreements and dominant positions.

---

[26] Only mergers and acquisitions involving firms with a minimum threshold turnover are regulated by the EU.

10.6.3 Price controls

Price controls are another form of regulation (and are therefore a direct control measure). They involve setting *maximum* or *minimum prices*, depending on the objective. If the aim is to guarantee a given income to the supplier of a good or service, the government will set a minimum price.[27] For anti-monopoly purposes, a maximum selling price will be set.[28] Price controls are an instrument (which is not alternative to anti-monopoly legislation or public enterprises) for increasing allocative efficiency (and/or 'χ' efficiency and, in some cases, dynamic efficiency).

Direct[29] control of prices can be accomplished in a number of ways. The main techniques are the following:

1 establishing a maximum profit margin;
2 fixing a rate of return (profit) on invested capital;
3 setting a maximum price (price cap).

1 The first technique involves setting a maximum percentage of profit over unit costs. This should restrain prices and, therefore, the exploitation of market power. However, since the regulatory authorities do not control unit costs, they do not actually control prices. In fact, the regulated firm will have an incentive to let unit costs rise, thus earning a larger total profit, given the margin fixed by the regulator.

2 Given capital and costs, fixing a limit on the rate of return on capital will determine the maximum unit price and thereby ensure allocative efficiency. However, the regulated firm will have an incentive to choose capital intensive techniques rather than the technique that ensures production efficiency as a way to increase total profits (the *Averch–Johnson effect*; see Averch and Johnson, 1962).

3 Given costs, setting a *price cap* implies a certain profit margin for each level of demand and, given capital and demand, a certain rate of return or profit. With this technique, the regulator aims to induce the firm to seek allocative efficiency (since the maximum price is fixed) and static and dynamic internal efficiency (since, given the price, the firm has an incentive to reduce costs). A dynamic version of this price control mechanism is the *RPI − X method*, where RPI is the annual rate of change in the retail price index and X is a percentage decided by the regulator. If, for example, annual inflation is 5 per cent

---

[27] Price controls are often used for this purpose in agriculture. The EU's Common Agricultural Policy still guarantees minimum prices to support farm incomes (although the level was reduced in a 1992 reform).

[28] Fixing maximum prices can also serve a macroeconomic purpose, such as ensuring price stability. We discuss this in chapter 15.

[29] Indirect control can be exerted by imposing a tax whose amount is inversely related to the volume of output. This raises allocative efficiency by encouraging the firm to increase production, which will lower the price for a given demand curve. Alternatively, the government could grant a subsidy directly linked to the level of output. The subsidy could be financed by auctioning the right to produce the good (the franchising mechanism we spoke of earlier).

and X is set at 3 per cent, the price set by the regulated firm[30] can increase by a maximum of 2 per cent per year. This means that the price of the regulated good must decline by 3 per cent annually in real terms, which the firm can accomplish by increasing productivity (the reason the formula was introduced). Given the level of costs that can be reached by increasing productivity, the regulator implicitly fixes a rate of return or profit in setting the size of X. Nevertheless, the regulated firm may still have an incentive to let costs rise in order to induce the authority to lower the value of X.

As a direct control measure, price regulation is potentially very effective. It is certainly effective in the short run in emergency situations if the administrative apparatus is efficient enough to ensure that it is implemented properly. In the longer run, its effectiveness greatly depends on solving a number of information problems. Let us see why.

The objective of regulating a private firm is to constrain its behaviour in some way (in our case, limiting the firm's ability to set prices) while allowing it to stay in business in the long run. To achieve this, the firm must be able to cover all its costs and earn a minimum rate of profit sufficient to ensure survival and, possibly, growth,[31] whatever price control method is used. On the other hand, the rate of profit must not be too high, since this would undermine the purpose of regulation. Regulation with price controls must therefore pass between the twin perils of Scylla and Charybdis: on the one side there is the risk that the firm will earn excessive profits; on the other, there is the danger that investment will be discouraged by a low rate of return or uncertainty about the price level to be set by the regulator. In order to avoid both risks, the regulator should know the firm's production costs. However, this is not always an easy task, even if the regulator has access to the firm's accounts, for many reasons: first, monitoring has costs itself; second, the firm could alter its production costs to subvert regulation by increasing them during the price revision period.[32]

Thus, price controls, which with full information might contribute to increasing efficiency, encounter difficulties when there is asymmetric information between regulator and firm, owing to the scope this gives the firm for strategic behaviour. For control to be effective, it is therefore essential to reduce the regulator's information disadvantage as much as possible (Baron and Besanko, 1984). If there are many firms in the market, the costs of each can be compared and under certain conditions it will even be possible to set prices efficiently with the maximum profit margin method by linking the price set by firm A to the costs of firm B and vice-versa, in the simple case of two firms (*yardstick competition*; see Shleifer, 1985).[33] Even if there is only one firm it is occasionally possible

[30] In the case of a firm producing more than one good, the constraint is normally placed on the increase in the price of a basket of the goods rather than each individual good. The formula referred to here was developed by Littlechild (1983) and has been widely used in the United Kingdom for privatised public utilities.

[31] In a time perspective we should also consider that, since it is possible that firms may be uncertain about the future rate of return allowed by regulators, there is a danger that investment will be below the socially efficient level (Vickers and Yarrow, 1988, especially pp. 427–8).

[32] This sort of regulation does appear to have had positive effects on efficiency and has given rise to an improvement in the accounts of regulated firms in the UK (see Veljanovski, 1991).

[33] However, this requires that at least some basic cost data be available to the regulator.

to obtain at least some information by comparing the same cost item among the various divisions of the firm. In a dynamic context, the regulator can try to learn about the firm's cost conditions gradually and choose the appropriate price-fixing mechanism in the light of this knowledge.

Price regulation has developed considerably in the last 10–15 years, often as a result of privatisation programmes. In the United States the most common method has been to set a rate of return on invested capital, whereas dynamic price caps have been the most frequently used method in the United Kingdom (for example, in the privatisation of British Telecom). Static price caps have been adopted in a number of countries.

10.6.4 Public enterprises

The *public-sector* (or *state-owned*) *enterprise* has traditionally been considered in European countries and in many developing nations an effective instrument for achieving a variety of specific objectives (allocative efficiency, full employment, sectoral, regional and general development, etc.) and increasing the general consistency of corporate behaviour with policy objectives (for example, promoting exports, abstaining from activities that replicate private-sector behaviour). In the United States and Japan, public enterprises have traditionally been assigned a smaller role.

The large number of privatisations in various countries since the mid 1980s is a tangible sign that, at least from a practical and contingent point of view, governments have lost confidence in public enterprises.[34] Table 10.1 gives some idea of the importance of the public sector in a selection of European countries at the beginning of the 1980s and the 1990s. The figures reflect the first wave of privatisations in France in 1986 and most of the privatisations in the United Kingdom. They do not show some large scale privatisations in Italy (which began in 1993) or the second wave of privatisations in France in 1993. Privatisation has also been accompanied by a shift in the attitudes of many experts with regard to the ability of public enterprises to achieve the objectives they have been assigned. The changes in the real-world situation and theoretical views are the product of a variety of factors. These include: the ideological and political changes of the period, which saw the triumph of 'Thatcherism' and 'Reaganism', the economic crisis and the associated fiscal crisis of recent years, and unsolved problems with controlling public enterprises.

Although all these are real problems, the swings of the pendulum of history (both economic history and the history of economic thought) have also been accentuated by the impulse of the 'fashionable'. Let us try to understand the economic arguments for and against using public-sector enterprises as an instrument of economic policy. For our purposes in this section, public enterprises should replace private-sector firms operating under natural monopoly conditions or operate alongside private firms under oligopoly[35] in order to increase allocative efficiency. In both cases the public enterprise

---

[34] We ignore here the pressing budget concerns that have prompted many governments to dispose of public property. On privatisation see Bös (1991).

[35] In the former case we would have the nationalisation of the firm (or industry); in the second, we would shift from private oligopoly to *mixed oligopoly*. The latter has only recently been modelled (see De Fraja and Delbono, 1989).

Table 10.1. *Public enterprises: employment, value added and gross capital investment as a percentage of the non-agricultural market sector, 1991.*

	Employment	Value added	Gross capital investment	Average of the three indicators			
				1991	1988	1985	1982
France	13.4	15.1	24.2	17.6	18.3	24.0	22.8
Germany[1]	8.3	10.0	14.9	11.1	11.6	12.4	14.0
Italy	13.5	20.0	23.5	19.0	19.6	20.3	20.0
United Kingdom	4.3	4.0	6.0	4.5	7.4	12.7	16.2
Spain	6.0	8.0	12.8	9.0	10.0	12.0	12.0
Portugal	10.6	21.5	30.0	20.7	24.0	22.7	23.9
Belgium	9.8	7.5	8.4	8.6	10.3	11.1	12.1
The Netherlands	6.1	8.0	9.2	7.5	9.6	9.0	9.0
Greece	14.7	17.0	30.0	20.6	20.8	23.2	22.3
Denmark	8.2	8.7	17.6	11.5	11.9	11.4	12.0
Ireland	8.7	11.5	16.9	12.4	14.4	15.3	15.1
Luxemburg	3.2	5.2	4.6	4.4	4.9	4.5	5.0
Europe[2]	8.9	10.9	15.6	11.8	13.3	15.3	16.4

Notes: [1] Provisional estimates excluding former East Germany.
   [2] Former East Germany not included.
Source: CEEP (1993).

should not aim to make a profit, and in the first situation could even operate at a loss.[36] Losses under such conditions should not be interpreted negatively, since they would be closely tied to the objective assigned to the public enterprise. It is often argued – especially in the current economic policy debate – that losses create distortions in the allocation of resources. From what has been said, we can infer that this is not true *per se*.

   Since the time of Marshall we have known that profit maximisation is a barrier to increasing output to the socially efficient level in industries facing decreasing costs. Public intervention and the associated losses (under the assumed conditions) make it possible to achieve an efficient allocation of resources, which the market is unable to guarantee. By contrast, setting higher prices in order to avoid losses, whether by a public or private firm, would lead to allocative inefficiency.[37]

[36] This would be the case of a public enterprise operating under the conditions shown in figure 6.3. The firm should set price equal to marginal cost; fixed costs (or the loss that the firm would incur with such price-setting behaviour) would have to be covered by a lump-sum tax to ensure allocative efficiency (see Hotelling, 1938).

[37] In the case of a single-product firm facing decreasing costs, the prices that ensure allocative efficiency, subject to the constraint of equating costs and revenues, are those equal to average costs. In the case of a multi-product firm, prices will still exceed marginal cost, but will be set in an inverse relation to the elasticity of demand of the different goods. These are called *Ramsey–Boiteux prices* (see Ramsey, 1927; Boiteux, 1956). However, these prices ensure efficiency subject to a constraint (breaking even), and are therefore suboptimal. Thus they should be used by public enterprises only when the latter are subject to budget limits (e.g., when the public debt is large) and must be self-sufficient.

Many public enterprises operate, or should operate, in industries facing decreasing costs. In fact, some of the critics that underscore losses by public enterprises contradict themselves by arguing that such firms should be present in (or perhaps confined to) innovative industries, which normally have (dynamic) economies of scale. The widespread conviction that operating at a loss by public enterprises is inefficient is therefore regrettable and incomprehensible in rational terms.

In truth, this view may be the product of the idea that losses are not the result of conscious decisions to increase allocative efficiency but are rather the result of management inefficiency (e.g., 'χ-inefficiency'), inefficiency caused by 'constraints' imposed by policymakers, improper relationships between public managers and politicians or even corruption. The fact is, however, that these sorts of problems can also arise with private firms, where they are concealed by setting monopoly prices: in other words, the exploitation of monopoly power has often allowed private firms to offset the high costs of their inefficient management with high revenues (even allowing a net profit).[38]

Inefficiency in public enterprises has also been attributed to the lack of incentives for public managers in the presence of a soft budget constraint and a multiple agency relationship and without the discipline exerted by the financial market on management. Such problems certainly afflict public enterprises, but the difference with private-sector firms seems one of degree rather than kind. Recall our discussion in sections 5.7.1 and 9.4 of the discretion of private managers. In order to limit this discretion, it was suggested that private firms should implement incentive schemes such as profit-sharing arrangements for their managers. There are also less well-known incentive schemes for the managers of public enterprises: for example, setting their pay as a direct function of profits and an inverse function of prices (see Finsinger and Vogelsang, 1985).[39]

Claims of the relative efficiency of private firms compared with public enterprises often do not stand up to scrutiny. Comparisons between the two are frequently made with regard to costs or operating profits. The latter has a bias, since it focuses on a variable, profit, that is the prime objective of private firms but an irrelevant or secondary consideration for public enterprises. Cost comparisons can also be biased for similar reasons. In any case, such assessments do not lead to unambiguous conclusions: in some cases the prevailing view of the inefficiency of public enterprises is vindicated, while in others there are no significant differences, as in the case of state-owned and private railways in Canada or public and private hospitals in the United States. In still other

[38] Obviously, this does not excuse the conduct of economic policymakers. They have not guaranteed the efficient operation of either public enterprises, by means of adequate supervision, or private enterprises, with the adoption, and implementation, of antitrust legislation or the proper use of price controls. The causes of this non-market failure are complex, having their roots in historical, social and political conditions.

[39] An important difference is the constraint imposed on public enterprises by equity considerations. For example, the pay of a public manager in the US cannot be much higher than that of the country's president (Stiglitz, 1988, p. 201). Less important is the argument that only private firms are concerned with bankruptcy. Difficulties at large firms, whether public or private, often prompt efforts to avoid insolvency, and, at least in theory, there is nothing to prevent a public enterprise from going bankrupt. The same effect on managers could also be achieved with the threat of privatisation. In the end, if a public enterprise is not able to carry out its assigned task, it is appropriate that it should be removed from the public sector or cease to exist altogether.

instances, public enterprises are clearly more efficient than private firms: although public social security systems are being threatened with dismantlement, it is not widely known that the administrative costs of these systems amount to less than 2 per cent of benefits paid, compared with 30–40 per cent for private insurance companies (Stiglitz, 1988, p. 196).

Assessing comparative studies of the performance of public and private enterprises nevertheless requires caution. Among other things, a systematic difference with regard to operating results is the tendency of private firms to abandon less profitable sectors: the fact is that some 'firms are government enterprises because they were running at a loss; they are not running at a loss because they are government enterprises' (ibid., p. 197).

Public enterprises are often viewed negatively not because public intervention is considered inappropriate or ineffective but because it is felt that there exist more effective control instruments. Some suggest using regulation rather than public enterprises because it does not give rise to incentive problems. Regulation in the form of antitrust legislation or price controls would prevent the extraction of monopoly profits by private firms, thus ensuring, if not Pareto efficiency, at least that efficiency constrained by the need to balance costs and revenues that guarantees a normal profit.[40] There are two arguments against this:

1 First, incentive problems also arise with regulation. The members of the regulatory authority charged with monitoring compliance with antitrust legislation or price controls might pursue their own ends, just like managers in public enterprises.
2 Second, although regulation is suited to achieving specific goals, public enterprises can pursue a variety of ends at the same time, as we noted at the beginning of this section.

However, the latter consideration, which is a point in favour of public enterprises, also reinforces the problem of the lack of management incentives. Although regulation and public enterprises both raise the same type of incentive problems when they have been assigned one objective, public enterprises give rise to much greater incentive problems when they have been entrusted with pursuing multiple generic goals. The possible ambiguity of the goals allows public managers greater discretion to pursue their personal interests.

The problem of incentives for public managers takes different forms in different cultural and social contexts. Incentives are never solely economic: professionalism, prestige, tradition and social control are some of the elements that may lessen the need for economic incentives and traditional forms of control (non-renewal of contracts or dismissal), which are simply other forms of incentive. In countries such as France, where there is a long tradition of good administration of public enterprises, it is possible to assign these firms a variety of objectives. In other countries (for example, Italy, where no such tradition exists) it is advisable to set out precise and limited objectives until such good administrative practices develop.

---

[40] We said earlier that in some cases public enterprises are also subject to this constraint.

10.6.5 Dynamic efficiency and industrial policy

The principal, and almost exclusive, criterion of the economic policy options outlined in this chapter has been (static) allocative efficiency.

Other important microeconomic problems arise when the objective is to increase dynamic efficiency. Here, too, we can speak of market failures that call for some form of public intervention. The theoretical foundations of these failures are often less apparent than those regarding the inability of the market to ensure allocative efficiency. The interested reader can consult specialised texts for a more extensive discussion of these issues (see, for example, Hay and Morris, 1991, chapter 18).

Dynamic efficiency is the ability to manage change and/or react to change introduced by others, making it possible to secure higher employment and faster income growth. The ability to do this is linked to many important features of the *productive structure* of an economy, i.e., the lasting rather than transitory aspects of an economic system. In addition to certain macroeconomic characteristics (such as the size of the economy, the degree of international openness, etc.), this includes microeconomic features (sectoral composition and regional division of production; technical, economic and financial concentration; production technologies used and the innovative content of products; entry and exit barriers; productive organisation; integration among firms). Note that some of the microeconomic features also have an impact on allocative efficiency.

We have already briefly discussed the effects of monopoly on innovation. Other microeconomic features of the productive structure appear to have a clearer impact on dynamic efficiency. An economy's capacity for growth and employment seems to depend directly on the sectoral composition of production: if an economy specialises in sectors in which world demand is growing more quickly at a given time, it will have greater scope for output growth and employment, *ceteris paribus*. Similarly, introducing innovative technologies (process innovation) can increase the rate of output growth, although in the short term it may accentuate employment problems. On the other hand, product innovation should have a positive impact on both objectives. The relationships between firms and between productive sectors can play a key role in determining innovative capacity (and even static efficiency). Technology sharing agreements, or even merely being located in the same area (for example, in an industrial district), in the same sector or in sectors linked by trade relationships, can help to increase static and dynamic efficiency.

The operation of market forces alone often does not guarantee the most efficienct productive structure, either because individual agents do not possess the necessary information to act appropriately, or because they are guided by personal rather than social interests or because their time preference rate is very high (which means that they do not take sufficient account of the interests of future generations). Of particular importance for regional or general development policies is the existence of *dynamic external economies*, i.e., the benefits or incentives that investment in one industry (e.g., electricity supply) generates for the growth of the market of other industries operating down-stream (e.g., electrical appliances) or up-stream (e.g., generator turbines) (see Rosenstein-Rodan, 1943; Nurkse, 1953).

Policies aimed at modifying the productive structure and, therefore, increasing allocative and dynamic efficiency are called *industrial policies*. They may be aimed at altering the sectoral composition of production, and/or inducing other changes in the productive structure, such as a change in technology, in the degree of integration, etc. (*restructuring*).

Many of the policies we have discussed in this chapter can be considered as specific kinds of industrial policy. Regulation in the form of antitrust legislation or price controls can often be a powerful stimulus to allocative and dynamic efficiency if it aims at both introducing innovations and eliminating the burden that monopolies in key sectors can impose on related industries. Public enterprises can be an effective instrument of industrial policy; in the 30 years after the second world war they were in fact conceived for this very purpose in various European countries (see Vernon, 1974). Even some policies for dealing with externalities and public goods can have a significant impact on industrial structure. Subsidies and tax incentives for investment, public procurement policies and trade policy (see section 17.11) are additional instruments, although we cannot deal with them here.

10.7 Summary

1 Microeconomic policy seeks to:
   (a) ensure the optimal operation of the market;
   (b) correct the market failures identified by microeconomic theory, which give rise to inefficiency and inequality.

2 The functioning of the market is 'guaranteed' by charging the government with the functions of assigning, enforcing and protecting rights. Carrying out these tasks involves additional functions, such as taxation.

3 Policies for correcting inefficiencies produced by externalities include:
   (a) taxing (subsidising) activities that generate external diseconomies (economies);
   (b) providing incentives for eliminating external diseconomies;
   (c) introducing tradable rights to produce diseconomies;
   (d) introducing regulations to prevent external diseconomies and generate external economies.

*4 Optimal policies to correct externalities can be devised from a microeconomic decision model.

*5 The production of public goods requires that we decide:
   (a) the socially efficient level of the good;
   (b) the procedures for financing its production;
   (c) the agent that should actually produce the good.
   The first and second elements of the decision process can be dealt with using the approach proposed by Wicksell–Lindahl, in the absence of free riding. Other, not entirely satisfactory, mechanisms have been suggested to take

account of free riding. Public goods do not necessarily have to be produced by the government.

6 Market power has uncertain effects on dynamic efficiency and negative effects on (Paretian) allocative efficiency. To counter the latter, it is necessary to increase potential and/or effective competition. Enhancing potential competition depends on lowering entry and exit barriers. Effective competition can be increased by using regulation to break up monopolies or auctioning the right of access to the market.

7 Given the limitations of increasing potential or effective competition, steps can be taken to ensure that the market power associated with scale economies or entry and exit barriers is not exploited. This can be done with various forms of regulation (antitrust laws, price controls) and the nationalisation of monopoly firms.

8 Antitrust legislation seeks to safeguard economic liberty and control the economic and political power of concentrations. It also aims to increase allocative efficiency by forbidding agreements that restrict competition and the formation and abuse of dominant positions (including those formed through mergers or other forms of concentration).

9 Price controls are a form of regulation that can involve:
(a) setting a profit margin;
(b) setting a rate of return on invested capital;
(c) introducing a price cap.

10 Public enterprises have traditionally been considered an effective tool for achieving a variety of specific objectives as well as ensuring greater generic consistency between corporate decisions and public objectives.

Pursuing allocative efficiency when facing scale economies means that the public enterprise will operate at a loss. Hence, losses do not in themselves imply inefficiency.

Incentive problems for public-sector managers are similar to those faced by private-sector firms.

Evaluating the performance of public enterprises does not present systematic differences with evaluating that of private firms.

11 The dynamic efficiency of an economic system is linked to the structural features of the system itself: e.g., the degree of international openness; the sectoral composition and regional division of production; technical, economic and financial concentration; production techniques; entry and exit barriers; organisation of production; integration between firms. Industrial policy affects these features.

10.8 Key concepts

Microeconomic policy
Minimal state
Tax subsidy
Tradable permit
Regulation
Pollution standard (environmental
  quality standard)
Pollution right
Personalised price
Dynamic efficiency
Potential, effective competition
Technical, economic, financial
  concentration
Competition for the market, for
  monopoly
Franchising
Dynamic economies of scale (scale
  economies)

Antitrust legislation
Agreements
Abuse of a dominant position
Minimum, maximum price
Common agricultural policy
Minimum wage
Profit margin
Rate of return, rate of profit
Price cap
Averch-Johnson effect
RPI - X method of price control
Public (state-owned) enterprise
Nationalisation
Privatisation
Mixed oligopoly
Ramsey-Boiteux price
Industrial policy
Restructuring

11 Redistributive policies and optimal taxation

Selective intervention?

This chapter examines government action aimed at obtaining a certain distribution of income (or wealth) considered to be optimal, i.e., at modifying the distribution produced by the operation of the market. The question of income distribution can arise independently or in relation to other economic policy problems whose solution requires using instruments that also have distributional effects. A special case of the latter arises when the government selects its criteria for allocating the tax burden, on which the final distribution of income and wealth depends. In all the cases mentioned, identifying the criteria that will determine how taxes are to be levied on different individuals so as to ensure an equitable distribution and an efficient allocation of resources involves the analysis of *optimal taxation.* An optimal tax is in fact that which maximises social welfare in terms of both equity and efficiency.

Section 11.1 aims to derive redistributive principles[1] from theories of justice. Section 11.2 illustrates the various tools of redistributive policy. Section 11.3 examines the conditions under which taxation based on ability to pay produces the same egalitarian results as utilitarianism. Section *11.4 derives the formal conditions of optimal taxation when the government has only partial information. Section 11.5 identifies the characteristics of the incentive-compatible tax structure in the case of private information. Section 11.6 discusses the consequences of our previous analysis in terms of the trade-off between efficiency and equity. Section 11.7 discusses optimal commodity taxation. Section 11.8 analyses the problems associated with tax incidence. Section 11.9 discusses alternative income support schemes, with specific reference to cash or in-kind transfers. Section 11.10 examines the features of actual welfare systems and section 11.11 reviews

---

[1] Having clarified the various possible contexts of public policy, for simplicity from now on we will refer to distributive and redistributive aims interchangeably, even if the proper use of the terms would imply that in the former case the government wants to ensure a certain distribution of income, possibly in a way independent of market forces, whereas in the latter it seeks to change the distribution produced by the operation of market forces.

empirical studies of the effects of taxes on labour supply and proposals for basic income and flat tax schemes.

11.1 Theories of justice and the principles of redistribution

The design of a policy aimed at redistributing income and wealth is closely related to (indeed clearly dependent on) the theory of justice accepted by policymakers.

Chapters 3, 4 and 5 showed that there are an infinite number of efficient allocations and that choosing among them requires some principle of equity.

The fundamental principles of equity, which can be traced to Aristotle (1980), are horizontal equity and vertical equity. *Horizontal equity* requires that individuals in the same position in all relevant aspects be treated equally. *Vertical equity* requires that individuals in different positions be treated differently.[2] Differences in income distribution can be justified on the basis of various characteristics of individuals:

- (a) differences in rights or in legitimate claims;
- (b) differences in effort, in productivity or in contribution;
- (c) differences in endowments;
- (d) differences in beliefs about the characteristics of goods;
- (e) differences in tastes or in the capacity to enjoy various goods;
- (f) differences in needs;
- (g) differences in capabilities and functioning.[3]

Our focus here will be on the redistributive implications of some theories of justice.

The *productivity principle*, advocated by Nozick, is at the basis of the entitlement theory, according to which everyone has an inviolable natural right to the product of his labour and capital, thus excluding any redistribution of income earned in compliance with the rules and procedures of a competitive market. The only acceptable redistribution policy would be that of voluntary transfers such as donations, charitable giving, patronage and the like. There is a tendency towards the conservation of individuals' initial endowments. In any case the (minimal) state should guarantee such endowments and the fruit of their utilisation.

A more moderate version of the productivity principle would still justify inequalities associated with differences in abilities or effort but not those due to circumstances in some way not directly dependent on the individual's choices (inheritance, education, family status, etc.). In these circumstances government action should aim at ensuring *equal opportunity*, e.g., by providing education also to young people who cannot afford to pay for it.

Advocates of the *redistribution principle* argue that differences in ability do not justify distributive inequalities, and redistribution policies should be used to adjust incomes to

---

[2] The relationship between horizontal and vertical equity is examined by Atkinson and Stiglitz (1980, pp. 354–5).

[3] This last difference has been added to the list of those suggested by Yaari and Bar-Hillel (1984) since it does not correspond precisely to any of the other differences mentioned by these authors.

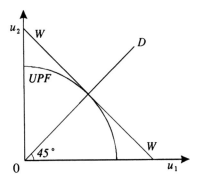

Figure 11.1

meet the needs of individuals or to allow all persons to achieve some (basic) functionings. The utilitarians, Rawls and Sen are the main proponents of the redistribution principle and of policies to redistribute income and wealth, although there are significant differences between them.[4]

As we have noted elsewhere, accepting a simple utilitarian SWF has egalitarian implications, which we can intuitively deduce from Pigou's equity principle. Figure 11.1 shows the egalitarian consequences of adopting a simple utilitarian SWF.

If we assume that the marginal utilities of the two individuals are (decreasing) functions of income only and that they are equal, the utility possibilities frontier (UPF) is symmetric with respect to the bisector, like the curve in figure 11.1. With a simple utilitarian SWF, the slope of the social indifference curves will be (minus) one. The point of tangency between the UPF and an isowelfare curve (WW) lies on the bisector $0D$. Social welfare is then maximised when the individuals have equal utility. However, since the individuals' marginal utility functions are equal and have income as their only argument, the previous result can be obtained only with equal incomes. In this simple version of utilitarianism, an equal distribution of income maximises social welfare. Different assumptions on working abilities, preferences or weights for the various individuals in the SWF will change the equilibrium outcome.[5]

The same result of equal income distribution could also be derived from Rawls' theory of justice if identical utility functions for the various individuals are assumed: resources would be transferred from the rich to the poor until the latter are no longer poor, i.e., when income is distributed equally. Also in this case any diversity in utility functions would change the result of an equal distribution of income.[6]

---

[4] After an early wave of interest following two papers by Dworkin (1981a, b), the debate on egalitarianism and redistribution has recently revived, producing a variety of positions. Fleurbaey (1995) has argued for equality of social outcomes, which should lead to a combination of Rawls' and Sen's theories. In his view, six individual outcomes would be important for Western societies: respect for the private sphere, health, education and information, wealth, collective decision-making power and social integration.

[5] The reader can check graphically this and the other results we are about to present. The consequences of different working abilities are examined by Atkinson and Stiglitz (1980, p. 351).

[6] However, recall that Rawls does not use utility functions in his theory.

According to Sen, we should ensure that individuals have equal capacity to carry out their functionings. If individuals are in the same situation (e.g., equal climate, metabolism, age, etc.) they should be treated in the same way, i.e., they should receive the same endowments of clothing, food and other goods. If they are in different situations, equality requires that goods be assigned differently.

11.2 Redistribution policies

Virtually all economic policy measures redistribute income or wealth. For example, although aimed at ensuring efficiency, antitrust regulations have redistributive effects; macroeconomic measures such as monetary, fiscal and incomes policies also have such effects, as we will see later.

The multiplicity of channels through which it is possible to affect income distribution, and the fact that redistributive goals are often disguised, require the government to identify the distributive consequences of adopting any economic policy measure as clearly as possible (Stiglitz, 1989). Bringing every redistributive activity out into the light of day is a necessary condition for distinguishing desirable and undesirable redistributions on the basis of justice and equity criteria (Bös, 1989). This also permits the identification of any unintended perverse consequences of the measures: some policies designed for a redistributive purpose in favour of some category of people (e.g., the poor) make this category worse off, since the operation of the market has not been properly taken account of (Baumol, 1986, chapter 1). Finally, it enables us to choose the redistributive measures with the smallest distortionary effects on efficiency (Stiglitz, 1989).

Although there are many redistributive measures, budget policy is the primary tool for achieving equity goals. We will discuss the macroeconomic aspects of budget measures in chapter 14. Our focus here will be to analyse their effects on income distribution, mainly at the individual (or household) level. The effects of budget measures do not primarily depend on the total volume of expenditures and revenues but rather on their composition and structure. For example, from a redistributive point of view it is not so much (or only) the level of taxes that counts,[7] but rather (or also) their composition and structure. As regards composition, for example, *direct taxes* (taxes on the income or wealth of individuals or firms) and *indirect* or *commodity taxes* (those on goods) have inherently different impacts on the distribution of income and wealth. As to the structure of taxes, it is important to know the tax schedule, i.e., the tax due and/or paid for each level of the tax base.

Taxation can be *proportional, progressive* or *regressive*. The average tax rate is the ratio between the total amount of taxes paid and the tax base (e.g., the level of income) possessed or earned by an individual. The marginal tax rate is the ratio between the increase in the value of taxes and the increase in the value of the tax base.

Taxation is proportional when the average and marginal tax rates are equal. The tax paid by each individual is $T_1 = t_1 Y$, where t_1 is the marginal and average tax rate and Y

---

[7] Obviously, the level is also important. For example, the level of employment and, therefore, various aspects of the income distribution depend on the level of taxation, *ceteris paribus*.

is the value of the individual's tax base. We will initially assume that income is the tax base.

Taxation is progressive when the marginal tax rate is higher than the average rate: the amount of tax paid increases more than proportionally with income. Taxes are regressive when the amount of tax paid increases less than proportionally with income.

An income tax can be made progressive in a number of ways, three of which are particularly important:

(a) by tax deductions (credits): in this case $T_2 = -G + t_2 Y$, where G is a tax deduction or tax credit for all earners having $Y > Y_0 = G/t_2$ and t_2 is the marginal tax rate, which is higher than the average rate, given by $T_2/Y \equiv -G/Y + t_2$;[8]

(b) by continuous progressivity, where the marginal tax rate increases with income: $T_3 = t_2 Y + t_3 Y^2$; the marginal rate is $t_2 + 2t_3 Y$ and increases with income;

(c) by tax brackets, where the marginal tax rate increases discontinuously with the different income brackets. Considering three income brackets, from 0 to Y_0, Y_0 to Y_1 and Y_1 to Y_2, for $Y = Y_2$ we would have $T_4 = t_0 Y_0 + t_1(Y_1 - Y_0) + t_2(Y_2 - Y_1)$, with $t_2 > t_1 > t_0$.[9]

The revenue generated by a proportional tax, T_1, and a tax made progressive with a tax allowance, T_2, is shown in figure 11.2(a). The slopes of the two lines give the marginal tax rates, t_1 and t_2, respectively. Figure 11.2(b) shows the average tax rates, $\bar{t}_1 = T_1/Y_1$ and $\bar{t}_2 = T_2/Y = t_2 - G/Y$. The marginal rate of the proportional tax is equal to the average rate, t_1. The average rate of the progressive tax converges asymptotically towards t_2, i.e., the marginal rate.

The concept of progressivity can be stated more generally with reference to any kind of tax. If T is the tax paid by an individual and Y is the value of the individual's tax base, we can say that a tax (or the entire tax system) is progressive, proportional or regressive if, respectively, T/Y increases, is constant or decreases as Y increases.

Redistribution through budget policy can be carried out not only with taxes but also with cash or in-kind transfers, as we briefly noted in section 5.7.2. Cash transfers involve payment of money, while in-kind transfers involve the direct provision of goods or services by the government (health services, food programmes, education) or vouchers for specific goods or services (medical coupons, food stamps, etc.) that can be used with private-sector suppliers to cover some or all of the cost.[10]

[8] Pure progressivity through a tax allowance simply means that tax is paid on the portion of income above Y_0. Incomes below Y_0 or the portion of income up to Y_0 are not subject to tax.
A different and more pronounced case of progressivity arises when the tax is levied symmetrically above and below Y_0. Above Y_0, the taxpayer will pay a positive tax (on the portion of income above Y_0). Below Y_0, not only will the individual pay no tax, he will also receive a subsidy (negative tax). In this case the formula holds for $Y \gtrless Y_0$.
[9] If $Y_1 < Y < Y_2$, $T_4 = t_0 Y_0 + t_1(Y_1 - Y_0) + t_2(Y - Y_1)$ and similarly for $Y \leq Y_1$.
[10] In some respects (see section 11.9) it is important to know whether the vouchers can be transferred (sold) to people other than the initial beneficiary. If this is not the case, vouchers can be considered as an in-kind transfer. If they can, they should be considered as cash transfers.

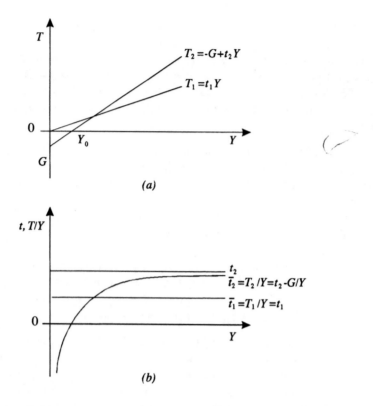

Figure 11.2

11.3 Utilitarianism, ability to pay and optimal taxation

According to utilitarians the principle of horizontal and vertical equity can be applied in terms of utility. In section 11.1 we were able to derive egalitarian consequences under certain circumstances concerning not only acceptance of a simple utilitarian SWF but also equality of the individuals' marginal utility functions. In principle, given any kind of utilitarian SWF and specific individuals' utility functions we could derive certain specific redistributive policies. However, we cannot ascertain which individuals enjoy a higher satisfaction and we are not in a position to tax them. We therefore need a practical criterion that incorporates our principles of horizontal and vertical equity in order to derive practical precepts for redistributive policies.

Imagine that we need to raise money for a government project. Our problem is to divide the burden among taxpayers in a way that ensures both horizontal and vertical equity. According to some authors, individuals can be characterised by their ability to pay; the same tax should then be levied on all individuals with equal ability to pay and a higher tax imposed on those with a greater ability to pay. Ability to pay can be measured through the concept of *comprehensive income*, which is equal to current consumption plus net capital gains (Haig, 1921; Simons, 1938).

Does it mean that freedom is not having an influence on income?

Under certain conditions, using the concept of comprehensive income will yield the same results as the utilitarian approach. To identify these conditions, consider two individuals with different pre-tax incomes. We need to ask whether and under what circumstances the taxes paid by the two should differ in order to ensure equal after-tax incomes. In addition to the hypotheses of identical (decreasing) marginal utility functions and their dependence on income alone (used earlier to show the egalitarian implications of utilitarianism), we assume that income is independent of taxation.[11] Under these hypotheses, it can be shown that at the optimum there will be an equal distribution of net incomes and the principle of tax equity used is that of *equal marginal sacrifice*.[12] Achieving equality of net incomes would obviously require progressive taxation.

Without these assumptions the optimal distribution would not be equal. In particular, it seems intuitively clear that the optimality condition would not require an equal distribution of net incomes if the marginal utility of income functions differed across individuals or if utility depended on leisure as well as income.

The above analysis is therefore based on a large number of simplifying hypotheses. An important role is played by the assumptions of the dependence of utility on income alone and the independence of income from the tax system. If these hypotheses were not satisfied, the optimal position would generally differ from that of an equal distribution of net incomes; moreover, the equilibrium level of total income would also change. *why?*

Both these hypotheses are unrealistic. First, we know that, according to neoclassical theory, utility is a function of both income and working time. In addition, taxation has an influence on income production: levying a tax on labour income reduces net income; this gives rise to both an income and a substitution effect. The *income effect* induces people to work more to satisfy their consumption needs, while the *substitution effect* acts in the opposite direction, since by lowering net income the tax reduces the opportunity cost of leisure, thus encouraging people to substitute leisure for work.[13]

Figure 11.3 shows the effect of an income tax on the number of hours an individual is willing to work under the assumption that there is no saving and, therefore, income equals consumption. The maximum number of hours that the individual can work in the time period is given by 0E. Obviously, working more means less leisure time. Line 0A is the budget constraint before the tax, while 0B is the constraint after the introduction of a proportional income tax. The indifference curves in terms of consumption and labour supply are depicted as rising since the former is a 'good' and the latter is a 'bad', according to standard neoclassical theory. Point D will lie to the right or left of C depending on whether the income or substitution effect dominates.[14] Note that the

[11] We were previously interested only in analysing the egalitarian implications of utilitarianism. We now tackle the problem of an equitable distribution of the tax burden over individuals' incomes. In the presence of a tax, (gross) income could depend on the tax rates. The new hypothesis is meant to exclude this dependence.

[12] According to this principle, the marginal utility of taxpayers' after-tax income, i.e., the sacrifice (utility loss) associated with the last penny of tax from each taxpayer, is equalised.

[13] Note that in the case of progressive income taxation, the income effect depends on the average tax rate, while the substitution effect depends on the marginal rate.

[14] We will examine the results of empirical studies later.

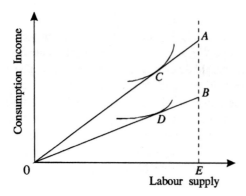

Figure 11.3

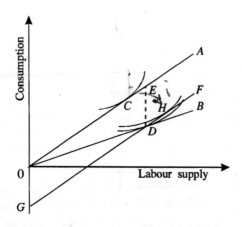

Figure 11.4

introduction of the tax alters the labour supply and reduces the utility of the taxpayer, who moves to a lower indifference curve. We can also show that the reduction in utility due to such a tax is greater than that induced by a lump-sum tax, assuming unchanged tax revenues. This can be attributed to the substitution effect, which generates a distortion in the labour supply.

The distortion is shown in figure 11.4. If an income tax is levied and the individual positions himself at D, tax revenue, or the loss of income (equal to consumption), is equal to DE. Instead of applying an income tax, we could impose a lump-sum tax generating the same revenue ($G0 = DE$). In this case the budget constraint would be GF and the welfare loss would be smaller, since the taxpayer would benefit by positioning himself at H, which is on a higher indifference curve than D. So an income tax distorts the supply of labour with respect to that under a lump-sum tax.

[15] A lump-sum tax causing the same utility reduction as an income tax would yield a higher revenue. This could be shown graphically in figure 11.4 by drawing a parallel to $0A$ tangent to the indifference curve passing through D. The vertical distance between D and such a parallel would represent the additional revenue.

In order to avoid such distortion,[16] taxes should not be levied in relation to an indicator of ability to pay, such as income, that not only depends on the choice of leisure time but also influences this choice through substitution effects. Taxes should instead be based on indicators of ability to pay, such as skill or talent, that do not play a significant role in this choice[17] while being specific to each individual. However, information on skill or talent is private, since it is known only to the individual and not the government. The more skilled or talented person might therefore attempt to avoid the tax by disguising his true level of ability, thus manipulating the redistribution mechanism. The tax must therefore necessarily be imposed on income or some other more easily verifiable indicator of the ability to pay. However, income is the result of both skill or talent and individual's decisions about how much labour to supply are affected by the tax, as we know from our previous analysis. The problem of optimal taxation of income (as an indicator of skill or talent) with private information about ability is that individuals have an incentive to misrepresent their ability, in particular by working less and earning less (i.e., substituting leisure for gross income)[18] in order to lower their fiscal burden (or to gain positive transfers). This will occur unless an incentive-compatible tax schedule is introduced, i.e., one that induces people to give a true representation of their ability.

This has two important implications: (1) it limits the extent of redistributive policies because of the difficulty of implementing such policies when the government has only partial information on individuals' abilities; and (2) it makes redistributive policies costly in terms of efficiency in the presence of asymmetric information about different individuals' ability to pay.

We will discuss the first of these consequences in the following two sections and the second in section 11.6.

*11.4 Optimal taxation with private information: incentive-compatible taxes

Following Mirrlees (1971), who first tackled this subject, let us suppose that there exists a continuum of individuals, each being paid a wage rate w according to his skill (or type), such that $0 < \underline{w} \leq w \leq \overline{w} \leq \infty$. The density function of the distribution of w (or types) is $f(w)$.

Suppose then that the government wants to raise revenue $R \geq 0$. The problem is how to distribute taxes across individuals. If $R = 0$ we have a case of pure redistributive

---

[16] Taxes can also distort the supply of savings, i.e., the temporal allocation of consumption. We will discuss this in section 11.7.

[17] This only holds in a relative sense: there is always the possibility that a person will decide to invest more or less in acquiring skills according to taxes levied. However, we can assume that this effect is of a lower magnitude and that taxing skill or talent does not significantly alter the individual's propensity to supply his labour services.

[18] This implies that in reality there can be two kinds of substitution effect caused by taxation: (a) one usually associated with the reduction in the opportunity cost of leisure; (b) one deriving from individuals' attempts to misrepresent their ability in a situation of asymmetric information.

taxation, i.e., the government wants to tax some individuals while subsidising others in order to maximise the value of a social welfare function.

If the government could observe the skill of each individual, in the purely redistributive case it could tax the most able and subsidise the least skilled. If this is not possible, abilities can be inferred indirectly from observed behaviour. In our case we suppose that they can be deduced from an individual's income, $Y = wL(w)$, where L is the quantity of labour supplied. However, as we know from the previous section, individuals could misrepresent their ability unless an incentive-compatible tax is devised. Incentive compatibility thus introduces a constraint on the redistributive activity of government.

In devising the tax-rate structure, the usual distortionary effects on efficiency that also arise in the case of full information have to be taken into account. Those who will be taxed (positively or negatively), as well as the average and marginal tax rates, will depend on considerations of both efficiency and equity, as reflected in the social welfare function.

Let us suppose that each individual lives for one period only and that he consumes all his income net of taxes. Consumption is thus $C = Y(w) - T[Y(w)]$, where $0 \leq T' < 1$.[19] Since $Y = wL(w)$, the budget constraint for an individual of type w is:

$$C = wL - T(wL) \tag{11.1}$$

Each individual maximises the following utility function with respect to L:

$$U[C(w), L(w)], \quad \text{subject to (11.1)} \tag{11.2}$$

If we substitute (11.1) into (11.2), the individual maximizes

$$U[wL - T(wL), L(w)] \tag{11.2'}$$

The first-order condition is:

$$U_C(1 - T')w + U_L = 0, \text{ where } U_C \equiv \partial U/\partial C, U_L \equiv \partial U/\partial L; T' = \partial T/\partial Y. \tag{11.3}$$

Considering that L is a function of w, we can also differentiate (11.2) with respect to w[20] and use (11.3), which gives:

$$U' = -LU_L/w, \text{ where } U' \equiv dU/dw \tag{11.4}$$

Since $U_L < 0, U' > 0$, which means that a person with a higher w should enjoy a higher utility if he is to maximise his satisfaction. This is important because, as we said, w

---

[19] We are considering a general case, which implies that there are no other restrictions on the form of the taxation function, $T[Y(w)]$. A simpler case is that of linear taxation, where the marginal tax rate is constant and there is an identical lump-sum transfer (or tax allowance) for all taxpayers. The progressive tax system introduced in section 11.2, $T_2 = -G + t_1 Y$, corresponds to the linear case. In this case the optimal values of the tax rate and the amount of the lump-sum transfer can be determined solving a standard maximisation problem.

[20] This differentiation shows how an individual's utility changes with his ability, which may be useful when one thinks, e.g., of the incentive for an individual to misrepresent it for tax purposes (by working less), in order to increase his utility.

This procedure, suggested by Tuomala (1990) among others, gives a good account of the meaning of the incentive-compatibility constraint, as we will see shortly.

can be misrepresented by the individual himself. He would be reluctant to reveal his higher skill if he did not derive a higher utility from this (in our case, for reasons related to the tax system). The individual would instead find it profitable to reveal a lower skill level by working less and earning less income. By hypothesis the government would have no way of detecting such behaviour, since ability is private information of individuals and can only be ascertained through their incomes. The condition $U' > 0$ can then be thought of as the *incentive-compatibility* (or *self-selection*) *constraint* that the government must satisfy.

The government aims at maximising social welfare:

$$W = \int_{\underline{w}}^{\overline{w}} G(U)f(w)dw \quad^{21}$$ (11.5)

by choosing an appropriate taxation function.[22]

Maximisation must satisfy condition (11.4) as well as the aggregate budget (or revenue) constraint. When the revenue to be raised is zero (pure redistribution), the budget constraint for the economy as a whole is given by:

$$Y = \int_{\underline{w}}^{\overline{w}} C(w)f(w)dw = \int_{\underline{w}}^{\overline{w}} wL(w)f(w)dw$$ (11.6)

We can solve this problem by applying Pontryagin's maximum principle (Intriligator, 1971). U is the state variable and $L(w)$ the control variable.[23]

Let us denote as $\gamma = \gamma(w)$ and $\lambda = \lambda(w)$ the costate variables relative to the national income constraint (11.6) and the self-selection constraint (11.4), respectively. The Hamiltonian can then be written as:

$$H = \{G(U) - \gamma[C - Y]\}f(w) - \lambda U'$$ (11.7)

or, substituting (11.2), as:

$$H = \{G\{U[C(w), L(w)]\} - \gamma[C(w) - L(w)w]\}f(w) - \lambda U'$$ (11.8)

Differentiating (11.8) with respect to L gives the following condition to be satisfied for dynamic maximisation:[24]

$$T'(1 - T') = U_C \gamma(w)\varepsilon^*/\lambda(w)f(w)w$$ (11.9)

[21] Utilitarianism means $G \equiv 1$ (identity function). The Rawlsian SWF has $G'(U) = 0$ for $U > U_{min}$ and $G(U) = U$ for $U = U_{min}$.

[22] Note that once we have chosen $T(Y)$, the labour-supply function is uniquely determined, since we know (11.2) and (11.1) holds. The opposite is also true. $T(Y)$ and $L(w)$ can therefore be thought of as interchangeable control variables.

[23] See the previous note.

[24] Readers interested in the details of the procedure are referred to Stiglitz (1987, pp. 1006–7) and, for a treatment that puts particular emphasis on the self-selection constraint, Myles (1995, section 3.3).

where $\varepsilon^* = \partial\ln(dU/dw)/\partial\ln L = \partial\ln - (LU_L/w)/\partial\ln L$ is the compensated elasticity of labour in the absence of taxation (Stiglitz, 1987). This result will be discussed in the next section.

11.5 The characteristics of the optimal tax

The model presented in the previous section and other similar models[25] enable us to draw the following conclusions about the optimal structure of tax rates:

1 In the presence of an incentive constraint a marginal tax rate above 100 per cent will never be optimal: no one would find it profitable to earn a higher gross income if this results in a lower net income; people of a given skill level will tend to reveal a lower skill level[26] by working, and thus earning, less. This result derives directly from the condition $U' > 0$ (see the comment to (11.4)).

2 The marginal tax rate will be lower the larger is the fraction of the population earning the income level that pays that marginal tax rate. The meaning of this is intuitively clear: to avoid large distortions when the number of people hit by the marginal tax rate is large, this rate must be reduced.

3 The marginal tax rate on the highest-ability individual should be zero.[27] This would reduce the disincentive effects of the tax – which are tied to the marginal rate – thus inducing the individual to tell the truth. The government can still impose a high average tax rate on the most able individuals in order to increase revenue, but this can be obtained by raising the marginal rates for lower-ability (and thus lower-income) groups.

4 The marginal tax rate is lower the higher is the productivity (w in the model presented in the previous section) of the group of people involved; in other words, the loss of output from distortionary taxation is larger for groups whose output per unit of labour is higher.

5 The marginal tax rate is lower the higher is the elasticity of the (compensated) labour supply (ε^* in (11.9)). In other words, since the tax reduces net income (or the consumption obtained from a certain amount of labour), the optimal marginal rate will be lower the greater is the disincentive it creates for the labour supply (Stiglitz, 1987).

We have thus obtained results that help us characterise the optimal tax schedule but do not define it in every detail. Further results cannot be obtained unless a specific social welfare function and individual utility function are selected. This has usually been done by numerical computation owing to the analytical complexity of the model.

Results of both theoretical analysis and numerical calculations seem to support the adoption of a tax system that is very different from the tax schedules applied in the real world.

The requirement of a marginal tax rate of less than 100 per cent, while intuitively

[25] Variations have been made by Sadka (1976) and Seade (1977).

[26] The reader should remember that skills are revealed through gross income.

[27] This result is difficult to derive (for more, see Stiglitz, 1987, pp. 1007–8; Sadka, 1976; Seade, 1977).

conceivable, is often not satisfied in reality.[28] The most striking requirement, however, seems to be that of a zero marginal rate for those with the greatest ability. This is far from reality, where in some cases (e.g., the Scandinavian countries) marginal tax rates are, or have until recently been, close to 100 per cent. However, the significance of theoretical results has to be examined carefully: in particular, the result of a zero marginal rate on the highest-ability individual may be only locally valid. In this case, contrary to what many say with regard to reforming actual tax systems, the above result would not mean that the marginal tax rates for levels of income near the top should be zero or close to zero. Numerical computations can be useful here. They in fact confirm that the result of a zero marginal rate at the upper end of the income scale is only locally valid and does not imply that incomes close to the maximum must be subject to low marginal tax rates (Tuomala, 1990).

Kanbur and Tuomala (1994) show that as the dispersion of skills increases the marginal tax rate at each income level increases, and this moves the top marginal tax rate up the income scale so that the marginal tax rate is increasing over the majority of individuals.

Numerical simulations also show that the degree of desired equity implicit in the chosen SWF has an impact on marginal tax rates, which increase in passing from a utilitarian to a more egalitarian SWF, such as the Rawlsian SWF (Atkinson, 1973).

Finally, high marginal tax rates can be justified if the elasticity of substitution between leisure and consumption is low, i.e., if the rate at which consumption can be exchanged for leisure (while keeping utility constant) is low. This is supported by both the numerical computations performed by Stern (1976) and the theoretical analysis of section *11.4 (see result 5 at the beginning of this section). This is the case if and when labour is performed for reasons of self-realisation, i.e., to achieve promotion or recognition for their own sake, regardless of monetary reward.

11.6 The trade-off between efficiency and equity

Stiglitz (1987) and Brito et al. (1990) define the characteristics of the UPF achievable in maximising social welfare when the incentive-compatibility (IC) constraint is satisfied, i.e., when the maximisation of social welfare takes place under the terms of section *11.4.

First, since this frontier is obtained by adding constraints connected with the existence of distortionary taxation and incentive compatibility to a normal maximising process of the sort considered in section *3.7,[29] it will lie within the unconstrained frontier (or better, the frontier that does not incorporate these additional constraints).

[28] This may happen at very low levels of income (the 'poverty trap'). Since eligibility for transfers often depends on the amount of earned income, high effective marginal tax rates (in some cases above 100 per cent) may be imposed on low incomes and reduce the labour supply. Take the simple case of pensions conditional on the absence of other sources of income (exceeding a certain – low – level) or of entitlement to free medical services below an income ceiling. Close to such levels individuals may find it profitable to reduce their labour supply (and thus their earnings) to qualify for the transfer. See Atkinson and Stiglitz (1980, lecture 2).

[29] Note that if we ignore the self-selection constraints, the maximisation processes followed in sections *3.7 and *11.4 are only apparently different. It can be shown that an allocation of goods that maximises a social welfare function is Pareto efficient (see Varian, 1992, p. 333).

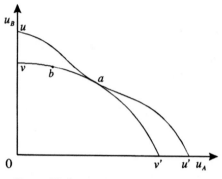

Figure 11.5

With reference to two individuals, the two frontiers are related as shown in figure 11.5 (given earlier in section 5.7.2 in a slightly different version), in which the outside curve uu' is the first-best UPF, while the inside curve, vv', which incorporates both the IC and the redistributive constraints, is the second-best frontier (*constrained Pareto-efficient frontier*).

Each point on the constrained UPF denotes an equilibrium for the two individuals in which the IC constraint is binding for at least one of them. If none of the two IC constraints are binding, the second-best frontier obviously coincides with the unconstrained Pareto-efficient frontier.

The 'standard' case, on which the literature has focused, is that where the binding constraint is that regarding the most talented individual. This arises when the government wishes to increase the welfare of the poor above the level that would prevail under perfect competition without redistribution. It is commonly argued in the real world and in much of the economic literature (the classic reference is Okun's 'leaky-bucket' example[30]) that redistribution involves costs that reduce efficiency. In addition to those related to the expenditure required to carry out the redistribution,[31] these costs are associated with the distortionary nature of the tax.[32]

Nevertheless, we need to understand exactly how the *unconstrained frontier* is obtained, since it is only with respect to this curve that the efficiency loss due to the redistribution can be defined. One often has the impression that such a frontier exists in an institutional void and in any case is an utterly abstract construction far removed from reality. In particular, it is not clear if it takes account of efficiency problems associated with, for example, malnutrition, slavery or the blatant infraction of social rules and customs – or human rights – concerning equality.

Improving equity can increase efficiency for a variety of reasons. First, the elimination of malnutrition and other forms of privation that weaken the body and limit the potential of human capital, curing diseases and supplying education all increase the social product (for a recent discussion, see Currie, 1995; Benabou, 1996). But inequality

[30] According to Okun (1975), transferring wealth from the rich to the poor is like carrying water in a leaky bucket: some of the contents are spilled during the transfer.
[31] These are usually assumed away in the first approximation, as we have done until now.
[32] A short review of existing empirical literature on the distortionary effects of taxation is deferred to section 11.11.

also has a negative impact on the social product if certain conventions of community life are violated: the belief that an unequal distribution of income violates some social convention is a cause of 'moral indignation' in the majority of community members. The inadequate distribution of consumption associated with 'excessive' income inequality will thus generate external diseconomies that may find expression in reduced productivity, social unrest (Caffè, 1948) or other forms of social disruption.[33]

For material or psychological reasons, then, equity may represent a necessary condition for the 'viability' of an economic system. However, it is impossible to specify fully the extent to which greater equality of income or wealth increases rather than decreases efficiency, precisely because of the conventional nature of equity itself.

Moreover, there is the problem that if, on the basis of the social welfare function, we desire a redistribution that brings us from point a to point b (which by assumption generates the maximum social welfare), the only feasible frontier is vv'. By construction, all other frontiers would not be feasible. Accordingly, any reference to uu' is simply an example of the Nirvana fallacy, *if we wish to implement the desired redistribution*.[34] Points on uu' different from a would never be attainable unless the economy happened to be in them spontaneously.

11.7 Optimal commodity taxation

As briefly noted earlier, in addition to direct taxes on income or wealth, there are indirect taxes on consumption or sales. Taxes on consumption goods can be levied at the time when such goods are produced and are then called *excise taxes*. They include taxes on goods such as cigarettes, petrol, alcohol, aeroplane tickets, and tariffs on imported goods. *Sales taxes* can be imposed at each intermediate stage or the final stage. The former are either *full-value* taxes or *value-added taxes* (the usual form adopted in the European Union countries). Taxes at the final stage are used in the United States mainly to finance state and local governments (*retail sales taxes*).

Since output in a closed economy equals demand (for consumption and investment) and the income of participants in the productive process, a uniform tax on (distributed) income is equivalent to a uniform tax on output (value-added tax) and a uniform tax on consumer and investment goods.[35]

---

[33] In this case, equity is intended as *fairness*, meaning the perception of what is considered equitable.

[34] Sandmo (1995) appears to argue along these lines.

[35] This requires some elaboration. As is well known, value added at each stage of production can be determined by subtracting the value of intermediate consumption (raw materials, services and components) from the value of the product. If, as in fact occurs, the productive process also makes use of fixed capital, the sum of the value added obtained by subtracting only the value of intermediate consumption from the value of the product is equal to the *gross* product. If we also subtract capital depreciation, we obtain *net* domestic product.

A tax on the value added of every firm as determined by subtracting intermediate goods and depreciation would be fully equivalent to an income tax, and we could thus speak of an 'income-type' value-added tax. If firms were allowed to subtract from the value of output not just the depreciation of capital goods but their entire value, in addition to intermediate consumption, investment would essentially be exempted from tax and consumption only would be hit. We would therefore have a 'consumption-type' value-added tax, as in the case of the European Union.

This equivalence between the various forms of tax might suggest that we can redistribute income by taxing goods rather than income. In effect, consumed or traded goods can be considered as an indirect indicator of ability to pay, hence the term 'indirect taxes' applied to taxes on consumption or trade.

One of the most important results in the theory of optimal taxation is the *Ramsey rule* (see Ramsey, 1927), which states that, if lump-sum taxes cannot be levied, an optimal commodity tax system (i.e., one that minimises the distortions) can nevertheless be devised. This system requires taxes to be proportional to the reciprocal of the compensated elasticity of demand, if supply is perfectly elastic: goods whose demand is most inelastic should be taxed more; the low elasticity of demand would reduce the distortions. However, the Ramsey rule was derived in a context which, in addition to very common assumptions (such as that of a competitive economy, labour as the only production input and constant returns to scale), also assumes a single individual (or population of identical individuals). This last assumption makes it impossible to apply the rule for redistributive purposes. In any case, considering that low price elasticity goods such as food are mainly consumed by the poor, an application of the *Ramsey rule* to the real world would imply a perverse redistribution.

However, Ramsey's analysis can be extended to take account of redistributive goals (Diamond and Mirrlees, 1971; Atkinson and Stiglitz, 1976). Pursuit of these objectives would require a more pronounced departure from the original Ramsey rule, the greater is our concern for redistributive goals: in particular, higher tax rates would be set on luxury goods such as jewellery, which are generally consumed by the rich, whereas lower rates would hit essential goods, which absorb a larger share of the income of the poor.

One argument in favour of commodity taxation is that ability to pay can be difficult to determine directly, i.e., through income. Thus, a sales or consumption tax can be added to (or substituted for) an income tax in order to prevent or reduce tax evasion.

However, the use of indirect taxation for redistributive purposes has a number of drawbacks. The first is the administrative complexity of managing the system of multiple tax rates implied by the Ramsey rule, which among other things means precisely defining the goods subject to each rate, a task that is not always possible.

A second problem arises because setting lower tax rates on certain goods normally benefits not only the consumers of those goods but also their producers; similarly, both the consumers and producers of goods hit with a higher tax rate are worse off. This introduces a degree of discrimination between the *producers* of goods subject to different tax rates, which, unlike discriminating between consumers, is not desired *per se* or is not, in any case, the objective of redistributing income for the equity reasons we are examining here.[36]

A third difficulty regards the distortionary effects of taxing goods. An income tax can distort consumer choices (since it influences individuals' decisions about how much time to spend working). A tax on a good (for example, on fish) will also be distortionary if it

---

[36] Discriminating between producers can instead be the objective of industrial or regional policy or of protectionism.

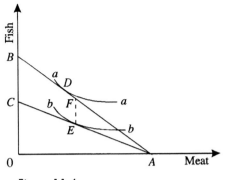

Figure 11.6

does not equally affect consumption of substitute goods. In general, consumption of the good hit by the tax will fall, since the tax normally leads to an increase in the final price of the taxed good[37] and the increase in price gives rise to a substitution effect between the taxed good and untaxed goods (such as meat, a substitute for fish), reducing consumption of the former. We show this effect in figure 11.6. The curve AB is the consumer's budget line before the introduction of a tax on fish and AC is the budget line after the tax, assuming that the price of fish increases as a result of the tax. The figure shows that taxing fish (and not meat) certainly reduces consumption of fish, while the effect on meat consumption may be uncertain.

The reduction in the consumption of the good hit by the tax gives rise to an inefficient allocation of consumption and, therefore, a loss of welfare for consumers of the taxed good.[38] Obviously, all taxes considered on their own (i.e., independently of any benefits that might derive from government spending financed by the tax) reduce welfare.

The *welfare loss* is clear because the individual moves from indifference curve aa to the lower indifference curve bb. However, it can be shown that a lump-sum tax generating the same revenue would reduce the individual's utility by less. In our example of a tax on fish, tax revenue is equal to EF if valued in terms of the difference in the quantity of fish that a consumer could purchase before the tax and the amount he could purchase after the tax, given the quantity of meat consumed after the tax.

If the same revenue were raised with a lump-sum tax, the consumer's welfare loss would be smaller, as we can see in figure 11.7, where the consumer's income is reduced by a tax $BG = EF$. We have added a budget line, GH, and an indifference curve, cc, to the indifference curves and budget lines of figure 11.6. The line GH is constructed by

[37] The extent to which a tax is shifted on to the price of the good depends on a large number of circumstances, such as the type of market and the elasticity of demand and supply. Under perfect competition, if demand is completely inelastic or supply is infinitely elastic, the tax will be borne entirely by the consumer, since the price of the good will rise by the amount of the tax (see section 11.8).

[38] As we know, the decline in fish consumption is attributable to two effects. The substitution effect causes fish consumption to fall, since the price of fish relative to that of meat increases as long as meat is not taxed. The tax also reduces income, which causes consumption of both fish and meat to diminish if these are normal goods.

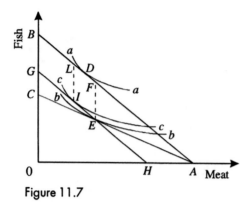

Figure 11.7

subtracting from income, $0B$, a lump-sum tax BG equal to the revenue raised through the consumption tax. Note that the new budget line GH leaves the individual on a higher indifference curve, cc, than that on which he would find himself if a consumption tax were imposed on fish. Thus a *deadweight loss* arises if a commodity tax is levied instead of a lump-sum tax.[39] A lump-sum tax causing the same reduction in welfare as a commodity tax would yield higher revenue. Referring to figure 11.6, this can easily be proved by drawing the parallel to the former budget constraint, AB, tangent to the indifference curve bb. In this case the consumer will enjoy the same satisfaction as with the tax on fish (staying on the same indifference curve), but tax revenue will be higher than EF. The extra tax revenue is a measure of the deadweight loss caused by a commodity tax.

The deadweight loss produced by the commodity tax can also be indicated in terms of the reduction in the consumer surplus associated with the price increase following the tax. Figure 11.8 shows this reduction, diagramming the consumer surplus before and after the introduction (in a competitive market) of a fish tax equal to AD that is entirely shifted on to final prices. PP' is the *compensated* demand curve for fish;[40] $A0$ is marginal cost, which for simplicity is assumed to be constant for every level of output. The marginal cost curve gives the supply curve for fish before the introduction of the tax. Equilibrium is at B. Levying a tax equal to AD shifts the supply curve upwards by the same amount, with the new equilibrium at E. Consumer surplus is reduced by $ABED$.[41] Part of this corresponds to the tax revenue ($AGED$), which might generate higher utility

[39] We can easily show that this is a necessary result. Since the budget line with lump-sum tax GH passes through E and is steeper than the budget line AC, it must be tangent to an indifference curve higher than bb, on which E lies.

[40] The compensated demand curve shows the quantity of fish demanded for every given price, assuming that as the price of fish increases the consumer is compensated for the consequent reduction in his real income, so as to stay on the same indifference curve. The compensated demand curve corresponds to the 'normal' demand curve adjusted for income effects and is steeper than the Marshallian curve (for normal goods). See Hausman (1981) for the construction of the curve.

[41] The reader will note that the reduction in consumer surplus is similar to that discussed in microeconomic textbooks with regard to monopoly pricing.

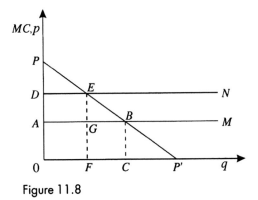

Figure 11.8

for our consumer or others as a result of the government spending it finances; the remainder of the lost surplus, equal to BEG, is the deadweight loss.[42]

11.8 Tax incidence

Any analysis of the redistributive effects of taxation must also consider who effectively pays the tax (the *de facto* taxpayer), who may not be the person on whom the tax is imposed (the *de jure* taxpayer): the latter could in fact shift the tax burden on to the former. Such tax shifting must be borne in mind when we decide to redistribute income.

Suppose, for example, that a tax is levied on consumers of labour (i.e., firms) in order to redistribute income. Under certain conditions this tax will be paid by labour producers (i.e., workers) rather than firms, undermining the desired redistributive effect. Let us see why.

Referring to figure 11.9, introducing a tax equal to BC per unit of labour employed will shift the labour demand curve by an amount equal to the tax itself. The demand curve for labour – which indicates the maximum net wage (equal to the marginal productivity of labour) that firms are willing to pay for each unit of labour – shifts downwards from DD to $D'D'$. This means that for any given quantity of labour firms operating in a perfectly competitive market will now pay at most a net wage equal to the previous maximum wage minus the tax for each labour unit if marginal productivity does not change.

However, the decline in the net wage causes the equilibrium labour supply to fall (from $0F$ to $0E$), so that the cost to firms of each labour unit is equal to the wage BE plus the amount of the tax, BC, for a total of CE; this is higher by CG than the pre-tax cost of labour, AF. Workers, who previously received a wage of $AF = EG$, now receive a net wage equal to BE. In this case, the tax is partly paid by the firm (CG) and partly shifted on to workers (BG).

The magnitude of this shift depends on a variety of factors, including the elasticity of

---

[42] The triangle BEG is sometimes called the *Harberger triangle*, after the economist who studied the problem under examination.

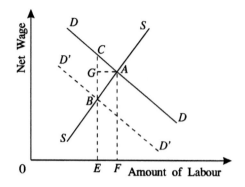

Figure 11.9

supply and demand. For example, the reader can check that in the case of perfectly inelastic supply (a vertical labour supply curve), the tax will be entirely borne by workers; the same will occur if demand is infinitely elastic. A larger fraction of the tax will be borne by firms when labour demand is inelastic or labour supply is elastic.

Our analysis so far has examined the effects of a tax on labour imposed on firms under perfect competition. However, the effects of a tax imposed on workers would be the same under the same market conditions. The tax would shift the labour supply curve upwards. Workers hit by the tax would attempt to shift the burden on to firms by increasing the supply price of labour by an amount equal to the tax, with the same consequences as before. In this case, however, the effects are produced by an increase in firms' marginal cost and the associated reduction in output, which causes its price to rise. This analysis shows that it makes no difference whether social security contributions (which are our labour taxes) are formally to be paid by workers or firms.

These results can change if markets are monopolistic or oligopolistic rather than perfectly competitive. Workers' ability to shift a labour tax on to firms will depend on their bargaining power *vis-à-vis* firms.

The concepts employed to analyse the effects of a labour tax can also be used to study the incidence of a tax on goods or, with the appropriate adjustments, on income from employment or capital. The reader should in any case note the fact that the considerations set out in this section have the obvious limitations (but also the advantage of clarity) of a partial equilibrium analysis.

11.9 Alternative redistribution and income maintenance schemes

We said that redistribution of income and wealth through fiscal policy is carried out by imposing taxes on the better-off and providing transfers to the poor. In addition to reducing inequalities, transfers can also be used to ensure that every individual (including the less talented) enjoys a minimum standard of living, using income maintenance systems. Normally, the two objectives – redistribution and income maintenance – are complementary; in fact, the former can be instrumental to the latter. Nevertheless, for reasons we will examine shortly, it may prove necessary to use equal transfers for everyone in order to guarantee a minimum standard of living, which would not reduce inequality.

Income maintenance programmes come in a variety of types. We will necessarily be selective in our discussion here. Of the following schemes, the first three are *welfare schemes*; the fourth is a *workfare scheme* (i.e., a programme requiring work from the beneficiary, according to the maxim 'you work for your welfare'):

(a) basic income schemes, in which people with an income below some standard level receive income supplements to bring them up to the minimum;

(b) schemes providing for positive income taxes on incomes above a given level and negative income taxes for those below that level;

(c) wage subsidy schemes, in which only those who work (and whose income is below a minimum level) receive a subsidy, which is reduced as income rises;

(d) schemes that require welfare recipients to work in government-provided jobs.

Apart from differences between the individual welfare schemes, it is important to understand the difference between welfare and workfare schemes and the situations in which the former are superior to the latter and vice versa. If income-generating abilities were observable and beyond individuals' control, the cost-minimising poverty-alleviation programme (PAP) would be a welfare – not a workfare – system, since workfare programmes reduce the individual's labour supply. In particular, under these assumptions a wage subsidy scheme would be optimal: low-ability individuals would be offered a cash transfer just large enough to lift them out of poverty while high-ability individuals would receive no benefits.

The abilities of each individual cannot be observed, however. They are 'private' information and high-ability individuals may find it worthwhile to claim a low-ability status in order to obtain a government transfer, as we saw in our discussion of optimal taxation. Announcing a programme of differentiated transfers that takes account of inequalities would encourage untruthful declarations of need. In the case of private information, assuming that a workfare scheme cannot be adopted, the optimal PAP would involve a transfer, equal to the difference between the minimum standard of consumption desired by the government and the maximum income that *could* be earned by the least able individuals, to people earning this level of maximum income. In order to encourage people to work, failure to reach this maximum income level would not give someone a right to an additional compensating transfer. Individuals with an income higher than the maximum income for the least able would receive a reduced benefit.

However, if workfare schemes are admitted, they offer an optimal solution since they are both a way of screening people's actual state of need (at least in part) and because they encourage efforts to find ways to reduce or eliminate that state of need (Besley and Coate, 1992).

All these schemes need to be administered, which implies sustaining costs. In some cases these are very high relative to the value of the transfer. To avoid such costs the government may resort to equal transfers for all, which – as we said – does not reduce inequality but can prevent poverty.

A second type of problem that must be solved by income maintenance and welfare programmes regards the choice between cash and in-kind transfers. We already know from section 5.7.2 that there are arguments in favour of in-kind transfers: by avoiding or reducing the role of the market, government redistributive activity will be more effective. With asymmetric information, in-kind transfers overcome the consequences of uncertainty.[43] Direct provision of goods and services by the government and other in-kind transfers for redistributive purposes can therefore increase social welfare.[44]

Conversely, cash transfers have perverse effects, all the more so the greater is the inequality of income distribution: equal cash transfers to people with different incomes will give rise to different levels of consumption for any given level of need; the better-off will consume more than the poor, which is exactly the opposite of what the government is trying to accomplish by redistributing income. In addition, there is no guarantee that a cash transfer will lead to greater consumption by the neediest individuals within a household.[45] Finally, owing to certain features of market economies (partial information and endogenous preferences in particular) we cannot be sure that goods for satisfying essential needs will be consumed.[46] The second and the third effects can be avoided at least partly with in-kind transfers. These can also be used to cope with the problems related to asymmetric information and administration costs that prompt recourse to equal cash transfers. In-kind transfers can thus be a substitute for an instrument (cash transfers) that accentuates inequality.

Choosing between the two types of transfer highlights the difference between negative and positive liberty (Dasgupta, 1989). Those who place greater emphasis on the former will tend to favour cash transfers, arguing that the individual must be protected from the external coercion implicit in choosing the quantity and type of goods provided in a system of in-kind transfers. Defenders of positive liberty will prefer in-kind transfers, at least in certain circumstances: Weitzman (1977) shows that the price system has greater comparative effectiveness in allocating a deficit commodity to those who most need it when income distribution is almost egalitarian. When this is not the case, allocation through the price system will result in a 'distortion', since high-income people will tend

[43] In terms of section *11.4, they enable us to overcome self-selection constraints.

[44] In addition to Blackorby and Donaldson (1988), cited earlier, see Boadway and Marchand (1995) and Blomquist and Christiansen (1995).

[45] We assume that cash transfers can only be paid to households, while in-kind transfers can be made directly to the various members of the household (for example, food can be provided to children through school lunch programmes).

[46] The easy availability of non-essential goods in developing countries (tobacco products and soda beverages are typical examples) and the persistent lack of essential goods is partly a reflection of this. Demand for non-essential goods arises because some individuals' incomes are above the subsistence level and spread to the poorer segments of society through ostentation and imitation, which are part of the mechanisms for forming endogenous preferences. Cash transfers can finance demand for such goods from poor people as well. Although the contrast between the availability of often superfluous goods and the lack of essential goods is striking in the developing world, it also exists in the more-developed countries. In both cases, the dualism (or distortion) between consumption of essential and non-essential goods is a serious flaw in market-based economies.

to have high consumption, while the opposite will tend to occur with low-income people, irrespective of needs, or even in the case where low-income people have greater needs. If income distribution is widely dispersed, rationing will be more effective in satisfying those who most need the scarce commodity.

11.10 The welfare state

The complex of government activities comprising cash transfers, health, education, food provision, housing and other essential services goes under the name of *welfare state* (see Lampman, 1984). The definition of welfare state is not entirely unambiguous, however. It is sometimes extended to include progressive taxation, government action to maintain full employment and even the collective bargaining system (see Freeman, 1995). The birth of the welfare state can be traced to the Beveridge Report (see Beveridge, 1942), the essential elements of which were implemented in the United Kingdom and, with variations, in other countries. The term was first introduced in 1914 to distinguish between the British wartime government and the imperialist German 'warfare' state, but came into common usage after Beveridge.[47]

In the following pages we will generally focus on the redistributive aspects of the welfare state. Nevertheless, its contributions to efficiency are anything but negligible. We will mention only a few: the fact that consumers usually have seriously deficient information about the prices and quality of some goods and services may make it necessary for the government to produce them directly, thus ensuring some minimal quality standard at a reasonable cost, as in the case of health services; asymmetric information, which gives rise to adverse selection and moral hazard, makes it advisable to restrict individuals' freedom of choice by, for example, imposing compulsory (and therefore general) insurance against adverse events, such as illness, accidents, disability, old age or unemployment, with only small distortionary effects on preferences and probably large efficiency gains. The possibility that an individual may be faced with an uninsurable risk (for example, chronic illness or unemployment), thus creating a situation of incomplete markets, may induce the government to step in and offer insurance services (Barr, 1992). In addition it enables us to overcome indivisibilities, budget constraints, capital market imperfections, social stratification and segregation (Galor and Zeira, 1993; Ledebur and Barnes, 1992; Rusk, 1993; Benassy, 1996). The welfare state can thus play an important role 'as a device for stimulating risk-taking, thereby liberating productive forces and increasing aggregate income' (Sinn, 1995).

Real welfare states differ as to the types and levels of intervention and the methods for financing them.[48] These differences can be attributed to differences in the systems of values prevailing in each country. There are basically four models of welfare state:

    (a) the conservative-corporatist model;
    (b) the liberal model, which can be divided into:

---

[47] On the intellectual roots of the welfare state see Sandmo (1991).
[48] The following survey of the various welfare state regimes draws extensively on Mishra (1993).

the pure liberal model;

the reform liberal model;

(c) the social democratic model;

(d) the catholic model.

The conservative-corporatist model, which was adopted in Austria, Germany and Italy until the second world war,[49] grants the right to benefit from the welfare state to those who are (or have been) employed. Redistribution is primarily carried out through the family and, in any case, the private sector (charity in particular). Government only intervenes in residual cases of need. The system tends to maintain distributive differences created by the market while attenuating the most extreme inequalities.

The liberal model, which has been adopted in the United States, Canada and Australia, also provides for government intervention at the margin: 'The state encourages the market, either passively, by guaranteeing only a minimum, or actively, by subsidising private welfare schemes' (Esping-Andersen, 1990). Assistance may be subject to *means testing*, which implies that transfers may not necessarily be universal. In the reform version of this model, of which the Beveridge Report is an example, redistributive measures are closely linked to other market failures.[50]

The social democratic model is exemplified by the welfare state in the Scandinavian countries, which seeks to promote equality not only between workers but between all citizens. The market and the family play only a marginal role.

The catholic model is a more recent addition. It differs from the conservative-corporatist model in that government intervenes only when the individual, the family and, finally, the local community (which includes the church and other voluntary organisations) fail to provide support.

The post-war expansion of the welfare state that has occurred in almost all countries, regardless of the model adopted, is attributable to a variety of factors. In addition to those associated with the developments of welfare economics and those that explain the increase in government spending as a result of the specific interests of politicians and bureaucrats (see sections 9.2 and 9.3), other possible factors underscored by some economists are:

(a) the asymmetry between the costs and benefits of redistributive policies: costs are often divided among many people (e.g., the employed, the healthy) and therefore constitute a relatively small burden for each individual, meaning that they are not seen as excessive and therefore do not elicit opposition. At the same time benefits often accrue to smaller groups (the unemployed, the disabled), which, since they expect high benefits, have a strong incentive to ask the government for them. This would explain why interest groups can form and are successful in inducing subsequent additions to the welfare state's tasks.

---

[49] For a comparative historical discussion of the welfare state, see Barr (1992) and, more extensively, Barr (1993).

[50] According to Beveridge, poverty is a consequence of 'accidents' (such as illness or unemployment) and, therefore, can be insured against. Since people tend to underestimate risk for various reasons, eliminating poverty requires that the government intervene to compel individuals to obtain insurance.

(b) the interaction between egalitarian policies, individual preferences and political attitudes. Redistributive policies induce changes in individual preferences (both in the sense of fostering greater egalitarianism and reducing incentives to work or take risks).[51] In both cases the government is induced to increase its redistributive role and broaden the sphere and reach of the welfare state (see, for example, Persson, 1995; Lindbeck, 1995).

The redistributive activity of the government has been severely criticised, not only because the value judgements that support it are open to debate but also because it is often considered to be ineffective. According to some calculations, the final distribution of income net of all taxes and transfers has not changed a great deal in certain periods and countries;[52] in some cases it has even worsened.[53]

Invariance of distribution does not prove the ineffectiveness of redistributive policies. Indeed, it can be argued that without government intervention there would have been a worsening of income distribution, where this has not changed, or that the deterioration experienced would have been even more pronounced. In other words, government action has been effective but insufficient. However, there is not enough evidence to support such a position, as plausible as it might sound in theory. An alternative argument is that, under pressure from individuals and interest groups, the coercive power of the government has been used to 'take from the poor and give to the rich', disguising redistribution under other forms of government activity (Stiglitz, 1989): in the redistributive struggle, the powers of the government have been used by the better-off to increase inequality.[54] In both cases, the foundation of government redistributive action is strengthened, even if the practical consequences are considerably different. If the first argument holds, all we need to do is increase government intervention. If the second argument is correct, increasing equity means changing spending procedures (more generally, the ways in which government action is decided), as well as the political relationships between social classes and groups. As to the former, the procedures of government intervention, which probably do not show the public the redistributive pressures exerted by wealthier groups or classes, should be amended. As to the latter, the balance of power between social groups must change to ensure that the interests of the neediest individuals prevail.

It is difficult to prevent the government from being captured by the rich without

---

[51] The reader should weigh this argument against the other suggested above, according to which welfare state is a device for stimulating risk-taking. Which one prevails in reality is a matter of empirical investigation.

[52] This was the case in post-war Britain up to the early 1970s (Nicholson, 1974).

[53] According to Morris and Preston (1986), the welfare state operated a redistribution in favour of the poorer segments of the population in the 15 years after 1968 in the UK. For similar conclusions see also Hills (1995).

[54] The importance of *rent seeking* is underscored by Krueger (1974). For a survey of the literature, see Mueller (1989, chapter 13).

According to Le Grand (1987) the welfare state has been captured by the middle class, which has had mixed consequences: these are negative from the point of view of the dispersion of transfers, which should be primarily or exclusively directed at the poor; at the same time, there has been a positive effect in terms of the pressure exerted to maintain high quality standards. This second point, together with the desirability of fostering social integration, is in reality a strong argument in favour of universal direct provision of services such as education, health and social security.

altering conditions, such as in education, that block less fortunate groups' access to power. Some recent studies suggest that the welfare state should be considered in a broad, systemic sense, and that its various components (progressive taxation, cash and in-kind transfers, collective bargaining) are closely linked and produce positive results only if all the elements are present (Freeman, 1995).[55]

While aware of the many policies with distributive effects and the fact that implementing one of these alone is not sufficient to have a decisive effect on equity, one important area of further study would be to identify the minimum conditions that must be satisfied by government action to guarantee individuals the possibility of enjoying a reasonable standard of living and, therefore, positive liberty (Helm, 1989).[56]

11.11 Criticism of redistribution policies, flat-rate taxation and the basic income

The debate on the effects of government redistributive policies has given rise to a large number of empirical studies. These show the conflicting effects of progressive taxation and transfers on labour supply. Focusing on the effects of a tax on labour supply, Browning and Johnson (1984) conclude that this generates a very large efficiency loss, but an earlier survey of existing studies (see Brown, 1980) suggested that income and substitution effects largely balance. Danziger, Haveman and Plotnick (1981) and Moffitt (1992) refer to a group of studies showing that welfare state transfers create labour disincentives of varying magnitudes (sometimes small, sometimes more significant). Eissa (1996) finds low effects on labour supply of the changes in marginal tax rates introduced by US tax reforms in the 1980s, suggesting that the apparent high responsiveness of taxable income to such changes (see, for example, Feldstein, 1995) should be attributed to factors other than elasticity of labour supply, such as tax shifting.

Despite the diversity of empirical results, recent years have seen the spread of a certain 'redistributive pessimism'. This gloom is largely unfounded, for the following reasons:

1 Even if we stick to labour supply in a static context we should not consider only the number of hours worked by the employed, which is the variable on which most empirical studies focus, but also the labour force participation rate. The effect of redistribution policies on the latter might not be negative: with so-called secondary workers (often women) a question of family decision-making arises, and it may be that a member of the family who does not work in the absence of taxation is induced to work once the income of the primary worker has been taxed; these decisions are, however, highly dependent on actual tax rules.

2 Second, there is no reason to focus only on labour supply, which is an indicator of allocative (static) efficiency, as do most of the empirical studies showing

---

[55] Both the positive and negative aspects of dynamic interaction between the various elements of the welfare state and the entire system of individual preferences were noted earlier.

[56] Recall Sen's arguments for ensuring certain 'functionings' and 'capabilities'.

negative effects of redistribution. Dynamic efficiency may be even more important and in a dynamic framework it is necessary to consider variables such as investment, saving, etc., on which redistributive policies can have a different effect. Let us consider, for instance, the effects on investment in an economy with imperfect capital markets. A tax levied on higher-income (wealthier) agents would reduce their incentive to invest. However tax-financed transfers could be used to ease the budget constraint of the lower-income (poorer) agents, thus raising their propensity to invest (Benabou, 1996). The net effect on growth of redistributive policies would not necessarily be negative, as predicted by the economists critical of those policies (Perotti, 1996).

3 Empirical findings often refer to specific situations and cannot easily be extended to other, more common frameworks (Atkinson, 1995a and b).

Nevertheless, there have been many proposals for changing the tax and transfer system in recent years as a result of the feared impact on labour supply, the desire to reduce the administrative costs associated with existing redistributive mechanisms and pressure from the most affected taxpayers.

Among these suggestions, two deserve special attention: the *basic income* (or *citizen's income*) and the *flat-rate income tax.*

The first was proposed in the 1970s and 1980s by a group of economists and sociologists led by James Meade who were sensitive to problems of equity but aware of the efficiency problems involved in managing the welfare state in the United Kingdom (see Meade, 1972). They proposed guaranteeing a basic income to every citizen, irrespective of other sources of income. The income could either be equal for all adults or vary in relation to age, regardless of job status (employed or unemployed) or marital status. The basic income would replace all existing social security benefits and tax allowances. In theory, this would reduce administrative costs and expenditure on the direct provision of essential public services by the government as well as the costs of any means testing currently used to establish eligibility for benefits.

The second proposal (see Hall and Rabushka, 1995) would replace the current income tax and social security contributions with a single marginal tax rate on all income above some threshold (flat-rate tax). This would reduce administrative costs, thus increasing efficiency. Efficiency would be further enhanced by the fact that reducing progressivity, an implicit effect of the flat rate, would not discourage work by high-income earners. Redistributive objectives can still be attained, either by granting a tax allowance or implementing the flat tax in conjunction with a basic income scheme; however, progressivity would be lessened.

Some therefore argue that objectives of efficiency and equity could be reconciled by taking both proposals together, although neither objective would be achieved entirely. The actual mix of these objectives that would result depends on the level of the basic income and the tax rate: the higher the basic income the greater would be the redistributive nature of the system, but the higher would be the tax rate needed to finance the minimum income and other expenditure of the minimal state. However, doubts have emerged about the feasibility of the proposal. For example, with reference to the United

Kingdom it has been noted that to ensure a satisfactory basic income, i.e., one that would replace existing transfers, a tax rate of at least 50 per cent would be required, which seems excessively high, especially for middle-income earners. In order to reduce the rate, some have argued for a sort of partial basic income, which would replace only some of the existing social insurance schemes. These efforts merit further study, both with regard to the actual structure of reform proposals and the costs and benefits for the various social groups. In the absence of further research, we are justified in questioning the feasibility of such reforms of the existing structure of government redistribution. Hastily formulated proposals of this sort might simply hide attempts to reduce the extent of progressivity or implement a regressive redistribution.

11.12 Summary

1 A supporter of the productivity principle approach would not be able to justify the redistribution of income as a policy objective, except perhaps in the form of ensuring equal opportunity.

2 There are many redistributive measures. Of special importance is budget policy (taxation, cash or in-kind transfers).

3 The optimal tax maximises social welfare in terms of both efficiency and equity. Redistributing income with taxation always generates distortions in the labour supply and/or saving. Such distortions are accentuated by private information.

4 Taking account of the incentive-compatibility constraint, it is possible to identify the characteristics of the optimal income tax structure in situations of asymmetric information.

5 However, the relationship between redistributive policies and efficiency is complex. In addition to the effects we have already examined, we must bear in mind the physical, psychological and social factors that may produce positive effects of redistribution on efficiency. Moreover, there are also reasons to believe that the unconstrained Pareto-efficient frontier is an example of the Nirvana fallacy.

6 Redistribution can also be carried out with indirect (commodity) taxation on goods, setting different tax rates on different categories of goods. These taxes are distortionary as well.

7 Redistribution policies must take account of the possibility that the *de jure* taxpayer will shift the tax on to others.

8 Cash or in-kind transfers can be used to redistribute income and ensure a minimum standard of living for every individual. They cause problems analogous to those created by taxes. The existence of asymmetric information is an argument in favour of in-kind rather than cash transfers.

9 The welfare state has both efficiency and redistributive aims. There are different reasons for the apparently limited impact of the welfare state on the distribution of income and wealth. Each one calls for a different change in the system.

10 Empirical studies of the distortionary effects of taxation have produced conflicting evidence. They therefore do not justify the proposals for a drastic reduction in the redistributive activity of government vigorously advanced by certain individuals and pressure groups. Providing a basic income in conjunction with a flat-rate income tax would meet the needs of both equity and efficiency but there are problems associated with the actual implementation of such a system.

11.13 Key concepts

Optimal taxation	Poverty trap
Horizontal, vertical equity	Constrained UPF
Productivity principle	Constrained Pareto-efficient frontier
Equal opportunity	Fairness
Redistribution principle	Commodity taxation
Direct, indirect tax	Okun's leaky bucket
Tax rate	Excise tax
Proportional, progressive, regressive tax	Tariff
Marginal tax rate	Sales tax
Average tax rate	Value-added tax
Tax deduction (credit)	Retail sales tax
Progressivity by tax deduction	Ramsey rule
Continuous progressivity	Tax shift
Progressivity by tax bracket	Deadweight loss
Subsidy	Compensated demand curve
Negative tax	Consumer surplus
Cash transfer	Tax incidence
In-kind transfer	*De facto* taxpayer
Tax revenue	*De jure* taxpayer
Ability to pay	Welfare, workfare scheme
Comprehensive income	Welfare state
Equal marginal sacrifice	Means test
Income, substitution effect	Rent seeking
Distortion	Basic income
Incentive-compatibility (constraint)	Citizen's income
Self-selection constraint	Flat-rate (income) tax (flat tax)

12 Social choice and cost–benefit analysis

12.1 Choice criteria in private and public projects

Welfare economics has other important practical applications in current public choices, in addition to those we discussed in the previous chapter. In particular, the government can use it to assess whether to undertake a project or programme or not and to choose among mutually exclusive projects or programmes. Evaluating a project for constructing public works, establishing staff training projects, subsidising private investment and regulating pollution are some of the areas in which welfare economics can make a major contribution. With reference to the evaluation of public sector projects, we can define a project as a change in the net supplies of commodities from the public sector. Mutually exclusive projects are those that serve (approximately) the same purpose, through alternative solutions (such as building a dam with different techniques). We will consider only *small* projects, which involve small changes in output and demand. When a project is large, measuring the change in welfare caused by the project requires us to take account of a large number of variables and introduces analytical complexities (see Starrett, 1988; Hammond, 1990).

In assessing the effects of any project and selecting one of various alternative solutions, a government agency will measure the costs and benefits of each and will reject those that are the least attractive, much the same as a private investor would do.

As a basis for an investment decision, a private entrepreneur prepares a list of costs and revenues for each alternative investment project. The procedure involves the following steps:

1 to identify the alternatives, which include the status quo (no action);
2 to identify the consequences of each alternative in physical terms (i.e., the quantity of inputs and outputs each project entails) in each period of the time horizon;
3 to estimate the costs and revenues in each period on the basis of these

276

quantities and the market prices of the inputs and outputs;

4 to refer the costs and the revenues to the same time period (discounting);

5 to add up the discounted costs and revenues and to calculate the expected rate of return (profit) for each project, so as to be able to choose the most profitable one.

The government can proceed in a similar manner to evaluate a project. However, in steps 2 and 3 government economic calculations differ from firms' evaluations. A firm carries out only a *financial* analysis of the project, which is limited to the monetary consequences of the project relevant to the firm itself. The government, in addition to the financial analysis, also considers all the direct and indirect consequences (*economic analysis*). Economic analysis serves to assess the validity of the project. Financial analysis can serve the purpose of indicating the need for financial resources for the firm or agency or body that will administer the project.[1] To underscore the difference between the private and government assessment of a project, when we discuss government action we speak of costs and benefits, rather than costs and revenues; assessing the costs and benefits of a project from a social point of view is therefore known as *cost–benefit analysis* (CBA).

Before examining the differences, let us first take a look at the similarities, with reference to steps 4 and 5.

Assume that steps 1, 2 and 3 have been completed. For each project m, we have a set of benefits, b_t^m, and costs, c_t^m, at time t. As we know from economic and financial analysis,[2] a good (or quantity of money or asset) available in different time periods can be considered as a different good. Nevertheless, the values of an asset in different times can be compared if they are adjusted to refer to the same time period (for example, the initial period).[3] This process is known as *discounting*. In the case of CBA, we discount costs and benefits.

The sum of the present values of the benefits of project m can be given as:

$$B^m = \sum_{t=0}^{n} b_t^m (1 + i)^{-t}$$

where i is the interest (discount) rate and $(1 + i)^{-1}$ is the discount factor.

Similarly for costs:

$$C^m = \sum_{t=0}^{n} c_t^m (1 + i)^{-t}$$

---

[1] The government can also carry out a *fiscal* analysis of a project, to assess its contribution to the budget, and a *political* analysis, to assess its impact on the probability of re-election or the aims of the political party or social group the government wants to serve; see chapter 9.

[2] See also section 5.5.

[3] An asset worth 100 at the beginning of the second period (or at the end of the first) is financially equivalent to an asset worth $100(1 + i)^{-1}$ at the beginning of the first period (time zero). The amount $100(1 + i)^{-1}$, invested for 1 year at interest rate i, earns $100(1 + i)^{-1} \cdot i$ in interest; adding up the interest and principal, the amount available at the end of the year is $100(1 + i)^{-1} + 100(1 + i)^{-1} \cdot i = 100(1 + i)^{-1}(1 + i) = 100$. Similarly, an asset worth 100 at the end of the second period is equal to one worth $100(1 + i)^{-1}$ at the end of the first period and $[100(1 + i)^{-1}](1 + i)^{-1} = 100(1 + i)^{-2}$ at the beginning of the first.

In this way the effects of project m can be summarised by the (absolute) *net present value*, NPV (or present discounted value), of its costs and benefits:

$$NPV^m = B^m - C^m$$

The NPV can be used as a yardstick for judging the desirability of a project: any project with a positive NPV at a given discount rate is viable and therefore *eligible* for support; we then choose the project with the highest NPV, among a number of mutually exclusive projects. Cost–benefit analysis can be applied with some difficulty to a choice of projects that are not mutually exclusive, e.g., a project for the reduction of pollution and a project for the construction of a dam. This would require a detailed specification of the social welfare function.

Nevertheless, this criterion is clearly inadequate for ranking projects, since it does not take account of project size, on which the absolute value of the costs and benefits depends: large-scale projects may have large net benefits in absolute terms but small net benefits in relation to invested capital. In order to take this factor into account, we normalise the absolute NPV to obtain the 'relative' NPV (NPV_r), which is equal to the NPV divided by the discounted costs:

$$NPV_r^m = \frac{B^m - C^m}{C^m} = \frac{B^m}{C^m} - 1^4$$

We then choose the project with the highest NPV_r.[5] This is our second possible criterion.[6] Shifting from NPV to NPV_r does not affect the eligibility of a project, since the relative NPV is greater than zero if and only if the absolute NPV is positive. However, the projects' ranking may differ.

We must emphasise that with both rules the final choice is crucially dependent on the discount rate, i. The economic attractiveness of projects with immediate (or nearly immediate) social costs and deferred social benefits increases as the discount rate declines, since the lower discount rate has a smaller negative influence on benefits (because of discounting). Since different projects have a different time distribution of costs and benefits, changing the discount rate may change their relative attractiveness.

---

[4] This relation makes it clear why this criterion is also referred to as the 'benefit–cost ratio' criterion.

[5] In reality, if the social costs are calculated properly, i.e., if they include the 'opportunity costs' associated with the scarcity of financial resources, there should be no reason to favour small-scale projects; the absolute NPV would reflect the different use of financial resources by projects of any dimension. Small projects have low financial costs, which, other circumstances being equal, tends to increase the absolute NPV; conversely, large projects have high financial costs, which tends to reduce the absolute NPV, *ceteris paribus*. However, using the relative NPV can be justified when the scarcity of financial resources results in their being rationed: with a given quantity of resources it may be worth our while to classify projects by their NPV_r, choosing among them so as to maximise total net benefits and use all the available resources.

[6] Note that for a private sector firm the NPV_r is none other than the expected rate of profit corresponding to the market interest rate. $B^m - C^m$ represents the discounted expected profits. C^m, the discounted value of the costs, is financially equivalent to the firm's capital: it is the sum available today that can be invested at the market interest rate i to obtain future payment flows that exactly match the costs to be borne at future dates.

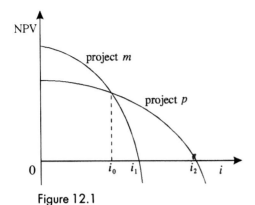

Figure 12.1

Figure 12.1 shows the importance of the discount rate in choosing among different projects.

For discount rates lower than i_0, project m is more attractive than project p in terms of NPV, but for $i > i_0$, the opposite holds; for $i > i_1$, project m has a negative NPV, as does project p for $i > i_2$.

A third decision criterion is the *internal rate of return* (IRR), which is the discount rate at which the sum of discounted benefits equals the sum of discounted costs. In other words the IRR is the discount rate at which the NPV is equal to zero. The IRR of project m is the discount rate i implicitly determined by the following equation:

$$\sum_{t=0}^{n} b_t^m (1 + i)^{-t} - \sum_{t=0}^{n} c_t^m (1 + i)^{-t} = 0 \qquad (12.1)$$

or

$$B^m - C^m = 0^7 \qquad (12.2)$$

Referring to figure 12.1, the IRR of project m is equal to i_1 and the IRR of project p is equal to i_2. These are the discount rates at which the projects' respective NPVs are equal to zero. If we use the IRR as a criterion, a project will be considered eligible if its IRR is higher than the social discount rate, which for the moment we will assume to be equal to the market interest rate. In choosing among more than one project, that with the highest IRR will be selected. In the example given in figure 12.1, this would be project p.

At first glance, this third criterion seems the most attractive since it does not require any prior selection of a discount rate in order to discount costs and benefits and calculate the net return of a project. However, problems can arise that may counsel against its use. We limit our comments here to the problem of multiple IRRs for a given project. Equation (12.1) is a polynomial equation of degree n in i, which in general

---

[7] The reader may have already encountered something similar to the IRR in Keynesian investment theory, where the marginal efficiency of capital is defined as the interest rate at which the sum of the discounted flows of net expected yields equals the cost of the investment. There are a number of differences between the two concepts that we cannot deal with here.

admits n distinct roots,[8] as shown in figure 12.2, where there are three (positive) IRRs, i_0, i_1 and i_2. In this case it is difficult to compare the IRRs of the different projects, or even assess the value of a single project.

Although the existence of multiple rates of return for a single project can be conceptually inconvenient, as long as all the roots are higher (lower) than the social discount rate we can still determine whether a project is (is not) eligible for consideration. Similarly, if project a has multiple rates of return that are all higher (lower) than those of project b, we can say that the former is (is not) preferable to the latter. However, there is no guarantee that this will happen, and we may even face paradoxical situations where, if the social discount rate lies between the minimum and maximum roots of the project, the project is simultaneously not eligible if we compare the social discount rate with the minimum rate of return (the minimum root) and eligible if we compare the social discount rate with the maximum rate of return. Similarly, the superiority of one project over another is uncertain if its rates of return are not all higher than those of the other.[9]

---

[8] As we know, the root is unique if there is only one change in the sign of the flow of net benefits (benefits net of costs) in the various periods (*Descartes' rule of signs*). This usually occurs if costs prevail in the initial periods and benefits prevail in later periods. Even if there is more than one sign inversion, it is possible to solve the problem of evaluating the IRR of the project if certain conditions hold (see, for example, Theichroew, Robichek and Montalbano, 1965; Gronchi, 1984).

[9] A second problem is pointed out by Boadway and Bruce (1984, pp. 295–7). We said that if the decision criterion is the IRR, we will choose the project with the highest IRR, regardless of the social interest rate (assumed to be equal to the market rate) and assuming that this is lower than the IRR. However, if at the market interest rate the NPV criterion orders the projects differently, it is possible to carry out a series of transactions on the capital market at this interest rate to obtain better results than those of the project selected using the IRR criterion. To this end let us suppose that the assessments of financial and economic analysis coincide and refer to figure 12.1. If we use the IRR criterion, we will choose project p; if we employ NPV, however, at an interest rate $i < i_0$ we will choose m. At this rate the net benefit flow of project m can be converted into a larger flow of net benefits than project p through appropriate financial transactions.

This can be shown with a simple example. The two projects have the following costs ($-$) and benefits ($+$):

	Year 0	Year 1	Year 2
Project m	$-$1,000	550	634
Project p	$-$1,000	1,150	00

From this we can deduce that $IRR^m = 0.12 < IRR^p = 0.15$. But, if $i = 0.05$, $NPV^m > NPV^p$. At this interest rate, it would be possible to exchange project m in the financial market for another project that is identical except that it involves borrowing 600 in year 1 (repaying 630 the following year). Call this project m'. It will have the following structure of costs and benefits:

	Year 0	Year 1	Year 2
Project m'	$-$1,000	1,150	4

This project is clearly superior to project p, which should have been preferred on the basis of the IRR criterion. The inconsistency is a consequence of the fact that the IRR criterion postulates the reinvestment of benefits within the cash-flow of the project at the same IRR, even if the market interest rate is different (in our case, it is lower than the IRR). The IRR approach thus neglects the financial aspects of the problem.

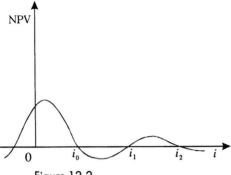

Figure 12.2

12.2 Identifying the effects of a project

We said earlier that the typical problems of calculating the social benefits of a project regard:

(a) identifying the quantitative effects of each project;
(b) assigning a value to those effects.

We will discuss these in order.

Forecasting the effects of a project is an extremely difficult operation that must be carried out with care. In particular, we must consider:

1 the direct and indirect effects of the project in terms of inputs and outputs of goods and services;
2 the effects of the project on incommensurable and intangible goods.

First, the relevant (direct or indirect) costs and benefits are those produced by the project in the economy as a whole. Direct effects are those generated by changes caused directly by the project in the demand for (input) or supply of (output) goods. Indirect effects are those that cause changes in the input or output of other, distorted, markets.

For example, the construction of a new underground line has direct effects in the form of purchases of cement, steel, labour and other goods and services, as well as the increased supply of underground transportation services. The indirect effects are a consequence of the fact that underground transportation is a substitute for congested road transportation. The reduction in road traffic induced by the increase in underground transportation services eases this congestion, i.e., *it reduces the external diseconomies of road traffic.*[10] Considering indirect effects is therefore the first difference between the social and private calculations of costs and benefits.

[10] This description accurately fits real-world cases, such as the well-known example of the construction of the Victoria line of London Underground. The indirect effects were in fact the largest benefits of the project. Note that the indirect effect is large and gives rise to a social benefit if and only if there is a large distortion in the affected market that is eliminated as an effect of the project: if the price in this market is not significantly distorted, there should not be any socially significant indirect effect since by hypothesis the social benefit (represented by the price of the good in the market considered) would be approximately equal to the social cost (the marginal cost of producing the good) for each additional unit produced and sold.

12.3 Evaluating the effects

Evaluating the effects of a project is an equally (or even more) complex operation in CBA. There are two specific questions to examine. The first regards choosing a numeraire for expressing benefits and costs. The second concerns the criterion for the valuation of the effects of the project.

As to the first question, instead of national currency, a foreign currency or consumption goods or investment goods can be taken as the numeraire. The choice among these different units of account is to be made according to the country's specific situation and policy objectives. If, for example, an underdeveloped country has a shortage of foreign currency, it can assess the benefits and costs of the project in terms of a foreign currency, e.g., dollars.

With reference to the second question, as a general criterion the society will find it advantageous to devote some of the available resources to a project if the benefits it derives from this project are larger than the benefits it could obtain from alternative uses of the same resources. The benefits of the project are measured by its beneficiaries' aggregate *willingness to pay*. The benefits of alternative projects that are forgone when resources are employed in the project in question represent what a society is *willing to pay* to have those resources diverted to alternative projects and are measured by the *opportunity cost* of these resources.[11]

To measure willingness to pay for benefits and opportunity costs we could use market prices in a competitive economy. As we know, if real markets were perfectly competitive, prices would represent both the benefits of a project, as valued by consumers, and its costs in terms of the goods society uses in that project, thereby foregoing the chance to use them in some other activity. (Recall that under perfect competition the price of *every good* is equal to its marginal cost.) However this is not the case in reality.

Indeed, there are several reasons why prices in actual markets cannot be taken as an appropriate measure of the willingness to pay and opportunity cost:

(a) the project under consideration is large enough to have an influence on the prices of outputs and/or inputs, but there are no distorted markets;
(b) some markets are distorted by monopoly, taxes, quotas, etc.; in addition, markets are incomplete;
(c) there are intangibles, i.e., immaterial benefits and costs that cannot be measured, since they have no market price;
(d) the distribution of income and wealth can have distortionary effects on individual valuations (and so on the prices) of goods.[12]

We deal with point (a) in this section, point (b) in the next and point (c) in section 12.5; section 12.6 will deal with 'distortions' deriving from the distribution of income and wealth.

---

[11] There is a problem in the assessment of willingness in the time horizon of the project: in fact, willingness may change through time.

[12] There is also the problem that prices reflect endogenous preferences or, in any case, preferences that are not shared by the government (as in the case of merit goods).

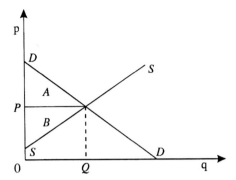

Figure 12.3

Before discussing the influence of a project's size, we have to define the concept of social surplus. This is the sum of the (private) consumer and the (private) producer surplus. As is well known, the former is the difference between what consumers are willing to pay and what they actually pay to secure a certain quantity of a good; the latter is what producers gain from selling the good at a price higher than the lowest price they are willing to accept (supply price). Consumer surplus and producer surplus can be represented, respectively, as areas A and B in figure 12.3, where DD and SS are the demand[13] and supply schedules.[14]

Both consumers and producers are willing to pay something to avoid a reduction in their surplus. Changes in the social surplus brought about by a change in price are then to be taken into account when measuring social benefits and costs.

Let us suppose now that a local government plans to increase the number of nursing homes it operates in a competitive market, assuming that the additional supply is small or, in any case, does not appreciably change the price of nursing services. This can be depicted as in figure 12.4, where DD is the demand schedule, SS is the supply schedule without the project, and $S'S'$ the supply schedule shifted to the right to account for the additional supply of nursing homes provided by the local government. The social surplus does not change as a result of the project since the price has not changed. The social benefit is then given by the area $MTQR$, which indicates the revenue to the local government for the sale of nursing services QR at the current price $0D$.

---

[13] The reader should note that this could be either the usual (*Marshallian*) *demand curve* or the *compensated* (*Hicksian*) *demand curve*. We can derive the traditional Marshallian consumer surplus from the Marshallian demand curve, while from the compensated demand curve we can draw either the 'compensating variation' or the 'equivalent variation'. There has been much debate on which of these measures should be used. The compensating variation seems to be the most widely supported by theoretical analysis, but the errors involved in using the traditional consumer surplus, which is simpler to calculate, are quite small (Willig, 1976; Just, Hueth and Schmitz, 1982).

[14] The position and shape of both the demand and supply curve can be derived in a number of ways (through observed behaviour; demonstrations or pilot programs; simulating the effects of the project; surveys offering contingent valuations, so-called because respondents are not actually required to pay their valuations of the goods; secondary sources of the kind used for intangibles – see section 12.5). On this the reader can consult Boardman *et al.* (1996).

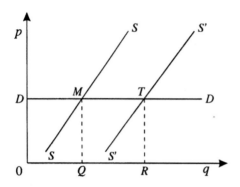

Figure 12.4

A similar situation applies if the local government buys additional quantities of an input that do not produce a change in the price of this input. In the case of the project to build and run additional nursing homes, the local government has to buy cement, furniture and so on as well as to hire nurses and other staff. If this does not change the price of cement and furniture or nurses' wages, and the relevant markets are competitive, the cost of the project is given by the sum of price times quantity of each good or service purchased.

In other terms, if markets are efficient and if the project does not affect the price of inputs, costs can be evaluated by simply multiplying the quantity of the inputs used by the project by the price of the input itself, since there is no change in the social surplus. In this case, which is most common when the inputs used in the project do not represent a significant proportion of the total quantity sold in the market, social costs correspond to budget expenditure.

If, however, the project causes a significant change in the price of outputs and inputs in competitive markets,[15] evaluating benefits and costs is a bit more complicated, since changes in the social surplus have to be accounted for, in addition to revenues and costs.

Let us first consider benefits. If the price of an output is significantly affected, we have the case shown in figure 12.5, where FG is the demand schedule, HI is the supply schedule without the project and LM that with the project. The price in the 'without-the-project' situation is $0D$; the price with the project is $0E$.

In this case both the consumer and producer surpluses change. The former increases by an amount equal to the area $ABED$. The latter decreases by $ANED$. (Notice that the supply curve relevant for the producer surplus is the original supply curve, which refers to *private* suppliers of the good). The net change in the social surplus is therefore ABN. In addition, benefits equal to $BSQN$ have to be considered, since consumers are willing to pay this amount to secure the additional quantity QS.[16]

With reference to costs, if the project has noticeable price effects on inputs, a change in

[15] As a matter of fact, we have said that CBA applies to small projects. So one can ask how these can cause significant changes in prices. This can really happen only with reference to one or a very few number of outputs or inputs.

[16] We leave it to the reader to evaluate benefits in the case where the project causes a change in the price of a producer good.

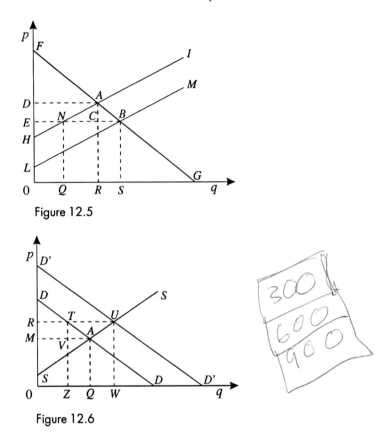

Figure 12.5

Figure 12.6

the social surplus occurs that has to be accounted for in *CBA*. Let us consider the case shown in figure 12.6. The shift in the demand curve of the good causes the price to rise from $0M$ to $0R$. This reduces the consumer surplus by the area $AMRT$. (The relevant demand curve is the original demand curve, which refers to *private* consumers.) The producer surplus increases by the area $AMRU$. There is a net increase in social surplus equal to TUA, and this has to be set against the cost of buying the quantity ZW(equal to the area $TUWZ$). The total cost of the project is thus $TAUWZ$. In this case the social cost is lower than the budget cost. The reader will note the redistribution of utility from consumers to producers.

12.4 Shadow prices

The need to use shadow prices arises when market prices do not reflect social values. As we said, in competitive markets the market price is also an indicator of the *cost* to society of using a good as an input in the project. By contrast, in non-competitive markets, the market price no longer reflects the cost to society since it is higher than marginal cost. It must then be replaced with a more accurate indicator of social value: the *shadow* (or *social*) *price*. This can be defined as the gain in the value of the (social) objective function from increasing expenditure on a given project by one unit (see section *12.9 for a more extensive discussion). As the objective in CBA is net social benefits, the shadow price of an output or input is the value of the marginal willingness to pay (for an output) or the production forgone in alternative projects, i.e., the opportunity cost (for an input). In general, shadow prices correspond to the prices that would prevail in an economy with complete markets where all markets were competitive. To calculate shadow prices, actual prices should be 'purged' of the surplus profit earned by firms as a result of their market power as well as of market failures and the existence of taxes or subsidies in the absence of market failures (see chapter 6).

However, we must consider that the difficulty of calculating shadow prices, which always involves approximations, means that it is advisable to use market prices where the distortions are not significant.[17]

As it is a measure of the opportunity cost, in principle the shadow price should be zero for resources that would otherwise remain unused; the opportunity cost of their use is, in fact, nil. However, we need to bear in mind the fact that in the real world there are situations where physical or human resources that would otherwise remain unused are used in conjunction with other *scarce* resources. This means that we must use different prices for each that reflect the different situations.

We can apply the concepts introduced here to a number of questions:

(a) determining the shadow prices of goods produced in non-competitive markets;
(b) determining the shadow prices of labour in the presence of involuntary unemployment;
(c) choosing the social discount rate.

12.4.1 Shadow prices in non-competitive markets

The market prices of goods used as inputs in a project will not reflect the social cost of using them if the market in which the prices are formed is not competitive. In CBA, we should consider the price corrected for the effects of market power. If we do not, our calculation of social value will be distorted. This would penalise projects that make use of goods whose prices are high due to the market power of their producers (even if using these goods does not excessively drain resources from alternative uses) rather than projects that make intensive use of scarce goods.

12.4.2 Shadow wages

A second important application of the concept of shadow prices is when we have involuntary or hidden unemployment.[18]

---

[17] The very difficulties associated with calculating shadow prices generate costs and inaccuracies that reduce the net benefit of using them in the first place.

[18] Recall that involuntary unemployment was defined as that occurring when the wage at which workers are willing to offer their services (the labour supply price) is less than or equal to the market wage of employed workers. Hidden unemployment is that which arises when the marginal product of labour is zero (see, for example, Lewis, 1954).

The unemployed labour used in projects subjected to CBA cannot be evaluated at the market price of labour, i.e., the prevailing wage. Since it is a good that is not fully used, its shadow price would be zero if we did not take account of the special features associated with the fact that labour is a cause of disutility.[19] Even if this is taken into account, the shadow wage may be lower than the current wage, since the latter may be the product of unions' monopoly power.

If we decide to take account of the disutility of labour in determining its shadow price in the presence of involuntary unemployment, the shadow price will be equal to the supply price of labour, which is equal to or less than the (net) market wage. However, if we did not accept, at least under these conditions, the neoclassical value judgements and hypotheses regarding the disutility of work, the shadow price of labour with involuntary unemployment would tend to be zero.[20]

Everything said so far holds if we assume that all of the jobs created by the project are filled by drawing from the ranks of the involuntary unemployed and that hiring them does not involve specific costs, such as moving expenses. If, however, the jobs created are filled by people who are already employed and decide to change their jobs, the shadow price of labour for these workers will be equal to the (pre-tax) market wage paid in their original job or even higher if this causes a reduction in output (e.g., agricultural production) with negative economic and social effects (see Harris and Todaro, 1970).

Since a real-world project will use both types of labour, the imputed shadow wage will be a weighted average of the wages of the two categories of worker: the current market – or even higher – wage for workers drawn from other jobs; zero or, at most, the supply price of labour for those drawn from the involuntary unemployed.

12.4.3 Choosing the social discount rate

Choosing the social discount rate is a very important step in CBA, and its impact increases the further costs and benefits are deferred into the future.[21]

As in the other cases, we can start with the market price, i.e., the market interest rate.[22] However, there are at least two reasons to choose a different rate.[23] The first regards the

[19] The emphasis placed on the disutility of labour in the presence of total involuntary unemployment (i.e., zero hours of work) of part of the labour force is excessive considering the various costs (including psychological costs) of forced idleness.

[20] Note that this is an especially controversial point. Among those in favour of imputing a shadow wage close to zero in the case of involuntary unemployment see Haveman (1977).

[21] Consider, for example, that the present value of 1 pound is equal to 0.5 pounds if the pound will be available in 23–24 years and the discount rate is 3 per cent; however, if the discount rate is 7 per cent, the present value falls by half in 10–11 years. If the pound were to become available in 23–24 years, its present value would be about 0.2 pounds, a fall of 80 per cent rather than 50 per cent.

[22] This section is very general. We therefore ignore certain aspects of reality, such as the fact that there are multiple market interest rates for different maturities or that consumer interest rates differ from producer's. This might lead us to adopt different interest rates, one for each 'maturity' (i.e., period) of the project. Market interest rates are also different for various risk prospects. For a treatment of risk see section 12.7.

[23] We must emphasise that the choice of the social discount rate depends on the choice of the numeraire, since the discount rate is nothing other than 'the rate of fall in the value of the numeraire against which goods are valued each year' (Drèze and Stern, 1987, p. 967).

market power of financial intermediaries and other distortions (e.g., those induced by taxation, credit rationing) that cause the interest rate to differ from its hypothetical level under perfect competition. The second regards future generations, which might not be adequately safeguarded even if capital markets are perfect: since future generations are unrepresented, the markets may express a large time preference for the present.

This latter issue is controversial, even outside the confines of CBA. Some argue that current generations take the interests of future generations into account in making their consumption decisions, if only because future generations are the descendants of current generations. However, this link is not always present. Childless individuals may express a greater time preference for the present since emotional considerations linking them directly to future generations are virtually absent and other considerations may be lacking. In addition, the current generation is influenced by factors (advertising, demonstration or imitation effects) that tend to increase current consumption. Note that such considerations are one-sided, since future generations, which would presumably choose to increase future consumption and reduce current consumption, cannot express their preferences.[24] Thus, markets tend to underestimate the value of the goods that, having deferred returns, enable such preferences to be satisfied (i.e., capital goods). From this point of view, future consumption can be considered as a form of merit good, which should be valued regardless of the preferences expressed by (current) consumers.

Some authors are critical of using a below-market rate for the social discount rate for a variety of reasons, including the fact that without total government control of investment the rate of return of public and private investments will not be equal, which causes production inefficiency. This is an important point that can be overcome in practice within the framework of a project analysis (see section *12.9), but it nonetheless gives us an idea of the theoretical difficulties that CBA can encounter.

12.5 Valuing non-marketed goods

Non-marketed goods include both tangible (i.e., material) and intangible (i.e., immaterial) goods.

Examples of tangible goods whose use is not traded in a market are motorways, bridges or other infrastructure that government could theoretically charge a price to use but, in the absence of congestion, generally supplies free, i.e., at a price equal to the marginal cost, which is zero if there is unused capacity. However, the fact that a public good is provided free does not exempt us from calculating its value (i.e., its benefit to society). We can do this by examining the hypothetical demand curve[25] for a particular good and calculate the willingness to pay for that good in the same way we do for marketed goods.[26]

---

[24] According to Pigou (1920, pp. 28–9) there is a 'natural tendency of people to devote too much of their resources to present service and too little to future service' (irrational discounting). Underlying this may be the 'limited generosity' of the human soul remarked on by Hume (1739).

[25] See note 13 in section 12.3.

[26] Recall that there is a free riding problem associated with expressing preferences but there are practical solutions for measuring willingness to pay (see section *10.5).

The problem of intangible goods is usually more difficult to solve because these goods are often even further removed from the market since they involve non-economic values. In particular, how do we place a value on human life, the environment or time?

12.5.1 Valuing life

Nearly every public project has considerable consequences in terms of costs and/or benefits for human life. Different versions of a basic project can be designed to provide different levels of safety. Choosing between these versions (or alternative projects) depends on the expected costs and benefits of each. We therefore need to assign a value to life precisely in order to safeguard it (as we might reasonably want to do), even if it is an incommensurable good in principle.

There are many techniques for valuing life. We will discuss only two: the direct or 'constructive' method and the indirect or 'hedonic price index' method.

With the first method, we measure the value of a life as the net discounted earnings of an individual over his expected life span. Only net earnings are considered; we therefore exclude those used to meet the costs of generating the earnings themselves. A problem with this method is that it identifies the value of a human life with the value of earnings, so that the value attributed to the lives of retired people or the disabled would be close to zero, which seems unjust and immoral.[27]

The indirect method makes use of the preferences revealed[28] by individuals with regard to alternatives with different probabilities of death. Those who place a greater value on living longer will choose less dangerous lines of work or goods and services (e.g., food, transportation), forgoing higher earnings or bearing higher costs in exchange. Wage or price differentials should be used with caution, however (see Viscusi, 1983), since they may be due to other unrelated factors (different disutility or social status of professions; different taste of foods; convenience of different types of transportation); there is also often a lack of information about the true probability of death associated with different jobs. 'Life preferences' revealed in the choice of work and goods and services are also influenced by individuals' state of need and, therefore, the income distribution. Consequently, the indirect method measures not only willingness to pay, but also ability to pay. Adopting this method, we will be forced to assign a lower value to the life of a pauper, who is more willing to accept a very risky job, than to that of a rich person, who will avoid risk like the plague. This considerably reduces the attractiveness of this method to those who consider that immaterial factors alone should be taken into account in valuing human life.

However controversial the methods used to measure it, the value of life is still a necessary element of CBA. Taking it into account favours projects with a lower probability of causing death, while ignoring it would have the opposite effect.

Even if a project does not place human life at risk, it may still affect the physical integrity or health of individuals. In other words, it may reduce or increase the probability of

---

[27] The direct method also raises technical problems, since the result is very sensitive to the discount rate adopted (Stiglitz, 1988).

[28] We can also consider declared rather than revealed preferences (see, for example, Jones-Lee, 1976).

injuries causing temporary or permanent disabilities, or adversely affecting people's health in some way. To value this we can use the same methods employed in valuing human life, supplementing them with a consideration of the additional costs to society of disability or illness.

If the effects on life, physical integrity or health (or other similar effects) are the main (rather than accessory) elements of alternative projects, as is the case in the field of health and safety, it may be appropriate to adopt a technique derived from CBA known as *cost-effectiveness analysis*. The objective of the project is taken as given (for example, a specific reduction in the number of fatal accidents due to some cause) and we focus on measuring the cost of alternative ways to achieve it. The advantage of this technique is that it avoids attributing a value to the benefits, which are only identified in qualitative and physical terms.

This technique can also be used for projects with objectives that are not identical but can be compared in physical terms. For example, Stiglitz (1988) cites a study in the United States to estimate the number of additional workers that would be protected against hearing loss by alternative noise reduction programmes. The study found that giving hearing protectors (ear plugs!) to workers would provide almost all the benefits of a general engineering-only noise standard (with the consequent drastic modifications of plant and equipment) at a much lower cost.[29]

12.5.2 Valuing the environment

The first step in identifying and valuing the effects of a project on the environment is the difficult task of defining the environment itself. We can rather vaguely define it as the set of conditions, objects and external circumstances on which the existence, health, satisfaction and ability of people to carry out certain functions depend.[30]

In principle, we can adopt the same criteria to value environmental damage as we did to value life, either by measuring individuals' reduced earning capacity as a consequence of environmental damage or, alternatively, assessing their willingness to pay to prevent such damage. The first method is usually more difficult to employ when the environmental impact of a project is diffuse. By its very nature, the environmental impact of a project is often precisely that, with widespread and long-lasting effects.[31]

Finally, it is possible to use another method for assessing the cost of environmental damage that is based on estimating the cost to society of preventing the damage or returning the environment to its original state. This cost assessment technique is particularly appropriate when we wish to compare alternative projects within the framework of a cost-effectiveness analysis.

To eliminate the many uncertainties surrounding the evaluation of the effects of a project on the environment, recourse has been made to the ambitiously named 'environ-

[29] Similar studies have been conducted for various disease screening programmes (see Drummond, 1980).

[30] This definition contains elements important to both direct and indirect social orderings, although the theoretical foundations of CBA are to be sought in the latter.

[31] Pollutants accumulate over time without degrading (*stock pollution*); the effects of a project, therefore, depend on previous levels of pollution and are difficult to measure in themselves (see Pearce, 1976).

mental impact study', which simply involves the determination of the qualitative or quantitative effects (in physical terms) of a project on the environment. This technique has come into widespread use in Europe in recent years, primarily under the impulse of EU legislation, and seeks to establish a basis for negotiation between the government and those intending to carry out a project with a significant environmental impact.

12.5.3 Valuing time

The impact of a project on individuals' leisure time must also be considered, since it can affect their utility level. For example, reducing workers' travel time by building a new underground line produces a social benefit.

Once again, however, the problem is one of measurement. We can use a variety of criteria, in particular willingness to pay. In the case we are dealing with, this is revealed by choosing faster, albeit more expensive, means of transport, such as taxis, private automobiles and so on. Obviously, this choice may also be influenced by other characteristics of alternative means of transport (comfort, safety), which must be taken into account in valuing the increased leisure time resulting from the project.

12.6 Distribution

We have noted on more than one occasion that market prices reflect the existing distribution of income and wealth. They will not appear as 'distorted' by the distribution, even in a competitive market, only if the existing distribution is the socially desirable one, whether as a result of chance or specific redistributive policies (obviously, by means of non-distortionary lump-sum transfers).

If the distribution is thought to be non-optimal, the costs and benefits of a project in terms of market prices can be corrected by using different weights for the different groups of income earners (at an extreme, we could use a different weight for each person). If, for example, there are ten income groups, the value of each cost and benefit should be attributed to these groups. We therefore calculate the net benefit for each group, which is then multiplied by the weight assigned to each by the policymaker. The sum of the net benefits to each group, corrected by the weighting factor, gives the net social benefit.

However, is this procedure in fact the best approach for taking account of distributive aspects? In the end, it is employed because the distribution is considered non-optimal. But if this so, why not implement direct, non-distortionary policies to achieve an optimal distribution? This is a valid point. Nevertheless, since it is normally not possible to redistribute wealth directly with non-distortionary instruments (lump-sum taxes), we can generally accept the merits of weighting the consequences of a project according to the groups affected. Moreover, as Stiglitz (1988, p. 274) argues, many public projects, such as education, have explicit redistributive purposes that make it necessary to use distributional weights.[32]

---

[32] For more on the correction of benefits and costs for income distribution see Layard (1980).

12.7 Uncertainty

Adding to the complexity of CBA is the fact that the magnitude of the costs and benefits of a project is usually uncertain. One way to deal with uncertainty is to calculate a *certainty equivalent* for each uncertain benefit or cost. Suppose we need to assess a project to build a dam. Owing to the uncertainty connected with determining geological conditions, the cost of some stage of construction might be either 1,000 or 2,000. We also assume that we can assign a probability to the two events, e.g., that they have the same probability, 1/2. The expected value of the cost, equal to $1/2 \cdot (1{,}000) + 1/2 \cdot (2{,}000) = 1{,}500$, underestimates the true cost if the person in charge of the decision process is risk-averse, as is normally the case. A risk-averter does not consider the prospect of paying a cost of 1,500 with probability 1 equivalent to that of paying 1,000 with a probability of 1/2 and 2,000 with a probability of 1/2. The utility associated with the latter is equivalent to that of a cost of *more* than 1,500 with probability 1 because the chance that the actual cost will be 2,000 weighs more *in terms of utility* (for a risk-averter) than the chance that the actual cost will be only 1,000. In other words, the certainty equivalent of the second possibility is greater than 1,500 – say 1,650 – where the difference of 150 represents the *risk premium*, i.e., the (additional) cost that someone would be prepared to bear in order to avoid the risk.

Similarly, if the benefits of a project are estimated to be either 1,000 or 2,000, each with a probability of 1/2, a risk averter would assign a certainty equivalent of *less* than 1,500, being willing to pay a premium (let us again say 150) in order to eliminate uncertainty.[33]

---

[33] The certainty equivalent can be derived from *expected utility*. Assume that an action (project) has outcomes y_i, with probability p_i, where i is an integer such that $1 \leq i \leq n$ indicates the state of nature that can occur. The expected utility of the action is:

$$U(y) = \sum_{i=1}^{n} p_i U(y_i) \tag{12.3}$$

If the agent is risk averse, we have:

$$U(y) = \sum_{i=1}^{n} p_i U(y_i) < U(\bar{y}) \tag{12.4}$$

where $\bar{y} = \sum p_i y_i$.

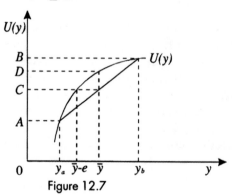

Figure 12.7

Thus, if some costs or benefits are uncertain, they should be replaced by their certainty equivalents, whereupon the choice of project can be made with the normal techniques.

12.8 The theoretical foundations of cost–benefit analysis

The main limitations of CBA are essentially a consequence of the fact that the reality affected by a project is imperfect.[34] Distortions distance the actual situation from the 'ideal' one – the yardstick of CBA – where Pareto efficiency conditions are assumed to be satisfied. These distortions are created by market power, externalities, taxes, etc. and are difficult to quantify, not only for purely practical reasons but also because it is necessary to distinguish between removable and irremovable distortions. With removable distortions, we can use shadow prices to simulate their removal. With irremovable distortions, the shadow prices for the indirect effects cannot be first-best prices and are more difficult to calculate.

Awareness of these problems has spurred research to identify:

(a) the conditions for the so-called '*decomposition*' or '*separability*' of the effects of a project, which enable us to isolate the effects of real-world distortions;

(b) the conditions and rules for overcoming distortions even if separability is not possible;

(c) practical methods for calculating shadow prices in the presence of distortions, founded, however, on the hypothesis that consumers can be treated as a single individual.

The first approach was taken by Davis and Whinston (1965) and Negishi (1972). We can say that using the shadow prices associated with Pareto efficiency is optimal if the project:

1 has no redistributive effect;

2 does not influence the production of, or demand for, goods affected by some distortion. Independence requires that the supply and demand for these goods be separate from the supply and demand for the direct inputs and outputs of the project (Starrett, 1988).

The certainty equivalent of the project is the value $\bar{y} - e$ (where e is a positive number) available with probability 1 that would be exchanged for the uncertain outcomes of y. If the agent is risk-neutral (risk-seeker), (12.4) will be satisfied with the equals (greater than) sign.

The concept of certainty equivalent is shown in geometric terms in figure 12.7. In the figure, $U(y)$ is the utility function of a risk-averse agent. The utility of a project that is expected to have revenues y_a and y_b with probability 1/2 is equal to $0C$ on the basis of (12.3) and is equal to that of $\bar{y} - e$, expected with certainty, where e is the risk premium. By contrast, the utility of $\bar{y}$, expected with certainty, is greater and is equal to $0D$. The greater the concavity of the utility function, the larger the risk premium. For more on these concepts, the reader can consult a microeconomics text such as Varian (1987), Varian (1992) or Mas-Colell (1995).

[34] The reader should recall however that the very imperfections of the market give rise to valuable indirect effects of the project (see section 12.2).

A more interesting result was reached by Diamond and Mirrlees (1971) for identifying the conditions for overcoming distortions even without separability in a model of public production with competitive price producers, unrestricted commodity taxation and full taxation of private profits. They identify the conditions for production efficiency when consumption is distorted by indirect taxes. These are similar to the Pareto conditions. In particular, the ratio between the shadow prices of each pair of government inputs must be equal to their relative producer prices in the private sector. This enables us to obtain Paretian production efficiency despite the presence of indirect taxes, which in theory are distortionary. In fact, it is the very possibility of levying different consumption taxes for each good that enables the government to control consumer prices, isolating the production efficiency conditions, which can still be the Paretian conditions.

The third strand of research, which seeks to identify practical methods for calculating shadow prices, has examined, for example, distortions caused by taxes that give rise to a difference between producer prices and consumer prices. Harberger (1969) showed that the shadow price can be expressed as a weighted average of the producer price and the consumer price of the good. His analysis does not hold in the presence of distributive effects, however (see Hammond, 1990).

*12.9 Shadow prices in a planning framework

In calculating shadow prices we can consider at least three different contexts.[35]

First, there is the shadow price in a *detached context*, which would be the value assigned to an extra unit of the good assuming that nothing else changes in the economy.

Second, we have the shadow price in a *project context*, in which the quantities of inputs and outputs of the project – considered to be independent – change, while other quantities are dependent on them through the operation of equilibrium conditions. If a project uses a larger quantity of some input with a given supply, the quantities of that input used elsewhere must fall.

Assume that the function to be maximised is $V(s)$, where s is a vector of social states that can be affected by a government project (considered as a set of inputs and outputs), represented by a vector (z); we therefore have $s = s(z)$. There are also constraints on resource availability, which can be shown as $F_i(s, z) \leq w_i, i = 1, 2, \ldots, k$, where w_i are parameters (the constraint constants, representing, for example, resource availability).

The objective of the project is:

$$\max_{s} V(s)$$

subject to

$$s = s(z)$$
$$F_i(s, z) \leq w_i$$

---

[35] Our discussion draws on Drèze and Stern (1987) and Starrett (1988), albeit with a number of modifications.

In this case the shadow price of an input (or output) in z is:

$$\frac{\partial V}{\partial s} \cdot \frac{\partial s}{\partial z}$$

which gives the marginal social value of the input (or output).

Third, we have shadow prices in a *programming context*, where all the constraints are taken into account. The constraint parameters are the independent variables and the dependent variables are represented by the arguments of the function that the policymaker wants to maximise. Since each parameter can change, the corresponding change in the objective function can be identified. This change in response to a unit change in the parameter is the shadow price of the parameter in a programming context.[36] For example, let $V(s, w)$ be the function the policymaker wants to maximise. The programming problem can be stated as:

$$\max_{s,w} V(s, w)$$

subject to

$$s = s(z)$$
$$F_i(s, z) \leq w_i$$

This is a more general problem than the previous one, since the w_i parameters can also change as a result of external shocks or specific shocks produced by the policymaker (reform policies).

In this case the shadow prices can be defined with reference not only to the planned quantities of the project's inputs or outputs but also to the level of the constraints or, more generally, to all the parameters that appear in the specification of the constraints. For example, the shadow price of parameter w_i is defined as $\partial V/\partial w_i$ and indicates the marginal social value of the parameter itself.[37]

12.10 Summary

1 An important practical application of welfare economics is cost–benefit analysis (CBA). This involves evaluating the costs and benefits of alternative government projects, much the same as private-sector firms do.

2 Choosing the best project can be carried out on the basis of:
    (a) the net present value (NPV) of the costs and benefits;
    (b) the internal rate of return (IRR).

[36] In other terms, the shadow price of parameter w_i measures the sensitivity of the objective function to changes in the parameter. It corresponds to the Lagrange multiplier associated with the ith constraint.

[37] See Drèze and Stern (1987, p. 919); Guesnerie (1977); Ahmad and Stern (1984); Newbery and Stern (1987).

3 The main differences between CBA and the estimations of a private firm regard:

    (a) the approaches to valuing costs and benefits;

    (b) the consideration of the positive and negative external effects of the project, as well as 'incommensurable' costs and benefits.

4 The general rule for the evaluation of costs and benefits is agents' willingness to pay. In particular, the valuation of the goods and services produced by the project and that of its inputs can be based on market prices (perhaps corrected by the change in the social surplus if the market prices are affected by the project) when markets are competitive; if this is not the case, the valuation of the costs and benefits must make use of shadow prices, which represent the true marginal social benefit or cost.

5 The shadow price corresponds to the price that would prevail under perfect competition with complete markets. Therefore, where the goods and services used in the project are produced in non-competitive markets, their prices must be purged of the extra profits attributable to market power.

6 Determining the shadow wage is especially important and particularly difficult when the project draws on unemployed workers.

7 Deciding which social discount rate to use is also important, since it influences the choice between projects whose returns are spread over different lengths of time. The reasons for not using the market interest rate regard the market power of financial intermediaries, as well as the existence of other distortions, and a desire to safeguard the interests of future generations.

8 Among non-marketed goods and services, valuing human life is particularly difficult. There are many methods for placing a value on life, although none is entirely satisfactory. However, the difficulty of determining such a value does not mean that we can do without it, precisely because we wish to protect life more effectively.

9 Cost–benefit analysis is complicated by uncertainty and the need to correct for distributive considerations.

*10 Additional complications are a consequence of the fact that the shadow prices for indirect effects are not first-best solutions and are more difficult to calculate in the presence of irremovable distortions. As a result, research has been conducted on:

    (a) the conditions for the decomposition of a project's effects;

    (b) the conditions for overcoming distortions;

    (c) practical methods for determining shadow prices in the presence of distortions.

*11 Shadow prices can be calculated in a detached, project or programming context.

12.11 Key concepts

Cost–benefit analysis
Discounting
Net present value
Project eligibility
Internal rate of return
Marginal efficiency of capital
Multiple roots
Descartes' rule of signs
Direct and indirect effects
Willingness to pay
Opportunity cost
Incommensurable
Demand price
Consumer surplus

(Marshallian) ordinary demand curve
(Hicksian) compensated demand curve
Producer price
Shadow (social) price
Intangible
Cost effectiveness analysis
Environmental impact study
Stock pollution
Certainty-equivalent
Risk premium
Conditions for decomposition,
    separability
*Detached, project, programming
    context.

PART V

MACROECONOMIC INTERVENTION IN A CLOSED ECONOMY

13 Macroeconomic objectives and monetary policy

13.1 Objectives, instruments and models of macroeconomic policy

Macroeconomic policy seeks to achieve objectives defined in terms of aggregate economic variables: full employment, price stability, balance of payments equilibrium, growth.

Since market failures in achieving these objectives are largely identified through macroeconomic theories, the latter underlie the analytical model that:

(a) enables us to identify variables that can be used as instruments;
(b) indicates the links between targets and instruments, thus permitting us to set instrument values at the optimal level.

We have seen that there have been attempts to undertake a microeconomic analysis of at least some of the problems considered here: unemployment is one example. This is the approach taken by many theories belonging to the 'classical' strand of economic thought. Some of these give no explanation for involuntary unemployment; others explain it, but only as the product of 'imperfections' (e.g., imperfectly flexible prices). Theories of this sort tend to suggest microeconomic solutions, such as reducing or eliminating the causes of price stickiness, rather than policies based on the adjustment of aggregate variables, such as government expenditure, tax revenue, liquidity, etc.

While the search for macroeconomic models constructed on microeconomic foundations is a worthy task, it must be said that currently available models of this kind are inadequate. Their shortcomings are such that Keynesian macroeconomic models still seem to offer more satisfactory explanations of reality. We will therefore rely primarily on such theories in identifying the most appropriate solutions to the macroeconomic aspects of market failure.[1]

---

[1] Nevertheless, references to microeconomic concepts will be helpful in some circumstances (e.g., monetary policy).

Since we will be giving more space to the solution to this sort of problem than we gave to that for microeconomic failures, we will be able to undertake a more thorough analysis of the institutional aspects of instruments. We therefore adopt a different approach from that used to assess microeconomic policies: with the latter, the instruments used for each target were indicated; for macroeconomic policies, we indicate the targets that can be achieved with each instrument. The macroeconomic instruments are: monetary policy, fiscal policy, price and incomes policy and exchange rate policy.

Although these instruments are aimed at macroeconomic targets, their effects are not necessarily spread equally over the entire economic system. On the contrary, they are often *selective*. For example, this is the case with a restrictive monetary policy, which has a greater negative impact on small firms; these usually pay higher interest rates, are credit rationed and can only make limited use of self-financing and cross-subsidisation.[2] Similarly, a revaluation or appreciation of the exchange rate will reduce exports more for firms producing high price elasticity goods than those producing innovative or high-quality goods, for which the price elasticity of demand is lower.

These selective effects are important and must be considered in formulating policy choices. However, for reasons of brevity we will not discuss them here, although the reader is invited to pursue the study of these issues.

13.2 The monetary economy

In chapter 7 we discussed the importance of money in the operation of the economy and argued that in order to understand the reasons for and nature of the instability of a capitalist system it is absolutely necessary to introduce the hypothesis of a monetary economy. Let us briefly review the characteristics of money before examining financial intermediaries.

It is well known that the first and most important function of money is its role as a *medium of exchange* or *means of payment*: compared with a barter economy, money reduces transaction and information costs (the time and effort spent searching for a suitable counterparty).

A second function of money is its role as a *unit of account*: it is the 'good' in which all prices are calculated and values are stated. Note that the good used as a means of payment may not necessarily be the same as that used as a unit of account.[3]

---

[2] We have *cross-subsidisation* when profits in one sector are used to finance investment in another sector in order to sustain the growth of the firm in this second area. The term is also used when profits from one line of business are used to cover losses in other activities resulting from, for example, aggressive pricing policies (predatory pricing practices) aimed at eliminating competition. Cross-subsidisation and self-financing can be used by large firms, especially when they are part of financial groups.

[3] With reference to modern economies, for example, accounts might be kept in dollars or gold while transactions are settled in yen, pounds sterling, German marks, French francs or Italian lire. The existence of different 'goods' for different monetary functions can cause problems if the ratio between them is not constant.

An example of a pure accounting currency is the guinea, an English gold coin that has not been minted since 1813 but remained in use as a unit of account in Great Britain until the 1970s. Some

Money's third function is to serve as a *store of value*, i.e., a means for transferring purchasing power in time, in association with or as an alternative to other financial and real assets.

Money has an essentially *fiduciary* nature. Throughout history, the attribution of a monetary function to one or another means has always been of a conventional and fiduciary nature:[4] 'the necessary condition for the performance of this exchange function is general acceptability in settlement of debt' and this 'falls within that perplexing but fascinating group of phenomena which is affected by self-justifying beliefs' (Newlyn, 1962, p. 2).

Once agents have come to trust some means, it is accepted as a medium of exchange and as a store of value, and transactions are stipulated in terms of it. The form of money has changed over time. The earliest forms were commodities (cattle, shells, etc.), followed by metal coins and then by paper money (banknotes) and bank money. In order to understand the evolution of money and especially the emergence of modern money (which is primarily bank money) we will introduce the concept of financial intermediation (see section 13.3). Acceptance of bank money is in fact prompted by the rise of institutions able to generate trust, such as financial intermediaries.

13.3 Financial intermediaries

In an economy the moment incomes are received and the moment they are spent do not coincide; if the division of labour is well-developed, the agents who own goods do not coincide with the agents who demand those goods either. In a monetary economy, 'the participants in the production process' receive a quantity of money[5] granting them purchasing power over goods. Some participants (typically, households) demand only part of the goods they are entitled to buy (consumption) while other agents (typically, firms) demand more than they have been assigned in the distribution of income, in order to expand their productive capacity (investment). We thus have some agents with a savings surplus and others with a savings deficit (or excess spending). Satisfying both the saving plans of one group and the spending plans of the other depends on the existence of financial instruments, primarily *direct credit*, through which agents with a surplus can temporarily transfer purchasing power to those in deficit.

However, direct credit, in the form of loans, bonds or shares (issued by firms and subscribed by households) has a limited range of action if, as happens in the real world, there is a considerable difference between the terms (interest rates and/or maturities)

---

prices were expressed in guineas, even though payment could only be made in the existing currency (pounds sterling and coins), at a ratio of 1.05 pounds to the guinea. The ECU is also a mere unit of account (see chapter 16).

[4] This is the case even when the use of a currency is imposed by an outside authority, such as the state or when this authority recognises some currency as *legal tender* for the settlement of debts. Such status may help a particular means of payment gain acceptance, although this is not fully guaranteed (or welcomed) in all circumstances.

[5] The actual type of money is irrelevant here. It may simply be some commodity to which monetary functions have been attributed.

requested by the two groups or if there are market imperfections. This is especially so if information costs are high, since agents do not have full information in a broad and differentiated market.

More specifically, the two sides will desire different loan maturities. Creditors will seek to shorten them as much as possible in order to reduce their exposure to insolvency risk, which rises as maturities lengthen. By contrast, borrowers will prefer to lengthen maturities until they match the time needed for the investment to produce the desired gains, in order to avoid the risk of not being re-financed when the initial shorter-term credit matures. Obviously, this fundamental divergence can be bridged by increasing the price paid by borrowers (i.e., raising the interest rate), which will incorporate a premium for the risk associated with a longer maturity. However, this solution would be very costly for debtors.

Financial intermediaries[6] – and with them *indirect credit*[7] – can lower the cost of credit for essentially three reasons:

1 There are economies of scale and scope in acquiring savings from surplus agents and channelling them to deficit agents. Economies of scale are linked not only to the reduction of management costs permitted by specialisation and standardisation of operations, but also to the existence of fixed costs for information on the *ex ante* riskiness of firms and specific investment projects as well as on the *ex post* risk associated with the actual use that has been made of the loan funds. This means that financial intermediaries are in some way involved in certifying borrower quality. Economies of scope are connected with the benefits (externalities) produced by lending in one field (e.g., short-term credit) for lending in another (e.g., long-term credit): this is clear from the fact that, for example, information costs are not only fixed (which gives rise to economies of scale) but are also joint costs for the different types of credit.

2 Intermediaries also have scope for *maturity transformation* thanks to the economies of scale associated with the law of large numbers: since not all suppliers of funds will demand repayment on maturity,[8] intermediaries can lend money for a longer period of time, keeping only a small precautionary reserve (*excess* or *free reserves*). Moreover, the insolvency risk of some borrowers can also be negatively correlated with that of others, thus lowering the overall level of risk.

3 The presence of financial intermediaries makes it easier to diversify the risk of individual portfolios. Owing to the relatively small size of their wealth, most surplus agents could at most lend to only a few borrowers. This would increase the insolvency risk they face compared with that of a more diversified portfolio, prompting surplus agents to demand a higher interest rate. Intermediaries make it possible to pool small individual savings and thereby diversify lending, reducing overall risk and, therefore, the interest rate.

The direct and indirect credit granted in a given economy constitutes the *financial*

---

[6] Among the initial contributions to the concept of financial intermediary was the Radcliffe Report (see the Committee on the Working of the Monetary System, 1959).

[7] From holders of surplus savings to financial intermediaries and then to those with a savings deficit.

[8] Or immediately, if the funds must be repaid on demand.

liabilities of that economy. For a closed economy, total financial assets must equal total financial liabilities. This remains true for an open economy if we include 'the Rest of the World' as an institutional sector.

Financial intermediaries, financial assets (or liabilities) and the related markets form the financial structure of an economy. The presence of financial intermediaries thus enriches not only the set of economic agents but also the ways financing can be provided. It generates a variety of financial instruments that differ in form,[9] maturity or other terms, as well as by issuer, i.e., the agent that assumes the liability either directly (if the agent operates in the deficit sector) or indirectly (if the agent is a financial intermediary).

The specialisation of financial intermediaries varies according to national characteristics and historical circumstances. Specialisation may take place according to borrowers' branch of activity (lending to agriculture, real estate, film companies, etc.), the maturity of the loans granted or received (short-, medium- or long-term credit) or the form of credit usually granted (in some countries, such as the United Kingdom, this led to the emergence of commercial banks, discount houses, accepting houses, etc.).

Of particular importance is the specialisation or *separation* between short-term credit and medium- and long-term credit that characterises *English-type banks*, in contrast to *universal* or *German-type banks*, in which there is no such separation. The universal bank was partly blamed for the financial instability of the 1920s, which saw the collapse of a number of such institutions. More recently, however, the universal bank model has been adopted even in EU countries that had previously favoured the other model.

13.4 Money as a liability of financial intermediaries

In the evolution from money with an intrinsic value (various forms of commodity money and specie in particular) to token money, money has become nothing more than a liability (with or without paper form) issued by a financial intermediary. Historical circumstances, often (but not always) associated with the shared belief in the reliability and solvency of a particular financial intermediary, have led to the acceptance of its sight or short-term liabilities as a means of payment.

There are two types of money and two corresponding types of financial intermediary: banknotes, which are created by central banks, and deposits, which are created by banks.

Banknotes are *legal tender*. After a period in which numerous issuing institutions co-existed, banknotes are now issued under a monopoly (originally as a government concession, now by law). Until 1914, and in some countries even after the first world war for a certain period, it was possible to convert banknotes into specie or bullion (see chapter 16). With the end of convertibility, the acceptance of banknotes was imposed by law (*fiat money*).[10]

---

[9] This may or may not be represented by a tradable security. If it is, we can speak of *securitisation*.

[10] The term fiat money indicates that, without the original fiduciary relationships, something becomes money as a result of government imposition; literally, it is 'created out of nothing'. Nevertheless, its acceptance and the spread of its use still depend to some degree on individuals' willingness to accept the currency on a fiduciary basis.

Bank deposits are the second type of financial liability used as money. In this case, their acceptance as money is still based on an entirely fiduciary relationship that has not been imposed by an outside authority. The circulation of bank deposits, necessary to their monetary role, takes place through cheques and giro transfers.

In recent years, banks have introduced new liabilities that have assumed an important role thanks to their considerable liquidity and can therefore be included in the definition of money: bank fund-raising through repurchase agreements and bank certificates of deposit; banker's acceptances.

Financial innovation is partly the result of private agents' attempt to elude credit regulations, such as compulsory reserve requirements and lending ceilings, which we will discuss later. In other cases, it involves creating new liquidity instruments to improve the performance of the financial system by meeting agents' needs more appropriately.

Repurchase agreements are temporary operations in securities consisting in the spot sale of government securities by one party to another and the simultaneous forward repurchase of the same securities by the original seller at a stated price. Banks can use repurchase agreements with their customers to raise funds.

Certificates of deposit are negotiable securities issued by banks representing time deposits.

Banker's acceptances, or bills drawn on a bank by a customer, are not a new instrument. However, since the mid 1970s they have been fairly widely used in some countries as a substitute for other forms of bank credit in order to avoid regulations limiting lending growth.

The existence of numerous liquidity instruments makes it necessary to introduce a variety of empirical definitions of money (*monetary aggregates*). The latter are often redefined to take account of financial innovation. We currently use a number of monetary aggregates, although definitions vary from country to country.

At the beginning of the 1990s, in the United States the aggregate M1 included current account deposits and traveller's cheques in addition to currency (i.e., banknotes and coins); M2 comprised M1 plus other chequeable assets, small-denomination certificates of deposit, overnight repurchase agreements and overnight Eurodollar funds; M3 comprised M2 plus other less liquid assets such as large-denomination certificates of deposit, long-term repurchase agreements and Eurodollar term deposits. In the mid 1990s in the EU countries there were still some differences in the published monetary aggregates (M0, M1, M2, M3, M4, 'extended' M), as well as in the asset composition of those called by the same name, especially for the narrow aggregates. For a full description see Monticelli and Papi (1996, appendix 1).

13.5 The central bank and monetary base

Banks to which the government privilege of issuing banknotes had been granted initially continued to perform ordinary banking activities. Subsequently, this privilege, the close relationship with government and the centralisation of metal reserves gave the banks of issue a special position compared with other banks. Nevertheless, they often continued to act as commercial enterprises and maintained their private-sector legal status (Goodhart, 1988).

For reasons that we will elaborate on later (see section 13.7), the evolution of financial systems mentioned in the previous section can give rise to increased risk of instability. In particular, there is a danger that banks' reserves might not be sufficient to cope with unexpected withdrawals. Insolvency can be avoided if the issuing institution provides banks with liquidity, acting as a *lender of last resort* or *banker's bank*. Central banks in the leading countries (e.g., the United States and the United Kingdom) perform this function. A major exception is Germany, where the Bundesbank has complete discretion in granting credit of last resort. This is because it was felt that preserving the stability of the financial system conflicted with the Bundesbank's primary objective of regulating the money supply, i.e., ensuring a stable value for the Deutsche Mark. The European Central Bank is largely based on the Bundesbank model, but it will provide lender of last resort services in certain cases (see Vives, 1992).

Central bank functions also include bank regulation and supervision to ensure compliance with sound management rules and thereby guarantee the stability of the financial system. The regulatory function complements the central bank's lender of last resort role. The existence of such a lender could create a form of moral hazard because the banks, feeling themselves protected ('insured') by the central bank, might engage in excessively risky transactions. Regulation and supervision by the central bank can reduce this risk.[11]

The regulatory function often includes requiring banks to maintain minimum *compulsory reserves* in addition to their excess reserves. The original aim of this regulation was to protect depositors, but compulsory reserves now have only the function of governing the money supply. The financial assets that can be used to constitute these reserves make up *monetary base* (or *high-powered money*). It includes all sight liabilities issued by the monetary authorities as well as others that can be readily converted into such liabilities.

Monetary base meets the need of the banks to maintain excess reserves as well as comply with the reserve requirement (see subsection 13.7). Moreover, since monetary base includes legal tender, it serves the public (i.e., the non-bank sector) as a stock of circulating currency. The *uses* of monetary base (which represent the demand for monetary base) are the free and compulsory reserves of banks and the currency in circulation held by the public.

The *sources* of monetary base creation – which determine its supply – correspond to the institutional sectors that act as counterparties in central bank lending operations: mainly, the foreign sector, the Treasury and bank refinancing.

1 The central bank creates monetary base through the foreign sector when it acquires official reserves (mainly gold and foreign reserve currencies), which constitute a loan to that sector or an asset (gold) that can be used in transactions with it. This happens when

---

[11] The need for regulation and supervision of the financial system by an external entity is examined by Goodhart (1988) in both analytical and historical terms.

there is a balance of payments surplus. Suppose that one good is imported with a value of 100 and another good is exported with a value of 150. In order to pay the foreign supplier, the importer must obtain foreign currency, which is held by the central bank; in exchange, he will surrender monetary base. Settling the transaction therefore leads to a simultaneous reduction in monetary base held by the public and the foreign reserves of the central bank. The opposite occurs for the export. The net result of the two transactions will be an increase in official reserves and the creation of 50 units of monetary base, which is equal to the balance of payments surplus.

Things may be more complex in reality when a (free) foreign exchange market exists, but we cannot be very specific on this point here since treatment of this market is deferred to chapter 16. All we can say at this stage is that the reasoning given in the text also holds when such a market exists if monetary authorities want to peg the exchange rate. In this case the central bank accommodates excess demand (supply) of a foreign currency by destroying (creating) monetary base.

2 Monetary base can be created by the Treasury, since the Treasury itself issues coins (and/or notes) and the central bank may grant it credit by purchasing government securities on the *primary market* (i.e., at issue) or in other ways (e.g., special loans).

The EU agreements signed in Maastricht prohibit central banks from financing the Treasury. In this regard, we need to clarify the nature of central banks' purchases or sales of government securities on the *secondary market* (*open market operations*, OMOs). The central bank can create or destroy monetary base with such operations: if it purchases government securities on the secondary market it creates monetary base; if it sells, it destroys monetary base. OMOs can be outright sales or purchases (when the effect of the change in monetary base lasts until the security matures). They can also be temporary operations (such as repurchase agreements).

OMOs in some ways resemble Treasury financing and we could therefore include this source of monetary base creation and destruction in the Treasury item. In other respects, however, they are an entirely distinct source. The fact is that OMOs have a dual nature: they are objectively a form of financing, albeit indirect, to the Treasury, but they are also a means for the central bank to regulate liquidity; the decision to purchase or sell government securities for this purpose may be a purely technical consequence of the size of the government securities market. Normally, the second function is thought to be dominant and OMOs are considered a source of monetary base separate from Treasury financing.

3 In its capacity as the 'banker's bank', the central bank creates monetary base through refinancing, i.e., providing finance to the credit system by rediscounting bills or providing advances against securities. The central bank can regulate access to credit of last resort by altering the terms on which it will supply this credit, primarily by changing the *minimum lending rate* (or *official discount rate*) and the rate on advances (*Lombard rate* in Germany). The central bank sets the terms of the credit it provides but the initiative in drawing on that credit is taken by the banks, which can decide whether or not to use the facility, depending on its terms and external circumstances. Consequently, the central

Table 13.1. *The balance sheet of a bank (I)*

Assets	Liabilities
BMB	*D*
CR	

bank's role in monetary base control emerges most clearly during moments of market tension, when the banks are forced to draw on central bank credit.

The total supply of monetary base through different sources should equal its total demand, i.e., its total uses. Obviously, changes in supply and demand should also be equal. They give the balance of monetary base, which can be expressed as follows: $BP_m + TFIN + BR = \Delta PMB + \Delta BMB$, where the symbols indicate, respectively, the overall balance of payments (in monetary terms), change in Treasury financing, change in bank refinancing, change in the monetary base held by the public, change in the monetary base (i.e., reserves) held by banks.

13.6 Banks and deposits

13.6.1 Banks' balance sheet and the deposit multiplier

As mentioned earlier, bank liabilities (deposits) are another means of payment (in addition to legal tender and, more generally, monetary base) and are conventionally assigned a pre-eminent role among the liabilities of financial intermediaries. However, this form of money is not independent of monetary base. To see this more clearly, let us first take a look at a simplified bank balance sheet.

In table 13.1 *BMB* is the stock of monetary base held by banks in the form of excess and compulsory reserves (bank monetary base or bank reserves); *CR* are loans to customers; *D* are deposits.[12] For simplicity, the balance sheet does not show other potentially significant items, such as securities and debts with the central bank (bank refinancing).

Let us now see how, under certain conditions, deposits depend on the amount of monetary base held by banks.[13]

First, we assume the following strict behavioural rules.

1 The public wants to maintain a fixed ratio between its holdings of monetary base (or currency in circulation), *PMB*, and deposits, *D*; let this ratio be *h*, such that:

$$PMB = h \cdot D \quad 0 \le h \tag{13.1}$$

---

[12] These include current account, or demand, deposits (checking accounts or sight deposits in the US) and time deposits (savings deposits in the US).

[13] In what follows we will refer to the banking system as a whole; alternatively we assume that only one bank operates.

2 Banks maintain a fixed ratio between monetary base held as excess and compulsory reserves, BMB, and deposits; let this ratio be j, such that:

$$BMB = j \cdot D \quad 0 < j < 1 \tag{13.2}$$

Let us now state the equilibrium condition between monetary base demand (i.e., its uses) and supply (the total of all its sources, MB):

$$MB = PMB + BMB \tag{13.3}$$

Substituting (13.1) and (13.2) into (13.3) we have:

$$MB = hD + jD = D(h + j) \tag{13.4}$$

from which:

$$D = \frac{1}{h + j} MB \tag{13.5}$$

Under the assumed conditions, there is a fixed ratio between monetary base and deposits and, in fact, if the total of h and j is (as it is in reality) less than 1, we can say that deposits are a multiple of monetary base. The ratio $1/(h + j)$ is therefore called the *deposit multiplier*.

If we define the money supply as currency in circulation (i.e., monetary base held by the public) plus deposits, we can express the money supply as a function of monetary base, thus enriching the usual *IS-LM* framework. If:

$$L_S = PMB + D \tag{13.6}$$

where L_S is the total money supply, recalling from (13.1) that $PMB = hD$, we obtain:

$$L_S = hD + D = D(1 + h) \tag{13.7}$$

But, since

$$D = \frac{1}{h + j} MB$$

we have:

$$L_S = \frac{1 + h}{h + j} MB \tag{13.8}$$

where $(1 + h)/(h + j)$ is the *money multiplier*, which is larger the smaller are h and j.[14]

We can easily supplement the *IS-LM* model by introducing an additional relation like (13.8). L_S is thus no longer an exogenous variable (possibly an instrument), but becomes an endogenous, 'irrelevant' variable. However, new variables are introduced that can be used as instruments: MB and j. Even h might be used as such, since the monetary authorities can influence it by, for example, introducing changes in the payment system, which, obviously, operate over the long run.[15]

---

[14] In the case of j, the inverse relation is clear. Readers familiar with calculus can also verify that the derivative of the multiplier with respect to h is positive.

[15] An example of developments that would lower h is the spread of bank branches and credit cards.

Table 13.2. *Stages of the deposit multiplication process (I)*

	Liabilities	Assets	
	Deposits	Monetary base	Loans
1	$D_1 = MB$	$BMB_1 = jMB$	$CR_1 = (1-j)MB$
2	$D_2 = (1-j)MB$	$BMB_2 = j(1-j)MB$	$CR_2 = (1-j)^2MB$
3	$D_3 = (1-j)^2MB$	$BMB_3 = j(1-j)^2MB$	$CR_3 = (1-j)^3MB$
n	$D_n = (1-j)^{n-1}MB$	$BMB_n = j(1-j)^{n-1}MB$	$CR_n = (1-j)^nMB$

The relationship between monetary base and deposits, which we have now derived in a mechanical way, can easily be grasped more intuitively. We continue to assume the second behavioural rule expressed by equation (13.2) and assume $h = 0$, i.e., that the public holds no monetary base, all of which instead goes to the banking system. In other words, the public uses bank money only.

Now suppose that a quantity MB of monetary base is created.[16] Since the public does not want to hold cash, the monetary base is deposited in a bank (the *primary deposit*, $D_1 = MB$). The bank must comply with the reserve requirement and in any case follows behavioural rule 2 above, and therefore retains $BMB_1 = j \cdot D_1 = j \cdot MB$, while lending $CR_1 = (1-j) \cdot MB$. The loan to the public is transformed into another deposit, D_2, of the same amount, i.e., $(1-j) \cdot MB$, since the public does not want to hold any monetary base, by assumption. The new deposit is called a *derived deposit*, since it is generated by a loan granted by the bank.

Having received an additional deposit and continuing to follow rule 2, the bank will hold monetary base equal to $BMB_2 = j \cdot D_2 = j \cdot (1-j) \cdot MB$ and make a loan equal to $CR_2 = (1-j) \cdot D_2 = (1-j)^2 \cdot MB$. The loan is again transformed into a deposit, $D_{3'} = (1-j)^2 \cdot MB$, of which the bank holds $BMB_3 = j \cdot D_3 = j \cdot (1-j)^2 \cdot MB$ and lends $CR_3 = (1-j) \cdot D_3 = (1-j)^3 \cdot MB$, and so on. In the nth round the bank will receive a deposit equal to $D_n = (1-j)^{n-1} \cdot MB$, retain $BMB_n = j \cdot (1-j)^{n-1} \cdot MB$ and lend $CR_n = (1-j)^n \cdot MB$. Its balance sheet will appear as shown in table 13.2.[17]

Each item in the balance sheet is given by the sum of a geometric progression with a ratio of $(1-j)$. Total deposits, D, are equal to:

$$D = D_1 + D_2 + D_3 + \ldots + D_n = $$
$$MB + (1-j)MB + (1-j)^2MB + \ldots + (1-j)^{n-1}MB$$

Recalling that the sum of such a progression is equal to

$$S_n = a_1 \frac{1-q^n}{1-q}$$

where a_1 is the first term and q is the ratio, in our example we have:

---

[16] MB can either be the absolute amount of or the change in monetary base.

[17] Unlike real balance sheets, liabilities are shown before assets in order to highlight the sequence of bank transactions.

Table 13.3. *The balance sheet of a bank (II)*

Assets		Liabilities	
BMB	1,000	D	5,000
CR	4,000		

$$D = MB\frac{1 - (1 - j)^n}{1 - (1 - j)}$$

For $n \to \infty$, $(1 - j)^n \to 0$, since $(1 - j) < 1$, and thus $D = MB/j$.

Similarly, we can show that $BMB = MB$ and $CR = MB(1 - j)/j = MB/j - MB = D - MB$.

Suppose that $MB = 1,000$ and $j = 0.20$. We therefore have $D = 1,000 \cdot 1/0.20 = 5,000$; $CR = 5,000 - 1,000 = 4,000$. The bank's balance sheet will appear as in table 13.3.

If we abandon the hypothesis of $h = 0$ and assume more realistically that $h > 0$, it is easily seen that the potential for creating derived deposits is reduced, since the amounts lent by the bank do not return entirely to the bank (or the banking system) in the form of deposits: a part, h, of the monetary base given by the bank to the borrower is retained by the latter.

The deposit multiplier given by (13.5), i.e., $1/(h + j)$, is larger the smaller are h and j. If h is small, this means that for a given increase in monetary base a larger share flows to the banks; that is, the larger is the percentage of monetary base on which the loan (and deposit) pyramid is constructed.[18] Similarly, a low j means a higher multiplier effect, since the banks recycle a larger percentage of the monetary base at their disposal through loans, which will again return to them in the form of deposits.

If $h = 0.1$, $j = 0.15$ and $MB = 100$, we have $D = [1/(0.1 + 0.15)] \cdot 100 = 4 \cdot 100 = 400$; $PBM = 0.1 \cdot 400 = 40$; $BMB = 0.15 \cdot 400 = 60$; $CR = D - BMB = 400 - 60 = 340$.

This last relation gives the condition for the accounting balance between bank assets and liabilities.

The reader will note that the public made an initial deposit $D_1 = [1/(1 + h)] \cdot MB$ (i.e., $D_1 = [1/1 + 0.1] \cdot 100 = [1/1.1] \cdot 100$)[19] and that the bank subsequently made a series of loans well in excess of the amount of this initial deposit (a total of 340). The bank received further deposits after the initial deposit as a *direct consequence of its lending*. This occurred because the public *preferred to hold part of its assets as bank liabilities rather than cash*.

In short, the ability to lend a larger amount than the initial deposit depends on the fact that each time the bank makes a loan the resulting loss of reserves is small, since a large

---

[18] This explains why the monetary instruments available to banks for excess and compulsory reserves are called 'monetary base'.

[19] The public thereby maintains a ratio of h between monetary base and deposits. If the public deposits $[1/(1 + h)] \cdot MB$, it will retain $[h/(1 + h)] \cdot MB$; the ratio between retained monetary base and deposits is equal to h, as can easily be verified.

part of the monetary base transferred to the borrower returns sooner or later to the bank itself, given the public's propensity to use bank money, i.e., deposits, as a means of payment.[20] Granting credit and creating money are two closely related activities in the economy of a bank: lending leads to the creation of bank money, i.e., deposits, because the public accepts these bank liabilities as a means of payment.

Note that the value of the deposit multiplier shown in (13.5) – where j is the reserve ratio desired by the bank, at a given lending interest rate – is the largest possible. In other words, it is a *potential multiplier* and not necessarily the *actual multiplier*. The entire process of deposit creation begins only as a result of bank lending. In addition, for the process to take place the willingness of banks to grant credit must be matched by the willingness of the public to borrow, as we have implicitly assumed. However, this does not always hold in reality. The demand for credit is a function of the terms on which it is offered, first and foremost the interest rate. If demand falls short of supply at the given interest rate, actual j will be higher than the desired j and the actual multiplier will be lower than the potential one.

On the other hand, the supply of credit is not automatically given either, as is assumed in equation (13.2). Since the reserve coefficient j includes not only the compulsory reserves, but also a percentage of excess reserves, it must depend on the interest rate on loans, which represents the opportunity cost to banks of holding free reserves. Supply and demand functions for credit should then be introduced.

Similar considerations hold for deposits: in the place of the rigid behaviour implicitly or explicitly assumed in our description of the multiplier process, we need to introduce demand and supply functions for deposits that depend on various factors, including any interest rate paid.

Dealing with this more complex situation does not fall within the scope of this book. Nevertheless, our discussion so far enables us to conclude the following:

1 The two main forms of money, monetary base and deposits, are linked because the monetary base available to banks is the basis of a process of credit and deposit creation.

2 In the analysis of the deposit multiplier presented here, the relation between monetary base and deposits is constant, but this hypothesis is acceptable only as an initial approximation. In reality, the link exists but is variable, since the coefficients in the multiplier can change as a function of the numerous factors underlying the demand and supply functions for credit and deposits. This explains why the so-called *new view* expressed by Tobin and others has criticized the use of the money multiplier (see Gurley and Shaw, 1960; Tobin, 1963). Note that only if there is a constant ratio between monetary base and deposits (aggregates that can be considered to represent outside money and

---

[20] The situation of non-bank financial intermediaries differs because they generally do not issue liabilities that can be used as a means of payment.

   Note that deposits are not necessarily preferred to cash because they yield a return. Often, for example, banks in the English-speaking countries do not pay interest and in fact charge fees for demand deposits, which are those that perform a primary monetary function. Demand deposits are mainly preferred for their convenience and safety.

inside money, respectively) will Patinkin's neutrality of money thesis hold (see section 7.4.3).

*13.6.2 A more complex analysis of the deposit multiplier

Assume rules 1 and 2 from the previous subsection hold and that additional monetary base equal to MB is created and is 'distributed' to the public (perhaps by dropping it out of a helicopter, as M. Friedman colourfully suggested, or, more seriously, with OMOs). If the public was initially in equilibrium, holding monetary base and deposits at a ratio of h, the increase in monetary base will move it into disequilibrium since monetary base has risen whereas deposits have not. The public will seek to return to its equilibrium position by observing rule 1, i.e., by transforming part of the new monetary base into deposits. It will retain a quantity of monetary base equal to $MB \cdot h/(1 + h)$ and make a deposit equal to $D_1 = MB/(1 + h)$. The ratio between the two will be h. The public will again be in equilibrium, but this will only be temporary, as we shall see.

Let us take a quick look at the bank's situation. Before receiving deposit D_1, the bank was in equilibrium. After receiving $D_1 = MB/(1 + h)$ and monetary base for an equal amount, the bank is no longer in equilibrium, since both variables have risen by the same amount rather than by the ratio prescribed by rule 2. The bank seeks to re-establish balance by following this rule, i.e., it retains $jD_1 = jMB/(1 + h)$ as reserves and lends the remainder: $CR_1 = (1 - j)D_1 = (1 - j)MB/(1 + h)$. At this point the public is again in disequilibrium and will seek to restore balance by following behavioural rule 1. Assume that the loan is disbursed as monetary base. This creates an excess of monetary base in the hands of the public, which re-establishes equilibrium by retaining a fraction $h/(1 + h)$ of the increase (equal to CR_1) and making a deposit $D_2 = CR_1/(1 + h)$. If, instead, the loan were disbursed – as is usually the case – by crediting the borrower's account, the public would have excess deposits and would re-establish equilibrium by withdrawing monetary base equal to $[h/(1 + h)]CR_1$. The increase in monetary base and deposits resulting from the two forms of lending is exactly the same.

Restoring the public's equilibrium leads to an increase in the ratio between reserves and deposits for the bank. It will again seek to restore equilibrium by putting a fraction of the monetary base received with deposit D_2 into reserves (retaining $BMB = jD_2$) and lending cash equal to $CR_2 = (1 - j)D_2$. The cash will in turn be recycled into the bank in the amount $CR_2/(1 + h) = D_3$.

Let us take a look at the bank's balance sheet (table 13.4).

Substituting the values of CR_1 and CR_2 shown under assets for CR_1 and CR_2 under liabilities, we have the situation given by table 13.5. Chain solving among the liabilities, we have:

$$D_1 = \frac{MB}{1 + h}$$

$$D_2 = \frac{1}{1 + h}(1 - j)\frac{1}{1 + h}MB = (1 - j)\frac{1}{(1 + h)^2}MB$$

$$D_3 = \frac{1}{1 + h}(1 - j)D_2 = \frac{1}{(1 + h)^3}(1 - j)^2 MB$$

Table 13.4. *Stages of the deposit multiplication process (II)*

	Assets	Liabilities
BMB:		$D_1 = MB/(1+h)$
	jD_1	$D_2 = CR_1/(1+h)$
	jD_2	$D_3 = CR_2/(1+h)$
CR:	$CR_1 = (1-j)D_1$	
	$CR_2 = (1-j)D_2$	

Table 13.5. *Stages of the deposit multiplication process (III)*

	Assets	Liabilities
BMB:		$D_1 = \dfrac{1}{(1+h)}MB$
	jD_1	$D_2 = \dfrac{1}{(1+h)}(1-j)D_1$
	jD_2	$D_3 = \dfrac{1}{(1+h)}(1-j)D_2$
CR:	$CR_1 = (1-j)D_1$	
	$CR_2 = (1-j)D_2$	

We can see that deposits are a geometric progression with a ratio of $(1-j)[1/(1+h)]$. The sum of this progression, whose first term is $MB/(1+h)$, for n approaching infinity is:

$$D = \frac{1}{[1-(1-j)/(1+h)]} \cdot \frac{MB}{1+h} = \frac{MB}{h+j} \tag{13.9}$$

Note that (13.9) is the same as (13.5).

13.7 Controlling monetary base and the money supply

In the two previous sections we identified the variables on which the money supply, L_S, depends.

We saw in chapter 7 that the money supply plays an important role in determining the level of economic activity and/or prices according to Keynesians and first generation monetarists. In particular, we know that in Keynes much of the instability of capitalism is linked to the existence of a monetary economy. Some authors argue that this is truer the greater the fiduciary nature of the monetary regime. They claim that in the case of commodity money, crises of confidence could not occur because the value of money was guaranteed by the intrinsic value of the commodity used as a medium of exchange. However, with the introduction of specie it became possible for the ratio between the nominal value of the coin and its intrinsic value to change, which introduced an element of arbitrariness and, hence, confidence. This change was accentuated by the introduction first of banknotes convertible into metal coins, then fiat money and, above all, bank money.

By increasing the fiduciary character of money, the developments in monetary systems we have discussed – prompted by the need for greater flexibility in money creation – undoubtedly increase the risk of instability. However, it is not true that systems based on commodity or metal money are immune from such instability. In the past, waves of inflation have been caused by events (for example, the discovery of America) that increased the supply of precious metals used as money. The opposite dangers – deflation and reduced economic activity – were avoided only because the growth of output and trade was accompanied by a parallel but incidental increase in the output of precious metals.[21]

We can conclude that, far from professing confidence in automatic monetary systems, policymakers should supervise the financial structure and, in particular, the money supply, contracting or expanding it according to circumstances.[22] In order to do so, however, it is essential to know which of the variables underlying the money supply can be controlled by the monetary authorities. We saw in the previous section that the quantity of money is an endogenous variable, since it depends on monetary base, the ratio between currency in circulation and deposits, and the bank reserve ratio. In order for the monetary authorities to control the money supply, they must be able to affect at least one of these variables. Those that seem most open to control in the short run are: (1) monetary base; and (2) the compulsory reserve ratio.

The controllability of these two variables and the consequences for the controllability of the money supply must be discussed in greater detail.

1 Let us first examine the controllability of monetary base. We can provisionally say that monetary base is controllable in principle if policymakers control at least one source of monetary base creation, so as to be able to offset any undesired creation or destruction of monetary base through other channels.

The foreign sector is not directly controllable if the exchange rate is rigidly pegged or if it fluctuates freely (for more on this see chapters 16 and 18) unless direct control measures such as administrative constraints on the movement of goods or capital are used.

By contrast, the Treasury source is controllable if there are no special requirements imposed on monetary authorities (as, for example, in Italy until November 1993, where the central bank was obliged to advance the Treasury up to 14 per cent of budget expenditure). Without such obligations, central bank purchases of government securities on the secondary market (open market operations) or even the primary market can be independently decided by the bank. Obviously, in managing such operations, the

---

[21] We refer in particular to the surprising stability of money during the gold standard era (from the second half of the 1800s to 1914), when banknotes were convertible into gold on the basis of the fixed gold content of the monetary unit.

[22] An important example of the need to adapt monetary action to circumstances is the expansionary action taken by the Federal Reserve in October 1987, which headed off a liquidity crisis in the presence of capital losses by banks and firms following an unexpected fall in share prices.

central bank will try to avoid any failure to place government securities, excessive falls in government securities prices or crises of confidence that undermine the soundness of the financial structure. If, however, the bank must purchase Treasury securities that fail to find buyers or must grant some form of advance to the Treasury, the central bank's only instrument for controlling the Treasury source would be open market operations (i.e., transactions on the secondary market).[23] However, it would be difficult to carry out open market operations under these conditions. Take, for example, the case where a new issue of government securities fails to be fully taken up. If the central bank is required to purchase these securities, it will be forced to issue monetary base. In theory it could offset the creation of monetary base by selling the securities on the financial market. This would be difficult in reality, however, given that the securities could not be placed on the primary market in the first place.

The central bank controls bank refinancing through changes in the interest rates charged on credit of last resort. It thereby influences the availability of reserves (i.e., monetary base) for banks. However, changing the official discount rate or that on advances is not always effective, especially for *expansionary* purposes: even if the monetary authorities lower these rates considerably,[24] the banks might not increase their recourse to central bank credit significantly if they already hold excess reserves of liquidity owing to modest credit demand. In this case demand for refinancing is inelastic to its price, i.e., the interest rate. The degree of controllability of this source of monetary base in a *restrictive* monetary policy is greater: the central bank can always raise the cost of refinancing (or set quantitative restrictions) to reduce monetary base creation to the desired level.[25] However, in this case lack of refinancing raises problems for the equilibrium of banks, and indirectly for other financial intermediaries, which could give rise to liquidity crises and thus undermine the confidence of depositors.

To sum up, the monetary authorities do not control the foreign sector unless they use direct controls, they substantially control the Treasury source if there are no requirements to finance the Treasury's borrowing requirement and they control bank refinancing, albeit with some difficulty when they wish to provide an expansionary boost.

The controllability of at least one source of monetary base creation should allow overall control, unless the uncontrolled sources are affected by very strong disturbances, in which case the controlled sources might prove insufficiently flexible in the short run.

This conclusion must be modified to take account of the exchange rate regime. Under fixed exchange rates, the foreign sector can destroy (or create) any amount of monetary base created (or destroyed) by other sectors under certain conditions. For example, suppose that monetary base is created through open market operations. Interest rates will fall, prompting a capital outflow if capital is sufficiently sensitive to interest rates.

[23] It was said earlier that open market operations are often considered a separate source of monetary base. In this case and in the absence of any requirement for central bank to finance the Treasury, the Treasury source would be controllable only in one way: the *possibility* that the bank could purchase government securities on the primary market.

[24] In any case rates are normally not negative. Although possible in theory, applying negative rates would amount to subsidising the banks.

[25] This is an example of the *asymmetry of the effects* of expansionary and restrictive monetary policies. This phenomenon has many other interesting features, as we will see shortly.

The balance of payments will deteriorate, causing a reduction in official reserves and destruction of monetary base (see section 18.2).[26]

Control of monetary base does not guarantee control over the money supply. Such control is possible only if the deposit multiplier is constant, i.e., if h and j are given, or if any change in their values is predictable. In reality, however, this is not necessarily so, for the following reasons:

(a) as we said earlier, both h and j (for the part constituted by excess reserves) are sensitive to interest rates on deposits and loans, respectively, which represent the opportunity cost to savers and banks of holding monetary base; the relationships between h and j, on the one hand, and their determinants, on the other, tend to be unstable;

(b) the coefficient j (again for excess reserves) is also determined by the demand for credit at a given interest rate. We saw that the multiplier mechanism for deposits requires that the public's demand for credit equal the banks' supply of credit. Only in this case will the actual multiplier be equal to the potential multiplier. This is less likely to occur when monetary base is expanded than when it is contracted. In the latter case, deposits must be reduced, by curbing lending, if the bank was operating at the limit in creating deposits, i.e., with an effective j equal to the desired value. By contrast, when monetary base is expanded, there is no guarantee that deposits will increase. This will only occur if credit demand – which is related to consumption and investment – increases, which the bank is not able to trigger (sometimes not even if it reduces its lending rate). Thus, j also tends to change in an unpredictable way.

2 Let us now examine the possibility of controlling the money supply through the compulsory reserve ratio. This is certainly controllable, since it can be subject to specific regulation. It is therefore a direct control measure prescribing a specific behaviour on the part of banks.

The impact of changing the reserve ratio on the money supply, analogously to adjusting monetary base, is highly influenced by a wide variety of circumstances. First, it has a greater effect in restrictive policies than in expansionary policies. In the former, it is much more likely that the effective deposit multiplier will be close to its potential, while in the latter it tends to be lower in the presence of inadequate credit demand.

Let us now see what can happen if the reserve ratio is increased, with monetary base unchanged. An increase means that, with the volume of deposits initially given, the banks must increase their holdings of monetary base in the form of compulsory reserves. If the banks do not have large excess reserves (as is likely in an expanding economy)[27] or other forms of liquidity, they will be forced to reduce their lending and thereby reduce the volume of deposits. This leads to a contraction in the monetary base required to be set aside as compulsory reserves, thus offsetting the effect of the increase in the reserve ratio. In this case the monetary restriction will be fully effective. Similarly, as we have

---

[26] This may take time, however, especially if capital is relatively immobile.
[27] It is in such circumstances that a tightening of the monetary policy stance may be needed.

already seen, a reduction in the banks' monetary base with no change in the reserve ratio leads to a reduction in lending and, therefore, in deposits. Once again, the effect will necessarily occur if banks do not have excess liquid reserves.

Now suppose that banks, while not holding large amounts of monetary base, do have other liquidity instruments that can be disposed of in the market or otherwise converted into monetary base (e.g., very short-term securities that the banks can decide not to renew at maturity). They may therefore decide not to reduce their lending, at least in the short run and with their 'best' customers, sacrificing short-run profits for long-run considerations (and profits). In these circumstances, changing the reserve ratio may be relatively ineffective and operate only with a considerable lag; regulating deposits (and the money supply) can only be achieved with other direct control instruments, such as *credit ceilings*, whereby banks are required to keep lending growth within certain limits, which may differ according to loan type (e.g., consumer credit, corporate lending, export credit) or borrowing sector (financial and commercial firms, industry, etc.). Banks that exceed the limits incur penalties.

13.8 (Final) objectives and agents of monetary policy

Monetary policy shares the same possible objectives as other macroeconomic policy instruments: price stability, balance of payments equilibrium, employment and growth.

The existence of complementarities between objectives facilitates monetary policy choices, as it does for other instruments. From this point of view, by maintaining the competitiveness of national goods and services, the pursuit of price stability (i.e., containing inflation) also tends to ensure balance of payments equilibrium and therefore exchange rate stability. Similarly, a certain degree of price stability may help to stimulate the formation of financial savings, facilitating long-term growth if this has been slowed by insufficient saving.[28]

However, there may be problems of substitutability between objectives, at least in the short run. Pursuing one may preclude, or make difficult, the achievement of another. The clearest case of substitutability regards price stability and balance of payments equilibrium, on the one hand, and employment, on the other. Substitutability creates problems for all instruments, but they may be especially serious for monetary policy, as we will see.

In general, substitutability means that we must make choices, and every choice involves some sort of sacrifice. Making a rational choice means defining the preference functions of policymakers and, therefore, the weights assigned to each objective, or their order of priority. This becomes more pressing when economic policy decisions are decentralised. We then must tackle the problem – which we briefly mentioned earlier and which will be examined in more detail in chapter 19 – of the appropriate assignment of instruments to targets; that is, deciding the specific objective that each instrument must seek to achieve exclusively or on a priority basis. There are now only a few cases in

---

[28] However, we saw in section 7.3 that a positive (but moderate) inflation rate has some advantages. These could also accrue in terms of higher growth rates.

contemporary economies in which the body responsible for fiscal policy (the Government and, in particular, the Treasury) is also responsible for monetary policy, giving instructions and orders to a central bank whose functions are essentially executive. More frequently, the central bank is entrusted with almost complete and independent responsibility[29] for monetary policy. In this context, the identification of the objectives of each authority (monetary and fiscal) is of special theoretical and practical importance.

Tradition[30] and much of economic theory assign the task of pursuing price stability and balance of payments equilibrium to the monetary authorities. Many economists agree on the ability to achieve equilibrium in the balance of payments. There is also an agreement that a restrictive monetary stance has powerful effects on the level (and rate of change) of prices, as well as on the level of income and employment, but, as we will shortly see, monetary policy is less powerful when it aims to stimulate an *increase* in income and employment beginning with an underemployment equilibrium. By contrast, monetary policy may play some role in long-term growth. This can be done in two quite different ways: (1) by ensuring monetary stability and thus providing an incentive for the formation of financial savings; (2) by using some degree of monetary instability to govern income distribution so as to foster investment and, consequently, growth. The choice between the two alternatives depends on the nature of expectations (rational, regressive, inelastic) and some features of the economic and social system. The emphasis given by some authors and in political debates to monetary stability as an absolutely necessary condition for growth seems therefore to be excessive.[31]

13.9 The operation of monetary policy: indicators and intermediate targets

Assume that all the sectors of the economy are initially in equilibrium. An increase in monetary base following open market purchases from banks has the immediate effect of increasing both the banks' excess reserves and securities prices, which reduces the latter's yield. Excess reserves and lower yields induce a substitution process in banks'

[29] On the degree of political independence (i.e., independence in choosing objectives) and economic independence (i.e., ability to choose instruments) of various central banks at the beginning of the 1990s consult Grilli, Masciandaro and Tabellini (1991). To meet the requirement for a monetary policy autonomous from fiscal policy imposed by the Maastricht agreements for European Economic and Monetary Union, all European central banks – including the Bank of England and the Bank of France, which have traditionally been less independent of the Government – have increased their independence. On the other hand, the Statute of the European Central Bank (see chapter 16) has been modelled on that of the Bundesbank and guarantees a very high level of independence for this institution. The problem of the political accountability of independent 'bodies' in a democratic system remains.

[30] Note, however, that many central banks were created 'out of the desire of the executive power to free itself of the tight control exercised by Parliament over its spending powers . . . for declared or disguised inflationary purposes' (De Cecco, 1995). The emphasis on monetary stability arises with the emergence of a broad social class of creditors (ibid., p. 26).

[31] This is consistent with the finding of an association between central bank independence and lower inflation and the lack of any systematic impact of that independence on real output growth (Grilli, Masciandaro and Tabellini, 1991).

portfolios, producing an increase in the supply of credit and a reduction in the lending rate. This may stimulate overall demand, causing an increase in deposits, which enables banks to balance their assets and liabilities. The increase in deposits and credit demand will be part of a more general process of change in the composition of the portfolios of households and firms. The final effect is usually an increase in demand and employment.

Depending on the economic situation, the increase in demand may or may not lead to an increase in prices. The change in the interest rate will also have an impact on the balance of payments, especially capital movements.

Tightening the monetary stance will have the opposite effect. However, in both cases (and especially in a restriction) monetary policy will affect real variables not only through changes in the *cost* of credit but also, or primarily, through changes in the *availability* of credit, for a number of reasons.

1 The increase in the market interest rate induced by the monetary tightening causes a fall in the prices of securities held by banks; they will therefore find it less attractive to raise funds through the sale of securities for their lending activities, which will have become more profitable owing to the rise in interest rates: selling securities would lead to capital losses. This disincentive effect on the supply of credit is called the *Roosa effect* (see Roosa, 1951) or the *lock-in effect* and helps explain the particular effectiveness of a restrictive monetary policy, which influences not only the *demand* for credit but also its *supply*.

2 The monetary restriction may increase uncertainty about the future and increase the demand for liquidity (see Kareken, 1975).

3 Faced with borrower insolvency risk and asymmetric information, *endogenous rationing* (rather than the exogenous rationing of the two previous examples) may take place: this occurs independently of external events such as a restrictive monetary policy. Whenever a bank faces excess credit demand, it will react not by raising interest rates but by offering credit to some and denying it to others. Under the assumed conditions, raising rates could have a negative effect on the bank's profitability, since:

(a) it leads to adverse selection of riskier customers; and

(b) it encourages some customers to undertake riskier projects (moral hazard).[32]

Our discussion so far shows the complexity of the operation of monetary policy. Before it can affect ultimate objectives (employment, the price level, balance of payments, growth), monetary policy requires time. It may also encounter obstacles and its effectiveness may not be easily discerned. In short, monetary policy is conducted in a highly uncertain environment, where it is important to follow the evolution of market

---

[32] We have been discussing *equilibrium rationing*, not dynamic rationing, which is associated with delays in the adjustment of bank interest rates to changing conditions in the money market. The importance of credit rationing can scarcely be overemphasised: it casts a very different light on the working of an economic system from that deriving from the traditional neoclassical theory (specifically, monetarist theory), in which there are hardly any binding constraints on the actions of individuals.

conditions and continually adjust actual target values to the desired level. This has prompted monetary authorities to direct their attention to variables that are intermediate between instruments and the ultimate targets of monetary policy.

It can be helpful to track the behaviour of variables that are either closely linked to instruments, in order to evaluate the magnitude of the stimulus or restriction, or closely tied to the ultimate targets, in order to assess the likely impact of the monetary action on the ultimate targets themselves, possibly in advance.

The former are known as *monetary policy indicators*. These are variables, such as money supply growth and the interest rate, that provide a summary assessment of the magnitude of the monetary expansion or restriction,[33] even when the policy action involves the use of numerous instruments.

Nevertheless, it may be difficult to find a reliable indicator that measures *only* the magnitude of the monetary policy action. The problem arises because, as we have seen, aggregates that reflect monetary measures alone do not exist. For example, the money supply is determined endogenously to some extent through the demand for credit, which also reflects the current state of economic activity and the outlook for the future. On the other hand, there are a variety of aggregates that enable us to measure the indicated variables (M0, M1, M2, etc.). Interest rates are also determined endogenously and there are many of them. In fact, we speak of the term structure of interest rates. The interest rates that serve as monetary policy indicators are normally short-term rates, for example rates on six-month Treasury bills or the overnight interbank rate (i.e., the rate on loans between banks maturing the first business day following the transaction). Note that in the presence of credit rationing, bank interest rates no longer function as a signal in the allocation of credit or as an indicator of the restrictiveness of the monetary policy stance.

In order to anticipate the effects of monetary measures on the ultimate targets it is helpful to aim at *intermediate targets*, i.e., variables that have an influence on the ultimate targets and are either affected by the monetary measures before the latter or can at least be learned before them, enabling the monetary authorities to regulate monetary policy promptly in subsequent periods.[34] For this reason, intermediate targets are frequently monetary or credit aggregates, which have both of these characteristics.[35]

One possible intermediate target is *domestic credit expansion* (DCE). The DCE aggregate is also called 'monetary credit', since it is equal to the monetary financing (i.e.,

[33] However, the reader should bear in mind that monetary policy action is much more varied and may not be narrowly confined to restriction and expansion, especially as it reflects long-term objectives. For example, reform of the payment system or compulsory reserve regulations can have a restrictive or expansionary effect in the short run but are introduced for long-run purposes.

[34] In the case of a fixed intermediate target, the monetary authorities should in principle act as if this target were in fact the true final target. In practice, however, not only do authorities monitor a variety of intermediate targets, they also monitor shifts away from the target values of both intermediate and final targets. For example, in April 1994 the Bundesbank lowered the discount rate despite the fact that its intermediate aggregate (M3) had expanded considerably more rapidly than the target rate because at the same time inflation (the ultimate target) had fallen significantly. The reason why in practice monetary authorities monitor a number of variables is that the relations between the different variables are uncertain and unstable.

[35] Monetary and credit statistics are normally available more quickly than data on the real economy.

financing with monetary base) of the Treasury plus bank lending to the private sector, which, as we know, also translates into changes in the money supply through the creation of derived deposits. Other widely used intermediate targets are the money supply (M2, M3 or other monetary aggregates), interest rates, credit targets (including various forms of credit and not only bank credit, as does DCE), and the exchange rate.

The choice of one or another intermediate target depends on numerous factors, each of which must be carefully assessed. There are three issues to consider in the various steps that link adjustment of the instruments to hitting the targets:

(a) the controllability of the aggregate being considered for use as an intermediate target;
(b) the stability of behavioural functions;
(c) the links between intermediate and ultimate targets.

The first problem concerns the nature of the relationship between instruments and intermediate targets. The stabler this is and the shorter the time that passes between the monetary policy action and its impact on the potential intermediate target, the greater the reliability of the variable as an intermediate target. In this sense, the 'closer' the target to the instruments, the greater the authorities' ability to control it. Monetary intermediate targets, such as DCE, are more easily controlled than credit targets.

The second problem regards the stability of the behaviour of the monetary system. This in turn raises two issues: the first regards complex substitutability relationships between different financial assets, while the second concerns the nature of the shocks that may affect the economic system (causing instability in behavioural functions).[36] Let us now address the latter problem and suppose the ultimate target is income. The government wants to minimise the divergence between actual income and its target value, which may be caused by real shocks to the system, i.e., changes in autonomous spending. We can show that in this case it is preferable to set an intermediate target in terms of the money supply, keeping it unchanged with respect to the change in autonomous spending caused by the real shock. This offsets the impact of the change in autonomous spending on income. For example, if the shock reduces autonomous spending, thus causing income to fall, the resulting fall in the interest rate in the presence of a constant money supply will cause investment to rise. This will attenuate the reduction in autonomous spending, containing the effects of the negative shock on income. If the government instead chooses to keep the interest rate[37] at a given level as its intermediate target, there would be no stimulus effect on investment and income would fall more markedly. The same would happen, *mutatis mutandis*, in the case of a positive real shock. The reader can verify our conclusions in terms of the *IS-LM* framework when the *IS* curve is shifted to the left (or right) following a negative (positive) shock. If the government sought to maintain a constant money supply as its

---

[36] Poole first introduced the concept of intermediate targets with reference to this problem (see Poole, 1970).

[37] In order to achieve this objective, the monetary authorities would have to change the money supply (or the true monetary instruments, i.e., monetary base and/or the reserve requirement) in such a way as to compensate for the change in the demand for money produced by the shock.

intermediate target, LM would not change; if instead its target were a constant interest rate, LM would flatten at the desired interest rate as a result of adjusting the money supply to match the change in demand for money.[38]

By contrast, in order to reduce fluctuations in the level of income, monetary shocks would have to be offset by changes in the money supply that would leave the interest rate unchanged. In this case, policymakers' intermediate target would have to be the interest rate rather than the money supply. Here too the reader can verify our conclusions within the IS-LM framework. With an autonomous increase in money demand, which tends to shift the LM curve to the left, the interest rate would rise and income would fall if the money supply remained unchanged. This can be avoided if the intermediate target is to hold the interest rate steady. The monetary authorities will provide enough monetary base to cause the money supply to increase by exactly as much as money demand.[39]

The final problem regards the relationship between intermediate and final targets. We have already said that it must be stable. Stability depends on the constancy of the parameters linking the relevant variables and of the functional form. Obviously, this can be assumed only in the short run and in the absence of unexpected shocks. Over the longer period, behavioural functions generally change.

The instability of the relationships between intermediate and final objectives has recently led some monetary authorities in Europe and North America to abandon the practice of fixing intermediate objectives. Instead, they have decided to announce and directly pursue final objectives such as inflation (hence the term *inflation targeting*).

13.10 Considerations on the effectiveness of monetary policy

In concluding the chapter, we briefly consider the effectiveness of monetary policy. Effectiveness has a quantitative dimension (which we discussed in theoretical terms in section 9.4) and a temporal dimension. We first examine the latter.

Monetary policy is affected by much the same observation lag as other discretionary instruments but its administrative and effect lags are different. The administrative lag of monetary policy is normally much shorter than that of other policy measures, especially all those that require some sort of political mediation in a representative democracy, fiscal policy first and foremost. The shortness of the administrative lag is therefore an advantage deriving from the independence of many central banks from political bodies, although there are also significant limitations and risks involved in such independence.[40]

---

[38] For more on this point, the reader can consult Poole (1970) or a macroeconomics textbook, such as Dornbusch and Fischer (1994).

[39] See Poole (1970) and Dornbusch and Fischer (1994).

[40] It is worth underscoring this point at a moment in time when the freeing of central banks from political interference is practically complete and has apparently received only uncritical agreement. There are two especially important points to bear in mind when judging the advisability of separating monetary and fiscal authorities. The first regards the fact that the monetary authorities are not elected (by citizens or their representatives); we mentioned this in section 13.8. The second

By contrast, the effect lag of monetary policy can be long and variable, at least for some targets. We have already noted the complexity of substitutability relations and the portfolio readjustment processes of banks and other agents. This means that with targets such as income, employment and price stability the effects of monetary policy may emerge quite slowly. By contrast, the time lag between the policy action and the emergence of its impact on targets such as the balance of payments can be shorter under certain conditions. For example, if the monetary authorities are able to influence interest rates, they can quickly eliminate a balance of payments deficit if capital is sufficiently mobile and there are no perverse effects on expected exchange rates (see chapter 17).

In any case monetary policy is ill-suited to *fine-tuning*. It instead requires large, if not massive, intervention[41] in order to be effective, especially if the financial markets are not deep or broad. In particular, massive intervention may have positive *announcement effects* that shorten the lag.

As we noted earlier, the effectiveness of monetary policy action depends on whether it is used for expansionary or restrictive purposes (asymmetry of effects), tending to be greater when a restrictive stance is adopted, for a number of reasons.

1 We have already remarked that the actual deposit multiplier tends to be higher for a reduction, rather than increase, in monetary base.

2 The existence of a 'floor' on the nominal interest rate has the same effect, since the interest rate cannot be negative and might not even be able to fall below some positive value if we find ourselves in a Keynesian *liquidity trap*. By contrast, there is no limit on the upward movement of the interest rate following a monetary tightening.

3 Credit demand may be inelastic with respect to the interest rate. This is not a very satisfactory explanation of the asymmetry of the effects of monetary policy action, since inelasticity should emerge for expansionary and restrictive policies alike. The matter is somewhat more complex in reality. It is not so much inelasticity that gives rise to asymmetric effects as it is the possibility of credit rationing: in this case a restrictive monetary policy does not cause an appreciable rise in the interest rate on bank credit (and therefore the elasticity of demand aspect seems irrelevant), but rather induces a reduction in the *supply* of credit to certain customers, who are rationed. Total supply is therefore reduced with certainty (even if demand does not fall). By contrast, an expansionary monetary policy action does not so much cause a fall in lending rates (and therefore once again the elasticity of credit demand is irrelevant) but rather prompts an increase in the supply of credit, perhaps to a level where it exceeds demand.

The monetary action thus has asymmetric results: it undoubtedly reduces the supply

point concerns the possibility that a non-cooperative game between the two authorities might lead to worse results than a cooperative game, both in theory and in the real situations in which the preference functions of the authorities are expressed. On the question of central bank independence see Eijffinger and Schaling (1993) and De Cecco (1995).

[41] The need for massive intervention may conflict with the continuous action required to maintain intermediate targets at the desired level.

of credit (and with it the volume of credit actually granted) when policy is restrictive; it increases supply when policy is expansionary, but demand does not necessarily match the higher supply (and so credit actually granted does not necessarily increase). Take the typical course of the business cycle: in order to slow demand expansion, the monetary authorities may reduce monetary base, which leads to credit rationing in a situation in which demand for credit is high. With the onset of a recession, the monetary authorities induce banks to increase the supply of credit but at this point credit demand is probably no longer rationed owing to the negative impact of the recession on the outlook for profitability.

13.11 Summary

1 Macroeconomic policy aims at ensuring the 'stability' of a market economy by adjusting aggregate variables. The main instruments of this policy are monetary policy, fiscal policy, incomes policy and exchange rate policy.

2 Money serves three essential functions: (a) means of payment or medium of exchange; (b) unit of account; (c) store of value.

3 In a monetary economy, agents with a surplus of financial savings finance agents with a deficit through direct and indirect credit. Direct credit is granted to a deficit agent directly by the surplus agent. Indirect credit is channelled through financial intermediaries.

4 In modern economies, money is a liability issued by a financial intermediary and accepted on a fiduciary basis as a medium of exchange and store of value. The constant process of monetary innovation is driven by a variety of factors (above all, reducing costs and avoiding constraints).

5 Central banks, which are granted the privilege of issuing legal tender, also act as lenders of last resort (banker's bank) and supervisors of banking activity.

6 Monetary base is composed of the financial assets that banks can use to meet reserve requirements. Its sources comprise the 'foreign' sector, the 'Treasury' sector, 'open market operations' and the 'bank refinancing' sector. Monetary base is held by the public and the banks.

7 The main operations for monetary base creation with the banks are the rediscounting of bills and advances backed by securities.

8 Deposits are a liability issued by banks and function as money (bank money). The quantity of deposits created within the banking system is a multiple of the monetary base held by the banks and depends on the behaviour of the banks themselves in addition to the behaviour of the public: banks supply credit that will be partially converted into deposits, owing to the public's willingness to hold bank liabilities in addition to currency.

9 The monetary authorities can affect the volume of bank money and the money supply through the control of monetary base and the compulsory reserve ratio. The money supply can also be regulated by setting a lending ceiling. A restrictive policy is more effective than an expansionary one and the actual deposit multiplier tends to be higher in the former case than in the latter. Under fixed exchange rates capital mobility reduces the degree of control that can be exercised over monetary base.

10 Monetary policy can be directed at achieving a number of ultimate objectives: price stability, balance of payments equilibrium, employment and growth. Recent monetary theory and practice assign monetary authorities with the task of pursuing the first two objectives.

11 Monetary measures can have expansionary or restrictive effects by triggering changes in the cost and availability of credit (rationing).

12 The monetary authorities usually pay attention to variables that stand between instruments and ultimate targets (indicators and intermediate targets) because of the complexity of monetary policy actions and their impact on ultimate targets.

13 The choice of the intermediate target depends on:
   (a) the controllability of the aggregate being considered for use as an intermediate target;
   (b) the stability of behavioural functions;
   (c) the links between intermediate and ultimate targets.

14 Monetary policy is to be preferred to other instruments for its very short administrative time lag. However its effect lag is long and variable.

13.12 Key concepts

Macroeconomic policy
Cross subsidisation
Selective effect
Money
Medium of exchange
Means of payment
Unit of account
Store of value
Commodity, token money
Inconvertible currency
Legal tender
Direct, indirect credit
Financial intermediary

Maturity transformation
Financial structure
English-type bank
Universal (German-type) bank
Separation of lending by term
Securitisation
Banks' precautionary (free, excess)
   reserves
Financial liability, asset
Repurchase agreement
Certificate of deposit
Banker's acceptance
Monetary aggregate

Lender of last resort, banker's bank

Reserve requirement

Monetary base, high-powered money

Sources, uses of monetary base

Primary (new-issues), secondary (old-issues) market

Open market operation

Official discount rate (minimum lending rate)

Rate on advances (Lombard rate in Germany)

Current account (demand) deposit

Checking account deposits

Time deposits

Savings deposits

Deposit, money multiplier

Compulsory reserve ratio

Excess reserves ratio

Primary, derived deposit

Potential, actual multiplier

Asymmetry of monetary policy

Lending ceiling

Political, economic independence

Roosa (lock-in) effect

Equilibrium, endogenous rationing

Monetary policy indicator

Intermediate target

Domestic credit expansion

Inflation targeting

Announcement effect

Fine tuning

Liquidity trap

14 Macroeconomic objectives and fiscal policy

The term *fiscal policy* refers to the government budget measures aimed primarily at changing income and employment in the short run. Since debate on fiscal policy is often obscured by improper reference to the institutions governing it, it can be helpful to first state the meaning of certain terms denoting the agents of fiscal policy. The general government sector consists of the following group of resident institutional units: (a) all units of central, state or local government; (b) all social security funds at each level of government; (c) all non-market non-profit institutions that are controlled and mainly financed by government units. The sector does not include public corporations owned by government units. However, unincorporated enterprises owned by government are included. Individual countries may be organised in such a way that some of the units indicated will be absent, e.g., states for countries that do not have a federal constitution (see Commission of the European Communities *et al.*, 1993). Our analysis will generally refer to the general government sector as a whole. This means that relationships within the sector (e.g., transfers from the central to local governments) will not be examined.

14.1 The budget and its components

Let us now provide a number of definitions. The fundamental budget accounting identity is:[1]

$$T - C_g - Tr_c - INT - I_g - Tr_k = B_t \tag{14.1}$$

---

[1] Note that the identity given in (14.1) can be expressed in any unit of account, as long as the same unit is used for all the terms: we can use current pounds sterling, pounds sterling at 1950 prices, dollars or some other unit. In order to reduce the number of symbols employed, we prefer to express all the values for the various budget items in real terms, i.e., in terms of quantities of goods and services that the corresponding monetary values would enable us to purchase.

The symbols stand for:

T = current revenues
C_g = government consumption
Tr_c = current transfers (transfer payments), excluding interest payments
INT = interest payments on the public debt
I_g = government investment, net of disinvestment
Tr_k = capital account transfers (transfer payments)
B_t = budget balance

We need to clarify the relationships between these variables and those that we have used so far, which we will continue to adopt in certain contexts: government spending on goods and services, G, and total transfers, Tr:[2]

$$G = C_g + I_g \tag{14.2}$$

$$Tr = Tr_c + INT + Tr_k \tag{14.3}$$

Let us give a more precise definition of a number of terms, beginning with government revenues, which include current revenues and those on capital account.

Current revenues are largely generated by direct and indirect taxes and social security contributions, with a small amount coming from other sources (e.g., profits from public-sector enterprises). The general use of these funds is fairly clear: apart from the obvious use of financing expenditure, the level of current revenues can be adjusted for countercyclical purposes. The composition of revenues can be adjusted to pursue redistributive goals.

Capital account revenues come from the sale of government property and public-sector enterprises and the repayment of loans. For simplicity we have subtracted them from the investment expenditures indicated below.

Let us now look at government expenditure.

1 Government expenditure on goods and services is composed of two parts:
 (a) *government consumption*, which includes wages and salaries plus spending on current purchases of goods and services; it is used for the current operation of the public sector;
 (b) *government investment* is aimed at increasing the stock of publicly-owned capital (buildings, schools, roads, etc.).
2 *Current transfers* proper include:
 (a) *transfers to households*, for redistributive purposes and to supply merit goods (e.g., benefits to certain categories of person, such as the disabled or veterans; covering social security expenditure in excess of contributions from firms and workers);
 (b) *transfers to firms*, which consist of production subsidies (e.g., exchange rate guarantees, subsidies to firms that undertake to provide certain transport

---

[2] In chapter 8 we referred to current transfers to households, denoted by Tr_h. These are part of current transfers, including interest.

services, etc.) for various purposes: improving the balance of payments, redistribution, increasing demand, etc.;

(c) *official transfers*, especially in the form of contributions to international organisations and aid to developing countries; in the first case, the transfers are part of membership of such organisations; in the second, they are a form of redistribution.

3 *Interest* is paid on government debt; it is a special component of current transfers that is best considered separately, as we will see. Interest transfers can have a redistributive effect if the distribution of taxes financing interest transfers among different income earners differs from that of public debt holders.

4 *Capital account transfers*: these consist of payments normally made to firms to boost private investment (for example, grants for regional development programmes).

The *overall budgetary balance* is the sum of the current and capital account balances. The *current balance* is analogous to private saving, as it is the excess of current revenues over current outlays, which can be used for expenditure on capital account.[3] For this reason, a current surplus denotes (positive) *public saving*. Public saving is often negative, however, since in many cases governments run current deficits.[4]

By subtracting interest outlays from *total* expenditure (which we indicate with $G_t = G + Tr$), we have *primary government expenditure* (G_p). Considering (14.2) and (14.3), we have:

$$G_p = C_g + I_g + Tr_c + Tr_k \tag{14.4}$$

If we subtract interest outlays from the current balance or the total balance – thus considering primary expenditure only – we have the *primary current balance* or the *total primary balance*, respectively. The primary current balance is therefore equal to $T - C_g - Tr_c$, while the total primary balance is $T - G_p = T - C_g - I_g - Tr_c - Tr_k$.

14.2 Income, employment and taxes

In this section we examine the effects of taxation on income and employment. First note that in a Keynesian model, taxation, T (net of transfers to households), enters the income circuit only indirectly, through its influence on consumption and/or investment:

$$C = f(Y, T) \quad I = g(i, T)$$

For simplicity, we will ignore its effects on investment. We can distinguish between: (a) *lump-sum taxation*; (b) *proportional taxation*; (c) *progressive taxation*.

---

[3] For households, current revenues are current income; current expenditures are consumption of non-durables and services; capital account spending comprises the purchase of consumer durables. (However, consumer durables, such as automobiles, furniture, appliances and so on, for which it is difficult to calculate the value of current services provided, are included under current spending. Spending on housing, for which it is easier to estimate the services provided, is included under capital spending).

[4] The trend in the 1990s seems to be towards a return of positive public saving.

14.2.1 Lump-sum taxation

We know from chapter 11 that it is very difficult to implement a true lump-sum tax. Our main interest in that chapter was individuals' scope for avoiding redistributive taxes in a situation of asymmetric information. For our present purposes we can abstract from such problems and make use of the concept of a lump-sum tax as a tax whose amount, T, is fixed and does not depend on individuals' behaviour. In particular, we will assume that this tax does not depend on national income, which is a variable that depends on individuals' behaviour.

With a lump-sum tax affecting consumption only, in a simple Keynesian model of the real economy we have:

$$Y = C + I + G$$
$$C = c(Y - T) \tag{14.5}$$
$$I = \bar{I}$$

from which we obtain:

$$Y = \frac{1}{1 - c}(\bar{I} + G - cT) \tag{14.6}$$

The lump-sum tax multiplier is therefore $- c/(1 - c)$, which is smaller (even in absolute value terms) than that for government expenditure, G, which is equal to $1/(1 - c)$. This means that a £1 increase in taxes leads to a reduction in income that is smaller than the increase in income produced by a £1 increase in government expenditure. This will be important in understanding the balanced-budget theorem (see section 14.5.1).

The smaller effect of taxation is due to the fact that the £1 tax does not enter the income circuit directly. It therefore translates into (less) demand only to the extent that it influences consumption (which is a direct component of total demand), i.e., for an amount equal to c.

14.2.2 Proportional taxation

If, in addition to the three equations of the model (14.5), we assume that $T = tY$, where the tax rate, t, is constant (i.e., proportional taxation), we have:

$$Y = \frac{1}{1 - c(1 - t)}(\bar{I} + G) \tag{14.7}$$

The effect on income of an increase in the tax rate is, obviously, always negative, since it increases the denominator of the multiplier $1/[1 - c(1 - t)]$.[5]

---

[5] The reader will note that all of the multipliers we have seen so far have been derived from a model that assumes that there is no money (or, better, the money supply changes so as to leave the interest rate unchanged as income varies) and a closed economy. If we drop these hypotheses (the first will be abandoned in this chapter), the expenditure and tax multipliers are lowered as a result of two factors: the first is linked to the change in the interest rate following a change in income; the second is related to the fact that part of domestic demand can be met by foreign production.

We can use the proportional taxation framework to analyse a problem that was much debated at the beginning of the 1960s and again in the 1980s: the effects on total tax revenues (or the government budget) of a reduction in the average tax rate.

In the early 1960s the issue was tackled within the framework of the potential output concept and the expansionary policies adopted in the United States by the Kennedy administration (see section 7.5). The question re-emerged years later, albeit in a considerably different context, in connection with the Reagan administration's attempts to stimulate income growth and reduce the federal budget deficit with tax cuts, counting on the expansionary supply-side effects on saving and labour, rather than the demand-side effects on consumption and investment.[6]

While the 1960s policy was successful, the more recent attempt failed, as the supply response to the tax cut proved to be much smaller than estimated, given the initial level of taxation. The failure of the supply-side policies of 1981–2 prompted the Reagan administration to take a more orthodox approach in subsequent years, adopting Keynesian measures based on increasing government spending. This produced considerable income and employment growth after 1982, despite a restrictive monetary policy. The consequence of the latter for the balance of payments was a large capital inflow and the accumulation of a massive foreign debt.

14.2.3 Progressive taxation

With progressive taxation, the average tax rate is no longer constant but is instead an increasing function of the taxpayer's income. The variability of the average tax rate implies that tax revenue depends on both the structure of taxation and personal income distribution.

Despite the greater complexity of the analytical treatment of this case, we can continue to use expression (14.7), albeit with a number of caveats, to examine the effects of progressive taxation on income .

First, we interpret t in (14.7) as the average effective tax rate, i.e., the average tax burden. In addition, for simplicity, we consider average (or per capita) income as the only relevant aspect of income distribution. If there are variations in autonomous spending that give rise to a change only in the number of income earners, leaving per capita income unchanged, the average rate will not change. By contrast, changes in autonomous spending that are also reflected in variations in the same direction in per capita income tend to alter the average tax rate, t, raising it if autonomous spending rises and vice-versa, all other conditions being equal. The multiplier will therefore fall or rise, respectively, in line with the rise or fall in autonomous spending. The final effect on income of a change in autonomous spending will therefore be less than that under proportional taxation.

It follows that progressive taxation is an important *automatic stabiliser*: the effects on real income of fluctuations in the value of the autonomous components of aggregate

---

[6] An essential reference for these policies is Fink (1982).

Table 14.1. *Effects of an increase in prices and income in the presence of progressive taxation*

(1) Time	(2) Nominal gross income	(3) Price level	(4) = (2)/(3) Real gross income	(5) Tax	(6) = (2)–(5) Nominal net income	(7) = (6)/(3) Real net income
t_0	1,000	100	10	200	800	8
t_1	2,000	200	10	200 + 300 = 500	1,500	7.5

demand are dampened by changes in the opposite direction of the multiplier caused by changes in the average tax rate.

Note that the stabilising effect may be amplified if we consider price changes, which we have so far left out of our analysis. We have in effect considered real variables only. Let us now examine the case of pure price movements.

Assume that we have a '*classical*' *business cycle* in which an increase (decrease) in the price level corresponds to a positive (negative) shock to the level of autonomous expenditure. Starting for simplicity from a situation of full employment,[7] an increase in demand will lead to a rise in prices and thus an increase in the nominal income of each taxpayer (if the income distribution does not change). Since progressive tax rates are set in relation to nominal income, which has increased for each taxpayer, the average tax rate will rise. Real disposable income will fall and consumption will decline, lowering overall demand.

The increase in taxes in real terms that results from the combination of a rise in prices and a progressive tax schedule is called *fiscal drag*. Let us take a look at a simple example to clarify the problem further. Assume a nominal gross income of 1,000 and a price level of 100 at time t_0. Further assume that the tax rate is 20 per cent for incomes between 0 and 1,000 and 30 per cent on the portion of incomes between 1,001 and 2,000 (*tax bracket progressivity*). A doubling of prices and nominal income at time t_1 leaves real income unchanged but will move income taxpayers into higher tax brackets (*tax bracket creep*) and will increase nominal tax revenues by a factor of 2.5, thus reducing net real income (or real disposable income) from 8 to 7.5 (table 14.1). Conversely, a reduction in nominal income (caused by or associated with a reduction in prices) will lower the tax burden, strengthening demand.

Fiscal drag also occurs outside the framework of a classical business cycle, but in this case does not act as an automatic stabiliser. Take a situation of *stagflation* like that experienced in a number of countries after 1973, when prices rose despite slack demand and steady or even rising unemployment. The price rise increased the tax burden, thereby accentuating the slowdown.

This depressive effect and pressure from the taxpayers who bear most of the burden may prompt policymakers to adopt a variety of relief measures: for example, tax refunds or indexation of tax brackets. In the former case, fiscal drag is offset by granting

---

[7] As with other assumptions, this is not necessary but it helps us make our point.

taxpayers a tax credit of comparable value. Indexing tax brackets is not a compensatory measure but rather an attempt to avoid fiscal drag in the first place. For example, let us suppose that there is initially a 15 per cent tax rate for incomes of between £10,000 and £20,000 and that the extreme values of the brackets rise at a rate equal to the rate of inflation. If inflation is 10 per cent, the subsequent year the 15 per cent rate will apply to incomes of between £11,000 and £21,000. Obviously, partial indexation schemes are also possible. Indexation has been introduced in various countries, such as the United Kingdom (in 1976), the United States (1986) and Italy (1989). In Italy tax credits had previously been used.

14.3 Expenditure financing

From a short-term aggregate perspective, according to Keynes, the economic impact of government expenditure does not depend on its precise content. However, this does not imply either that we must accept inefficiency and patronage or that in a capitalist system any type of expenditure is feasible.

Spending can be financed with taxes – with a balanced budget – or in deficit (*deficit spending*). In the latter case, spending can be financed either by issuing government bonds (holding monetary base unchanged) or creating additional monetary base. The effects of the various options are different.

14.3.1 Balancing the budget

If expenditure is tax-financed, an increase in spending still has an expansionary effect, since it acts directly on national income, while the simultaneous increase in taxes affects disposable income, and hence consumption, and only through this national income (see section 14.2).

An increase of £1 in government spending gives rise to an immediate increase of £1 in income; an increase of £1 in taxes gives rise to an immediate decrease of £c of consumption and, therefore, income. Since c, the marginal propensity to consume, is usually less than 1, there is an immediate net increase in income, which will be followed by additional increases thanks to the multiplier process. In short, the spending multiplier is larger than the tax multiplier, as shown by (14.6) (repeated here for convenience):

$$Y = \frac{1}{1-c}(\bar{I} + G - cT) \tag{14.6}$$

where the expenditure multiplier is $1/(1-c)$ and the tax multiplier is $-c/(1-c)$.

If we assume a change in government spending *and* taxation, the corresponding change in income will be:

$$\Delta Y = \frac{1}{1-c}(\Delta G - c\Delta T) \tag{14.8}$$

If the increase in spending is entirely financed by taxes, i.e., if $\Delta G = \Delta T$, from (14.8) we have:

$$\Delta Y = \frac{1-c}{1-c}\Delta G$$

from which we derive:

$$\frac{\Delta Y}{\Delta G} = 1$$

So, a £1 increase in government spending financed by an equal increase in taxation raises income by £1. This result, known as the *balanced budget theorem* or the *Haavelmo theorem*, shows that any income target can be achieved without adding to the budget deficit, but only with a change in the level of government expenditure equal to the desired change in income; in other words, all the additional demand would come from the public sector. Ideological opposition to such a prospect helps explain why deficit spending is used at least on a temporary basis in market economies, even those which have mandated a balanced budget rule.

14.3.2 Deficit financing

Expenditure normally provides a larger boost to income and employment if it is not financed with taxes. This is the reason Keynes favoured deficit spending over tax-financed spending to escape from the Great Depression of the 1930s.

In the 1970s and 1980s many countries used deficit financing of government expenditure for a wide variety of reasons. In some cases it was difficult to control spending, on the one hand, and increase taxation, on the other, owing to obstacles associated with the structure of modern societies, such as the existence of a multitude of interest groups wielding considerable economic and political power. This is the reason for the *asymmetry of fiscal policy*, which is related to the decision-making process: an expansionary policy (reduction of tax revenues, increase in spending) is easier to adopt than a restrictive policy.[8] In addition, the institutions that emerged after the second world war provided for automatic stabilisers, such that the first real recessionary impulse (which came in the wake of the 1973–4 oil crisis) would generate large budget deficits. The increase in budget deficits that occurred in the 1970s and 1980s was not only a consequence of structural factors or automatic stabilizers. The oil crisis itself and the ineffectiveness of other policies (such as the supply-side measures in the United States) prompted the adoption of discretionary measures that also increased deficits. An additional influence was the restrictive monetary policy stance taken in the United States and, at the same time, in Germany beginning at the end of the 1970s, which increased the interest that had to be paid on the public debt.

A final factor in the increase in public deficits is tax evasion, avoidance and erosion.

[8] This sort of asymmetry is different from monetary policy asymmetry (see chapter 13) and that associated with exchange rate policy (see chapter 17): here the asymmetry involves the greater ease with which expansionary policy measures can be *adopted* compared with restrictive ones, not differences in their effectiveness, as in the case of the other two policies.

Tax evasion refers to illegal actions to reduce one's tax obligations. *Tax avoidance* involves reducing one's tax obligations by taking full advantage of the provisions of the tax code, through such devices as: (a) income shifting to lower-income taxpayers, if the tax system is progressive; (b) tax deferral (in particular, payment of taxes on capital gains can be deferred in a number of ways); (c) tax arbitrage, i.e., exploiting differences in tax rates on different kinds of income, individuals or countries.[9] The provisions of the tax code that give rise to tax avoidance are often 'technical' in nature and the consequences may well be unintended. There are other provisions, however, which purposely grant tax exemptions in order to encourage the development of an industry, a region or certain social groups (e.g., the poor or the disabled). Such tax provisions are called *tax expenditures*, since they are a substitute for direct government expenditure or subsidies.[10] In this case we speak of *erosion of the tax base*. Tax evasion and tax avoidance have tended to increase in connection with the globalisation of markets and production (see Unctad, 1994). Tax expenditures have also risen in recent years for a number of reasons, ranging from the decline in growth rates and the rise in unemployment rates in many countries to the increased pressure of interest groups.

Government expenditure, revenues and deficits in the G7 countries in a selection of years since 1970 are given in table 14.2.

Let us now return to equation (14.1). If the budget is balanced we have $B_s = 0$. If total expenditure exceeds revenues, i.e., there is a budget deficit, $B_s < 0$. As we said, the deficit can be financed in two ways: through the creation of monetary base, ΔMB, or by issuing government debt, ΔB. Taking account of the possibility of deficit financing, the following budget identity can be derived from (14.1) and (14.4):

$$T - G_p - INT + \frac{\Delta MB}{p} + \frac{\Delta B}{p} = 0 \tag{14.9}$$

where ΔMB and/or ΔB are positive values.

Note that the additional monetary base and the new government debt have been deflated (remember that we decided to express the budget identity in terms of real variables in section 14.1).

We will examine the two methods of deficit financing separately, since they have considerably different natures and effects.

---

[9] For some of the tax avoidance devices mentioned in the text, see Stiglitz (1988). Special mention should be made of *transfer pricing*, a tax avoidance (and in some case, a tax evasion) method that exploits differences in tax treatment in different countries. Transfer prices are those applied to transfers of goods or services within a financial group. For example, if the parent company of the group sells a semi-finished product (or the right to use a patent) to a foreign subsidiary in a country where taxes are lower, it will set a lower price on the transfer in order to reduce its profit (taxed at a higher rate) and increase the profit of the subsidiary (taxed at a lower rate in the foreign country), thus minimising its tax liability.

[10] Provisions may also be designed to help other people in special positions (e.g., the head of state, MPs, etc.) or powerful lobbies. A special form of tax expenditure is the partial or total exemption of interest on certain categories of bonds (usually government securities).

Table 14.2. *Total expenditure, current revenues and overall general government budget balances as a percentage of GDP in the 7 leading industrial countries, 1970–95*

	1970*	1975*	1980	1985	1990	1995
United States						
Total expenditure	31.6	34.6	31.4	32.9	32.8	33.3
Current revenues	28.9	28.8	30.0	29.7	30.1	31.3
Budget balance	−1.1	−4.1	−1.4	−3.2	−2.7	−2.0
Japan						
Total expenditure	19.4	27.3	32.0	31.6	31.3	35.6
Current revenues	20.6	24.0	27.6	30.8	34.2	31.7
Budget balance	+1.7	−2.8	−4.4	−0.8	+2.9	−3.9
Germany						
Total expenditure	38.6	48.9	47.9	47.0	45.1	49.5
Current revenues	38.3	42.7	45.0	45.8	43.1	45.9
Budget balance	+0.2	−5.6	−2.9	−1.2	−2.1	−3.5
France						
Total expenditure	38.5	43.4	46.1	52.1	49.8	53.7
Current revenues	38.5	39.7	46.1	49.3	48.3	48.8
Budget balance	+1.1	−2.2	0	−2.9	−1.6	−5.0
Italy						
Total expenditure	34.2	43.2	41.9	50.9	53.2	51.9
Current revenues	30.4	31.2	33.3	38.3	42.3	44.7
Budget balance	−4.0	−12.9	−8.6	−12.6	−10.9	−7.2
United Kingdom						
Total expenditure	38.8	46.6	43.0	44.0	39.9	43.4
Current revenues	40.2	40.5	39.6	41.2	38.6	37.6
Budget balance	+2.9	−4.6	−3.4	−2.8	−1.2	−5.7
Canada						
Total expenditure	34.8	40.1	38.8	45.3	46.0	46.2
Current revenues	34.2	36.1	36.1	38.5	41.9	42.1
Budget balance	+0.8	−2.5	−2.8	−6.8	−4.1	−4.2
Average						
Total expenditure	32.3	37.7	36.2	38.2	37.6	39.9
Current revenues	30.8	32.2	33.4	34.8	35.5	36.1
Budget balance	0	−4.4	−2.7	−3.4	−2.1	−3.5

Note: *The figures for this year are not strictly comparable with those for 1980 onwards owing to different definitions of the government sector and some aggregates.
Source: OECD (1990, 1996).

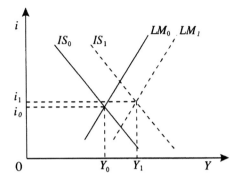

Figure 14.1

14.3.3 Monetary base financing

The first difference between the two methods is their cost to the government. Debt financing is obviously expensive. Monetary base financing, on the other hand, is often less expensive or even without costs.[11] It generates no costs if it is carried out by directly printing money (ignoring printing costs), while it involves minimal costs if effected by means of credit agreements between the government and the central bank, which set a below-market interest rate, thus generating a hidden revenue equal to the difference between the cost of funds raised through government securities issues and the cost of central bank financing. This hidden revenue is called *seignorage*.[12]

The term is also used to mean the creation of monetary base in excess of that needed to keep the purchasing power of the currency stable. This creates a sort of *inflation tax*, which benefits the government (as it does any other debtor), since inflation reduces the real value of debt if, being unexpected, it does not lead to an increase in nominal interest rates.

The second difference between monetary and debt financing is in the magnitude of their expansionary effect on income. In terms of the *IS-LM* framework, monetary financing of expenditure would shift both the *IS* and *LM* curves to the right (figure 14.1). Note that while an increase in income is certain, the effect on the interest rate is ambiguous.

We will provide a formal derivation of the condition for the invariance of the interest rate in a note to the following subsection. However, we can say right now that this condition is generally difficult to meet. The change in monetary base needed to keep the interest rate constant can be larger or smaller than the additional expenditure to be

---

[11] A differential cost to consumers could arise from monetary base financing if this stimulates demand to such an extent as to cause inflation (or higher inflation than debt financing).

[12] The term was originally used to indicate the privilege connected with the minting of metal coins with a face value greater than their (positive) intrinsic value. Subsequently, it indicated the profit earned by the central bank as a result of its ability to issue paper money (with no intrinsic value at all) in exchange for financing the government. Seignorage is also used to indicate the benefits accruing to a reserve currency country (see chapter 16).

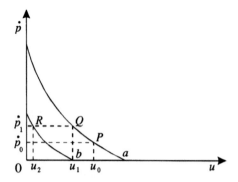

Figure 14.2

financed. A monetary policy that seeks to maintain a constant interest rate is called an *accommodating monetary policy*. If such a policy is adopted, an expansionary fiscal policy has full effect and the pre-eminent role assigned to it by Keynes is justified. From this point of view, close coordination of fiscal and monetary policy is vital for obtaining higher income and employment. By contrast, an independent central bank that did not adequately expand the money supply in the presence of an increase in government spending could be harmful, since this would trigger a rise in the interest rate, with adverse effects that we will examine in greater detail in the next subsection.

Monetary financing can lead to inflation in the presence of full employment or sectoral bottlenecks, or if wage rates, profit margins and other income are an increasing function of the level of economic activity. The inflationary effect, emphasised by the monetarists, is a real possibility in these conditions. If present, policymakers' short-run options would be higher income and employment together with inflation or lower income and employment together with greater monetary stability.

This trade-off is partly a consequence of the fact that the structure of the economic system should be considered given in the short run. In addition to implementing appropriate short-term measures, effective policymaking will be directed towards changing the economic structure, so as to reduce the constraints that bear on short-term decisions.

Consider the following example, which uses the concept of a 'transformation' curve between objectives (see section 8.3), with unemployment and inflation rates as our policy objectives. Referring to figure 14.2, policymakers must choose a point on the Phillips curve a.

Beginning at P, for example, where the unemployment rate is u_0 and the inflation rate is $\dot{p}_0$, policymakers must decide if an expansionary fiscal policy (e.g., an increase in expenditure financed with monetary base) is advisable, being aware that this may cause inflation to increase. This possibility prompts a measure of caution and leads them to choose point Q, where the unemployment rate is u_1, only slightly less than u_0 and inflation is $\dot{p}_1$. Unemployment lower than u_1 would mean higher inflation, which is judged to be unacceptable. If, however, policymakers were able to shift the Phillips curve from a to b, it would still be possible to have an inflation rate of $\dot{p}_1$ with unemployment of $u_2 < u_1$ with an expansionary fiscal policy.

Policymakers can shift the 'transformation' curve[13] downwards with:

professional training policies (obviously, in sectors and jobs where bottlenecks exist);

labour flexibility policies (in addition to those regarding employment conditions, this includes measures to improve transportation and communications, develop the housing market, etc.);

policies to increase productivity (reorganisation of production, innovation policies) and output (incentives to supply, directives to public enterprises) in certain sectors (those affected by bottlenecks, which can cause prices to rise, or those whose products are widely used as inputs by other sectors).

14.3.4 Debt financing

The Keynesian arguments for deficit spending have been criticised, especially by monetarists. The latter have raised the possibility that deficit spending may have no expansionary effect. In their view, monetary financing of public expenditure would only create inflation (see section 7.4.4), while government spending would crowd out private investment if it were financed with government debt.

To understand the monetarist critique, let us first examine what would happen if the increase in debt-financed government spending occurred in the presence of a horizontal LM curve, i.e., if the increase was matched by an accommodating monetary policy, expanding the money supply enough to keep the interest rate unchanged. In this case, an increase in spending equal to ΔG would produce an increase in income $\Delta Y = AB$ (figure 14.3, panel a, where LM is horizontal). In other words, we would have an increase in income equal to the increase we would obtain in a Keynesian model that considered only the real economy.

If monetary policy is not accommodating (figure 14.3, panel b, where LM is not horizontal), the increase in income generated by the increase in spending will be smaller, equal to AD; i.e., the multiplier $\Delta Y/\Delta G$ is lower owing to the *crowding-out effect* of the unchanged money supply. Here, the increase in income leads in sequence[14] to a rise in the transaction demand for money, an excess of money demand over money supply, a rise in the interest rate, a decline in investment and, therefore, a brake on the increase in income itself.

The braking effect can be identified in a analytical framework with reference to a simple Keynesian model:

---

[13] Shifting the curve downwards gives policymakers a wider range of choice, since the objectives are expressed as 'bads' to be minimised. If the objectives were formulated in terms of 'goods', widening the range of choice would mean shifting the transformation curve upwards.

[14] Note that the reference to a sequence is for illustrative purposes only. In reality, the Keynesian reference model is a static one.

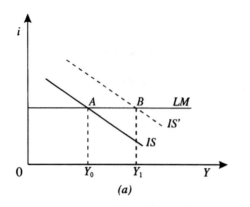 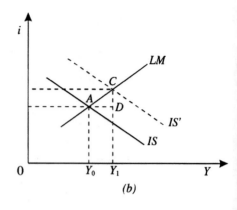

(a)   (b)

Figure 14.3

$$Y = C + I + G$$
$$C = cY$$
$$I = I_0 - ai$$

$$\frac{L_s}{p} = L_d \qquad\qquad\qquad\qquad (14.10)$$

$$L_d = L_d^1 + L_d^2$$
$$L_d^1 = kY$$
$$L_d^2 = L_0 - vi$$

where the symbols have the usual meaning.
Solving with respect to Y,[15] we have:

$$Y = \frac{1}{1 - c + ak/v}\left[I_0 + G + \frac{a}{v}\left(\frac{L_s}{p} - L_0\right)\right] \qquad (14.11)$$

The crowding-out effect is expressed by the positive term ak/v, which increases the denominator of the multiplier, reducing its value. The reader can verify that the value of the multiplier will be smaller the more sensitive is transaction demand for money to income (the coefficient k), the less sensitive is speculative demand to the interest rate (v) and the more sensitive is investment to the interest rate (a).[16]

---

[15] Substitute the sixth and seventh equation in (14.10) into the fifth, and the fifth into the fourth; then solve the fourth for i and substitute its value into the third; substituting the latter together with the second into the first, we obtain expression (14.11).

[16] Note that the crowding-out effect is always operative, even when government spending is partially or entirely financed with monetary base. The effect would not operate only if the money supply changed so as to keep the interest rate constant. Assume the limiting case where the increase in government spending is financed entirely with monetary base, i.e., $\Delta G = \Delta MB/p$. The resulting rise in income is not equal to $1/(1 - c)\Delta G$. It must be derived from (14.11), taking account both of ak/v in the denominator of the multiplier and the fact that as G varies, so does L_s, since G is monetary financed. More precisely, since, by using the money multiplier formula:

The substitution of private investment with government spending is a case of *financial crowding out*,[17] associated with the increase in the interest rate as a result of the non-monetary financing of government spending (or, more generally, a non-accommodating monetary policy).

Empirical studies have not lent much support to the hypothesis of financial crowding out. The *crowding-out ratio*[18] has often proved very small or even nil, as in France (0), and the US and Canada (0.12). One exception is Japan, where it has been estimated at 0.63 (see Price and Chouraqui, 1983, p. 29, table 8).

These issues have been at the heart of a wide-ranging and complex debate, on which we will offer only a few brief remarks to give an idea of the complexity of the issues involved.

According to the new classical macroeconomists, an increase in government spending financed by issuing debt would give rise to full real crowding out, since individuals – predicting that the government will have to raise future taxes to repay the debt – prepare for this by reducing current consumption. Current income will not be affected by government expenditure. To state this position in other terms, government securities do not constitute net wealth: an increase in government debt in private individuals'

$\Delta L_s/p = [(1+h)/(j+h)] \cdot \Delta MB/p = [(1+h)/(j+h)] \cdot \Delta G$, from (14.11) we derive:

$$\Delta Y = \frac{1}{1-c+ak/v}\left[\Delta G + \frac{a}{v}\frac{\Delta L_s}{p}\right] = \frac{1}{1-c+ak/v}\Delta G\left(1+\frac{a}{v}\frac{1+h}{h+j}\right)$$

We can now determine the condition under which monetary financing of spending will not cause the interest rate to change (the problem we mentioned with reference to figure 14.1). In order for there to be no change in the interest rate, transaction demand for money and the money supply must change by the same amount, i.e., $k\Delta Y = \Delta L_s/p$, which requires, using the previous expression and the money multiplier formula:

$$k\frac{1}{1-c+ak/v}\Delta G\left(1+\frac{a}{v}\frac{1+h}{1+j}\right) = \frac{1+h}{h+j}\frac{\Delta MB}{p}$$

Recalling that $\Delta G = \Delta MB/p$, by hypothesis, and for simplicity indicating the income and money multipliers with u and z respectively, the invariance condition for the interest rate is:

$$ku\left(1+\frac{a}{v}z\right) = z$$

or

$$ku + \frac{ak}{v}uz = z$$

In the special case where the crowding-out effect is zero, the condition would reduce to $ku = z$.

[17] This differs from *real crowding out*, which may be caused by a number of factors: proximity to the full employment barrier or the existence of sectoral bottlenecks; substitution of government consumption for private consumption; depressive effects on investment due to a possible increase in uncertainty as a result of government spending; a reduction in exports and an increase in imports under flexible exchange rates and capital mobility (see chapter 18). One possible substitution of public consumption (more generally, government spending) for private consumption (generally, private spending) will be shortly examined in this section.

[18] This is defined as $(u^* - u)/u^*$, where u^* is the government spending multiplier with an accommodating monetary policy and u is the same multiplier with a non-accommodating monetary policy.

portfolios would be offset by the perception of an equivalent increase in the present value of their debts owing to expectations of higher future taxes. This assumption of consumer 'ultrarationality', which is already debatable on theoretical grounds, does not appear to find sufficient support in the real world either. In any case the proposition it has generated is known as *Ricardian equivalence* or *Barro-Ricardo equivalence*,[19] meaning that debt financing of government spending is equivalent to tax financing.

In contrast to the hypothesis of ultrarationality, others argue that the effectiveness of debt financing could be enhanced by the interest-bearing nature of government debt, which would increase disposable income, thus helping to boost the expansionary effects of government spending (Blinder and Solow, 1973). This effect would disappear as soon as a deficit reduction policy were adopted, because the higher taxes would offset the increase in disposable income resulting from interest payments to holders of government securities.[20]

14.4 Public debt

14.4.1 Historical developments in selected countries

Public debt will grow over time if budget deficits persist. This has occurred in many countries in the post-war period, as shown by table 14.3.

14.4.2 The determinants of the growth in public debt

Let us take a look at the reasons for the rise in the ratio between nominal public debt, B, and nominal GDP, pY, first from an abstract point of view and then in more concrete terms.

The ratio $B/(pY)$ increases over time if the numerator increases more rapidly than the denominator, i.e., if, approximately:

$$\dot{B} - \dot{p} - \dot{Y} > 0 \tag{14.12}$$

where a dot over a variable indicates its rate of change per unit of time. Thus, $\dot{B} = (\Delta B/\Delta t)/B$. If we always refer to changes over the unit of time considered, we can write $\dot{B} = \Delta B/B$.[21]

On what does ΔB depend?

1 Assume that we start with a primary balance equal to zero, i.e., $G_p - T = 0$. In this

---

[19] It was first formulated by David Ricardo and restated by Barro (1974). In a more recent paper Barro admits that the way public expenditure is financed can affect the level of income through labour supply effects (see Barro, 1989).

[20] An excellent survey of the various positions in the debate on debt financing of government spending is given by Stevenson, Muscatelli and Gregory (1988, section 6.3).

[21] Let us denote $B/(pY)$ with z, i.e., we have $z = B/(pY)$. Taking the log of this expression and differentiating with respect to time, we obtain $\dot{z} = \dot{B} - \dot{p} - \dot{Y}$. We can state that if $\dot{z} > 0$ if $\dot{B} - \dot{p} - \dot{Y} > 0$; but if $\dot{z} > 0$, the ratio of debt to nominal GDP increases. Hence, the condition for an increase in the ratio is $\dot{B} - \dot{p} - \dot{Y} > 0$. This condition holds for continuous changes in the variables, but is only approximately valid for discrete changes.

Table 14.3. *The public debt in various European countries, 1981–96 (percentage of GDP)*

	1981	1985	1990	1995	1996*
Belgium	93.2	123.1	130.9	133.7	130.0
Denmark	51.1	72.0	59.6	71.9	69.8
France	22.2	31.0	35.4	52.8	55.4
Germany	35.4	41.7	43.8	58.1	60.7
Greece	28.3	51.6	90.1	111.8	111.8
Ireland	76.6	103.3	96.5	81.6	73.3
Italy	59.9	82.4	98.0	124.9	123.7
Luxembourg	13.0	12.9	4.4	6.0	6.8
The Netherlands	50.9	71.5	78.8	79.7	78.5
Portugal	41.6	72.3	68.6	71.7	70.3
United Kingdom	54.5	53.8	35.3	54.1	55.3
Spain	21.4	43.7	45.1	65.7	69.3

Note: *Forecast March 1997.
Source: Based on data from *European Economy* (1994), until 1990, and from European Monetary Institute (1997) for subsequent years.

case public debt can increase only as a result of interest payments (equal to iB) on the existing stock of debt, if there is no monetary financing. The rate of increase in public debt will then be iB/B, or i. Expression (14.12) can be rewritten as:

$$i - \dot{p} - \dot{Y} > 0 \tag{14.12'}$$

But $i - \dot{p}$ is the real (*ex post*) interest rate. We can therefore say that with no primary deficit (or surplus) and no monetary financing the ratio of public debt to GDP increases if the real interest rate is higher than the GDP growth rate.

2 Suppose instead that we have a primary deficit. If it were entirely financed with monetary base, public debt would not be increased by the primary deficit and the conclusion under point 1 would still hold. If the primary deficit were only partly financed with monetary base, there would be an additional source of debt growth: the debt could in fact increase even if the real interest rate were equal to, rather than higher than, the rate of GDP growth. By contrast, the existence of a primary surplus would slow the growth in the debt, even eliminating it if appropriate real interest rates and GDP growth rates prevailed.

This brief analysis can help us understand the sharp increase in the ratio of public debt to GDP in the 1980s. During this period the real interest rate was well above the rate of GDP growth, for at least two reasons:

    (a) the monetary tightening in the US at the end of the 1970s caused world interest rates to rise;

    (b) the rate of GDP growth slowed down in Europe as a result of a tight monetary policy and participation in the Exchange Rate Mechanism (ERM) (see chapter 16).

14.4.3 Limits to debt growth

Are there limits to the growth of public debt? Obviously, the problem must be stated in relative, rather than absolute, terms. We therefore need to identify the most suitable yardstick. In our earlier discussion, we compared the size of public debt with GDP at current prices. This was done simply for 'normalising' purposes. Since each new issue of securities is denominated in money at current purchasing power, the nominal value of the debt tends to increase over time; we can see if the debt is growing in real terms by dividing this value by the current price level. Dividing the real value of the public debt by real GDP, we can determine the relative increase in the two variables, the same as we would, say, in comparing the growth rate of consumption and investment with income.

    Beyond this, we cannot attribute any other economic meaning to the ratio of public debt to GDP. The question about limits to the growth of public debt is relevant insofar as that growth has economic repercussions, such as insolvency risk. From this point of view, a more significant ratio would be that between public debt and the total assets (or liabilities) of the economy. The concentration of debtors, of which an increase in this ratio would be an indicator, is in fact dangerous in itself.

    Nevertheless, the ratio of public debt to total assets is not used for a variety of reasons, including greater calculation difficulty. Instead, we use the ratio of public debt to income in order to have at least a rough idea of current trends and the risk of default. The underlying issue can be stated as follows: if a high debt/GDP ratio rises continuously rather than stabilising or falling, there are two possible outcomes. One is the insolvency of the debtor (the government); the other is credit rationing (or complete denial of credit) by the creditor (i.e., the market).[22] There have been real-life instances of both, although they have been associated with 'revolutions' or 'breakdown' in the countries concerned.

14.4.4 Debt reduction policies

Apart from debt repudiation, a variety of instruments can be used to influence the variables on which the dynamics of the debt/GDP ratio depend, as discussed in section 14.4.2.

Income growth policies
Measures designed to promote income growth (the denominator of the ratio) may be difficult to implement because under our assumption of a large public debt we cannot use traditional fiscal tools to stimulate global demand (increasing expenditure and

---

[22] Insolvency can take a number of forms: the government may *repudiate* the debt, *fund* it (i.e., convert maturities from short-term into long-term, or even perpetual) or introduce some other change in the terms of the loan (e.g., the interest rate). Credit rationing may occur in the form of only partial placement of new issues or as attempts by the public to *monetise* existing public debt.

reducing taxes), since this would increase the deficit. Growth can be fostered by restructuring government spending and taxes (without increasing the deficit). Government spending can be made more efficient and a growth-oriented industrial policy can be implemented. Taxation can be directed to enhancing incentives for private economic activity (see chapter 11). Growth can also be enhanced by using other policy tools, both microeconomic, such as regulation, and macroeconomic, such as an easy monetary policy, an incomes policy (see chapter 15) and devaluation or depreciation of the domestic currency (see chapter 17).

Policies for the primary balance

Although not strictly necessary, a primary surplus certainly facilitates the reduction of the debt/GDP ratio. Improving the primary balance is an explicit objective of any policy aimed at stabilising this ratio. In order to generate a primary surplus, policymakers can either reduce primary spending or increase revenues.

1 *Expenditure policies*. Reducing spending is one theoretically possible step, but this can produce a considerable welfare loss for the public as well as undermine the growth potential of the economy unless the quality of public services can be significantly improved.
2 *Revenue policies*. Increasing revenues would also help increase the primary surplus and so help reduce the debt/GDP ratio. However, raising tax revenue has an adverse impact on income, thus reducing the denominator of the ratio. As with expenditure, the most appropriate solution seems to be the reorganisation and improved operation of the administrative machinery of government, which should reduce tax evasion, avoidance and erosion. A role in this can be played by closer international coordination.

Privatisation of public-sector enterprises is seen as a possible source of revenues to reduce the borrowing requirement and a way to increase the efficiency of the productive system, with a beneficial effect on income growth. However, this second aspect of privatisation is controversial since it is debatable whether the efficiency of the private sector is clearly superior to that of the public sector, as we saw in chapter 10.

Interest rate policies

Lowering the real interest rate paid on public debt may contribute to lowering the debt/GDP ratio. This can be accomplished in at least two ways.

1 The public debt can be managed in such a way as to reduce the real cost of the debt, especially by adjusting the terms applied to debt issues or improving issuing techniques and the functioning of the secondary government securities market.
2 A more general solution to lowering the real interest rate involves the relationship with world financial markets. With a fixed (or managed) exchange rate, a country's interest rates are more closely linked to those abroad the greater is international capital mobility. Reducing capital mobility may make it feasible

to undertake policies aimed at keeping domestic rates lower than those abroad, without triggering undesired increases in the exchange rate (depreciations). This can be done by imposing constraints on capital movements or a tax on capital invested abroad, as suggested by Tobin. We will return to this question in part VI.

14.5 Summary

1 Fiscal policy involves tax and expenditure measures. It is normally aimed at achieving income and employment objectives.

2 Taxation can come in the form of lump-sum taxation, proportional taxation or progressive taxation. The latter serves as an automatic stabiliser. Tax revenue increases if prices rise in the presence of progressive taxation (fiscal drag). The stabilising effect of progressive taxation can be amplified by procyclical price movements. Fiscal drag has perverse effects in the presence of stagflation.

3 In the 1970s and 1980s growth in government expenditure in the industrial countries was often more rapid than the increase in tax revenue for a number of reasons. In recent years this has primarily been due to interest payments on public debt.

4 Expenditure can be financed with taxes (balanced budget) or in deficit. The balanced budget theorem stresses the possibility of achieving any income objective without adding to the budget deficit.

5 According to Keynes, deficit spending has a larger impact on income. Deficit spending can be financed either with monetary base or government bonds.

6 Monetary base financing is less expensive (seignorage) and has a larger impact on income, since it gives rise to a simultaneous rightward shift of the *IS* and *LM* curves. Close to the full employment level, the effect on income may also be associated with inflationary tensions.

7 Debt financing leaves the quantity of monetary base unchanged and causes interest rates to rise; consequently, government expenditure crowds out private investment (financial crowding out).

8 Real crowding out mainly takes place: when the economy is close to full employment; when government spending replaces private spending, which could occur if the 'ultrarationality' hypothesis holds (Barro-Ricardo equivalence); and when public spending is a substitute for exports under flexible exchange rates and capital mobility.

9 The ratio of public debt to GDP increases when the real interest rate is higher than the rate of GDP growth in the presence of a primary balance or deficit.

10 There are no definite limits to the increase in the debt/GDP ratio, which is not,

however, the best indicator of a government's insolvency risk. Policies aimed at reducing this ratio comprise measures for income growth, reduction of primary expenditure and interest rates and increasing revenues.

14.6 Key concepts

Fiscal policy

Public consumption

Transfers to households, firms

Official transfers

Current transfers

Capital account transfers

Interest

Public investment

Current (account) revenue

Capital (account) revenue

Primary expenditure

Public saving

Budgetary balance

Lump-sum, proportional, progressive tax

(Lump-sum) tax multiplier

Supply-side policy

Classical business cycle

Fiscal drag

Tax-bracket creep

Stagflation

Asymmetry of fiscal policy

Public (government) debt

(Public) expenditure multiplier

Deficit spending

Balanced-budget (Haavelmo) theorem

Tax erosion

Tax avoidance

Tax evasion

Transfer pricing

Tax expenditure

Seignorage

Accommodating monetary policy

Real, financial crowding out

Ultrarationality

Ricardian, Barro-Ricardian equivalence

Debt repudiation

Debt funding

Monetisation of public debt

15 Incomes and price policies

15.1 Introduction

In chapter 7 inflation was characterised as the outcome of a competition in which agents seek to increase their share of income by increasing the price of the good or service they sell. The connection between the distribution of income and the price level should therefore be clear.

The objective of incomes policy is to contain increases in the general price level by controlling distributive variables, which are essentially the wage rate and/or the profit margin. Take the wage rate, for example. It represents income for a worker and a cost for a firm. An incomes policy may seek to limit wage increases in order to keep labour costs – and costs in general – low and thus reduce the possibility of price increases. In the next section we develop this simple concept in an abstract context, referring to a closed economic system in which there is one good and only two categories of income: wages and profits. We then distinguish between different types of incomes policy on the basis of their degree of coerciveness (section 15.3). Section 15.4 analyses the many problems that arise with the direct *control* of wages and/or other incomes (statist policies), while section 15.5 examines the possibilities and limitations of 'market-based' incomes policies. Section 15.6 is devoted to 'institutional' incomes policies and section 15.7 analyses the role of productivity-boosting measures in relation to incomes policies. The last section offers a brief survey of incomes policy experiments in the real world.

15.2 Income distribution, full cost and incomes policy

For simplicity, we consider a closed economy producing only one good; there is no fixed capital and there are only two types of income recipient: workers and capitalists. The total value of output will therefore be equal to:

$$pY = W + R \tag{15.1}$$

where p and Y are the price and quantity of the good, W is total wages and R total profits, both expressed in money terms.

Total wages are obtained by multiplying the nominal wage rate, w, by the number of employed workers, N. If we take this relation into account and divide both sides of the previous expression by Y, we have:

$$p = \frac{wN}{Y} + \frac{R}{Y} \tag{15.2}$$

Now consider that total profits can be expressed in a variety of ways. For example, they can be given as the *rate of profit* times capital employed or the *mark-up rate* times prime costs. In the second case, since costs are represented by wages only, if we indicate the profit margin with g we have $R \equiv wNg$. Equation 15.2 can therefore be rewritten as:

$$p = \frac{wN}{Y} + \frac{wNg}{Y} = \frac{wN}{Y}(1 + g) \tag{15.3}$$

Equation (15.3) is simply a mark-up equation, expressing the *full-cost principle*. Considering that *average labour productivity* is $\pi = Y/N$, by substitution we have:

$$p = \frac{w}{\pi}(1 + g) \tag{15.4}$$

Deriving this simple relation from the identity between output and distributed income underscores the link between price setting and income distribution. We will consider additional aspects later.

Let us now examine (15.4). In dynamic terms price changes can be expressed as:

$$\dot{p} = \dot{w} - \dot{\pi} + (1 \dotplus g) \tag{15.5}$$

Sufficient conditions for no inflation (i.e., $\dot{p} = 0$) are that $\dot{w} = \dot{\pi}$ and $(1 \dotplus g) = 0$. In other words, there will be no rise in prices if the percentage change in the nominal wage rate is equal to that in productivity *and* the profit margin does not change. A change in the wage rate equal to that in labour productivity is on its own neither a necessary nor a sufficient condition.

If both sufficient conditions for no inflation held, distributive shares would not change. The share of wages in income is equal to $W/pY = wN/pY = w/p\pi$. This does not change if $\dot{w} - \dot{p} - \dot{\pi} = 0$. If $\dot{w} = \dot{\pi}$ and $\dot{p} = 0$, this condition is met and the ratio remains constant. The invariance of the share of wages in total income means that the share of profits is also unchanged, since these are the only categories of income.

To sum up, price invariance requires certain forms of behaviour on the part of both categories of income recipient. If the change in the wage rate is equal to that in productivity and the profit margin does not change, distributive shares do not change. Obviously, constant prices are not inconsistent with a change in distributive shares. We said that $\dot{w} = \dot{\pi}$ and $(1 \dotplus g) = 0$ are only sufficient conditions: prices can still be constant if the change in the wage rate is different from that in productivity (thus permitting changes in distributive shares) as long as the profit margin changes in the opposite direction by an amount equal to the difference between wage and productivity growth. For example, there will be no change in prices if $\dot{w} = 10\%$, $\dot{\pi} = 6\%$ and $(1 \dotplus g) = -4\%$.

This reconfirms our depiction of inflation as the product of a competition to increase one's share of total income. Inflation ceases if this competition ends and the various classes of income recipient maintain (or are induced or forced to maintain) their share of income, or if they agree on how shares should change, offsetting an increase for one group with a decline for the other group.

Before examining the ways incomes policy can be implemented, we should emphasise the limitations of the simple framework we have adopted so far. First and foremost, note that we have assumed a one-good (or one-industry) economy without fixed capital where productivity is the same for all firms. In a many-industry world, productivity changes differ across industries, which gives rise to the problem of which change in productivity should be used as a benchmark for changes in nominal wage rates. We address this question in section 15.4. In addition, the multiplicity of goods forces us to consider other variable costs, such as those of raw materials, in the mark-up formula.[1]

The existence of fixed capital in real life means that we must interpret the profit margin, g, as a *gross* margin, so as to cover the depreciation costs of capital itself. Changes in the gross margin do not necessarily indicate equal changes in the net margin; nor does a constant gross margin imply a constant net margin and therefore a constant share of profits in income.

Moreover, in reality there is at least one other class of income recipients in addition to workers and capitalists: recipients of rent, or *rentiers*. The form and importance of rent can change over time, so prices may change even when the shares of wages and profits are unchanged. Part of income (more precisely, part of GDP at market prices) is also appropriated by the government in the form of direct and indirect taxes (net of subsidies). Changes in taxation can therefore also give rise to changes in the prices of goods and services. The theory of tax shifting can help us predict these effects (see Stiglitz, 1988, chapter 17).

Finally, an open economy poses an additional problem, since price changes in the domestic currency of imported raw materials and semi-finished goods also give rise to price changes in the final product.

We can conclude by recalling that many conditions (or rules) must be satisfied for prices to remain constant. The most frequently used rules (or guidelines) of incomes policy are those that require wage rates to increase at the same rate as average labour productivity and no change in the profit margin. These are not the only possible rules, however, nor do they guarantee no inflation if other conditions are not met (e.g., if there is a change in taxation or the share of rent in national income or in the prices of imported raw materials).

---

[1] Moreover, logical difficulties arise in using the mark-up formula to explain price setting by a firm that produces more than one good. These are a consequence of the fact that the price of each product is made to depend on labour productivity, but this cannot be calculated if we do not know the prices of the various goods.

15.3 Coercion and incomes policies

Incomes policies can be distinguished according to their relative coerciveness into three basic types: statist, market and institutional.

Statist incomes policies impose specific behaviour – by way of regulation, moral suasion or mere jawboning – on workers and/or capitalists with regard to changes in wages or profit margins: for example, a *wage freeze* ($\dot{w} = 0$) is a statist policy where government rules replace the free decisions of workers and capitalists. They are therefore direct control measures.

By contrast, *market incomes policies* involve the government's use of a system of incentives or disincentives (rather than prescriptive rules) to steer the autonomous choices of income recipients in an anti-inflationary direction. For example, an agreement between workers and capitalists to hold prices steady might be rewarded with tax concessions.

Institutional policies seek to instil cooperative *industrial relations*, i.e., relations between capitalists and workers regarding wages and work rules, by establishing a structure of appropriate institutional mechanisms such as arbitration procedures, 'social agreements', etc. Institutional policies are essentially reforms that aim to change the nature of the competition (or game) between the various income recipients.

15.4 Statist policies

Since they consist of direct control measures, statist policies should offer the advantage of immediacy and effectiveness. In practice, however, many problems can arise. We will distinguish such difficulties according to whether the policies affect wages only or also comprise other forms of income.

Wage policies, which have the advantage of being easier to implement, do not guarantee an anti-inflationary outcome. We know from equation (15.5) that any rule governing wages (e.g., limiting growth in the wage rate to productivity growth) may not ensure price stability as long as profit margins can still be widened. In fact, the latter can be set arbitrarily in the absence of government or market constraints (e.g., strong international competitive pressures, which might force a narrowing of margins).

The possibility of price increases occurring even with constraints on wage rises may be increased by the conditions in which the incomes policy rules must actually be formulated, especially by the presence of different industries with differing levels and rates of growth of productivity. In this case, two different rules are possible:

(a) the wage rate in each industry should change by the same percentage as productivity in that industry; or
(b) the wage rate in all industries should change by the same percentage as the change in the *average* productivity of the economy as a whole.

Rule (a) is better suited to avoiding changes in the general price level: if profit margins remained unchanged, prices would not rise in any industry. However, a labour union sensitive to problems of equity among workers would find it difficult to accept such a rule. The more equitable second rule has greater problems of effectiveness. In industries with slower productivity growth, the wage rate would rise faster than productivity, since its growth would be linked to the rise in average productivity for all industries. With no change in profit margins, prices would rise. This increase will result in a *general* increase in the price level unless it is offset by a reduction in prices in industries with faster productivity growth. Such a reduction is possible in theory, as long as profit margins do not change in these industries, since the wage rate would be increasing less rapidly than industry productivity. However, it is unlikely that the required conditions can be met as there are strong inertial factors inhibiting any reduction in prices.[2] The likely consequence of rule (b) is therefore an increase in the general price level associated with an increase in prices in industries with a low rate of productivity growth and no change in prices in more dynamic industries.

It must also be noted that a coercive incomes policy limited to wages only may not have significant and immediate effects if its announcement provokes a reaction from workers supported by a highly combative and powerful union. In addition to the coercive nature of the policy, the union may object to its partial nature, which offers the prospect not so much of a frozen distribution (which might in any case be considered unsatisfactory) but rather a worsening of wage earners' share of income, if average profit margins are increased.

Let us now examine the problems that arise in relation to more complete (or general) forms of incomes policy.

The usual reason cited for limiting policy measures to wage income is the simplicity of measuring wages compared with the difficulty of ascertaining profits, which is often only possible after a detailed examination of jealously guarded company information. This difficulty has prompted efforts to supplement wage policies with price control measures: while it is difficult to determine profit margins, prices are 'visible and measurable'. However, there are also a multitude of different prices, the types of good sold change and classifications are more difficult and uncertain than for wages. There is also a difference between the position of wage earners and entrepreneurs: the former are paid on the basis of prices *agreed* during wage bargaining; the latter obtain their income from prices *set* in a relatively free manner, albeit with certain limitations imposed by the existence of actual or potential competitors. Thus changes in wages are slower, more difficult and transparent, while changes in profits are more rapid, freer and difficult to observe (partly due to qualitative and quantitative differences in products). This explains the difficulties of price control policies as a substitute for controlling profit margins, but these should not be overstressed. In fact it is possible to identify a relatively limited number of goods whose prices play a key role in the overall price structure, such that exercising close control over them would ensure control over the general price level (Rothschild, 1973).

Given the difference in the ability of wage earners and entrepreneurs to set the price of the good they supply, effective price control can play an important role in persuading workers to accept wage control policies.

---

[2] In addition to the factors determining price stickiness (e.g., menu costs), this is due to the resistance of oligopolistic firms to price reductions for fear of triggering a price war with competitors, who might interpret the cut as a sign of aggression.

It is often argued that another obstacle to a *general* incomes policy is that price controls reduce the efficiency of the economy by constraining 'market forces'. In particular, constant profit margins do not provide an incentive to increase productivity. More generally, 'freezing' distributive shares conflicts with the motivations and the operation of a market economy. There is some element of truth in this argument. However, the problem is largely an abstract one. In the real world of non-competitive markets, *administered prices* – in the sense of prices being set at the discretion of firms on the basis of their market power (see section 10.6.3) – are the norm and they are quite different from those of the Walrasian equilibrium, which would reflect scarcity and guarantee allocative efficiency. In this reality, directives and intervention in the price sector are not necessarily more problematic than intervention in the wage sector, even though there may be substantial differences in their implementation (Rothschild, 1973). In fact, a *government* price policy might at least act as a counterweight to the market power of large oligopolistic firms.

15.5 Market-based policies

There are two types of market-based incomes policies.

1 One is founded on the idea that inflation is an external diseconomy, like pollution. The government can therefore set a total amount of the diseconomy that can be produced and assign rights to produce the diseconomy to individual firms up to that point, leaving them free to choose between exercising the right directly or selling it to someone else. In other words, *tradable price-increase permits* can be created. If, for example, the limit on price increases is 1 per cent and a firm does not raise its prices at all, it can sell the right to other firms. This mechanism can also be used to restrain that special kind of price which is the wage rate, thus creating tradable wage-increase permits.

Proposals of this sort, which have been advanced by leading scholars (see Weitzacker, 1975; Lerner, 1978; Lerner and Colander, 1980), seek to reconcile the macroeconomic objective of price stability with microeconomic flexibility for firms, introducing rewards for virtuous behaviour and penalising inflationary conduct. Nevertheless, if productivity growth differs across industries and is largely independent of firm behaviour, this sort of policy may excessively punish industries that are already disadvantaged by a low rate of productivity growth. Moreover, the difficulties of implementing such proposals are at least as formidable as those facing statist policies. This may help explain the absence of any practical attempts to implement them.

2 The second type of market-based policy seeks to create incentives for not increasing prices and disincentives for increasing them through the tax system. Such measures are called *tax-tied incomes policies* or *tax-based incomes policies* (TIPs) (Wallich and Weintraub, 1971).

If incentives are granted to firms or workers that do not increase their prices (or do not raise them above some threshold), we have so-called *reward TIPs*. If instead sanctions are imposed for excessive price increases, we have *penalty TIPs*. The objections to this sort of policy are similar to those for price-increase permits (for more on this, see Seidman, 1978).

15.6 Institutional policies

We can try to avoid the inflationary consequences of the distributive conflict by establishing certain rules of the game, i.e., we can introduce regulations or practices that foster cooperative behaviour. We have already said that institutional policies seek to transform the nature of the distributive game from non-cooperative to cooperative. This can be done in three ways:

1 First, the government can introduce an explicit requirement for cooperation or in any case impose a 'last resort' cooperative solution, such as *arbitration*.
2 An alternative solution would be to engage in an *economic exchange* that, for example, ensures certain levels of taxes, subsidies, various measures with regard to incomes, labour and industrial policies for employers and workers that reach a non-inflationary agreement on wages and/or behave in a non-inflationary way. Another possibility would simply be to announce different government policies in response to different behaviour by employers and workers. More generally, an institutional incomes policy could be applied within the framework of a planned economy. For example, the plan could forecast some level of private investment, set the level of government investment and the rate of wage increase that, ensuring a flow of savings equal to investment, would avoid both cost-push and demand-pull inflation. The content of such an incomes policy would be very different from that normally attributed to it. It would be a much more complex mechanism ensuring both the desired level of investment and monetary stability.
3 A third approach involves a *political exchange* consisting in the government's promise to act in certain ways in areas that are not strictly economic (e.g., civil rights) or that involve the general political programme of the government itself, or even in drafting a '*social pact*' (or *social agreement*) that sets out lines of action in economic and social matters agreed to by the social partners.

The feasibility of implementing the various forms of institutional policy depends on a wide variety of economic, social and political circumstances. We have indicated the policies in increasing order of difficulty of implementation. Some argue that a key element in instituting effective institutional incomes policies is *neo-corporatism*, which is a situation characterised by centralisation of bargaining, a general attitude of consensus between labour and employers, and government involvement in wage negotiations. The findings of some econometric studies reveal the existence of a negative relationship between the degree of neo-corporatism and the Okun misery index (Tarantelli, 1983): this means that a high level of neo-corporatism is successful in lowering the inflation rate (given the unemployment rate) or the unemployment rate (given the inflation rate). Later studies have been contradictory, both confirming and rejecting these findings (Calmfors, 1993).

15.7 Incomes policy and productivity policies

Except in some of its versions, such as the economic and political exchange models, incomes policy does not seek to change many aspects of the existing situation, in particular the rate of productivity growth. This variable has an important role in determining the consistency of wage growth with price stability. For example, if productivity increases by 2 per cent, an equal rise in the wage rate and an unchanged profit margin will ensure price stability. If productivity rose by 4 per cent, it would be possible to increase the wage rate by more than 2 per cent and/or increase the profit margin without inflationary consequences.

Accordingly, we can broaden the choice set of incomes policy to comprise measures aimed at increasing the rate of productivity growth. In order to identify these measures we must first examine the factors on which productivity depends. These can be factors internal and external to the firm.

Among the internal factors, some are controlled by workers, others by the firm. The former include the level of work effort and any preparation and professional training undertaken at the worker's initiative. The latter include professional training provided by the firm, work organisation, capital and technology. Some of these factors can then be the object of negotiations over incomes policy between workers and employers, since such factors are under their control. More specifically, a union may accept a temporary ceiling on wage increases, taking the productivity gains obtainable in the short term as given, but at the same time it may ask for a commitment from firms to introduce organisational and technological innovations that will ease the productivity constraint on wage rises in the future.

Among the external factors that influence labour productivity are those associated with interfirm and intersectoral relationships. For example, the availability of inputs of goods and services as well as the terms of their supply (e.g., quality and cost) can be important factors. Thus the overall productivity of, say, the manufacturing sector depends on the availability of cheap and efficient transportation and communications networks, schools and universities, research centres, information services, financial services, etc. Since it is not possible for the market to guarantee all the conditions necessary for the optimal development of these activities, government intervention – in particular, through industrial policy – may be necessary, as we argued in section 10.6.5. This form of intervention can play an ancillary role to incomes policy.

15.8 Incomes policy in the real world

The various forms of incomes policy we have discussed here have been implemented on numerous occasions in the post-war period. Above all, governments have established non-coercive guidelines backed up by *moral suasion* as well as the threat of some form of retaliation (restrictive measures, as in Sweden, or exclusion from government procurement contracts, as in Austria or the United States). There have also been examples of negotiation and more-or-less formal exchanges between wage moderation and expansionary policies, such as in the United Kingdom in the 1960s and 1970s and France in the 1960s.

Incomes policies were implemented intermittently up to the early 1980s in many countries. The Netherlands' experiment in incomes policy was exceptional, since it lasted from 1948 to the 1960s. The number of countries resorting to such policies has fallen in the 1980s.

Let us take a closer look at some of the more interesting cases.

In the United States, the Kennedy administration introduced voluntary wage and price guidelines in 1962. The government hoped to obtain the cooperation of unions and firms, in part encouraged by moral suasion. Kennedy got the steel industry unions to comply with the limit on wage increases by assuring them (after a three-month-long strike) that the steel companies would not raise prices. Nevertheless, after the agreement with the union was reached, the steel companies raised their prices significantly, prompting the government to threaten severe retaliatory measures (enforcement of antitrust legislation, exclusion from military procurement contracts). The clash continued the following year, until the president's assassination, with Kennedy's (vain) attempt to swing public opinion against the companies. The guidelines remained in force until 1968 and the Johnson administration proved more effective in exerting informal pressure on the industries involved, especially aluminium producers in 1965.

Australia has a federal arbitration commission and regional commissions that can take binding decisions on wage matters. The federal commission is in fact a court. Australia has also experimented with more complex forms of incomes policy, developing a sort of 'social agreement'.

Austria has a centralised bargaining structure, the Parity Commission for Wages and Prices, in which the government, unions and firms participate on equal footing. The Commission operates on the basis of two guiding principles: first, wage increases must be related to productivity growth; second, for goods not directly subject to government price controls (certain essential goods and services), firms whose costs have risen more rapidly than productivity can request a price increase. After verifying the validity of the request, the Commission can recommend full or partial acceptance, or reject it altogether. Firms are free to increase prices even if the Commission rejects their request, but they may be subject to government retaliation in the form of taxes or other punitive measures (e.g., exclusion from government procurement contracts).

In France, as part of the V plan in 1964, it was decided to consider wage and price problems explicitly. The prospect of a high rate of growth in national income was offered in return for wage moderation. The government and firms also drafted 'programme agreements', which gave particular attention to the pricing policies of firms. Incomes policies have become less and less incisive since the end of 1960s.

In the United Kingdom between 1948 and 1950 the Labour government negotiated a voluntary policy of wage restraint with the trade unions. Later, between 1974 and 1979, an attempt was made to draft a 'social contract' between trade unions and the Labour government. The unions were granted a role in the formulation of economic policy – especially industrial relations legislation – in exchange for wage moderation. The failure of the contract for economic and political reasons contributed to Labour's defeat in the 1979 elections.

In Italy, as the scope of price policy gradually narrowed over time, greater recourse was made to wage containment policies. In recent years, the automatic mechanism for indexing wages to prices has been eliminated, the period between collective bargaining rounds has been lengthened and it has been agreed that wage increases must be consistent with the government's target rate of inflation, with some possibility, however, of later recouping the difference between actual and target inflation in order to safeguard the purchasing power of wages.[3]

15.9 Summary

1 The objective of incomes (and price) policy is to avoid any increase in the general price level by controlling distributive variables. These are essentially the wage rate and/or the profit margin.

2 The most frequently adopted incomes policy rules provide for growth in the wage rate equal to that in average labour productivity and no change in profit margins.

3 Depending on the degree of coercion involved, incomes policies can be described as statist, market or institutional.

4 Statist policies involve direct control measures and, as such, should have large and immediate effects. In practice, there are many problems regarding the variables to be controlled and the specific rules governing wage growth in the presence of sectoral productivity differences.

5 One type of market-based incomes policy consists in assigning firms a tradable permit to raise their prices. A second type attempts to create incentives not to raise prices using fiscal measures.

6 Institutional policies seek to place industrial relations on a cooperative basis by establishing rules to regulate them (e.g., arbitration, economic exchange, political exchange).

7 The range of incomes policies can be extended by including measures aimed at increasing the rate of productivity growth, which depends on factors internal and external to the firm.

8 The many real-world examples of attempts to implement incomes policies have not always produced satisfactory results with regard to controlling inflation.

---

[3] More information on incomes policy in the US, Australia and the European countries can be found, respectively, in Pencavel (1981), Burrell and Stutchbury (1994) and Dore *et al.* (1994). Flanagan *et al.* (1983) is also a good reference for European experience with incomes policy in the 1960s and 1970s.

15.10 Key concepts

Price and incomes policy

Rate of profit

Average labour productivity

Guideline

Statist, market, institutional incomes
  policies

Industrial relations

Wage freeze

Agreed, set prices

Administered price

Price increase permit

Tax-tied incomes policy (TIP)

Reward, penalty TIP

Arbitration

Economic, political exchange

Neo-corporatism

Moral suasion

Social pact, agreement

Target rate of inflation

PART VI

MACROECONOMIC INTERVENTION IN AN OPEN ECONOMY

16 Monetary systems and exchange rate regimes

16.1 Balance of payments disequilibria and their causes

The balance of payments is a systematic record of the economic transactions[1] in a specific period of time between the residents of a country and non-residents. Such transactions normally give rise to outflows and inflows of foreign exchange.[2] A debit entry is recorded for any transaction involving an outflow of foreign exchange (imports of goods and services, *unilateral* (or *unrequited*) *transfers* abroad, capital outflows); a credit entry is recorded for any transaction involving an inflow of foreign exchange (exports of goods and services, unrequited transfers from abroad, capital inflows).[3]

The balance of payments is divided into two sections: the *current account* and the *capital account*. The current account records imports and exports of goods and services[4] and unrequited transfers.[5] Within the current account, the record of goods transactions gives the *trade balance*, while other transactions are called '*invisible items*' or '*invisibles*'. The capital account records short-, medium- and long-term capital flows, which can be divided into: bank capital and other short-term assets; short-, medium- and long-term trade credit; official and private-sector loans; foreign direct investment (purchase or sale of shares and equity interests that ensure the control of firms located abroad); portfolio investment (purchase or sale of shares and equity interests that does not lead to control

[1] According to the balance of payments manual of the International Monetary Fund, an economic transaction is a transfer of economic value, with or without consideration, between one economic agent and another. An economic value is a good, service, income or financial item (IMF, 1993).
[2] Foreign exchange consists of banknotes and other financial assets representing a claim on residents of a foreign country expressed in the currency of that country.
[3] In reality, the recording rules are more complex (see Gandolfo, 1995).
[4] Services include freight and insurance, investment income (interest and dividends), compensation of employees (temporarily abroad) and tourism receipts.
[5] Unrequited transfers can be official (contributions to and from international organisations, such as the European Union; government aid to developing countries, etc.) or private (gifts, remittances from emigrants, who are considered non-residents).

of the firm, purchase of bonds or government securities). The sum of flows in the two sections gives the net outflow or inflow of foreign exchange, i.e. *the balance of payments deficit* or *surplus* and therefore the variation in the country's foreign reserves.[6] The quantity of monetary base[7] in circulation in the economy changes correspondingly. For example, when an exporter receives foreign currency, this increases the official reserves of the country since it is transferred to the central bank by the exporter in exchange for national currency.

Balance of payments deficits and surpluses should both be considered disequilibrium positions, albeit for different reasons. First, a deficit signals a reduction in the official reserves and, with this, a decline in the possibility of sustaining additional deficits in the future, which might not be financed.[8] By contrast, a surplus can be difficult to sustain in the long run for the different, although less pressing, reason that it would give rise to excessive monetary base creation.[9]

More generally, however, the balance of payments can be seen as a mirror of relations between a given country and the rest of the world. From this point of view, the excess of exports over imports reflects an excess of savings over domestic investment.[10] With a current account surplus, equilibrating the balance of payments would require a deficit on capital account, i.e., a net outflow of capital representing a loan through which the country makes its excess savings available to the rest of the world. By contrast, positive net imports and an overall balance of payments equilibrium indicate that the country is borrowing savings from the rest of the world. Obviously, equilibrium in the balance of payments with a current account deficit[11] is difficult to sustain in the long run, since it implies that the country is not able to foster independent growth, remaining dependent on the rest of the world for the savings needed to support domestic investment (for an opposing view, see Bazdarich, 1978).

Monetary union between two or more countries would eliminate the formal balance of payments problem, as well as that of managing the official reserves (as far as their relations are concerned), but it would leave untouched the problem of the performance of the real economy in each country. Thus, German monetary unification (parallel to political unification) did not eliminate the importance of tracking movements of goods

---

[6] More generally, taking account of gold and other instruments of international liquidity available for use by the central authorities of a country in meeting balance of payments needs, we speak of the country's *official reserves*.

[7] With pegged exchange rates the monetary authorities are compelled to buy or sell foreign currency against monetary base to avoid unwanted exchange rate changes.

[8] For the concept of 'sustainability' of current account deficits, see Frenkel *et al.* (1996).

[9] Under certain conditions, this can be offset through other sources of monetary base creation or destruction, as we will discuss later (see chapter 18).

[10] As we know from national accounting, $S - I = X - M$, or, specifying the public sector, $S - I = X - M + G - T$, where S, I, X, M, G and T respectively stand for saving, investment, exports, imports, government spending and taxes (net of domestic government transfers; see chapter 14).

[11] In this case, the balance of payments is not in *full* equilibrium, which requires that both accounts balance.

and services between the various *Länder*,[12] precisely because they are indicative of savings flows: for example, eastern Germany has been a net importer, absorbing savings from the rest of the world, especially western Germany.[13] Sustaining this situation depends on a constant net inflow of capital or unrequited transfers from abroad, with western Germany once again playing a key role. However, such a situation cannot continue for long: other areas find it difficult to maintain a steady flow of unrequited transfers (in effect, donations). Inflows of private capital generate income that in the long term should create sufficient productive capacity to reverse the sign of net imports of goods and services; were relative underdevelopment to last, their persistence would be difficult to explain.

16.2 The balance of payments, the foreign exchange market and the exchange rate

For simplicity we will initially refer to a world with only two countries, the home country and the 'Rest of the World'.

The balance of payments was introduced in section 16.1: all economic transactions that normally give rise to payments and receipts in foreign currency are usually recorded. The residents of the home country that need to make payments to non-residents will demand foreign currency; conversely, residents that receive payments in foreign currency will supply it. This is the foreign exchange market, where, like all other markets, a price, called the exchange rate or, more precisely, the *nominal bilateral exchange rate*, is determined.

The nominal bilateral exchange rate is the price of a currency in terms of another currency. There are two ways to express this price. With the first, the reference unit is the foreign currency and its price is expressed in terms of the domestic currency: this is the *price-quotation system*, which indicates the variable price in terms of the domestic currency for one unit of foreign currency. The second method, known as the *volume-quotation system*, expresses the variable quantity of foreign currency that can be purchased with a unit of domestic currency. Unless otherwise indicated we will adopt the price-quotation system, which is used by most countries (the United Kingdom is the major exception). Thus, a rise in the exchange rate in the United States (e.g., from $0.665/1 DM to $0.700/1 DM, assuming the Rest of the World uses the German mark, DM, as its currency) indicates a fall in the value of the dollar with respect to that of the mark (i.e., a depreciation of the dollar). If the $/DM exchange rate rises, the DM/$

---

[12] It did make it more difficult, however. Since the balance of payments between the two parts of the country is no longer compiled, the task is entrusted to the sources and uses of resources account, which reproduces the fundamental macroeconomic identity between demand for goods and services (divided into its components) and supply and can be compiled for the individual regions of a country.

[13] With reference to eastern Germany, the rest of the world includes western Germany as well as foreign countries.

exchange rate, which gives the number of marks needed to purchase $1, falls, i.e., the mark appreciates.

Obviously there are more than two countries in the real world and it may therefore be useful to calculate an average of nominal bilateral exchange rates (e.g., $/DM, $/£, $/yen) in order to have a synthetic indicator. If n is the total number of countries, the *nominal effective exchange rate* is a weighted average of the $n - 1$ nominal bilateral exchange rates with the home country's currency. The weights can reflect the level of international trade between the country under consideration and the other $n - 1$ countries.

Returning to our initial hypothesis of two countries, we now need to have at least an approximate understanding of the forces that determine the level and changes in the nominal exchange rate and what variables the exchange rate is capable of influencing.

We said that the exchange rate is determined in the foreign exchange market, which reflects the balance of payments. Referring to our previous example, the depreciation of the dollar that occurs when the exchange rate rises from $0.665/1 DM to $0.700/1 DM is a consequence of the worsening of the balance of payments of the United States. Assume that the initial exchange rate of 0.665 corresponds to balance of payments equilibrium (which means that demand for foreign currency equals supply). If the demand for foreign currency subsequently increases relative to supply, the exchange rate cannot remain at its initial level. It must increase instead. Note that any deterioration in the balance of payments (even if we do not begin in equilibrium) leads to a depreciation of the currency. Similarly, improvements will lead to an appreciation. In addition, the worsening (or improvement) in the balance of payments influences the exchange rate independently of the composition of the overall balance, i.e., the relative size of the current and capital account balances.

Although the changes in the exchange rate are triggered by variations in all the items of the balance of payments, they influence only some transactions, more specifically foreign trade, having an effect on the competitiveness of domestic goods and services.[14] The role of the exchange rate in this is easily understood. Assume that the price of a good or basket of goods produced in the home country (the US) is $0.665, and the price of the same good produced in the Rest of the World is DM 1. If the exchange rate were exactly $0.665/DM 1, in the absence of any barriers to international trade it would make no difference whether we bought the good produced in the US or that produced abroad. If, however, the exchange rate were higher (say $0.8/DM1), both US residents and non-residents would benefit by buying American goods, thus increasing US exports. A lower exchange rate would reverse the situation in favour of goods produced abroad, generating US imports.

From this example we can deduce that the exchange rate influences competitiveness if prices are given in the two countries. Let us now assume that the exchange rate remains at $0.665/DM1. If the price level in the United States falls below $0.665 and/or the price level abroad rises above DM1, consumers will gain by purchasing from the US, which

---

[14] We will see later that this statement is only valid as a first approximation: actual changes in the exchange rate may have an influence on expected changes in the same variable and, thus, on capital movements (see section 17.1.2).

will boost its exports and reduce imports, thus increasing net US exports.[15] We therefore need an indicator that simultaneously takes account of the nominal exchange rate and domestic and foreign prices. Such an indicator is in fact easy to devise: we take the price of foreign goods expressed in the domestic currency ($), which is given by the price of foreign goods in foreign currency (marks), p_w, multiplied by the nominal exchange rate ($/DM), e, and divide it by the dollar price of domestic goods, p. This gives us the *real bilateral exchange rate*, e_r:

$$e_r = \frac{p_w \cdot e}{p} \tag{16.1}$$

The price level in the two countries is usually measured in terms of wholesale or producer price indices.[16]

More realistically, if there are numerous foreign countries rather than the single country we have assumed here, e will be the effective exchange rate rather than the bilateral exchange rate. In this case, e_r will represent the *real effective exchange rate*.

From (16.1) we can derive that the change in the real bilateral exchange rate[17] is approximately:

$$\dot{e}_r = \dot{p}_w + \dot{e} - \dot{p} = \dot{e} - (\dot{p} - \dot{p}_w) \tag{16.2}$$

where a dot above the variable indicates its rate of change per unit of time.

The terms in parentheses denote *relative inflation*. It is clear that if relative inflation is lower than the change in the nominal exchange rate, there will be an increase in the

---

[15] We will see later that this statement, too, is valid under some conditions. In addition, in the real world, imperfections, differences in the quality of domestic and foreign goods, etc. introduce friction that makes it possible for some imports to persist even in the presence of a currency depreciation and for the increase in exports to lag behind.

[16] Sometimes the real exchange rate is defined as $p/(p_w \cdot e)$.

The index of unit labour costs is sometimes used in order to underscore some of the factors that cause changes in competitiveness. This precludes consideration of factors that are not included in the labour cost index. Differences between the real exchange rate constructed with the labour cost index and the rate based on producer prices reflect the behaviour of these other variables. For example, in France the real exchange rate measured in terms of unit labour costs rose by 5 percentage points between 1987 and 1991, denoting a moderate increase in that country's competitiveness; the increase in terms of producer prices was much smaller, about 2 points, indicating small gains in competitiveness. Over the same period, in Italy the real effective exchange rate measured in terms of unit labour costs fell by 11.3 per cent, indicating a sharp decline in competitiveness; the fall was only 4.3 per cent if measured on the basis of producer prices, signalling a smaller loss of competitiveness. Canada recorded results similar to Italy's. The difference between the two indices in the three countries could first be attributed to differences in the behaviour of other variable costs not included in the index of unit labour costs. This is unlikely since it is difficult to imagine that the costs of raw materials and energy in the three countries behaved differently from those of their main trading partners. It is more likely that the differences in the behaviour of the two indicators of competitiveness were produced by the behaviour of profit margins (increasing in France, decreasing in Italy and Canada).

[17] If we want to calculate the change in the real effective exchange rate, the change in the nominal bilateral exchange rate ($\dot{e}$ in (16.2)) should be substituted for the change in the nominal effective exchange rate.

home country's competitiveness; in this case the real exchange rate will increase.[18] This represents a 'depreciation' in the real exchange rate, which will have the same effect as a 'depreciation' in the nominal exchange rate (i.e., an increase in the rate) when prices are constant: i.e., the competitiveness of the home country's goods will increase.

Our discussion so far has focused on the causes and effects of changes in the nominal exchange rate, assuming that there are no limits to such changes. If there are in fact no limits, we generally speak of *floating exchange rates*; if there are limits (or no variations at all), we speak of *fixed exchange rates*. To understand the operation of the foreign exchange market, with specific reference to the conditions that may limit exchange rate fluctuations, we need to specify the nature and operation of the different monetary systems. We will examine this in the following sections of this chapter.

By monetary system we mean the set of rules that govern the monetary aspects of the operation of an economic system and/or its relationship with other economies. More specifically, a monetary system is a specification of rules that:

(a) define the monetary unit, i.e., the instrument used as legal tender, which is (usually) also the unit of account;
(b) regulate the issue of money;
(c) define the currency's relationships with foreign currencies in terms of its value, circulation and convertibility.

Points (a) and (b) regard the domestic aspects of a monetary system. Point (c) concerns its international aspects. When we speak of an international monetary system, we refer to the set of rules regarding the international aspects (which are usually fairly independent of those governing domestic aspects) adopted by some groups of countries.

In the following sections we will examine the main monetary systems, with specific reference to their international aspects. We will generally describe the structure and operation of each system in abstract terms and then examine real-life systems based on these models. Bear in mind that a real monetary system may often have features that do not exactly fit one of the abstract reference systems described here. In other words, there may not necessarily be a one-to-one correspondence between abstract and real-life systems. This is understandable given the fact that the content of the rules underlying each system are the product of a mix of ideas and interests whose shape is largely determined by the vicissitudes of history. Identifying types of monetary system is to a certain degree an *ex post* rationalisation of highly diverse realities.

16.3 The gold standard

The value of a monetary unit can be linked to that of a commodity, especially a precious metal, if the monetary unit is defined in terms of that good and certain additional conditions are met. Linking a currency's value to a commodity is one attempt to ensure

---

[18] Suppose that prices increase by 5 per cent in the home country and by 2 per cent abroad. This means that relative inflation is 3 per cent. If the nominal exchange rate depreciates by more than 3 per cent (say 4 per cent) the home country increases its competitiveness.

the stability of that value and to remove control of money creation from the arbitrary decisions of some authority.[19] This does not mean, however, that the attempt is always successful or that a monetary unit not linked to a commodity cannot be stable, as we will see in greater detail later.

The basic elements of the *gold standard* are the following:

(a) in a country that adopts the gold standard, banknotes are issued by the central bank and can be exchanged for goods (whether they are called dollars, pounds, francs, etc.), therefore constituting that country's currency;

(b) the gold 'content' (i.e., equivalence) of the monetary unit is defined (for example, a mark 'contains' 0.5 grams of gold, a dollar is equivalent to 1 gram of gold, etc.);

(c) the central bank holds a gold reserve, either coins or bars, that is some proportion of the quantity of currency issued; legal tender can be converted into gold on request or, vice-versa, the central bank can exchange banknotes for gold on the basis of the gold content of the currency;

(d) gold can be freely imported or exported.

As mentioned, our focus here is the international dimension of monetary systems. If a number of countries simultaneously adopt the gold standard, these international aspects can be immediately identified as follows.

Since the monetary units of each country are all defined in terms of a homogenous common base, gold, the relative value of these units can be determined by dividing their respective gold contents. For example, using our earlier example of the mark and the dollar, the relative value of these currencies is equal to $0.5/1 = 0.5$: a dollar has twice the gold content of a mark and therefore has twice its value. This ratio, called the *mint parity*, is an abstract relative price, i.e., a relative reference price. The actual price of the mark in terms of dollars – which is the nominal bilateral exchange rate of the mark in terms of dollars – may move away from the parity depending on the actual supply of and demand for marks against dollars.

However, a special feature of the gold standard is that the fluctuations around the parity are *objectively* limited, for the following reasons. An American who needs to make a payment in marks will always be able to do so by purchasing gold and sending it to Germany, where it can be converted into marks, rather than purchasing marks in the US and sending them abroad. This means that the exchange rate (in our example, the price of a mark in terms of dollars) cannot exceed what is called the *gold-export point*, which is equal to parity plus the cost of shipping the gold (transport, insurance and forgone interest[20]): above this value, it is profitable to convert dollars into gold (given the gold content of the dollar), ship the gold abroad and have it converted into marks instead of purchasing marks on the foreign exchange market. Conversely, if the exchange rate falls below the *gold-import point*, which is equal to parity minus the gold shipment costs, for

---

[19] Precious metals, and gold in particular, are preferred not only because of their chemical and physical properties but above all because of the *relative* stability of their value.

[20] The loss of interest is due to the fact that the capital represented by the gold sent abroad does not bear interest while it is in transit.

an American it becomes more profitable to accept gold in payment from abroad rather than foreign currency (in our case, marks). Since the shipping costs of gold are usually small with respect to the value of the goods shipped, the gold standard is essentially a *fixed* exchange rate system.

In such a system, equilibrating the current account of the balance of payments is entrusted to price movements (in addition to variations in income, as we will see) within the countries affected by the imbalance, rather than changes in the nominal exchange rate as happens in monetary systems where the nominal exchange rate can vary significantly. Without changes in the nominal exchange rate, it is price changes that ensure the variation of the real exchange rate that may be needed to adjust the current account.

Price movements in countries that have adopted the gold standard are automatic: a balance of payments surplus in country A means that its stock of gold will increase, leading to an increase in the money supply and, under certain conditions, a rise in prices. The opposite will occur in country B. This will discourage exports by A and boost its imports, thus re-establishing equilibrium.[21] The same result can also be achieved through changes in incomes under certain circumstances. We will examine the adjustment mechanisms in greater detail in section 17.3.

The gold standard is largely of historical interest. Gold has had a monetary role since ancient times, but the foundations of a true gold standard were laid in the United Kingdom only in 1821, when the Bank of England was legally required to redeem its notes in gold and restrictions on the melting of coins and gold shipments were lifted. The gold standard later acquired an international role between 1870 and 1880, when it was adopted by a sufficiently large number of countries. With the increase in monetarily financed government spending at the outbreak of the first world war in 1914, and the consequent difficulty of maintaining convertibility, nearly all countries abandoned the gold standard, only to reintroduce it for a few years during the interwar period (see Grubel, 1984; Bordo and Schwartz, 1984).

The UK's attempt to return to the gold standard in the mid 1920s would probably have met with greater success without the mistake that was made in setting the gold 'content' of the pound too high and the effects of other external circumstances. The decision to adopt the pre-war gold content, despite the increase in currency in circulation and a higher price level, implied a monetary restriction and a general fall in prices (and wages). Such a fall in prices and wages is always a threat to economic activity and is in any case difficult to achieve when faced by powerful labour unions and the resistance of firms. Under these conditions, the most likely outcome was a fall in output and employment, which is what actually happened, as predicted by Keynes, who considered the gold standard a 'barbarous relic' (see Keynes, 1924, p. 138). When the impact of adverse external circumstances was added, including the consequences of the world depression that began in 1929, keeping the gold standard in the UK became impossible and the devaluation of the pound in September 1931 marked its demise.

Some economists and politicians still admire the gold standard today. They under-

---

[21] This mechanism of automatic adjustment is call the *price-specie flow mechanism*.

score its stability and automatic nature, which they credit for the economic growth achieved before 1914. In reality, these presumed merits are attributable to a series of fortunate circumstances as well as the careful monetary policy of the central banks and the trade policy of the period. In fact, others argue that the gold standard played a key role in causing the Great Depression (Eichengreen, 1992).

16.4 The gold exchange standard

Under the gold exchange standard, at least one country adopts the gold standard while the others:

(a) set the gold 'content' of their currencies;
(b) hold the currency of the gold-standard country (rather than gold or in addition to it) as the reserve backing for their national currency;
(c) permit the conversion of the national currency into the *reserve currency* at a constant, fixed value, which represents the *parity* between the two currencies, i.e., the ratio between their respective gold contents (similar parities can be defined between the currency of the country under consideration and those of other gold-standard countries).

If the gold-standard country were the United States (as it was), the dollar would serve as the reserve currency for other countries (e.g., France) and, in a pure gold exchange system, the French franc could be converted into gold by virtue of its convertibility into dollars, since this could in turn be converted directly into gold. In practice, conversion of national currency into gold may be limited to central banks only. Conversion of the national currency into foreign currency can also be subject to restrictions. For example, rather than circulating freely, use of reserve currencies may be limited to settling foreign transactions (*non-resident convertibility*).

The gold exchange standard can economise on the use of gold, which proves useful if this is scarce. It also has the advantage of allowing countries that adopt it to hold interest-bearing reserves, as (unlike gold) the foreign currency assets held as reserves normally earn interest.

However, the system may become unstable if the countries adopting this system want to keep gold among their reserves when the solvency of the gold-standard country becomes uncertain, as we will see later in this section. In this case the countries that have adopted the gold exchange standard could convert their reserves of foreign currency into gold, triggering a sort of 'run' on the central bank of the gold-standard country.

If a gold exchange system allows all agents to convert domestic currency into gold, it works in exactly the same way as the gold standard. In particular, the exchange rate between the currencies of two countries that adopt the gold exchange standard is set around their parity. However, the parity in this case is an *adjustable peg* rather than an unchangeable value. Changes in the parity may be accompanied by significant variations in the exchange rate, producing changes in the trade balance. We speak of a *devaluation* when the parity of the currency considered (e.g., the French franc) with the reserve currency (e.g., the dollar) is increased, i.e., one needs more francs to acquire one dollar (the value of the dollar in terms of francs is higher). If this parity is lowered, we have a *revaluation*.

If convertibility is restricted in some way, the fluctuations of the exchange rate around its parity can be quite large and can only be avoided through the active intervention of the monetary authorities to absorb the excess demand or supply of foreign currency causing the fluctuations: if the exchange rate rises above a given upper limit as an effect of excess demand for the foreign currency, the monetary authorities will supply that foreign currency; vice-versa, they will buy foreign currency if the exchange rate falls below a given lower limit.

This was the situation with the International Monetary Fund (IMF) system, established in 1944 at Bretton Woods (USA), which operated as a gold exchange standard until 1971. Only central banks were allowed to convert dollars into gold and in many countries private agents could buy foreign currency (in particular, dollars) only to make payments to non-residents.[22] Participating countries committed themselves to: (a) setting the gold content of their currency; (b) intervening to limit fluctuations in the exchange rate to a maximum of 1 per cent above or below parity; (c) paying a quota to the Fund that could be used for loans in case of need; (d) complying with other rules designed to avoid frequent and widespread changes in parities.

Changing parities was only allowed to overcome a *fundamental disequilibrium* (i.e., a severe and persistent imbalance). In the absence of such a situation, each country had to tackle balance of payments difficulties with other economic policies (which we will discuss in the next chapter).[23] While waiting for the effects of these *adjustment* policies to operate, it was nevertheless possible for deficit countries to obtain loans.[24]

This system had a greater basis in convention than the gold standard, and conventions need a durable preliminary agreement. It is again clear, in this as in other areas, why no institutions are perfectly suited to all occasions. For example, the gold exchange standard, which did not work well between the wars, was quite successful after the second world war until 1971.

---

[22] This ensured the *multilateralism* of trade, i.e., the possibility of offsetting any deficit that a country might have with respect to another with its surplus *vis-à-vis* a third country, thus overcoming the tendency towards *bilateralism* (i.e., balancing trade country by country) that had distinguished the period between the two world wars, which reduced allocative efficiency.

[23] The burden of the structural adjustment should in principle be borne both by debtor countries (those with balance of payment deficits) and creditor countries (the others). This was done to avoid the deflationary effects that would have resulted from placing the burden on debtor countries only, which might have meant adopting deflationary policies as an instrument to re-establish equilibrium. It was Keynes, fearing a repetition of the depression of the 1930s, who insisted on the necessity of a symmetric adjustment that nevertheless found little application: in reality, it was the debtor countries that made the greatest adjustments.

[24] Loans could (and still can) be granted by the IMF to meet temporary balance of payments imbalances by drawing on the members' quotas or by borrowing from a member. In addition, there were (and still are) long-term loans available for specific projects, usually on normal bank terms, from the International Bank for Reconstruction and Development. This institution, more commonly known as the World Bank, is the second of the institutions created at Bretton Woods.

One problem with the gold exchange standard is that the constancy of the gold content of the reserve currency underpins confidence in the system. This creates a conflict since, if the gold content is kept constant, there is a risk of an international liquidity shortage as international transactions grow. If sufficient liquidity is provided, however, it may prove difficult to maintain the gold content of the reserve currency (*Triffin's dilemma*). In general, there is no guarantee whatsoever that the quantity of the reserve currency issued by the gold-standard country and circulating in the rest of the world will match other countries' demand for reserves, i.e., the demand for reserve currency related to international transactions (Triffin, 1960).[25] If the gold-standard country decides to regulate the money supply to adjust it to the level of international transactions, it loses a further degree of freedom (in addition to that of altering the gold content of its currency) in the use of its economic policy instruments. Bear in mind that the reserve currency enters circulation in the rest of the world only if the gold-standard country runs balance of payments deficits.[26] Such deficits may or may not occur. Even if they do, they may not be sufficiently large if difficulties arise in regulating the balance of payments or the gold-standard country's economic interests or other policy aims take precedence. However, if the balance of payments deficit over a certain span of time is sufficiently large to ensure adequate international liquidity, confidence in the stability of the value of the reserve currency *may* be undermined. This occurs precisely because the amount of reserve currency held by the central banks of the rest of the world is too large in relation to the gold reserves of the gold-standard country, creating concern about its ability to redeem banknotes for gold upon request. Conversely, if the amount of reserve currency supplied through balance of payments deficits is regulated so as to avoid these risks, it might be insufficient to ensure steady trade growth.

The former situation did in fact occur in the post-war period. After a span in which there was a dollar shortage, the opposite situation emerged during the 1960s in connection with large US balance of payments deficits. While these solved the international liquidity problem much more effectively than the creation of Special Drawing Rights (see next section), it also generated growing worries about dollar convertibility. On 15 August 1971, President Nixon was forced to suspend the convertibility of the dollar into gold, thus bringing an end to the gold exchange system embodied by the IMF.

---

[25] For more on the determinants of the demand for international reserves see Gandolfo (1995, section 20.2).

[26] For this reason some speak of the *seignorage* of the gold-standard country, by analogy with the situation inside a country when it issues money whose nominal value exceeds its intrinsic value or when non-interest bearing (rather than interest-bearing) liabilities are issued in exchange for goods and services. The analogy is justified by the fact that the reserve currency country can exchange non-interest bearing liabilities (banknotes) or low-interest liabilities for an excess of imported goods and services (for more on this see Grubel, 1984). However, this and other benefits (which we will discuss in chapter 17) are offset by disadvantages, some of which we mentioned in the text (the impossibility of changing the currency's parity to secure the desired balance of payments equilibrium, the necessity of subordinating domestic economic policy to the objective of maintaining adequate international liquidity).

16.5 Centrally created reserves

An alternative to the monetary systems we have examined so far would be to establish an international monetary organisation to act as a central banker for the world, much the same as the national central banks. This organisation would be responsible for creating the international liquidity it judged necessary to achieve some world-level objective (e.g., global income growth) as a true fiat money.

In a world of independent nation states, such a supranational central bank could only be established cooperatively. Even if an agreement were reached, however, the lack of effective executive powers would make such a system difficult to design and implement. Since states tend to reserve the right to regulate domestic liquidity directly or to determine the level of the exchange rate (as well as other non-monetary economic variables), an international central bank would only be able to create international money used exclusively by national central banks to settle debts between themselves. The quantity of domestic currency would continue to be regulated by each national central bank.

Any international agreement would have to clarify:

(a) the alternative methods for distributing international money among the various countries (the distribution of seignorage);
(b) the criteria for deciding how much reserves to create and their possible uses, in order to maintain the value of the fiat money stable and ensure balance of payments adjustment (Grubel, 1984).

This system, which would represent an advanced stage of the transformation of the international monetary system towards the centralisation and discretionary regulation of the currency, has found only partial application.

At the IMF's 1967 meeting in Rio de Janeiro – i.e., still within the framework of the IMF system – it was decided to create a special unit of account known as *Special Drawing Rights* (SDRs), whose initial value was equal to that of the dollar.[27] SDRs, which are still in use, have no paper form, existing only as accounting credits. Countries with balance of payment deficits can make payments or intervene in foreign exchange markets by exchanging SDRs for other members' currencies. The countries accepting SDRs (normally those in surplus) can use them to settle any future deficits, earning interest in the meantime.

Many obstacles had to be overcome to reach the stage of issuing SDRs. The obstacles were a sign of the resistance to the centralised creation of international liquidity as fiat money, resistance that still exists today (see Salin, 1990; Schröder, 1990). The hostility to such a system derives from fears that at both the international and national levels creating non-convertible money produces inflationary pressures. The surprising feature of this resistance to a true international means of payment is that it emerged in a period in which the various countries continued to make widespread use of the dollar, whose

[27] In 1974, after two devaluations of the dollar and the switch to a floating rate regime, SDRs were transformed into a basket currency whose value depended (and still depends) on the weighted value of a selection of major currencies.

creation was inevitably linked to the specific needs of the United States and thus its domestic economic policy and general political orientation.[28]

16.6 Floating exchange rates

Systems in which the value of a currency is allowed to float like other market prices differ completely from those we have seen so far. As with any other price, fluctuations in the exchange rate should be able to ensure equilibrium in the relevant market (the foreign exchange market in our case): if demand for foreign currency (e.g., dollars) exceeds supply, the exchange rate (i.e., the price of the dollar in the domestic currency) will rise, thus curbing demand and expanding the supply of dollars (*depreciation* of the currency); if demand for foreign currency falls short of supply, the exchange rate will fall (*appreciation*).

Under a floating exchange rate system (or fixed-rate systems that allow parity adjustments), international adjustment is partly or mainly entrusted to fluctuations in the exchange rate: a balance of payments surplus (deficit) will cause the currency to appreciate (depreciate). This will affect the current account in such a way as to return the overall balance of payments to equilibrium (whatever the balance on capital movements).

Note that a variation in the exchange rate will produce a simultaneous change of the same magnitude in the relative prices of all goods in the two countries (the price of bread in country A compared with its price in country B, as well as the relative price of iron in the same countries, etc.). By contrast, the changes in relative prices that occur under a fixed exchange rate system following the variation in the price level in each country may differ, since in the real world the prices of some goods (e.g., bread) vary more easily and rapidly than prices of other goods (e.g., iron).

The advantage of such a floating rate system is that it streamlines the duties of policymakers, who, being freed of the burden of equilibrating the balance of payments, do not have to undertake specific interventions or accumulate reserves to finance future deficits. Nevertheless, leaving exchange rate movements entirely to market forces has a number of drawbacks. For this reason, real-life floating exchange rate regimes have tended to be *dirty* (or *managed*), i.e., not fully free.

One of the arguments in favour of floating (or *flexible* or *fluctuating*) exchange rates is that fixed exchange rates encourage speculators by 'guaranteeing' them large profits (Friedman, 1953). When a change in a parity is thought to be highly likely (and the extent of the speculation itself may contribute to this), the fixed level of the exchange rate becomes a sort of bonus for speculators (the narrower the fluctuation band, the larger the bonus). They can acquire the foreign currency at a (low) fixed price, i.e. one that is independent of the demand for the currency and then sell it at a higher price, after the devaluation. This would not happen in a flexible exchange rate system, where the exchange rate is not (officially) kept fixed.

For example, the lira/dollar parity in the IMF system was Lit 625/$1, with a

---

[28] For the problems associated with SDRs, see Van Ypersele (1977).

fluctuation band of $\pm$ 1 per cent; dollars could be bought in Italy at a maximum price of 631.25 lire, a price that would not rise in reaction to the increase in speculative purchases. If a 5 per cent devaluation of the lira against the dollar were forecast, the expected gain to speculators would have been 4 per cent, excluding transaction costs. If the fluctuation band had been 3 per cent, the expected maximum gain to speculators forecasting a 5 per cent devaluation would have been 2 per cent, since the exchange rate would have increased to $625 + 0.03(625) = 643.75$ as an effect of speculative purchases of dollars.

Widening the fluctuation band would not have been sufficient to fend off large-scale speculative movements triggered, for example, by expectations of an even larger devaluation. In this case only a freely floating exchange rate would have enabled the lira to depreciate sufficiently to reduce the profitability of speculation, in parallel with speculative activity. However, in a flexible exchange rate system another factor may also encourage speculation. As a currency depreciates under the pressure of speculative purchases of the foreign currency, the initial forecast of the future exchange rate does not remain unchanged; i.e., the expected exchange rate for a given date (e.g., two months hence) is not independent of the current exchange rate and its most recent fluctuations.

Floating exchange rates present clear disadvantages in terms of the uncertainty of the price of foreign currencies, potentially hindering trade and medium- and long-term capital movements, which are not speculation-induced, as well as non-speculative short-term flows.[29] However, it should be noted that exchange rate uncertainty is often a reflection of other factors and that, if the underlying tensions were not smoothly channelled into the current exchange rate, they might build up and explode, causing sharp and possibly traumatic fluctuations in the parity.

A further issue is the degree of discipline that the different exchange rate regimes exert over the conduct of private and public agents. Some economists argue that fixed rates should be favoured, since they act as a tighter constraint on the agents of a country than floating exchange rates. To understand this argument, first consider the position of private agents such as firms. If the exchange rate is fixed, they will find it difficult to increase their prices by more than their competitors in both domestic and international markets. They will therefore have an incentive to contain costs, resisting pressure for wage increases and improving their static and dynamic efficiency. Policymakers will also be encouraged to implement policies to increase the competitiveness of domestic goods, since they would otherwise risk a deterioration in the balance of payments. The country will thus be forced to adjust its domestic situation to that prevailing abroad. Fixed exchange rates are therefore a powerful tool of (implicit) international coordination and should therefore be favoured. By contrast, other economists favour a floating rate regime because it gives a country greater autonomy: balance of payments adjustment under floating rates occurs directly in the external transactions market and does

---

[29] Uncertainty can be eliminated by appropriate hedging on the forward exchange rate market. Anyone who wants to ensure that a future purchase (or sale) of a given currency is executed at a certain exchange rate will turn to the forward market. This can be expensive, however.

Frankel (1992) considers the different factors that affect the volume of foreign trade and argues that the negative effect of exchange rate uncertainty is very small.

not lead to appreciable changes in domestic prices or incomes, as would happen in the case of a fixed exchange rate regime.

Two aspects of this debate should be singled out. One regards the disciplinary role to assign to external rules. We will deal with this in the next section and later in this chapter with reference to the EMS. The other regards the actual ability of floating rates to confine the adjustment to the external transactions market, which can be limited by the links between exchange rates, on the one hand, and prices and incomes, on the other. We will defer further discussion of this issue to the following chapter.

As we can see, the picture is highly varied and there are no clearly superior solutions except in relation to the objectives posed and the specific situation.

A floating exchange rate system is now in place worldwide and was accepted by the IMF in the 1970s after the suspension of dollar convertibility and after an attempt to maintain a system of fixed exchange rates (albeit not linked to gold) with wider fluctuation bands. Some countries had sought to introduce floating rates for international capital movements only,[30] keeping fixed rates for current transactions. However, this *dual* (or *two-tier*) *foreign exchange market* did not last long owing to the lack of a sharp distinction between current transactions and capital movements.[31]

16.7 Fixed versus flexible exchange rates: reflections from experience

In many countries the change to a floating exchange rate regime was made necessary by the practical impossibility of keeping exchange rates within their fluctuation limits as official reserves were used up. The experience gained in these years can help assess the relative merits of the two systems and the validity of a number of hypotheses about the determinants of exchange rate fluctuations. Nevertheless, the fact that exchange rate movements have never been completely free means that we must exercise a certain degree of caution in reaching our conclusions.[32] By the same token, in at least part of the period in which floating rates prevailed (the 1970s), international economic relationships were considerably influenced by such a complex variety of factors that it is difficult to identify their respective individual influences.

First and foremost, it does not seem that floating rates had a significant negative impact on the volume of international trade and capital movements, despite the possible indirect consequences of incentives to adopt protectionist measures in reaction to the sharp depreciation of some currencies.

If kept for too long, as in certain cases in the EMS (which we will examine later in this

---

[30] It was thought that floating rates would discourage speculative capital flows and excessive currency depreciation, for the reasons set out earlier in this section.

[31] Capital can be transferred by anticipating or delaying current payments (leads and lags) and over- or underinvoicing of international trade transactions (see section 17.5).

[32] In other words, we are not comparing fixed exchange rates with floating exchange rates but rather fixed rates and managed floating rates. According to Friedman, this sort of fluctuation may turn out to be the worst of all possible worlds, since speculators must predict not only the underlying behaviour of equilibrium exchange rates but also the policy stance of monetary authorities.

chapter), fixed parities (and, hence, exchange rates) can have severe adverse consequences for some economies. On the other hand, the greater autonomy lent to countries'
economic policies by floating rates did not manifest itself or, in any case, did not
guarantee higher levels of income and employment. According to some, the trade-off
between employment and inflation proved illusory, at least during the 1970s, for reasons
unrelated to the exchange rate system. Others argue that many governments were
simply not willing to exchange lower unemployment rates for higher inflation, at least
after the second oil crisis. In any case, whether or not the domestic constraints were
objective or subjective, any greater autonomy did not translate into an incentive to
pursue expansionary policies.

The point of disagreement between the opposing advocates of fixed and floating
exchange rates on which the experience of the last 20 years shines most light is the
presumed ability of floating rates to discourage speculative capital movements. In fact,
this has not always been the case and, on the contrary, speculation has often been fuelled
by the variation in the exchange rate that it helped trigger in the first place. There were
therefore many cases of persistent exchange rate *overshooting*, giving rise to *currency
cycles*.[33] For example, both the nominal and real effective exchange rates of the dollar
appreciated by one-third in the five years following 1980. Over the same period the real
DM/$ exchange rate rose by about 60 per cent. Currency cycles may be caused by
economic policy choices or autonomous shocks, or even be produced by the self-
fulfilling expectations of private agents (*bootstraps*): some forecasts may prove true only
because they induce the behaviour needed for the expectation to be realised. The size of
the transactions is essential: if major traders expect the dollar to appreciate, their large
purchases of dollars will fulfil those expectations. Self-fulfilling behaviour may even be
spurred on by the prospect of breaching what are viewed as 'key' exchange rate levels. In
any case, in the short to medium term the existence of currency cycles appears to conflict
sharply with the *purchasing power parity theory*, according to which movements in
(nominal) exchange rates reflect changes in relative inflation, i.e., in inflation differentials
between the different countries.[34]

16.8 The European Monetary System

16.8.1 Objectives

In April 1972 a number of European countries had reacted to the widening of exchange
rate fluctuation bands around the world by narrowing the bands between their currencies (the *snake*). In 1979, they decided to strengthen and extend this agreement, which
had proved to be more difficult to implement with the emergence of an international
system of floating rates, by establishing a fully fledged European Monetary System
(EMS) of fixed exchange rates.

In addition to their shared desire to create an area of monetary stability, and therefore
economic and political stability within the European Economic Community, the coun-

---

[33] On the dollar cycle, see Gerlach and Petri (1990).
[34] This theory, which was originally formulated by Cassel (1918), implies that variations in real
exchange rates are zero. We will return to it in section *18.6.

tries had different motives that nonetheless converged on a system of fixed exchange rates: low-inflation countries, i.e., those in the German mark area, wanted to use the system to prevent competitive devaluations (or depreciations) by high-inflation countries. On their part, the latter sought to introduce an external element of discipline on the behaviour of unions[35] or to increase the credibility of their anti-inflation policies.[36]

The final structure of the system is the result of a compromise between the various interests and largely reflects political considerations (Coffey, 1984, p. 17; Van Ypersele, 1984, p. 16).

The EMS is essentially composed of two elements:

(a) the European Exchange Rate Mechanism (ERM), which is intended to reduce fluctuations in the exchange rates between EU currencies. Not all EU members participate in the ERM;

(b) a mechanism for providing credit to countries with balance of payments difficulties. All EU members participate in this.

The compromise nature of the EMS is evident in the fact that in setting limits on exchange rate fluctuations, an additional mechanism, based on the ECU, was added to that already operating with the snake, which was based on bilateral parities. We will examine both in detail, beginning with the second, simpler, mechanism.

16.8.2 The bilateral parity grid

A 'grid' of bilateral parities was first established; that is, a central rate was set for each pair of currencies.[37] The system initially called for a fluctuation band of only $\pm$ 2.25 per cent ($\pm$ 6 per cent for a few currencies).[38] On 2 August 1993 the band was widened to $\pm$ 15 per cent for all countries in order to counter increased speculative attacks.

The participating countries *can* intervene before the margins are reached (*intramarginal intervention*) by purchasing or selling any of the currencies of the participating countries, but only with their prior consent. Once the exchange rate between any two currencies has reached the limit of the fluctuation band, the monetary authorities of both countries are *required* to intervene (*marginal intervention*), each trading the currency of the other in order to increase the effectiveness of their intervention.[39] The country whose currency is at the upper limit of the band can obtain the currency to sell

[35] The game was in fact more complex. Firms, and often the central bank, also had the objective of preventing the government and Parliament from running up budget deficits.

[36] These higher-order 'objectives' will be discussed later.

[37] Since the EMS is not based on gold, it is more appropriate to speak of central rates rather than parities, since these are defined as the ratio between the gold contents of two currencies.

[38] With discrete variations in the exchange rates the margins are not perfectly symmetrical, with the lower being narrower than the upper (Gandolfo, 1995).

[39] When the central rate for the franc/mark is 3.35386, with a fluctuation band from 2.88810 to 3.89480, if the franc approaches its upper limit (and the mark correspondingly declines towards its lower limit) the Bank of France could intervene by using dollar reserves (rather than marks) to buy francs; similarly, the Bundesbank could buy dollars (rather than francs) and sell marks. If the exchange rate is at the margin, however, both would have to sell marks and buy francs.

from the other central banks by means of a very short-term financing facility, with no limit on drawings.

The mechanism to ensure that exchange rates remain fixed operates asymmetrically in practice. Intramarginal and marginal interventions are more costly for countries with a balance of payments deficit than for those with a surplus, since the former may use up their reserves and find it difficult to borrow, while the latter face only the possibility of an unwanted increase in the domestic money supply, which they could in any case offset with sterilisation (see sections 18.1 and *18.2). However, the asymmetry goes beyond this. It is accentuated by the fact that the tensions that push a currency (e.g., the French franc) towards the upper limit of the fluctuation band and another (e.g., the mark) towards the bottom are not necessarily caused by the behaviour of the country whose currency is depreciating, i.e., by French economic policies. They may also be caused by the behaviour of the other country, Germany, which by adopting an excessively restrict-ive policy stance accumulates balance of payments surpluses that lead to an appreci-ation of the mark and a depreciation of the franc. And if the restrictive stance is adopted by the economically more important country, its currency will appreciate *vis-à-vis* a number of smaller countries.

In fact, our example broadly describes actual events in the history of the 'snake' (later repeated under the EMS): constant pressure for the appreciation of the mark against the other currencies was generated by Germany's economic policies, which were firmly oriented towards achieving monetary stability. The burden of adjustment policies was actually placed on currencies which depreciated against the mark and the 'snake' had a markedly deflationary effect (De Grauwe, 1987; Wyplosz, 1990). This argument was used by the French (and to some extent the Italians) in the negotiations for the establishment of the EMS and was accepted to a certain degree. This led to the creation of a second fluctuation mechanism based on the European Currency Unit (ECU), which should have been the biggest innovation of the EMS with respect to the 'snake'.

16.8.3 The ECU and the divergence indicator

The ECU was created as a basket currency containing the currencies of the EEC member states. It was intended to serve three purposes: (a) as a basis for a symmetric fluctuation mechanism; (b) as an instrument for repaying loans from the central banks within the framework of the EMS and (c) as a reserve asset. The quantity of each currency in the basket was initially revised every five years so as to avoid excessive variations in overall weights, which should reflect the relative importance of each country within the Community.[40]

[40] If the quantity of the various currencies were kept unchanged in the presence of systematic changes in central rates, the weight of the currencies that systematically revalue would grow continuously, at the expense of those that regularly devalued. It was therefore decided that a five-year revision should be carried out to compensate for the loss of value of the devalued currencies by increasing their weight in the basket. This decision was criticised by some, since it had the effect of depreciating the basket itself and increasing uncertainty about the value of the ECU. In order to avoid this problem, the Treaty on European Union (which we discuss in section 16.8.5) froze the quantities of the currencies in the basket.

The value of the ECU (i.e., the exchange rate of the ECU) in terms of each currency i can be written as:

$$\text{ECU}_i = \sum_{j=1}^{n} a_j e_{ij} \quad i = 1, 2, \ldots, n \tag{16.3}$$

where a_j is the quantity of currency j in the basket of n currencies, and e_{ij} is the bilateral exchange rate, i.e., the value of currency i in terms of currency j.[41]

In (16.3) both the bilateral exchange rates and the exchange rates with the ECU can be either market rates or central rates. Suppose, for example, that the ECU is composed of only three currencies, the mark, the franc and the lira, and contains 1.75 marks (DM), 0.4 francs (FF) and 187.5 lire (Lit). Let the bilateral central rate for Lit/DM be 750, that for Lit/FF be 250 and, therefore, that for FF/DM be 3. The central rate of the ECU in lire can be obtained from (16.3):

$$\text{ECU}_{\text{Lit}} = a_{\text{DM}} \cdot e_{\text{DMLit}} + a_{\text{FF}} \cdot e_{\text{FFLit}} + a_{\text{Lit}} \cdot e_{\text{LitLit}} =$$
$$= 1.75 \cdot 750 + 0.4 \cdot 250 + 187.5 \cdot 1 = 1,600$$

Similarly, the central rate of the ECU in marks is:

$$\text{ECU}_{\text{DM}} = a_{\text{DM}} \cdot e_{\text{DMDM}} + a_{\text{FF}} \cdot e_{\text{FFDM}} + a_{\text{Lit}} \cdot e_{\text{LitDM}} =$$
$$= 1.75 \cdot 1 + 0.4/3 \cdot 187.5 \cdot 1/750 = 2.1\overline{3}.$$

We leave it to the reader to verify that the value of the ECU in francs is 6.40.[42]

Let the market exchange rates be Lit 760/DM 1, Lit 253.$\overline{3}$/FF 1 and FF 3/DM 1. The value of the ECU in lire calculated on the basis of the market exchange rate will be:

$$\text{ECU}_{\text{Lit}} = 1.75 \cdot 760 + 0.4 \cdot 253.\overline{3} + 187.5 \cdot 1 = 1,618.8$$

while the value of the ECU in marks and francs will be 2.1$\overline{3}$ and 6.39 respectively.[43]

The difference between the value of the ECU in terms of central rates and that calculated with reference to market rates is an indicator of the divergence of the values of the various currencies from the central rates. Since it takes account of the differences between the market value and central rates *for all currencies*, it is a more balanced *indicator of divergence* than the fluctuations in bilateral rates. It enables us to identify the *divergent currency* with respect to the full basket of currencies, which is impossible to do

[41] Obviously $e_{ij} = 1$ if $i = j$; that is, the value of a currency in terms of itself is equal to 1.
[42] Note that each country only declares the central rate with the ECU, not bilateral rates. Thus, in (16.3) we do not know the exchange rates on the right-hand side but rather those of the left-hand side and the quantities a_j. Nevertheless, once the central rate of the ECU in each currency is given, we can derive the bilateral rates between the currencies by dividing the values of the central rates. For example, if the central rates of the ECU in francs and marks are set at 6.4 and 2.1$\overline{3}$, the rate of the mark in lire is 6.4/2.1$\overline{3}$ = 3.
[43] These are hypothetical, not actual values of the ECU in lire, marks or francs. In other words, these are the values towards which the actual values of the ECU in terms of lire, marks or francs (i.e., the prices of ECU in the foreign exchange markets) should tend, all the more so the less imperfect are the foreign exchange markets.

using fluctuations around the bilateral parities.[44] The indicator of divergence in terms of ECU was adopted as an additional way of signalling the need for intervention in the foreign exchange market. It is the basis for determining a *threshold of divergence*, beyond which there is a *presumption* that the divergent country will intervene in the foreign exchange market to avoid further divergence and that it will adopt appropriate monetary and fiscal *adjustment* policies. The divergence threshold is set at 75 per cent of the maximum margin of fluctuation. Moreover, in recognition of the fact that the currencies with a smaller weight in the ECU would be subjected to unwanted pressure by fluctuations of the others, it was also decided to confine the fluctuations of the latter within narrower limits. Accordingly, specific divergence thresholds were set as an inverse function of the weight of the currencies.[45]

This mechanism should have ensured greater symmetry than that based on the parity grid in signalling tensions and allocating the burden of adjustment, thus constituting a more balanced instrument for initiating coordination of the economic policies of the ERM countries.

In practice, this system, defined as a system of 'individualised' intervention limits (Coffey, 1984), has not worked for a variety of reasons. First, as we mentioned, the system only incorporates a presumption that countries will intervene, not an obligation. Second, the system also suffers from a number of technical limitations (see, for instance, Spaventa, 1982). Third, the symmetry it is supposed to ensure was opposed by those who fear its potential inflationary effects.[46] The fourth reason is that while the ECU was conceived as a means of payment and reserve asset in addition to its role as a unit of account, in reality it has primarily been used as the latter. Since central bank interventions in the foreign exchange market are not carried out in ECU, but rather in the individual national currencies, it was a natural step to comply with the fluctuation limits that have practical relevance for intervention with regard to individual currencies, i.e., the limits in terms of bilateral parities. Finally, the frequency of intramarginal intervention has meant that the divergence threshold is rarely reached, which contributes to the impression that the mechanism is not operating (Tsoukalis, 1993, p. 200).

---

[44] For example, if the franc is at the upper limit of its fluctuation band with respect to the mark, the mark will simultaneously be at the lower limit of its band with the franc, since $e_{ij} \cdot e_{ji} = 1$ as a consistency condition (see Gandolfo, 1995, p. 6). Thus we cannot tell which is the divergent currency. This can only be done by looking at the overall performance of the franc and the mark with respect to the other currencies. The divergence indicator provides just such a measure of overall performance.

[45] The divergence threshold for currency j is $0.75 \cdot d \cdot (1 - w_j)$, where d is the maximum margin of fluctuation allowed for that currency and wj is the weight of the currency j in the ECU. An additional correction was needed because some of the currencies in the ECU can float freely. For more on the operation and the problems of the EMS, see Giavazzi and Giovannini (1989), Fratianni and Von Hagen (1991) and Gros and Thygesen (1992).

[46] The mechanism is theoretically capable of signalling divergences attributable to both debtor countries and creditor countries. Thus, the burden of adjustment would not fall more heavily on the former. This explains why Germany – champion of the fight against inflation – was the main opponent of the ECU. A related reason for Germany's opposition is that the ECU would have reduced the mark's role as an 'anchor', which has also been officially acknowledged in the Delors Report (see Commission for the Study of Economic and Monetary Union, 1989, p. 12).

16.8.4 Objectives and achievements

To what extent have the various goals set by EMS participants been achieved? The answer depends on the objective.

If we consider the aim of extending and strengthening currency coordination and we take the variability of exchange rates as an indicator of coordination, such variability has been reduced more among ERM participants than among other OECD countries. This is especially true after 1983, when the high frequency of realignments declined with respect to that in the initial period, at least until 1992–3 (when there were five realignments).

As regards eliminating the asymmetry of the 'snake', we previously noted that this objective was generally not achieved. Only Germany was in a position to decide its monetary policy independently, while the others normally adjusted their own policies accordingly, if they were not at least temporarily insulated by controls on capital movements (Giavazzi and Giovannini, 1989, p. 75).

Nevertheless, the asymmetric operation of the EMS seems to have laid the foundation for reaching the objective set by some countries of exerting external discipline on the behaviour of certain agents. Since monetary policy in the EMS has essentially been dictated by Germany, which has set price stability as its primary objective, the domestic behaviour of agents in the other countries has had to fall into line. This explains the reminders that have repeatedly come from policymakers (especially central banks) in high-inflation countries of the obligations imposed by EMS membership; these reminders have sometimes been a powerful tool in arguing against domestic wage settlements or fiscal policies that are felt to be inflationary. The question of how successful this external discipline was (especially between 1987 and 1992) in influencing union and government action and, conversely, to what extent it imposed an excessive sacrifice in terms of high interest rates and, therefore, a worsening of public debt problems still needs to be addressed in a dispassionate fashion, especially in the light of the devaluations that subsequently occurred in 1992–3.[47]

Some argue (Giavazzi and Pagano, 1988) that membership in the EMS lent *credibility* to the anti-inflationary policies of certain countries, acting as a guarantee of high-inflation countries' commitment to implementing such policies by tying the hands of their policymakers and lowering the public's inflationary expectations. Whether this actually occurred is not at all clear:[48] the frequency of parity realignments until 1983 is itself indicative of the fact that the commitment was not so credible after all. The situation may have changed to some extent after 1987.[49]

The EMS may have served to reduce the magnitude of the devaluations that high-inflation countries might have resorted to in order to maintain their competitiveness. Two facts support this hypothesis: the progressive reduction in the variability of

---

[47] The costs of this policy choice have been considered in detail by a 'neutral' observer in Dornbusch (1988).

[48] Weber (1991) made an attempt at measuring credibility, obtaining largely negative results.

[49] The hypothesis of the EMS as an instrument of credibility is linked to the complex issue of the time inconsistency of government action, which we will examine in chapter 19.

exchange rates;[50] and the growth in the trade surpluses of Germany and other low-inflation countries with the other ERM countries.

Fratianni and von Hagen (1990, 1991) argue that the EMS also helped to absorb external shocks, especially those originating in the United States, by inducing the European countries to coordinate their economic policies.

16.8.5 European Economic and Monetary Union

European Economic and Monetary Union (EMU) will be implemented on the basis of the principles set out in the Delors Report of 1989 as well as subsequent decisions of the European Union, which have partially modified the framework provided by the Report.

The Report established three stages for monetary union. The first began in 1990 and, among other things, provided for the elimination of restrictions on capital movements between the member states. Stage 2 began in 1994 with the creation of the European Monetary Institute, which has been charged with strengthening the coordination of monetary policies and preparing for the final stage. Stage 3 will begin on 1 January 1999 and will involve:

(a) full and irreversible convertibility of currencies;
(b) absence of any restrictions on capital transactions and the full integration of EU money and financial markets;
(c) the elimination of fluctuation margins and the irrevocable locking of exchange rates between the EU currencies and between these and the euro, the future European currency.

In addition:

(d) the ECU will cease to exist as an official basket currency and will be replaced by the euro at par;
(e) the euro will enter circulation by 1 January 2002 at the latest and will replace national currencies by 1 July 2002;
(f) monetary policy will be decided by a European System of Central Banks, composed of the national central banks and the European Central Bank, whose mandate will be to ensure price stability.[51]

Stage 3 will involve only those countries that have met the convergence standards laid down at the Intergovernmental Conferences in Maastricht (the Netherlands) in 1991 (which produced the Treaty on European Union, the so-called Maastricht treaty),[52] which regard:

[50] This is true with reference to both nominal and real exchange rates until 1992–3. It is however difficult to judge the performance of the EMS afterwards in the light of its inability to cope with the speculative attacks which forced the pound sterling and the lira out of the ERM and led to large depreciations of these currencies. The ERM may have simply allowed unsustainable tensions to accumulate. This problem is examined further in sections *16.8.6 and 18.5.

[51] It was agreed that a system of fixed exchange rates (the so-called EMS 2) will continue to link the currencies of the participants in monetary union and those initially excluded from participation.

[52] The Maastricht agreements amended the Treaty of Rome, which established the European Economic Community.

1 price stability;
2 the convergence of long-term interest rates;
3 the sustainability of governments' financial position;
4 exchange rate behaviour consistent with the aim of exchange rate stability.

Let us examine these in order.

1 *A high degree of price stability.* In particular, the rate of increase in consumer prices in a country must not exceed by more than 1.5 percentage points average inflation in the three best performing countries in terms of inflation.

2 *Convergence of long-term interest rates.* The long-term interest rate of a country must not exceed by more than 2 percentage points that in the three countries with the lowest inflation. This condition should be seen as complementing the previous one: a country might keep its inflation rate low by means of direct control measures that have no lasting effect; in this case expectations of higher future price increases would emerge, which would cause long-term interest rates to rise. However, it seems rather odd to entrust the markets with such an important role in the valuation of future inflation. In the light of our analysis so far, we cannot exclude the possibility that the markets may be distorted by erroneous and biased assessments and that they generate self-fulfilling forecasts.[53]

3 *Sustainability of the government financial position.* Indicators of sustainability are the ratio of the stock of government debt to GDP, which should not exceed 60 per cent, and the ratio of the government budget deficit to GDP, which should not exceed 3 per cent. Apart from questions about the reasons for choosing these values rather than others,[54] a more general problem regards the motives and the effects of setting upper limits on the indicated ratios.

The arguments in favour of doing so seem to be based on the assumption that an expanding government debt generates negative externalities with regard to:
    (a) interest rates;
    (b) the proper functioning of financial markets;
    (c) the conduct of an independent monetary policy.

As regards the first issue, it is argued that if a EMU participant had an increasing ratio of government debt to GDP it would be forced to make repeated recourse to the EU

---

[53] For arguments very similar to those advanced here see Kenen (1992); for a defence of the Maastricht criteria, see Gros and Thygesen (1992, p. 389).

[54] The debt/GDP ratio was chosen because it was the average of such ratios for the various member states at the time the Maastricht agreements were reached; the deficit/GDP ratio was chosen so as to maintain the average ratio between debt and GDP given certain forecasts about real GDP growth and inflation. A certain amount of discretion has been left to the Council of Economic and Financial Ministers (ECOFIN) in applying these standards.

    The *stability agreement* reached at the Dublin European Council in December 1996 decided that countries participating in Stage 3 of EMU should tend to have surplus or balanced budgets. The maximum deficit/GDP ratio allowed will be 3 per cent. Countries that do not observe this limit will be subject to heavy penalties.

capital markets, thus exerting upward pressure on interest rates, with deflationary consequences. However, this assumes that the capital markets are unable to discriminate between different categories of borrower, in particular between countries with a large government debt and others, and demand a higher risk premium from the former only.

The second argument becomes relevant at this point. It is argued that the threat of default by a highly indebted government would create disorder in the financial markets. This would force countries with little debt to guarantee the debt issued by their highly indebted brethren. This could increase the risk of default by countries with little or no debt, leading to a general increase in interest rates and thus a reduction in demand and employment.

The third argument regards the effects of interest rate externalities on the conduct of monetary policy by the European Central Bank (ECB): a general increase in EU interest rates as a result of the excessive growth of government debt in a given country might induce the member states to request a more relaxed monetary stance on the part of the ECB, which, in acceding to the request, would fail to carry out its primary responsibility of guaranteeing monetary stability.

This convergence criterion may find some justification in economic theory. However, as we know (chapter 14), the sustainability of government debt and budget deficits is extremely difficult to determine at both the theoretical and empirical levels. Fixing any limit on these variables can therefore be considered arbitrary. In addition, setting such standards reduces the independence of national legislatures even before the conditions for political union have been established. Finally, setting upper limits on the size of government deficits conflicts with the need for fiscal flexibility to counter exogenous depressive shocks that may affect certain member states with particular severity.

4 *Exchange rate stability.* A country must have observed the normal fluctuation margins and not devalued its currency for at least two years. Although this seemed the least controversial of the criteria when the Maastricht agreements were signed, given the virtual absence of realignments since 1987, it has since become the most problematic issue after the flurry of realignments in 1992–3 and the suspension of the participation of the pound and the lira in the ERM. In addition, this condition seems capable of triggering self-fulfilling speculative movements, as we will see in more detail in section *18.5.

The path to monetary union differs from that recommended by some experts and member states. For example, the United Kingdom had proposed the mechanism of *currency competition,*[55] arguing that Stages 2 and 3 of EMU and the related institutional structures could have been avoided, allowing the free circulation of existing national

---

[55] This is based on an extreme vision of the virtues of the market. Gros and Thygesen (1992, p. 333) correctly underscore its roots in the conception of the market (formulated by Von Hayek) as a 'discovery device', owing to its ability to provide information at low cost and to foster the rapid adjustment of the economy to changing circumstances (dynamic efficiency) (Hayek, 1978). Among the advocates of competing currencies, see Vaubel (1977, 1990); for an opposing view, see Kenen (1990).

currencies and letting the market choose the soundest monetary unit. The most stable currencies would be rewarded, with their use spreading to the international level and even to domestic transactions in other countries, while the least stable would be relegated to marginal uses. For example, if the German mark showed greater stability, it would be preferred by agents to other EU currencies both for international and domestic transactions. However, the existence of external economies[56] produced by the use of one currency raises fundamental objections to this alternative.

The path taken by EMU with the creation of the euro is very similar to a system of *parallel currencies*, consisting in the creation of a new monetary unit which will circulate for a short time alongside existing national currencies before replacing them. According to the proponents of that system, a new currency should have been created beginning with Stage 2 of EMU, but the proposal was initially rejected for fear that an additional instrument of liquidity would have inflationary consequences.

Apart from more technical questions arising in connection with the specific arrangements of the EMU (for which see De Grauwe, 1996; Thygesen, 1996), other problems can arise as to the *economic* costs and benefits of monetary integration, both from an abstract point of view and with particular reference to Europe.

As to the former, the net economic benefits of a monetary union are higher the greater the degree of openness of the economies involved and capital and labour mobility, the lower are price and wage rigidities. As to the extent to which the conditions for a beneficial monetary integration (*optimum currency area*) are met in the case of the European Union, concern has been expressed about low labour mobility and some price and wage rigidity. (On both sets of issues the reader is referred to De Grauwe, 1994.)

*16.8.6 Nominal and real exchange rates in the EMS

Over the entire period in which the EMS has been in operation, especially the period in which exchange rates were virtually fixed (between January 1987 and September 1992), the small variation (or even no change) in nominal exchange rates led to a real appreciation of the currency in countries (for example, Italy, Ireland and, for a certain period, France) where inflation was above the European average and a depreciation in other countries, such as Germany, where relative inflation was negative. This generated large current account deficits for the high-inflation countries and equally large surpluses for the low-inflation countries.

In the deficit countries, overall equilibrium in the balance of payments was achieved thanks to high interest rates that attracted net capital inflows. The consequent

---

[56] The existence of external economies means that the cost of holding and using a currency declines as its use spreads. For example, a universal currency would have very low costs, since it could be used in all countries for all transactions and would not involve any conversion costs; by contrast, the cost of using a currency that is accepted only in certain shops or certain transactions would be very high. These are the network externalities we discussed in section 6.7. This explains why in all countries the final monetary authority is a public or semi-public institution. The alternative explanation of the public nature of monetary authorities offered by the advocates of competing currencies is that government monopolises monetary functions in order to extract the related 'seignorage'.

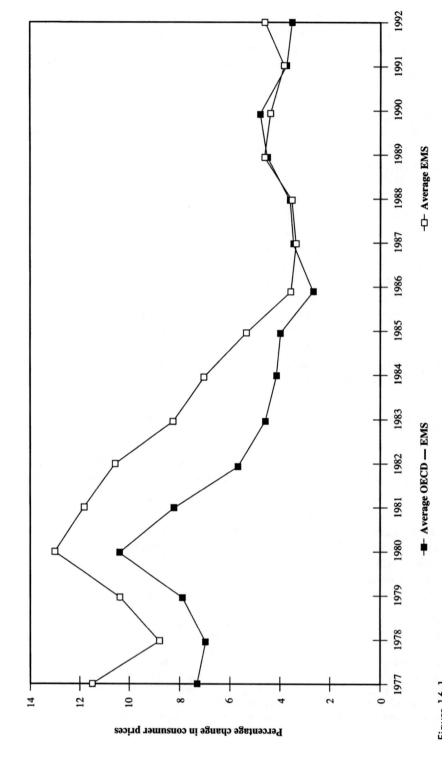

Figure 16.1
Source: OECD (1994)

expansion of foreign debt was reflected in an increase in payments abroad for invest-ment income and, hence, in an increase in the current account deficit.

The policy of fostering an appreciation in the real exchange rate, often called a *hard exchange rate* policy, was aimed at imposing discipline on the behaviour of public and private agents (see section 16.8.4). Policymakers expected that achieving this goal would reduce relative inflation and, therefore, lead to the stabilisation of the real exchange rate over time.[57]

The real appreciation of weak currencies has, however, lasted for a long period. The unexpected persistence of the appreciation can be explained in a number of ways. Some argue (Miller and Sutherland, 1991; see also Giavazzi and Spaventa, 1990) that it was due to the long lags in the effects of the hard exchange rate policy, which is more effective in the financial market than the labour market owing to the different ways expectations are formed in the two markets or to the hysteresis effects of inflation (e.g., owing to indexation of nominal wages). However, considering the fact that nominal interest rate differentials with Germany remained large in countries with current account deficits, like Italy, it seems difficult to imagine that even before the realignments of 1992–3 the financial markets believed the commitment to fixed nominal exchange rates and/or the possibility of maintaining them.[58]

Both the fact that inflation differentials with Germany did not narrow significantly for a number of countries, such as Italy, and the reduction that other countries, such as France, were able to achieve can account for the increase in unemployment in ERM countries between 1986 and 1992, in contrast to the decline (at least until 1990) recorded in other OECD countries.

In countries such as Italy, the appreciation in the real exchange rate explains at least part of the weakening of demand growth and, therefore, the increase in unemployment. On the other hand, countries, like France, that were able to reduce their inflation rate to a level even below that in Germany, could do so only by adopting severe domestic deflationary measures, which again explains the rise in unemployment. Meanwhile, Germany adopted consistently restrictive measures. This illustrates the generally defla-tionary situation in the ERM economies. This is testified to above all by the consider-able reduction in inflation, which from a starting point above levels in other OECD countries fell to virtually the same level in more recent years (figure 16.1). Deflation is even more evident in real terms, with a much sharper increase in unemployment in the ERM countries than in the other OECD countries (figure 16.2).

---

[57] The hard exchange rate policy would have also increased the country's competitiveness, in due course, since it would have stimulated both process innovation (with the reduction of costs and therefore prices) and product innovation (with qualitative improvements that would have increased non-price competitiveness). The exchange rate policy adopted by Germany in the 1970s has been cited in support.

[58] Before the EMS crisis of 1992, Gros and Thygesen (1992, p. 177) had noted that the persistence of large nominal interest rate differentials between Italy and Spain, on the one hand, and Germany, on the other, was indicative of the fact that the markets still perceived lira and peseta liabilities as high risk investments. In other words, the markets did not think that the commitment of Italian and Spanish authorities to avoiding realignments in the central rates of their respective currencies was credible.

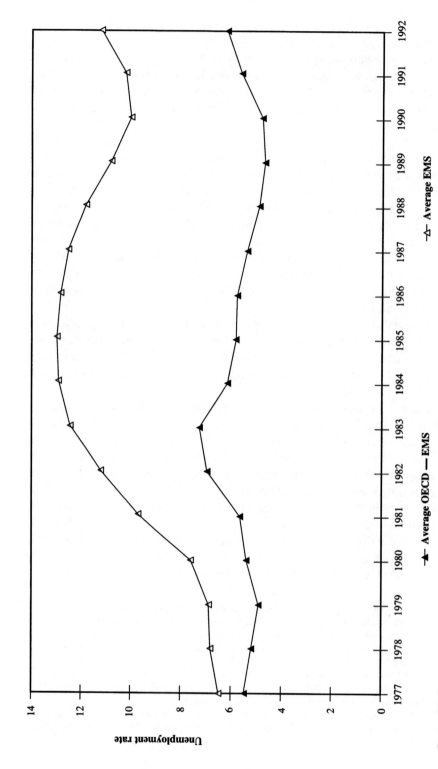

Figure 16.2
Source: OECD (1994)

A rise in the natural rate of unemployment owing to greater labour market rigidity in Europe has been cited (De Grauwe, 1990) to explain the increase in unemployment in the EMS countries. In the light of our discussion here, we can legitimately cast doubt on the importance of this line of reasoning, which at most may help explain the hysteresis in the rate of unemployment in terms of the deflationary effects of the hard exchange rate policy.

16.9 International payments imbalances over the last two decades

Despite the considerable tensions that emerged over the period and the absence of any considered and substantial reform, the international payment system was able to continue functioning without any further traumatic breakdowns after that of August 1971. This does not mean that problems did not arise, but rather that they were solved in some way, albeit often with partial, fortuitous or provisional adjustments. The problems that have emerged in the last two decades can be grouped into those specific to relationships between some groups of countries and those that regard all countries. Among the former are: the problem of disequilibria in countries that import raw materials (and oil in particular) owing to the rise in their prices during the 1970s; the problem of the foreign debt of developing countries; and that of the foreign debt of the East European countries. The more general problem concerns the strains that have been caused by speculative capital movements.

The sharp rise in raw materials prices in the 1970s created large balance of payments disequilibria. The IMF partially dealt with these by providing new special *facilities* and increasing the limit on *drawings* on existing mechanisms.[59] The *conditional* nature of the credit, however, hindered more extensive use of the Fund as an intermediary to *recycle* the balance of payments surpluses accumulated by oil-exporting countries.

Thus, recycling was largely left to private institutions: banks and other intermediaries in the Eurocurrency market. In fact, the low (at times even negative) real interest rates prevailing in this market as a consequence of an excess supply of funds stimulated recourse to these forms of private credit by many developing countries during the 1970s. However, the lack of attention paid by both borrowers and lenders to borrowers' real capacity to service their foreign debt (payment of interest and principal) helped push their debt situation towards the 'verge of unsustainability' even before 1979. In the first half of the 1980s a combination of circumstances led to a crisis in the financial situation of the developing countries and, with them, that of the lenders. First, the monetary restriction in the United States in 1979 caused real interest rates to rise sharply. The consequent appreciation of the dollar further increased the burden of debt servicing by requiring larger outlays of domestic currency to repay the principal. In addition, the recession that had hit the creditor nations in the early 1980s made it even more difficult

---

[59] Limits are now revised annually. For example, in 1993 each country could receive annual credit from the Fund up to 168 per cent of its quota, with a cumulative limit of 400 per cent of the quota.

to repay principal and interest.[60] The foreign debt crisis, which burst into the open with Mexico's declaration of a moratorium on debt payments in 1982, was only partially solved with the financial assistance of the Fund. In more recent years, a more comprehensive solution seems to have been found in measures that include:

(a) voluntary debt reduction by creditor countries through the granting of a subsidy for interest payments by international organisations (the Brady Plan);
(b) *debt buy-backs* at highly discounted prices (up to 90 per cent) by some developing countries;
(c) *debt–equity swaps*, where debt is converted into shares, or *debt–nature swaps*, where debt is exchanged for land for investment in environmental projects.[61]

At the end of the 1980s, foreign debt also became a problem in the former Soviet-bloc countries. Unlike the 1980s debt crisis in the developing countries, the problem did not pose a real threat to the stability of the international financial system. Most bank loans were backed by official guarantees and accompanied by sufficient provision for default. In addition, exposures, which were small in relation to lenders' capital and reserves, were not highly concentrated (Bank for International Settlements, 1992, p. 71). Nevertheless, foreign debt has for some time continued to severely affect the economic policy choices of the Eastern and Central European countries. For example, serious problems have been caused by the drastic reduction in capacity[62] (with consequent shortages of even essential goods) and the simultaneous need to channel some output towards foreign markets in order to permit at least some debt servicing.

Let us now examine the general problem posed by speculative capital movements. These are in large part fuelled by the existence of large international money markets that are not subject to any form of regulation, such as the *Eurodollar* market. This market, which emerged in the 1960s and grew rapidly in the following years (see McKinnon, 1979, for a detailed discussion of the reasons for this growth), deals in US dollar deposits with banks of any nationality located in Europe. Analogous balances in other foreign currencies with banks resident in Europe are also possible and constitute the *Eurocurrency* market. More generally, deposits in a currency different from that of the country

---

[60] A country in recession tends to reduce its imports. In our case the recession that hit creditor countries caused a reduction in the exports of debtor developing countries. Note that balance of payments equilibrium requires that the deficit on capital movements and investment income (in our case associated with repayment of principal and interest) be offset by a surplus on (other) current transactions, essentially positive net exports. But this was precisely the problem in the developing countries. Note that only equilibrium (or a surplus, which would have even more drastic consequences) of the balance of payments of the developing countries would allow the debt to be repaid: a deficit would soon run down these countries' reserves and would not in any case be sustainable in the medium to long term.

[61] In some cases these operations were used to encourage the return of flight capital that had left the country for economic or political reasons: thus, for example, someone who had exported capital from a developing country could acquire – usually at a discount – an existing credit with the country and then convert the credit into local currency with the central bank, using this to purchase shares or other equity interests within the country itself (debt–equity swap). In the case of debt–nature swaps, the purchaser of the foreign debt is an environmental association.

[62] This is due to a wide variety of factors, ranging from the disorganisation (or even chaos) caused by political upheaval to the fact that the sudden international opening of these countries has made production with often outdated (or, in any case, different) techniques unprofitable.

(European or otherwise) where they are held are known as *xeno-currencies*.

How do these markets function? Assume that IBM has deposited $1 billion with Wells Fargo, a US bank, but feels that the interest rate it earns is too low. It may be more profitable for IBM to transfer the deposit to Barclays Bank in England by drawing a cheque for the amount against its balance with Wells Fargo for deposit with Barclays. This operation (or, alternatively, a giro transfer from IBM's account with Wells Fargo to its account with Barclays) does not give rise to a physical transfer of funds, as it simply involves making accounting entries in the appropriate accounts: debiting IBM and crediting Barclays Bank in Wells Fargo's accounts; debiting Wells Fargo and crediting IBM in Barclays' accounts. The latter can transfer access to the dollar balance with Wells Fargo to some other European bank, again without any material movement of funds, in order to earn an acceptable interest rate. The scope for creating further interbank deposits is practically unlimited if:

(a) there are no reserve requirements for the dollar deposits received by Barclays and other banks in Europe (hence *Eurobanks*);
(b) the dollar deposits remain within the Eurobank system.

The first condition is normally met, since many monetary authorities do not require banks to meet reserve obligations for foreign currency deposits. The second condition is met to a varying degree, which cannot be known *a priori*: the deposit creation process ends when a Eurobank makes a loan to a customer who converts his credit with Wells Fargo into cash rather than redepositing it with another Eurobank,

The size of the Eurocurrency market can be measured with reference to gross and net stocks: gross stocks include interbank deposits, while net stocks exclude them, comprising only transactions between Eurobanks and the sources or final beneficiaries of the funds outside the Eurobank system itself.

What characterises the market is not the specific nature of the operations – which are no different from normal bank transactions – but rather the absence of any regulation by the monetary authorities. This reduces the cost of fund-raising and allows banks to offer higher deposit rates and lower lending rates, thus stimulating the formation and growth of markets. The *spread* between lending and deposit rates can be very small (1/8%, 1/4%) and still be profitable.

The Eurocurrency markets are very sensitive to economic policies (and more generally, economic conditions), especially in the countries that issue the currency in which the deposits are denominated, and tend to reduce the effectiveness of the policies themselves. For example, a tight monetary policy in the United States or some other country will induce US operators to raise funds on the Eurodollar market, thereby circumventing the monetary tightening; similarly, an expansionary policy in the US or another country may be undermined by an outflow of funds from that country. In addition, all countries (especially in Europe) are exposed to the backlash of events in these markets, which can cause sudden large flows of funds connected with arbitrage and speculative activities, fuelled by even small interest rate differentials or expectations of exchange rate changes. On the other hand, on various occasions (e.g., during the oil crisis) the Eurocurrency market has enabled some countries to finance large balance of payments deficits.

These markets therefore have both positive and negative effects that countries cannot ignore. Among the problems that await solution within the framework of a reform of the international monetary system is the adequate regulation of the Eurocurrency market.

The Eurocurrency market has been flanked by the development of a *Eurobond* market, which involves transactions in bearer bonds denominated in currencies different from that of the country in which they are issued or marketed. This market is not a simple extension of the Eurocurrency market to different maturities. In the Eurocurrency market, it is the banks, which are the major operators in it, that bear the risk of default, whereas in the Eurobond market – as with securities transactions of any sort – the risk is borne only by the lender (Giddy, 1983, p. 4).

16.10 Summary

1 The balance of payments records international economic transactions. Balance of payments surpluses and deficits are both disequilibrium positions. Current account surpluses and deficits represent excessive or insufficient saving with respect to domestic investment and are difficult to sustain in the long run.

2 The foreign currency payments and receipts recorded in the balance of payments fuel the foreign currency market, which in a two-country world forms a price called the nominal bilateral exchange rate. In a world with more than two countries, the nominal effective exchange rate can be defined as the weighted average of the different bilateral rates.

3 The real exchange rate is an indicator of the competitiveness of domestic goods that takes account of the nominal exchange rate and domestic and foreign prices.

4 The behaviour of exchange rates is influenced by the type of monetary system adopted. With regard to international aspects, the most important monetary systems are: the gold standard; the gold exchange standard; systems of centrally created reserves; floating or flexible exchange rate systems.

5 The gold standard is a fixed exchange rate system; more precisely, it allows only small movements around the parity.

6 The gold exchange standard – which economises on the use of gold – is also a fixed exchange rate system under certain conditions, but it admits adjustable parities. It is more heavily reliant on convention than the gold standard.

7 A system of centrally created reserves requires an international monetary organisation to act as a central bank for the world, operating in a similar manner to a national central bank in a single country.

8 A floating exchange rate regime ensures balance of payments adjustment through exchange rate movements. Among the merits attributed to this system is that the flexibility of exchange rates discourages speculation. Drawbacks include the adverse impact on trade of uncertainty about the price of foreign currencies.

9 The experience of the last few decades shines light on the debate between the advocates of fixed and floating exchange rates: exchange rate flexibility has not been able to discourage speculation, giving rise instead to currency cycles. The increased autonomy of countries has proved illusory. On the other hand, it does not appear that floating rates have had a significant negative effect on the volume of international trade.

10 The final objectives of the members of the EMS appear to have been to: (a) ensure an area of economic and political stability; (b) reduce the opportunities for competitive devaluations by high-inflation countries; (c) exert external discipline over these countries.

11 The EMS is composed of the Exchange Rate Mechanism (ERM), which is intended to reduce exchange rate fluctuations, and credit facilities for countries with balance of payments difficulties.

12 The system has two mechanisms to ensure the stability of exchange rates. The first is a bilateral parity grid in which exchange rate fluctuations may occur within a band. The second, based on the ECU (a basket currency), is intended to ensure greater symmetry and provides for divergence thresholds for exchange rates. When a rate moves beyond its threshold, there is a presumption of intervention by the deviant country. Only limited use has been made of this second mechanism.

13 Realignments of central rates were frequent until 1983. They subsequently became quite rare before resurging in 1992. The variability of nominal and real exchange rates between ERM currencies has been less than that between other currencies.

14 The final stage of European Economic and Monetary Union will involve only those countries that have satisfied the convergence criteria established at Maastricht. The definitive fixing of exchange rates between participating currencies and between the latter and the euro, the European currency, is scheduled for 1 January 1999. The euro will replace the national currencies on 1 July 2002.

*15 The policy of relative stability of nominal exchange rates (the hard exchange rate policy) followed by high-inflation countries has had deflationary consequences that, together with the restrictive stance taken by Germany, have produced a much larger rise in unemployment than that recorded in non-ERM countries. However, it has reduced inflation to levels comparable with those in non-ERM countries.

16 International payments imbalances following 1971 have had two important specific effects (associated with the oil crisis and the foreign debt of the developing countries) and one general effect (deriving from the growth of Eurocurrency markets).

16.11 Key concepts

International economic transaction
Foreign exchange, foreign currency
Exports, imports of goods, services
Balance of trade
Unilateral (unrequited) transfer
Invisibles
Current account
Capital movements, flows
(Foreign) direct investment
Portfolio investment
Balance of payments surplus, deficit
Official reserves, official reserve assets
Balance of payments equilibrium,
    disequilibrium
Full equilibrium
Nominal bilateral, effective exchange rate
Price-quotation system
Volume-quotation system
Appreciation, depreciation
Real bilateral, effective exchange rate
Relative inflation
Gold standard
Mint parity
Gold-export point
Gold-import point
Fixed, floating (fluctuating, flexible)
    exchange rate
Gold exchange standard
Non-resident convertibility
Reserve currency
Adjustable peg
Devaluation, revaluation
Seignorage
Centrally-created reserves
International Monetary Fund (IMF)
Bilateralism (bilateral trade),
    multilateralism (multilateral trade)
Fundamental disequilibrium
Sterilisation
Dollar shortage
Special Drawing Rights
Basket currency or composite currency
Fiat money

Dirty (managed) float
Speculation
Dual (two-tier) foreign exchange market
Fluctuation margin, band
'Snake'
Overshooting
Currency cycle
Bootstrap
Purchasing-power-parity theory
Exchange rate mechanism (ERM)
Bilateral parity grid (grid of bilateral
    central rates, parities)
Narrow, wide band
Marginal, intramarginal intervention
Weight, quantity of currencies in the
    basket
Threshold of divergence, divergence
    indicator
Divergent currency
Presumption of intervention
(Parity) realignment
Credibility
European Economic and Monetary
    Union (EMU)
Treaty on European Union (Maastricht
    agreements, treaty)
European System of Central Banks
Currency competition (as a discovery
    device)
Parallel currency
Optimum currency area
*Hard exchange rate
*Hysteresis
Facility
Drawing
Recycling
Buy-back
Debt-equity swap
Debt-nature swap
Eurodollar, eurocurrency, xeno-currency
Eurobank
Spread
Eurobond

17 Balance of payments policies

17.1 Theory of the balance of payments

In section 16.1 we saw that the balance of payments is composed of two parts: the current account and the capital account. In the coming pages we will analyse the determinants of the two parts separately before turning to the determinants of the balance of payments as a whole.

17.1.1 The current account

Excluding unrequited transfers, which often involve non-economic considerations, the current account is made up of imports and exports of goods and services.

Let us take a world consisting of two 'countries', say the Netherlands (the home country) and the Rest of the World (the foreign country); we refer to the imports and exports of the home country.

Imports are normally made to depend on the level of demand (demand factors). In its simplest form, we have $M = mY$, where M denotes imports in real terms, m is the propensity to import and Y the level of domestic real income. The variable m is considered given in a first approximation, but in reality it depends on *structural factors*, which only change in the long run,[1] and on *factors of competitiveness*, i.e., the quality and other similar characteristics of goods (*non-price competitiveness*)[2] and the prices of domestic goods compared with those of foreign goods (*price competitiveness*).

Structural factors and most factors of non-price competitiveness are influenced by industrial policies, antitrust legislation, etc., which normally do not change in the short

---

[1] For example, other things being equal, a 'small' country or one lacking raw materials like the Netherlands will have a higher propensity to import.

[2] For example, the technology incorporated in a product, which affects its quality and its image, as well as the quantity and type of associated services offered, payment terms, etc.

run. Price and demand factors are normally affected by short-run macroeconomic policies.[3] Let us focus on price factors, which can be represented by the general price level (measured, for example, by the producer price index) in the home country, p, and that in the Rest of the World expressed in the foreign country's currency, p_w, as well as the nominal exchange rate, e. Given the exchange rate, the quantity imported will rise if p rises and decline if p_w rises. If p and p_w are given, we can assume that imports will fall as e rises.[4]

We can therefore write $m = m(\overset{+}{p}, \overset{-}{p}_w, \overset{-}{e})$ and then

$$M = m(\overset{+}{p}, \overset{-}{p}_w, \overset{-}{e})Y \tag{17.1}$$

where the signs of the partial derivatives are shown above the independent variables: for example, $(\partial m/\partial p > 0)$.[5] If we wish to introduce the real exchange rate e_r defined in section 16.2, we can write $M = m'(\overset{-}{e}_r)Y$.

We can also write a similar expression for exports, bearing in mind that the exports of the Netherlands, X, are simply the imports of the Rest of the World, M_w, which we can treat as we did with the imports of the Netherlands:

$$X = M_w = m_w(\overset{-}{p}, \overset{+}{p}_w, \overset{+}{e})Y_w \tag{17.2}$$

where M_w, m_w and Y_w are the imports, propensity to import and aggregate demand of the Rest of the World; the arguments of this propensity to import are again marked with the signs of the partial derivatives. Obviously, the signs of prices and the exchange rate are reversed in (17.2) with respect to those in (17.1), since the position of the Rest of the World is symmetric to that of the domestic country.

Introducing the real exchange rate, e_r, we would have: $X = m'_w(\overset{+}{e}_r)Y_w$.

In introductory macroeconomics textbooks a simple specification of the functions (17.1) and (17.2) is given: as to imports, $M = mY$, where m is constant; as to exports, $X = \bar{X}$. We want now to show how these simpler specifications can be related to ours. In the case of the import function there is no problem: the specification is the same; the only difference is that m is taken as constant by introductory textbooks. With reference to (17.1), the demand of the Rest of the World must be considered given, at least in a first approximation, since it cannot be influenced by a small country such as the Netherlands by means of changes in its domestic income and, therefore, its imports. If m_w is also considered constant, as is done in the first approximation for m in the import function when *it is assumed that structural and competitiveness factors are substantially constant*,

---

[3] Prices are also influenced by the policies cited earlier for non-price factors of competitiveness.

[4] As explained later in this chapter this is a shaky assumption. It is true that a higher exchange rate – i.e., a higher number of guilders for one unit of the foreign currency – has to be paid to buy foreign goods. A reduction in the physical quantity of imports will ensue. However, the value of imports denominated in the domestic currency will decline only if the proportionate decline in the physical quantity is higher than the proportionate increase in the domestic price of imports (see section 17.9).

[5] For readers who have not studied calculus, this simply means that an increase in domestic prices causes a rise in imports, *ceteris paribus*: a positive derivative means that the dependent and the independent variable we are considering move in the same direction; e.g., as p rises, m and, then, M rise.

(17.2) reduces to $X = \bar{m}_w \cdot \bar{Y}_w = \bar{X}$, where $\bar{m}_w$ and $\bar{Y}_w$ are the given values of the two variables. The apparent asymmetry between the functional form of exports ($X = \bar{X}$) and that of imports used in introductory textbooks ($M = mY$, with m constant) is thus explained. In reality, both depend on income, but in the case of exports the relevant income is that of the Rest of the World, which, for our small exporting country, is given. Exports can therefore be considered exogenous. The reader should bear in mind the fact that in the simpler specification of the import and export functions (i.e., $M = mY$, where m is constant, and $X = \bar{X}$), all possible causes of change in the propensity to import, both long and short run, including competitiveness factors, are ignored.

If we come back to (17.1) and (17.2) the current account balance in real terms of the Netherlands can be expressed as:

$$CA = X - M = f(\overset{+}{p}, \overset{+}{p}_w, \overset{+}{e}, \bar{Y}, \overset{+}{Y}_w) \tag{17.3}$$

or

$$CA = f'(\overset{+}{e}_r, \bar{Y}, \overset{+}{Y}_w)$$

It therefore depends on competitiveness factors (p, p_w, e) and demand factors (Y, Y_w).[6] In particular, a rise in the exchange rate always improves the current account balance in real terms. In what follows we will usually assume that p, p_w, Y_w are given; we could then express CA as a function of the nominal exchange rate and the domestic income only, i.e., $CA = g(\overset{+}{e}, \bar{Y})$.

17.1.2 Capital movements

Capital movements depend on long-term interest rate differentials (portfolio investment, long-term loans and credits), short-term interest rate differentials (short-term loans and speculative flows), as well as expected changes in exchange rates (especially, but not solely, for short-term and speculative flows). Direct investment is influenced by other variables and circumstances that are more difficult to represent in aggregate terms: differences in profit rates, the position of firms in their markets and related strategic matters, the size and rate of growth of the countries in question, etc. (Acocella, 1992a, 1992b).

If for simplicity we overlook direct investment and assume that in each country long-term rates are closely linked to short-term rates and their relationship does not change over time,[7] the balance of capital movements, KA, will only depend on interest rates (short or long-term) in the two countries and expected changes in the exchange rate:

$$KA = g(\overset{+}{i}, \overset{-}{i}_w, \bar{e}^e) \tag{17.4}$$

where i and i_w are interest rates in the Netherlands and the Rest of the World,

---

[6] However, recall the influence of structural and non-price competitiveness factors, which are not made explicit in (17.3) and in the expressions from which it is derived.
[7] We also assume that the expected change in the exchange rate is constant over time, so that it affects short- and long-term capital movements in the same way.

respectively, and $\dot{e}^e$ is the expected rate of change in the exchange rate of the guilder;[8] the signs of the partial derivatives are shown above the variables. In what follows we will usually consider i_w and $\dot{e}^e$ as given. In this case we could express the capital account as $KA = g'(i)$.

17.1.3 The balance of payments

The overall balance of payments is the sum of the current account and capital account balances. It can be written as:

$$BP = CA + KA = \psi(\overset{-}{p}, \overset{+}{p_w}, \overset{+}{e}, \overset{-}{Y}, \overset{+}{Y_w}, \overset{+}{i}, \overset{-}{i_w}, \overset{-}{\dot{e}^e}) \tag{17.5}$$

The balance of payments thus depends on:

(a) the balance on current account, which is a function of:
price competitiveness factors (p, p_w, e), i.e., the real exchange rate, e_r;
demand factors (Y, Y_w);
(b) the balance on capital account, which depends on interest rate differentials and the expected change in the exchange rate $(i, i_w, \dot{e}^e)$.

If we consider $p, p_w, Y_w i_w, \dot{e}^e$ as given, we have: $BP = h(e, Y, i)$.

These elements of the theory of the balance of payments will be helpful in understanding the possibilities for automatic adjustment of the balance and the factors that economic policymakers can act on to redress imbalances.

17.2 Balance of payments equilibrium and disequilibrium

By balance of payments equilibrium we mean a situation in which the sum of the current account balance and the capital account balance is equal to zero.

Equilibrium of the balance of payments is a long-run economic policy objective, in the sense that a country must seek on average to offset deficits it may run in some periods with surpluses from other periods. The pursuit of continuous surpluses is feasible in

---

[8] The so-called *uncovered* (i.e., without cover on the forward market) *interest-rate parity* of capital movements can be written as: $i = i_w + \dot{e}^e$. It assumes perfect substitutability between domestic and foreign financial assets with the same yield in a given unit of account (currency); see Gandolfo (1995).

We can easily demonstrate the validity of the indicated equilibrium condition. Take two financial liabilities issued by the same debtor but denominated in two different currencies, guilders and marks. Over a certain time span (one year, for example) they should pay the same return in a given currency. If the nominal values of the two liabilities in guilders and marks are shown by K_{FL} and K_{DM}, respectively, and e^e is the expected exchange rate at the end of the year, (K_{FL}/e^e) gives the equivalent in marks of the capital value of the liability in guilders. Indicating the rate of change in a variable over the time period with a dot, $\dot{K}_{DM}$ gives the rate of return in marks of the liability denominated in marks and (K_{FL}/e^e) gives the rate of return in marks of the guilder-denominated liability. The indifference condition between the two liabilities can therefore be written as $\dot{K}_{DM} = (K_{FL}/e^e)$. However, the rate of return in marks of the mark-denominated liability is given by the prevailing interest rate in Germany, i_D, while $(K_{FL}/e^e) \cong \dot{K}_{FL} - \dot{e}^e$, where the rate of return in guilders of the guilder-denominated liability is equal to the rate of interest in the Netherlands, i. Thus, the indifference condition between the two liabilities can be written as $i_D = i - \dot{e}^e$, or $i = i_D + \dot{e}^e$.

appearance, while persistent deficits are not, since they would eventually exhaust the country's foreign reserves and make further net payments abroad impossible. An exception to this is when the country is itself the issuer of a reserve currency that is accepted without limits by the other country (for instance, under a gold exchange standard in which the convertibility of the reserve currency is, for whatever reason, always credible).

Upon closer analysis, however, running a constant surplus is not feasible either, since it implies a persistent deficit for the other country, which is not technically possible in general, as we have said. Therefore, when we speak of persistent surpluses, we mean a country that runs a balance of payments surplus for a long but not infinite period.

A surplus is certainly preferable to a deficit, but it may be awkward for two reasons:

(a) it implies deficits for other countries, which may be important when a country's international stance is markedly cooperative (although this is quite rare);
(b) it may give rise to domestic inflationary pressures; recall that a balance of payments surplus is a source of monetary base: if it proves difficult to sterilise through other sources (see section 18.3), monetary base may expand fast enough to generate inflation.

A country may also seek to limit, if not eliminate, balance of payments surpluses for another reason. In reality, if it wants to increase the world market shares of national firms it can try, on the one hand, to achieve a surplus on current account and, on the other, to pursue a deficit on capital account (especially in terms of direct investment). Thus the deficit on capital account will at least in part offset positive current account balances.

We said that balance of payments equilibrium is a long-run objective. In the short term, the aim may be different. Depending on the circumstances, the variety of objectives can include: reducing the deficit, balancing international transactions or running a surplus. We will therefore analyse the following problems: assuming there is a balance of payments disequilibrium (surplus or deficit):

(a) are there forces working for automatic adjustment?
(b) if not, or if they are not sufficiently strong, what *adjustment policies* are possible?

We examine the first problem in the next section and the second problem in the sections that follow.

17.3 Automatic adjustment mechanisms

Automatic adjustment mechanisms can operate for both the current account and the capital account. These mechanisms are normally analysed separately, with the former usually receiving more attention, a practice we will follow here.

The capital account can adjust if capital movements are sufficiently mobile. Given exchange rate expectations, the net inflow of capital induced when domestic interest rates are higher than foreign rates will cause domestic rates to fall and foreign rates to rise, eliminating the initial differential. In reality, this has a simultaneous effect on the current account, and we should therefore examine the overall process of balance of payments adjustment. Somewhat greater detail of this process can be obtained from the analysis of a model of flow disequilibria of the sort suggested by Fleming and Mundell, which will be presented in section 18.1.

Under floating exchange rates, adjustment of the current account is assured by the flexibility of the exchange rate, which affects competitiveness. Under a fixed exchange rate regime, two adjustment mechanisms operate, both of which affect the current account. The first is based on price changes, which – like exchange rate movements – cause variations in the competitiveness of domestic and foreign goods; the second is based on income changes. We will examine these in order.

17.3.1 Price changes

Price changes were emphasised by the classics with reference to actual situations (such as the gold standard and the relative flexibility of prices) and theories (such as the quantity theory of money) with which they were familiar. The hypothesis of a gold standard system is not essential to the operation of the mechanism;[9] the other hypotheses – those underlying the quantity theory of money – are, however.

Assume there are only two countries, A and B. Beginning in equilibrium, country A for some reason accumulates a balance of payments deficit. Conversely, country B will run a surplus. A's loss of gold will reduce its money supply and, if the conditions for the validity of the quantity theory are met, prices will decline. The exact opposite will occur in country B. Consequently, the prices of goods produced by country A will decline with respect to those produced by country B. Other things being equal, this change in relative prices will generally improve the current account of A (see (17.5)). This process will continue until the balance of payments equilibrates.

This mechanism could also operate in monetary systems other than the gold standard, as long as they ensure that the price changes we have described occur in at least one of the two countries. Since price flexibility in modern economies is asymmetric, i.e., prices rise more easily than they fall, it would be sufficient for prices to rise at an adequate rate and by an adequate amount in the country running a surplus; i.e., for there to be an appropriate inflation differential between the two countries (in our example, prices in A must rise less rapidly than in B).[10]

However, bear in mind that the problems facing the operation of this mechanism are not simply a consequence of the specific features of modern economies. Adjustment has never occurred without difficulties and social costs, even when economies did not have the technological, financial and institutional rigidities they do today. Moreover, adjustment takes time. For these reasons, even when policymakers had confidence in the mechanism and some of the conditions for its operation were satisfied, adjustment *policies* were nonetheless undertaken. Faced with a decline in gold reserves (or even the

---

[9] There must be a link between international gold movements, generated by balance of payments disequilibria, and changes in the domestic money supply. A gold standard is a sufficient but not necessary condition for the existence of such a link.

[10] Another kind of asymmetry can arise in the case when the domestic country is small. Changes in the quantity of money (and in the level of domestic prices) tend to equilibrate the balance of payments also in the absence of significant money (and price) changes in the Rest of the World.

mere expectation that they would decline), central banks usually reacted by raising the discount rate in order to attract foreign funds immediately. In due course this policy measure also had a dampening effect on domestic economic activity, thus reducing imports. Such a policy action seems to have been even more effective than the automatic adjustment mechanism we have described. Nevertheless, it also has social costs, in that it depresses domestic demand (and employment).

17.3.2 Income changes

A different automatic mechanism relies on changes in income associated with balance of payment disequilibria.

Let us again consider two countries, A and B. Assume that the balance of payments is initially in equilibrium and that there is an exogenous increase in A's exports. This will cause B's current account balance to deteriorate and will improve A's, if demand in A remains unchanged. However, this occurs only in part. Let us examine the reasons for this. The increase in A's exports will cause A's income to rise, since exports are a positive component of aggregate demand.[11] The increase in income will cause imports to rise in turn, according to (17.1). The country thus moves from equilibrium to surplus (owing to the increase in exports) and then to a decline in the surplus (owing to the increase in imports). The opposite happens in country B, where the rise in A's exports causes an initial balance of payments deficit. If the level of autonomous expenditure on domestic output in B decreases simultaneously by the same amount, there will be a decline in income that will produce a fall in imports, while exports will rise as an effect of the higher imports by A, where demand has increased.

This mechanism probably acts more rapidly than that based on price movements (since downward price flexibility usually takes a long time), but it does not guarantee perfect adjustment under the conditions normally assumed in Keynesian models[12] and,

---

[11] In an open economy, we have: $Y = C + I + G + X - M$; taking account of the relevant behavioural functions in a simple Keynesian model that considers only the real economy and ignores price factors ($C = cY; I = \bar{I}; M = mY$) we have the following reduced form:

$$Y = \frac{1}{1 - c + m}(\bar{I} + G + X)$$

We will see later that the more complicated versions of the Keynesian model do not ignore price factors. Nevertheless, the direct relationship between exports and income remains valid.

[12] Full adjustment would occur only if the marginal propensity to consume were equal to unity, an assumption which is normally rejected by Keynesian models for stability considerations. This can be shown with a simple form of such models: in order for the initial increase in exports, ΔX, to lead to full adjustment, there must be an equal increase in imports:

$$\Delta X = \Delta M \tag{17.6}$$

Considering that:

$$\Delta M = m\Delta Y \tag{17.7}$$

$$\Delta Y = \frac{1}{1 - c + m}\Delta X \tag{17.8}$$

and substituting (17.7) and (17.8) into the previous condition imposing adjustment, we have: Dividing both terms by ΔX, we have:

above all, it generates social costs associated with the variations (especially reductions) in income and employment caused by its operation. In the previous example, country B experiences a reduction in employment owing to the increase in import demand until the adjustment is complete. If there is underadjustment, the reduction in employment will never be fully absorbed.

17.4 Adjustment policies and the causes of disequilibrium

Both automatic adjustment mechanisms of the balance of payments described above can operate in the real world. Indeed, they may do so at the same time. We have separated them for analytical reasons only and will continue to do so in this section.

In the light of our discussion, the Keynesian mechanism has the advantage of probably being more rapid, but it may not allow full readjustment and, above all, it imposes relatively high social costs. The price movement mechanism is hindered by the imperfect (downward) flexibility of prices – which takes time – and the absence of the conditions on which the quantity theory is based (constant velocity of circulation, full employment).

Accordingly, achieving balance of payments equilibrium under fixed exchange rates requires specific government intervention. However, the form of such intervention must be tailored to the causes of the imbalance. We first examine those regarding the capital account (section 17.5) and subsequently move on to those involving the current account (section 17.6 for imbalances caused by the level of demand and section 17.7 for those relating to competitiveness).

Before beginning this discussion, it is helpful to consider that, in general, understanding the factors on which the balance of payments depends would enable policymakers to adjust any imbalance whatsoever (for example, one caused by poor competitiveness) with measures aimed at any of the variables on which the balance depends (for example, increasing the differential between domestic and foreign interest rates). In this case they could offset the current account deficit caused by poor competitiveness with a surplus on capital account.[13] Nevertheless, it is always advisable to target the same factors that caused the imbalance in the first place: in our example, we should take steps to redress the competitiveness problems.

$$\Delta X = m \Delta X / (1 - c + m) \tag{17.9}$$

Dividing both sides by ΔX and rearranging, we have

$$1 - c + m = m \tag{17.10}$$

i.e., $c = 1$ if we desire full adjustment.

If $c < 1$, as is normally assumed, there would be underadjustment. However, it is possible to have full adjustment or even overadjustment (i.e., situations in which an initial shock of ΔX triggers a larger rise in imports: $\Delta M > \Delta X$), if there is a positive (and sufficiently high) marginal propensity to invest (Gandolfo, 1995, section 13.2).

[13] However, there are limits to the effectiveness of certain policies in certain situations. We will see later that policies to increase competitiveness through changes in the exchange rate are ineffective if there is excess demand.

17.5 Policies for adjustment on capital account

In the absence both of barriers to capital movements and differences in the riskiness of debtors, equilibrium on the foreign exchange market is achieved when the domestic interest rate is equal to the foreign interest rate, increased by the expected rate of change in the exchange rate. The latter represents the specific risk[14] faced by an agent who purchases an asset denominated in the foreign currency:

$$i = i_w + \dot{e}^e \qquad\qquad (17.11)$$

If the exchange rate is expected to remain stable, this condition reduces to the elimination of interest rate differentials.[15] If world interest rates are higher (lower) than domestic ones, there will be capital outflows (inflows).

Given the foreign interest rate, simple monetary policy operations will allow the capital account to improve: in the case of a deficit, for instance, policymakers can reduce the quantity of monetary base and thus the money supply in order to obtain an increase in the domestic interest rate and an improvement in the capital account; they should do the opposite if they want to reduce the capital account balance. However, we have already noted the drawbacks of this measure, which causes income in the deficit country to fall as the interest rate rises. Under certain circumstances, or if there are no alternatives to a restrictive monetary policy stance, these drawbacks cannot be avoided. In other circumstances, they can be avoided by resorting to other instruments, such as controls on capital movements, which we will discuss shortly. Of course, the latter policy instrument has negative effects as well. Accordingly, the choice of one or the other policy option cannot be decided *a priori* by rejecting direct controls out of hand, although this is often done. Instead, a variety of circumstances need to be assessed, such as the severity of unemployment, the sensitivity of investment to the interest rate, the degree to which capital movements are speculative in nature, the effectiveness of capital controls, etc.

The most interesting aspects of adjustment policies for the capital account come into play in the presence of expectations of a change in the exchange rate. If these were entirely exogenous to the behaviour of policymakers, no specific issues would arise. In the real world, however, this hypothesis does not hold. There are many links between public policy and expectations of exchange rate variations. First, monetary policy itself, with which policymakers can influence domestic interest rates, also has an impact on exchange rate expectations. Take a situation where the foreign interest rate is equal to the domestic rate and investors expect the domestic currency to depreciate. In this case, there would be an outflow of capital, which could be stemmed by adopting a more restrictive monetary policy stance. Now, the restriction should raise domestic interest rates by less than the size of the initial expected depreciation, since it is likely that the

---

[14] The risk is 'specific' in that it is not related to different degrees of creditworthiness of debtors in the two countries (assumed equal) but simply to the possibility of variations in the exchange rate. The agent is assumed to be risk-neutral, so as not to seek forward cover.

[15] Obviously, as with our previous conclusions, this is strictly dependent on the hypotheses we have made (generally, absence of barriers to capital movements and equal riskiness of debtors, in addition to expectations of a stable exchange rate for the specific condition just introduced in the text).

restriction itself will influence expectations, reducing them. Similarly, other government policies can affect exchange rate expectations and facilitate the adjustment of capital movements.

Nevertheless, these considerations hold only within certain limits. First, they are valid only if the expected exchange rate variations are small; when they are large, corrective monetary action is practically impossible. For example, consider a situation where a 10 per cent devaluation of a currency within at most ten days is expected with near certainty. Buying foreign currency today and repurchasing the domestic currency after the devaluation will generate an expected capital gain of 10 per cent within ten days, which is equal to an annualised gain of at least $(365/10) \cdot 10\% = 365\%$! In order to counter such expectations and the consequent investment behaviour, the monetary authorities would have to raise interest rates to a level close to the expected (annualised) return generated by the devaluation.[16] However, such action will probably be ineffective[17] if the expected devaluation is large. It may even be counterproductive: the abnormality of the measure may create alarm or at the very least confirm investors' expectations. If these investors include powerful financial intermediaries, or even other types of firms with large cash holdings, they may be encouraged to bet on a 'sure thing' by investing their capital abroad for speculative purposes.

Another limit on using a tight monetary policy to reduce expectations of devaluation consists in the possible repercussions on the budget: a rise in interest rates increases interest payments on the public debt.[18]

Let us now consider the effects of EMS membership on a country with a large public debt and high (cost-push) inflation. Some argue that such membership would increase the 'credibility' of the country, in particular reducing expectations of a devaluation. Nevertheless, financial markets do not believe in agreements and treaties if these are not backed up by daily action and, in any case, good balance of payments performance. Assuming that the government does not use fiscal policy to reduce the (primary) budget deficit and incomes policy to lower labour costs – policies that would also produce an improvement in the current account – the credibility of its commitment to maintaining its parity in the ERM depends on a restrictive monetary policy stance. However, raising interest rates, which may in itself enhance credibility, has a negative impact on the budget, thus possibly undermining credibility on that side. The effect on the public finances of a restrictive monetary policy is therefore uncertain.[19]

The more general problem is that international capital movements:

(a) have become excessively sensitive, especially to expectations of exchange rate variations;

[16] This is exactly what the Swedish central bank did during the exchange rate crisis of September 1992, raising interest rates to an annualised 500 per cent.
[17] In fact, the Swedish krona had to be devalued.
[18] Moreover, high interest rates that even produce capital account surpluses (and therefore foreign debt) may have an adverse impact on the current account as a result of the increased outlays of foreign currency for payment of interest on that debt (see sections 7.5 and *18.6).
[19] Such situations have in fact occurred in the real world. The case that most closely fits the assumed conditions was that of Italy in 1992, but the same sort of problem arose in France and in other countries in 1992–3.

(b) are now so large that they can themselves ensure that the expected event occurs, whether the forecast is well-founded or not, as long as agents have sufficient financial resources, as is the case with large multinational firms.

These observations are the basis of fairly widespread proposals to limit the freedom of international capital movements with direct controls (such as administrative rules imposing information requirements, limits on foreign exchange outflows, etc.) or indirect controls (imposing an explicit tax – called the *Tobin tax*[20] – or an implicit tax by requiring a non-interest-bearing deposit equal to the entire capital outflow or some fraction thereof[21]). The effect of these limitations – initially suggested by Tobin (1978) and more recently reproposed by other authors, such as Eichengreen and Wyplosz (1993) – would create a diaphragm or wedge between domestic interest rates and foreign interest rates, enabling policymakers to keep the former lower than the latter without triggering capital outflows. Nevertheless, much attention must be paid to the possibility that agents will find ways to circumvent the controls (for example, through the overinvoicing or *underinvoicing* of exports of goods and services).[22] To be effective in the long term, such controls must be pervasive and in some cases require the cooperation of foreign countries. They would nonetheless be effective in the short term, helping to avoid unexpected speculative crises: arranging evasion and avoidance of controls takes time, enabling policymakers to adopt appropriate corrective measures.

17.6 Adjustment policies for excess or insufficient demand

Recall from equation (17.3) that the balance of the current account is an inverse function of the level of domestic demand and a direct function of foreign demand.

The home country's policymakers cannot affect foreign demand, if not through appeals to the Rest of the World (in practice, the leading foreign countries) to expand its economy, acting as a *locomotive* for the home economy.[23]

On the other hand, policymakers can take measures to affect the level of domestic demand, restricting (expanding) it to reduce a current account deficit (surplus) if the current account imbalance is the result of excess (insufficient) domestic demand with respect to productive capacity.

The instruments for implementing such variations in domestic demand are those we have examined at length in previous chapters, fiscal and monetary policy in particular.

---

[20] Tobin sought to throw 'sand in the wheels' of international financial markets.

[21] This would reduce the return on investment abroad. Such a control, which can also be viewed as a form of prudential supervision, was adopted in Italy in the 1970s and in Spain in 1992. It does not conflict either with the Maastricht agreements or the Single European Act (Eichengreen and Wyplosz, 1993, p. 77).

[22] It is possible to export capital by overinvoicing imports and/or underinvoicing exports. In the case of multinational firms, these transactions are simple indeed, since transfers of goods and services are not at arm's length, i.e., they do not take place between independent trading partners but rather between different units of the same company: it is therefore easier to adjust the prices of internal transfers (as the reader will recall, these are called *transfer prices*).

[23] We are assuming fixed exchange rates or flexible exchange rates when these are not completely isolating.

The only difference with regard to the problems now under examination is that whereas earlier we viewed increases in demand as desirable *per se*, we have now considered them as an intermediate target with respect to the final objective of adjusting the current account.

In reality, increases in demand and current account adjustment can both be final objectives. In this case, they may conflict (or be inconsistent). For example, in the presence of unemployment, the use of demand-restricting measures to adjust a current account deficit would worsen the employment problem; similarly, measures aiming at raising aggregate demand, thereby reducing unemployment, would cause a worsening of the current account. The situation is difficult to solve with short-run, aggregate policies: structural measures for unemployment and/or the balance of payments are needed.

17.7 Policies for competitiveness

From equation (17.3) we know that apart from demand factors, current account disequilibria can also depend on excessive or insufficient competitiveness. Let us examine the matter in more detail. Take a homogeneous good produced in both the Netherlands and the Rest of the World, limiting our examination to competitiveness factors only. If we consider competitiveness factors only and assume away any kind of transportation costs or market 'imperfection', and no capacity constraints to meeting demand, international arbitrage implies:

$$p = p_w \cdot e \tag{17.12}$$

i.e., there is no advantage to exporting or importing if the price of the domestic good in guilders is equal to the price of the foreign good in dollars times the exchange rate (which corresponds to the price of the foreign good in guilders).[24] If the left-hand side of (17.12) is greater than the right-hand side, Dutch goods are less competitive; if it is smaller, they are more competitive. Therefore, a current account imbalance due to excess or insufficient competitiveness (meaning that (17.12) is not satisfied) can be eliminated, thus re-establishing the equality in (17.12), by adjusting each of the three variables in the equation or their underlying factors:

(a) p or, better, the factors on which this variable depends (essentially wages, productivity and profit margins) can be adjusted;
(b) e, i.e., the nominal exchange rate, can be adjusted: under a fixed exchange rate regime, this can be done by devaluing (setting a higher parity or central rate) or revaluing (setting a lower parity or central rate) in the case of insufficient or excessive competitiveness, respectively; in a system of managed floating rates it is done by letting the currency depreciate or appreciate;
(c) it would appear impossible to affect p_w, since the factors underlying the dollar

---

[24] Obviously, these conditions are not met in reality and only for simplicity do we assume that they are.

  The true significance of condition (17.12) is to highlight factors which have an influence on the current account: a fall in p or a rise in p_w and e will all tend to stimulate exports and depress imports.

price of the foreign good are beyond the reach of Dutch policymakers; however, the same effect can be attained through protectionist policies (such as levying a tariff) that increase the price of the foreign good, rather than acting directly on the exchange rate.[25]

We discussed the policies regarding point (a) in chapter 15. Those in point (c) are examined in section 17.11. More space is devoted to the adjustment of the exchange rate in section 17.8, where we discuss its controllability, and sections 17.9 and 17.10, where we examine the effectiveness of exchange rate adjustments.

17.8 The controllability of the exchange rate

Controllability is related to the exchange rate regime. First we examine the case of fixed exchange rates. In all fixed exchange rate systems (gold standard, gold exchange standard, EMS), if the exchange rate is actually fixed (i.e., if the fluctuation limits are close to the parity or central rate), in what sense is the exchange rate a controllable variable and therefore a practicable policy instrument? In other words, does not the fixity of the exchange rate conflict with its controllability? The problem appears substantive but is in fact only semantic. In this case, control is exercised through the variable to which the exchange rate is linked, i.e., the parity or the central rate:[26] policymakers change the exchange rate (or rather, the band within which it can fluctuate) by altering the parity or central rate (with a devaluation or revaluation).

A similar problem arises with floating exchange rate regimes. In theory, in such systems the exchange rate is completely free to move in both directions (free floating). If the exchange rate is free floating, how can it be an instrumental variable? Flexibility and controllability would seem irreconcilable. Nevertheless, controllability (or effective control) implies that the exchange rate is not entirely free floating, or rather it does not react only to market forces but also reflects government intervention. In the real world, floating exchange rate regimes have never been entirely free (or 'clean') floating; they have instead tended to be managed regimes, as we noted in chapter 16.

17.9 The effectiveness of exchange rate adjustment

17.9.1 Demand elasticity conditions

Effectiveness means that changes in the exchange rate induced by government action[27] have an effect on some variable, specifically the level of income and/or the variables making up the balance of payments, notably the current account. In what follows we will refer specifically to the balance of payments, setting aside the effects of changes in the

---

[25] Instead of acting on the underlying variables of price competitiveness *in absolute terms*, we can take measures to affect *changes* in the variables if we are interested in *changes* in the current account balance.

[26] It is also possible to influence the level of the exchange rate to some degree within the allowed fluctuation margins by appropriate intervention in the foreign exchange market.

[27] In what follows we will refer to the effects of such action simply as depreciation or appreciation of the currency. This may be the effect of government intervention in the foreign exchange market, in a floating regime, or of a devaluation or revaluation, in a fixed exchange rate regime.

exchange rate on aggregate demand. The reader will note, however, the link between the two targets from what we will say later. Let us refer to the balance on current account in nominal terms, CA_m, which can be expressed as:

$$CA_m = p_x q_x - (p_m e)q_m \tag{17.13}$$

where p_x and p_m are the prices of imports and exports in the currency of the country of origin (p_x in domestic currency, p_m in foreign currency); e is the quantity of domestic currency per unit of foreign currency; q_x and q_m are physical quantities of exports and imports, respectively.[28]

For an intuitive grasp of some of the conditions (elasticity conditions) that must be met for a rise in the exchange rate (depreciation) to improve the current account balance in nominal terms, let us begin with a situation where the current account is in equilibrium ($CA_m = 0$) and p_x and p_m are given and constant even after changes in the exchange rate. We will later discuss the justification of the latter assumption.

Setting the right-hand side of (17.13) equal to zero, we can write the initial balance of the current account as:

$$\frac{p_x q_x}{p_m e q_m} = 1 \tag{17.14}$$

or

$$\frac{p_x}{p_m e} \cdot \frac{q_x}{q_m} = 1 \tag{17.15}$$

Equation (17.15) gives us the terms of the problem exactly.

An increase in e will normally cause q_x to rise and q_m to fall, but it will also simultaneously reduce the price of domestic goods with respect to the price of foreign goods expressed in the domestic currency. That is, it will worsen the terms of trade, $TT = p_x/(p_m e)$,[29] since e has increased while p_x and p_m have been assumed to remain constant.

---

[28] It is implicitly assumed that the reference currency is the domestic currency. Using the foreign currency as the reference would not alter our conclusions.

The reader may ask what the relationship between q_x and X, and q_m and M is. We have said that q_x and q_m are physical quantities of exports and imports. X and M are values, expressed in terms of the common unit of all the components of aggregate demand, which usually is the GDP price deflator, p. In other terms, $X = p_x q_x/p$; $M = p_m e q_m/p$. $\left(\text{In the special but often assumed case } p_x = p \right.$ and $p_m = p_w$, we would have $X = q_x$; $M = \dfrac{p_w \cdot e}{p} q_m.\Big)$

The reader should note that $CA = CA_m/p$. Since p is assumed to be constant (or to vary parametrically), if a depreciation improves the current account in monetary terms, then it improves the current account in real terms as well.

[29] The terms of trade are defined differently from the real exchange rate, despite their apparent formal similarity to the inverse of the latter. The variables p_x and p_m indicate the prices (or unit values) of exports and imports rather than the general price level (as measured by producer or wholesale prices or other indices of tradable goods), as is the case with the real exchange rate. The difference reflects the different analytical purposes of the two indicators: the real exchange rate is an indicator of potential competitiveness and the prices it refers to are prices that can be applied in international trade, if profit margins in the domestic and foreign market are the same. The terms of trade are a relative price, and the prices whose ratio determines the terms of trade are those used in actual (as opposed to potential) international trade. They are therefore in some sense an *ex post* indicator of

From (17.14) we can state that if exports, q_x, did not react to the depreciation (i.e., if the elasticity of foreign demand with respect to the price of the domestic good, ε_x, were zero), the entire burden of improving the current account would be borne by the denominator and q_m would have to fall by a larger percentage than that by which e increases; that is, the elasticity of imports would have to be greater than $1(\varepsilon_m > 1)$ for it to improve the current account balance.[30] If, however, the volume of imports did not change at all with respect to changes in the exchange rate ($\varepsilon_m = 0$), the burden of balancing the increase in e in the denominator of (17.14) would fall entirely on q_x, which would have to increase by a greater percentage (i.e., $\varepsilon_x > 1$).[31] However, if we allow for a positive elasticity of both exports and imports, the condition for the improvement of the current account following a depreciation or devaluation is obviously that $\varepsilon_m + \varepsilon_x > 1$.[32] This is known as the *Marshall–Lerner condition* for the effectiveness of a depreciation (devaluation).

We have so far either implicitly or explicitly introduced a variety of assumptions that we should examine closely:

competitiveness. (In both cases the ratios are not used in terms of the absolute values of the variables but rather in terms of their index numbers, i.e., to express changes in competitiveness.)

[30] We can refer indifferently to the elasticity of imports to the exchange rate or to prices in the domestic currency, since it is assumed that the price of foreign goods in foreign currency, p_m, is constant. In this case the price of these goods in domestic currency changes by the same percentage as the exchange rate.

[31] We can speak indifferently in terms of the elasticity of exports with respect to the exchange rate or to prices in foreign currency since the increase in the exchange rate enables domestic producers to lower the foreign currency price of exports by an amount equal to the depreciation of the currency, leaving the domestic currency price of exports unchanged, as we have assumed. In other words, we assume that the export price in domestic currency, p_x, remains unchanged while the exchange rate increases, which means that the foreign currency price of exports will fall by the same proportion. Thus, speaking of the elasticity of exports to the exchange rate or prices is the same thing.

[32] The formal demonstration is fairly simple. With $CA_m = 0$ initially, we can write:

$$\frac{p_x q_x}{p_m e q_m} = 1 \qquad (17.16)$$

If p_x and p_m remain constant and e increases, the improvement in the balance means that:

$$\dot{q}_x - \dot{e} - \dot{q}_m > 0 \qquad (17.17)$$

where the dots over the variables indicate the rate of increase per unit of time. Divide (17.17) by $\dot{e}$. We then have:

$$\frac{\dot{q}_x}{\dot{e}} - \frac{\dot{q}_m}{\dot{e}} > 1$$

but

$$\frac{\dot{q}_x}{\dot{e}} = \frac{dq_x}{q_x} \Big/ \frac{de}{e} = \varepsilon_x$$

and

$$\frac{\dot{q}_m}{\dot{e}} = \frac{dq_m}{q_m} \Big/ \frac{de}{e} = -\varepsilon_m$$

Therefore, we must have $\varepsilon_m + \varepsilon_x > 1$. For a generalisation of the problem and some reservations about the significance of these conditions for an improvement in the current account, see Gandolfo (1995).

(a) p_x and p_m are given;
(b) there are no constraints on the supply of export goods (as well as the supply of foreign goods for import);
(c) prices and quantities exported and imported adjust instantly;
(d) there are no effects on expectations regarding future exchange rate variations.

Let us examine the problems raised by these assumptions in order.

17.9.2 The pass-through of exchange rate variations to prices

The hypothesis that p_x and p_m are given is meant to express the idea that the prices of internationally traded goods are constant in domestic currencies and, as exchange rates change, prices on foreign markets change accordingly. If our home country is the Netherlands, as in the previous example, a given increase in the exchange rate of the guilder would lower the dollar prices of Dutch goods by the same amount as the rise in the exchange rate; similarly, it would leave the dollar prices of foreign goods unchanged and increase their prices in guilders. This can only happen if we make certain assumptions about the features of the different markets. For example, the dollar price of Dutch goods will fall in exactly the same proportion as the depreciation if there is perfect competition among the Dutch producers of each exported good that represents a significant part of the world supply of the good.[33] By contrast, the dollar prices of goods imported into the Netherlands will remain unchanged if the domestic market accounts for only a small fraction of the world market for these goods. Obviously, if these assumptions do not hold, then the depreciation may not be entirely passed through to the foreign currency prices of exports or the guilder prices of imports.

It is entirely possible that these conditions do not hold in the real world. Given that markets are usually not perfectly competitive, firms have the power to pass the depreciation through to foreign currency prices on the basis of a number of factors.

Let us take a more detailed look at some elements that must be considered in the process of deciding how much of the depreciation to pass through.

For example, take a Dutch firm that sells its product in the United States at a unit price of $100. At the initial exchange rate of Fl 2/$1, this will generate a unit revenue of Fl 200. If the guilder depreciates by 10 per cent, the firm must decide how much of the depreciation it must (and can) pass through to the dollar price, lowering it so as to increase foreign demand. This decision will be dictated by company objectives (e.g., maximising profits). The firm will consider the fact that the larger the pass-through, the lower the unit revenues in guilders and the lower the *unit* profit, other things being equal. On the other hand, a larger pass-through will increase foreign demand. The greater the elasticity the lower the need to have a larger pass-through to boost demand. The firm must therefore weigh both effects, which have an opposite impact on profits.

The pattern of production costs introduces a further element. If there are scale

---

[33] The requirement that the good represents a large part of the total world supply can be thought of as being met for such goods as tulips (for the Netherlands), whisky (for the UK), champagne (for France), olive oil and pasta (for Italy), etc.

economies, a larger pass-through will not necessarily lower unit profit, since the increase in demand – and therefore production – caused by the pass-through will lower average costs, which will increase unit profit. In this case, even the complete pass-through of the depreciation to the foreign currency price could increase the unit profit and therefore benefit the firm, prompting it to alter the allocation of resources between goods produced for the domestic market and those produced for export in favour of the latter.

There may also be cases in which the complete pass-through of the depreciation may prove advantageous even if it does not increase unit profits, since it increases the demand for the domestic firm's good. Assume that the firm has excess capacity owing to weak domestic and foreign demand and is therefore 'rationed' on the demand side. The depreciation offers an opportunity to increase foreign demand, which will rise as a direct function of the size of the pass-through. It is likely that unit profits will also rise owing to the scope for lowering the unit incidence of fixed costs (since productive capacity is being more completely used). But even if this does not occur, the increase in foreign demand, by eliminating rationing, may still be beneficial since it will increase total profits, even with unchanged unit profits. This is the case in a depression, when the problem is to use the available resources as completely as possible and not change their allocation, making it more attractive to sell abroad than on the domestic market.

We can therefore conclude that the pass-through is larger the lower is the price elasticity of foreign demand, the higher are the scale economies and the level of domestic and foreign demand in individual sectors and in the economy as a whole.

17.9.3 The elasticity of supply

Let us now consider the implicit assumption that there are no supply side constraints on exports (or imports), i.e., that supply elasticity is infinite in both countries. This means that if demand is sufficiently elastic (i.e., the Marshall–Lerner condition is met), supply will always adjust to it – without any change in supply prices, which are assumed to be constant – and the current account will improve.

In order for the increase in demand generated by the devaluation to be fully met, supply must be elastic in all relevant sectors (or markets). High supply elasticity at the aggregate level and not just in individual markets presupposes the only partial use of physical resources and labour; otherwise, supply may not be able to adjust sufficiently to the increase in demand, making the depreciation ineffective.

To examine the consequences of insufficient supply elasticity, we must abandon our assumption that p_x and p_m and the general price level in the two countries are constant. An increase in the exchange rate gives rise to an increase in demand, which in full employment will lead exclusively to an increase in all prices, including those of exports. In a situation of demand-pull inflation (either already under way or incipient), adjusting the exchange rate will therefore be ineffective. In other words, devaluing the currency or letting (making) it depreciate will not improve the current account for an economy with full employment. On the contrary, in such a situation the deficit may be at least partly due to the pressure of domestic demand, which a depreciation would only increase, accentuating demand-pull inflation. Policymakers must therefore use depreciation or devaluation with care. The incentive to recoup competitiveness lost as a result of domestic inflation is strong. However, if this was caused by the pressure of demand, depreciation would be an inappropriate response, as it would trigger a vicious circle of inflation–depreciation–inflation.

The adverse effect of an increase in the exchange rate on domestic prices can be channelled through costs as well as demand. The increase in the exchange rate is reflected in a rise in the prices of imported goods, and if these are used in the production of domestic goods – as in the case of raw materials – the production cost of domestic goods will rise. This effect will be accentuated (dampened) by excess (insufficient) domestic demand with respect to the country's productive capacity. The recent experience of two European countries, the United Kingdom and Italy, is exemplary. Both saw their currencies depreciate sharply from September 1992 onwards. Despite a depreciation of the pound of more than 12 per cent in terms of the effective exchange rate, inflation in the United Kingdom fell from 6.5 per cent to 3.4 per cent between 1991 and 1993; similarly, despite an effective depreciation of the lira of 18 per cent, inflation fell from 7.75 per cent to 4.3 per cent over the same period.

Apart from other specific circumstances of each of these countries, the reduction of inflation was made possible by the low level of domestic and foreign demand. This hindered a complete pass-through of the depreciation to the prices of imported goods in both the UK and Italy and led to a narrowing of profit margins on domestic goods in domestic markets, which was compensated for by an increase in profit margins in foreign markets owing to a partial pass-through.

17.9.4 The effect lag: the j-curve

In addition to the size of the effects, an increase in the exchange rate raises the problem of the time needed for these effects to operate. The initial impact of a depreciation on the balance of payments can be 'perverse', since the reaction of export and import quantities to the change in competitiveness emerges with a lag (for various reasons: time needed to recalculate prices, contracts with pre-established terms, etc.), whereas the terms of trade worsen immediately owing to the increase in the exchange rate, if p_m and p_x remain constant. For a better understanding of these effects, consider equation (17.15). An increase in e causes the first ratio to increase immediately, i.e., worsens the terms of trade (if all agents keep prices in their domestic currencies, p_x and p_m, constant) and leaves q_x and q_m unchanged. If we begin with equilibrium on current account, as is assumed in (17.15), after the devaluation we will have $(p_x/p_m e)q_x/q_m < 1$, or $p_x q_x < p_m e q_m$.[34]

Only after a certain period of time will the beneficial effects on quantities emerge and – if the conditions outlined in the previous subsections are met – more than offset the adverse effects on the terms of trade. If we wished to show the balance of payments over time in diagram form, the curve would initially be decreasing and then increasing, giving rise to a j-shaped curve (hence the term 'j-curve' or 'j-effect').[35]

[34] Obviously, if we begin with a current account deficit, the immediate effect of the devaluation will be a worsening of the deficit.

[35] For empirical evidence on the j-curve see Wood (1991).

17.9.5 The effect on capital movements

We have so far considered the effects of exchange rate changes with exclusive reference to the current account. However, such effects are not limited to exports and imports of goods and services: changes in the actual exchange rate can influence the expected exchange rate and hence capital movements. *Under certain circumstances*, a depreciation may induce expectations of further depreciation and therefore cause a capital outflow;[36] in other circumstances the opposite can occur: a depreciation considered sufficiently large or excessive might give rise to expectations of a future appreciation.

The main conclusion we can draw is that adjusting the exchange rate is effective only in certain situations of balance of payment disequilibrium: depreciation is appropriate when competitiveness is being lost owing, for example, to changes in unit labour costs and/or other costs and profit margins that are higher at home than abroad. In the case of a current account deficit caused by excess demand, the proper response would be the adoption of restrictive fiscal and monetary policies. If policymakers wished to devalue under such circumstances, this would have to be accompanied by restrictive fiscal and monetary measures freeing resources for production to meet increased foreign demand. Similarly, depreciation is not an appropriate response to a deficit caused by capital movements and may actually have undesired adverse effects on the capital account.

The analysis of the effects of a depreciation on the current account can be used to assess the consequences for other policy objectives. We have already briefly mentioned the positive effects on income of an increase in net exports. At the same time, there may be adverse inflationary effects owing to the impulse imparted to demand and the increase in the cost of imported goods.

17.10 The asymmetric effects of a variation in the exchange rate

The effects of a change in the exchange rate have so far implicitly been assumed to be symmetric. This is only a rough initial approximation, however. Consider the entry and exit decisions of an individual agent with regard to the foreign market as the exchange rate changes (figure 17.1).

We can assume that entering the foreign market is only worthwhile for exchange rates $e \geq e_0$, given production costs and demand prospects in term of foreign-currency prices. As the exchange rate rises exports will increase, as shown by the solid line, which therefore represents the *potential* pattern of exports, i.e., that before entering the foreign market.

Once the agent has entered the foreign market, the pattern may change and, if the exchange rate falls below e_0 but remains above, say, e_1, it may still be worthwhile to remain in the market in the short run, albeit supplying fewer goods (hysteresis). If the exchange rate falls below e_1 it may be more profitable to abandon the market, even in

---

[36] We will apply these considerations in section 17.11.5.

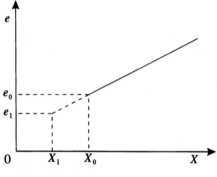

Figure 17.1

the short run. The agent's decision to remain in the market if $e_1 \leq e < e_0$ depends on the existence of *sunk costs* (for example, tangible and intangible fixed costs incurred on first entering the foreign market) that would have to be written off if the firm abandoned the market.[37] By incurring sunk costs to penetrate a foreign market a firm can establish a kind of *beachhead* in that market. The firm will not find it profitable to leave the market since it would lose its initial investment (Baldwin, 1988).

In this case the behaviour of the firm would be shown by the broken line in figure 17.1. The firm would remain in the foreign market in the short run, in the hope that a depreciation would bring the exchange rate back above e_0, which would allow it to stay in the market in the long run. Studies have shown that under certain conditions the exit value of e_1 (i.e., the value of e below which firms decide to exit the foreign market) may be much lower than that predicted by traditional Marshallian theory, since firms may be induced to stay in the market by high variability in the exchange rate as well as the prospect of facing very high new sunk costs to re-enter the market (Dixit, 1989, 1992).

17.11 Exchange rate variations, subsidies and tariffs

We have seen that the exchange rate affects the competitiveness of a country's goods and services compared with those of the Rest of the World. The same effects of an increase in the exchange rate – that is, a simultaneous boost to exports and damper on imports – can be obtained with generalised export subsidies and tariffs.[38]

Subsidies can take a variety of forms (credit or tax subsidies[39]) but they all normally

---

[37] Obviously, these costs are specific to the firm (plant or other fixed capital suitable for certain purposes; advertising). Often only a very small part of these costs can be recovered by transferring the related rights to other firms.

[38] However, note that the effects of the simultaneous use of generalised subsidies and tariffs are equal to those of a devaluation only for the current account (and, consequently, income). In addition to the effects on the current account, as we know, exchange rate changes will also have an effect on capital movements, since they can influence expectations of future exchange rate changes. Moreover, subsidies and tariffs are often selective rather than generalised, i.e., they are adopted for specific goods.

[39] Credit subsidies may involve a reduction in the interest rate or even just a larger credit facility in a situation of credit rationing. Tax incentives normally involve exemptions or reduction of tax rates.

translate into larger profits. In the case of export subsidies, the benefit is reaped by firms that sell their goods in foreign markets: the unit profit after the subsidy is increased by at least a part of the amount of the subsidy, which will encourage firms to shift resources to the production of goods for export.

Tariffs or duties also come in a variety of forms and can be used for different purposes. They are indirect taxes that normally raise the price of foreign goods in the domestic market. As taxes, they are naturally a source of tax revenues. However, this is rarely their primary purpose except for developing countries. Usually, they are used to protect domestic producers of goods and services from foreign competition. As such they are instruments of *customs protection*, together with *import quotas*, which are limits on the quantity or value of imports.

Other instruments can be used for protection in addition to tariffs, quotas, export subsidies and devaluations. The last few decades have seen the spread of many highly sophisticated *non-tariff barriers*, which normally come in the form of procedures and regulations that are apparently designed to serve other purposes (hygiene, safety, environmental protection, etc.) but in reality represent obstacles, delays and extra costs for foreign producers. These hidden forms of protection also include national preferences in the awarding of public works contracts and production subsidies, which may allow domestic firms to face foreign competition.[40]

17.11.1 Free trade and protectionism as alternative trade policies

As a *trade policy* alternative to free trade, protectionism has been both the subject of an extensive theoretical debate that marked the very birth of economic science and the focus of a variety of government actions over the ages.

To limit ourselves to the modern era, examples of such policy measures include the Navigation Act of 1651, with which Cromwell made use of vessels of the English

---

[40] The European Single Market, which was launched on 1 January 1993, was intended to eliminate these forms of non-tariff barriers, as tariffs and quotas had already been eliminated with the formation of the Common Market in 1958 (see Cecchini, 1988).

On a more global scale, since 1995 the World Trade Organisation (WTO) has been operating to foster world trade. It has taken on the role of the stillborn International Trade Organisation envisaged by the Bretton Woods agreements of 1944, constituting the third, missing, pillar of the post-war world economic system. The WTO has the function of monitoring the implementation of rules governing the protection of intellectual property and international trade in goods and services, of managing the system for the multilateral resolution of trade disputes, of verifying the compatibility of regional trade agreements with the principles of liberalisation and of promoting free trade in sectors that are still protected (especially agriculture, textiles, international financial services and trade in services).

The General Agreement on Tariffs and Trade (GATT), established in 1947, was the predecessor of the WTO. It was conceived as a provisional agreement to eliminate trade discrimination, especially through the elimination of quantitative restrictions on trade (quotas), the reduction of tariffs and the elimination of trade discrimination (with the use of the *most-favoured-nation clause*; this automatically extends any more favourable concessions that each party to a trade agreement may subsequently grant other nations to the other parties to the agreement). Elimination of quantitive restrictions and tariff reduction were obtained through eight successive multilateral negotiations which began in Geneva in 1947; the most recent ones have been the Kennedy Round, the Tokyo Round and the Uruguay Round.

Table 17.1. *Comparative costs*

	Wine	Cloth
UK	20	40
Portugal	10	30

merchant marine mandatory for all the country's imports and exports. This was a powerful instrument for advancing English economic power against the superior might of the Dutch. Once it had established its hegemony, Britain adopted and promoted free trade. Especially important moments of this policy were the abolition of the Corn Laws restricting trade in grain in 1846 (although Ricardo had advocated their repeal many years earlier) and the Franco-English trade agreement of 1860, which had a liberal orientation, partly owing to the inclusion of a most-favoured-nation clause.

A constant feature of the history of economic development would seem to be that countries become industrial powers thanks (in part) to protectionism. In addition to England, similar situations can be found in France (with the mercantilist policies of Colbert), Germany, Italy and the United States in the last quarter of the nineteenth century, and in Japan after 1945. The newly industrialising economies of East Asia are a striking exception, having enjoyed rapid growth since the end of the 1970s thanks to markedly free trade policies.[41]

The scientific foundation of free trade lies in the advantages of specialisation at the international level, advantages that were underscored by David Ricardo with the *comparative-cost principle*: if two countries have different relative abilities to produce two goods (which is reflected in their comparative costs of production), both countries could be better off if each specialises in producing the good whose cost is *comparatively* lower and trades the quantity of that good in excess of domestic demand to secure the other good from the other country. Take the production costs in table 17.1 (expressed in labour units, according to the labour theory of value adopted by the classical economists) for the two goods, wine and cloth, in the two countries, the United Kingdom and Portugal.

The comparative costs can be defined as $20/40 = 1/2$ (or 0.5 units of wine for 1 unit of cloth) in the UK and $10/30 = 1/3$ in Portugal. Wine costs relatively less in Portugal than in the UK and therefore Portugal could profit from specialising in that good. The UK, on the other hand, should specialise in cloth. Although cloth costs more in the UK than in Portugal in absolute terms, it costs only twice the cost of wine in the UK, whereas it costs three times the cost of wine in Portugal. It can be demonstrated that despite the fact that costs for both goods are higher in the UK than in Portugal, both countries will benefit by specialising as long as the international terms of trade between the two goods lie between the domestic terms of trade in each of the two countries under autarky (see Gandolfo, 1994).

All subsequent theories substantially incorporate the Ricardian principle. The most

---

[41] However, this growth has been sustained in most cases by clearly statist domestic policies. See Lall (1994).

recent also adopt more realistic hypotheses of scale economies and imperfect competition (see Helpman and Krugman, 1985).

Nevertheless, the Ricardian principle suffers from many implicit and explicit limitations mainly associated with the static nature of the analysis and the assumption of full employment.[42]

The economic arguments in favour of protectionism are largely based on these limitations.[43] We discuss them in sections 17.11.2–17.11.5. The non-economic arguments that are usually advanced in support of protectionism hark back to Adam Smith. In fact, the founder of modern economics and father of liberalism argued that 'defence is of more importance than opulence'. On this argument, we can justify the protection of certain 'industries' (agriculture, basic industries, some services) despite the fact that their production may be unprofitable from a strictly economic point of view.

17.11.2 Protecting 'infant industries'

The need to nurture *infant industries* has been cited as a reason for protection at least since John Stuart Mill, who argued that the temporary imposition of a protective tariff is justified by the attempt to naturalise 'a foreign industry in itself perfectly suitable to the circumstances of the country. The superiority of one country over another in a branch of production often arises only from having begun it sooner', consisting of 'a present superiority of acquired skill and experience' (Mill, 1848, p. 918). A country that protects an infant industry may acquire the same skills and experience over time, thus enabling it to compete on an equal footing (or even gain an edge).

This is especially the case when there are *dynamic economies of scale* to be gained as producers *learn by doing*: their special importance lies in the fact that they are not linked to the quantity produced per unit of time, but rather to cumulative output over time. Their presence produces a *learning curve* of the sort shown in figure 17.2. It indicates average cost, AC, as a function of total output since production began.[44]

Country 1, which has yet to begin production of the good in question, could produce at cost AC_0, which is higher than that in countries 2 and 3, which have lower costs thanks to the time they have spent producing the good (and, perhaps, to the size of their market). The advantage of protection is that the scope for foreign producers to expand their share of the domestic market is curbed, allowing domestic producers to increase their market share and raise their total output more rapidly. Even if after a certain number of years country 1's production costs fell only to the level in country 3 and no

---

[42] These have been partly overcome by later work, although these theories in turn have their own limitations.

[43] Other limitations of the theory in favour of free trade are related to the incentive incompatibility of the measures directed at compensating the agents losing from free trade (Hammond and Sempere, 1995).

[44] This curve was initially introduced for the aeroplane industry. It was noticed that the number of hours of labour – which was taken as a measure of average costs – fell drastically as production passed from the construction of prototypes to mass production and then as the *total* number of planes increased. Cumulative production thus assumed the role of a proxy for accumulated experience.

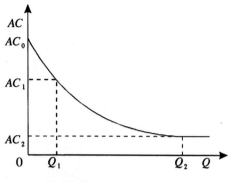

Figure 17.2

more, protection would still have been advantageous if the presence of the industry has generated positive spillover effects for country 1's economy. Such effects are associated with close interindustry linkages that can help spread knowledge, stimulate innovations and determine their orientation through the relationships arising between innovators and the users of innovations.

Country 1 may derive further benefit from protection if its production costs are lower than those in other countries, due, for example, to lower wages or rents, or narrower profit margins. In this case, the learning curve of country 1 may be below that shown in figure 17.2 (which earlier was assumed to hold for both country 1 and the other countries). In this case, country 1 could produce the good at a lower cost than country 3 even before having achieved a cumulative output of OQ_2.

Die-hard free traders have argued that at least where there are no spillover effects, the prospect of profits deriving from the gradual reduction of production costs as producers learn their craft should be enough on its own to induce new firms to enter the market, making any protectionist incentives unnecessary. However, in addition to ignoring spillover effects, which may cause a divergence between private and social returns, this position also fails to take account of the risky outlook for sufficiently large profits, which in any case would be deferred in time: the imperfections of financial markets, by raising the cost of capital or rationing credit, especially for riskier activities, often discourage innovation and/or the entrance of goods that are not immediately profitable into the market.

The difficulty of identifying infant industries that will become viable in the future or produce positive spillover effects and the possibility that firms may sit comfortably behind the protective tariff barrier well beyond the time necessary for the new industry to take off should be borne in mind. However, this does not lessen the importance of this argument in favour of protection, whose scope has actually been broadened in recent times. It was made with reference not to specific industries but to manufacturing in general in underdeveloped countries, where the problem is not individual infant industries but rather entire infant economies, to cite Myrdal (1956, 1957). The problem in developing countries is to install manufacturing industries as soon as the production of primary goods has developed sufficiently to meet the country's basic needs.

The latter seems a necessary but not sufficient condition for economic development, which must be completed by the growth of industry. One reason for this is that as soon

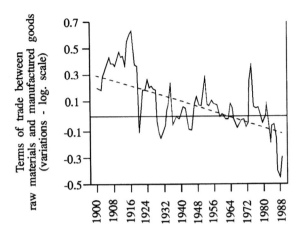

Figure 17.3

as the country moves from production of subsistence commodities to primary production for the market, it risks specialising in an activity where the terms of trade with
respect to manufactured goods worsen continuously, as was argued by Prebisch (1950)
and Singer (1950) and verified by numerous studies (most recently, Ardeni and Wright,
1992, from which figure 17.3 is drawn). In addition, manufacturing is the area where the
greatest productivity gains are to be made.[45]

Nevertheless, recent studies have shown that the considerable change in the composition of developing countries' exports (towards a greater proportion of manufactured
goods) has only attenuated the worsening of the terms of trade between primary
products and manufactures: between 1970 and 1987, there was an annual decline of 1 per
cent in the terms of trade between the manufactures of developing countries and similar
products of the developed world, while the terms of trade between primary products and
manufactures fell by more than 2 per cent annually (Sarkar and Singer, 1991). This
occurred despite the more rapid productivity growth in the developed countries, which,
ceteris paribus, could have led to a fall in the prices of their goods. This means that (a) the
remuneration of factors in the developing countries declined with respect to that in the
advanced nations and (b) the problem of the sectoral structure of production is only one
of the difficulties facing the developing economies. Other equally important problems
regard the structure of trade, finance and services, the size of economic activities and
market regimes.

17.11.3 Protection as a tool for improving the terms of trade

A second economic argument in favour of protection is the possibility for a country to
improve its terms of trade if certain demand and supply conditions are met.

---

[45] This statement does not contradict our earlier statement regarding the worsening of the terms of
trade to the detriment of agriculture and the benefit of manufacturing. The main reason for this is
the different market regime for the two types of good (Kaldor, 1971). Manufactured goods are
normally traded under oligopolistic conditions and productivity gains usually lead to increases in
the incomes of 'factors' (wages and profits) rather than lower prices (Sylos Labini, 1962).

We said that a tariff is an indirect tax and, as such, may be shifted on to the price of goods. The more elastic is demand, the less likely the shift is. A low elasticity of supply also tends to reduce the shifting of the tariff on to the price. If the price does not rise, the tax is borne by the foreign supplier. Let us now examine the conditions for the shifting of the tariff on to the foreign supplier in more detail. The influence of demand elasticity seems to be clear. Consider instead the meaning of supply elasticity. First, this should be taken with reference to the price net of the tariff, which represents the net unit revenue for the exporting firm. Inelastic supply thus means that the firm does not change its supply despite the reduction in price: after a tariff is introduced, the firm is willing to sell the same quantity at a lower price. This may be due to the importance of the market for the exporting firm[46] and the fact that the good is produced under significant economies of scale.

If the foreign exporter keeps the price unchanged after the introduction of the tariff, the tariff-imposing country's terms of trade improve. Recall that $TT = p_x/(p_m \cdot e)$. Both p_x and the price (in domestic currency) of imports, $p_m e$, remain unchanged, but the latter is inclusive of the tariff, which is collected by the importing country. From the point of view of the country as a whole, we must consider the price of imports *net of the tariff*, which has fallen. The tariff improves the terms of trade even in the more frequent situation when it is partially shifted on to prices. The possible positive effects of a tariff on the terms of trade are shown in diagrammatic form and in a general equilibrium setting in the appendix to this chapter (see section *17.12).

17.11.4 Protection from cheap labour and social dumping

Developed countries often argue for protection against cheap foreign labour to defend their industry – in particular the labour-intensive branches of it – that are threatened by the low cost of labour abroad, which makes inadequately protected domestic industries uncompetitive.

In reality, this position fails to take account of the fact that the lower labour costs of less developed countries largely correspond to lower productivity, so that labour costs per unit of output are often not much different and in any case not as dramatically low as the labour costs *per se*. It is thus a justification that is not always founded on reality and is often advanced only to promote purely sectoral interests. Although it is understandable that these are defended at the government level in the short run to avoid dangerous and painful falls in employment, it is less justifiable to do so in the long run. The task of avoiding this situation must be entrusted to a full employment macroeconomic policy and an industrial policy to ensure rapid productive reconversion and restructuring in response to changes in the international division of labour.

An argument in favour of protection similar to the one just developed is that protection is needed to counter *social dumping*, i.e., the possibility for countries (often less developed countries) with poor workplace standards and protection to compete successfully with other (often developed) countries. This is the subject of a heated debate, for more on which we refer the reader to World Bank (1995).

---

[46] J. S. Mill made this argument, as he did with infant industries.

17.11.5 Protection as an employment policy

If an economy suffers from unemployment, protection can help push it back to full employment.

Looking at the reduced form of any Keynesian model for an open economy, we can see that the value of the multiplier rises if the propensity to import declines, a result that can be obtained through protectionist policies. If there is unemployment, the same initial level of autonomous spending will give rise to a higher level of aggregate demand and employment because of the increase in the multiplier.

Protection and the reduction of the propensity to import lower (raise) the level of the country's imports if the consequent increase in income is proportionately smaller (larger) than the reduction in the propensity to import. But the imports of one country are the exports of the Rest of the World. Thus, protection can cause a decline (or a rise) in the autonomous spending of the Rest of the World and, therefore, in its income and employment. If the imports of the domestic country (the Rest of the World's exports) decline, we have a *beggar-thy-neighbour policy*. Such a result is less likely if protection is undertaken together with expansionary policies in the domestic country. Keynes examined the matter with reference to the United Kingdom between the two wars. Although initially arguing from a free-trade position, Keynes came to suggest some form of protection, such as import duties, as a way to ease the balance of payments constraint that would have arisen owing to expansionary fiscal and monetary policies. In his view, lowering the propensity to import would prevent an increase in imports – and a worsening of the current account balance – in the presence of an increase in government spending and aggregate demand (see section 18.1). The level of imports could remain constant owing to the effect of the reduction in the propensity to import and the simultaneous increase in domestic demand, thus leaving other countries unaffected. Protection in conjunction with expansionary monetary or fiscal policies would *simultaneously* achieve full employment and balance of payments equilibrium.

This is the substance of Keynes' position. It matured slowly and unwillingly over the years, but it was strenuously defended in the end. In particular, he came out in favour of subsidies and tariffs as an alternative to devaluation, taking account of Britain's special position as an international financial centre: a devaluation would have weakened or undermined that position, thus reducing net foreign capital inflows.[47]

*17.12 Appendix. The optimum tariff

This section gives a diagrammatic presentation of our analysis in section 17.11.3 with regard to the possibility of improving the terms of trade by imposing an import tariff. We will also identify the optimum tariff.

In order to do this we need to introduce the concept of *offer curve*. Let there be two

---

[47] Consider the fact that devaluation can induce expectations of future devaluation and therefore give rise to net outflows (or smaller inflows) of capital (section 17.9.5). It is therefore absolutely necessary for a country that is a financial centre and wishes to continue to operate as such to ensure the stability of its exchange rate. For Keynes' argument in favour of protection see Milone (1993).

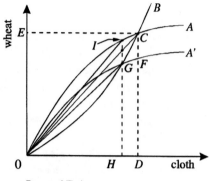

Figure 17.4

internationally traded goods: wheat, which is produced by country 2 and imported by country 1, and cloth, which is produced by country 1 and imported by country 2. In figure 17.4, the curves $0A$ and $0B$ are the offer curves of country 2 and country 1 respectively. Examine curve $0A$.

It indicates the maximum amount of wheat that country 2 is willing to exchange for any given quantity of cloth from country 1. The downward concavity of the curve is due to the fact that country 2 is willing to exchange a gradually smaller amount of wheat for each additional unit of cloth as the quantity of cloth imported increases, owing to the decreasing marginal utility of wheat and cloth. In other words, the price of wheat in terms of cloth asked by country 2 increases as the amount of cloth increases. This price is given by the segment that joins the origin with the point on the offer curve considered: if country 2 imports $0D$ of cloth, the price is given by the slope of the segment $0C$. If this country imports $0H$ of cloth, the price is given by the slope of the segment $0I$, which is steeper.

Similarly, $0B$ indicates the maximum quantity of cloth that country 1 is willing to trade for any given quantity of grain from country 2.

The imposition of a 20 per cent tariff by country 2 means that agents in this country, who were willing to exchange $0E = CD$ of wheat for $0D$ of cloth, beginning in equilibrium, are now willing to exchange 20 per cent less wheat (DF) for the same amount of cloth, as they must pay CF for the tariff. In fact, they would now give 20 per cent less wheat than before for *any* given amount of imported cloth. The offer curve of country 2 shifts downward, which leads to a new international trade equilibrium at point G. As is easily seen, country 2's terms of trade have improved with respect to the pre-tariff position: the slope of $0G$ is less than that of $0C$, which denotes the fact that country 2 now exchanges a smaller amount of wheat for each unit of imported cloth. The tariff therefore redistributes the earnings of international trade if the elasticity conditions of supply and demand discussed in section 17.11.3 are satisfied.[48]

If this is the effect of the introduction of a *given* tariff, we might ask how we can

[48] The introduction of a tariff on cloth by country 2 will, in general, cause the absolute price of cloth to rise by an amount that depends on the elasticities of cloth demand and supply, as we discussed in section 17.11.3. Only in the limiting case we examined would the price remain unchanged. The reader interested in pursuing this topic further is referred to Gandolfo (1994).

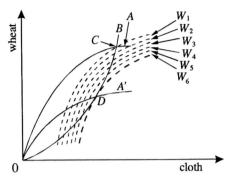

Figure 17.5

identify the *optimum tariff*, i.e., the tariff that best improves the terms of trade. Optimality means making reference to a social preference function having country 2's cloth imports and wheat exports as its arguments.

Importing cloth has a positive effect *per se* on the social welfare of country 2, which acquires a wider range of goods. Conversely, exporting wheat lowers country 2's welfare, since it reduces the availability of that good. The social indifference curves of country 2 are therefore increasing, as shown in figure 17.5. They are also concave, since the volume of wheat exports needed to maintain welfare unchanged decreases as the quantity of cloth available increases. Obviously, social welfare increases if we move from an indifference curve such as W_1 to a curve such as W_6, i.e., if we move south-east.

Without a tariff, country 2 is on indifference curve W_1. We said above that the country can improve its terms of trade by imposing a tariff: this lowers its offer curve, bringing the country to a higher-level indifference curve, such as W_2 or W_3. The country can maximise its welfare if it chooses the tariff level by taking the offer curve of country 1, $0B$, as a constraint in its optimising problem. In other words, country 2's welfare is maximised if it chooses a tariff that will position it at the point where one of its social indifference curves is tangent to country 1's offer curve, $0B$. This is shown at point D in figure 17.5.

Note that the optimum tariff is higher the less elastic is the offer curve of the other country, i.e., the larger the increase in price in terms of wheat that country 1 requires for increasing quantities of cloth exports, or the more country 1 is willing to lower the price in terms of wheat if the other country demands a smaller amount of cloth. In the limiting case where country 1's offer curve is a straight line beginning at the origin – which is the case when country 1 is small – the price requested would not change. In other words, country 1 would be willing to keep the price of cloth in terms of wheat unchanged as cloth exports increased. In this case the optimal tariff would be zero.

The preceding analysis is based on the hypothesis that country 1 does not react to the introduction of a tariff, perhaps for non-economic reasons. If, however, country 1 does react, a tariff war could ensue, although – it is to be hoped – this would be confined to the economic sphere and would end with a final equilibrium position somewhere in the area between 0 and C bounded by the curves $0A$ and $0B$. For country 2 such a position may or may not be superior in terms of social welfare to point C, which denotes a free-trade situation. It will be superior if the ability, or desire, of country 1 to retaliate is limited. This possibility represents an exception to the argument that free trade will produce an optimum.

17.13 Summary

1 The current account balance in real terms depends on various factors, including price competitiveness (indicated by the real exchange rate) and income factors. The capital account balance depends on interest rate differentials and expectations of exchange rate variations.

2 Balance of payments disequilibrium is represented by either a deficit or a surplus. Capital mobility can contribute to automatically equilibrating the balance of payments.

3 Current account imbalances tend to be eliminated automatically by exchange rate variations under a floating rate regime. Under fixed exchange rates, equilibrium is attained through price movements (which are slow, however) or changes in income (with possible depression in the deficit country).

4 The imperfection of automatic current account adjustment mechanisms or the existence of a collateral depressive effect on income under fixed exchange rates are an incentive to search for appropriate discretionary adjustment measures.

5 In the presence of excess or insufficient demand, discretionary adjustment measures consist of, respectively, restrictive or expansionary monetary and fiscal policies.

6 Insufficient or excessive competitiveness can be eliminated by acting on domestic prices (or the factors on which they depend) or the nominal exchange rate (with depreciations or appreciations, respectively), or by imposing a tariff on foreign goods.

7 If capital is insufficiently mobile, restrictive or expansionary monetary action may be needed to increase or reduce the domestic interest rate in order to compensate a deficit or a surplus in the capital account. Expectations of exchange rate variations and associated speculative movements can undermine discretionary policy measures.

8 The impact of exchange rate variations on the current account in nominal terms depends on the elasticity of demand for exports and imports (the Marshall–Lerner condition), the degree of 'pass-through', the elasticity of supply and the speed of the variations. Exchange rate changes can have an impact on capital movements, influencing expectations of future changes. These effects are uncertain.

9 Exchange rate variations can have asymmetric effects. In particular, entry by firms into foreign markets may occur at a high exchange rate, while exit can occur at a low rate, owing to the presence of sunk costs.

10 The effects of a devaluation on the current account are equivalent to those of the simultaneous use of import tariffs and export subsidies. Tariffs, subsidies and devaluation are some of the instruments available to a protectionist policy for domestic goods.

11 Free trade and protectionism are alternative trade policies. The scientific foundation of free trade lies with advantages of specialisation identified by Ricardo with the comparative-cost principle.

12 The Ricardian principle suffers from numerous limitations associated with the existence of infant industries, with the possibility of improving the terms of trade, with the need to protect domestic workers (in the short run) against cheap foreign labour and with the need to ensure full employment and balance of payments equilibrium simultaneously.

17.14 Key concepts

Balance of payments
Current account
Capital account, capital movements
Structural determinants
Competitiveness factors (price, non-price)
Demand factors
Covered, uncovered interest rate parity
Equilibrium, surplus, deficit
Overadjustment
Tobin tax
Non-interest bearing deposit
Overinvoicing
Exchange-rate controllability
Demand elasticity
Marshall–Lerner condition
Terms of trade
Pass-through
Supply elasticity
Vicious circle of
   inflation-depreciation-inflation
J-curve, j-effect

Asymmetry of the effects of exchange rate
   variations
Sunk cost
Beachhead effect
Trade policy
Credit, tax subsidy
Quota
Non-tariff barriers
Free trade
Protection, protectionism
Colbertism
Most-favoured-nation clause
Comparative-cost principle (theory)
Infant industry
Dynamic economies of scale
Learning curve
Protection from cheap labour
Social dumping
Beggar-thy-neighbour policy
*Optimum tariff
*Offer curve

18 Economic policies in an open economy

18.1 The Mundell–Fleming model

The Mundell–Fleming model (see Mundell, 1963 and Fleming, 1962) goes beyond the initial Keynesian hypothesis of a closed economic system and generalises the *IS-LM* analytical framework. This is done by introducing:

(a) net exports (i.e., exports net of imports, $X - M$) as an additional positive component of aggregate demand. The export and import functions are those given in section 17.1;

(b) an external-payments 'market' in addition to the goods and money markets.

Let us first examine the changes that occur to the *IS-LM* framework when we introduce net exports. In the simplest case, where $X = \bar{X}$ and $M = mY$, adding these components of demand to the usual elements (also expressed in their simplest form) transforms the equilibrium of the goods market as follows:

$$
\begin{aligned}
Y &= C + I + G + X - M \\
C &= cY \\
I &= I(i) \\
G &= \bar{G} \\
X &= \bar{X} \\
M &= mY
\end{aligned}
\tag{18.1}
$$

From this we obtain by substitution:

$$
Y = \frac{1}{1 - c + m}[I(i) + \bar{G} + \bar{X}]
\tag{18.2}
$$

From (18.2) we can obtain a relationship between i and Y of the same form as the normal

428

IS curve in a closed economy.[1] However, the *IS* schedule in an open economy has the following notable features:

(a) for a given *I* and $\bar{G}$, the curve tends to shift to the right with the increase in $\bar{X}$, which is an additional exogenous component of demand;

(b) it is steeper than the *IS* curve for a closed economy, since the multiplier is reduced by the diversion of some demand towards foreign goods; this is reflected in a positive propensity to import.

If we take price competitivity factors into account, we have $M = m(p, p_w, e)Y$ and $X = m_w(p, p_w, e)Y_w$, instead of the simple forms of the import and export functions used in (18.1). *IS* then becomes sensitive to domestic and foreign prices (although the latter are largely beyond the control of the home country) and the exchange rate. A rise in domestic prices tends to shift the *IS* schedule to the left, owing both to the real balance effect and the adverse impact the rise would have on exports; it also causes *IS* to become steeper by increasing the propensity to import. A rise in the exchange rate and/or foreign prices would have the opposite effect. International openness does not cause changes in the money market, which means that the *LM* schedule can be drawn in the usual way.

Let us now consider the third market, external payments, which is characteristic of an open economy.

First, recall the theory of the balance of payments outlined in the preceding chapter. We know that the following relation holds:

$$BP = \psi(p, p_w, e, Y, Y_w, i, i_w, e^e) \tag{18.3}$$

This representation of the factors on which the balance of payments depends can be simplified for the purposes of the present analysis. Some variables are entirely (p_w, Y_w, i_w) or largely (e^e) outside the control of policymakers in the home country and must therefore be considered given.[2] Domestic prices can change, but we will initially assume that they are also given, as is normally done with the *IS-LM* model. The balance of payments can therefore be written as:

$$BP = h(Y, i, e) \tag{18.4}$$

Balance of payments equilibrium in the light of equation (18.4) can be shown diagrammatically on the (Y, i) plane used for the *IS* and *LM* schedules (figure 18.1), setting $BP = 0$ in (18.4) and considering *e* as given.

The *BP* curve in this figure represents the combinations of *Y* and *i* that ensure balance of payments equilibrium, or external balance $(BP = 0)$. We can intuitively construct the

---

[1] Since the *IS-LM* model assumes constant prices, the real interest rate is equal to the nominal interest rate; we can therefore use either. Prices variability poses problems that, for simplicity's sake, we will not examine. No basic macroeconomics texts (of which at least partial knowledge is assumed here) deal with the problem. From here on, we will therefore refer to the two interest rates indifferently even in the few cases in which we introduce price changes into our discussion.

[2] It would be possible to examine the consequences for *BP* of alternative values for the variables. In this case we say that we are analysing parametric variations in the variables considered. We will briefly discuss this issue later on.

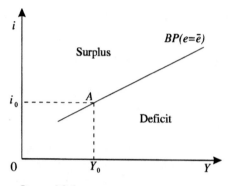

Figure 18.1

curve as follows. Let A be a combination of Y and i, Y_0 and i_0, that ensures equilibrium in the balance of payments for a given e ($e = \bar{e}$). If Y rises above Y_0, imports rise and the current account balance deteriorates, all the more so the higher the propensity to import. To keep the balance of payments in equilibrium the domestic interest rate, i, must rise in order to attract larger net inflows of capital. BP will therefore have a positive slope, with the curve being flatter the lower the propensity to import and the more sensitive capital flows are to the interest rate. With perfect capital mobility – i.e., when domestic and foreign financial assets are perfect substitutes and there are no obstacles to the international movement of funds – the curve will be horizontal at a domestic interest rate exactly equal to the world interest rate. In other words, with perfect capital mobility there is only one interest rate that ensures a balance of payments equilibrium for any level of income. In this case the conditions for balance of payments equilibrium are 'completely dominated by the rate of interest and the capital account' (Dernburg, 1989, p. 109). If the domestic interest rate exceeds the world rate (even by an infinitesimal amount), there will be unlimited capital inflows, causing a balance of payments surplus whatever the current account balance. The opposite will occur if the domestic rate is lower than the world rate.

By contrast, BP is vertical if there is no capital mobility. In this case, balance of payments equilibrium is independent of i and corresponds to a single value for Y. This can easily be shown if we consider the simple specification of the export and import functions given by the last two relations of (18.1). We have $X - M = \bar{X} - mY$, where m is given. There is one and only one level of Y that ensures $\bar{X} - mY = 0$.

Returning to figure 18.1, points above and to the left of BP represent a balance of payments surplus: for each level of income there is an interest rate above that for which $BP = 0$ (or, for each given interest rate, the level of income is less than that which insures $BP = 0$) and therefore $BP > 0$. Points below and to the right of BP correspond to a balance of payments deficit.

This discussion holds for a given exchange rate. If the exchange rate were to rise (following depreciation or devaluation), and the Marshall–Lerner conditions are satisfied, balance of payments equilibrium would occur at a lower interest rate (for a given income level) or a higher income (for a given interest rate); BP would therefore shift

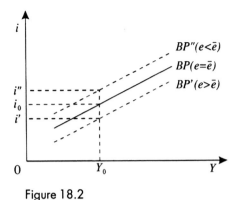

Figure 18.2

downwards and become flatter. The downwards shift is due to the fact that – if the appropriate conditions discussed in the previous chapter hold – a devaluation increases exports while decreasing imports (for a given level of income), thus generating a balance of payments surplus: a higher income level is then needed to ensure higher imports and, therefore, balance of payments equilibrium for any given level of the interest rate. The reduction in the slope of the curve corresponds to a reduction in the propensity to import. By contrast, BP would be higher and steeper if the currency were to appreciate or to be revalued. (The diagrams that follow ignore changes in the slope of BP brought about by variations in the exchange rate or other prices.)

In figure 18.2 the curve BP'' corresponds to an exchange rate lower than $\bar{e}$ and BP' to a higher rate. For a given income level Y_0 and an exchange rate $\bar{e}$, external balance would require $i = i_0$; with an exchange rate higher than $\bar{e}$ (which reduces imports and boosts exports) and an unchanged level of income Y_0, equilibrium would require a lower net inflow (or larger net outflow) of capital and hence $i' < i_0$. The opposite occurs if $e < \bar{e}$.

More generally, recall that the position and slope of BP in the (Y, i) plane also depend on the other variables of equation (18.3) as well as the structural factors discussed earlier. Thus, for example, a fall in domestic prices[3] tends:

(a) to lower BP by raising exports; and
(b) to flatten BP by reducing the propensity to import.

A similar effect is produced by a rise in foreign prices, while an export subsidy has the same effect as (a) and the imposition of a tariff has the same effect as (b). An increase in foreign income also lowers BP. For countries that produce and export goods with high income elasticity and import goods with low income elasticity, the BP curve shifts gradually downwards in a world with rising income.

The crucial point regards the effect on the real rate of interest. As we have seen, when prices are constant, $i = r$; when prices can vary, the nominal rate of interest normally varies as well. This makes it difficult to use the IS-LM framework in a context of

---

[3] A decline might be the result of an increase in productivity and/or a reduction in wage rates or profit margins.

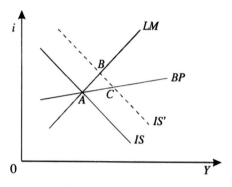

Figure 18.3

changing prices since the effects on the goods market equilibrium are transmitted through the real interest rate while those on the money market equilibrium operate through changes in the nominal interest rate.

Let us now consider the goods market, the money market and the balance of payments together. Point A in figure 18.3 shows the simultaneous equilibrium of the three markets.[4] In general, starting in such equilibrium, a change in the equilibrium conditions in one of the three markets (which implies a shift in one of the three curves) causes at least one of the other two to move into imbalance. For example, if IS shifts upwards following an increase in government spending, we move to point B, at B the money market would be in equilibrium but not the balance of payments; at C the opposite would be the case.

The imbalance thus created can essentially be eliminated in one of the following ways:

(a) the system may tend to revert (to some extent) to its original position; or
(b) it may move[5] towards a new equilibrium position.

Which alternative will actually occur depends on both the type of imbalance created (monetary, real or external) and the exchange rate regime (fixed or floating). We will discuss this aspect more fully in our examination of fiscal and monetary policy. For the moment we will examine shifts in BP caused by changes in the exchange rate.[6]

We have seen that a devaluation (or depreciation) normally causes BP to shift downwards. This is not the only effect, however, since the rise in the exchange rate also produces an increase in autonomous spending (higher exports) and therefore causes IS to shift as well.

Referring to figure 18.4, let us assume that we are in a fixed exchange rate regime and

---

[4] The steeper slope of LM with respect to BP reflects the hypothesis (which does not always hold in the real world) of considerable international capital mobility.

[5] The reader must bear in mind that although we use expressions that in a strict sense should only be used with regard to dynamic analysis, ours is a purely comparative statics analysis.

[6] More generally, such shifts can be caused by all the other factors that determine the position of BP in the (Y, i) plane, including changes in the structure of the economic system. In the case here, we assume that variations in the exchange rate do not cause domestic prices to vary in order to avoid the difficulties that may emerge in the Mundell–Fleming model when prices are not held constant.

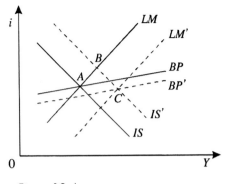

Figure 18.4

the initial simultaneous equilibrium position is at A. If the appropriate conditions are met, a currency devaluation improves the balance of payments, thus causing BP to move to BP'. At the same time, the increase in exports following the devaluation increases aggregate demand, thus shifting the curve for goods market equilibrium to IS'. With the money supply unchanged, we move along LM to B. But even under the previous exchange rate there was a balance of payments surplus at B and the imbalance increases further at the new exchange rate. Holding other conditions unchanged and assuming there is no sterilisation, this will expand monetary base and therefore the money supply, since the increase in foreign reserves is converted into domestic currency. This lowers the equilibrium interest rate corresponding to the new, higher level of demand. Hence, LM will also shift right until the balance of payments surplus is eliminated, which happens at the new equilibrium point C. However, adjustment takes time and may encounter numerous obstacles, as was discussed in non-formal terms in the previous chapter. The possibility that a devaluation might cause a rise in domestic prices will be discussed in terms of the Mundell–Fleming model in section 18.5. The reader can try to diagram the consequences of a devaluation (or depreciation) beginning in a situation of balance of payments disequilibrium.

We can now examine diagrammatically the importance of a devaluation (or other protectionist measures)[7] if we wish to implement a non-beggar-thy-neighbour expansionary policy (see section 17.11.5). Assume there are no international capital movements, which allows us to focus on movements of goods and to capture the effects of a devaluation on the income of both the country involved and the rest of the world as well as on the balance of payments. Under this assumption, the BP schedule is vertical, as in figure 18.5. The system is initially in equilibrium at A. If Y_A does not correspond to full employment, the monetary or fiscal authorities could attempt to boost income to its full employment level, $\bar{Y}$, with measures aimed at shifting LM or IS. If monetary or fiscal measures alone are adopted, the economy would then be at B or C, respectively. However, in both cases government action would produce a balance of payments deficit: the increase in income would cause imports to rise, while exports would remain

[7] As we said in the previous chapter, the devaluation itself may serve to protect domestic goods.

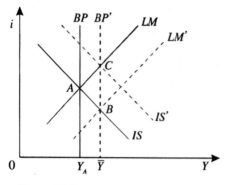

Figure 18.5

unchanged. The resulting deficit is not sustainable in the long run in the presence of limited foreign reserves.

The only way to sustain such an expansionary policy in the long run is to 'ease' the balance of payments constraint. This can be accomplished by either a devaluation or other protectionist measures, which reduce the propensity to import of the country involved and/or raise it in the rest of the world in the case of a devaluation. Suppose that the government adopts an expansionary fiscal policy that shifts *IS* to *IS'*. If the currency is simultaneously devalued, *BP* will move to *BP'*.[8] The new equilibrium between imports and exports is now reached at a higher level of the two quantities, which means that not only is the country exporting more than before, it is also importing a larger quantity of foreign goods. In this case, the devaluation (or other protectionist measures) would not shift domestic problems (the elimination of unemployment) on to trading partners. In some circumstances it could even help to increase income and employment in other countries.

18.2 Fiscal and monetary policy under fixed exchange rates

In addition to analysing the effects of exchange rate variations, the Mundell–Fleming model can be used to evaluate the impact of fiscal and monetary policy in an open economy under both fixed and floating exchange rate regimes. The effects of monetary and fiscal policies on income and employment under the two exchange rate systems differ profoundly.

In brief, with fixed exchange rates (and high international capital mobility) fiscal policy will have full control over aggregate demand and monetary policy will be relatively ineffective, all the more so the greater is the mobility of capital. The opposite is the case if exchange rates float. We will attempt to understand why this is so, examining fixed exchange rates in this section and floating rates in section 18.4.

We must first make clear that in a fixed exchange rate regime, balance of payments surpluses or deficits caused by fiscal or monetary policy cannot cause changes in the

---

[8] For the sake of simplicity, we ignore the effects of the devaluation on *IS*, which we can consider to be included in the rightward shift of the curve.

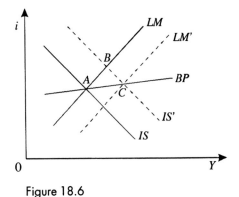

Figure 18.6

exchange rate, causing variations in monetary base instead, if no sterilisation is carried out.[9]

1 Let us consider an expansionary *fiscal policy*; for example, an increase in government spending that is not financed with monetary base. This measure will have two effects on the balance of payments: first, the current account balance will worsen, owing to the resulting rise in income; second, there will be an improvement in the capital account, owing to the rise in the interest rate following the increase in income with no expansion of the money supply. The net effect will depend on the responsiveness of the different markets.

We initially consider the case of an improvement in the balance of payments resulting from a situation in which the international financial market is more responsive than the international goods market. There will therefore be an increase in monetary base to facilitate the expansion triggered by government spending. This is shown in figure 18.6.

The initial point of simultaneous equilibrium is *A*. *BP* is flatter than *LM* owing to the considerable responsiveness of international capital movements to changes in the interest rate. The increase in government expenditure will shift *IS* to the right, moving its intersection with *LM* to *B*, which, since it is above *BP*, denotes a balance of payments surplus. The surplus gives rise to an increase in monetary base and thus shifts *LM* to the right, to *C*, where the surplus is eliminated and general macroeconomic equilibrium is restored, although at a higher level of income.

If the negative effect on the balance of payments of the current account deterioration should predominate, owing to a lack of capital mobility, *BP* would be steeper than *LM* and the situation would be that shown in figure 18.7. Point *B* now denotes a balance of payments deficit. The deficit causes a contraction in monetary base and, therefore, shifts *LM* upwards to *C*, where there is a new equilibrium for all markets at a higher income level, despite the crowding out effect deriving from the contraction in the money supply.

A shared feature of these two situations is the positive effect on income of an

[9] We will discuss this in detail in section 18.3. For the moment it is enough to know that sterilisation basically consists in open market operations that offset changes in monetary base through the foreign sector.

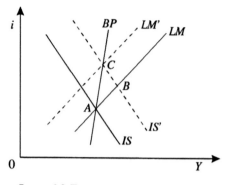

Figure 18.7

expansionary fiscal policy under a fixed exchange rate system, which is reinforced by high capital mobility and dampened by low capital mobility.

2 By contrast, *monetary policy* is relatively ineffective in increasing income under fixed exchange rates. Take an increase in monetary base, which causes the money supply to expand and, therefore, interest rates to fall. The consequent stimulus to investment would be large if the reduction in the interest rate were lasting. This does not happen, however, since the effect is only temporary. On the one hand, the lower interest rate will cause a deterioration in the capital account, while, on the other, any increase in income deriving from the increase in investment will worsen the current account balance. Upward pressure will be exerted on the exchange rate. However, under a fixed exchange rate regime the exchange rate cannot rise. To stop the exchange rate from rising above its fluctuation limit the monetary authorities normally have to intervene in the foreign exchange market, selling foreign currency and buying domestic currency, which gives rise to a progressive reabsorption of the liquidity created initially.[10] This is the reason it was argued that the exchange rate regime can influence the ability to control the creation of monetary base (see section 13.7). In the present example of fixed exchange rates, monetary base creation tends to be endogenous rather than exogenous – since it is created by the operation of the economy itself – and therefore cannot be controlled by the monetary authorities. Controllability declines as the sensitivity of capital movements to the interest rate increases. The size of the balance of payments deficit associated with a given action to reduce the interest rate is in fact larger (and the larger and more rapid will be the related contraction of monetary base) the greater the mobility of capital.[11] The situation is shown in figure 18.8.

[10] Nevertheless, large capital outflows would not be sustainable, owing to the limited size of reserves.
[11] The relationship between the money market and the balance of payments has been studied by the advocates of the so-called 'monetary theory of the balance of payments'. According to this strand of economic thought, for a country with a fixed exchange rate system, a balance of payments surplus (deficit) reflects excess demand for (supply of) domestic money. Agents will get rid of, say, an excess supply of money by increasing aggregate demand, which will generate a balance of payments deficit. In the absence of sterilisation, changes in foreign reserves associated with balance of payments disequilibrium – which, as we have said, is a reflection of a disequilibrium in the money

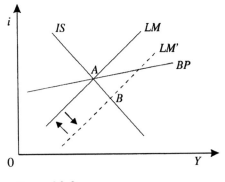

Figure 18.8

The *LM* curve initially shifts to the right to *LM'*. At *B* income is higher and the interest rate is lower. Nevertheless, owing to these effects, at *B* there would be a balance of payments deficit and a consequent tendency towards the depreciation of the currency. Intervention by the monetary authorities to avoid the depreciation would return *LM* to its original position.

18.3 Sterilisation under fixed exchange rates

Fixed exchange rates mean that monetary base tends to be an endogenous rather than exogenous variable. In other words, it is the balance of payments that determines monetary base and hence the money supply: liquidity expands or contracts depending on whether there is a surplus or deficit. However, we noted in chapter 13 that in theory it is possible to offset monetary base creation or destruction via one source by appropriate intervention through other sources. In the case where the unwanted monetary base creation or destruction takes place through the external source, compensatory action usually consists of open market operations. This is known as *sterilisation* of the changes in monetary base induced by balance of payments disequilibria.

There are two possible situations:

market – tend to be self-eliminating. Let us take the case of a balance of payments deficit, which is a symptom of excess money supply. This deficit will reduce international reserves and destroy monetary base, thus reducing the excess money supply. Under flexible exchange rates, the adjustment of the money market occurs through changes in the exchange rate rather than flows of foreign reserves. On this view, real factors (changes in preferences, increases in income, trade policy measures, etc.) would influence the balance of payments and/or the exchange rate only to the extent that they have an effect on the money market. The literature of the monetary approach emphasises that in the long run in a small economy with fixed exchange rates the money supply tends to take on the characteristics of an endogenous variable: the monetary authorities do not control the overall size of monetary base but rather only its division into domestic and external components. A number of the most important contributions to the vast literature of the monetary theory of the balance of payments and the exchange rate are contained in Frenkel and Johnson (1976, 1978).

1 there is a balance of payments deficit that destroys an excessive quantity of
monetary base. In this case, sterilisation seeks to reconstitute the monetary
base destroyed;

2 there is a balance of payments surplus that creates unwanted monetary base.
Here, sterilisation seeks to destroy the excess monetary base.

In both cases the effectiveness of sterilisation may depend on the time horizon
considered.

1 Take the first case, where the balance of payments deficit has been caused, for
example, by an expansionary monetary policy. Referring to figure 18.8, the deficit
destroys the monetary base created by the expansion, undermining the policy. In the
short term, the money supply can be kept at the desired level by appropriate sterilisation
measures (i.e., open market operations to restore monetary base destroyed through the
external channel). However, the availability of foreign exchange reserves places a limit
on such action. Let us see why. Beginning in equilibrium (point A in figure 18.8), the
monetary authorities expand monetary base, which in a system of fixed exchange rates
gives rise to a balance of payments deficit. In order to keep the exchange rate at the fixed
level, foreign exchange reserves are sold and monetary base is reduced. If they wish,
policymakers can restore monetary base by purchasing securities in the open market,
which will again cause a balance of payment deficit, sale of reserves and the acquisition
of monetary base by the public. Yet again, the destruction of monetary base can be
sterilised by further purchases of securities and so forth. Monetary base can continue to
be created as long as foreign exchange reserves hold out, but no longer. This is the
reason why in the long-run monetary policy is ineffective in the presence of imperfect
capital mobility and sterilisation.

If capital is perfectly mobile, BP is flat, i.e., it is infinitely elastic with respect to the
interest rate, and we have the situation shown in figure 18.9. Even if the monetary
authorities attempt to create monetary base, which shifts LM to the right to LM', their
efforts will be immediately nullified by the large capital outflows induced by even the
smallest decline in the interest rate. Staying in a position like B is impossible. Sterilisation of the balance of payments deficit, and hence monetary policy, become impracticable even in the short run. The LM schedule immediately shifts back to its original
position and the final equilibrium will be the same as the initial one, i.e., A.

2 Let us now examine the case in which sterilisation is intended to destroy excess
monetary base created by a balance of payments surplus. The reason for this may be, for
example, the desire of the authorities to pursue a tight monetary policy, even with an
expansionary fiscal policy (in which case the policy stance would be non-accommodating, dampening the expansion induced by fiscal policy; see chapter 14).

Referring to figure 18.6, sterilisation will cause the system to remain at B, where we
have a balance of payments surplus and an increase in income with respect to the level
preceding the introduction of the expansionary fiscal policy. However, the rise in income
is limited by the tight monetary policy.

There are limits to sterilisation in this case as well, which basically come in two forms:

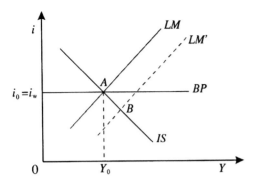

Figure 18.9

(a) Sterilisation of a persistent surplus is not possible, since sterilisation is carried out by selling government securities to the private sector. It would be necessary to raise the interest rate to induce the public to accept a larger quantity of securities and reduce the quantity of money in their portfolios. Such action would become unsustainable over time and the monetary authorities would be forced to allow monetary base to expand. There are a variety of reasons for this: the central bank's portfolio of securities may not be large enough to sustain continuous open-market operations; or the high level of interest rates may give rise to excessive growth of the public debt.

(b) Sterilisation is impossible even in the short run if capital is perfectly mobile, i.e., if there is perfect substitutability between domestic and foreign securities (and no capital controls): any attempt by the monetary authorities to sell government securities will exert upward pressure on the interest rate, prompting unlimited inflows of foreign capital; the consequent balance of payments surplus will be extremely large, as will be the corresponding creation of monetary base. Government securities are purchased by foreign investors with foreign currency, not monetary base. The destruction of monetary base becomes a truly Sisyphean task. However, the limit on the *destruction* of monetary base is less stringent than that on its *creation* in the previous example of sterilisation with perfect capital mobility, since while foreign exchange reserves can increase without limit, the value of reserves cannot be negative. So, there is asymmetry between countries with balance of payments surpluses and deficits from the standpoint of sterilisation as well.

18.4 Fiscal and monetary policy under floating exchange rates

With floating exchange rates and capital mobility, monetary policy can be effective in controlling the level of aggregate demand. By contrast, fiscal policy is rendered totally or partially ineffective by the appreciation of the currency.

In order to understand the operation of the two policies in a flexible exchange rate

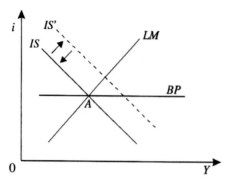

Figure 18.10

environment, we must bear in mind that the incipient balance of payments surplus or deficit[12] that they can produce leads to a change in the exchange rate rather than a change in monetary base, as it does under fixed exchange rates, as a result of central bank intervention to keep the exchange rate within fluctuation limits. Thus, an incipient worsening of the balance of payments, far from causing monetary base destruction (with restrictive effects), gives rise to a depreciation (with expansionary effects). The opposite occurs if the balance of payments tends to improve. We will first examine fiscal policy in greater detail before taking a closer look at monetary policy.

1 An increase in debt-financed government spending will cause both income and interest rates to rise. This will worsen the current account balance and improve the capital account balance, respectively. If capital movements are sufficiently responsive to cause an incipient improvement in the overall balance of payments, the currency will appreciate, as it is no longer constrained within the limits of the fixed exchange rate system. The resulting loss of competitiveness will reduce net exports and income. The pressure on the currency to appreciate will be stronger the greater is capital mobility (i.e., the inflow of capital induced by a given change in the interest rate) and the greater is the tendency of the interest rate to change following the initial increase in autonomous spending.

Figure 18.10 shows the impact of *fiscal policy* in the case of perfect capital mobility. In this case, fiscal measures are entirely ineffective. The pressure to appreciate is so strong that only a reduction in net exports equal to the initial increase in autonomous spending will restore equilibrium at *A* (complete crowding out). Only then will the demand pressure that gave rise to the initial increase in interest rates disappear. Note that if capital is highly mobile, even if the final equilibrium is almost exactly equal to the initial equilibrium in terms of the income level and interest rates, the composition of demand

---

[12] We refer to an 'incipient' imbalance since, at least in theory, in the regime we are dealing with now exchange rate variations automatically produce external balance. Economists sometimes refer to an *ex ante* imbalance, i.e., to the imbalance that would tend to be created *before* changes in the exchange rate produce the adjustment of the balance of payments (see Dernburg, 1989, pp. 117–18).

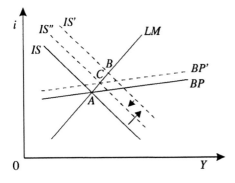

Figure 18.11

and the balance of payments has changed: the government expenditure component of demand has increased, while foreign demand has fallen, and the net balance on current account has declined, while that on capital account has increased.

If capital is not perfectly mobile, fiscal policy may be effective to some degree: the less mobile is capital, the greater the effectiveness. Examine figure 18.11, which shows a fairly flat BP, indicating high but not perfect capital mobility. With an expansionary fiscal policy, IS shifts to IS' and the system moves from A to B. At B, there is an incipient balance of payments surplus owing to the high interest rate, and the surplus will cause the currency to appreciate.

Given the increase in the interest rate, the size of the net inflow of capital will depend on the mobility of capital. The less mobile is capital, the smaller the inflow and consequently the smaller the appreciation of the currency. The appreciation will cause a reduction in net exports and therefore in aggregate demand (IS' will therefore move backwards to IS'') and shift the equilibrium conditions for the balance of payments: at a given interest rate, the appreciation of the currency will make equilibrium possible only at lower levels of income. BP will therefore move upwards to BP'. The final point of simultaneous equilibrium in the three markets will be C, with a lower income level than B (owing to the fall in net exports) but higher than the initial level at A.

If capital mobility is so low that BP is steeper than LM, fiscal policy can be quite effective. Examine figure 18.12. An expansionary fiscal policy will shift IS towards IS' and the system will move from A to B, where B denotes a balance of payments deficit owing to the dominance of the adverse effects of the expansion of demand (which have a direct impact on net exports) over the beneficial effects of the expansion (which operate on capital movements through the interest rate). The beneficial effects are small owing to the limited mobility of capital. The trend towards a balance of payments deficit causes the currency to depreciate, which boosts net exports, shifting IS' to IS''.

2 The effectiveness of *monetary policy* in a flexible exchange rate system stems from its tendency to cause a balance of payments disequilibrium that is not followed by central bank intervention to peg the exchange rate (as in the fixed exchange rate system, which gives rise to changes in monetary base in the opposite direction from that of the

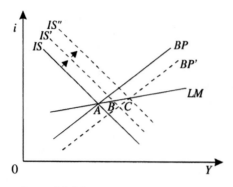

Figure 18.12

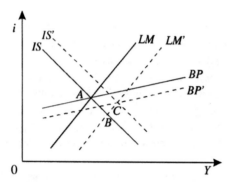

Figure 18.13

monetary policy stance). Since the exchange rate is free to fluctuate, the tendency towards an imbalance will only modify the exchange rate itself, with effects that operate in the same direction as monetary policy. A monetary expansion will cause interest rates to fall and, therefore, tend to worsen both the current account balance (owing to the expansionary effect on income) and the capital account balance. The result will be a depreciation of the currency, which will also have an expansionary effect. The expansionary impact of monetary policy on income in a flexible rate regime is greatest when capital is perfectly mobile: any monetary base creation places downward pressure on the interest rate; in this case, even a small fall in the interest rate will give rise to capital outflows large enough to cause the currency to depreciate significantly and, therefore, shift *IS* considerably.

We can summarise the effects of monetary policy by referring to figure 18.13. The increase in the money supply shifts *LM* to *LM'* and the system moves from *A* to *B*, where there is an incipient balance of payments deficit that causes the currency to depreciate. The depreciation causes *IS* to shift to *IS'* and *BP* to move to *BP'*. Point *C* is the final equilibrium point for the three markets.

The claim that a country gains independence under a flexible exchange rate regime means it can separate its monetary policy stance from balance of payments objectives –

Table 18.1. *Effectiveness of expansionary fiscal policy on income under different exchange rate regimes and different degrees of capital mobility*

Fixed exchange rates		Floating exchange rates	
Capital mobility	No capital mobility	Capital mobility	No capital mobility
Highly effective: capital mobility also causes monetary expansion	Effective, albeit less so than under capital mobility	Not very effective: capital mobility causes the currency to appreciate. With perfect mobility, there is complete crowding out of foreign demand.	Effective: the depreciation of the currency reinforces the fiscal stimulus.

which are now achieved through exchange rate variations – and assign it to domestic goals. However, the greater effectiveness of monetary policy is counterbalanced by the reduced effectiveness of fiscal policy, at least when capital is sufficiently mobile.

Tables 18.1 and 18.2 summarise the effects on income of fiscal and monetary policy, respectively, in the two exchange rate systems and with differing degrees of capital mobility. For reasons of clarity, we refer to expansionary policies only.

18.5 Applying the Mundell–Fleming model to the 1992–3 EMS crisis

An interesting application of the Mundell–Fleming model that can be used to analyse the EMS crisis in 1992–3 concerns the effects of German unification in 1990. Our presentation follows Eichengreen and Wyplosz (1993).

The unification of Germany unmasked the backwardness of public and private capital in the former German Democratic Republic. It caused supply to collapse with the dismantling of existing plant and led to an increase in demand for capital goods to be used in reconversion and restructuring. This excess demand caused income to increase and, in the absence of an accommodating monetary policy,[13] also led to a rise in domestic interest rates and an inflow of foreign capital. In a *flexible exchange rate* regime, the resulting incipient improvement in the balance of payments would have led to an appreciation of the currency in both nominal and real terms (possibly with no change in prices in Germany or the rest of the world), thus achieving a new equilibrium: Germany's current account balance would have worsened due to the appreciation and

---

[13] This was dictated by the German monetary authorities' desire to maintain the stability of the value of the mark. The reader should consider that very different consequences would result in the absence of such a monetary policy stance.

Table 18.2. *Effectiveness of expansionary monetary policy on income under different exchange rate regimes and different degrees of capital mobility*

Fixed exchange rates		Floating exchange rates	
Capital mobility	No capital mobility	Capital mobility	No capital mobility
Completely ineffective: capital mobility causes capital outflows and considerable destruction of monetary base	Limited and temporary effectiveness: the impact of the monetary action on the balance of payments is limited to the current account	Very effective: capital mobility causes the currency to depreciate, providing an expansionary stimulus to autonomous spending as well	Effective: the depreciation is relatively small, being largely due to the impact on the current account

the increase in demand, while there would have been a net inflow of capital. The effects of the excess demand shock would have been distributed between Germany and the other countries. These effects can be seen with the help of figure 18.11. The domestic results of the positive demand shock, consisting in a shift of *IS* to the right, are: (i) an increase in income and the interest rate and (ii) the nominal and real appreciation of the currency. The latter moderates the increase in the country's income and fosters an increase in income in the rest of the world.

If, however, the country operates in a *fixed exchange rate* regime, as is the case in the EMS,[14] the real appreciation of the mark can be obtained by a one-off nominal revaluation or an increase in the price (or inflation) differential between Germany and the other EMS countries with no change in the nominal exchange rate.

Figure 18.6 can help illustrate this point. The positive demand shock shifts *IS* to the right, with a rise in the interest rate and the emergence of a balance of payments surplus. As we know, in normal circumstances *B* is not stable because with fixed exchange rates the surplus translates into an expansion of monetary base, with a consequent rightward shift of *LM* as well, and final equilibrium is reached at *C*. However, since monetary policy tends to be non-accommodating (as initially assumed), the monetary authorities will seek to sterilise the monetary base created through the external surplus. As a result the system will remain in a position (such as *B* in figure 18.6) that does not represent a simultaneous equilibrium of all markets. Policymakers could seek a position of simultaneous equilibrium either by abandoning sterilisation (at the cost of monetary instability) or by revaluing the nominal exchange rate. From the point of view of the goods market equilibrium, this would temper the expansionary effects of the demand shock while restoring balance of payments equilibrium at a higher level of interest rates and

[14] The relevance of fixed exchange rate effects (which arise with EMS countries) is indeed greater than that of floating exchange rate effects (which arise *vis-à-vis* other countries) since most of Germany's international transactions take place with other EMS countries.

income.[15] In diagrammatic terms the revaluation of the nominal exchange rate would partly shift *IS* backwards and move *BP* upwards, just as we saw with flexible exchange rates (see figure 18.11). Note that the nominal revaluation (or appreciation) of the currency implies an equivalent real appreciation if the inflation differential between Germany and the rest of the EMS countries is nil. It is the real appreciation of the currency, i.e., Germany's loss of competitiveness, that permits external balance even with an increase in the interest rate. However, we can obtain the same real appreciation as would be produced by a nominal revaluation or appreciation if, for example, the nominal exchange rate and (the rate of change in) prices in Germany remained unchanged *and* (the rate of change in) prices in the other countries fell,[16] i.e., with a worsening of the inflation differential with the other European countries.

A nominal revaluation of the mark, which seems to have been preferred by the German monetary authorities, was apparently not carried out owing to the opposition of France and the United Kingdom. An increase in the price level (or inflation rate) in Germany with no change in prices (or inflation rates) in the other countries would have satisfied our alternative condition for adjustment, but would have required an accommodating monetary policy on the part of the Bundesbank, which was unthinkable. Thus, only a fall in prices (or inflation rates) in the other countries could have shifted the inflation differential with the EMS partners towards higher relative inflation in Germany, and in this way led to a real appreciation of the mark that would have been capable of reducing the German current account balance sufficiently to meet excess demand in Germany.

According to Eichengreen and Wyplosz (1993), at the beginning of autumn 1992 this change in the relative competitiveness of the EMS members was already well advanced in at least two of the countries where competitive problems were most acute, Italy, Spain and the UK, which shared the same problems. Italy was a partial exception: since the beginning of that year it had begun to show signs of such a change, which were then followed in July by the adoption of an incomes policy (see section 15.8).

It is therefore difficult to argue, according to these authors, that the EMS crisis of September 1992 was caused by the financial markets' perception of a failure to adjust to the shock of German unification. If this had been the case, it would have cast further doubt on the forecasting abilities of these markets, which first failed to speculate promptly against the currencies that lagged behind in adjusting to the shock and then decided to act just when the adjustment seemed well under way.[17]

---

[15] If capital is highly mobile, as was the case in this period and as is reflected in figure 18.6, the net effect of the increase in both of these variables would be an improvement in the balance of payments.

[16] This situation can be examined in terms of the Mundell–Fleming model without causing the problems associated with price changes (see note 1 to this chapter). Domestic prices in the country in question (Germany) are constant and only prices abroad change, which implies no changes in German nominal interest rates.

[17] Some argue that the 1992 crisis can be explained by the lack of convergence between the most relevant 'fundamentals', those connected with international competitiveness and trade balances; in particular, the lack of convergence is attributable to the ineffectiveness of the hard exchange rate policy as an instrument of industrial policy to stimulate technological innovation and improve competitiveness (see section *16.8.6).

If, despite the delay, the speculative attack against sterling and the lira in September 1992 can be justified in terms of the above model on the basis of the perception that the United Kingdom and Italy had not completely adjusted, the target and dynamics of subsequent attacks are difficult to reconcile with this explanation. For example, the peseta was at the upper margin of its fluctuation band in the EMS until just a few days before the speculative wave hit it; this means that the foreign exchange market had a positive assessment of the change in Spain's competitiveness before suddenly altering its view.

A more consistent explanation would seem to be that self-fulfilling predictions gave rise to these speculative movements despite the absence of problems with the economic 'fundamentals' (in particular, the required changes in real exchange rates). A speculative attack can be launched even if economic fundamentals and policy attitudes are consistent with balance of payments equilibrium.[18] Imagine a speculative movement strong enough to swamp the attempts of the monetary authorities of some countries to resist it, forcing them to realign their currencies. If the fundamentals do not justify the speculative attack and the monetary authorities do not alter their policies – in particular if a devaluing country does not adopt a more permissive policy stance – sooner or later the unjustified devaluation will generate a balance of payments surplus, which could lead to a return to the old parity, thus demonstrating how unfounded the initial attack had been. If, however, the monetary authorities decide to adopt a more expansionary policy after the attack, the devaluation would not produce a balance of payments surplus: in fact, the negative impact of monetary policy on capital movements could, at least initially, prevail over the positive effects of the devaluation on the current account, thus confirming the devaluation itself and the speculative attack that prompted it.

But why should the monetary authorities change their policy stance? For members of the European Union, one reason may lie in the attempt of some central bank to gain credibility by pegging the domestic currency. Less importance is thus given to other objectives, such as full employment, in the short run. However, where pegging the exchange rate is no longer feasible, other objectives become overriding.

What are the implications of our analysis for the events in the EMS in 1992–3?

A preliminary word is in order. The abandonment of the parities, whatever the cause of the speculative attack, was made possible by the disappearance of the 'dikes' created to defend them. In particular, the system of *unlimited* very-short-term credit, which was supposed to be granted by the country whose currency was appreciating (Germany) to support marginal intervention, did not work. The reason for this failure lies in the German monetary authorities' preference for an independent policy aimed at ensuring domestic monetary stability.

This provides even clearer confirmation of a fundamental principle of international economics: the inconsistency between free movement of capital and goods, fixed exchange rates and monetary independence. A transition towards EMU without major foreign exchange rate turbulence therefore calls for the easing of at least one of these

---

[18] Empirical tests of this hypothesis (although not conclusive ones) are given in Eichengreen, Rose and Wyplosz (1994).

three constraints. Since easing the peg of exchange rates is not really desired by European countries, one can only choose between relaxing monetary policy independence or free movements of capital (or goods). The former seems to be the actual route followed, with the various European countries renouncing their monetary independence *vis-à-vis* German monetary policy. As an alternative, however, capital mobility could be reduced in order to dampen speculative attacks. One way to stem large speculative flows would be measures to influence the decisions of more cautious investors,[19] such as the Tobin tax or a deposit requirement against the purchase of foreign exchange (see section 17.5).

18.6 The limitations of the Mundell–Fleming model and ways to overcome them

The Mundell–Fleming model suffers from a number of limitations that must be borne in mind to avoid unwarranted conclusions. There are essentially four types of limitation:

1 the model assumes that both domestic and foreign prices are given;
2 only credit and debit flows with the rest of the world are considered, independently of their relationships with stocks;
3 the model considers the overall equilibrium of the balance of payments, not its full equilibrium;
4 expectations of exchange rate variations are not considered.

1 The Mundell–Fleming model takes as given the domestic price level, in addition to the external price level, which is in any case an exogenous variable for a small domestic economy. Nevertheless, it is not difficult to make fruitful use of the model even if prices are allowed to change, bearing in mind the following:

(a) an increase in domestic prices may shift both *IS* and *LM* to the left. The shift of the former may be due to the real balance effect;[20] but this effect may be offset or dominated by the Fisher effect;[21] moreover, the shift to the left is due to the effects on the current account.[22] The shift in *LM* is due to the reduction in the real money supply caused by the rise in prices. This is the equivalent of a restrictive monetary policy stance;
(b) *BP* will shift upwards if domestic prices rise, similar to the effect of an appreciation in the nominal exchange rate.

Assuming that the current account and real balance effects prevail over the Fisher

---

[19] Speculative operations are started by a few agents who then mobilise the resources of many others who were initially more cautious.
[20] If nominal wages adjust to price changes with a lag, there will be a fall in real wages and, consequently, in the economy's overall propensity to consume (if wage earners have a higher propensity to consume than capitalists), which makes the slope of *IS* steeper.
[21] Recall our discussion in section 7.4.3.
[22] The increase in the propensity to import will make *IS* steeper, thus having the same effect as that of the reduction in the propensity to consume.

effect for *IS*, all our previous conclusions will still hold, albeit usually to a somewhat attenuated degree. For example, the positive effects of the devaluation on income that were discussed in section 18.1 (see figure 18.4 in particular) are dampened by the rise in domestic prices caused by the devaluation, which shifts the curves of the three markets backwards to an extent that depends on the price rise. In a fixed exchange rate regime, an expansionary fiscal policy will also cause a potentially inflationary increase in income. If domestic prices rise, *BP* will shift upwards and *IS* and *LM* will move to the left, thus containing the expansion. On the other hand, an expansionary monetary policy under fixed exchange rates will worsen the balance of payments even further as a result of the price increase it could produce. The deterioration in the balance of payments will be temporary, and the resulting reduction of monetary base should in theory cause prices to decline.[23]

In a floating exchange rate system, there is an interesting interaction between prices and the exchange rate that may be triggered by fiscal or monetary policy. Take an expansionary fiscal policy when capital is highly mobile. This will improve the balance of payments, triggering an appreciation in the nominal exchange rate. A decline in prices will result[24] that curbs the negative effect of the appreciation on the balance of payments and the real equilibrium. The net impact on income will be larger than in the case of constant prices, albeit relatively small. In the case of an expansionary monetary policy the positive effect on income may be attenuated by the increase in prices that normally accompanies the expansion and the depreciation of the nominal exchange rate.

We will further consider the possibility that prices may change in a different context in the following section.

2 In our discussion of the effects of domestic interest rate variations on capital movements we implicitly used a flow rather than stock model. Foreign investment was considered as a flow that lasts as long as there is a positive differential between domestic and world interest rates.[25] However, foreign investment can be considered as the effect of the adjustment of the stock of financial capital invested at home and abroad. Take an initial situation of equilibrium in the portfolio of domestic and foreign investors. For simplicity, we can assume that the domestic interest rate is equal to the world rate. A decline in the domestic interest rate will trigger a portfolio adjustment with an increase in holdings of foreign assets and a reduction in domestic assets, giving rise to net capital outflows. However, this impact effect may not continue for the entire period in which the interest rate differential persists. In other words, such capital flows represent a temporary process of *stock adjustment*.

Considering the riskiness as well as the rate of return of various assets may reduce the elasticity of capital movements: the fact that assets are denominated in different currencies reduces their substitutability owing to the specific risks associated with the individ-

---

[23] However, recall that price movements are normally asymmetric, being more elastic upwards than downwards (price rigidity). This might imply a lower level of final real output.

[24] This implies that the real exchange rate appreciates less than the nominal rate.

[25] We are assuming no change in the expected exchange rate. If we drop this assumption, the flow will arise or persist when the differential net of the expected variation in the exchange rate is positive.

ual currencies, making demand less sensitive to variations in interest rates. The outcome of these considerations is that *BP* tends to become steeper.

In addition, higher and higher domestic rates are required to sustain a permanent net inflow of capital, given the world interest rate: the effect of changes in the interest rate on capital movements therefore tends to be temporary; an increase in the rate results in a temporary improvement in the balance of payments through the capital account.

When we consider stocks, changes in interest rates may also have an impact on the current account owing to variations in interest payments abroad, which are included under the 'investment income' item. These effects run in the opposite direction to those on the capital account and are lasting: the rise in the interest rate attracts foreign capital for a period, thus increasing total outstanding foreign debt, on which it will be necessary to pay interest at a higher rate until the debt is redeemed. These effects imply a shift to the left in the *BP* curve.

3 The latter considerations introduce the third limitation of the Mundell-Fleming model: the fact that it considers the overall equilibrium of the balance of payments rather than full equilibrium. Overall equilibrium can be attained with various combinations of balances on the two accounts:

(a) a current account surplus and a capital account deficit;
(b) a current account deficit and a capital account surplus;
(c) balance on each account (full equilibrium).

The sustainability and the domestic effects of (a) and (b) differ significantly. We discussed sustainability under point 2). Domestic income and employment are usually higher in (a) than in (b). A current account surplus and a lower domestic interest rate both have positive effects on those variables.

4 The final limitation of the standard Mundell–Fleming model regards the hypothesis that investors do not expect changes in the exchange rate. Some argue that this assumption should be dropped because it is inconsistent with many real-life situations, especially regarding the policies we have discussed, such as monetary policy. In the previous section, in fact, we saw that exchange rate expectations can play a role.

*18.7 Exchange rate volatility and overshooting

Let us first take a long-run perspective and assume full employment and perfect substitutability between domestic and foreign assets. We will also limit our analysis to monetary policy, which is the simplest to follow. If the monetary authorities induce a permanent increase in the money supply and there is perfect and instantaneous price flexibility, there will be no effect on any variable except prices. If we begin in equilibrium, this position can only be maintained with a price increase proportional to the nominal increase in the money supply, so as to leave the real money supply unchanged.

Now suppose price increases lag behind. In this case, for a certain period of time the

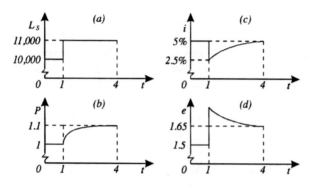

Figure 18.14

real money supply will increase and the domestic interest rate will consequently fall. What happens to the exchange rate? If the foreign interest rate remains unchanged, the decline in the domestic rate will trigger capital outflows[26] and the currency will depreciate. Some economists (see Dornbusch, 1976, in particular[27]) argue that the initial depreciation will be too large (exchange rate *overshooting*), i.e. the exchange rate will rise above the level it will have when prices have fully adjusted to the increase in the money supply (the long-run level). Following Dornbusch, let us examine the reasons for overshooting, referring to figure 18.14.

Assume that in period 1 the equilibrium exchange rate between the German mark and the dollar is 1.5 (part (d) of the figure) and there is an interest rate of 5 per cent in both countries (part (c)), with no expectations of changes in the exchange rate. A 10 per cent increase in the German money supply at the end of period 1, e.g., from 10,000 to 11,000 (as shown in part (a)) will lead to a 10 per cent increase in prices after, say, three years (e.g., from 1 to 1.1; see part (b)) and therefore an equal depreciation of the mark, with the exchange rate rising to 1.65 after the same time lag. However, we can imagine a situation in which prices initially rise only slightly. Suppose for simplicity that they increase very little at the beginning of period 2. The real quantity of money has therefore increased. The interest rate in Germany will fall to, say, 2.5 per cent and remain lower than the foreign rate until the final adjustment of prices. This means that there will be a capital outflow, causing a depreciation. The idea is that during this initial phase the exchange rate overshoots the final 'target' of 1.65. The subtle reasoning behind this conclusion is that if the exchange rate in period 2 were not higher than 1.65, in period 3 and 4 the international capital market could not be in equilibrium since, as we have said, in this period the domestic interest rate is still lower than the world rate. Only expectations of an appreciation in the subsequent period will allow equilibrium to be reached. But such expectations are justified only if the currency has depreciated too much at the beginning of period 2.

Many aspects of this argument are extremely interesting, since it offers a possible

---

[26] In addition to effects of the same sign on the current account.
[27] An extension is contained in Frenkel (1981).

explanation for the 'volatility' of exchange rates that underlies the currency cycles we discussed in section 16.7. In our opinion, however, the basic hypotheses of the overshooting model are unrealistic, and therefore open to criticism. This is especially the case with:

(a) the full employment assumption (although this can easily be removed; see Dornbusch, 1980);

(b) the related assumption that the change in the money supply induces a proportional change in prices in the long run;

(c) the assumption that price changes in a country give rise in the long run to corresponding variations in the nominal exchange rate, leaving the real exchange rate constant: in other words, an increase in prices in Germany is presumed to give rise to a proportional increase in the mark/dollar exchange rate (depreciation of the mark). This is none other than the purchasing power parity theory that we briefly introduced in section 16.7, with all its considerable limitations;[28]

(d) the hypothesis that markets must always be in equilibrium. This is a methodological problem that is relevant to much of economics, and is very difficult to address.

These long-run hypotheses correspond exactly to the monetarist model[29] with the additions made necessary by the consideration of an open economy (e.g., the purchasing power parity theory). The critique of this approach (see chapter 7) therefore applies here.

18.8 Summary

1 The Mundell–Fleming model extends the *IS-LM* analytical apparatus to the case of an open economy, introducing:
   (a) net exports as an additional component of aggregate demand;
   (b) an external payments market in addition to the goods market and money market.

2 The *BP* curve represents the combinations of income and interest rates that ensure external equilibrium when the exchange rate, foreign prices and domestic prices are given. The curve shifts as these variables change. In particular,

---

[28] The idea behind this theory is that prices (in the absolute version of the theory) or changes in prices (in its relative version) of a good (or a basket of goods) in two countries should be equal when measured in the same currency owing to the operation of international arbitrage mechanisms.
   The reasons this theory does not hold are basically the following:

   (a) there are barriers of different varieties to international trade;
   (b) the consumption basket in the two countries may be different;
   (c) markets are imperfect and there are different substitute goods in different countries;
   (d) some goods are *non-tradable* at the international level and therefore cannot be the object of arbitrage transactions except indirectly (e.g., through the movement of people in the case of tourism).

[29] De Grauwe (1983, section 15.5) makes a similar observation.

beginning in a situation of unemployment, a devaluation can ease the balance of payments constraint, making expansionary monetary and fiscal policies possible.

3 Monetary and fiscal policies have significantly different effects in fixed and floating exchange rate regimes.

4 In fixed rate systems fiscal policy is very effective, all the more so the greater the mobility of capital, which causes a change in the money supply (more precisely, it increases the money supply in the case of an expansionary policy). By contrast, monetary policy is completely ineffective in the presence of high capital mobility, which causes large and immediate capital outflows (in the case of an expansionary policy stance) or inflows (with a restrictive stance) and, therefore, considerable monetary base destruction or creation. Monetary policy can be somewhat effective, but only temporarily, in the case of low capital mobility.

5 In a floating exchange rate system, fiscal policy is less effective, all the more so the greater is capital mobility, which causes the currency to appreciate. With perfect mobility, foreign demand is crowded out. Conversely, monetary policy is very effective, all the more so the greater is capital mobility. In the case of an expansionary policy, capital mobility leads to an increase in income through the depreciation of the currency.

6 Under fixed exchange rates, monetary base tends to be an endogenous variable depending on the external balance. To avoid unwanted destruction or creation of monetary base through the foreign sector it is theoretically possible to sterilise changes in monetary base. This is not possible in certain circumstances, such as when there is perfect capital mobility.

7 An interesting application of the Mundell–Fleming model to the events in the EMS in 1992–3 shows the necessity for a country such as Germany, hit by a positive demand shock, to cause a nominal or real appreciation or revaluation of its currency. Given the reluctance of other countries to accept a revaluation of the mark and Germany's unwillingness to allow domestic prices to rise, a real appreciation should have come about through a reduction in prices (or rather, a reduction in the relative rate of increase in prices) in the other ERM countries. This real appreciation appeared to be well under way in 1992 before the onset of the foreign exchange crises that led to a flurry of realignments. The foreign exchange crises of 1992–3 were probably the effect of unjustified speculative attacks rather than the markets' perception of a lack of adjustment. High capital mobility, which makes such attacks possible, should therefore be slowed down by mechanisms such as the Tobin tax.

8 The limitations of the Mundell–Fleming model regard:
(a) the assumption of given prices;
(b) its reference to flows rather than stocks;

(c) its focus on the overall equilibrium of the balance of payments only;

(d) the neglect of expectations of exchange rate variations.

These limitations can be overcome with varying degrees of difficulty.

*9 Differences in the reactivity of exchange rates and the prices of goods and services make exchange rate overshooting possible.

18.9 Key concepts

Mundell–Fleming model

External balance

Real, nominal interest rate

Simultaneous equilibrium

Capital mobility

Monetary theory of the balance of payments

Sterilisation

Real crowding-out of the foreign component of income

Self-fulfilling prediction

'Fundamentals'

Unlimited very-short-term credit

*Overshooting

*Volatility

*Non-tradeable good

PART VII

PROBLEMS OF 'REGIME' IN GOVERNMENT ACTION, DOMESTIC AND INTERNATIONAL

19 Consistency in public choice

19.1 Time inconsistency: fixed rules and discretionary intervention

We have already discussed the meaning of rules and discretionary intervention (section 8.4.2) as well as some of the arguments in favour of rules (e.g., Friedman's 'simple rule').[1] Essentially, three arguments are advanced in support of rules:

(a) the length and variability of the time lag with which the various policies (in particular, monetary policy) take effect means that it is possible that discretionary action could exacerbate cyclical trends;
(b) expansionary discretionary measures are ineffective beyond the short run, producing only inflation in the long run;
(c) simple rules are inexpensive in terms of the administrative apparatus required to implement them.

The idea that the performance of the economy should not depend on the will and the errors of policymakers and be freed of the cost of government administration has found expression in the search for automatic measures that are more complicated than Friedman's rule (i.e., rules acting at the level of market regime, such as perfect competition, and/or monetary systems, such as the gold standard) or more 'formal' (monetary and fiscal constitutions). The supposed merits of such regimes and systems were examined at length in previous chapters. Our concern here will be to analyse the implications of the choice between automatic rules and discretionary intervention in a multi-period decision environment. This will enable us to discuss some additional economic foundations of proposals for a monetary and fiscal constitution.

Let us first examine a situation in which there are no (automatic) rules. The time

---

[1] A survey of the debate on rules and discretionary intervention in recent years is given in Argy (1988).

horizon is two periods and in each the government may choose the action that maximises its objective function.

Assume that the objective is the growth rate of output and policymakers wish to pursue this target through a policy designed to boost innovation. To stimulate technical progress, the government may initially promise inventors that they will be granted the right to the exclusive exploitation of their invention (patentability). However, once the inventions have been created (which we assume to occur by the end of period 1), the economy would benefit if everyone could use them freely, given the (allocative) inefficiency of monopoly. A policy of patent protection would therefore be *time inconsistent*; that is, it would be optimal in period 1 but no longer so in period 2, when private agents interested in producing inventions have already made their choices. Breaking the promise[2] to protect inventions, which is possible when government choices in period 2 are discretionary and not constrained by a rule, would generate a better outcome for the government. However, private agents are thus assumed to be myopic, i.e. they are induced to carry out research and development for their inventions, trusting that the patent protection promised at time 0 will be maintained in period 2. If, however, agents have rational expectations (more generally, forward-looking rather than backward-looking), discretion in government action does not ensure an optimal outcome: private agents, aware of the government's incentive to renege on its promise of patent protection, will not undertake any innovative activity.

This reasoning was initially advanced by Kydland and Prescott (1977) to argue that in the presence of rational expectations the optimal policy is not a time-consistent one chosen discretionally in each period but rather an *a priori* rule that constrains future government action, inhibiting any change in that initial choice.[3]

The constraint on future government action (pre-commitment) may be based on *custom, convention* or *law*,[4] adhered to by government in order to establish a *reputation* and strengthen its *credibility*. Thus, the daily practice of government activities that are consistent with previous commitments, repeated government affirmations of the inevitability of certain policies and the passage of laws with constitutional status or that delegate decisions to someone who does not suffer from the same temptation of opportunism (central banks, agencies) are different but not mutually exclusive ways of committing to a certain policy.

Although important, Kydland and Prescott's contribution does not demonstrate the superiority of fixed rules over discretionary policies. Discretionary policy is not simply

---

[2] In the case of a threat the concept of subgame perfection, which is usually thought to be the same as time consistency, would be relevant (see Guiso and Terlizzese, 1990).

[3] Bear in mind that the rule must be fixed, i.e., a rule that provides for one action only and not one that determines the action on the basis of the prevailing circumstances or available information in the subsequent period. This sort of rule, known variously as a *non-contingent, non-causal, no-feedback* or *open-loop rule*, contrasts with flexible rules (*contingent, causal, feedback* or *closed loop*), which is the more general case of discretionary action.

[4] These terms represent the hierarchy of social institutions established by Max Weber (1922): custom (habits, etc.) is behaviour that has become habitual following protracted practice; conventions represent behaviour followed in order to avoid the disapproval of the social group to which one belongs; law is a behaviour followed in order to avoid specific punishments and penalties.

that system in which policymakers have complete freedom of choice in the next period; the most general form of discretionary policy is the *flexible rule* (or strategy) that from the very beginning provides for the possibility of acting differently in the second period. It has been demonstrated that this sort of flexible rule is always superior to fixed rules under uncertainty (Buiter, 1981).

Returning to our patent protection example, a guarantee to protect the inventor based on a flexible rule that allows the duration of the protection to vary according to certain circumstances (e.g., the importance of the invention) produces better results than a fixed rule if there is uncertainty about the nature of the invention. Such a flexible rule would be time-consistent, since the actual decisions will be taken (within the time limit set) in the second period in the light of the information available at that time concerning the importance of the inventions realised. However, the rule does not give rise to credibility problems or at least does not create larger credibility problems than those posed by fixed rules, which may in any case always be changed at some later time, since the terms of the future decision are set in the first period and are well-known to private agents.

The literature in this area has identified other cases of time-inconsistent policies. A particularly interesting example, discussed in Kydland and Prescott (1977) and later by other authors (e.g., Barro and Gordon, 1983) is choosing between unemployment and inflation.

Assume two short-run expectations-augmented Phillips curves (f_1 and f_2 in figure 19.1) and a long-run Phillips curve ($\bar{u}$, which according to the authors is vertical). The preferences of policymakers are also defined and are expressed as a map of indifference curves, W_1, W_2 and W_3.

Consider the choices of government[5] and workers in a 2-period setting. In period 1 the government elects to choose point A, which is on indifference curve W_2, and announces that it will remain at A – i.e., will not introduce an expansionary and inflationary policy – in period 2 as well, after the unions have decided their wage policy. If the unions believed this promise, they would choose a policy of wage moderation (the relevant Phillips curve being f_1) that would allow the economy to remain at A. However, once the unions have chosen this strategy, the government would no longer have an incentive to remain at A in period 2, which is a second-best situation. Instead, the government could increase its utility by moving to the social indifference curve W_3, which is closer to the origin, at B (a first-best position) by adopting expansionary measures that reduce unemployment and raise the inflation rate. However, having rational expectations, the unions are aware of this possibility. Since they know the government will have an incentive to diverge from its announced non-inflationary policy, they will incorporate their inflation forecasts into their choices and seek large wage increases from the beginning of period 1. The relevant Phillips curve then becomes f_2. In this case, in period 2 the government should not expand the economy (i.e., let it move away from $u = \bar{u}$), which brings the economy to C, a third-best position. If the

---

[5] Here government means any policymaker, which may be fiscal policy authorities or, as is assumed in much of the literature, the monetary authorities.

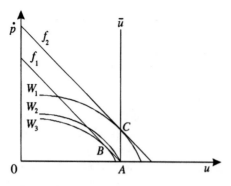

Figure 19.1

government adopted an expansionary policy, the economy would not move to C (where an indifference curve is tangent to the augmented Phillips curve) but rather to the left of that point along f_2, which would be suboptimal with respect to C.

Point C is therefore reached as the outcome of a time-consistent policy, in which each agent chooses the best alternative in each period, taking previous decisions as given but forming rational expectations about the future. However, it is precisely these rational expectations that induce some agents (in our case, the unions) to take actions that limit the possible future choices of other agents (the government), leading to suboptimal results. Note that C provides less welfare than A, which is reached with a firm and credible commitment of the government to forgo expansionary policies of the kind mentioned earlier.

The suboptimality of time-consistent policies supports the adoption of rules. However, the constraint that such rules impose may be extremely burdensome if unexpected adverse events occur (e.g., a fall in world demand). In this case, the ability to react flexibly – through discretionary policies – may offer greater advantages than precommitment (Fischer, 1990; Bernanke and Mishkin, 1992). In other words, an initially desirable objective may lose its attraction with the passage of time. Time inconsistency is not necessarily an ill. Those who consider it so are perhaps influenced by the myth of Ulysses, who had himself bound to the mast in order not to succumb to the Sirens' song. Unfortunately, we lack a frame of reference to distinguish between good time inconsistency and bad time inconsistency and there is a risk that certain justified time-inconsistent policies will be cited in support of irrevocable commitments (monetary and fiscal rules or constitutions), with hidden goals that are anything but neutral as regards the distribution of income and social impact.

Thus the question of the relative advantages of rules and discretion is not just an abstract quandary; rather, to a degree it reflects the different weight assigned to different policy objectives and different real-world circumstances. In particular, those who attribute considerable importance to monetary stability will try to rein in the competition that may give rise to inflation by means of rules that limit government action. Those who fear a fall in demand and employment will argue that rules limiting the freedom of government action make a recovery impossible and should thus be abandoned in favour of discretionary policies.

19.2 Consistency and domestic decentralisation: the appropriate assignment of instruments to targets

In our discussion of the reduced-form decision model (section 8.5.2) we saw that each instrument influences all the targets. Therefore, in general we cannot assign individual instruments exclusively to individual targets. This means, for example, that the exchange rate lever cannot be used to reach balance of payments equilibrium alone, since in addition to exports and imports it affects other target variables, such as inflation. Failing to consider these additional effects when setting the value of the exchange rate would mean ignoring its full impact, concentrating on one aspect only (perhaps the main element but certainly not the only one). As we can see from the inverse reduced form (equations (8.6)), the value of each instrument should be chosen by taking account of both objectives simultaneously. A simultaneous solution is clearly a centralised solution, at least as far as *decision* is concerned. Execution can nevertheless be delegated to separate bodies responsible for the various policies (exchange rate policy, fiscal policy, monetary policy, etc.).

However, we must consider the fact that we often know only approximately the parameter values of the model describing the economy, so that we can only determine the order of magnitude of the effects of each instrument. In other words, we may only know that one instrument is more effective than another in achieving a given objective, without being able to calculate its exact effects. In this situation, a simultaneous solution of the policy problem is difficult to formulate and even in a centralised context policymakers must proceed by trial and error, by adjusting one instrument at a time.

In addition, in the real world, each of several institutions may be charged with independently *choosing* the level of one instrument in order to achieve its target: for instance, the central bank decides the quantity of monetary base to create in order to hit its target (e.g., price stability), while Parliament establishes the amount of public expenditure or the level of taxation needed to achieve its objective (e.g., employment).

There are two aspects to this problem:

(a) first, we must determine the conditions in which such decentralisation of economic policy decisions can be considered rational in economic terms;

(b) second, we need to determine which objective to assign to each of the bodies that control the various instruments of government action.

A decentralised approach, if feasible, could offer the advantages of lower costs associated with specialised functions of policy management. We will shortly show that in the Mundell–Fleming setting the decentralised solution is possible and that, in theory, it gives the same result as the centralised approach if:

(a) the instruments have different degrees of effectiveness on the objectives; i.e., if one instrument is more effective than another for one objective and less effective for others;

(b) each instrument is adjusted by the relevant authority in relation to the objective for which it is relatively more effective (*appropriate assignment* of instruments to objectives).[6]

For example, let there be two objectives (full employment income, or internal balance, and balance of payments equilibrium or external balance) and two instruments (government expenditure and liquidity). If the effectiveness of monetary policy in impacting income, compared with the effectiveness of fiscal policy, is less than its effectiveness over the balance of payments (again relative to that of fiscal policy), then monetary policy should be assigned to the balance of payments objective (i.e., it should be adjusted with a view to reaching the desired value for the external balance) and fiscal policy should be assigned the income objective.

Let us examine the problem in more detail in intuitive terms. Assume that the desired target values are $Y = \bar{Y}$ and $BP = 0$, where the symbols have the usual meanings and $\bar{Y}$ denotes full employment income. At time t_0, $BP = 0$ and $Y < \bar{Y}$. The monetary authority (say, the central bank), appropriately assigned to ensuring external balance, has no reason to take action. By contrast, the Treasury, which has been assigned responsibility for fiscal policy in pursuing internal balance, should adopt expansionary measures, increasing government spending. Assume that this policy is fully effective and produces $Y = \bar{Y}$ at time t_1.

The increase in income leads to a worsening of the current account, however; if capital is not highly mobile (as we assume in order to replicate the original Mundell analysis), a balance of payments deficit will result ($BP < 0$). At this point it is the central bank's turn to intervene by restricting liquidity so as to foster an inflow of foreign capital. But the monetary squeeze also has a depressive effect on income. The fall in imports associated with the reduction in income, together with a larger inflow of foreign capital, will return the balance of payments to equilibrium ($BP = 0$). Nevertheless, as a result of the restrictive monetary stance, income at t_2 will be below the desired level ($Y < \bar{Y}$).

At t_2 we are therefore in a situation that resembles that where we began at t_0. In the periods after t_2, each of the two policy authorities will continue to act in the same manner. The question we must ask is whether there will be convergence towards the desired position (where we have $Y = \bar{Y}$ and $BP = 0$ simultaneously); that is, whether the corrective interventions of the authorities gradually become smaller.

The answer is yes, given that the instruments – as posited – have been assigned appropriately: to correct an imbalance (in income or balance of payments) the relatively more effective instrument has been used for the unmet target. We know that each instrument influences both targets; nevertheless, since using the liquidity instrument to

---

[6] This is also known as the *Mundell principle* (or the *effective-market classification principle*), as it was introduced by Mundell (1962). The sufficient conditions for the appropriate assignment of instruments to targets within the framework of dynamic models are analysed in Aoki and Canzoneri (1979). For a clear statement of the conditions for the validity of the principle and, more generally, for an analysis of problems of centralisation and decentralisation see Johansen (1978, chapter 7) and Vandenbroucke (1985).

correct a balance of payments deficit had a larger impact (compared with the fiscal instrument) on that target than for the income target, the (negative) effect of the liquidity squeeze on income was less than the beneficial impact on the balance of payments. Thus, liquidity has the maximum positive impact on the balance of payments, with the smallest disturbance effect on income (assuming we begin with income in equilibrium), precisely because liquidity is relatively less effective in influencing income.

The validity of this reasoning is strictly dependent on our hypotheses about the functioning of the economy; that is, on the model. In particular, it is assumed that the exchange rate is fixed. With this hypothesis, fiscal policy is more effective than monetary policy for domestic equilibrium, as was argued in section 18.2.[7] It is also assumed that interest rate differentials generate lasting outflows of capital, rather than temporary flows associated with stock adjustment.[8] In addition, the position of policymakers in the rest of the world is taken as given, not depending on the choices made by domestic policymakers. This is a reasonable assumption only if the economy in question is very small. Actually, when a country of some size changes its policy stance, especially monetary policy, it may have an effect on interest rates in the rest of the world, which normally responds by adjusting its own policy. More generally, if the reference model were to change, the conclusions regarding the *type* of appropriate assignment could change as well. For example, this is the case of the New Cambridge School, which adopts a different model of the economy and reaches opposite conclusions to the foregoing regarding the pairing of monetary and fiscal policy with internal and external balance targets (see Cripps and Godley, 1976; Fetherston and Godley, 1978).

A second limitation of our previous argument is the assumption that there are no costs or barriers to the use of the various instruments. In particular, they must be completely flexible and available for immediate use (effect lags must not be excessive).[9]

A further limitation stems from our assumption that there are only overall internal and external balance targets, whereas in the real world the composition of both aggregate demand and the balance of payments is not irrelevant. For example, with reference to the latter, we have already seen that an overall balance deriving from a capital account surplus and a current account deficit can raise problems for policymakers, since the surplus may represent additional debt for the country. As to internal balance, it can make a difference (especially in terms of the economy's capacity to grow) whether an income target is obtained with a larger or smaller investment component.

---

[7] This makes it easier to satisfy the required condition that fiscal policy is more effective than monetary policy for internal balance as compared with their relative effectiveness for external balance.

  The assumption of fixed exchange rates can create problems in defining monetary base as a policy instrument since we know that this regime tends to make monetary base an endogenous variable (also through sterilization), all the more so the higher is capital mobility. The assumption of low capital mobility hence serves the purpose of strengthening the control of monetary authorities over monetary base.

[8] This was discussed in detail in section 18.6.

[9] Once we recognize that there are costs associated with the use of instruments, the decentralised-assignment rules become inappropriate (see more extensively Vandenbroucke, 1985).

A diagrammatic and formal exposition of the Mundell principle is given in the following section.

*19.3 A formal analysis of appropriate assignment

The relationships between objectives (income and balance of payments) and instruments (government expenditure and monetary base) can be expressed in reduced form as follows:

$$Y = h(G, MB) \tag{19.1}$$

$$BP = f(G, MB) \tag{19.2}$$

We will first construct an iso-target curve for the two objectives in the indicated order. Take a pair of values for G and MB that satisfy (19.1) for $Y = \bar{Y}$. Let these be G_0 and MB_0. Let us now ask how G must change if MB is increased and we want to keep $Y = \bar{Y}$. Clearly, G should decrease to offset the expansionary effect of an increase in MB. This implies a decreasing slope for the iso-income curve (the locus of the combinations of G and MB that maintain Y constant), or that the instruments are *substitutes* with regard to the income target.

In addition, the more effective government expenditure is in determining income, compared with its effect on monetary base, the smaller the contraction (expansion) of spending needed to compensate a given expansion (contraction) of monetary base. This means that the resulting iso-income curve (see figure 19.2)[10] will not be very steep; i.e. the slope, given by $(dG/dMB)_{Y=\bar{Y}}$, is relatively small (in absolute value).

Referring to figure 19.2, note that the points above and to the right of the curve are points of excess demand (inflationary gap), since at least one of the two instruments is set at a level above that needed to produce $Y = \bar{Y}$. The points below and to the left of the curve indicate a recession (deflationary gap).

We will now construct the iso-target curve for the balance of payments. Suppose that the desired target ($BP = 0$) can be achieved by setting $MB = MB_1$ and $G = G_1$ (see figure 19.3). If monetary base increases, the balance of payments will show a deficit, which could be offset by a reduction in government expenditure that improves the current account balance.[11] Thus, government expenditure and monetary base are substitutes rather than complements for external balance as well. However, the iso-target curve for external balance is steeper (in absolute value) than the iso-target curve for internal balance. If our previous considerations hold, adjusting monetary base is considerably more effective than adjusting government spending in influencing the balance of payments. Therefore, a given increase in monetary base will produce a significant balance of payments deficit, which must be offset by a large reduction in

---

[10] For simplicity we assume that the relationship between G and MB is linear.

[11] The reader should remember that because of the assumption of relatively immobile capital, reducing G does not cause a reduction of i so great as to cause a large capital outflow. Hence, the improvement in the current account is not counterbalanced by a significant capital account deterioration, thus leading to a net improvement in the balance of payments.

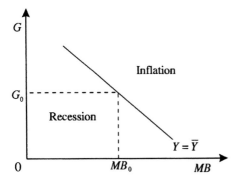

Figure 19.2

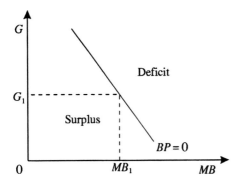

Figure 19.3

government expenditure. On the other hand, an equal increase in monetary base will have little[12] expansionary impact on income and must therefore be offset by a smaller reduction in government expenditure, since the latter is relatively more effective in affecting the level of income. Points above and to the right (below and to the left) of the curve indicate a balance of payments deficit (surplus).

We can now bring these arguments together (see figure 19.4).

As we said in chapter 8, an economic policy problem with fixed targets normally has one solution if the number of instruments is at least equal to the number of targets. In our case, there will normally be one pair of values, G^* and MB^*, that give $Y = \bar{Y}$ and $BP = 0$ simultaneously. Our discussion of the appropriate assignment of instruments to objectives shows that we can separately adjust the two instruments – each of which is aimed at 'its' target – to reach this solution: if the relative slope of the two iso-target curves is that shown in figure 19.4, we can attain $Y = \bar{Y}$ and $BP = 0$ if government expenditure is assigned the task of maintaining internal balance (the objective for which it is relatively more effective) and monetary policy is paired with external balance (for which it is best suited).

---

[12] The terms 'large' and 'little' are meant in relative terms, i.e., with comparative reference to the two targets.

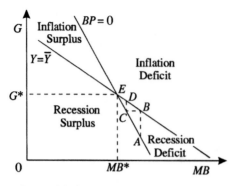

Figure 19.4

We can determine diagrammatically whether there is a tendency towards the desired position if we begin in a different initial position. Let the initial position be A, where $BP = 0$ and $Y < \bar{Y}$. The Treasury increases G, while the central bank keeps MB unchanged. We will therefore reach point B, where $Y = \bar{Y}$, but $BP < 0$, since the expansion of domestic demand has caused imports to increase, whereas the increase in the interest rate (caused by the boost in aggregate demand with unchanged monetary base) has not attracted enough capital from abroad. At this point the central bank will tighten its stance, reducing MB and bringing the system to C, where $BP = 0$; income still falls short of its target level $\bar{Y}$, but the deflationary gap has been narrowed with respect to that in A. Continuing in the same fashion, both policymakers reach their desired position at E, where $BP = 0$ and $Y = \bar{Y}$. (The reader could arrive at the same conclusions in diagrammatic terms using the IS-LM-BP apparatus instead of the iso-target curves used here.)

In formal terms, we indicate the slopes of the two curves with $(dG/dMB)_{Y=\bar{Y}}$ and $(dG/dMB)_{BP=0}$. These slopes represent the marginal rates of substitution between the two instruments for each of the objectives. We can therefore state that government expenditure and monetary base should be assigned to income and balance of payments respectively if the iso-income curve is flatter than the iso-balance of payments curve. Considering that both curves have a negative slope, this assignment is therefore justified if the relative value of the slopes of the two curves respects the following inequality:

$$(dG/dMB)_{Y=\bar{Y}} > (dG/dMB)_{BP=0} \qquad (19.3)$$

Now, we can show that:[13]

---

[13] Consider (19.1) as an implicit function of the two instruments:

$$Y(G, MB) = 0 \qquad (19.1')$$

Totally differentiating (19.1'), we have:

$$\frac{\partial Y}{\partial G}dG + \frac{\partial Y}{\partial MB}dMB = 0$$

from which we can easily obtain (19.4).

We can proceed in a similar manner with (19.2), considering it as an implicit function:

$$BP(G, MB) = 0.$$

$$(dG/dMB)_{Y=\bar{Y}} = -\frac{\partial Y/\partial MB}{\partial Y/\partial G} \tag{19.4}$$

and

$$(dG/dMB)_{BP=0} = -\frac{\partial BP/\partial MB}{\partial BP/\partial G} \tag{19.5}$$

Substituting (19.4) and (19.5) into (19.3) we have:

$$-\frac{\partial Y/\partial MB}{\partial Y/\partial G} > -\frac{\partial BP/\partial MB}{\partial BP/\partial G}$$

or

$$\frac{\partial Y/\partial MB}{\partial Y/\partial G} < \frac{\partial BP/\partial MB}{\partial BP/\partial G} \tag{19.6}$$

The left-hand side is a measure of the relative effectiveness of the two instruments on income. Similarly, the right-hand side is a measure of the relative effectiveness of the two instruments on the balance of payments.

Inequality (19.6) is simply the formal expression of the condition for the appropriate assignment of instruments. We can therefore say that pairing fiscal policy with internal balance and monetary policy with external balance is justified if the impact of monetary policy on income compared with that of government expenditure on the same variable is smaller than the impact of monetary policy on the balance of payments compared with that of government expenditure on the same objective.[14]

Despite the convergence towards the desired solution, there may be a form of overshooting even if the appropriate assignment criterion is followed when the adjustment of the decentralised authorities takes place (as it normally does) in discrete rather than continuous terms (Dernburg, 1989, pp. 333 ff.). For example, let there be two instruments, the exchange rate, e, and the level of government expenditure, G, to achieve two targets, $BP = 0$ and $Y = \bar{Y}$.

The iso-target curves will be like those shown in figure 19.5, as the reader can easily verify by repeating the reasoning of the previous section. Note that the instruments are substitutes for the income target but, if low capital mobility is assumed, complements for the balance of payments target.

If the slope of $Y = \bar{Y}$ is greater in absolute value than that of $BP = 0$, it will be appropriate to assign government expenditure to internal balance and the exchange rate to external balance. Beginning at A, where there is a balance of payments surplus, the exchange rate is revalued to achieve external balance and the system moves to B. At B, government expenditure is increased to counter the recession and the system moves to C, and so forth. The figure shows that the process converges on P, where government expenditure is G_p and the exchange rate is e_p. However, each time one instrument is over-adjusted in relation to the variation needed to achieve the two targets

---

[14] A full formal demonstration of the fact that satisfying condition (19.6) ensures the stability of the solution is given in Gandolfo (1995, section A15.4).

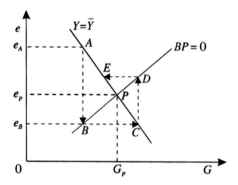

Figure 19.5

simultaneously.[15] For example, in moving from A to B, the exchange rate is revalued by too much, being set at e_B rather than e_p, which is the desired final value for both the target variables. The same applies to government spending in the successive adjustments.

This is a serious problem for economic policy since it implies the inefficient use of instruments. However, if instruments were adjusted continuously over time (that is, with small but immediate variations), the probability of having convergence without overshooting rises (for more on this see Dernburg, 1989, sections 12.3 and 12.4).

19.4 Implicit international coordination and the redundancy problem

Let us first examine one of the problems that often arises if there is no explicit international coordination: the so-called *redundancy problem* or *nth-country problem*.

Let there be n countries, which constitute the 'world' we wish to examine. There are therefore n balances of payments, but only $n - 1$ of them are independent and represent possible targets for the policymakers in the respective countries (Walras' law). The value of the nth balance of payments cannot be fixed independently of the sum of the other $n - 1$ balances: it will be equal in size and opposite in sign to this sum, since for the world as a whole we must have:

$$\sum_{i=1}^{n} BP_i = 0 \tag{19.7}$$

Therefore, if each of the policy authorities of $n - 1$ countries independently uses an instrument (say, monetary policy[16]) to achieve their desired balance, the nth country will not be able to choose its own preferred balance. If a country *autonomously* decided to take a passive stance, accepting the imbalance produced by the joint action of the other

[15] Note that overshooting cannot occur when the instruments are substitutes with respect to both objectives, as in the case of the monetary and fiscal policies used for the income and balance of payments targets. Similarly, it cannot occur when the instruments are complementary with respect to both targets.

[16] Exchange rate adjustments could also be used.

countries, a sort of implicit coordination would arise, and that country would be the nth country. Without such a decision, some form of coordination would be needed to arrive at:

(a) an explicit agreement on the size of the balances of all n countries, such as to satisfy (19.7); or

(b) an explicit agreement under which one country will take a passive position (acting as the nth country), accepting an imbalance equal to the sum of the imbalances of the other $n - 1$ countries but of the opposite sign, *whatever* that imbalance may be: the nth country will run a balance of payments deficit if the others wish to run surpluses and are in a position to do so.

The first form of explicit coordination requires negotiations that are likely to be arduous. The second form may appear even more difficult to achieve, given the passive stance requested from the nth country with regard to its balance of payments. However, the nth country is not necessarily at a disadvantage; in fact, it may be in a privileged position: freed of the task of pursuing its balance of payments objective, it can use monetary policy for domestic economic purposes. Certainly, the balance of payments targets of the other $n - 1$ countries may imply a balance of payments deficit for the nth country, but there is no reason for the latter to be concerned by this if the other countries accept without limit its liabilities (i.e., its currency) in settlement of its deficit. In other cases, the economic structure and social conditions of the nth country may be such that it tends to run a balance of payments surplus.

So, the nth country is free to decide its own monetary policy so as to achieve its inflation and employment targets,[17] entirely (or largely) ignoring its balance of payments. The other $n - 1$ countries will have to adjust their monetary instruments to set the interest rate that (given the other variables) will ensure attainment of the desired balance of payments.

Who acts as the nth country depends on historical considerations (which country issues a reserve currency), political factors (the leadership role that the country is able to perform) and economic conditions (the size of the country and the objectives of the monetary authorities). As regards the latter, in certain circumstances the other $n - 1$ countries will appreciate the intention and ability of a country to pursue expansionary policies that will provide a boost for them as well. This was essentially the situation under the Bretton Woods system: after an initial period of dollar shortage, the expansionary policy stance of the United States contributed to generating balance of payments deficits for that country, consistent with the desire of the other countries to build up dollar-denominated reserves. As we saw in section 16.4, however, in these circumstances there would be a risk that problems of confidence will emerge, since the dollar was accepted as an instrument of international liquidity in part because of its convertibility into gold and in part because of the fact that it preserved its real purchasing power over time.

In more recent years, some authors (see Giavazzi and Giovannini, 1989, p. 195) have

---

[17] We know from section 18.2 that in a fixed exchange rate regime monetary policy is not effective in pursuing these objectives. However, this does not apply if capital is not very responsive to interest rate differentials and, most important, if the home country is a large one.

identified Germany as the nth country within the EMS, since this country has decided its monetary policy in a largely independent manner and the other member states have had to set interest rates accordingly to obtain their desired external balances. However, this similarity between Germany in the EMS and the nth country should not lead us to overlook the profound differences between this situation and that of the United States.[18]

19.5 The case for international coordination[19]

Following Cooper (1969), we define international coordination as a situation in which each country adjusts its policy instruments so as to achieve the objectives of the rest of the world as well as its own.

The need for coordination may arise when the following two circumstances exist:

(a) there is interdependence between the different economies; and
(b) the non-coordinated action of the various countries would produce suboptimal outcomes.

Economic interdependence between different economies is expressed through the international movement of goods, labour and capital. Technological progress, especially in the area of communications and transportation, has greatly increased the international mobility of goods and 'factors' and the degree of international openness of economies (World Bank, 1995).[20] Thus, events in one country, including those induced by government action, have repercussions in other countries. These repercussions can be positive or negative and therefore constitute externalities similar to those we discussed in chapter 6 (*spillover*). In some cases the concepts of external economies and diseconomies can be applied directly: pollution, for example, or the spread of knowledge through different means of communication. In other cases, the effects are better represented in macroeconomic terms. In this section, we focus on macroeconomic effects.

Let us examine how these effects can emerge. Let there be two countries only, Germany and the United Kingdom. Let us assume that the two economies are approximately the same size, there is only one policy instrument available (government expenditure) and there are flexible targets. More precisely, they seek to maximise a welfare function whose arguments are income and the balance of payments. For simplicity, we assume that welfare increases with both arguments of the function, at least within a certain range, as far as the balance of payments is concerned.

Given the policy followed by the United Kingdom, which we assume has government

---

[18] The difference between the EMS and the IMF is underscored in De Cecco (1990), who argues – among other things – against the attempt to create an asymmetric monetary pole within the EMS in conflict with the policy direction given by the United States.

[19] International coordination poses many problems. For reasons of space, we must limit our discussion here. A minor problem is semantic. However, it is worth stressing that in most of the literature the terms 'coordination' and 'cooperation' are used interchangeably. We will follow this habit here.

[20] In the case of goods and services, the degree of international openness of a country is measured as the ratio of its total international trade $(X + M)$ to GDP. This ratio has greatly increased over time owing to the fact that international trade has grown more rapidly than GDP.

expenditure of G_{UK}^0, Germany adopts a fiscal policy that will cause income to grow but will not worsen (too much) the balance of payments.[21] Let G_D^0 be the level of this optimal policy; any more expansionary policy, *ceteris paribus*, will reduce German welfare. There is a similar situation in the UK: given the level of German government expenditure (e.g., G_D^0), the UK will set its own expenditure at a level, G_{UK}^0, that maximises its welfare function.

These are the optimal policies for each country *given* the non-expansionary behaviour of the other. However, for each country the optimal level of government expenditure would be higher if the other were to adopt a more expansionary policy: the UK could raise government expenditure above G_{UK}^0, thus increasing income without worsening the balance of payments if Germany were to adopt a more expansionary policy ($G_D > G_D^0$). In this case, the increase in UK imports caused by the expansionary policy would be balanced by the rise in German imports (which represent UK exports) due to Germany's expansionary policy. The reason this does not occur is the lack of coordination: if each country fears that the other will not expand its economy enough, the outcome may be that neither expands.[22] Obviously, in the real world there are other facets to the problem. For example, asymmetry in the size of the economy or in the degree of international openness can make coordination difficult.

Thus in theory it is possible to increase the welfare of both countries, thereby achieving a Pareto-superior outcome, by employing some form of policy coordination.

The *transmission* of the effects of one country's policy to the other country may be negative rather than positive, as it was in our example. That is, the macroeconomic external effect may be negative rather than positive, meaning that the policy would be of the beggar-thy-neighbour sort. Examples of this are public or private actions that increase pollution or, in certain circumstances, devaluations or other protectionist policies.[23]

Cooperation can be beneficial even if the two countries assign different weights to the various objectives. This is clearer if we consider the fact that coordination enables us to shift the efficiency frontier (i.e., the 'transformation' curve between two targets) outwards. We will return to this issue in the following section.

The cases we have just examined regard a situation of *pure discretionary coordination* (the term was introduced by Schultze, 1988): the various countries decide on a case-by-case basis to internalise the externalities or benefit from macroeconomic interdependence and each country gains without losing anything. There are then cases of *discretionary coordination through compromise*, in which each country gains with reference to one objective but loses with respect to another, while still achieving a net gain.

Coordination can be implemented with *ad hoc concertation* (e.g., negotiations over

---

[21] More precisely, we have an optimal policy when the marginal rate of substitution between the two objectives is equal to their marginal rate of 'transformation'.

[22] This is the classic prisoner's dilemma we discussed in section *6.6. In other cases, the situation may appear not as a prisoner's dilemma but as some other game, e.g., the stag-hunt game. This depicts a situation where n hunters surround a stag. If one defects to catch a passing rabbit, the stag will escape, with some gain for the defecting hunter and none for the others. If they all hunt for the stag, they will share it equally. Each hunter prefers $1/n$ of a stag to one rabbit. According to Carraro (1989) this is an appropriate game to model international policy coordination.

[23] See section 17.11.5, however.

tariff levels), or through the adoption of rules that give rise to *institutionalised cooperation* (e.g., an agreement to maintain fixed exchange rates, perhaps with the help of *ad hoc* institutions). This second form of cooperation normally involves creating rules or regimes that enable the countries to avoid at least some of the inefficiencies of unilateral solutions (Guerrieri and Padoan, 1988), thus providing a certain and lasting form of cooperation. The gold standard, the Bretton Woods system, the EMS and the rules laid down at Maastricht for participation in Stage 3 of EMU are examples of this sort of coordination. Unlike the Maastricht agreements, the other systems did not offer precise policy prescriptions. Instead they adopted a shared intermediate target (exchange rate stability), which was expected to have beneficial consequences for the operation of the different economies (e.g., in order to avoid beggar-thy-neighbour policies).[24]

There are reasons for preferring institutionalised cooperation to *ad hoc* solutions. For example, the latter is more vulnerable to pressure from various interest groups. The need to repeat *ad hoc* negotiations before each concerted action also makes this approach inefficient, all the more so if there are problems of political instability in the negotiating countries, with the related turnover of negotiators.

On the other hand, an awareness of the difficulty of renegotiating rules established within the framework of institutionalised cooperation (rules that in theory should be complied with for an indefinite, or at least lengthy, period) may accentuate the difficulties of this sort of coordination. In addition, *ad hoc* (and hence discretionary) intervention may be required whenever the system has to cope with events that are not provided for in the rules of institutionalised cooperation or specific circumstances force policymakers to take different action than that contemplated by those rules.[25] Finally, such rules require regular review, which cannot be ignored simply to avoid slow and difficult negotiations. Without such revision, the discretion and flexibility needed to adapt to the evolution of the historical context would be provided by the technocrats of the institutions themselves, which could produce distortions.[26]

*19.6 International coordination in formal terms

We first analyse problems of coordination, which differ depending on whether targets are fixed or flexible. Let us first consider fixed targets. We know that a country,

[24] Two more precise rules suggested as instruments of international coordination are: the *McKinnon monetary rule* (each country varies its money supply as an inverse function of the exchange rate) and J. Williamson's proposal for a *target zone*, where exchange rates would be flexible within fairly broad bands but countries would have to undertake corrective action as they approached the margins (see McKinnon, 1988; Williamson, 1985, and, for a discussion of these proposals, Fischer, 1988).

[25] Institutionalised cooperation often provides for exceptions – or safeguard clauses – to the normal rules. For example, Article 73 of the Treaty of Rome establishing the European Economic Community, which is still in force, allows a member state to adopt discretionary protectionist measures whenever capital movements jeopardise the operation of its capital markets.

[26] An example of such distortions is perhaps the decision to allow access to IMF resources for deficits caused by capital outflows. Access was first denied and then granted by the Fund bureaucrats without any change in the Fund's Articles of Agreement, with significant practical consequences.

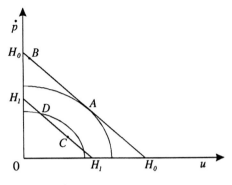

Figure 19.6

regardless of international coordination, can achieve any set of fixed targets as long as there are at least as many instruments as targets and as long as the targets are feasible (i.e., are within the set bounded by the 'transformation' curve). International coordination is beneficial simply because the frontier of possible targets (the 'transformation' curve) is shifted outwards (if the targets are 'goods') or inwards (if they are 'bads') for each country. This makes it possible to improve the attainable level of at least one of the two targets, leaving the other unchanged; alternatively, in the case of flexible targets, it will be possible to move to a higher indifference curve.

Take the case of the Phillips curve (e.g., for the United States), which we assume can be drawn like $H_0 H_0$ in figure 19.6. Let A be the initial position of the US, which corresponds, by hypothesis, to the values of the targets that maximise its welfare. An expansionary policy would move the US *along* the curve to B, which is suboptimal. On closer examination, however, we see that the *position* of this curve depends on the level of demand in the Rest of the World: if foreign demand were higher, under flexible exchange rates the curve would shift downwards to, say, $H_1 H_1$.[27] The increase in foreign demand could worsen the terms of trade of the Rest of the World (through depreciation of the exchange rate) while improving those of the US. Since the consumption basket of workers also includes foreign goods, which would become less expensive, workers could be satisfied with a smaller nominal wage increase for each given level of unemployment, since their real wages would increase by the same amount that they would have if the Rest of the World had not adopted expansionary policies.

With the new Phillips curve $H_1 H_1$ resulting from the expansion of demand abroad, it will be possible, e.g., to reach C (if the US does not expand) or D (if it does). Both are Pareto-superior to A (remember that since we are dealing with 'bads', curves closer to the origin ensure greater welfare). Note that this is the case whatever the shape of the indifference curves (apart from their slope, which must be negative), which reflects the weights assigned to the two targets. The basic idea is that easing the constraint, which is reflected in the lowering of the Phillips curve, can benefit the country in any case.

---

[27] For simplicity, we assume that the magnitude of the expansion is given. For brevity, we do not examine the change in the transformation curve under fixed exchange rates.

Table 19.1. *The benefits of cooperation in a 'prisoner's dilemma' setting*

		Rest of the World	
		Expand	Don't expand
United States	Expand	(D, D')	(B, C')
	Don't expand	(C, B')	(A, A')

The problem of coordination can be formulated in terms of game theory. If each country acts in a non-cooperative fashion, we may be faced with a prisoner's dilemma situation. If, instead, the game is cooperative, both countries may be able to achieve a better outcome. Let us see why.

First assume that all of the considerations we have made with regard to the US apply to the rest of the world as well: the position of the latter can be plotted in exactly the same way as that of the US in figure 19.6. In order to distinguish the two positions, the points referring to the rest of the world will be marked with primes. Thus, A' will be the initial position of the rest of the world if both it and the US adopt restrictive policies. B' is the rest of the world's position if it expands while the US maintains its restrictive stance. C' is the position of the rest of the world if it does not expand and the US does, while D' denotes the rest of the world's position if both adopt expansionary policies. The outcomes of the different possible combinations are given in table 19.1. As we can see from figure 19.6, the preference ordering of the various positions for the US is: C, D, A, B, where C provides the highest welfare and the other positions offer decreasing levels of satisfaction. Similarly for the rest of the world.

Game theory shows that in a non-repeated game the non-cooperative equilibrium (A, A')[28] is suboptimal. One of the ways to reach the efficient solution is to repeat the game: if the game is repeated an infinite number of times, it is possible that a Pareto-superior outcome ((D, D') in our example) will be reached. The repetitive nature of the relationship between the two countries may induce each of them to adopt a cooperative attitude and, therefore, build a reputation as being cooperative and as being willing to punish non-cooperative behaviour in others, even when this is not beneficial in the short run.[29] This is, therefore, a form of cooperation that, like that in section 19.4, emerges implicitly from the unilateral actions of the various countries. However, bear in mind that the benefits of such cooperative behaviour decrease as the number of countries increases: a small country may have a strong incentive to adopt a non-cooperative stance (e.g., not expanding) that would enable it to achieve C, which is superior to D.

Introducing time and the related problems of time consistency may make the outcome of cooperation negative. Rogoff (1985),[30] for example, considers a situation in

---

[28] A 'cooperative' game is one in which the players can make binding commitments. In such games the coordination of strategies is thus supported by the possibility of enforcement guaranteed by appropriate institutions.

[29] The classic example is a trade war by means of tariff reprisals.

[30] For a critique, see Carraro and Giavazzi (1991). The analysis employs game theory.

which domestic wages in each country depend on the expected price level. Without cooperation between monetary authorities, each will adopt restrictive policies to avoid the formation of inflationary expectations stimulated by the possibility of a depreciation (or devaluation). If the various central banks cooperate, they can take an expansionary stance without fear of causing a depreciation, since all would expand at the same time. However, stronger demand would have inflationary effects. Fearing such effects, workers would increase their wage demands, thus fuelling inflation. The solution would be for the central banks to commit themselves to not expanding the money supply excessively once wages have been set. In the indicated setting, this is the only form of cooperation that will produce an outcome superior to that of independent policies. A set of more or less explicit assumptions are crucial to such a result. Among these, policymakers are assumed to ignore inflationary expectations created among workers when they agree to expand their economies. This is a special case of a more general situation: cooperative solutions can be inferior if some policymakers do not know the 'true' model of the economy (Frankel and Rockett, 1986).

The uncertainty of the advantages of cooperation (as well as other economic policy measures in different contexts) underscores the need for extreme care in modelling any given problem: since different models can yield different conclusions, the results can be considered 'robust' only when they are supported by a wide range of models, as they do not change in relation to changes in the underlying hypotheses. Moreover, an effort must be made to capture the aspects of reality felt to be most significant, avoiding *ad hoc* hypotheses adopted merely for the sake of analytical expediency.

19.7 Summary

1 Kydland and Prescott examine the choice between rules and discretion in a multi-period framework. In the presence of rational expectations the optimal policy is not a time-consistent policy, but rather one decided *a priori* with a rule that forces the government to respect the initial choice. Nevertheless, the constraint imposed by such a rule may prove burdensome in the event of unexpected adverse circumstances.

2 The basis of planning lies in the consistent use of the different instruments in attaining the desired objectives, given that each instrument influences all objectives. The need to search for the values of instruments that simultaneously ensure the achievement of all objectives clearly justifies a centralised solution. However, in the real world the choice of different policy instruments is often entrusted to different bodies, each of which aims at a specific target. The decentralisation of policy responsibility is possible and in principle will produce the same result obtained with centralised policy control, even if obtained by trial and error, if the effectiveness of instruments differs in relation to the various instruments and if each instrument is assigned to the objective for which it is relatively most effective.

*3 In certain cases of decentralisation, overshooting may occur even if there is convergence towards the final simultaneous solution. In other words, the correction adopted by each policy authority may be excessive in relation to that required in the case of a simultaneous solution.

4 In a world of n countries, the nth country cannot independently choose its desired balance of international transactions, given the value of the other $n - 1$ balances. If a country decides (either independently or through explicit coordination with other countries) to accept whatever balance is produced by the joint action of the other countries, this country acts as the nth country. There are two reasons why a country might choose to follow this path:

(a) the country that takes on this role will not be penalised by the impossibility of influencing its balance of payments since the other countries are willing to accept the currency of the nth country in settlement of any deficit;

(b) the nth country can freely choose its own monetary policy. Once it is no longer aimed at ensuring external stability, this instrument can be directed at attaining monetary stability or employment objectives.

5 International coordination requires each country to adjust its policy instruments to achieve not only its own objectives but also those of the rest of the world. The need for coordination derives from interdependence between economies and the possibility of achieving Pareto-superior results.

*6 Game theory shows cases in which international coordination (which can be represented in terms of a cooperative game) is beneficial or detrimental.

19.8 Key concepts

Time consistency, inconsistency
Forward, backward-looking
Pre-commitment
Contingent, causal, feedback, closed-loop
    rule
Non-contingent, non-causal,
    no-feedback, open-loop rule
Custom
Convention
Law
Credibility
Reputation
Tying one's hands
Flexible rule
Commitment
Centralisation, decentralisation
Simultaneous solution

Appropriate assignment of instruments
    to targets
Mundell principle
Principle of efficient market classification
Stock adjustment
Iso-target curve
Implicit function
Redundancy problem
Nth-country problem
Spillover
Transmission of effects
McKinnon monetary rule
Target zone
Safeguard clause
Cooperative game
Coordination

References

The date of the first edition of a work is quoted usually for works published before
1939. However, page references are to the most recent edition indicated.

Acocella, N. (1992a). 'The Multinational Firm and the Theory of Industrial Organization',
in A. Del Monte (ed.), *Recent Approaches to the Theory of Industrial Organization*,
London: Macmillan.
(1992b). 'Trade and Direct Investment Within the EC: the Impact of Strategic
Considerations', in J. Cantwell (ed.), *Multinational Investment in Modern Europe*,
Cheltenham: E. Elgar.
Acocella, N. and G. Ciccarone (1994). '*Stagflation as a Nash Equilibrium Outcome*',
Dipartimento di Economia Pubblica, Università di Roma 'La Sapienza', Working
Paper no. 1, July.
(1997). 'Trade Unions, Nonneutrality and Stagflation', *Public Choice*, 91: 161–78.
Ahmad, E. and N. H. Stern (1984). 'The Theory of Reform and Indian Indirect Taxes',
Journal of Public Economics, 25: 259–98.
Akerlof, G. (1970). 'The Market for Lemons, Uncertainty and the Market Mechanism',
Quarterly Journal of Economics, 84: 488–500.
Alchian, A. (1950). 'Uncertainty, Evolution and Economic Theory', *Journal of Political
Economy*, 68: 211–21.
(1987). 'Property Rights', in J. Eatwell, M. Milgate and P. Newman (eds.), *The New
Palgrave. A Dictionary of Economics*, London: Macmillan, Vol. III.
Alesina, A. (1987). 'Macroeconomic Policy in a Two-Party System as a Repeated Game',
Quarterly Journal of Economics, 102: 651–78; repr. (1994) in Persson, J. and G.
Tabellini, Vol. II.
Alesina, A., G. D. Cohen and N. Roubini (1992). 'Macroeconomic Policy and Elections in
OECD Democracies', *Economics and Politics*, 4: 1–30.
Alesina, A. and G. Tabellini (1990). 'A Positive Theory of Fiscal Deficits and Government
Debt', *Review of Economic Studies*, 57: 403–14.
Alt, J. E. (1991). 'Leaning into the Wind or Ducking out of the Storm: US Monetary Policy
in the 1980s', in A. Alesina and G. Carliner (eds.), *Politics and Economics in the '80s*,
Chicago: University of Chicago Press.
Alt, J. E. and K. A. Chrystal (1983). *Political Economics*, Brighton: Wheatsheaf Books.
Aoki, M. and M. Canzoneri (1979). 'Sufficient Conditions for Control of Target Variables

and Assignment of Instruments in Dynamic Macroeconomic Models', *International Economic Review*, **20**: 605–16.

Ardeni, P. G. and B. Wright (1992). 'The Prebisch-Singer Hypothesis: A Reappraisal Independent of Stationary Hypothesis', *Economic Journal*, **102**: 803–12.

Argy, V. (1988). 'A Post-war History of the Rules vs Discretion Debate', *Banca Nazionale del Lavoro Quarterly Review*, no. 165: 147–77.

Aristotle (1980). *The Nichomachean Ethics*, ed. by D. Ross, Oxford: Clarendon Press.

Arrow, K. J. (1951). *Social Choice and Individual Values*, New York: Wiley and Son (2nd rev. edn, New Haven: Yale University Press, 1963).

(1953). 'Le Rôle des Valeurs Boursières pour la Répartition la Meilleure des Risques', *Econométrie*, **11**: 41–7; English translation (1963–4) 'The Role of Securities in the Optimal Allocation of Risk-Bearing', *Review of Economic Studies* 31: 91–6; repr. (1974) as 'Essay 4' in K.J. Arrow, *Essays in the Theory of Risk-bearing*, Amsterdam: North-Holland.

(1962). 'The Economic Implications of Learning by Doing', *Review of Economic Studies*, **29**: 155–73.

Arrow, K. J. and G. Debreu (1954). 'Existence of an Equilibrium for a Competitive Economy', *Econometrica*, **22**: 265–90.

Arrow, K. J. and F. Hahn (1971). *General Competitive Analysis*, Edinburgh: Oliver & Boyd.

Atkinson, A. B. (1970). 'On the Measurement of Inequality', *Journal of Economic Theory*, **2**: 244–63.

(1973). 'Maximum and Optimal Income Taxation', D.P. no. 47, University of Essex, Dept. of Economics.

(1995a) *Public Economics in Action: The Basic Income/Flat Tax Proposal*, Oxford: Clarendon Press

(1995b). 'The Welfare State and Economic Performance', *National Tax Journal*, **48**: 171–98.

Atkinson, A. B. and J. E. Stiglitz (1976). 'The Design of Tax Structure: Direct versus Indirect Taxation', *Journal of Public Economics*, **6**: 55–75.

(1980). *Lectures on Public Economics*, New York: Mc-Graw Hill.

Auerbach, A. J. and M. Feldstein (eds.) (1987). *Handbook of Public Economics*, Amsterdam: North-Holland.

Averch, H. and L. Johnson (1962). 'Behaviour of the Firm Under Regulatory Constraint', *American Economic Review*, **52**: 1052–69.

Axelrod, R. (1984). *The Evolution of Cooperation*, New York: Basic Books.

Azariadis, C. (1975). 'Implicit Contracts and Underemployment Equilibria', *Journal of Political Economy*, **83**: 1183–202.

Baily, M. N. (1974). 'Wages and Employment under Uncertain Demand', *Review of Economic Studies*, **41**: 37–50.

Baldwin, R. (1988). 'Hysteresis in Import Prices: The Beachhead Effect', *American Economic Review*, **78**: 773–85.

Bank for International Settlements (1983). *53rd Annual Report*, Basle: Bank for International Settlements.

(1986). 'Recent Innovations in International Banking', Basle, April.

(1992). *62nd Annual Report*, Basle: Bank for International Settlements.

Baron, D. P. and T. D. Besanko (1984). 'Regulation, Asymmetric Information and Auditing', *Rand Journal of Economics*, **15**: 447–70.

Barr, N. (1992). 'Economic Theory and the Welfare State: A Survey and Interpretation', *Journal of Economic Literature*, **30**: 741–803.

(1993). *The Economics of the Welfare State*, 1st edn 1987, Stanford: Stanford University Press.

Barro, R. J. (1974). 'Are Government Bonds Net Wealth?', *Journal of Political Economy*, **82**: 1095–118.

(1989). 'The Ricardian Approach to Fiscal Policy', in R. Barro (ed.), *Modern Business Cycle Theory*, Cambridge, Mass.: Harvard University Press.

Barro, R. J. and D. Gordon (1983). 'Rules, Discretion and Reputation in a Model of Monetary Policy', *Journal of Monetary Economics*, **12**: 101–21; repr. (1994) in Persson, J. and G. Tabellini, Vol. I.

Barro, R.J. and H. I. Grossman (1971). 'A General Disequilibrium Model of Income and Employment', *American Economic Review*, **61**: 82–93.

Barry, B. (1965). *Political Argument*, London: Routledge & Kegan.

Baumol, W. J. (1986). *Superfairness*, Cambridge, Mass.: MIT Press.

Baumol, W. J., J. Panzar and R. D. Willig (1982). *Contestable Markets and the Theory of Industry Structure*, New York: Harcourt Brace Jovanovich.

Bazdarich, M. J. (1978). 'Optimal Growth and Stages in the Balance of Payments', *Journal of International Economics*, **8**: 425–43.

Bénabou, R. (1996). 'Inequality and Growth', NBER Working Paper 5583.

Benassy, J. P. (1992). *The Economics of Market Disequilibrium*, New York: Academic Press.

Bentham, J. (1789). *An Introduction to the Principles of Moral and Legislation*, London: Payne; repr. (1907), Oxford: Clarendon Press.

Bergstrom, T. (1971). 'On the Existence and Optimality of Competitive Equilibrium for a Slave Economy', *Review of Economic Studies*, **38**: 23–36.

Berlin, I. (1969). 'Two Concepts of Liberty', in I. Berlin, *Four Essays on Liberty*, Oxford: Oxford University Press.

Bernanke, B. and F. Mishkin (1992). 'Central Bank Behaviour and the Strategy of Monetary Policy: Observations from Six Industrialized Countries', in O. J. Blanchard and S. Fischer (eds.), *NBER Macroeconomics Annual 1992*, Cambridge, Mass.: MIT Press.

Besley, T. and S. Coate (1992). 'Workfare vs. Welfare: Incentive Arguments for Work Requirements in Poverty Alleviation Programs', *American Economic Review*, **82**: 249–61.

Beveridge, W. (1942). *Social Insurance and Allied Services*, CMND 6404, London: HMSO.

Binmore, K. (1989). 'Social Contract I: Harsanyi and Rawls', *Economic Journal*, Conference issue, **99**: 84–102.

Black, D. (1948). 'On the Rationale of Group Decision-Making', *Journal of Political Economy*, **66**: 23–34.

(1958). *The Theory of Committee and Elections*, Cambridge: Cambridge University Press.

Blackorby, C. and D. Donaldson (1988). 'Cash Versus Kind, Self-Selection and Efficient Transfers', *American Economic Review*, **78**: 691–700.

Blanchard, O. J. and N. Kiyotaki (1987). 'Monopolistic Competition and the Effects of Aggregate Demand', *American Economic Review*, **77**: 647–66.

Blanchard, O. J. and L. Summers (1986). 'Hysteresis and the European Employment Problem', *NBER Macroeconomic Annual*.

Blinder, A. S. (1987). *Hard Heads, Soft Hearts: Tough-Minded Economics for a Just Society*, Reading, Mass.: Addison-Wesley.

Blinder, A. S. and R. M. Solow (1973). 'Does Fiscal Policy Matter?', *Journal of Public Economics*, **2**: 319–37.

Blomquist, S. and V. Christiansen (1995). 'Public Provision of Private Goods as a

Redistributive Device in an Optimum Income Tax Model', *The Scandinavian Journal of Economics*, **97**: 547–67.

Boadway, R. W. (1979). *Public Sector Economics*, Cambridge, Mass.: Winthrop Publ.

Boadway, R. W. and N. Bruce (1984). *Welfare Economics*, Oxford: Blackwell.

Boadway, R. W. and M. Marchand (1995). 'The Use of Public Expenditure for Redistributive Purposes', *Oxford Economic Papers*, **47**: 45–59.

Boardman, A. E., D.H. Greenberg, A. R. Vining and D. L. Weimer (1996). *Cost-Benefit Analysis: Concepts and Practice*, Upper Saddle River: Prentice-Hall.

Boitani, A. (1984). 'Two Views on Oligopoly and Stagnation', *Economic Notes*, no. 3: 128–54.

Boiteux, M. (1956). 'Sur la Gestion des Monopoles Publics Astreints à l'Equilibre Budgétaire', *Econometrica*, **24**: 22–40.

Borda, J. C. (1781). *Mémoire sur les Elections au Scrutin*, Histoire de l'Académie Royale des Sciences, Paris.

Bordo, M. and A. Schwartz (1984). *A Retrospective on the Classical Gold Standard*, 1821–1931, Chicago: University of Chicago Press.

Bös, D. (1989). 'Comments', in J. E. Stiglitz.

(1991). *Privatization. A Theoretical Treatment*, Oxford: Clarendon Press.

Bowles, S. (1985). 'The Production Process in a Competitive Economy: Walrasian, Neo-Hobbesian, and Marxian Models', *American Economic Review*, **75**: 16–36.

Bresciani Turroni, C. (1937). *The Economics of Inflation*, London: Allen & Unwin (1st Italian edition 1931).

Brito, D. L., J. H. Hamilton, S. M. Slutsky and J. E. Stiglitz (1990). 'Pareto Efficient Tax Structures', *Oxford Economic Papers*, **42**: 61–77.

Brown, C.V. (1980). *Taxation and Incentives to Work*, Oxford: Oxford University Press.

Browning, E. K. and W. R. Johnson (1984). 'The Trade-off between Equality and Efficiency', *Journal of Political Economy*, **92**: 175–203.

Brunner, K. (ed.) (1981). *The Great Depression Revisited*, The Hague: Nijhoff.

Brusco, S. (1986). 'Small Firms and Industrial Districts: The Experience of Italy', in D. Keeble and E. Wever (eds.), *New Firms and Regional Development*, London: Croom Helm.

Buchanan, J. M. (1965). 'An Economic Theory of Clubs', *Economica*, **32**: 1–14.

Buchanan, J. M. and G. Tullock (1962). *The Calculus of Consent: Logical Foundations of Constitutional Democracy*, Ann Arbor: University of Michigan Press.

Buiter, W. H. (1980). 'The Macroeconomics of Dr. Pangloss. A Critical Survey of the New Classical Macroeconomics', *Economic Journal*, **90**: 34–50.

(1981). 'The Superiority of Contingent Rules over Fixed Rules in Models with Rational Expectations', *Economic Journal*, **91**: 647–70; repr. (1989) in W. H. Buiter, *Macroeconomic Theory and Stabilization Policy*, Manchester: Manchester University Press.

Burrel, S. and M. Stutchbury (1994). *Australia Rebuilds. The Recovery We Had To Have*, Sidney: Financial Review Library.

Caffè, F. (1948). 'La Politica delle Priorità e il Pensiero degli Economisti Inglesi', *Critica Economica*, no. 5.

(1966). *Politica Economica. Sistematica e Tecniche di Analisi*, Torino: Boringhieri, Vol. I.

Cagan, P. (1956). 'The Monetary Dynamics of Hyperinflation', in M. Friedman (ed.), *Studies in the Quantity Theory of Money*, Chicago: University of Chicago Press.

Calabresi, G. (1968). 'Transaction Costs, Resource Allocation, and Liability Rules. A Comment', *Journal of Law and Economics*, **11**: 67–73.

Calmfors, L. (1993). 'Centralisation of Wage Bargaining and Macroeconomic Performance. A Survey', *OECD Economic Studies*, no. 21: 161–91.

Campiglio, L. (1990). 'Income Distribution, Public Expenditure and Equality', *Labour*, 4: 97–124.

Cararro, C. (1989). *Modelling International Policy Coordination*, mimeo, November.

Cararro, C. and F. Giavazzi (1991). 'Can International Policy Co-ordination Really Be Counterproductive?', in Carraro C. and F. Giavazzi (eds.), *International Economic Policy Co-ordination*, Oxford: Blackwell.

Cararro, C. and D. Siniscalco (eds.) (1993). *The European Carbon Tax: An Economic Assessment*, Dordrecht: Kluwer Academy Publications.

Cassel, G. (1918). 'Abnormal Deviations in International Exchanges', *Economic Journal*, **28**: 413–15.

Cecchini, P. (1988). *The European Challenge 1992. The Benefits of a Single Market*, Aldershot: Wildwood House.

Ceep (1994). *Annales*, Paris.

Chichilnisky, G. and G. M. Heal (1983). 'Necessary and Sufficient Conditions for a Resolution of the Social Choice Paradox', *Journal of Economic Theory*, **31**: 68–87.

Chrystal, K. A. and S. Price (1994). *Controversies in Macroeconomics*, 3rd edn, Hertfordshire: Wheatsheaf.

Ciocca, P. and G. Nardozzi (1996). *The High Price of Money. An Interpretation of World Interest Rate*, Oxford: Clarendon Press.

Claassen, E. M. (ed.) (1990). *International and European Monetary Systems*, New York: Praeger.

Clarke, E. H. (1971). 'Multipart Pricing of Public Goods', *Public Choice*, **11**: 17–33.

Clower, R. (1965). 'The Keynesian Counterrevolution: A Theoretical Appraisal', in F. H. Hahn, F. and P. R. Brechling (eds.), *Theory of Interest Rates*, London: Macmillan.

Coase, R. H. (1937). 'The Nature of the Firm', *Economica*, 4: 386–405; repr. (1953) in K. E. Boulding and G. J. Stigler (eds.), *Readings in Price Theory*, London: Allen & Unwin, and (1988) in R. H. Coase.

    (1960). 'The Problem of Social Cost', *Journal of Law and Economics*, 3: 1–44; repr. (1988) in R. H. Coase.

    (1988). *The Firm, the Market and the Law*, Chicago: University of Chicago Press.

Coffey, P. (1984). *The European Monetary System. Past, Present and Future*, Dordrecht: Nijhoff.

Colander, D. *et al.* (1996). *Beyond Microfoundations. Postwalrasian Macroeconomics*, Cambridge: Cambridge University Press.

Coles, J. L. and P. J. Hammond (1995). 'Walrasian Equilibrium without Survival: Existence, Efficiency and Remedial Policy', in P. Pattanaik and K. Suzumura (eds.), *Choice, Welfare Development: A Festschrift in Honour of Amartya Sen*, Oxford: Clarendon Press.

Commission of the European Communities (1989). *Interim Report on a Specific Community Action Programme to Combat Poverty*, Brussels: European Commission.

Commission of the European Communities, IMF, OECD, UN and World Bank (1993). *System of National Accounts*, 1993, rev. edn, Brussels: Commission of the European Communities.

Commission for the Study of Economic and Monetary Union (1989). *Report on Economic and Monetary Union in the European Community*, Luxembourg: Office for the Official Publications of the European Communities (Delors Report).

Committee on the Working of the Monetary System (1959). *Report*, CMND 827, HMSO.

Condorcet, M. De (1785). *Essai sur l'Application de l'Analyse à la Probabilité des Décisions Rendues à la Pluralité des Voix*, Paris: L'Imprimerie Royale.

Cooper, J. and A. John (1988). 'Coordinating Coordination Failures in Keynesian Models', *Quarterly Journal of Economics*, **103**: 441–63.

Cooper, R. N. (1969). 'Macroeconomic Policy Adjustment in Interdependent Economies', *Quarterly Journal of Economics*, **83**: 1–24.

Cooter, R. (1982). 'The Cost of Coase', *Journal of Legal Studies*, **11**: 1–33.

Coricelli, F. (1990). 'Industrial Relations and Macroeconomic Performance: An Application to Spain', IMF Working Paper, October.

Corlett, W. J. and D. C. Hague (1953). 'Complementarity and the Excess Burden of Taxation', *Review of Economic Studies*, **21**: 21–30.

Cornes, R. and T. Sandler (1986). *The Theory of Externalities, Public Goods, and Club Goods*, Cambridge: Cambridge University Press.

Cornwall, R. R. (1984). *Introduction to the Use of General Equilibrium Analysis*, Amsterdam: North-Holland.

Cozzi, G. (1997). 'Exploring Growth Trajectories', *Journal of Economic Growth*, **2**: 1–14.

Cripps, T. F. and W. Godley (1976). 'A Formal Analysis of the Cambridge Economic Policy Group Model', *Economica*, **43**: 335–48.

Crocker, D. A. (1992). 'Functioning and Capability. The Foundations of Sen's and Nussbaum's Development Ethics', *Political Theory*, **20**: 584–612.

Cross, R. (1988). *Unemployment, Hysteresis and the Natural Rate Hypothesis*, Oxford: Blackwell.

Currie, J. (1995). 'Socio-Economic Status and Child Health: Does Public Health Insurance Narrow the Gap?', *The Scandinavian Journal of Economics*, **97**: 603–20.

Cuthbertson, K. and M. P. Taylor (1987). *Macroeconomic Systems*, Oxford: Blackwell.

Cyert, R. M. and J. G. March (1963). *A Behavioral Theory of the Firm*, Englewood Cliffs: Prentice Hall.

Dales, J. H. (1968). *Pollution, Property and Prices. An Essay in Policy-Making and Economics*, Toronto: University of Toronto Press.

Danziger, S., R. Haveman and R. Plotnick (1981). 'How Income Transfers Affect Work, Savings and the Income Distribution: A Critical Review', *Journal of Economic Literature*, **19**: 975–1028.

Dasgupta, P. (1980). 'Decentralization and Rights', *Economica*, **47**: 107–24.
    (1989). 'Positive Freedom, Markets, and the Welfare State', in D. Helm.

Dasgupta, P. and D. Ray (1986). 'Inequality as a Determinant of Malnutrition and Unemployment: Theory', *Economic Journal*, **96**: 1011–34.

Davidson, P. (1982–3). 'Rational Expectations: A Fallacious Foundation for Studying Crucial Decision Making Processes', *Journal of Post-Keynesian Economics*, **5**: 182–98.

Davis, O. A., M. H. De Groot and M. J. Hinich (1972). 'Social Preference Orderings and Majority Rule', *Econometrica*, **40**: 147–57.

Davis, O. A. and A. B. Whinston (1965). 'Welfare Economics and the Theory of Second Best', *Review of Economic Studies*, **32**: 1–14.

De Cecco, M. (1990). 'The EMS and Other International Monetary Regimes Compared', in P. Ferri (ed.), *Prospects for the European Monetary System*, New York: St. Martin's Press.
    (1995). 'Central Bank Cooperation in the Inter-War Period: A View from the Periphery', in J. Reis (ed.), *International Monetary Systems in Historical Perspective*, Basingstoke: Macmillan.

De Fraja, G. and F. Delbono (1989). 'Alternative Strategies of a Public Enterprise in

Oligopoly', *Oxford Economic Papers*, **41**: 302–11.

De Grauwe, P. (1983). *Macroeconomic Theory for the Open Economy*, Aldershot: Gower.

——(1987). 'International Trade and Economic Growth in the European Monetary System', *European Economic Review*, **31**: 389–98.

——(1990). 'The Cost of Disinflation and the European Monetary System', *Open Economies Review*, **1**: 147–73.

——(1994). *The Economics of Monetary Integration*, 2nd edn, Oxford: Oxford University Press.

——(1996). 'The Dynamics of Convergence toward European Monetary Union: A Comment', in 'European Monetary Union: The Problems of the Transition to a Single Currency', *Banca Nazionale del Lavoro Quarterly Review*, Special Issue, March: 33–45.

Demsetz, H. (1968). 'The Cost of Transacting', *Quarterly Journal of Economics*, **82**: 33–53.

Dernburg, T. F. (1989). *Global Macroeconomics*, New York: Harper and Row.

Desai, M. (1989). 'Potential Lifetime (plt): A Proposal for an Index of Social Welfare', in F. Bracho (ed.), *Towards a New Way to Measure Development*, Caracas: Office of the South Commission.

——(1990). 'Poverty and Capability: Towards an Empirically Implementable Measure', in London School of Economics, 'Development Economics Research Group', Discussion Paper.

——(1991). 'Human Development: Concepts and Measurement', *European Economic Review*, **35**: 350–57.

Diamond, P. A. (1967). 'The Role of a Stock Market in a General Equilibrium Model with Technological Uncertainty', *American Economic Review*, **57**: 759–76.

Diamond, P. A. and J. A. Mirrlees (1971). 'Optimal Taxation and Public Production', *American Economic Review*, **51**: 261–78.

Dixit, A. (1989). 'Entry and Exit Decisions under Uncertainty', *Journal of Political Economy*, **97**: 620–38.

——(1992). Investment and Hysteresis, *Journal of Economic Perspectives*, **6**: 107–302.

——(1996). *The Making of Economic Policy: A Transaction-Cost Politics Perspective*, Cambridge, Mass.: MIT Press.

——(1997). 'Power of Incentives in Private versus Public Organizations', *American Economic Review*, **87**: 378–82.

Dixit, A. and J. Londregan (1995). 'Redistributive Politics and Economic Efficiency', *American Political Science Review*, **89**: 856–66.

Domar, E. D. (1946). 'Capital Expansion, Rate of Growth and Employment', *Econometrica*, **14**: 137–47.

——(1947). 'Expansion and Employment', *American Economic Review*, **37**: 34–55.

Dore, R. (1992). 'Japanese Capitalism, Anglo-Saxon Capitalism; How Will the Darwinian Contest Turn Out?', London School of Economics, Centre for Economic Performance, Occasional Paper 26.

Dore, R., R. Boyer and Z. Mars (eds.) (1994). *The Return to Incomes Policy*, London: Pinter.

Dornbusch, R. (1976). 'Expectations and Exchange Rate Dynamics', *Journal of Political Economy*, **84**: 1161–76; repr. (1988) in R. Dornbusch, *Exchange Rates and Inflation*, Cambridge, Mass.: MIT Press.

——(1980), *Open Economy Macroeconomics*, New York: Basic Books.

——(1988). 'The European Monetary System, the Dollar and the Yen', in F. Giavazzi, S. Micossi and M. Miller (eds.), *The European Monetary System*, Cambridge: Cambridge University Press.

Dornbusch, R. and S. Fischer (1994). *Macroeconomics*, 6th edn (1st edn 1978), New York:

McGraw Hill.

Downs, A. (1957). *An Economic Theory of Good Decision-Making in Democracy*, New York: Harper & Row.

(1967). *Inside Bureaucracy*, Boston: Little, Brown and Company.

Drèze, J. H. (1993). *Money and Uncertainty: Inflation, Interest, Indexation*, Paolo Baffi Lectures on Money and Finance, Banca d'Italia, Roma: Edizioni dell'Elefante.

(1995). 'Forty Years of Public Economics', *Journal of Economic Perspectives*, 9: 111–30.

Drèze, J. and N. Stern (1987). *The Theory of Cost–Benefit Analysis*, in A. J. Auerbach and M. Feldstein.

Drummond, M. F. (1980). *Principles of Economic Appraisal in Health Care*, Oxford: Oxford University Press.

Duesenberry, J. (1967). *Income, Saving and the Theory of Consumer Behaviour*, Oxford: Oxford University Press.

Duffie, D. and H. Sonnenschein (1989). 'Arrow and General Equilibrium Theory', *Journal of Economic Literature*, 27: 565–98.

Dupuit, J. (1844). 'De l'Utilité et de sa Mesure', *Annales de Ponts et Chaussées* (English translation: 'On the Measurement of Utility of Public Works', *International Economic Papers*, 1952, 2: 83–110).

Dworkin, R. (1981a). 'What Is Equality? Part 1: Equality of Welfare', *Philosophy and Public Affairs*, 10: 185–246.

(1981b). 'What Is Equality? Part 2: Equality of Resources', *Philosophy and Public Affairs*, 10: 283–345.

Eatwell, J. (1987). 'Walras' Theory of Capital', in J. Eatwell, M. Milgate and P. Newman, *The New Palgrave. A Dictionary of Economics*, London: Macmillan, Vol. IV.

Economides, N. (1996). 'The Economics of Networks', *International Journal of Industrial Organization*, 14: 673–99.

Eichengreen, B. (1992). *Golden Fetters. The Gold Standard and the Great Depression 1919–1939*, Oxford: Oxford University Press.

(1993). 'European Monetary Integration', *Journal of Economic Literature*, 31: 1321–57.

Eichengreen, B. and C. Wyplosz (1993). 'The Unstable EMS', *The Brookings Papers on Economic Activity*, no. 1: 51–124.

Eichengreen, B., A. K. Rose and C. Wyplosz (1994). 'Speculative Attacks on Pegged Exchange Rates: An Empirical Exploration with Special Reference to the European Monetary System', NBER Working Paper 4898.

Eijffinger, S. and E. Schaling (1993). 'Central Bank Independence in Twelve Industrial Countries', *Banca Nazionale del Lavoro Quarterly Review*, no. 184: 49–89.

Eissa, N. (1996). 'Tax Reform and Labor Supply', in J.M. Poterba (ed.), *Tax Policy and the Economy* 10, NBER, Cambridge, Mass.: MIT Press.

Esping-Andersen, G. (1990). *The Three Worlds of Welfare Capitalism*, Princeton: Princeton University Press.

Etzioni, A. (1985). 'Opening the Preferences. A Socio-Economic Research Agenda', *Journal of Behavioral Economics*, 14: 183–205.

European Monetary Institute (1997). *Annual Report* 1996, Frankfurt, April.

Farrell, M. (1959). 'The Convexity Assumption in the Theory of Competitive Markets', *Journal of Political Economy*, 67: 377–91.

Feldstein, M. (1995). 'The Effect of Marginal Tax Rates on Taxable Income: A Panel Study in the 1986 Tax Reform Act', *Journal of Political Economy*, 103: 551–72.

Fetherston, M. and W. Godley (1978). 'New Cambridge Macroeconomics and Global Monetarism: Some Issues in the Conduct of UK Economic Policy', *Carnegie*

Rochester Conference Series on Public Policy, **9**: 33–65.

Fink, R. (1982). *Supply-Side Economics*, Washington: University Publications of America.

Finsinger, J. and I. Vogelsang (1985). 'Strategic Management Behavior under Reward Structures in a Planned Economy', *Quarterly Journal of Economics*, **100**: 263–9.

Fischer, S. (1988). 'International Macroeconomic Policy Coordination', in M. Feldstein (ed.), *International Economic Cooperation*, Chicago: University of Chicago Press.

—— (1990). 'Rules versus Discretion in Monetary Policy', in B. Friedman and F. Hahn (eds.), *Handbook of Monetary Economics*, Amsterdam: North-Holland, Vol. II.

Fishburn, P.C. (1973). *The Theory of Social Choice*, Princeton: Princeton University Press.

Fisher, F. M. (1983). *Disequilibrium Foundations of Equilibrium Economics*, Cambridge: Cambridge University Press.

Fisher, I. (1932). *Booms and Depression*, New York: Adelphi.

—— (1933). 'The Debt-Deflation Theory of Great Depression', *Econometrica*, **1**: 337–57.

Fitoussi, J. P. (1983). 'Modern Macroeconomic Theory: An Overview', in J. P. Fitoussi (ed.), *Modern Macroeconomic Theory*, Oxford: Blackwell.

Flanagan, R.J., D.W. Soskice and L. Ulman (1983). *Unionism, Economic Stabilization and Incomes Policies: European Experience*, Washington: The Brookings Institution.

Fleming, J. M. (1962). 'Domestic Financial Policies under Fixed and under Floating Exchange Rates', *IMF Staff Papers*, **9**: 369–80.

Fleurbaey, M. (1995). 'Equal Opportunity or Equal Social Outcome?', *Economics and Philosophy*, **11**: 25–55.

Foley, D. (1970). 'Economic Equilibrium with Costly Marketing', *Journal of Economic Theory*, **2**: 276–91.

Frankel, J. A. (1992). *Monetary Regime Choices for a Semi-Open Economy*, Berkeley: University of California.

Frankel, J. A. and K. Rockett (1986). 'International Macroeconomic Policy Coordination when Policy-Makers Disagree on the Model', NBER Working Paper 2059.

Franzini, M. (1993). 'Corrupt Transactions', Paper presented at the Workshop on Economics and Politics, International School of Economic Research, Certosa di Pontignano, Siena, Italy, mimeo.

Franzini, M. and M. Messori (1991). 'Introduzione: Coordinamento e Mercato', in M. Franzini and M. Messori (eds.), *Impresa, Istituzioni e Informazione*, Bologna: Clueb.

Fratianni, M. and J. Von Hagen (1990). 'Asymmetries and Realignments in the EMS', in P. De Grauwe, L. Papademos (eds.), *The European Monetary System in the 1990's*, London: Longman.

—— (1991). *The European Monetary System and European Monetary Union*, San Francisco: Westview Press.

Freeman, R. B. (1995). 'The Large Welfare State as a System', *American Economic Review*, **85**: 16–21.

Frenkel, J. A. (1981). 'Flexible Exchange Rates, Prices, and the Role of "News": Lessons from the 1970s', *Journal of Political Economy*, **89**: 665–705.

Frenkel, J. A. and H. G. Johnson (eds.) (1976). *The Monetary Approach to the Balance of Payments*, London: Allen & Unwin.

—— (1978). *The Economics of the Exchange Rates: Selected Studies*, London: Addison-Wesley.

Frenkel, J. A., Razin, A. and Yuen, C.-W. (1996). 'Fiscal Policies and Growth in the World Economy', 3rd edn, Cambridge, Mass.: MIT Press.

Friedman, B. M. (1979). 'Optimal Expectations and the Extreme Information Assumptions of Rational Expectation Macromodels', *Journal of Monetary Economics*, **5**: 23–41.

Friedman, J. W. (1990). *Game Theory with Applications to Economics*, Oxford: Oxford

University Press.

Friedman, M. (1953). *Essays in Positive Economics*, Chicago: Chicago University Press.
(1968). 'The Role of Monetary Policy', *American Economic Review*, **58**: 1–17.

Frisch, R. (1949). 'A Memorandum on Price-wage-tax Subsidy Policies as Instruments in Maintaining Optimal Employment', UN Document E (CN1/Sub 2), New York, repr. as Memorandum from Universitets Socialokomiscke Institutt, Oslo.
(1950). 'L'Emploi des Modèles pour l'Elaboration d'une Politique Economique Rationnelle', *Revue d'Economie Politique*, **60**: 474–98; 601–34.
(1959). 'Practical Rules for Interview Determination of One-Sided and Two-Sided Preference Coefficients in Macroeconomic Decision Problems', in Memorandum of the Institute of Economics, Oslo University.

Fudenberg, D. and J. Tirole (1991). *Game Theory*, Cambridge, Mass.: MIT Press.

Galor, O. and Zeira, J. (1993). 'Income Distribution and Macroeconomics', *Review of Economic Studies*, **60**: 35–52.

Gandolfo, G. (1994). *International Economics I. The Pure Theory of International Trade*, 2nd rev. edn (1st edn 1986), Berlin: Springer-Verlag.
(1995). *International Economics II. International Monetary Theory and Open-Economy Macroeconomics*, 2nd rev. edn (1st edn 1987), Berlin: Springer-Verlag.

Gans, J. S. and M. Smart (1996). 'Majority Voting With Single-Crossing Preferences', *Journal of Public Economics*, **59**: 219–37.

Gerber, E. R. and J. E. Jackson (1993). 'Endogenous Preferences and The Study of Institutions', *American Political Science Review*, **87**: 639–56.

Gerlach, S. and P. A. Petri (eds.) (1990). *The Economics of the Dollar Cycle*, Cambridge, Mass.: MIT Press.

Giavazzi, F. and A. Giovannini (1989). *Limiting Exchange Rate Flexibility. The European Monetary System*, Cambridge, Mass.: MIT Press.

Giavazzi, F. and M. Pagano (1988). 'Capital Controls in the EMS', in D. E. Fair and C. de Boissieu (eds.), *International Monetary and Financial Integration. The European Dimension*, Dordrecht: M. Nijhoff.

Giavazzi, F. and L. Spaventa (1990). 'The New EMS', in P. De Grauwe and L. Papademos (eds.), *The European Monetary System in the 1990s*, London: Longman.

Gibbard, A. (1973). 'Manipulation of Voting Schemes: A General Result', *Econometrica*, **41**: 587–601.

Giddy, I. H. (1983). 'The Eurocurrency Market', in A. M. George and I. H. Giddy (eds.), *International Finance Handbook*, New York: Wiley & Sons, Vol. I.

Glomm, G. and B. Ravikumar (1992). 'Public versus Private Investment in Human Capital: Endogenous Growth and Income Inequality', *Journal of Political Economy*, **100**: 813–34.

Glyn, A. and R. B. Sutcliffe (1972). *British Capitalism, Workers and the Profit Squeeze*, Harmondsworth: Penguin.

Goodhart, C. A. E. (1988). *The Evolution of Central Banks*, Cambridge, Mass.: MIT Press.

Gorman, W. M. (1956). 'The Demand for Related Goods', *Journal Paper*, J / 3129, Ames (Iowa): Iowa Experimental Station.

Graaff, J. De V. (1957). *Theoretical Welfare Economics*, Cambridge: Cambridge University Press.

Gravelle, H. and R. Rees (1992). *Microeconomics*, 2nd edn, London: Longman.

Green, J. and J. J. Laffont (1979). *Incentives in Public Decision-Making*, Amsterdam: North-Holland.

Greenwald, B. and J. Stiglitz (1993). 'New and Old Keynesians', *Journal of Economic*

Perspectives, **7**: 23–44.

Grilli, V., D. Masciandaro and G. Tabellini (1991). 'Political and Monetary Institutions and Public Finance Policies in the Industrial Countries', *Economic Policy*, **6**: 342–92; repr. (1994) in Persson, J. and G. Tabellini, Vol. II.

Gronchi, S. (1984). 'On Karmel's Criterion for Optimal Truncation', Quaderni del Dipartimento di Economia Politica dell'Università di Siena 26.

Gros, D. and N. Thygesen (1992). *European Monetary Integration*, London: Longman.

Grossman, G. and E. Helpman (1991). *Innovation and Growth in the Global Economy*, Cambridge, Mass.: MIT Press.

Grubel, H. G. (1984). *The International Monetary System. Efficiency and Practical Alternatives*, 4th edn, Harmondsworth: Penguin.

Guerrieri, P. and P. C. Padoan (1988). *The Political Economy of International Cooperation*, London: Croom Helm.

Guesnerie, R. (1977). 'On the Direction of Tax Refom', *Journal of Public Economics*, **7**: 179–202.

Guiso, L. and D. Terlizzese (1990). 'Time Consistency and Subgame Perfection: The Difference between Promises and Threats', Temi di Discussione 138, Banca d'Italia.

Gurley, J. G. and E. S. Shaw (1960). *Money in a Theory of Finance*, Washington: The Brookings Institution.

Hahn, F. (1971). 'Equilibrium with Transactions Costs', *Econometrica*, **39**: 417–39.

—— (1982). 'Reflections on the Invisible Hand', *Lloyds Bank Review*, no. 144: 1–21.

—— (1985). 'Some Keynesian Reflections on Monetarism', in F.Vicarelli (ed.), *Keynes' Relevance Today*, London: Macmillan.

Hahn, F. and R. Solow (1995). *A Critical Essay on Modern Macroeconomic Theory*, Oxford: Blackwell.

Hahnel, R. and M. Albert (1990). *Quiet Revolution in Welfare Economics*, Princeton: Princeton University Press.

Haig, R. M. (1921). *The Federal Income Tax*, New York: Columbia University Press.

Hall, R. E. and A. Rabushka (1995). *The Flat Tax*, 2nd edn, Stanford: Hoover Institution Press.

Hammond, P. J. (1979). 'Straightforward Individual Incentive Compatibility in Large Economies', *Review of Economic Studies*, **46**: 263–82.

—— (1987). 'Markets as Constraints: Multilateral Incentive Compatibility in Continuum Economies', *Review of Economic Studies*, **54**: 399–412.

—— (1990). 'Theoretical Progress in Public Economics: A Provocative Assessment', *Oxford Economic Papers*, **42**: 6–33.

—— (1995). 'Social Choice of Individual and Group Rights', in W.A. Barnett, H. Moulin, M. Salles and N.J. Schofield (eds.), *Social Choice, Welfare, and Ethics*, Cambridge: Cambridge University Press.

Hammond, P. J. and J. Sempere (1995). 'Limits to the Potential Gains from Economic Integration and Other Supply-Side Policies', *Economic Journal*, **105**: 1180–204.

Hansen, B. (1958). *The Economic Theory of Fiscal Policy*, London: Allen & Unwin.

Harberger, A. C. (1969). 'Professor Arrow on the Social Discount Rate', in G. G. Somers, W. D. Wood (eds.), *Cost-Benefit Analysis of Manpower Policies*, Industrial Relations Centre, Queen's University, Kingston (Ont.).

Hardin, G. (1968). 'The Tragedy of Commons', *Science*, **162**: 1243–8.

Harris, J. R. and M. P. Todaro (1970). 'Migration, Unemployment and Development: A Two-Sector Analysis', *American Economic Review*, **60**: 136–42.

Harrod, R. F. (1938). 'Scope and Method in Economics', *Economic Journal*, **48**: 383–412.

(1939). 'An Essay in Dynamic Theory', *Economic Journal*, 49: 14–33.

(1951). *The Life of J. M. Keynes*, London: Macmillan.

Harsanyi, J. (1953). 'Cardinal Utility in Welfare Economics and the Theory of Risk-Taking', *Journal of Political Economy*, 61: 434–5; repr. (1976) in Harsanyi.

(1955). 'Cardinal Welfare, Individualistic Ethics and Interpersonal Comparisons of Utility', *Journal of Political Economy*, 63: 309–21; repr. (1976) in Harsanyi.

(1976). *Essays on Ethics, Social Behavior and Scientific Explanations*, Dordrecht: Reidel.

(1977). *Rational Behavior and Bargaining Equilibrium in Games and Social Situations*, Cambridge: Cambridge University Press.

Hausman, J. A. (1981). 'Exact Consumer's Surplus and Deadweight Loss', *American Economic Review*, 71: 662–76.

Haveman, R. H. (1977). 'Evaluating Public Expenditures under Conditions of Unemployment', in R. H. Haveman and J. Margolis, *Public Expediture and Policy Analysis*, Chicago: Rand McNelly.

Hay, D. A. and D. J. Morris (1991). *Industrial Economics and Organization. Theory and Evidence*, Oxford: Oxford University Press.

Hayek, F. A. Von (1945). 'The Use of Knowledge in Society', *American Economic Review*, 35: 519–30; repr. (1948) in F. A. Von Hayek, *Individualism and Economic Order*, Chicago: University of Chicago Press.

(1960). *The Constitution of Liberty*, Chicago: University of Chicago Press.

(1978). 'Competition as a Discovery Procedure', in F. A. Von Hayek, *New Studies in Philosophy, Politics, Economics and the History of Ideas*, London: Routledge & Kegan (1st German edn., 1968).

Heal, G. (1973). *The Theory of Economic Planning*, Amsterdam: North Holland.

Heller, W. P. (1972). 'Transactions with Set Up Costs', *Journal of Economic Theory*, 4: 465–478.

Helm, D. (1989). 'The Economic Borders of the State', in D. Helm (ed.), *The Economic Borders of the State*, Oxford: Oxford University Press.

Helpman, E. and P. R. Krugman (1985), *Market Structure and Foreign Trade*, Cambridge, Mass.: MIT Press.

Henry, J. F. (1990). *The Making of Neoclassical Economics*, London: Unwin Hyman.

Hibbs, D. A. (1977). 'Political Parties and Macroeconomic Policy', *American Political Science Review*, 71: 1467–87.

(1992). 'Partisan Theory after Fifteen Years', *European Journal of Political Economy*, 8: 361–73.

Hicks, J. R. (1937). 'Mr. Keynes and the "Classics": A Suggested Interpretation', *Econometrica*, 5: 147–59.

(1939). 'The Foundations of Welfare Economics', *Economic Journal*, 49: 696–712.

Hills, J. (1995). 'Funding the Welfare State', *Oxford Review of Economic Policy*, 11: 27–43.

Hirschman, A. O. (1970). *Exit, Voice and Loyalty. Responses to Decline in Firms, Organizations and States*, Cambridge, Mass.: Harvard University Press.

Holcombe, R. G. (1994). *The Economic Foundations of Government*, London: Macmillan.

Hollander, S.(1987). *Classical Economics*, Oxford: Blackwell.

Hotelling, H. (1938). 'The General Welfare in Relation to Problems of Taxation and of Railways and Utility Rates', *Econometrica*, 6: 242–69.

Hughes-Hallett, A. J. (1989). 'Econometrics and the Theory of Economic Policy: the Tinbergen-Theil Contributions 40 Years on', *Oxford Economic Paper*, 41: 189–214.

Hughes Hallett, A. J. and H. Rees (1983), *Quantitative Economic Policies and Interactive Planning*, Cambridge: Cambridge University Press.

Hume, D. (1739). *Treatise of Human Nature*, London: Everyman Library.

Hunt, E. K. (1980). 'A Radical Critique of Welfare Economics', in E. Nell (ed.), *Growth, Profits and Property*, Cambridge: Cambridge University Press.

Hurwicz, L. (1972). 'On Informationally Decentralized Systems', in C. B. McGuire and R. Radner (eds.), *Decision and Organization*, Amsterdam: North-Holland.

Ingbermann, D. E. and R. P. Inman (1988). 'The Political Economy of Fiscal Policy', in P.G. Hare (ed.), *Surveys in Public Sector Economics*, Oxford: Blackwell.

Inman, R. P. (1987). *Markets, Governments, and the 'New' Political Economy*, in A. J. Auerbach and M. Feldstein.

International Monetary Fund (1993). *Balance of Payments Manual*, 5th edn, Washington.

Intriligator, M. (1971). *Mathematical Optimization and Economic Theory*, Englewood Cliffs: Prentice-Hall.

Johansen, L. (1977). *Lectures on Macro-Economic Planning, Part I*, Amsterdam: North-Holland.

(1978). *Lectures on Macro-Economic Planning, Part II*, Amsterdam: North-Holland.

Jones-Lee, M. W. (1976). *The Value of Life. An Economic Analysis*, Chicago: University of Chicago Press.

Just, R. E., L. D. Hueth and A. Schmitz (1982). *Applied Welfare Economics and Public Policy*, Englewood Cliffs: Prentice-Hall.

Kaldor, N. (1939). 'Welfare Propositions of Economics and Interpersonal Comparisons of Utility', *Economic Journal*, **49**: 549–52.

(1971). 'Conflicts in National Economic Objectives', *Economic Journal*, **81**: 1–16.

(1976). 'Inflation and Recession in the World Economy', *Economic Journal*, **86**: 703–14.

Kalecki, M. (1933). *Proba Teorji Konjuktury*, Warszawa: Ibkge; 1st chapter repr. (1966) in M. Kalecki, *Studies in the Theory of Business Cycle*, Oxford: Blackwell.

(1943). 'Political Aspects of Full Employment', *Political Quarterly*, October; repr. (1971) in M. Kalecki, *Selected Essays on the Dynamics of the Capitalist Economy 1933–1970*, Cambridge: Cambridge University Press.

(1954). *Theory of Economic Dynamics*, London: Allen & Unwin.

Kanbur, S. M. R. and G. D. Myles (1992). 'Policy Choice and Political Constraints', *European Journal of Political Economy*, **8**: 1–29.

Kanbur, S. M. R. and M. Tuomala (1994). 'Inherent Inequality and the Optimal Graduation of Marginal Rates', *Scandinavian Journal of Economics*, **96**: 275–82.

Kareken, J. (1975). 'Lenders Preferences, Credit Rationing and the Effectiveness of Monetary Policy', *Review of Economics and Statistics*, **39**: 292–302.

Kay J. and J. Vickers (1990). 'Regulatory Reform: An Appraisal', in G. Majone (ed.), *Deregulation or Reregulation? Regulatory Reform in Europe and the US*, London: Pinter.

Kenen, P. B. (1990). *Currency Unification, Currency Competition and the Private Ecu: Second Thought. Comment*, in E. M. Claassen.

(1992). 'EMU after Maastricht', in Group of Thirty, O. P., 36, Washington.

Keynes, J. M. (1924). *Tract on Monetary System*, London: Macmillan.

(1935). 'Letter to R. F. Harrod, 27.8.1935'; repr. (1973) in *The Collected Writings, The General Theory and After, Part I, Preparation*, London: Macmillan, Vol. XIII.

(1936). *The General Theory of Employment, Interest and Money*, London: Macmillan; repr. (1973) in *The Collected Writings*, London: Macmillan, Vol. VII.

(1940). *How to Pay for the War*; repr. (1972) in *The Collected Writings*, London: Macmillan, Vol. IX.

Kirman, A. (1989). 'The Intrinsic Limits of Modern Economic Theory: The Emperor Has

No Clothes', *Economic Journal*, Conference Issue, **99**: 126–39.

(1992). 'Whom or What Does the Representative Consumer Represent', *Journal of Economic Perspectives*, **6**: 117–36.

Knight, F. H. (1952). 'Institutionalism and Empirism in Economics', *American Economic Review*, **42**: 45–55.

Krueger, A. (1974). 'The Political Economy of the Rent-Seeking Society', *American Economic Review*, **64**: 291–303.

Kydland, F. E. and E.C. Prescott (1977). 'Rules Rather than Discretion: The Inconsistency of Optimal Plans', *Journal of Political Economy*, **85**: 473–92; repr. (1994) in Persson, J. and G. Tabellini, Vol. I.

Laffont, J. J. (1976). 'Decentralization with Externalities', *European Economic Review*, **7**: 359–75.

Laffont, J. J. and J. Tirole (1991). 'The Politics of Government Decision-Making: A Theory of Regulatory Capture', *Quarterly Journal of Economics*, **106**: 1089–127.

Lall, S. (1994). 'Does the Bell Toll for Industrial Strategy?', *World Development*, **22**: 645–54.

Lampman, R. J. (1984). *Social Welfare Spending: Accounting for Changes from 1950 to 1978*, New York: Academic Press.

Lancaster, K. J. (1966). 'A New Approach to Consumer Theory', *Journal of Political Economy*, **74**: 132–57.

Lange, O. (1936). 'On the Economic Theory of Socialism', *Review of Economic Studies*, **4**: 53–71 and 123–42.

Layard, R. (1980). 'On the Use of the Distribution Weights in Social Cost–Benefit Analysis', *Journal of Political Economy*, **88**: 1041–47.

Layard, R., S. Nickell and R. Jackman (1991). *Unemployment. Macroeconomic Performance and the Labour Market*, Oxford: Oxford University Press.

Ledebur, L. and Barnes, W. (1992). *City Distress, Metropolitan Disparities and Economic Growth*, National League of Cities Research Report.

Le Grand, J. (1987). 'The Middle-Class Use of the British Social Services', in R. E. Goodin and J. Le Grand (eds.), *Not only the Poor: The Middle Classes and the Welfare State*, London: Allen & Unwin.

(1991). 'The Theory of Government Failure', *British Journal of Political Science*, **21**: 423–42.

Leibenstein, H. (1950). 'Bandwagon, Snob and Veblen Effects in the Theory of Consumers' Demand', *Quarterly Journal of Economics*, **64**: 183–207.

(1966). 'Allocative Efficiency against "X-Efficiency"', *American Economic Review*, **56**: 392–415.

Leijonhufvud, A. (1968). *On Keynesian Economics and the Economics of Keynes. A Study in Monetary Theory*, Oxford: Oxford University Press.

Leontief, W. (1964). 'Modern Techniques for Economic Planning and Projections', in W. Leontief, *Essays in Economics, Theories and Theorizing*, Oxford: Blackwell, Vol. I.

(1976). 'National Economic Planning; Methods and Problems', in W. Leontief, *The Economic System in an Age of Discontinuity*, New York: New York University Press.

Lerner, A. P. (1934). 'Economic Theory and Socialist Economics', *Review of Economic Studies*, **2**: 51–61.

(1937). 'Statics and Dynamics in a Socialist Economy', *Economic Journal*, **47**: 253–70.

(1944). *The Economics of Control. Principle of Welfare Economics*, New York: Macmillan.

(1978). 'A Wage-Increase Permit Plan to Stop Inflation', *The Brookings Papers on Economic Activity*, **2**: 491–505.

Lerner, A. P. and D. C. Colander (1980). *MAP, A Market Anti-Inflation Plan*, New York:

Harcourt Jovanovich.

Lewis, W. A. (1954). 'Development with Unlimited Supply of Labour', *The Manchester School of Economic and Social Studies*, **22**: 139–91.

Lindbeck, A. (1976). 'Stabilisation Policies in Open Economies with Endogenous Politicians', *American Economic Review*, **66**: 1–19.

—— (1995). 'Welfare State Disincentives with Endogenous Habits and Norms', *The Scandinavian Journal of Economics*, **97**: 477–94.

Lindbeck, A. and D. J. Snower (1984). 'Involuntary Unemployment as an Insider-Outsider Dilemma', Seminar Paper no. 282, Institute for International Economic Studies, University of Stockholm, repr. (1986) in W. Beckerman (ed.), *Wage Rigidity and Unemployment*, London: Duckworth.

Lindhal, E. (1919). *Die Gerechtigkeit der Besteuerung*, Lund: Gloerup (English translation (1967) 'Just Taxation, A Positive Solution', in R. A. Musgrave and A. Peacock (eds.), *Classics in the Theory of Public Finance*, New York: St. Martin's Press).

Lipsey, R. G. and K. Lancaster (1956). 'The General Theory of Second Best', *Review of Economic Studies*, **24**: 11–32.

Little, I. M. D. (1949). 'The Foundations of Welfare Economics', *Oxford Economic Paper*, **1**: 227–46.

Littlechild, S. (1983). *Regulation of British Telecommunications Profitability*, London: HMSO.

Lucas, R. E. (1973). 'Some International Evidence on Output-Inflation Tradeoffs', *American Economic Review*, **63**: 326–34.

—— (1976). *Econometric Policy Evaluation: A Critique*, in K. Brunner and A. Meltzer (eds.), *The Phillips Curve and Labour Markets*, Carnegie-Rochester Conference Series on Public Policy, Amsterdam: North-Holland, Vol. I.

—— (1977). 'Understanding Business Cycle', in *Journal of Monetary Economics*, **5** (Supplementary Series): 7–29; repr. (1981) in R. E. Lucas, *Studies in Business Cycle Theory*, Oxford: Blackwell.

—— (1988). 'On the Mechanism of Economic Development', *Journal of Monetary Economics*, **22**: 3–42.

MacRae, C. D. (1977). 'A Political Model of the Business Cycle', *Journal of Political Economy*, **85**: 239–63.

Maddison, A. (1991). *Dynamic Forces in Capitalist Development. A Long-Run Comparative View*, Oxford: Oxford University Press.

Maddock, R. and M. Carter (1982). 'A Child's Guide to Rational Expectations', *Journal of Economic Literature*, **20**: 39–51.

Madse, H. J. (1981). 'Partisanship and Macroeconomic Outcomes: A Reconsideration', in D. A. Hibbs and H. Fassbender (eds.), *Contemporary Political Economy*, Amsterdam: North-Holland.

Magill, M. and M. Quinzii (1996). *Theory of Incomplete Markets*, Cambridge, Mass.: MIT Press.

Malinvaud, E. (1977). *The Theory of Unemployment Reconsidered*, Oxford: Blackwell.

—— (1984). *Mass Unemployment*, Oxford: Blackwell.

Mankiw, N. G. (1985). 'Small Menu Costs and Large Business Cycles: A Macroeconomic Model of Monopoly', *Quarterly Journal of Economics*, **100**: 529–38; repr. (1991) in N. G. Mankiw and D. Romer (eds.), *New Keynesian Economics*, Cambridge, Mass.: MIT Press.

Marris, R. (1964). *The Economic Theory of 'Managerial' Capitalism*, London: Macmillan.

Marshall, A. (1890). *Principles of Economics*, 1st ed. (9th ed., 1920), London: Macmillan.

Martimort, D. (1996). 'The Multiprincipal Nature of Government', *European Economic Review*, **35**: 673–86.

Martin, S. (1993). *Advanced Industrial Economics*, Oxford: Blackwell.

Marx, K. (1867). *Das Kapital, Kritik der Politische Okonomie*, Hamburg: Meisner (English translation (1967), *Capital*, New York: International Publishers).

Mas-Colell, A., M D. Whinston and J. R. Green (1995). *Microeconomic Theory*, Oxford: Oxford University Press.

Mayer, T. (1959). 'The Empirical Significance of the Real Balance Effect', *Quarterly Journal of Economics*, **73**: 275–91.

McCubbins, M. D. (1991). 'Party Governance and U.S. Budget Deficits: Divided Goverment and Fiscal Stalemate', in A. Alesina, G. Carliner (eds.), *Politics and Economics in the Eighties*, Chicago: University of Chicago Press.

McDonald, I. M. and R. M. Solow (1981). 'Wage Bargaining and Employment', *American Economic Review*, **71**: 896–908.

McKenzie, L. W. (1951). 'Ideal Output and the Interdependence of Firm', *Economic Journal*, **61**: 785–803.

McKinnon, R. I. (1979). *Money in International Exchange. The Convertible Currency System*, Oxford: Oxford University Press.

(1988). 'Monetary and Exchange Rate Policies for International Financial Stability: A Proposal', *Journal of Economic Perspectives*, **2**: 83–103.

McMurrin, S. M. (ed.) (1987). *Liberty, Equality, and Law: Selected Tanner Lectures on Moral Philosophy*, Salt Lake City: University of Utah Press.

Meade, J. E. (1951). *The Theory of International Economic Policy*, Oxford: Oxford University Press.

(1955). *Trade and Welfare*, Oxford: Oxford University Press.

(1972). 'Poverty in the Welfare State', *Oxford Economic Papers*, **24**: 289–326.

Migué, J. L. and G. Bélanger (1974). 'Towards a General Theory of Managerial Discretion', *Public Choice*, **17**: 27–34.

Mill, J. S. (1848). *Principles of Political Economy*, London; repr. (1970) Harmondsworth: Penguin.

Miller, M. and A. Sutherland (1991). 'The Walters Critique of the EMS: A Case of Inconsistent Expectations', *Manchester School of Economics and Social Studies*, **59** (supplement): 23–37.

Milone, L. M. (1993). *Libero Scambio, Protezionismo e Cooperazione Internazionale nel Pensiero di Keynes*, Roma: La Nuova Italia Scientifica.

Minsky, H. P. (1975). *John Maynard Keynes*, New York: Columbia University Press.

Mirrlees, J. (1971). 'An Exploration in the Theory of Optimum Income Taxation', *Review of Economic Studies*, **38**: 175–208.

Mishra, R. (1993). 'Typologies of the Welfare State and Comparative Analysis: The 'Liberal' Welfare State', paper presented at the Seminar on Comparative Research on Welfare States in Transition, Oxford, 9–12 Sept.

Modigliani, F. (1944). 'Liquidity Preference and the Theory of Interest and Money', *Econometrica*, **12**: 45–88.

Moffit, R. (1992). 'Incentive Effects of the U.S. Welfare System: A Review', *Journal of Economic Literature*, **30**: 1–61.

Monticelli, C. and L. Papi (1996). *European Integration, Monetary Co-ordination and the Demand for Money*, Oxford: Clarendon Press.

Morris, C. N. and I. Preston (1986). Taxes, Benefits and the Distribution of Income, 1968–83, *Fiscal Studies*, **7**: 18–27.

Moulin, H. (1988). *Axioms of Cooperative Decision Making*, Cambridge: Cambridge University Press.

Mueller, D. C. (1989). *Public Choice II*, Cambridge: Cambridge University Press.

Mundell, R. A. (1962). 'The Appropriate Use of Monetary and Fiscal Policy for Internal and External Stability', *IMF Staff Papers*, 9: 70–9; repr. (1968) in R. A. Mundell, *International Economics*, London: Macmillan.

(1963). 'Capital Mobility and Stabilisation Policy under Fixed and Flexible Exchange Rates', *Canadian Journal of Economics and Political Science*, 29: 475–85; repr (1968) in R. A. Mundell, *International Economics*, New York: Macmillan.

Musgrave, R. A. (1959). *The Theory of Public Finance*, 1st edn., New York: McGraw Hill.

Muth, J. F. (1961). 'Rational Expectations and the Theory of Price Movements', *Econometrica*, 29: 315–55.

Myles, G. D. (1995). *Public Economics*, Cambridge: Cambridge University Press.

Myrdal, G. (1953). *The Political Element in the Development of Economic Theory*, London: Routledge & Kegan.

(1956). *An International Economy. Problems and Prospects*, London: Routledge & Kegan.

(1957). *Economic Theory and Underdeveloped Regions*, London: Duckworth, (London: University Paperbacks, Methuen and Co., 1969).

(1958). *Value in Social Theory*, New York: Harper.

Negishi, T. (1972). *General Equilibrium Theory and International Trade*, Amsterdam: North-Holland.

Newbery, D. M. G. and N. H. Stern (1987). *The Theory of Taxation for Developing Countries*, Oxford: Oxford University Press.

Newlyn, W. T. (1962). *Theory of Money*, Oxford: Clarendon Press.

Nicholson, J. L. (1974). 'The Distribution and Redistribution of Income in the U. K.', in D. Wedderburn (ed.), *Poverty, Inequality and Class Structure*, Cambridge: Cambridge University Press.

Niskanen, W. (1971). *Bureaucracy and Representative Government*, Chicago: Aldine.

(1975). 'Bureaucrats and Politicians', *Journal of Law and Economics*, 38: 617–44.

Nordhaus, W. (1975). 'The Political Business Cycle', *Review of Economic Studies*, 42:169–90.

North, D.C. (1990). 'A Transaction Cost Theory of Politics', *Journal of Theoretical Politics*, 2: 355–67.

Nozick, R. (1974). *Anarchy, State and Utopia*, New York: Basic Books.

Nurkse, R. (1953). *Problems of Capital Formation in Underdeveloped Countries*, Oxford: Oxford University Press.

Nussbaum, M. N. (1992). 'Human Functioning and Social Justice. In Defence of Aristotelian Essentialism', *Political Theory*, 20: 202–46.

Oakland, W. H. (1987). *Theory of Public Goods*, in A. J. Auerbach and M. Feldstein.

OECD (1990). *Economic Outlook*, December.

(1993). *Economic Outlook*, December.

(1994). *Economic Outlook*, December.

(1996). *Economic Outlook*, June.

Okun, A. M. (1962). 'Potential GNP: Its Measurement and Significance', in American Statistical Association, 'Proceedings of the Business and Economic Statistics Section'; repr. (1970) in A. M. Okun, *The Political Economy of Prosperity*, Washington: The Brookings Institution.

(1975). *Equality and Efficiency*, Washington: The Brookings Institution.

Olson, M. (1965). *The Logic of Collective Action: Public Goods and Theory of Groups*, Cambridge, Mass.: Harvard University Press.

(1982). *The Rise and Decline of Nations*, New Haven: Yale University Press.

Ordover, J. A. and A. Weiss (1981). 'Information and the Law: Evaluating Legal Restrictions on Competitive Contracts', *American Economic Review*, **71**: 399–404.

Osborne, M. J. (1995). 'Spatial Models of Political Competition Under Plurality Rule: A Survey of Some Explanations of the Number of Candidates and the Position They Take', *Canadian Journal of Economics*, **28**: 261–301.

Pagano, U. (1992). 'Organizational Equilibria and Production Efficiency', *Metroeconomica*, **43**: 227–47.

Pareto, V. (1906). *Manuale di Economia Politica*, Milan: Società Editrice Libraria; (English edition 1971), *Manual of Political Economy*, New York: A.M. Kelley (English translation from French edition of 1927, Geneva: Librairie Droz; 1st French edn 1909).

Parrinello, S. (1993). 'Non Pure Private Goods in the Economics of Production Processes', *Metroeconomica*, **44**: 195–214.

Pasinetti, L. L. (1981). *Structural Change and Economic Growth*, Cambridge: Cambridge University Press.

  (1993). *Structural Economic Dynamics: A Theory of the Economic Consequences of Human Learning*, Cambridge: Cambridge University Press.

Patinkin, D. (1956). *Money, Interest and Prices*, Evanston: Roe Peterson; 2nd edn (1965), New York: Harper & Row.

Pattanaik, P. K. and K. Suzumura (1994). 'Rights, Welfarism, and Social Choice', *American Economic Review*, **84**: 435–9.

Pearce, D. (1976). 'The Limits of Cost-Benefit Analysis as a Guide to Environmental Policy', *Kyklos*, **29**: 97–112.

Pencavel, J. (1981). 'The American Experience with Incomes Policy', in J. L. Fallick and R. F. Elliot (eds.), *Incomes Policy, Inflation and Relative Pay*, London: Allen & Unwin.

Perotti, R. (1996). 'Growth, Income Distribution and Democracy: What the Data Say', *Journal of Economic Growth*, **1**: 149–87.

Persson, M. (1995). 'Why are Taxes so High in Egalitarian Societies?', *The Scandinavian Journal of Economics*, **97**: 569–80.

Persson, J. and G. Tabellini (eds.) (1994). *Monetary and Fiscal Policies*, Cambridge, Mass.: MIT Press, 2 Vols.

Petit, M. L. (1990). *Control Theory and Dynamic Games in Economic Policy Analysis*, Cambridge: Cambridge University Press.

Phelps, E.S. (1970). 'Introduction: the New Microeconomics of Unemployment and Inflation Theory', in E.S. Phelps *et al.* (eds.), *Microeconomic Foundations of Employment and Inflation Theory*, New York: Norton.

Phillips A. W. (1958). 'The relation between unemployment and the rate of change of money wage rates in the United Kingdom, 1861–1957', *Economica*, **25**: 283–99.

Pigou, A. C. (1920) *The Economics of Welfare*, 1st edn (4th edn, 1932), London: Macmillan.

  (1928). *A Study in Public Finance*, 1st edn (3rd edn, 1947), London: Macmillan.

  (1941). *Employment and Equilibrium*, London: Macmillan.

  (1951). 'Some Aspects of Welfare Economics,' *American Economic Review*, June.

Poole, W. (1970). 'Optimal Choice of Monetary Policy Instruments in a Simple Stochastic Macro Model', *Quarterly Journal of Economics*, **84**: 197–216.

Prebisch, R. (1950). *The Economic Development of Latin America and Its Principal Problems*, Lake Success: United Nations.

Preston, A. J. and A. R. Pagan (1982). *The Theory of Economic Policy. Statics and Dynamics*, Cambridge: Cambridge University Press.

Price, R. W. R. and J. C. Chouraqui (1983). 'Public Sector Deficits: Problems and Policy

Implications', *OECD Economic Outlook, Occasional Studies*, June.

Pyke, F., G. Becattini and W. Sengenberger (1990). *Industrial Districts and Inter-Firm Cooperation in Italy*, Geneva: International Institute for Labour Studies.

Rae, D. W. (1969). 'Decision Rules and Individual Values in Constitutional Choice', *American Political Science Review*, 63: 40–56.

Ramsey, F. P. (1927). 'A Contribution to the Theory of Taxation', *Economic Journal*, 37: 47–61.

Rasmusen, E. (1994). *Games and Information*, 1st edn 1989, Oxford: Blackwell.

Ravagnani, F. (1994). 'Decisions on Production and the Behaviour of Savers in Recent General Equilibrium Models', Dipartimento di Economia Pubblica, Università di Roma 'La Sapienza', Working Paper no. 2.

Rawls, J. (1971). *A Theory of Justice*, Cambridge, Mass.: Harvard University Press.

Regan, D. H. (1972). 'The Problem of Social Cost Revisited', *Journal of Law and Economics*, 15: 427–37.

Riker, W. H. (1982). *Liberalism against Populism. A Confrontation between the Theory of Democracy and the Theory of Social Choice*, San Francisco: Freeman.

Robbins, L. (1932). *An Essay on the Nature and Significance of Economic Science*, 1st ed. (2nd edn, 1935), London: Macmillan.

Robinson, J. (1937). *Essays in the Theory of Employment*, London: Blackwell.

(1943). 'Planning Full Employment', *The London Times*, Jan. 22 & 23; repr. (1951) in *Collected Economic Papers*, Oxford: Blackwell, Vol. I.

(1962a). *Essays in the Theory of Economic Growth*, London: Macmillan.

(1962b). 'Latter-Day Capitalism', *New Left Review*, July–August: 37–46; repr. (1965) in *Collected Economic Papers*, Oxford: Blackwell, Vol. III.

(1964). *Kalecki and Keynes*, in *Essays in Honour of M. Kalecki*; repr. (1965) in J. Robinson, *Collected Economic Papers*, Oxford: Blackwell, Vol. III.

Roemer, J. E. (1994a). *A Future for Socialism*, Cambridge, Mass.: Harvard University Press.

(1994b). The Strategic Role of Party Ideology when Voters Are Uncertain about How the Economy Works, *American Political Science Review*, 88: 327–35.

Rogoff, K. (1985). 'Can International Monetary Policy Coordination Be Counterproductive?', *Journal of International Economics*, 18: 199–217.

Rogoff, K. and A. Sibert (1988). 'Elections and Macroeconomic Policy Cycles', *Review of Economic Studies*, 55: 1–16.

Romani, F. (1984). 'I Limiti della Politica Economica', *Rassegna Economica*, no. 2. (Rep. 1985, Società Italiana degli Economisti, *I Limiti della Politica Economica* Milano: Giuffrè).

Romer, D. (1993). 'The New Keynesian Synthesis', *Journal of Economic Perspectives*, 7: 5–22.

Romer, P. (1986). 'Increasing Returns and Long-run Growth', *Journal of Political Economy*, 94: 1002–37.

(1987). 'Growth Based on Increasing Returns Due to Specialisation', *American Economic Review*, 77: 56–62.

(1990). 'Endogenous Technological Change', *Journal of Political Economy* (supplement), 98, no. 5 (part 2): S71–S102.

Roosa, R. V. (1951). *Interest Rates and the Central Bank*, in R. V. Roosa, *Money, Trade and Economic Growth: in Honour of John Henry Williams*, New York: Macmillan.

Rosen, S. (1985). 'Implicit Contracts', *Journal of Economic Literature*, 23: 1144–75.

Rosenstein-Rodan, P. N. (1943). 'Problems of Industrialization of Eastern and South Eastern Europe', *Economic Journal*, 53: 202–11.

Rothschild, E. (1994). 'Adam Smith and the Invisible Hand', *American Economic Review, Papers and Proceedings*, **84**: 319–22.

Rothschild, K. (1973). 'Politica dei Redditi o Politica Economica', in D. Cavalieri (ed.), *La Politica dei Redditi*, Milan: Franco Angeli (Italian translation from 'Einkommenspolitik oder Wirtschaftspolitik', pp. 63–80, in *Probleme der Einkommenspolitik*, Kiel: Institut für Weltwirtschaft an der Universität).

Roubini, N. and J. Sachs (1989). 'Political and Economic Determinants of Budget Deficits in the Industrial Democracies', *European Economic Review*, **33**: 903–33.

Rusk, D. (1993). *Cities without Suburbs*, Baltimore: Johns Hopkins University Press.

Sadka, E. (1976). 'On Income Distribution, Incentive Effects and Optimal Income Taxation', *Review of Economic Studies*, **43**: 261–8.

Salin, P. (1990). *The Role of the SDRs in the International Monetary System. Comment*, in E. M. Claassen.

Salvati, M. (1985). 'Commento alla Relazione di Franco Romani', in Società Italiana degli Economisti, *I Limiti della Politica Economica*, Milano: Giuffrè.

Samuelson, P. A. (1947). *Foundations of Economic Analysis*, Cambridge, Mass.: Harvard University Press.

   (1954). 'The Pure Theory of Public Expenditure', *Review of Economics and Statistics*, November; repr. (1969) in K. J. Arrow, T. Scitovsky (eds.), *Readings in Welfare Economics*, Homewood: Irwin.

   (1963). 'Problems of Methodology. Discussion', *American Economic Review*; repr. (1966) in *Collected Scientific Papers*, Cambridge, Mass.: MIT Press.

Sandmo, A. (1991). 'Economists and the Welfare State', *European Economic Review*, **35**: 213–39.

   (1995). 'Introduction: The Welfare Economics of the Welfare State', *The Scandinavian Journal of Economics*, **97**: 469–76.

Sarkar, P. and H. W. Singer (1991). 'Manufactured Exports of Developing Countries and their Terms of Trade since 1965', *World Development*, **19**: 333–40.

Satterthwaite, M. A. (1975). 'Strategy-Proofness and Arrow's Conditions: Existence and Correspondence Theorems for Voting Procedures and Social Welfare Functions', *Journal of Economic Theory*, **10**: 187–217.

Scherer, F. M. (1980). *Industrial Market Structure and Economic Performance*, Boston: Houghton Mifflin Co.

Schröder, J. (1990). *The Role of the SDRs in the International Monetary System*, in E. M. Claassen.

Schultze, C. L. (1988). 'International Macroeconomic Coordination. Marrying the Economic Models with Political Reality', in M. Feldstein (ed.), *International Economic Cooperation*, Chicago: University of Chicago Press.

Schumpeter, J. A. (1934). *The Theory of Economic Development*, Cambridge, Mass.: Harvard University Press.

   (1943). *Capitalism, Socialism and Democracy*, London: Allen & Unwin.

   (1954). *History of Economic Analysis*, New York: Oxford University Press.

Schwartz, A. J. (1975). 'Review of Kindleberger's *The World in Depression*', *Journal of Political Economy*, **83**: 231–7.

   (1981). 'Understanding 1929–1933', in K. Brunner (ed.), *The Great Depression Revisited*, Boston: Kluwer-Nijhoff.

Scitovsky, T. (1941). 'A Note on Welfare Propositions in Economics', *Review of Economic Studies*, **9**: 77–88.

Seade, J. (1977). 'On the Shape of Optimal Tax Schedules', *Journal of Public Economics*, **7**:

203–35.

Sebastiani, M. (1994). *Kalecki and Unemployment Equilibrium*, New York: St. Martin's Press.

Seidman, L. S. (1978). 'Tax-Based Incomes Policy', *Brookings Papers on Economic Activity*, **2**: 301–61.

Sen, A. K. (1970a). *Collective Choice and Social Welfare*, Edinburgh: Oliver and Boyd.

(ed.) (1970b). *Growth Economics: Selected Readings*, Harmondsworth: Penguin.

(1979). 'Utilitarianism and Welfarism', *Journal of Philosophy*, **76**: 463–89.

(1980a). 'Equality of What?', in S. McMurrin (ed.), *The Tanner Lectures on Human Values*, Salt Lake City, University of Utah and Cambridge: Cambridge University Press, Vol. I; repr. (1982) in A. K. Sen.

(1980b). 'Description as a Choice', *Oxford Economic Paper*, 1980, **32**: 353–69; repr. (1982) in A. K. Sen.

(1982). *Choice, Welfare and Measurement*, Oxford: Blackwell.

(1984). 'Goods and People' in A. K. Sen, *Resources, Value and Development*, Cambridge, Mass.: Harvard University Press.

(1985). *Commodities and Capabilities*, Amsterdam: North-Holland.

(1987). *On Ethics and Economics*, Oxford: Blackwell.

(1992). *Inequality Re-examined*, Oxford: Clarendon Press.

(1995). 'Rationality and Social Choice', *American Economic Review*, **85**: 1–24.

Sengenberger, W. and F. Pyke (eds.) (1992). *Industrial Districts and Local Economic Regeneration*, Geneva: International Institute for Labour Studies.

Shapiro, C. and J.E. Stiglitz (1984). 'Equilibrium Unemployment as a Worker Discipline Device', *American Economic Review*, **74**: 433–44.

Shleifer, A. (1985). 'A Theory of Yardstick Competition', *Rand Journal of Economics*, **16**: 319–27.

Simon, H. A. (1976). 'From Substantive to Procedural Rationality', in S. Latsis (ed.), *Method and Appraisal in Economics*, Cambridge: Cambridge University Press.

Simons, H. C. (1938). *Personal income taxation*, Chicago: University of Chicago Press.

Singer, H. W. (1950). 'The Distribution of Gains between Investing and Borrowing Countries', *American Economic Review*, **40**: 473–85.

Singh, A. (1971). *Takeovers. Their Relevance to the Stock Market and the Theory of Firm*, Cambridge: Cambridge University Press.

Sinn, H. W. (1995). 'A Theory of the Welfare State', *Scandinavian Journal of Economics*, **97**: 495–526.

Smith, A. (1776). *An Inquiry into Nature and Causes of the Wealth of Nations*, 1st edn London: Straham & Cadell (quotations from the edition by R.H. Campbell, A.S. Skinner and W.B. Todd, Oxford: Clarendon Press, 1976).

Solow, R. (1956). 'A Contribution to the Theory of Economic Growth', *Quarterly Journal of Economics*, **70**: 65–94.

Spaventa, L. (1982). 'Algebraic Properties and Economic Improperties of the "Indicator of Divergence" in the EMS', in Cooper R. N. *et al.* (eds.), *The International Monetary System Under Flexible Exchange Rates: Global, Regional and National. Essays in Honor of Robert Triffin*, Cambridge, Mass: Ballinger.

Spiller, P. T. (1990). 'Politicians, Interest Groups and Regulators: A Multiple-Principals Agency Theory of Regulation, or "Let Them Be Bribed" ', *Journal of Law and Economics*, **33**: 65–101.

Spulber, D. F. (1989). *Regulation and Markets*, Cambridge, Mass.: MIT Press.

Staniland, M. (1985). *What is Political Economy? A Study of Social Theory and*

Underdevelopment, New Haven: Yale University Press.

Starrett, D. A. (1972). 'Fundamental Non-Convexities in the Theory of Externalities', *Journal of Economic Theory*, **4**: 180–99.

—— (1988). *Foundations of Public Economics*, Cambridge: Cambridge University Press.

Steindl, J. (1952). *Maturity and Stagnation in American Capitalism*, Oxford: Blackwell, 2nd edn, New York: Monthly Review Press, 1976.

—— (1981). 'Ideas and Concepts of Long Run Growth', *Banca Nazionale del Lavoro Quarterly Review*, **136**: 35–48.

Stern, N. H. (1976). 'On the Specification of Models of Optimum Income Taxation', *Journal of Public Economics*, **6**: 123–62.

Stevenson, A., V. Muscatelli and M. Gregory (1988). *Macroeconomic Theory and Stabilisation Policy*, New York: P. Allan.

Stigler, G. J. (1966). *The Theory of Price*, 3rd edn (1st edn 1946), New York: Macmillan.

Stiglitz, J. E. (1987). *Pareto Efficient and Optimal Taxation and the New New Welfare Economics*, in A. J. Auerbach and M. Feldstein.

—— (1988). *Economics of the Public Sector*, 2nd edn, New York: Norton & Co.

—— (1989). *The Economic Role of the State*, Oxford: Blackwell.

—— (1991). 'Alcuni Aspetti Teorici delle Pirvatizzazioni: Applicazione all'Europa Orientale', *Rivista di Politica Economica*, **81**: 199–224.

—— (1994). *Whither Socialism?*, Cambridge, Mass., MIT Press.

Stiglitz, J. E. and A. Weiss (1981). 'Credit Rationing in Markets with Imperfect Information', *American Economic Review*, **71**: 393–410.

Summers, L. H. (1983). 'The Nonadjustment of Nominal Interest Rates: A Study of the Fisher Effect', in J. Tobin, (ed.), *Macroeconomics, Prices and Quantities. Essays in Memory of Arthur M. Okun*, Oxford: Blackwell.

Sydsaeter, K. and P.J. Hammond (1995). *Mathematics for Economic Analysis*, Englewood Cliffs: Prentice Hall.

Sylos Labini, P. (1962). *Oligopoly and Technical Progress*, (1st Italian edn., 1956), Cambridge, Mass.: Harvard University Press.

Tabellini, G. and A. Alesina (1990). 'Voting on the Budget Deficit', *American Economic Review*, **80**: 37–49; repr. (1994) in Persson, J. and G. Tabellini, Vol. II.

Tarantelli, E. (1983). 'The Regulation of Inflation in Western Countries and the Degree of Neocorporatism', *Economia* (*Portuguese Catholic University*), **7**: 199–238.

Taylor, M. J. (1969). 'Proof of a Theorem on Majority Rule', *Behavioral Science*, May.

Temin, P. (1976). *Did Monetary Forces Cause the Great Depression?*, New York: Norton.

Theichroew, D., A. Robichek and M. Montalbano (1965). 'An Analysis of Criteria for Investment and Financial Decisions under Certainty', *Management Science*, **12**: 151–79.

Theil, H. (1954). 'Econometric Models and Welfare Maximization', *Weltwirtschaftliches Archiv*, **72**: 60–83.

—— (1956). 'On the Theory of Economic Policy', *American Economic Review*, **46**: 360–6.

—— (1964). *Optimal Decision Rules for Government and Industry*, Amsterdam: North-Holland.

Thygesen, N. (1996). 'Should Budgetary Policies Be Coordinated Further in Economic and Monetary Union and Is That Feasible?' in 'European Monetary Union: The Problems of the Transition to a Single Currency', *Banca Nazionale del Lavoro Quarterly Review*, Special Issue, March: 5–31.

Tiebout, C. M. (1956). 'A Pure Theory of Local Expenditures', *Journal of Political Economy*, **64**: 416–22.

Tinbergen, J. (1952). *On the Theory of Economic Policy*, Amsterdam: North-Holland.

(1954). *Centralization and Decentralization in Economic Policy*, Amsterdam: North-Holland.

(1956). *Economic Policies. Principles and Design*, Amsterdam: North-Holland.

Tirole, J. (1994). 'The Internal Organization of Government', *Oxford Economic Papers*, **46**: 1–29.

Tobin, J. (1963). 'Commercial Banks as Creators of Money', in D. Carson (ed.), *Banking and Monetary Studies*, Homewood: Irwin.

(1978). 'A Proposal for International Monetary Reform', *Eastern Economic Journal*, **4**: 153–9.

(1980). *Asset Accumulation and Economic Activity*, Oxford: Blackwell.

Triffin, R. (1960). *Gold and the Dollar Crisis*, New Haven: Yale University Press.

Tsoukalis, L. (1993). *The New European Economy. The Politics and Economics of Integration*, 2nd rev. edn, Oxford: Oxford University Press.

Tullock, G. (1965). *The Politics of Bureaucracy*, Washington: Public Affairs Press.

Tuomala, M. (1990). *Optimal Income Tax and Redistribution*, Oxford: Clarendon Press.

Unctad (1994). *World Investment Report 1994*, New York.

United Nations (1990). *Human Development Report 1990*, Oxford: Oxford University Press.

(1993). *Human Development Report 1993*, Oxford: Oxford University Press.

(1994). *World Social Situation in the 1990s*, New York: United Nations Publications.

United States, Bureau of the Census (1993). *Poverty in the United States: 1992*, Washington: US Government Printing Office.

United States (1996). Economic Report of the President, Transmitted to the Congress, February.

Vandenbroucke, F. (1985). 'Conflicts in International Economic Policy and the World Recession: A Theoretical Analysis', *Cambridge Journal of Economics*, **9**: 15–42.

Van den Doel, H. and B. Van Velthoven (1993). *Democracy and Welfare Economics*, 2nd edn, Cambridge: Cambridge University Press.

Van Ypersele, J. (1977). 'A Central Position for the SDR in the Monetary System', *Banca Nazionale del Lavoro Quarterly Review*, no. 123: 381–97.

(1984). *The European Monetary System*, Brussels: European Communities.

Varian, H. R. (1987). *Intermediate Microeconomics. A Modern Approach*, New York: Norton and Co.

(1992). *Microeconomic Analysis*, 3rd edn., New York: Norton and Co.

Vaubel, R. (1977). 'Free Currency Competition', *Weltwirtschaftliches Archiv*, **113**: 435–61.

(1990). 'Currency Unification, Currency Competition and the Private ecu: Second Thoughts', in E. M. Claassen.

Veljanovski, C. (ed.) (1991). *Regulators and the Market. An Assessment of the Growth of Regulation in the UK*, Institute of Economic Affairs, London.

Vercelli, A. (1991). *Methodological foundations of macroeconomics: Keynes and Lucas*, Cambridge: Cambridge University Press.

Vernon, R. (1974). *Big Business and the State. Changing Relations in Western Europe*, London: Macmillan.

Vicarelli, F. (1984). *Keynes. The Instability of Capitalism*, Philadelphia: University of Pennsylvania Press.

Vickers, J. (1995). 'Concepts of Competition', *Oxford Economic Papers*, **47**:1–23.

Vickers, J. and G. Yarrow (1988). *Privatization. An Economic Analysis*, Cambridge, Mass.: MIT Press.

Viner, J. (1950). *The Customs Union Issue*, New York: Carnegie Endowment for International Peace.

Viscusi, W. K. (1983). *Risk by Choice. Regulating Health and Safety in the Workplace*, Cambridge, Mass.: Harvard University Press.

Vives, X. (1992). 'The Supervisory Function of The European System of Central Banks', *Giornale degli Economisti e Annali di Economia*, **51 (9–12)**: 523–32.

Von Neumann, J. and O. Morgenstern (1944). *Theory of Games and Economic Behavior*, Princeton: Princeton University Press.

Wallich, H. and S. Weintraub (1971). 'Tax Based Incomes Policies', *Journal of Economic Issues*, **5**: 1–17.

Waterson, M. (1988). *Regulation of the Firm and Natural Monopoly*, Oxford: Blackwell.

Weber, A. A. (1991). 'European Economic and Monetary Union and Asymmetries and Adjustment Problems in the European Monetary System: Some Empirical Evidence', *European Economy*, special edition, no. 1: 185–207.

Weber, M. (1922). *Wirtschaft und Gesellschaft*, Mohr: Tübingen (English translation (1968) *Economy and Society; An Outline of Interpretative Sociology*; translation of the 4th German edn, New York: Bedminster Press).

Weitzman, M. L. (1977). 'Is the Price System or Rationing more Effective in Getting a Commodity to Those Who Need It Most?', *Bell Journal of Economics*, **8**: 517–24.

—— (1982). 'Increasing Returns and the Foundations of Unemployment Theory', *Economic Journal*, **92**: 787–804.

Weitzacker, C. C. (1975). 'Political Limits of Traditional Stabilization Policy', mimeo, May.

Wicksell, K. (1896). *Ein neues Prinzip der gerechten Besteuerung*, Jena; repr. (1994) as 'A New Principle of Just Taxation' in R. Musgrave and A. T. Peacock, *Classics in the Theory of Public Finance*, 2nd edn, New York: St. Martin's Press.

Williamson, J. (1985). *The Exchange Rate System*, rev. edn, Washington, DC: Institute for International Economics.

Williamson, O. E. (1975). *Markets and Hierarchies: Analysis and Antitrust Implications*, New York: The Free Press.

—— (1985). *The Economic Institutions of Capitalism*, New York: The Free Press.

—— (1989). 'Transaction Cost Economics', in R. Schmalensee and R. Willig (eds.), *Handbook of Industrial Organization*, Amsterdam: North-Holland, Vol. I.

Willig, R. (1976). 'Consumer's Surplus Without Apology', *American Economic Review*, **66**: 589–97.

Wolf, C. (1979). 'A Theory of Nonmarket Failure', *Journal of Law and Economics*, **22**: 107–39.

—— (1988). *Markets or Governments: Choosing between Imperfect Alternative*, Cambridge, Mass.: MIT Press.

Wood, G. (1991). 'Valuation Effects, Currency Contract Impacts and the J-Curve: Empirical Estimates', *Australian Economic Papers*, **30**: 148–63.

World Bank (1992). *World Development Report 1992: Development and the Environment*, Oxford: Oxford University Press.

—— (1995). *World Development Report 1995: Workers in an Integrating World*, Oxford: Oxford University Press.

Wyplosz, C. (1990). 'Macroeconomic Implications of 1992', in J. Dermine (ed.), *European Banking in the 1990s*, Oxford: Blackwell.

Yaari, M. E. and M. Bar-Hillel (1984). 'On Dividing Justly', *Social Choice and Welfare*, **1**: 1–24.

Young, A. (1928). 'Increasing Returns and Economic Progress', *Economic Journal*, **38**: 527–42.

Author index

Subject index

ability to pay, 252–5, 262
abuse of a dominant position, 235–6
ad hoc concertation, 471
adjustable peg, 371
adverse selection
  credit and, 112–13, 307, 321
  defined, 112–14
  welfare state and, 269
  see also agency problems
advertising
  as an instrument of persuasion, 96
  information content of, 96
agency problems
  between employee and employer, 83–4, 113,
    155
  credit and, 112–13, 307, 321
  defined, 112
  examples, 112–13
  government and, 206–17, 237–9, 241–2
  insurance and, 112–13
  solutions, 113–14
aggregate demand; *see* effective demand
aggregate supply; *see* supply curve, aggregate
agreements among firms, 73, 95–6, 235–6, 243
animal spirits, 137
anti-monopoly policy; *see* antitrust legislation;
    price control; public enterprise; trade
    policy
antitrust legislation
  content of, 235–6
  dynamic efficiency and, 244
  market failure and, 92, 93, 96
  public enterprise and, 241, 242

appreciation
  asymmetric effects of exchange rate variations,
    415–16
  balance of payments equilibrium and, 408–9,
    431
  of nominal exchange rate, 365–6
  of real exchange rate, 367–8
  see also depreciation; floating exchange rates;
    also under specific monetary systems
appropriate assignment of instruments to
    objectives, 176, 192, 461–7
arbitrage, 393
arbitration, 353, 356, 358
automatic stabilisers, 187–8
Averch–Johnson effect, 237

baby Bells, 233
balance of payments
  automatic adjustment, 401–4
  defined, 363
  determinants, 397–400
  disequilibrium
    causes, 404
    defined, 364, 400–1
  equilibrium
    defined, 400–1
    full, 364, 449
  monetary theory of, 436–7
  policies for adjustment, 404–9
    for competitiveness, 408–9
    for excess or insufficient demand, 407–8
    on capital account, 405–7
  theory of, 397–400

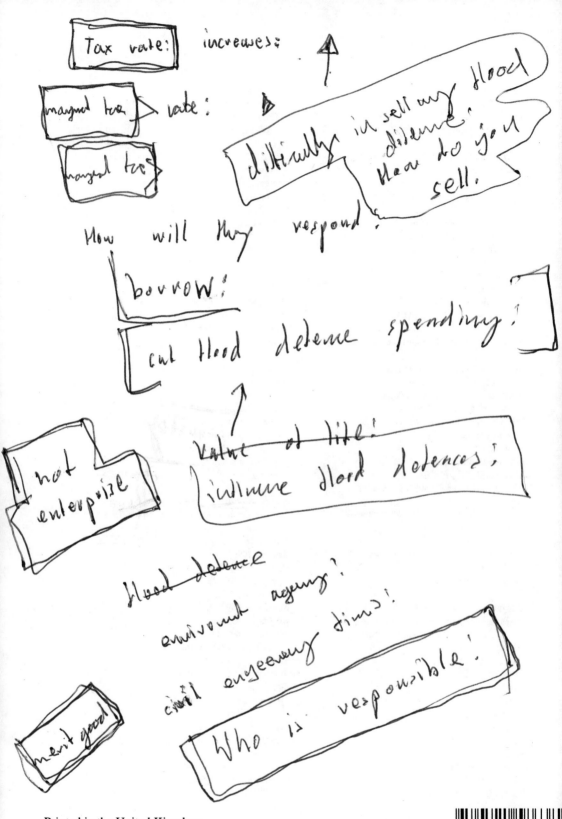

Printed in the United Kingdom
by Lightning Source UK Ltd.
122308UK00001B/19-24/A

9 780521 586382